Muslim Perceptions *of* Other Religions

MUSLIM PERCEPTIONS *of* OTHER RELIGIONS

A Historical Survey

Edited by
Jacques Waardenburg

New York   Oxford

OXFORD UNIVERSITY PRESS

1999

Oxford University Press

Oxford New York
Athens Auckland Bangkok Bogotá Buenos Aires Calcutta
Cape Town Chennai Dar es Salaam Delhi Florence Hong Kong Istanbul
Karachi Kuala Lumpur Madrid Melbourne Mexico City Mumbai
Nairobi Paris São Paulo Singapore Taipei Tokyo Toronto Warsaw

and associated companies in
Berlin Ibadan

Published by Oxford University Press, Inc.
198 Madison Avenue, New York, New York 10016

Library of Congress Cataloging-in-Publication Data
Muslim perceptions of other religions : a historical survey /
edited by Jacques Waardenburg.
p. cm.
Includes bibliographical references
ISBN 0-19-510472-2
1. Islam—Relations. 2. Islam—History.
I. Waardenburg, Jean Jacques.
BP171.M86 1998
297.2'8—DC21 97-29982

9 8 7 6 5 4 3 2 1

Printed in the United States of America
on acid-free paper

For H.M.D.
since 1975

PREFACE

In the course of history, Islam as a religion and as a religious community has come into contact with a number of other religions in the East and West. Muslims have met non-Muslims and their cultures in different situations and at different times and places. Throughout this history there have been Muslim authors who wrote of what they knew and thought about other religions and their adherents. It is a legitimate scholarly question how, in different circumstances, they saw people with other religions or none at all, and to seek an answer through the study of texts which have reached us from the past.

This book presents some results of such research. Part I, written by the editor, is of a general nature and surveys the field. Parts II and III contain essays by different authors on specific subjects in the medieval and modern periods of the history of Islam. They were originally read and discussed at a symposium organized at the University of Lausanne in December 1991. Unfortunately, the publication of the definitive texts took much more time than I had expected; in the meantime four participants have published five books related to the subject: Camilla Adang, *Islam Frente a Judaïsmo: La polémica de Ibn Hazm de Córdoba* (Madrid: Aben Ezra Ediciones, 1994); Adang, *Muslim Writers on Judaïsm and the Hebrew Bible: From Ibn Rabban to Ibn Hazm* (Leiden: E. J. Brill, 1996); Christine Schirrmacher, *Mit den Waffen des Gegners: Christlich-muslimische Kontroversen im 19. und 20. Jahrhundert* (Berlin: Klaus Schwarz, 1992); Isabel Stümpel-Hatami, *Das Christentum aus der Sicht zeitgenössischer iranischer Autoren: Eine Untersuchung religionskundlicher Publikationen in persischer Sprache* (Berlin: Klaus Schwarz, 1996); Steven M. Wasserstrom, *Between Muslim and Jew: The Problem of Symbiosis under Early Islam* (Princeton: Princeton University Press, 1995).

The historical and social relations between religious communities are attracting increasing scholarly attention. I hope that this book with its bibliography will encourage others to continue research in this relatively new field. It is not just the religions themselves—the interpretations their adherents have given them and the norms they have derived from them in the course of time—that are worthy of attention. The views, appreciations, and judgments that these adherents have given of each other and their behavior are equally a valid subject of investigation. This holds especially true for Islam, today's second largest religion, about which most people have opinions but only a few knowledge and insight.

Thanks are due to all those who gave this research project scholarly, moral, and financial support. Without a subsidy from the Swiss National Science Foundation and the Swiss Academy for the Humanities and Social Sciences the symposium would not have taken place. Without much patient work by Hilary Kilpatrick and Isabel Stümpel the text and the bibliography would not have been readable. And without the active participation of colleagues who prepared papers and took part in the discussion, the whole enterprise would have been but one man's dream. The dream started in 1965 when the late Gustav E. von Grunebaum encouraged me to study the medieval Muslim contribution to the development of Religionswissenschaft. I have extended this subject to cover the whole field of Muslim views of other religions in the course of history, collecting a vast documentation on the subject. The symposium of December 1991 has been one of the results of what may be called a lifelong dream, "Religions in the Mirror of Islam"—more or less the reverse of my doctoral dissertation, "Islam in the Mirror of Western Orientalists."

Lausanne, Switzerland J. W.
August 1998

CONTENTS

INTRODUCTION

In recent years, the ways in which artists, authors, and scholars have described people from cultures other than their own or in which one culture has viewed another one have been attracting increasing scholarly interest. This interest is twofold: first to establish which aspects of the other culture were seen and described, and second, to determine the extent to which the views of that other culture reflect particular values and ways of thinking that are specific to the author's own culture or society.

The underlying question here is to what extent a certain openness toward people from other cultures exists among given groups or individuals, if they are willing and able to learn from these other cultures, and what exactly they are prepared to learn. The attention paid to other cultures, of course, is not only a matter of the mind. It also has to do with intersocietal relations generally, including economic and political relations. But it is connected, too, with man's fundamental need for communication and with his gift of imagination.

Whereas Western views of Islam have received increasing scholarly attention during the last decades, this is much less the case with Muslim views of other cultures and religions. Yet since its inception the Muslim civilization has been in continuous relationship with other cultures and civilizations. It extends from the Atlantic to the Pacific Oceans and through regions which have long been carriers of culture. As a consequence, Muslims have come into contact with many religions. One may think not only of various forms of Christianity and Judaism inside and outside the Middle East but also of Zoroastrianism and Manicheism, Hinduism, and even Buddhism, not to speak of nonliterate religions in many parts of Asia and Africa.

A number of texts have come down to us about these cultures and their religions, written by Muslim theologians and jurists, travelers and historians, and men of letters, as well as other people of imagination. These texts testify to voluntary and involuntary meetings that have taken place between Muslims and other peoples. They are the sources of this book.

Part I, "Muslim Studies of Other Religions," is meant to open up this area as a field of research. Jacques Waardenburg surveys the field's broad outlines and supplies information especially on those issues that are hardly treated in the more specialized essays of Parts II and III.

Part II, "Medieval Times," treats specific subjects from the very beginnings of Islam to the sixteenth century. Jane McAuliffe examines the way in which the Christians are viewed in the Qur'ān and specific Qur'ānic commentaries. To a large extent, these texts have conditioned the ways in which Muslims perceived and perceive Christians. Ahmad Shboul gives an account of early medieval Arab-Muslim perceptions of Byzantine Christian religion and culture, whereas Andrea Borruso treats similar perceptions of Latin Christian religion and culture around the eleventh century C.E. Next, medieval Muslim perceptions of Judaism are treated. Camilla Adang analyzes medieval polemics particularly against the Jewish Scriptures, while Steven Wasserstrom discusses some documents from Mamluk times. Particular circles in medieval Muslim civilization viewed other religions in particular ways. Carl-A. Keller opens up the various ways in which mystics viewed other religions. Charles Genequand presents views about such religions as developed by some prominent thinkers. More specifically, Christoph Bürgel treats Zoroastrianism and the ways in which it is referred to in medieval Persian and Arabic literature. And at the end of Part II, Hilary Kilpatrick highlights the ways in which authors of *belles-lettres* texts (*adab*), especially Abu'l-Faraj al-Isfahānī, treated encounters between Muslims and non-Muslims in sometimes unexpected situations.

Part III contains essays dealing with "Modern Times," from the nineteenth century to the present. It opens with accounts of Persian and Arabic writings especially of the twentieth century. Isabel Stümpel concentrates on a selection of Persian writings about Christianity. Patrice Brodeur discusses Arabic writings on religions other than Islam by three Egyptian authors. As in former times, India has remained a meeting place of religions. Sheila McDonough traces intellectual developments in the Muslim community and its new forms of self-awareness after Mughal times until the partition of 1947. Ashgar Ali Engineer critically describes how the situation of the Muslim minority in India has evolved since independence. This part ends with three essays indicating different orientations in the perception of other religions. Christine Schirrmacher concentrates on the ways in which modern Muslim apologetics and polemics against Christianity were influenced by German critical Bible research. Karel Steenbrink sketches how the various religions in Indonesia are perceived in a framework of religious harmony, and how on the basis of the Panjasila a kind of theology of religions is developing. Ekkehard Rudolph analyzes different positions taken by Arab Muslims about the possibility and nature of a dialogue with Christians.

The book ends with a selective Bibliography divided into four periods, a distinction being made for each period between texts in translation and studies. At the end there is a list of some modern Muslim writings in Arabic, Persian, and Turkish. The materials were collected and the selection was made by Jacques Waardenburg.

We tried to concentrate on subjects on which substantial research has not yet been carried out. Thus, apart from the information given in Part I, the reader will be referred to the available literature for instance on the status of the *dhimmīs* or on the work of well-known authors such as Ibn Hazm, al-Bīrūnī, al-Shahrastānī, al-Masʿūdī, and Ibn Khaldūn. The same holds true for the polemics against the Manicheans and Zoroastrians, Arab accounts of the Crusades or Muslim views of Jews and Hindus, not to speak of the innumerable subjects of twentieth century interaction between Muslims and non-Muslims.

This book, then, is meant to encourage further research in the broad field of Muslim interactions with communities adhering to religions other than Islam. Both the ways in which Muslims perceived and perceive other religions and cultures and the ways in which non-Muslims did and do the same with Islam have become relevant topics of study. It seems that there has been more interaction and that there have been more natural and unconstrained relationships between Muslims and other people than has been assumed until now. And whether or not a person, group, or society opens or closes itself to other cultures is largely dependent on its articulation of identity and contextual factors such as power relationships and needs of economic or physical survival.

That such research, especially when religious issues are concerned, puts high demands on the researcher is evident. It should be carried out without political, confessional or ideological bias, in a scholarly spirit of impartial search for the truth about relations between people coming from different cultures and religions. Academic studies of this kind test the possibilities of a true science of religions.*

* For the current situation of the study of religions as carried out in various Muslim countries, see Jacques Waardenburg, "Observations on the Scholarly Study of Religions as Pursued in Some Muslim Countries," *Numen* 45 (1998), pp. 235–257. One may hope that a workshop will be organized in a Muslim country where scholars and researchers from the Muslim world can present and freely discuss their research and teaching on this subject.

CONTRIBUTORS

Camilla Adang has carried out Islamic and Judaic studies at the University of Nijmegen and the Hebrew University of Jerusalem. She obtained her M.A. and Ph.D. degrees at the University of Nijmegen in 1985 and 1993, respectively. Here she taught Hebrew, Arabic, and Islam. During 1993–1996 she carried out research at Tel Aviv University on Muslim-Jewish coexistence in the medieval period; she also taught Islamic history and religion. In 1997 she carried out research on the subject in Madrid. Since 1998 she has again been teaching at Tel Aviv University. Her publications include *Islam frente a Judaísmo: La polémica de Ibn Ḥazm de Córdoba* (1994) and *Muslim Writers on Judaism and the Hebrew Bible: From Ibn Rabban to Ibn Hazm* (1996).

Andrea Borruso obtained his doctorate in Arta in 1971. Since 1974 he has taught Islamic studies at the University of Palermo where he served as director of the Institute of Oriental Studies in 1980–1981 and 1988–1992. Since 1992 he has been professor of Arabic language and culture at the University of Palermo. His research interests include literature and culture of the Arabs in the medieval period. Among his publications are *Islam e Occidente* (1984) and *Saggi di cultura e letteratura araba* (1995), as well as translations of theater plays of Tawfīq al-Hakīm (1980–1988) and Ibn Hamdīs (1987 and 1994), of the autobiography of Ahmad Amīn (1996), and of Ibn Sīnā's *Poem of Medicine* (1996).

Patrice C. Brodeur first studied at McGill University, Montreal, where he obtained his M.A. degree in Islamic Studies in 1989. His thesis was entitled "Contemporary Muslim Approaches to the Study of Religion: A Comparative Analysis of Three Egyptian Authors." He continued at Harvard University where in 1992 he received an A.M. degree in religious studies. At present he is a doctoral candidate at Harvard University. His research interests include the study of contemporary Islam especially in terms of "self" and "other" and interreligious dialogue.

J. Christoph Bürgel studied Islamics at the Universities of Frankfurt, Ankara, Bonn, and Göttingen. In 1960 he received his Ph.D. at the University of Göttingen and worked subsequently at this university (1960–1969) where he submitted his Habil. thesis on the art of healing in medieval Islam. In 1970 he was appointed to the new chair of Islamic studies at the University of Bern where he built up the Institute of Islamic Studies. He has given numerous lectures in the United States and in European and Muslim countries. His fields of research are Arabic, Persian, and Urdu literature, and Islamic cultural history including the history of the sciences in the Islamic world. He has been awarded several prizes for his scholarly work and translations. He retired in 1995. Among his numerous publications are *The Feather of Simurgh* (1988) and *Allmacht und Mächtigheit: Religion und Welt im Islam* (1991), as well as translations of Hāfiz (1972, 1975), Rūmī (1974, 1992), and Nizāmī (1991).

Asghar Ali Engineer was trained in the Islamic religious sciences and is a graduate in civil engineering. He was awarded an honorary doctorate at Calcutta

University in 1993 for his work on communal harmony and interreligious understanding in India. Living in Bombay he is vice president of the People's Union for Civil Liberties, chairman of the Vikas Adhyayan Kendra (Center for Development Studies), chairman of the Committee for Communal Harmony (EKTA), founder and chairman of the Centre for Study of Society and Secularism and convenor of the Asian Muslims' Action Network (AMAN). He has lectured at a number of universities outside India and published numerous articles and some 40 books on Islam, contemporary problems of Muslims, Muslim women's rights, and communal and ethnic problems in India and South Asia. Among his recent books are *Communalism in India: A Historical and Empirical Study*; *Kerala Muslims in Historical Perspective*; and *Rethinking Issues in Islam*.

Charles Genequand studied Arabic language, literature, and medieval thought at the Universities of Geneva and Oxford. In 1977 he obtained his D. Phil. at Oxford with a study on Averroes. Since 1990 he has been a professor of Arabic language and literature, as well as Islam, at the University of Geneva. His main areas of research are the Aristotelian tradition in Islam, Islamic gnosis, the Alexander Romance in Arabic literature, and the Muslim heresiographers. In 1984 his book *Ibn Rushd's Metaphysics* was published. Among his articles in English are "Platonism and Hermetism in al-Kindī's *Fī al-Nafs*" and "Metaphysics" in *Routledge History of World Philosophies*, vol. 1.

Carl-A. Keller studied theology and Oriental languages (several Indian languages, Arabic) at the Universities of Zurich and Basel and received his doctorate at the latter university in 1946. He worked from 1946 until 1952 in the service of the Church of South India, and between 1952 and 1956 he was a Protestant minister in German-speaking Switzerland. He was appointed at the University of Lausanne first as professor of Old Testament (1956) and then of Science des Religions (1964), teaching Hebrew as well. He also lectured on this discipline, as well as Arabic and Islam, at other universities in Switzerland. His main research interest is the mystical aspects of religions. He retired in 1987. Among his books published are *Communication avec l'Ultime* (Selected papers, 1987), *Approche de la mystique*, 2 vols. (1989/90; 2nd ed. 1997), and *Rāmakrishna et la tradition de l'amour* (1997).

Hilary Kilpatrick studied Arabic and Persian at Oxford University where she obtained her D. Phil. in 1971. She has lived in Lebanon (1967–1968) and Egypt (1969–1970). She taught Arabic language and literature at the universities of St. Andrews (1972–1973), Nijmegen (1977–1987), and Bern (1988–1990). Presently, she is completing a study of Abu'l-Faraj al-Isfahānī's *Kitāb al Aghānī* (10th c.) with the working title "Making the Great Book of Songs." She was a member of the editorial board of the *Journal of Arabic Literature* from 1992 to 1996 and is now an editor of *Arabic and Middle Eastern Literatures*. Besides a number of articles on classical and modern Arabic literature, her book publications are *The Egyptian Novel: A Study in Social Criticism* (1974) and a translation of fiction by Ghassan Kanafani (4th ed. 1991).

Jane Dammen McAuliffe studied at the University of Toronto where she obtained an M.A. in religious studies (1979) and a Ph.D. in Islamic studies (1984). She is professor of Islamic studies at the University of Toronto, having taught at Emory University, Atlanta, Georgia, from 1986 to 1992. Her publications include *Qur'ānic Christians: An Analysis of Classical and Modern Exegesis* (1991) and *ʿAbbāsid Authority Affirmed: The Early Years of al-Mansūr*, a translation of vol. 28 of al-Tabarī's *Ta'rīkh al-rusul wa'l-mulūk* (1995). She is the editor of *With Reverence for the Word: Medieval Scriptural Exegesis in Judaism, Christianity and Islam* (forthcoming). She is preparing a monograph on Qur'ānic authority and is general editor of the *Encyclopaedia of the Qur'ān*.

Sheila McDonough studied at McGill University, Montreal, where she obtained a Ph.D. in Islamic studies in 1963. She has taught religious studies and Islam at Concordia University, Montreal, and is at present emeritus professor. Her research interest is Islam in modern and contemporary time, with special reference to South Asia. Her book publications are *The Authority of the Past: A Study of Three Muslim Modernists* (1970), *Mohammed Ali Jinnah: Maker of Modern Pakistan* (1970), *Muslim Ethics and Modernity: A Comparative Study of the Ethical Thought of Sayyid Ahmad Khan and Mawlana Mawdudi* (1980), and *Gandhi's Responses to Islam* (1994).

Ekkehard Rudolph studied Islamic history and culture at the University of Halle (1977–1982) and worked at the Arabic manuscript department of the former Ducal Library in Gotha (1982–1985). He resumed his Islamic studies at the University of Bonn (1986–1990) where he obtained his doctorate in 1990 with a thesis on Arab Muslim evaluations of Western orientalism. He was researcher at the University of Lausanne (1991–1993) and worked at the secretariat of the German National Commission for UNESCO (1994–1996). In 1996–1997 he did research on the situation of Islamic studies in Germany for the German Orient Institute in Hamburg. His other research interests are in intercultural dialogue and mutual perceptions of Islam and the West. As a contribution to it, he has edited *Das arabische Almanach* (Berlin) since its beginning in 1991. His book publications are *Westliche Islamwissenschaft im Spiegel muslimischer Kritik* (1991) and *Dialogues islamo-chrétiens 1950–1993: Introduction suivie d'une bibliographie étendue des sources arabes* (1993). He is the editor of *Mittelmer Partnerschaft: Verzeichnis der Institutionen in der Bundesrepublik Deutschland* (1997).

Christine Schirrmacher studied Islamics and Religionswissenschaft at the Universities of Giessen and Bonn. At the latter university she obtained her doctorate in Islamic studies in 1991, with a dissertation on some Muslim-Christian controversies in the nineteenth and twentieth centuries. She has taught Islamic studies at Philadelphia Theological Seminary. Her dissertation was published as *Mit den Waffen des Gegners: Die christlich-muslimische Kontroverse im 19. und 20. Jahrhundert* (1992).

Ahmad Shboul studied Islamic history at the University of Jordan in Amman and at the University of London where he obtained his doctorate in 1972 with a dissertation on al-Masʿūdī. He taught history at the University of Jordan and subsequently held research fellowships at the Universities of Edinburgh, the Australian National University in Canberra, and Dumberton Oaks in Washington, D.C. He joined the University of Sydney in 1976 where he is now associate professor working in the area of Arab, Islamic, and Middle Eastern studies. His research interests are in the fields of Arab Islamic cultural history, especially in early Islamic Syria, and in Arab-Byzantine cultural relations. He is currently working on a research project on sociocultural change and continuity in early Islamic Damascus and Syria. Apart from a number of articles, he has published *Al-Masʿudi and his World: A Muslim Humanist and His Interest in Non-Muslims* (1979).

Karel A. Steenbrink studied theology, Arabic, and Islam at the University of Nijmegen where he received his doctorate in 1974 with a dissertation on Islamic education on Java. He studied Indonesian, and later also Javanese, in Indonesia. He held teaching positions at the State Institutes of Islamic Studies in Jakarta and Yogyakarta from 1981 until 1988. Since 1989 he has been a senior researcher at the Institute of Ecumenical and Missiological Research, connected first with the University of Leiden and since 1993 with that of Utrecht. In 1992–1993 he was a visiting professor at the Institute of Islamic Studies of McGill University, Montreal. He is much involved in interreligious dialogue and at present editor of the Dutch periodical *Begrip* for Muslim-Christian understanding. His book publications include *Pesantren, madrasah, sekolah: Recente ontwikkelingen in Indonesisch Islamonderricht* (On recent developments in Islamic education in Indonesia; 1974), *Dutch Colonialism and Indonesian Islam: Contacts and Conflicts, 1596–1950* (1993), and *Islamietische mystiek uit Indonesië* (Islamic mysticism in Indonesia; 1994). He also published two books in Indonesian, *Studies in 19th Century Islam in Indonesia* (1984) and *Orientalism and the Study of Indonesian Islam: A Critical Assessment* (1988).

Isabel Stümpel studied Islamics including Arabic, Persian, and Turkish, as well as Religionswissenschaft at the University of Freiburg (Germany) where she obtained her doctorate in 1994 with a dissertation on Iranian perceptions of Christianity during the last hundred years. She was research assistant in Islamic studies in Lausanne during 1989–1995. Since 1996 she has been lecturer in Persian and Persian Islam at the University of Frankfurt. Her research interest is in the field of Persian literature and Islam, and she is preparing her Habil. thesis in this field. She has published *Das Christentum aus der Sicht zeitgenössischer iranischer Autoren: Eine Untersuchung religionskundlicher Publikationen in persischer Sprache* (1996).

Jacques Waardenburg studied theology, phenomenology, and history of religions at the University of Amsterdam (1949–1954), where he specialized in Islam and obtained his doctorate in 1961 with a dissertation on the work of five orientalists. He spent two years in the Middle East (1959–1960 and 1963–1964) and was research associate at the Institute of Islamic Studies of McGill University, Montreal (1962–1963). After teaching Arabic and Islamic history at the University of California at Los Angeles (1964–1968), and Islam and the phenomenology of religion at the University of Utrecht (1968–1987), he was professor of Science des religions at the University of Lausanne (1987–1995). Among his book publications are *L'islam dans le miroir de l'Occident* (3rd ed. 1970), *Classical Approaches to the Study of Religion* (2 vols. 1973–1974), *Reflections on the Study of Religion* (1978), *Religionen und Religion: Systematische Einführung in die Religionswissenschaft* (1986), *Islamisch-christliche Beziehungen: Geschichtliche Streifzüge* (1992), *Islam et Occident face à face: Regards de l'histoire des religions* (1998), and *Islam et sciences des religions: Huit leçons au Collège de France* (1998).

Steven M. Wasserstrom studied at the University of Toronto where he received his Ph.D. in 1986 with a thesis on Muslim-Jewish relations in the medieval period. At present he is associate professor of Judaic studies at Reed College in Portland, Oregon. He has an award-winning book, *Between Muslim and Jew: The Problem of Symbiosis under Early Islam* (1995). He is presently completing *Religion after Religion: Gershom Scholem, Mircea Eliade and Henry Corbin at Eranos.*

I

MUSLIM STUDIES OF OTHER RELIGIONS

I

The Early Period

610–650

JACQUES WAARDENBURG

The Qur'ān on Other Religions

The Qur'ānic view of other religions has attracted increasing interest in recent years. It has been the subject of a number of publications by Muslims and non-Muslims, theologians and scholars of religions, philologists and historians—some favoring interreligious relations, others expressing reservations about them. Since the Qur'ān is the founding Scripture of Islam and because Qur'ānic verses (*āyāt*) are considered Words of God, knowing what the Qur'ān says about other religions and understanding what is meant by these passages is indispensable if one wants to grasp the relations between Muslims and non-Muslims. Throughout Islamic history Muslim exegetes have paid attention to this problem, sometimes showing much ingenuity in discussing it.

Our approach is of a historical nature. We are only concerned here with the texts' literal meaning and the historical context within which they arose, or, as Muslims put it, within which they were revealed. Our basic hypotheses are, first, that this context was largely constituted by the various kinds of interaction which Muhammad had with other believers and, second, that this interaction falls into three successive phases—at the beginning with the polytheists in Mecca, then with the Jews in Medina, and finally with the Christians in northwestern Arabia. Other scholars as well, whether Muslim or not, have adopted a similar historical approach but we hope to contribute something new.

When using Qur'ānic texts as sources for our investigation we do not discuss questions such as whether the Qur'ān is Revelation, or in what sense it is Revelation. We take the texts seriously as they are, but we do not feel called upon to discuss questions that are basically of a theological nature. While respecting the Muslim faith, we address ourselves as a researcher to other researchers, on the level of historical scholarship. We hope, however, that this approach will encourage further studies of the Qur'ānic texts and their meaning, as far as attitudes to other believers are concerned. We also trust that such Qur'ānic studies will not preclude similar investigations, based on historical method and evidence, of the ways in which the other believers have formulated their own beliefs and practices themselves.

A number of Qur'ānic verses reflect the intense discussions and debates which Muhammad had in Mecca and Medina. He had these discussions both with Arabs who clung to their religious and cultural traditions, which Muslim authors characterized as "ignorance" (*jāhiliyya*), and with Jewish and Christian Arabs, whom the Qur'ān characterizes as "People of the Book" (*ahl al-kitāb*). Much attention has been paid to the nature of pre-Islamic beliefs and practices in Arabia, to the origin and history of the Jews living in Arabia in Muhammad's lifetime, and to the beliefs and practices of the Christians at the time. Much attention has also been given to the meanings of a number of Qurʾānic concepts and representations—their use, for instance, in pre-Islamic poetry and in Jewish, Christian, or other texts and representations current at the time. Certain elements of what have been vaguely called monotheistic oral traditions of Judeo-Christian origin and even Zoroastrian and Manichean elements have been traced in early Islam. We leave the intricate problem of historical influences here out of consideration.

Much less interest has been shown, however, in the discussions and debates which Muhammad carried on with pagan Arabs and with Jews and Christians. How did Muhammad perceive Judaism and Christianity? Which arguments did he use in order to convince pagan Arabs, Jews, and Christians of the correctness of his message and preaching and of the falsity of a great number of their religious beliefs and practices? What exactly did he want to refute and why? The Qurʾān contains much material on this "interreligious dialogue," not in the terminology of rational, theological thought but rather in the spontaneous utterances of an inspired prophet addressing people from various religious traditions and trying to convince them by means of arguments which continuously appeal to reason.

Polytheists

The battle which the prophet waged against the prevalent polytheism in Arabia of his time left its traces in the Qurʾān. The Qurʾān calls it *shirk* or *ishrāk*, meaning "associationism, assigning associates to Allāh," and the people concerned *mushrikūn*, meaning "associationists." They commit the worst sin possible in that they recognize *shurakāʾ* ("associates") side-by-side with Allāh (literally, "the God"). Throughout the Qurʾān there is a fundamental opposition between the *hanīf*, monotheist, on the one hand (and every Muslim is, by definition, necessarily a *hanīf*), and the *mushrik*, "associationist" or polytheist, on the other hand. In the debate between the *hanīf* Muhammad and the *mushrikūn* around him, particularly in Mecca, reasonable argumentation plays an important role. The Qurʾān describes a similar debate in earlier times between the *hanīf* Ibrāhīm (Abraham) and the surrounding *mushrikūn*, including his own father.

Attributing associates to God (the Arabic verb *ashraka*)[1] is the worst sin imaginable (*ithm ʿazīm*, S. 4:48). It is precisely the distinctive nature of God that he has no child, no associate, and does not need a protector (*walī*) from abasement (S. 17:111). Muhammad himself receives the strict order not to appeal to any other god than Allāh (S. 28:88), to turn away from associationists (S. 15:94), to have no doubts of the falsity of the gods to whom others pray in their idolatry (S. 11:109). He is forbidden to worship those to whom others pray outside of Allāh (S. 40:66–68).

God regularly sent warners and prophets to mankind so that believers would arise who would surrender to God and follow his laws. But, there were often downfalls when new believers or their descendants no longer followed the path of the true religion and no longer believed in God as the only God. People fell back into a state of ingratitude and unbelief (*kufr*), which resulted in a negation of the oneness and uniqueness of God. Such a *kufr* manifests itself in *shirk*: either explicitly as in the worship of idols, or implicitly as in the recognition of other, independent manifestations of the sacred apart from God, whether in the inner or outside world. Any religious surrender to anything other than God, or any religious attachment outside of God, is an offense to the true religion. Associating anything to God makes one's religion "impure," which goes against man's calling to make one's religion "pure" (*akhlasa al-dīn*, S. 98:4).

The very act of *ashraka* is attributed in the Qurʾān to *zann* (S. 10:67). *Zann* is a subjective opinion imbued with imagination, and hence uncertainty. It is the opposite of solid knowledge (*ʿilm*, S. 51:10–12) which is acquired by experience and reason, revelation and reflection. In the same way as *zann* causes *shirk*, man's *ahwāʾ* (desires leading to wrong imagination) cause his being to go astray (*dalāl*) from God and from true reality. The Qurʾān suggests that "associationism" has psychological roots: *shirk* is a consequence of *zann* and a cause of *dalāl* (S. 26:22–23, S. 22:12, S. 6:74). When someone commits the sin of *shirk*, he not only dishonors God but distorts and falsifies reality, committing, in effect, a religious and metaphysical falsehood.

The expression *al-mushrikūna* often occurs in the Qurʾān. On a social level, this word may have indicated the opponents of the new Muslim community and its leader; on a religious level, the word referred to those who had committed a deadly sin. The term, which consequently has both a sociopolitical and a religious meaning, does not necessarily point to a given group of individuals. As other Qurʾānic general concepts, *al-mushrikūna* conceptually embraces all those whom Muhammad saw as the fundamental antagonists of monotheism. It is the Qurʾānic understanding that those who commit the sin of *shirk* are unable to recognize the absolute oneness and uniqueness (*tawhīd*) of God.

Characteristic of such "associationists" is that in their sacrifices and worship they do not offer everything to God but they give a part of it to *shurakāʾ*, gods beside God. These gods do not create anything but they themselves have been created; they neither give life nor take it away nor do they have the capacity to resurrect life (S. 25:2), thus they have no useful purpose. Such *shurakāʾ* take the form of idols (*awthān, asnām,* S. 29:17) or of intercessors (*shufaʿāʾ*). People who accept such "masters" besides God say that they worship them with the hope that their status will be raised and that they will enter into a more immediate relationship with God (S. 39:3)[2] or because they ask them for help (S. 36:74). In a situation of crisis people may call to God but when the crisis is over, they once again address the *shurakāʾ* as well as God. The associationists consider the spirits (*jinn*) as associates of God (S. 37:158), whereas they are only his creatures. They also think that angels are divine beings, whereas, in reality, they are simply God's servants (S. 43:19). They say that God begat a child or children (*ittakhadha al-rahmān waladan*, S. 19:88, 21:26, 18:4), which is not true (S. 112:3). Characteristic of the "associationists" is also that they are divided into different religious groups (S. 30:31–32), as if there were some intrinsic connection between polytheism on the one hand and sectarianism on the other (S. 30:31–329).

The judgment on such polytheists (*mushrikūn*) is exceedingly negative and can be summarized as follows. At the end of time they will be under the power of Satan, and on Judgment Day those beings which the polytheists associated to God will abandon them (S. 6:94). When the *shurakāʾ* abandon the *mushrikūn*, who had put their confidence in them, the latter are lost (S. 2:166). When they pray to the *shurakāʾ*, even with the ironical encouragement of Allāh, there is no response. And when they declare that they had never been "associationists" (*mushrikūn*), the answer is clear: "They lie to themselves!" (S. 6:22–24). At the Last Judgment, the *shurakāʾ* themselves will testify against the polytheists who worshipped them (S. 19: 81, 82); they will declare themselves nonresponsible for the fact that the people worshipped them. Whether it was all a human illusion, a scheme organized by Satan or even the *shurakāʾ* themselves is not clarified. What is certain, however, is that the final reckoning is made before God and the polytheists, along with their *shurakāʾ* (S. 37:22–23, 21:98–99), will be sent to hell.

In the debate with the polytheists, the Qurʾān uses different types of arguments. The arguments of authority remind the polytheists that God is Lord of all creation and all beings and that the Day of Judgment will come (S. 18:102). The arguments of questioning, as put in the mouth of Ibrāhīm for instance, show that the polytheists cannot escape from their own self-made traps. Other arguments, often in parable form, are aimed at making the polytheists reconsider their position by reflecting on their unavoidable death and God's power at the moment of resurrection. Sometimes there is a complicated exchange of arguments on both sides as in S. 38:4–11 or S. 25:42 where the Meccans admit that Muhammad nearly succeeded in averting them from their gods! There are also arguments which put the polytheists before otherwise unsolvable questions, by means of a paradox or psychological unmasking, as in S. 25:43, "What do you think of someone who has made of his desire or wish his god?" Or, as stated in S. 23:91, 21:22, 13:16, a multiplicity of gods would lead to chaos in heaven as well as on earth. Beyond all these arguments and above all who discuss and debate, the last word is given to God on the Day of Judgment (S. 22:17). With subtlety, the Qurʾān admonishes the believers not to insult the *shurakāʾ* to whom the polytheists pray, since they could be tempted to abuse Allāh.

In terms of belief, the polytheists are guilty of the one unforgivable sin of *shirk* or *ishrāk*. They have to convert from this sin and recognize God as being one and unique. A continuous effort is made on the part of Muhammad to make the polytheists understand the *āyāt*, the "signs" of God contained in the Qurʾān, in nature and history. Furthermore, they are threatened with what will happen to them on the Day of Judgment.[3] In the end there will be a grandiose battle undertaken in the name of God, an ideological, political, and military battle to persuade and strike down this terrible enemy of Islam: not so much atheism but polytheism. Only a radical conversion to the one and unique God will be able to tear them away from their ancient religious bonds. All arguments used presuppose that the polytheists are able to exercise their faculty of reason and that the existence of God is a given. For Muhammad the omnipotence of God and the powerlessness of everything outside of Him is evident, something to which his commands testify.

This may help clarify in part why the arguments used in the Qur'ān are all impregnated with a particular absolutist tone. Is it the real discussions carried out by Muhammad, or the inspired character of the recited texts, or rather the deeper level of human emotion expressed in a particular rhetoric which are at the root of this absolute tone which cannot but help move the hearer? As far as the precise historical reality of Muhammad's discussions and the precise identity of these *mushrikūn* are concerned, however, the Qur'ānic discourse does not give us much information. Yet, in certain cases, it is certain that *mushrikūn* means Christians, among others.

People of the Book

The second category of non-Muslims mentioned in the Qur'ān are the "People of the Book" *(ahl al-kitāb)* consisting specifically of Jews and Christians who, according to the Qur'ān, received revealed Scriptures just as the Muslims received the Qur'ān. Through Moses, the Jews received the *Tawrāt*; through Jesus, the Christians received the *Injīl*—both in exactly the same way as the Muslims, through Muhammad, received the *Qur'ān*. All three Scriptures, as brought by the three prophets, go back to an original heavenly Book (*kitāb* or *umm al-kitāb)*.[4] This Book was revealed in the past to Moses and Jesus whose followers constitute two religious communities called "People of the Book." We shall first look at the main judgments contained in the Qur'ān regarding the People of the Book in general, before going on to mention some specific arguments brought out against the Jews and Christians.

It is first of all stressed that the behavior of Muhammad and his community toward these people, as long as they are not malevolent, should be one of good faith. There should be discussions with these communities and both parties should witness their faith in the form of the revelation they have received, for it is the same God that is shared by the People of the Book (S. 29:45). The Muslims should attempt to come to an understanding with them regarding the worship of God, without association (*shirk)* and without looking at humans as masters instead of God. In the event that the People of the Book should turn away, the Muslims should witness that one has to abandon oneself to God (S. 3:57). Both the People of the Book and the polytheists should be called upon to accept the divine message of submission to God (*islām*) so that even if people turn away, the message still reaches them (S. 3:19). On the other hand, there are texts saying that the faithful should not take Jews and Christians as friends (S. 5:56) or put their trust in those people outside of their own community (S. 3:114). S. 8:29 even goes so far as to say that those People of the Book who do not believe or act according to their religion do not belong to the true religion and should be fought against until they are subjected and forced to pay tribute (S. 9:29). This verse occurs in a part of the Qur'ān which is dated at the end of Muhammad's prophetical activity, a short time before his death.

The People of the Book are called upon to accept the new Revelation, so that the questions on which they disagree among themselves will be decided (S. 3:22). Why do the People of the Book who already possess knowledge of Revelation not accept the new Revelation (S. 2:83)? The answer is simple: because the present Revelation brings to light their opposition and unbelief (S. 5:72). Muhammad came so that the People of the Book would not be able to say that a messenger or warner had not been sent to them. Subsequently, the People of the Book are called upon to live and act according to the prescriptions outlined in the new Revelation.

Three texts do not restrict the People of the Book to Jews and Christians but also add the Sabians and in one case the Zoroastrians, too. If the Jews, Christians, and Sabians believe in God and if what they do is correct, they will be rewarded on the Day of Judgment (S. 2:59, 5:73). S. 22:17 adds to these three communities of the People of the Book the Zoroastrians (*majūs*): on the day of Resurrection God will distinguish between three groups and decide accordingly. These groups are the faithful (Muslims), the People of the Book (Jews, Christians, Sabians, and Zoroastrians), and the polytheists. In other words, all except the pagan Arabs can be rewarded on the Last Day if they have been faithful to God and have acted correctly. The solution for the problem of different kinds of faith in God is thus seen to be eschatological, at the end of time.

Jews and Christians are both reproached with claiming exclusive access to Paradise and therefore quarreling with one another; the final truth will not manifest itself until the Day of Judgment however, that is, eschatologically. In S. 2:114–115 mention is made of the fact that Jews and Christians exert pressure on Muhammad to join them: they do not recognize Muhammad's authentic prophetical inspiration. In response to this observation, it is added that those people who read their own Scripture diligently will certainly believe in the Qur'ānic revelation.

S. 2:129–135 describes how the new religious community obtains its independence from Jews and Christians by referring to the pure monotheistic religion of Ibrāhīm; the claim of the People of the Book that Ibrāhīm and his descendants would have been Jews or Christians themselves is refuted. Ibrāhīm was neither Jew nor Christian but rather a monotheist (*hanīf*) who had given himself to God (*muslim*). Ibrāhīm is highly valued in the Qur'ān as the true monotheistic patriarch whose descendants, not only the faithful (Muslims) but also the Jews and Christians, should recognize Ibrāhīm as true monotheist (*hanīf*) and each other as his spiritual descendants. Seen from this perspective, the Qur'ān calls on Jews and Christians to put their faith anew in God, to submit themselves to the teachings of their own Scriptures and to return to the pure, monotheistic religion of Ibrāhīm the *hanīf* which now takes shape among the faithful (Muslims).

God's alliance with the children of Israel and with the Christians is highly estimated; unfortunately both Jews and Christians have neglected the obligations implied in the alliance. The fact that the People of the Book have kept part of their Scriptures hidden from themselves necessitated the mission of Muhammad. The claim of Jews and Christians to be God's chosen people is rejected with rational arguments (S. 5:15–22).

The long passage of S. 9:29–35, which dates from the end of Muhammad's activity, calls Muslims to fight the People of the Book and submit them to Muslim rule. S. 9:30 reproaches the Jews and Christians for saying so shamelessly that a human being, ʿUzair by the Jews and Jesus by the Christians, would have been a son of God; in this respect the People of the Book are like the polytheists and are to be cursed. Moreover, they have taken their religious leaders to be masters instead of God, therefore sinning against the command to serve only the one and unique God (S. 9:31). In the next verse (32) the People of the Book are said to want to block God's salvation which was sent to humanity. In this passage the true religion is clearly defined as the community of faithful Muslims. This community is not only independent of the existing older communities (compare S. 2:129) but is also described as superior to all other religious communities. This religious superiority can translate itself into political superiority, that is authority, as well, which implies subjection and humiliation of these other communities. It is added in verse 34 that many of the religious leaders of the People of the Book take material advantage of their people and keep them from following the will of God. However, their punishment is inevitable.

The previous Scriptures are repeatedly declared to have been sent by God (S. 6:92, 2:91, 95, 3:2,75, etc.). Consequently, S. 10:94 proposes to consult the People of the Book to take away their possible doubts concerning Muhammad's mission and revelation. In S. 29:45 the recognition by Muslims of the previous Scriptures is seen to be an excellent starting-point for discussion with the People of the Book. It is assumed that Muhammad's prophethood was previously announced in special *aʿlām* (announcement) texts, both in the *Tawrāt* of Moses and the *Injīl* of Jesus (S. 7:156). In any case, possession of Scripture carries an extremely positive religious value in the Qur'ān. It is perhaps not superfluous to say that many of the texts addressed to the People of the Book are in fact addressed specifically to the Jews whereas only a few of them are meant specifically for the Christians. Like the category of the *mushrikūn*, the category of the *ahl al-kitāb* covers various concrete groups that are not always identifiable with precision. We shall now briefly review the main arguments against the two specific groups of Jews and Christians as they appear in the Qur'ān.

The Jews

When referring to the Jewish community, the Qur'ān uses two different terms: the children of Israel (*banū isrāʾīl*) standing for the ancient Israelites, and the Jews (*yahūd*) standing for the Jewish people at the time of Jesus and in particular those contemporaries of Muhammad living in Medina.

Various positive appreciations of the Jewish community and their Scripture brought by Moses are contained within the Qur'ān. Those People of the Book who are faithful will be rewarded on the Day of Judgment (S. 2:59, 5:73), as sharply distinguished from the *mushrikūn* (S. 22:17). Some People of the Book recognize truth in the Qur'ān saying, "We were already abandoning ourselves to God (*muslim*) before the Qur'ān was there" (S. 28:52,53). Among the children of Israel there were not only quarreling groups (S. 32:25, etc.); there were also believers among them (3:106, etc.). There exists among the Jews a pious community of upright men and women (S. 3:109–110) as there was also a good community among the people of Moses (S. 7:159). Special mention is made of a group with a moderate standpoint (S. 5:70b).

The Jews have been divided into different communities (S. 7:167). Some of them can be trusted in business where others cannot (S. 3:68). They are longing for the goods of this world rather than for eternal life (S. 7:168); more than other people they tend to cling to this life (S. 2:90); they have murdered their prophets (S. 3:177) and have a long register of sins (S. 2:79, etc.).

In his grace, God, through Moses, gave the children of Israel their Scripture and saved them from Pharaoh (S. 6:155, 7:101–133). He declared them a chosen people (S. 44:31). Jesus was sent to them and fulfilled the *Tawrāt* (S. 3:44a), bringing the *Injīl* into existence (S. 5:50) and announcing the coming of a prophet after him (S. 61:6). It is expressly stated that the God of the People of the Book and of the faithful Muslims is the same (S. 29:45). No harm can come to pass which has not already been foretold in the Heavenly Book which existed before creation itself (S. 57:22).

In response to these acts of grace, however, the children of Israel were disobedient to God and committed many sins, most notably the worshipping of the golden calf (S. 2:86–87). They turned away from God, but He had mercy on them nevertheless (S. 2:61). Only a small group among them kept the prescriptions to which they had bound themselves before God (S. 2:77).

Now God sends a new revelation which confirms the *Tawrāt* and both *Tawrāt* and *Injīl* (S. 46:11, etc.). From this new revelation the children of Israel can learn most from to solve their disagreements with one another (S. 27:78). The Qur'ān also gives information about the fire of hell, so that the People of the Book will not doubt any longer (S. 74:31).

However, the Jews do not accept the new revelation; their behavior toward God is reprehensible. They do not believe in God's signs (S. 63, 93); they even barter them away (S. 5:48). The Jews have little faith (S. 2:82); part of them reject the Scripture sent by God (S. 2:95). They quarrel among themselves even after having received the Scripture and clear proofs (S. 2:209). They lie to God (S. 4:53) and are also hostile toward God, his prophets, and angels (S. 5:91–92). However, they still claim to be friends of God (S. 62:6), his sons, and also his chosen ones (S. 5:21). As a consequence, God sends his punishment: his wrath was sent against them (S. 58:15), He cursed them and hardened their hearts (S. 5:16).

The Jews obscured the truth of their Scripture through lies and kept it a secret (S. 3:64, 2:141), so that a new prophet had to come in order to clarify to them their act of secrecy (S. 5:18). They did not act according to the prescriptions of their Scripture (S. 2:79, 5:70). They even claim that a text which they fabricated themselves is revelation (S. 2:73). They changed the text of their Scripture so that people would think that words that were their own originated in Scripture; claiming that it came from God whereas in reality it only came from them. They therefore willingly tell a falsehood against God (S. 3:72). They behave badly toward Muhammad (S. 3:183), they listen to lies and tell lies themselves (S. 5:45); they do not want the Lord to reveal anything to the Muslim community that is holy to themselves (S. 2:99). Some of them would like to mislead the faithful Muslims, but it is in fact they themselves who are deceived without being conscious of the fact (S. 3:62, 65–66).

The Christians

Like Moses, Jesus is highly praised as a prophet.[5] Like the Jews, the Christians are disobedient to their alliance with God. However, the tone of accusation in the Qur'ān toward the Christians is much milder than that addressed to the Jews, and the conflict between Muhammad and the Christians was certainly not nearly as intense as his conflict with the Jews.

Leaving aside the texts related to Jesus (*al-masīh*) which consider him as an eminent prophet, there are a number of texts in which Christians are evaluated positively. S. 57:27 mentions certain positive character traits, in particular among those who have chosen the religious life; living as monks was not prescribed by God, however, and their choice remains their own responsibility. Other positive judgments are given in S. 9:113 where it may also concern monotheistic piety of the *hanīf* type; S. 24:36–37, S. 3:109–111, and S. 28: 52–55 may refer to Christian but could also refer to Jewish groups.

On the other hand, the Christians are reproached having forgotten their spiritual rules and prescriptions and hence living in animosity with one another. Such conflicts have been aroused by God as a punishment, and they will continue until the Day of

Resurrection when an account will be made of their deeds (S. 5:17). All of this implies that the Christians have broken their alliance with God. S. 5:19 and S. 5:76 reject the idea that God is a human being, the son of Mary, Jesus, *al-masīh*; they state that God's omnipotence puts Jesus above all human beings.

Jesus was a created being (S. 3:52) and a servant of God (S. 43:59). The Jews tried to kill Jesus with their plan of crucifixion but unsuccessfully (S. 4: 152–157, S. 3:48). Furthermore, the Qur'ān proclaims itself to be against the following theses ascribed to Christianity: that God is one of three (S. 5:77, S. 4:169), that Jesus and his mother Mary are gods (S. 5:116), that the Christians give "associates" to God (S. 9:31, 17:111, 19:36, 23:93, 25:2), that *al-masīh* is the son of God (S. 9:30), and that God has a son, a child, or children (S. 19:36 and 4:169; other similar verses are directed primarily to pagan Arabs holding such beliefs).

In conclusion, we can say along with W. M. Watt[6] that the Qur'ān rejects the idea of:

- Jesus and Mary as gods (S. 5:116–120)
- man as a "son" of God (S. 19:36)
- tritheism (S. 5:77, 4:169)
- complete identity between Jesus and God (S. 5:19, 76)
- *al-masīh* being independent of God (S.9:30, 5:116)

In summary, we can say that the Qur'ān directs reproaches at the Christians but explicitly or implicitly recognizes positive religious values in them. As in the case of the texts on the Jews, in the case of the texts on the Christians there is less judgmental concern of the two religions of Judaism and Christianity in their assumed "pure" state since they are recognized to have a prophetic origin. The judgments concern rather what the Jews and Christians have made of the religions given to them; that is, their behavior and beliefs. Asking for the Qur'ānic view of the Christian religion, one only finds texts which refute certain doctrines[7] concerning the person of Jesus, the nature of God, and God's relationship to Jesus. As soon as the Christians, according to Muhammad, erred, the latter felt obliged to protest.

One of the most interesting aspects of the Qur'ānic texts concerning Muhammad's debates with the Jews and Christians[8] seems to be the fact that during those debates Islam had not yet crystallized into a complete and "fulfilled" religion. During the Qur'ānic period, prophetic revelations made up the core of the religion; specific doctrinal positions began to take form only later. Consequently, the Qur'ānic texts concerning Jews and Christians are to be seen first as a response to—and a protest against—their ways of life and their pretensions as they existed during Muhammad's lifetime.

It may legitimately be asked whether the development of the Qur'ānic concept of Islam as a religion is not somehow linked to the development of the Qur'ānic concepts of Jews and Christians and their religions. This seems at least plausible when taking into account the Qur'ānic texts concerning Muhammad's discussions and debates with the Jews and Christians. In any case, the definitive Qur'ānic judgment of Jews and Christians appears to be eschatologically suspended. It is simply left to God's final judgment at the end of history.

Muhammad and Other Believers

As in the other sections of Part I, the treatment of relevant texts is followed—or sometimes preceded—by a survey of the historical relationships between the Muslims and the religious community concerned. Consequently, after having dealt with the Qur'ānic view of other religions, we shall briefly describe the relations which Muhammad, the prophet and founder of the Muslim community, entertained with other religious communities, as far as this can be historically known.

In the following pages, we shall be concerned with the historical periods in which Muhammad interacted with the polytheists in Mecca, the Jews in Medina, and the Christians in northwestern Arabia, in that order. These interactions constitute the historical context of the Qur'ānic texts already treated. They are, as Muslims would put it, the *asbāb al-nuzūl* (occasions of revelation) of the *āyāt* about polytheists, Jews, and Christians. There were other moments as well, as in the case of Muhammad's encounter with a delegation of Christians from Najrān in southwestern Arabia, but they are not treated here.

Our approach, a purely historical one, has been adopted by a number of historians, whether or not Muslim. We hope to be able to offer something new, however. As a matter of fact, we shall attempt to describe certain aspects of the historical development of Islam during Muhammad's lifetime that are closely connected with the encounters of the growing Muslim community with other religious communities. As a consequence, we must also deal with some aspects of the biography of Muhammad.

For this kind of historical research it is not relevant to discuss questions such as the prophethood of Muhammad or the relation between the religious and sociopolitical aspects of his action. We simply inquire about what happened historically, as far as it can be ascertained. While respecting Muslim perceptions of Muhammad, we study him here as a mature, responsible, and gifted person who was aware of the choices he had to make, not as a passive being simply subject to the laws and customs of his time. We submit our findings for further scholarly discussion and hope that this approach can contribute to further historical research into the many encounters that have taken place between Muslim and other communities. In such research we also have to bear in mind the views which both parties had of each other and themselves in given situations.

In the previous pages we briefly summarized the main ideas and judgments contained in the Qur'ān regarding polytheists and the People of the Book. It is now time to put these ideas and judgments in the historical context of the successive relationships which Muhammad had with Meccan polytheists, Jews in Medina, and Christians in northwestern Arabia.[9] On closer observation, these relationships also represent the principal phases of the development of Islam, starting as a prophetic message and evolving into a historical religion. The key to this development seems to have been the interaction which took place between the prophetic leader with his community on the one hand and existing religious communities on the other. The encounter between Muhammad and the religious beliefs and practices surrounding him is particularly relevant for the growth of Muhammad's prophetical preaching and acting, his founding of a new community, and the institutionalization of Islam as a historical religion. This seems to have taken place through the development of Islam as a religion in three phases: from a movement of religious purification to a movement of reform and, finally, to a "completed" religion shortly before Muhammad's death in 632 C.E.[10]

Muhammad and the Polytheists in Mecca

The fact that Muhammad started preaching a new religious message in Mecca implies that he had explicitly set himself apart from the world, with its assumptions and rules, with which he was familiar. His message was primarily directed at the *mushrikūn* (polytheists), that is to say specifically the Meccans whom he identified as such. The ensuing interaction with the Meccan milieu, apart from the political ramifications which we leave aside, was extremely important for the development of Islam.

As W. Montgomery Watt demonstrated, Allāh was a god recognized by the Mecccans as *rabb al-bayt*, lord of the city, but not as the only divine being.[11] But to Muhammad, Allāh became *rabb al-ʿālamīn*, a universal god, benevolent creator, sustainer and judge, outside of whom nothing divine could exist. This message, together with that of the coming resurrection, judgment, and afterlife, led to violent debates between Muhammad and the Meccans. He reproached them for not being able or willing to recognize God and his oneness and to draw the consequences of that. Instead of powers such as fate and time, or fertility, Muhammad taught that it was this almighty *al-ilāh* (Allāh) who decided on the major determinants of life. Over and against the prevailing confidence in a good life on earth and material well-being during that life, Muhammad preached man's status as a creature and his dependence on his Creator. He preached a morality of divine commands instead of tribal tradition, the sanction of eschatological reward and punishment instead of tribal honor, religion rather than tribal and other factional interests as a basis for human solidarity. These notions of divine commands, a judgment at the end of time, and one religious community of all the faithful were most probably new to the Meccans, or if certain ideas and practices from other religions may have been half-known at the time, they were now being presented in a new, "Arabicized," form. As a result, the new religious movement was launched.

In response to disbelief in his prophethood, Muhammad elaborated a more historical dimension for his activity by giving, in an almost mythical fashion, accounts of stories of prophets of the past. These stories contained both Arabic elements like the punishment stories (*mathānī*) and figures from the patriarchal period of the Judeo-Christian tradition. Such prophets of the past in whose line Muhammad stood could serve as an argumentative tool in sermons and debates and they also had the potential to link the Arab prophet with a patriarchal past.

The religious basis of the new movement, and in particular prophetic authenticity and authority, were elaborated in various terms, the most important being that Muhammad's recitations (*qur'āns*) were revelations given through an angel. They had a mysterious origin, being signs or symbols (*āyāt*) of something hidden (*ghayb*) beyond the visible world.

There are many aspects to this particular belief in revelation,[12] but the most important one, as far as our subject is concerned, is that, through it, Muhammad assumed prophetic authority not only in his words, like the typical Old Testament prophets, but also in his deeds, like Moses and the patriarchs. His claim, moreover, that his message was basically the same as that of the previous prophets, not only gave his activity a supplementary charismatic quality, but it also provided a link with the Judeo-Christian religious tradition, and it gave his message a certain universality. Those who joined the movement entered the community of believers of the one universal monotheistic religion in its Arab branch. The Arabs thus had their own revelation in Arabic, and they had their "heavenly" religion just as the Jews and Christians had theirs.

The refusal of the majority of the Meccans and their leaders to drop their religious tradition and abjure other divine powers alongside of Allāh, whose veneration was part of their tradition, led to intense debates with the prophet who was unrelenting on the subject. He rejected any compromise, arrived at a position of absolute monotheism and separated the movement of the believers (*mu'minūn*) rigorously from all polytheists (*mushrikūn*) with their basic sin of *shirk* or *ishrāk* from which society had to be purified. At this significant point the earlier openness and receptivity on the part of the prophet stopped and the demand of purification from—and fight against—idolatry in all its forms became one of the striking features of the Islamic religion. Paradoxically enough, the Meccan opposition caused the new religion—which stressed the need for repentance with a view of the oncoming Judgment, the fight for the oneness of God as a necessary belief to be held in his honor—to grow. The opposition also forced Muhammad to give the necessary theological, historical, and social weight to the message he conveyed.

When Mecca finally opened its doors to Muhammad and Islam in 630 C.E./8 A.H., a number of ancient Arab practices and ideas were retained, provided they did not constitute *shirk*. The transfer of certain traditional practices, such as the *hajj*, even though with a change of meaning, was the last important contribution which the ancient Meccan religion made, before its demise, to the formation of Islam. In various ways, the interaction between Muhammad and the polytheists in Mecca clearly and decisively shaped the new religion.[13]

Muhammad and the Jews in Medina

Although hardly any Jews appear to have lived permanently in Mecca itself, Jewish religious ideas and practices were certainly not unknown and a number of elements of what may be called Jewish-Christian oral traditions must have reached Muhammad both before and after the beginning of his prophetic activity.[14] He must have known the notion of a universal religion with the worship of one single God, the existence of sacred scriptures in languages other than Arabic, the idea that such scriptures were based on revelation and that revelations were transmitted by prophets. Already in the early sūras we find eschatological representations, certain cult practices, and references to biblical stories containing Judaic elements which may have reached Muhammad directly or via Christian channels. Given that the prophet was convinced that his inspirations had the same origin as those of the prophets before him, there was no harm in looking for further information as is clearly stated in S. 25:4–6 and S. 16:103. As Watt has observed,[15] Muhammad, facing particular problems, gave a definitive Arabian formulation to certain truths held in the Judeo-Christian tradition, insofar as he had had an immediate and original experience of such truths himself. With their new formulation ancient truths obtained a new, Arabian meaning within the framework of Muhammad's overall message which he conveyed to the Arabs in both word and deed.[16]

The fundamental notions of the continuity of revelation and the unity of all revelations—and the religions resulting from them—had also practical implications. They made it possible and legitimate for Muhammad to adjust the cultic regulations of the Muslim community, in certain respects, to Jewish ones when the prospect of going to Yathrib (Medina) presented itself. One could speak of an "ecumenical" effort in matters of ritual: Friday (the preparatory day for Shabbāt) became the day for public worship, Jerusalem became the *qibla* of prayer, the fast of ʿAshūrā parallelled that of 10 Tishrī, and the midday *salāt* was added so that there would be three daily prayers in the Muslim as well as the Jewish community. Muslims obtained permission to eat the food of the People of the Book and to marry their women. Evidently, Muhammad hoped intensely that he would be recognized by the Jews in Medina as a prophet. His open attitude at the time should be seen, however, not simply as a result of tactical policy making; it was also the logical consequence of the universalist assumptions underlying his own religious message. We have to see Muhammad's appeal to the Jews to reconcile themselves with the Muslims on the basis of their common faith in one God in a similar light.[17]

It was through his contact with Medinan Jews, some of whom converted, that Muhammad received further information about Judaism. Apparently, Muhammad had held that the Jews and Christians of his time were two offshoots from the ancient Banū Isrā'īl. He learned now, for instance, that the Jews had their *Tawrāt* and the Christians their *Injīl*, that Mūsā had been the founder of Judaism and had preceded ʿĪsā who, as the last prophet, came from the Jews, and that Ibrāhīm had preceded both of them. In this way he learned more about Judaism and certainly became aware of the importance which a particular religious tradition and history holds to those who keep to it.

The Jews, however, did not cooperate in the way Muhammad had hoped for, and they undermined his authority by denying the divine origin of his revelations and consequently the authenticity of his prophethood. This was possible precisely because Muhammad—out of prophetic conviction but without empirical evidence—held that his own revelation was in essence identical with the revelation held by the Jews. When the latter denied this, Muhammad had to react. He made some changes in ritual practice away from that of Judaism and started to see Ibrāhīm as his great example and to fashion Islamic monotheism according to his understanding of Ibrāhīm's monotheism. His way of incorporating elements of Ibrāhīm, known in Mecca as the builder of the Kaʿba, clearly made Islam more acceptable to the Arabs while retaining a universal, monotheistic framework. The results, in polemic and action, of the confrontation between the Jewish claim to be the chosen people and Muhammad's claim to be the chosen prophet are well known and need not be elaborated here.

Muhammad's interaction with the Jewish tribes in Medina had profound consequences for the further development of Islam. Besides the halakic-biblical elements already absorbed earlier in Mecca, we have seen that certain Jewish ritual regulations provided a model for the ritual innovations made by Muhammad in the period of assimilation which started shortly before the Hijra. However, in the period of Jewish opposition, starting about a year and a half after the Hijra, this model was abandoned. Muhammad's negative experience with the Jews caused him to be disillusioned in his assumption of the unity of the monotheistic religions, at least on an empirical level. Consequently, he seems to have retained the idea of the unity of revelations rather than that of religions. The Jews and the Christians developed their religions in ways contrary to the revelations given to Moses and Jesus which were fundamentally identical. This was the context in which the accusation was developed that the Jews and the Christians had corrupted the Scriptures which Moses and Jesus had received by way of revelation.[18] As a result, Muhammad could now legitimately distance himself from the Jews of Medina and their religion. He then brought together all the arguments that could be used to support this separation.

Apart from what Muhammad learned from Judaism and partly incorporated into the new religious movement, his experience with the Jews certainly reinforced his prophetic self-consciousness. It forced him to reconsider his own position, the meaning of his preaching and action, and the significance of the new movement, in terms not only of the past but also of the future. He now moved toward completely identifying the *hanīfiyya* with the religion of Ibrāhīm, that is to say the *millat Ibrāhīm*. Through the figure of Ismāʿīl and the idea of the *millat Ibrāhīm*, the notion of a chosen people and its historical role was now as it were transferred and applied to the Arabs and to the Muslim community at large.[19]

It may have been precisely his encounter with the particularity of Judaism that stimulated Muhammad's elaboration of—and stress on—the universality of his message and religion, with the movement resulting from it. Significantly, the new religious movement took the name of "Hanīfiyya," stressing monotheism, before becoming known as "Islam," stressing surrender to God. Both names imply universality. Just as the Meccans' resistance had induced a strict monotheistic universalistic stance, so the Jewish opposition in Medina resulted in a growing universalization of the nascent religion.

Muhammad and the Christians in Northwestern Arabia

Alongside the notion of one almighty God and a number of biblical stories, certain beliefs and practices seem to have been especially strong among the Christians in Mecca where Muhammad grew up and along the caravan routes where he traveled. They are the idea of Resurrection and the Day of Judgment, representations of the Hereafter, certain ethical and ascetic values, and practices of worship. These elements appear in the Qur'ān already in the first two Meccan periods, together with references to patriarchal figures, apocryphal stories of Mary and Jesus, and the notion of angels and other spiritual beings. As in the case of Judaism, elements obtained from Christian communities could be assimilated into Islam on the assumption of the continuity of revelation and the unity of the revelations and the religions resulting from them.[20]

Muhammad had probably already been making open or implied statements hostile to certain Christian beliefs in the Meccan period, when he felt that true monotheism, to which he was passionately attached, was violated. But his attitude in Mecca on the whole was open and favorable with regard to the devotional attitudes and moral virtues which struck him among the Christians, as expressed for example in S. 57:27 and 5:82–84. Before the *hijra*, adherents of the community were sent to Christian Ethiopia for security reasons and apparently he had made approaches to Christian tribes before deciding to go to Yathrib (Medina). In the first Medinan years, during his conflict with the Jews, Muhammad compared the Christians most favorably with the Jews and used stories about ʿĪsā and the way he had been treated as part of what may be called an ideological attack on the Jews. But after his victory, first over the Jews and then over the Meccans in 630 C.E./8. H., there was a remarkable change in his attitude toward the Christians and Christianity which is clear in the well-known passage (S. 9:29–33) to wage war against them. How is this change to be explained historically?

A Historical Explanation

A first explanation is that Muhammad, when expanding to the north, was confronted with tribes that were mostly Christian and linked to what may be called the Byzantine defense system. According to this view, Muhammad's attack on Christianity was primarily of a political nature, so as to detach these tribes from their Christian overlords by making an ideological attack on their religion as part of a full-fledged war. It is questionable, however, whether there might not have been better political or other means available to win these tribes over to the prophet's side, rather than attacking their religion, which was likely to enhance their resistance. Thus we have to look for another explanation, without denying the fact that Muhammad made political use of Islam in his struggle against the Christian tribes.

A historical explanation of the change in Muhammad's attitude has to take into account certain Qur'ānic data. One notable aspect of the Qur'ānic texts directed against the Christians and Christianity is their doctrinal interest, a feature that was scarcely present in Muhammad's refutation of the polytheists and the Jews. Another particularity is that certain Christian doctrines are mentioned and subsequently refuted, whereas other doctrines are not mentioned at all. Why would Muhammad have been so badly informed about Christianity?[21] A third striking fact is that, contrary to the Qur'ānic texts directed against the polytheists and Jews, which seem to correspond with real debates in which Muhammad used any arguments he could find within the arsenal of beliefs of the other party, the Qur'ānic texts against the Christians are rather incidental and give the impression of someone shouting at a distant enemy rather than being involved in lengthy debates.

It would indeed seem that the new attitude taken by the prophet against Christians was due to several historical factors. Muhammad's disillusionment with the idea of the unity of the monotheistic religions, to which his experience with the Jews in Medina testified, certainly played a role as did his new understanding and conceptualization of Islam as an expression and elaboration of the *millat Ibrāhīm*. The old name of the movement, the *hanīfiyya*, stressing monotheism, suggests not only a religious purification movement against polytheism but also somewhat of a reform movement with regard to the *ahl al-kitāb*. Once this monotheistic religious reform movement had become established, following the victories over the Jews and the Meccans, Muhammad gave new attention to the Christians. When he attacked what he held to be the false doctrines of Christianity, it was not because he had studied that religion, but simply because he was struck by those doctrines held by the Christians which he saw to be contrary to the *hanīfiyya*, the religion of Ibrāhīm (*millat Ibrāhīm*). Over and against Christianity, he then qualified Islam as the "religion of truth" or "true religion" (*dīn al-haqq*, S. 9:29) and further institutionalized it.

In Medina, Muhammad had the opportunity to get to know the Jews in the area just as he had known the Meccans since his childhood. We must assume that he was less familiar with the life of the Christians with whom he probably had not lived. He rather saw their religion from a distance, first respecting and even admiring what he witnessed of their devotion and virtues, while later combatting what he saw as opposed to his own idea of religion.

Politically speaking, Muhammad could use his "true religion" (*dīn al-haqq*) against the Christians in times of warfare, just as he could very well use the Ibrāhīm story against the Jews in the period of political conflict. Our contention, however, is that Muhammad's view of the "religion of Ibrāhīm" (*millat Ibrāhīm*) and the "true religion" (*dīn al-haqq*) represents an autonomous religious structure which goes beyond and precedes the political use made of it.

The key to the problem of why the Qur'ān provides so little information about Christianity, and provides even information which does not represent orthodox Christianity, is that Muhammad was simply not interested in it. Muhammad was neither a scholar of religion nor a theologian but a prophetical reformer. As a reformer he only stressed those elements of the Christian religion that were objectionable in his view. These elements were mainly of a doctrinal nature. Just as he had been struck by the idolatry of the Meccans and hurt by the pretensions of the Jews, he was shocked by certain theological constructs of the Christians. In all three cases he directed his reform activities against the aspects he found to be objectionable and fashioned Islam—the primordial religion of mankind—as a protest against them.

We have now gathered the necessary elements to explain Muhammad's change of attitude in his dealings with Christian tribes in the north. The earlier treaty with Judhām suggests that the prophet was first prepared to enter into alliances with Christian tribes, as he had done from time to time with other tribes and groups without making specific religious demands. Then, precisely between the defeat at Mu'ta (Sept. 629) and the expedition to Tabūk (starting in Oct. 630) he changed his policy. He now concluded alliances only on the basis of acceptance of Islam. Christian tribes were now put before the dilemma of accepting or avoiding war. And in case they wanted to avoid war, they were either to accept Islam or to submit to the prophet's political authority with the payment of an annual tribute. And whereas the southern Christian tribes who refused to become Muslims, like the Christians of Najrān, avoided war by opting for a treaty settlement,[22] the northern Christian tribes who also refused to become Muslims opposed Muhammad's troops with armed resistance.

It is important to keep in mind that the command of war as contained in the Qur'ān (S. 9) was most certainly not directed at the Christian tribes for being Christians but rather against tribal enemies who happened to be Christians. In this war Muhammad seems to have used politically the idea of the "true religion" (*dīn al-haqq*) as a war ideology. In a similar way he had used politically the idea of the "religion of Ibrāhīm" (*millat Ibrāhīm*) as an ideology of combat against his Jewish opponents in Medina a few years earlier. It must be assumed, however, that the monotheistic idea of the Hanīfiyya, as well as the idea of the religion of Ibrāhīm and also the idea of Islam as the true religion, *had already been conceived by Muhammad before his actual political and military conflicts with the Jews and the Christians.* These ideas, however, found a political or "ideological" application here.

A Broader Explanation

The command of war against the Christians in S. 9:1–37 should be seen in a broader context. It is linked with a similar command against the Jews, with the argument that neither of them were true monotheists. It is also linked with the general command proclaimed in March 631 to wage war against all Arabs who had remained pagans. In other words, the unbelief of the *ahl al-kitāb* in the new *dīn* and their unwillingness to submit to it, is equated with the unbelief of the pagan Arabs. This is a logical conclusion from the standpoint of a purification and reform movement which has arrived at a stage in which it wants to impose a new social and political order.

Summarizing the argument, the new attitude taken by Muhammad toward Christian tribes is not specifically directed against the Christians. It is rather a consequence of his fundamental decision to impose the new *dīn* as a religious, social and political order on all Arabs in the Arabian peninsula and to subject them. Different as they were from the pagans, Christians and Jews were not forced to adopt Islam themselves. They were forced, however, to recognize the dominance of this *dīn* as the new overall base of society imposed by the present political authority and they had to pay tribute accordingly.[23]

The religious movement which had started in Mecca as a purification movement and which had become a religious reform movement and potential religion in Medina had now been completed or "fulfilled" as a full-fledged *dīn* in the true meaning of the word at the time. That is to say, a religion with a strong sociopolitical dimension, or the other way round, a sociopolitical order on a religious foundation.

Summing Up

When trying to sum up the consequences of the interaction between Muhammad and the Christians in Arabia at the time, the first thing we must point out is the fact that the Christians whom Muhammad was forced to deal with were not a community with which the prophet lived, unlike the polytheists in Mecca and the Jewish tribes in Medina. They were dispersed, they had different political allegiances, they belonged to different churches and sects, and they had differing forms of piety. In part as a consequence of this state of affairs, there was much less immediate interaction between Muhammad and the Christians than with the polytheists in Mecca or the Jews in Medina.

The interaction with the Christians must have had certain consequences for Islam. The creating, sustaining, and judging aspects of God were stressed and its eschatology was developed strongly. Certain devotional practices along with a particular ascetic life style could provide a model for the pious. It has been observed that such elements were so to say "in the air" in Mecca and in other places in Arabia at the time, as is witnessed by the presence of *hanīfs*. This fact may explain a certain openness on Muhammad's part toward the religious practice and way of life of the Christians. During the Medinan conflict Muhammad compared the Christians favorably with the Jews, notwithstanding the fact that neither group recognized him as a prophet. At that time the Christians were less closed off religiously and less dangerous politically than the Jews, and he was impressed by their virtuous life.

While appreciating the religious practice of the Christians, the prophet refuted current Christian doctrines of the relationship between God and Jesus and with man in general. This may be considered as a logical consequence both of the absolute monotheism which had characterized Islam from the beginning and of the way in which Islam had developed throughout the conflicts with the Meccan polytheists and the Medinan Jews. From a purification and reform movement it had become a complete *dīn*. The very resistance of the Christian Arab tribes in the north certainly accelerated the ideological use of the new religion against them. The refutation itself, however, not only of Christianity but of all that seemed to be contrary to strict monotheism, went beyond politics. It was, in fact, a logical consequence of the fact that the prophet had identified his *hanīfiyya* with the monotheistic *millat Ibrāhīm* and that he came to consider it as the *dīn al-haqq* in the full sense of the word.

In short, we would say that the new religious movement presented itself successively in at least three principal ways: as a religious purification movement of polytheism, as a religious reform movement of Judaism and Christianity, and as the proclamation of the true universal monotheistic religion in its Arabian form with a complete sociopolitical order. All three tenets, as well as the fact that the movement had now established itself with its own power base, affected Muhammad's attitude toward the Christians in the north. The resistance of the Jewish and Christian tribes may indeed have been a factor that contributed to the transformation of Islam from a reform movement to a new religion with universal claims, including that of being the true religion (*dīn al-haqq*), distinct from empirical Judaism and Christianity. Paradoxically, the Christianity of the northern Arab tribes may thus have indirectly contributed to the full development of the new religion among the Arabs and also to the sense of competition which this religion developed alongside the claims of Christianity.

Looking at the interaction of the new Islamic religious movement with the major religious communities with which Muhammad had to do, one is struck on first sight by the important role sociopolitical factors played. Yet on closer analysis, one has to recognize another dimension as well, which determined the significance and weight of these interactions. Muhammad simultaneously acted on earth and pronounced a series of *āyāt*, which were held to be revealed and consequently lent religious authority to at least certain of his worldly activities. In his deeds he behaved as a statesman; but he was a prophet as far as his revelatory experience was concerned. The implication for Muhammad's dealing with other religions is clear. *Every encounter with another community took place on two levels*: a settling of affairs on a sociopolitical level and an interaction of religious ideals and practices. This interaction was paralleled by particular inspirations or revelations of the prophet.

If Muhammad had not considered himself to be a prophet nor had been considered by his followers as such, he would have been obliged to deal with other religious communities on a mundane level only, without any religious dimension. It was precisely his recognized prophethood that made possible this functioning on two different levels, a sociopolitical and a religious-ideological one, at the same time.

In an analogous way, Islam's interactions after Muhammad's death with other religions, religious communities, and more or less secular societies would take place at the same time on both a worldly and a religious level.

NOTES

1. The verb *sharaka* with its various verbal forms occurs 70 times in the Qurʾān, the masdar *shirk* 5 times, the participles in the plural *shurakāʾ*, and *mushrikūna* 35 and 44 times, respectively. See, for what follows, Toshihiko Izutsu, *Ethico Religious Concepts in the Qurʾān* (Montreal: McGill University Press, 1966).

2. A specific explanation of the idolatry of the Banū Isrāʾīl is given in S. 7:134: When the latter arrived in a country where the people had *asnām*, they asked Moses to make them a god like the gods of the other peoples.

3. The supposed proximity of the Day of Judgment where the hypocrites and the idolaters will receive their punishment (S. 33:73; 48:6) from the One and only God gives to the Qurʾānic threats a particular seriousness. Especially in Muhammad's earlier preachings the eschatological dimension is very strong.

4. By *kitāb* is meant not a closed "book" but rather a document that functions as a contract and that ascertains and regulates relationships—in particular a juridical relationship—to God; the basic version of this contract is with God in heaven. The *kitāb* contains the fundamental rules which should be kept by the community and the individuals. See D. Künstlinger, "'Kitāb' and 'ahlu l-Kitābi' im Kuran," *Rocznik Orientalistyczny*, IV (1926), pp. 238–247, in particular p. 246.

5. This account is kept to a minimum. For detailed information, see Jane Damman McAuliffe, *Qurʾanic Christians. An Analysis of Classical and Modern Exegesis* (New York: Cambridge University Press, 1991). See also McAuliffe, "Christians in the Qurʾān and Tafsīr" (chapter 5 in this volume). "ʿIsā" by G. C. Anawati in the *Encyclopaedia of Islam*, new ed., vol. 4 (Leiden: E. J. Brill, 1978), pp. 81–86. See also, for instance, Geoffrey Parrinder, *Jesus in the Qurʾān* (New York: Barnes and Noble, 1965).

6. W. Montgomery Watt, "The Christianity criticized in the Qurʾān," *Muslim World*, vol. 57 (1967), pp. 197–201. Compare Watt, *Muhammad at Medina* (Oxford: Clarendon Press, 1956), pp. 317–320.

7. Whereas the Jews are criticized in the Qurʾān for certain kinds of behavior, the Christians are criticized because of certain doctrinal tenets. Compare Rudi Paret, *Mohammed und der Koran* (Stuttgart: Kohlhammer, 1957), p. 128.

8. Jacques Waardenburg, "Koranisches Religionsgespräch," in *Liber Amicorum: Studies in Honour of Professor Dr. C. J. Bleeker* (Leiden: E. J. Brill, 1969), pp. 208–253. Compare, for instance, Ernest Hamilton, "The Qurʾanic dialogue with Jews and Christians," *Chicago Theological Seminary Register*, vol. 80 (1990), pp. 24–38.

9. Muhammad's contacts with polytheists, Jews, and Christians elsewhere, inside or outside Arabia, are not considered here. Also his possible contacts with Zoroastrians and Manicheans are left out of consideration.

10. We are concerned here with situations of encounter and processes of interaction rather than with direct historical influences. Needless to say, the historical relations between different religious groups at the time were extremely complex and the textual evidence is scarce. There has been much discussion about the presence of Christianity in Arabia and the influence of Judeo-Christian traditions in the region at the time. See, for instance, Shlomo Pines, "Notes on Islam and on Arabic Christianity and Judaeo-Christianity," *Jerusalem Studies in Arabic and Islam*, vol. 4 (1984), pp. 135–152.

11. W. Montgomery Watt, *Muhammad at Mecca*, esp. pp. 23–29, and "Belief in a 'High God' in pre-Islamic Mecca," *Journal of Semitic Studies*, Vol. 16 (1971), pp. 35–40. Compare Watt, "The Qurʾān and belief in a 'High God'," *Der Islam*, vol. 56 (1979), pp. 205–211.

12. On Muhammad's idea of revelation, see for instance Tor Andrae, *Mohammed: The Man and His Faith* (New York, Harper Torchbook, 1960), pp. 94–113. This is a translation of the German edition, *Mohammed, sein Leben und Glaube* (Göttingen, 1932) which was itself translated from the Swedish original. Compare also Thomas O'Shaughnessy, s.j., *The Koranic Concept of the Word of God*, Biblica et Orientalia, vol. 11 (Rome: Pontificio Istituto Biblico, 1948).

13. Muhammad's interaction with Bedouin *mushrikūn* played a role too, but this has been left out of the account here.

14. A. J. Wensinck, *Muhammad and the Jews of Medina* (Berlin: Adiyok, 1982); original Dutch edition *Mohammed en de Joden te Medina* (Leiden: E. J. Brill, 1908; 2nd ed., 1928). Compare Barakat Ahmad, *Muhammad and the Jews: A Re-examination* (New Delhi: Vikas, 1979). See also Gordon Darnell Newby, *A History of the Jews of Arabia: From Ancient Times to Their Eclipse under Islam* (Columbia: University of South Carolina Press, 1988).

15. Watt, *Muhammad at Mecca*, pp. 80–85. The originality of the Qurʾān, formally speaking, is given precisely with its Arabic presentation of religious information within one corpus of texts.

16. In the history of religions, attention should be given to establishing both historical and social facts and to discerning the meaning of these facts in the given historical and social context for particular groups and persons who interpret them. During the acceptance of specific elements from elsewhere within a particular religious tradition, their meaning nearly always changes. Even the most direct factual influences or borrowings often imply considerable changes in meaning. All such changes of meaning need careful study. Islam may then turn out to be much more original than has been commonly assumed.

17. S. 29: 46: . . . *wa-ilāhunā wa-ilāhukum wāhidun* . . . The nature of this appeal, and its later interpretation, deserves further study, as well as the responses to it on the part of Jews and Christians then and in later times.

18. The accusation is well known in the history of polemics between monotheistic religions with scriptures. The Christians had already accused the Jews of falsifying or false reading of their scriptures with regard to messianic announcements. Mani had written down and illustrated his revelations himself in order to counter such accusations. Similarly, ʿUthmān ordered variant Qurʾān texts to be destroyed.

19. There has been much discussion about Muhammad and the figure of Abraham. See Youakim Moubarac, *Abraham dans le Coran* (Paris: Vrin, 1958).

20. Muhammad considered that his mission had been foretold in the previous revelations of the *Tawrāt* and the *Injīl*. During a journey Muhammad made as a young man, the Christian hermit Bahīrā is supposed to have recognized in him the expected and last prophet sent to the world. See, for example, Stephen Gero, "The legend of the monk Bahīrā, the cult of the Cross, and iconoclasm," in *La Syrie de Byzance à l'islam, VIIe–VIIIe Siècles*, Colloque 1990 (Damas: Institut Français de Damas, 1992), pp. 47–58.

21. The lapidary and biased information which is given in the Qurʾān about Christianity and Judaism is not just a scholarly problem. It has also caused concern among Christians and Jews, especially when they set out to pursue a dialogue with certain Muslims who, rather than inquiring about their actual beliefs and practices, believe that the Qurʾān gives all the knowledge that is needed about the beliefs and practices of Christianity and Judaism. Compare Note 5.

22. On the Christians of Najrān, see, for instance, Werner Schmucker, "Die christliche Minderheit von Najrān und die Problematik ihrer Beziehungen zum frühen Islam," in *Studien zum Minderheitenproblem im Islam*, vol. 1 (Bonn: Selbstverlag des Orientalischen Seminars der Universität Bonn, 1973), pp. 183–281. Peace treaties concluded by Muhammad—for instance, the Covenant of Medina, the Treaties with the Meccans at al-Hudaybīya, with the Jews of Khabar, with the Christians of Najrān, etc.—later served as models for treaties during and after the Arab conquest. Compare Wilson B. Bishai, "Negotiations and peace agreements between Muslims and non-Muslims in Islamic history," in *Medieval and Middle Eastern Studies in Honour of Aziz Suryal Atiya*, ed. Sami A. Hanna (Leiden: E. J. Brill, 1972), pp. 50–61.

23. Jews and Christians would later be expelled from the Arabian peninsula. See Seth Ward, "A fragment from an unknown work by al-Tabarī on the tradition 'Expel the Jews and Christians from the Arabian Peninsula/lands of Islam'," *Bulletin of the School of Oriental and African Studies*, vol. 53 (1990), pp. 407–420. Compare André Ferré, "Muhammad a-t-il exclu de l'Arabie les juifs et les chrétiens?," *Islamochristiana*, vol. 16 (1990), pp. 43–65.

2

The Medieval Period

650–1500

JACQUES WAARDENBURG

Muslim Interest in Other Religions

Not only among the ancient Greeks and Romans, with Herodotus, Plutarch, and Tacitus, but also in medieval Islamic civilization an interest existed in the religions of other civilizations and in religious history. In Europe it was, with a few exceptions such as Roger Bacon (1214–1294) and some missionary minds like Ramon Lull (ca. 1232–1316), only at the time of the Renaissance and of the voyages of discovery that people showed a real interest in the mythology and religions of the Ancients, and the beliefs and religious practices of the newly discovered countries and peoples. Given that medieval Muslim scholars showed an interest in foreign religions, what can we say about the "study of religions" in medieval Islamic civilization?[1]

There were many difficulties and limitations with regard to such a study at the time. First, there were technical difficulties. There was very little knowledge of languages other than Arabic and Persian. The lack of diffusion of foreign manuscripts—that is, texts from outside Islamic countries but also from the religious communities within the *dār al-islām*—added to the difficulties. There was a lack of knowledge of the history of civilizations before the outset of Islam and outside of the Islamic world. The way in which non-Muslims were perceived depended mainly on the restricted information that was available and on the limited direct contacts between Muslims and non-Muslims.

There were also limitations of a different sort which arose out of the predominant life and world views of the time. Such views were both "Islamic"—that is, nourished by the Qur᾿ān and the Sunna which were further elaborated intellectually—and "medieval" in a broad sense of the word. I would not like to propose that such views were imposed by Islam as such, but rather that they were due to medieval people's interpretation of Islam, which was variable depending on the milieu, time, and place. On the whole, any Muslim interest in non-Muslims, their ideas and practices, seems to have been practical rather than inquisitive. This outlook was culturally reinforced since Muslims at the time saw others from their own vantage point of being "lords of the two worlds" who had very little to learn from others.

Some Basic Distinctions

Let us recall some basic medieval Islamic distinctions regarding non-Muslims. They are derived from certain general views on man and the world which largely go back to Qur᾿ānic notions and ideas. I will refer to three of these distinctions.

First, the Qur᾿ān makes a sharp distinction between believers and unbelievers, Muslims and non-Muslims. There are at least three ways in which non-Muslims differ from Muslims: (1) they do not confess the one and unique God; (2) they do not recognize Muhammad as the conclusive and all-encompassing prophet; (3) they do not accept the Qurʾān as the definitive Revelation. All of these criteria are, of course, closely linked. Non-Muslims do not confess, recognize, and accept things which Muslims do; such a refusal of what is offered to them is considered to be "ingratitude" or unbelief (*kufr*).

Second, the Qurʾān distinguishes between two different categories of non-Muslims—namely Jews and Christians, Zoroastrians and Sabians on the one hand and polytheists (*mushrikūn*), with more primitive forms of religion, on the other. The criterion is theological: everything depends on the question of whether or not a community has received a revelation, what kind of a revelation it was, and what the community has done with the given revelation. Any revelation is transmitted by a prophet, who can either be a *nabī*, simply warning of the Judgment to come, or a *rasūl*, a messenger transmitting a recited revelation in the form of a sacred book (*kitāb*). His hearers will have to choose either to accept or to reject the book, to hear or not to hear the warning, or even to keep intact or to falsify (*tahrīf*) the revelation. Of those who received a revelation, the Jews and Christians in particular are called the "People of the Book" (*ahl al-kitāb*), possessing a revealed or "heavenly" religion. For a Muslim, all revelation was fulfilled in Muhammad as the "seal of the prophets" and his transmission of the Qurʾān is seen to be the last and definitive revelation for humanity.

Third, the Qurʾān makes another distinction among non-Muslims, which more or less runs parallel to the distinction just mentioned. There are those who believe in the one and unique God (i.e., monotheists), and then those who believe in more than one God or who ascribe a divine quality to people or things separate from God (i.e., the polytheists, *mushrikūn*). The criterion for this distinction is again of a theological nature, since it is the recognition of the God proclaimed by the prophets that is decisive. One can respond to the truth which was conveyed and believe but one can also refuse it. The distinction, interestingly enough, does not coincide completely with the distinction made earlier between a revealed and a polytheistic religion, since in principle there can be monotheists within polytheism, or believers among unbelievers.

These basic distinctions derived from the Qurʾān are fundamental for understanding medieval Muslim conceptions of non-Muslims. They also gave rise to some general normative ideas which may help us understand why Muslims perceived non-Muslims the way they did:

1. Non-Muslims are judged by Muslims primarily in light of what is accepted by the latter as revelation (i.e., the Qurʾān), hence in a religious light.
2. This revelation is considered not only to provide the formal standards and categories by which non-Muslims are to be evaluated but also to provide substantial knowledge about them and their religious beliefs.
3. Certain earlier revelations in the course of history, preceding that to Muhammad, which were not fully heard or widely respected but are at the origin of all monotheistic religion, are recognized as valid.
4. There is recognition of a kind of "primordial religion" (*Urreligion*), a primal and fundamental consciousness of God (*fitra*), which has been implanted in each human being at birth. Humanity can choose to follow this consciousness or neglect it. Islam is the true expression of this eternal, primordial religion.
5. A nonreligious person or a polytheist is not recognized and should become a believer. Jews and Christians, Zoroastrians and Sabians can continue to live according to the beliefs of their respective, recognized religions, but within Muslim territory (*dār al-islām*) they must submit to the given Muslim political authority and, without coercion, be encouraged to become believers.

In addition to these normative ideas concerning doctrine (elaborated in *tafsīr* and *kalām*), two other medieval Islamic distinctions can be traced to the Qurʾān and have been elaborated in *fiqh*. They concern political organization and social behavior.

The first distinction is between *dār al-islām*, territory under Muslim political authority, and *dār al-harb*, the world outside Muslim territory. According to this view, as the latter name indicates, there is a conflictual relationship, a "cold" or "hot" war situation between Muslim territory governed by an *imām* (caliph) and the outside world. A similar "imperial" vision of the world can be found in medieval Byzantine and Latin Christian thought; here it was centered around the office of the Emperor. In medieval Islamic thought, it was the caliph who was the central political authority figure. He was a wordly ruler responsible, among many other things, for enabling the Sharīʿa to be applied and specifically for carrying out the *jihād*.

The second distinction is that made within the *dār al-islām* itself, between Muslim believers and *dhimmīs* ("protected people") who are not Muslims but whose religion is recognized. Interestingly enough, the basic concern is less the rapid conversion of all people within the *dār al-islām* than the ruling that all should recognize the caliph's authority and accept the validity of the *Sharīʿa* in a Muslim territory, even though the *Sharīʿa* does not apply to non-Muslims (*dhimmīs*) personally or to their relations among themselves. However, polytheists (*mushrikūn*) cannot be *dhimmīs*: no *mushrikūn* are allowed within the *dār al-islām*; only monotheists and in particular *ahl al-kitāb* can be *dhimmīs*. The *dhimmīs* were subject to a special taxation (*jizya*), and they kept an internal autonomy within Muslim territory as socioreligious communities possessing their own laws and jurisdiction. Nevertheless, certain explicitly formulated social duties and other consequences of their lower socioreligious status effectively made them second-class citizens in Muslim society.

Of course, the *dhimmīs* were viewed by Muslims from an Islamic standpoint. The latter, for instance, hardly knew the meaning of the Christian church and had no conception of the tension which exists between "heavenly" church and "earthly" society in all Christian communities, including the *dhimmīs*. Not only in normative *Sharīʿa* but also in social practice the communities of the *dhimmīs* were considered and treated as adhering to a distortion of Islam and of Islamic beliefs and practices. The polytheists (*mushrikūn*) were described and treated as a kind of counter-image, the very reverse of the Islamic ideal.

The Muslim *mutakallimūn*, *ʿulamāʾ*, and *fuqahāʾ* — theologians and doctors of religious law—developed a coherent normative system by means of which non-Muslims were perceived, judged, and treated and which contained the basic categories for the description and evaluation of religions other than Islam. Discussions took place and variations were allowed within the framework of this normative system.

Development of Muslim Attitudes to Other Religions

We will now tentatively survey the main attitudes which developed in medieval Islamic civilization with regard to the interest in other religions. We are particularly concerned with the social conditions and the cultural context within which Muslim interest in religious history and the plurality of religions arose. As a civilization and as a religion Islam has had numerous contacts and encounters with different religions, and the nature of these contacts could not but influence Muslim attitudes toward adherents of these religions. Political and social conditions played a major role, as did the views that Muslims had of themselves and of their religion. One should note that there is a nearly constant and self-perpetuating relationship between the notion a believer has of his own religion and the attitude he takes toward other religions and religion in general.

On the whole, we can distinguish at least seven major attitudes to other religions which developed in the course of time in medieval Islamic civilization. They can be sketched as follows.

1. Those who had no curiosity or desire for further knowledge could simply dismiss the earlier religions as having been superseded, if not as complete nonsense. This may have been the attitude of the first Arab conquerors or rulers, for instance, who had other interests and simply left the religions of the conquered territories as they were. These religions were unable to stimulate any intellectual curiosity or interest among the invading soldiers, settlers, and traders.

2. Given a slowly rising number of converts to Islam in the conquered territories one could express concern, or even suspicion and distrust, toward foreign doctrines and ways of life which might enter the Muslim community by way of these new converts. This negative attitude could lead here and there to a hunt for heretical movements which might disturb the social order and of course to suspicion of those who were interested in foreign doctrines. As Ibn al-Muqaffaʿ (d. ca. 756) and Abū ʿĪsā Muhammad ibn Hārūn al-Warrāq (d. 861) were to experience, this attitude of suspicion on the part of the religious as well as some political leaders, not only blocked any authentic intellectual interest but also threatened those who harbored any such serious interest sometimes with the death penalty.

3. With the growth of discussions on an intellectual level on faith, doctrine, and religious practice within the Muslim community itself, one had to be informed of the opponent's doctrines in order to be able to refute them, such as the Muʿtazilites did. Consequently, the various opinions and doctrines to be found within the Muslim community were described. Such descriptions of deviating "sects" were given both by Sunnī and by Shīʿī authors. In the course of time they were expanded so that eventually other religions were included among them. One sees this already in the *Maqālāt al-islāmiyyīn* of al-Ashʿarī (d. 935) or in the *Al-farq bayna 'l-firaq* of al-Baghdādī (d. 1037). Within medieval Islamic civilization the study of other religions arose in this way from the study of Islamic sects. The main purpose of these descriptions, however, was to gain knowledge of other religions only as false systems and sources of falsehood to be refuted. This is particularly evident in the *Kitāb al-fisal wa 'l-ahwā' wa 'l-milal wa 'l-nihal* of Ibn Hazm (d. 1064).

4. A more positive interest in foreign doctrines was first found among those who, for some reason or other, converted to Islam but continued, quite naturally, to appreciate their ancient cultural and spiritual heritage. This could lead on the one hand to non-Islamic doctrines being inserted into comprehensive synthetic systems of more or less esoteric philosophies. It is difficult to find precise information about such sectarian groups and their universalist teachings, but there are certain references to Ismāʿīlī groups cherishing ancient gnostic doctrines. On the other hand, this could lead to the study of foreign doctrines for their own sake.

Here we come across an interesting rule: namely, that the very interest in foreign doctrines—that is to say, doctrines other than what the Muslim community as such believed—is to be found at the earliest date among those who were outside the established religious system. This interest was much weaker among those who adhered to Islam as it was usually defined according to tradition (*sunna*), those who wanted to make it into a distinctive system to be defended. It is no accident that this interest could be found in Shīʿī circles. One may think of the lost writings of al-Nawbakhtī (d. 912) and Ibn Bābūya (d. 1001), of alleged Shīʿī sympathizers such as al-Shahrastānī (d. 1153) and Abū-Maʿālī (who wrote his book in 1092), and also of certain insights and doctrines of the Ikhwān al-Safā' (10th c.) and the Ismāʿīlīs.

5. A different attitude found in medieval Islam goes back to the notion that all things true and good in other religions and cultures were evidently already present in Islam itself. Such elements, even if they are to be found elsewhere, may then still be called "Islamic." In other words, elements of Islam could be found outside the historical community of Muslims. This idea often served in practice to legitimate the various assimilation processes from other cultures which enriched medieval Islamic civilization with so many practical, intellectual, and also religious views, prescriptions and customs which cannot be found in the proper sources of Islam. It is difficult to find an outspoken representative of this attitude who studied other religions at all, since he would probably consider them as variations of Islam. The Islamic idea is here taken to include the positive elements of other cultures.

6. At the apogee of classical medieval Islamic civilization (ninth–thirteenth centuries C.E.) the cultivated Muslim public had a pronounced interest in the history and geography of the world known at the time. This public required information on other cultures, and it was most likely due to this rising general cultural interest that encyclopedic works were composed by authors like al-Masʿūdī (d. 956–957) and Ibn al-Nadīm (author of the *Fihrist* written in 987–990). In this way, knowledge of non-Muslims, insofar as it was not harmful to Muslim self-understanding, was more or less harmoniously integrated into the general Muslim life and world view of the time. In the tenth–twelfth centuries, and here and there also in later periods, there existed among educated Muslims a sense of one universal world in which adherents of different religions lived side by side, accepting the reality of religious plurality.

7. Finally, we should mention in classical Islamic civilization the attitude of Muslims versed in mysticism and who adhered to the wider idea of the universality of divine revelation to humanity. One may think here of the great mystical poet Jalāl al-Dīn Rūmī (d. 1273). This religious universality provided an openness toward "other" believers, and as a spiritual attitude it could lead to religious studies. Such an attitude, which was evidently only found among individual persons and in certain religious circles—and which probably had little impact on society as a whole—nevertheless upheld and nourished the idea of the essential unity of all revelations and religious traditions, despite their external differences.

Sources for the Study of Muslim Views of Other Religions

The following is a brief survey and selection of the various kinds of sources available for the study of medieval Islamic perceptions of other religions.

Descriptive Texts

1. First there are *historical works*, where we find descriptions of religious history from a Muslim perspective, which span this history before the beginnings of Islam. The major elements of this Islamic view of history are given in the Qurʾān, in particular the prophets mentioned there who were sent to bring a message of warning, a law or scripture to the people.

We see this scheme elaborated in the so-called Universal Histories which treat the history of the world from the creation onward. One thinks of the works of al-Yaʿqūbī (d. 923) and al-Masʿūdī (d. 956 or 958), which concentrate on the prophets and on the non-Muslim religious communities to which they spoke in the past. The characteristic features of these communities largely depended not on broader historical realities but on the preaching of the prophets and the response of the people addressed. History is viewed here from a theological standpoint, which emerges from the prophet's message of divine revelation. In the series of prophets Abraham, *khalīl Allāh* ("friend of God"), occupies a place of honor. Both his personal history and the history of his people constitute in the Muslim view the very "infrastructure" of the relations between the Jewish, Christian, and Muslim monotheistic communities. It would be difficult, if not impossible, to understand Muslim perceptions of other religions if we did not take this fundamental view of religious history into account. In medieval times and even later, Muslim world historiography was based both on this normative framework deduced from the Qurʾān and on factual information obtained by scholars.

It is significant that the prophetical religious history of humanity is not seen in a completely negative light. The prophetical religions were seen to be, to the extent that they rejected idolatry, not wholly false. The revelations on which they were based were thought to be inherently true but to have been tainted by people in the course of history, resulting in a betrayal of the divine, revelatory, primordial religion (*Urreligion*) common to all. In order to restore and further this primordial, monotheistic religion, Muhammad was sent to bring a conclusive revelation. Once memorized and written down, the Qurʾānic revelation channeled by Muhammed, unlike earlier prophecies, was held to have remained authentic and pure.

According to the medieval Muslim view, the truths contained within the Qurʾān do not differ from the truths of the preceding prophetic religions. The same revelation, meant to restore the innate religious disposition (*fitra*) to mankind, is supposed to be behind all the monotheistic traditions. The medieval Muslim view of history, as a consequence, is not one in which different religions succeed each other in a continuous history. It is, rather, the history of the one religion which has been revealed intermittently and which perpetuates itself through multiple histories. This primordial religion was in particular realized in history through the "heavenly" or "revealed" prophetical religions with their historical variations. We are concerned here with a particular theological view of history which provided the normative framework within which individual historians worked. The history of nonprophetical religions such as, for example, those of ancient Greece and Egypt, evoked much less interest.

2. For the *religions contemporary with Islam* and mostly beyond the borders of the *dār al-islām* itself, Muslims owed their knowledge largely to travelers whose *travel accounts* were used and synthesized by geographers. Such travelers were neither professional discoverers nor primarily interested in religions. When we think of Ibn Fadlān (traveled in 921–922), Abū Dulaf Misʿar (d. 942), and the unknown authors of the *Kitāb akhbār al-Sīn wa-ʾl-Hind* (851) and the *Kitāb ʿajāʾib al-Hind* (ca. 950), we are mainly looking at people whose interest in intellectual matters was limited. They were attentive to those customs which were opposed to their accustomed way of life—for example, statues of divinities in India or funeral customs in China. The farther the country was, the greater the taste for the miraculous.

Muslims recognized the greatness of other contemporary civilizations in South Asia and the Far East. Al-Bīrūnī (d. after 1050), in his description of India, perceived Hinduism, religiously and culturally, as something astonishing; Ibn Battūta (d. 1377) liked to entertain his readers with his travel adventures. However, nonliterate religions, as in Africa for instance, were not viewed favorably by Muslims and could even be seen as bordering on the ridiculous.

A notable case to be mentioned are the accounts brought into Muslim territory regarding the Christians in the Byzantine Empire, Italy, and northern Spain.[2] We have reports of battles against the Rūm, and poetry in connection with the *jihād* on the Muslim-Byzantine frontier at our disposal, as well as descriptions of Constantinople and Rome as they were seen by ambassadors and prisoners, tradesmen and free travelers, who visited these Christian territories for various reasons. Hārūn b. Yahyā (d. end 9th c.) and Ibrāhīm b. Yaʿqūb (traveled c. 965) are both brought to mind in this regard. On the whole, however, Europe evoked little interest.

Also of a special nature are Muslim accounts of the crusaders—for example, the customs and behavior of the Franks at the time of Salāh al-Dīn (d. 1192). Yet with respect to their religion, which was assumed to be known and looked upon with contempt, little was said with the exception of some matters pertaining to morality.

In fact, all of these reports by direct observers show little interest in other religions. Religious facts were only noted down if they happened to draw the attention or stirred up the imagination of the Muslim visitors. Geographers such as Ibn Rusta (wrote ca. 905) and al-Muqaddasī (ca. 985–990) synthesized sundry travel reports into their books about the known world at the time. They did not give much data about other religions.

3. Besides historical literature and travel accounts, the broad field of the *literature* of medieval Muslim civilization (mostly *adab*) is another source for the study of Muslim perceptions of other believers.[3] In Arabic poetry and prose there are numerous references to adherents of other religions; the same holds true for more popular literature such as the *Thousand and One Nights*. One should also explore Persian, Turkish, Swāhilī, and other Muslim literatures in which non-Muslims are referred to. Not only descriptions of perceived reality but also the imaginative dimension of Muslim writings are resources for the study of how non-Muslims were perceived and imagined in the medieval Muslim world.

4. There are other writings as well which are of great interest. We have accounts of philosophical and other schools of thought outside Islam.[4] The *Fihrist* written in 987–990 by Ibn al-Nadīm shows to what extent Muslim culture was interested in the outside world, the world before and outside the bounds of Islam. It contains reports of the Zoroastrians[5] and the Manicheans and is a work to which the modern discipline of the history of religions is indebted. Another work of importance is the *Murūj al-dhahab* ("Golden Meadows") of al-Masʿūdī (d. 956/7).

Among these sources there are some extensive medieval Muslim *accounts of other religions* which are of particular interest and which we shall examine in a following section.

Texts concerning Jewish and Christian dhimmīs

A special category of texts is the literature treating the *dhimmīs* living in the *dār al-islām*. If we can see a certain lingering curiosity in the descriptions of non-Muslims outside of the *dār al-islām*, we must note the marked absence of such a curiosity when Muslims wrote about Jewish and Christian *dhimmīs* living in Islamic territory. We can clearly see that Muslims wished to carve out a distinct and separate existence from the *dhimmīs* whom they tolerated but fundamentally held in contempt. The presence of the *dhimmīs* implied social and economic possibilities but also problems which gave the writings concerning them a pragmatic and utilitarian tendency.

Jews and Christians living in the same town or countryside as Muslims were not the object of interest or study; their religions were supposed to be sufficiently known. In their unavoidable presence, all attention was directed to practical matters: taxes they must pay, rules of conduct to which they must adhere, juridical problems to be solved, the public order to be maintained, laudable cases of conversion, and so on. They were, after all, people who had either been defeated in battle or who had surrendered in time, and in either case, they lived under Muslim political authority and were considered second-class citizens. Muslims could not help but notice the silent resistance on the part of the *dhimmīs* to attempts to convert them and to Muslim political authority; they were sensitive to any sign of arrogance or rebellion. Thus heretical views within the Muslim community could easily be ascribed to *dhimmī* and other foreign influences which, it was suspected, had infiltrated Islam with the entry of the new converts. There was a noticeable suspicion of Jewish influences of various kinds, especially in religious matters. Such influences in hadīth literature were called *isrāʾīliyyāt*.

The juridical *fiqh* literature about the status and treatment of *dhimmīs*, including relevant *fatwās* given to specific problems that occurred in the relations between Muslims and dhimmīs is a wide field of research. It has to be explored not only to know better how prescriptions about the *dhimmīs* were developed in the Sharīʿa but also to find out what medieval Muslims knew about the Christian and Jewish communities, their organization, communal rules, and customs. Administrators had to know the *dhimmīs* to be able to impose the *dizya* on them. A special topic is to what extent and how exactly interactions between Muslims and *dhimmīs* took place. Apparently, both sides avoided too close relationships.

Polemical Literature

Polemical literature constitutes another source for any study of medieval Muslim perceptions of other religions. The starting point of the large number of polemical texts written by medieval Muslim authors against other religions is the fundamental opposition between Islam, based on revelation, and other religions without reliable revelation, and between the Muslims and other religious communities. This opposition is stressed over and over again, with regard to both doctrines and practices; anything essential that Muslims and non-Muslims might have in common is omitted.[6]

Such polemical literature which largely serves to ascertain one's identity over others, also abundantly developed between the different schools of thought within the Muslim community itself. Here we are primarily concerned, however, with polemics directed against Christianity and Judaism, Zoroastrianism or Mazdeism, Manicheism, and other foreign religions. This literature has been studied already for its technical arguments, for a better knowledge of Islamic doctrines, and for its impact on medieval Islamic civilization itself. But for our purposes it is of particular interest in the following respects.

Behind these debates one finds basic positions and judgments on the Muslim side regarding truth, positions from where doctrines held to be outside that truth were denounced, confronted, and refuted. Throughout the polemical literature we can distinguish typical Muslim expressions of truth, often intellectually elaborated with technical precision, spiritually rather dry and narrow but useful for polemical purposes. Such ideas of truth have had far-reaching consequences, not only for Muslim evaluations and judgments of non-Muslims but also for the limits within which Muslim authors were able to understand at all what non-Muslims thought and did, and why.

Viewed from this angle, this literature is disappointing. In the refutations as well as in the various debates, which in their written form are mostly fictitious, we almost invariably find stereotyped arguments on both sides rather than a real discussion. Such arguments mainly function, whether used personally or communally, to define and strengthen the position of the community against the opposing party; there is no common search, no dialogue. This literature constitutes a genre in itself, with a clear taste for the art of rhetoric and for arguments that are supposed to be convincing through the beauty of their coherence and suggestive force.

Throughout this medieval polemical literature, however, we note the inability of the authors to grasp what really moves the non-Muslim believers and to arrive at what we would presently call understanding others from their own point of view. The level on which the arguments are carried forth demonstrate that in the majority of cases it was only doctrinal and factual issues which were seen to have any value and which were treated according to established rules. This kind of polemical literature represents a largely negative dialogue. From another point of view, however, this literature is useful because it throws light on the cultural and social climate in which the polemic functioned. It certainly played an important role in the Muslim community's sense of truth and self-identity through debate and controversy. Real knowledge of the other party was of secondary importance; as a rule, such polemical treatises were hardly read by those to whom they were addressed. When we look at the polemical literature as a social phenomenon, the point is not so much the contents but the occasions on which, the precise reasons why and aims for which particular tracts were written by particular individuals for specific groups.

One should add that there was a marked tendency to identify and define oneself in terms of contrasts. This tendency is at variance with the other assumption mentioned earlier: the ideal that all believers are deeply united through their belief in the one God and the existence of a shared, primordial, monotheistic religion.

Spiritual Religious Texts

Quite opposed to the confrontational texts just described are a certain number of what may be called spiritual texts which offer a mystical, gnostic, or philosophical interpretation of religions other than Islam.[7] Such interpretations remained the privilege of small religious and philosophical groups, sometimes accused of heresy, who were on a search for what may be called the universal and who often had an esoteric character. With the exception of great mystics like Ibn al-ʿArabī (1165–1240) and Jalāl al-Dīn Rūmī (1207–1273), they remained outside the mainstream Muslim community, perhaps because of their penchant toward universality. With their spiritual inclinations, however, they did little to set forth a real knowledge of other religions. They mainly wanted to appropriate tenets of these religions for their own religious purposes rather than learn about them for the sake of a better understanding of people who were different from themselves.

Four Scholars Concerned with the Study of Other Religions

Medieval Muslim authors gave some very interesting accounts of other religions, and we shall devote this section to four which are particularly important. So far we have traced the major medieval Muslim distinctions concerning non-Islamic religions, and the main attitudes taken toward them. We have also surveyed the various kinds of sources at our disposal for the study of medieval Muslim views of other religions. We shall now look at four medieval Muslim scholars who studied other religions, three of whom have acquired a reputation beyond the borders of Islam itself and may be considered as forerunners of the modern study of religions.

Ibn Hazm

Ibn Hazm[8] was born on the 4th of November, 994 in Cordoba, Spain. He was possibly of Iranian descent; other sources suggest that he came from a family of former Mozarabs and that his great-grandfather had converted from Christianity to Islam. His father was *wazīr* to the regent al-Mansūr (d. 1002) and to his son, the *hājib* al-Muzaffar (d. 1008). As a result, Ibn Hazm received an excellent education and moved within the highest circles of court and culture. As a member of the Moorish aristocracy and a fervent partisan of the Spanish Umayyad caliphate, a difficult and uncertain time began for him with the turbulent political situation after 1008, culminating in the fall of the caliphate in 1031. After spending some time in prison and as a refugee on Majorca, Ibn Hazm retired to his family estate where he devoted himself to scholarship and writing. He died on the 15th of August, 1064. Ibn Hazm was hated by the *ʿulamāʾ* because of his violent attacks on the traditional religious authorities of the Ashʿarī school of *kalām* and on all four recognized *madhāhib* of law; he himself was a Zāhirī. With his polemical writings he made himself many enemies and as a result his works—he was said to have left about 400 works written on about 80,000 leaves—were publicly burned in Seville. Much was thus lost to us forever.

Ibn Hazm must have had a strong and sensitive personality and an immense erudition with wide horizons. His was an exceedingly sharp intelligence which was directed, in an original and fearless way, toward what he held to be true according to logic and Zāhirī interpretation of religious texts, that is to say, taking the literal meaning of texts. Besides being a theologian, jurist, and politician, Ibn Hazm was also a writer of essays and a poet—author of the well-known *Tawq al-hamāma* ("The Neckring of the Dove")—and polemicist. He had an immense thirst for knowledge. His convictions and his theology challenged the religious thinking of his time. With his immense knowledge, his superior mind, and last but not least, his passionate temperament, whether in love or in hatred, Ibn Hazm remained a man of incredible intellectual courage, lonely in his intellectual and spiritual wrestling and isolated within his society.

The famous work on religions written by Ibn Hazm is his *Kitāb al-fisal* (or: *al-fasl*) *fī ʾl-milal wa-ʾl-ahwāʾ wa-ʾl-nihal*[9] which he started to write most likely between 1027 and 1030. It consists of two parts: one about non-Muslim religions, the other about Muslim sects. It also contains a special refutation of the Scriptures of Judaism and Christianity—probably a second work, inserted later into this book—which may be called a forerunner of modern Bible criticism. What interests us here in particular is the first part of the book, since it contains a systematic description and a refutation of the religions outside Islam which Ibn Hazm knew, treated in a logical order.

In his introduction, Ibn Hazm indicates how highly he esteems reason. Subsequently, he applies this reason to what he considers to be the six principal forms of philosophical and religious thought. We mention them here since they give a good idea of Ibn Hazm's strict reasoning.

First, there is the skepticism of the sophists who deny all truth, saying there can be no positive, real truth. However, that statement itself has been accepted by them as "truth."

Second, there is the atheism of certain philosophers who do indeed recognize the existence of real truth but who deny the existence of God; they believe in the eternity of the world.

Third, there are those philosophers who recognize the existence of God. God is Lord in their opinion, but he is not the creator of the world. Hence they affirm both a God and an eternal world.

These three forms of thought deny the foundation of religion, and Ibn Hazm attempts to refute their false propositions and wrong assumptions about the world and God logically.

Fourth, there are the polytheists who do indeed admit that there is truth and that the world may not be eternal but created, but they accept more than one Lord of the world. Included in this group are also the supposedly polytheistic Christians. Ibn Hazm tries to prove that the idea of number cannot be applied to the idea of God, since the two ideas represent two orders of reality which are incompatible. He turns himself then to the task of refuting the main doctrines of Christianity: the trinity, the incarnation, and Christ's divinity. He thus upholds monotheism.

Fifth, there are those monotheists who, like the rationalists and those whom he calls the "Brahmans" (*barāhima*), accept truth, look at the world as created, and recognize one God as creator and Lord, but who do not want to speak of prophetic revelation. Ibn Hazm attempts to show the necessity of divine revelation with special reference to the role of the prophets. There are three prophetic religions: Judaism, Christianity, and Islam. The question still remains, however, as to which is the true one. Before he starts answering this question, however, Ibn Hazm refers to some special forms of religion: belief in the transmigration of souls, astrology, magic, animism, and so on. He also discusses the philosophical doctrine of time and space being eternal like God and the idea that the celestial sphere, in itself eternal and different from God, determines the world. Such doctrines, in his view, are contrary to monotheism itself.

Sixth and last, there are the monotheists who accept truth, who take the world to be created, who recognize God as Lord and creator of the world, and who also accept prophetic revelation. These are the Jews and the anti-Trinitarian Christians, but they are limited in that they only accept certain prophets. Ibn Hazm then tries to refute their views: since they do not recognize a continuous chain of prophets, they have lost the divine revelation in its completeness as it manifested itself in the course of history. The contradictions in their Scriptures are important proofs of their deficiency; moreover, these monotheistic Scriptures have been definitively abrogated, according to Ibn Hazm's reading of the Qurʾān. In his refutation of the revelatory character of the Old and New Testament texts, Ibn Hazm applies a vehement internal textual criticism to the Bible and refutes any claim to "revelation" made by Jews and Christians. Hence only Islam remains as the one true prophetic religion. To complete his case, Ibn Hazm also refutes Christian objections to Islam.

Besides the literalism in which Ibn Hazm confronts the texts, it is striking to see the nearly complete absence of any historical treatment in the *Kitāb al-fisal*. The author pays no attention to the origin and rise of religious ideas or to the historical development of the religions he writes about. He is uniquely concerned with the doctrinal base and contents of the religions he discusses.

After having given a descriptive rendering of the doctrines of a religion, he takes a fundamentally critical stance in his polemical writing and applies a truly "modern" scriptural criticism to the sacred texts of that religion, in particular Judaism and Christianity. He thus demonstrates an extraordinary critical sense which he combines with a thorough skepticism about all religions outside of Islam. His brilliant intelligence, which at times takes the shape of hard rationalism, is applied to refuting not only intellectual mistakes and indifference to truth but also popular credulity and superstition, as well as false religious authorities.

Ibn Hazm had great influence on later Muslim polemicists against Judaism and Christianity; his arguments, especially in refuting the revelatory character and authority of the Bible, have been repeated again and again. He was answered by his contemporary Ibn al-Nagrīla (933–1056) who was *wazīr* at the time in Granada and much later by Salomo Ibn Adret (d. 1310), both belonging to the Jewish community. In return he gave a crushing rebuttal of Ibn al-Nagrīla, which approaches what would be called today anti-Semitic vehemency.

Al-Bīrūnī

Al-Bīrūnī[10] was born on the 4th of September, 973, in a suburb (*bīrūn*) of Kāth, capital of Khwārizm, south of Lake Aral. He descended from an Iranian family from the border area between the Iranian world and the steppe inhabited by Turkic nomads. Here he lived and worked for the first 15 years of his life. From about 988 onward he worked for a number of years in Jurjān, south of the Caspian Sea, in a region of ancient Iranian culture, where he was attached to the court of the Ziyārid sultan Qābūs ibn Wushmagīr. He carried out a correspondence with Ibn Sīnā (980–1037) in Bukhārā.

Here he wrote a lengthy work of fundamental importance on the institutions of ancient peoples and religions, the *Kitāb al-āthār al-bāqiya ʿan al-qurūn al-khāliya*.[11] Al-Bīrūnī returned to Khwārizm before 1008, where he worked for seven years at the court of the *khwārizmshāh* Abū ʿl-ʾAbbās Maʾmūn b. Maʾmūn.

However, calamity struck after the *khwārizmshāh* was assassinated in 1016–1017, and the country was conquered by sultan Mahmūd of Ghazna. In the year 1017 al-Bīrūnī was taken as a prisoner or hostage to Ghazna in Sijistān. A few years later the sultan took al-Bīrunī with him on his conquests to India, and left him somewhere in northwest India (now Pakistan) for a number of years in a capacity which is unknown. During these years, al-Bīrūnī sought to get to know the country where he was living and became well acquainted with it, but he probably traveled no further than Lahore. It seems that he received considerable instruction from Hindu pandits and may have learned some Sanskrit. In these years he wrote his *Kitāb taʾrīkh al-Hind*[12] which was finished in the year 1030, shortly before the death of sultan Mahmūd. This famous work which was to make him immortal appeared anonymously and, contrary to the customs of the time, was not dedicated to anyone. This may indicate a tense relationship between al-Bīrūnī and Mahmūd of Ghazna under whose patronage he worked. In the same year al-Bīrūnī also finished the great astronomical calendar-study which immortalized him as a scientist, the *Kitāb al-qānūn al-Masʿūdi fi ʾl-hayʾa wa-ʾl-nujūm*.[13] This book was dedicated to Mahmūd's son and successor, sultan Masʿūd who is mentioned in the title.

As a result of his reconciliation with sultan Masʿūd, al-Bīrūnī was allowed to return to Ghazna where he wrote a number of works, apparently untroubled by further difficulties. When he died some time after 1050, most likely in Ghazna, he left behind some 180 works, of which 20 concerned India, including several translations of Sanskrit works. Abu Rayhān al-Bīrūnī must be considered an intellectual genius in the history of mankind. In the Muslim tradition he carries the honorific title of *al-ustādh*, the Master.

The *Kitāb taʾrīkh al-Hind*, with which we are concerned here, is a unique attempt on the part of a Muslim scholar to become acquainted with a completely different culture and worldview on the basis of personal observations, questions, and the study of Sanskrit texts. Out of the 80 chapters of the book, 10 deal with religion and philosophy, 14 with festivals and folklore, 6 with literature and the study of metres in poetry, 14 with geography and cosmography, no fewer than 31 with chronology and astronomy (which was the scholar's proper field), and 4 with astrology among the Hindus. Chapter 10, for instance, treats the source of the Hindu "Law" and the Indian "prophets"; chapter 11, the beginning of polytheism with a description of different statues of deities; chapter 63, the Brahmins and their way of life; chapter 64, the rites and customs of the lower castes. In the book no fewer than 35 Sanskrit sources are used in addition to a description of different aspects of Hindu culture and a survey of theological and philosophical doctrines. The work remained unknown for a long time but has fortunately been discovered and made accessible in a text edition and an English translation of Eduard C. Sachau.

What is of special interest to us are al-Bīrūnī's empirical investigations into Indian culture.[14] During his probably forced residence in India, al-Bīrūnī apparently did not enjoy any special protection on Sultan Mahmūd's part. His own misery, caused by Mahmūd, may have made him sympathetic to Hindus who, as is well known, received an extremely harsh treatment from Mahmūd who had destroyed a number of sanctuaries. Since al-Bīrūnī had come with the conquerors, however, he must have been suspect among the Indians and his relationship with Hindu scholars may have remained cool, notwithstanding his friendly intentions. Since, moreover, he could not go to the real centers of Hindu scholarship in Benares and Kashmir, al-Bīrūnī had to be content with the information given by those people whom he could meet and question.[15] Nevertheless, his personal curiosity and his own fascination with India, especially its philosophy and its latent monotheism behind a palpable polytheism, enabled him to overcome many obstacles and led him to remarkable results.

Al-Bīrūnī's method is neither apologetic nor polemical but rather observing and descriptive. He remains at a distance from the material and does not identify himself with it. His aim is, as he states in the Introduction to his book, to render what Hindus themselves wrote or personally told him, so that it is not he himself who describes doctrines, behavior, and Sanskrit renderings but rather those with whom he was in contact. Each chapter sets forth the problem of the subject treated along with the Hindus' doctrines and opinions and al-Bīrūnī's own observations. Several of the early chapters contain references to ancient Greek and Sūfī concepts and practices which al-Bīrūnī compares to their Indian counterparts with the purpose of clarifying Indian practices and making them more comprehensible.

One can observe in al-Bīrūnī himself two different sets of values. On the one hand, he stresses the superiority of Islam in matters such as the equality of all men versus the inequality of the caste system which he finds reprehensible. He emphasizes the virtues of the personal law contained in the Sharīʿa in opposition to the Hindu law, and the cleanliness and moderation of Muslims in comparison with the unclean customs he found among the Hindus. On the other hand, throughout his description of India al-Bīrūnī significantly depreciates the Arabs. He affirms especially that the Arabs who destroyed the ancient Iranian culture were no better than the Zoroastrian Iranians and had customs which were no better than the Hindu ones. He must have been proud to be of Iranian stock.

Prominent traits of al-Bīrūnī are his spirit of discovery, his scholarly curiosity, the clear and open way in which he expresses himself and his respect for truth. It is this respect for truth which prompts him to unmask cheating and swindling, to separate chaff from wheat, and continually to appeal to logic, reason, and the laws of nature. In his study of Hinduism there are elements that have become fundamental in present-day studies of religions, especially in the task of acquiring correct information and attempting to render the given information more comprehensible by means of comparison.

Alessandro Bausani offered some valuable critical remarks on al-Bīrūnī's view of India and its unavoidable limitations.[16] He calls Al-Bīrūnī's approach static, rather theoretical, and bookish. Al-Bīrūnī overstresses the asymmetry and the lack of order of the Hindus, particularly in their spiritual life. He sees the Hindu world as simply the reversed image of the Muslim world and discerns a sort of "perversity" in the Hindu mind, leading to a disharmonious worldview of unity, which for him is nothing but muddled confusion.

What al-Bīrūnī did not see was the more impersonal character of the Hindu divinities as compared to the more personal character of the Semitic divinity. With his rational mind, al-Bīrūnī did not have much feeling for the meaning of symbols for Hindus and pantheists; in fact, he was rather insensitive to symbolism in general. Al-Bīrūnī also did not perceive that Hinduism, as compared with Semitic Islam, accentuates knowledge more than behavior and action, and fundamental philosophy more than basic religious feeling and emotions. Being himself an intellectual, he was struck by Hindu popular religion; he did not and could not have an open mind for the positive values of nonliterate people and their religion.

According to Bausani, the following assumptions are typical of al-Bīrūnī and his view and description of India:

1. The existence of a common *fitra* (innate religious disposition) among all mankind and all civilizations, implying a certain natural theology.
2. The stress on faith in one and the same God, in connection with the common *fitra*; this faith also demonstrates the link between Islam and Hinduism.
3. The predominant idea of an impersonal and philosophical God as it was developed in Greek philosophical speculation. Hence al-Bīrūnī's irritation with illiterate, sensuous folk religion and anthropomorphic gods; he offers a euhemeristic explanation of polytheism, deducing it from the veneration of human beings, and he embodies traditional Semitic antipantheistic views.
4. The desire to reconcile on the highest level the thought of the Brahmins with al-Bīrūnī's own philosophy; this also contributes to the sharp distinction he makes between popular religion and philosophy.
5. A typical rationality to be found in his elaboration of certain concepts and in his idea that true religion cannot be contrary to reason. Consequently, he was not only unable to see the positive aspects of nonrational popular religion, but he also judged the Hindu mind as irrational, perverse, and arbitrary.
6. A certain empiricism based on an elementary notion of common sense. This prevents al-Bīrūnī from being on the spiritual wavelength of the ideal and of metaphysics.
7. A basic philosophical orientation and a fundamental Sūfī grounding. This makes it impossible for al-Bīrūnī to grasp the real contrast between Islam and Hinduism.

These various observations make it clear that also in al-Bīrūnī's scholarly work, which rises so far above the work of other medieval scholars in this field, a definite set of Muslim norms and values remains palpable. Nevertheless, his attitude toward other religions betrays an openness and inquisitiveness that testify to a modern mind in search of universal truth, living in medieval Muslim civilization.

Franz Rosenthal draws attention to some other general views contained in al-Bīrūnī's *India*.[17] First, al-Bīrūnī thought that Indian civilization, though different from Greek civilization, was comparable to it and that both had been in agreement in the distant past. He believed that there was a basic original unity of higher civilization, and he wanted to open the eyes of educated Muslims to Indian culture besides Greek science and philosophy.

Second, al-Bīrūnī held that both in India and in Greece there had been and still were philosophers who, through their power of thought and reason, arrived at the truth of the one God which, on a philosophical level, corresponds with the basic message brought by all prophets.

Third, he contended that this kind of universal monotheistic thought is only within reach of the literate elite, the *khawāss*; on the contrary, the illiterate masses, the *ʿawāmm* not only outside but also within Islam, tend to give way to the innate human inclination toward idolatry.

Fourth, as a consequence, al-Bīrūnī extended his affirmation of God's universality to the point where he contended that Greeks and Hindus also knew of God as the One. Through mystical experience they sought spiritual unification (*ittihād*) leading, beyond scholarly knowledge, to the true insight of the mind.

Arthur Jeffery and W. Montgomery Watt analyzed al-Bīrūnī's contribution to the study of religions as a scholarly discipline taking religions as subjects of empirical research.[18]

Al-Shahrastānī

Al-Shahrastānī[19] was born in 1086 in Shahrastān, a town in Khurāsān, on the fringes of the desert near Khwārizm. After having finished his studies in Nīsābūr he continued to live in his home town. The only interruption was the *hajj* which he accomplished in the year 1116, after which he stayed for three years in Bagdad. He then returned to Shahrastān where he lived until his death in 1153. He left several works of a theological nature as well as his famous *Kitāb al-milal waʾl-nihal*[20] which he wrote around 1125, ten years after his return from Bagdad.

Al-Shahrastānī must have been a pleasant person, irreproachable in his way of life and endowed with an excellent, albeit perhaps not very original mind. Although an Ashʿarī theologian, he appears to have sympathized with Ismāʿīlī ideas for a certain time. It is known that he, unlike many of his colleagues, had little interest in juridical questions. On the other hand, he was a talented author with a clear and readable style. He is said to have had a thirst for knowledge.

What he writes in his *Kitāb al-milal waʾl-nihal* is for the most part a presentation of what was already known at the time but he does it objectively, without a consciously apologetic attitude. As he himself states, his presentation is "without hatred against the one, and without preference for the other." He used existing sources without giving further specification; he chose his materials with care and sought to classify them appropriately. He was especially concerned with describing doctrines and systems. The book presents practically no history, indication of historical data or biographical details of people.

The *Kitāb al-milal waʾl-nihal* consists of two parts. The first part treats people with a religion, that is, those who have received a revelation. They are, for the most part, sects within Islam and then those non-Muslims who possess Scriptures and who are recognized as such by Islam, mainly Jews and Christians. Those who have a doubtful or even falsified scripture like the Zoroastrians and the Manicheans are also mentioned. The second part treats people who have no "revealed religion," that is, people "who follow their own inclinations" (*ahl al-ahwāʾ*). The first are the Sabians who venerate stars and spiritual beings; exceptionally, al-Shahrastānī includes a religious dialogue between a Muslim and a Sabian. Second, there are the philosophers who constitute by and large the greater part of the *ahl al-ahwāʾ*. Third, there are the polytheists: the pre-Islamic Arabs as well as the Hindus (Brahmins, Vaishnavas, and Shaivas), the Buddhists, the star- and idol-worshippers, as well as some more philosophers.

As previously stated, the book is a compilation of existing knowledge. There arises, therefore, the problem of al-Shahrastānī's sources, which has been much discussed and to which different solutions have been proposed. However, the problem has not yet been adequately solved, largely because certain probable sources no longer exist. Curiously, al-Bīrūnī was apparently unknown to al-Shahrastānī. Consequently, on first sight the book amounts to a patchwork of existing fragments written by others earlier and then rounded off and polished into a self-contained survey. On second sight, however, there is a certain system in it, as was shown by Bruce B. Lawrence.[21] By applying certain models in his descriptions al-Shahrastānī rehabilitates the Indian religions.

It is no accident that al-Shahrastānī treats *Sabianism*[22] in the second part of his book, where the Indian religions are treated also. For him, it serves as a kind of "model" for a sort of religion that is situated, so to say, between monotheism and polytheism. Sabianism would have been an ancient religion and there have been varieties of it, like the ancient Sabians themselves, the Greek Sabians, the Indian Sabians, and the later Sabians in Harrān. Al-Shahrastānī considers the Sabians to have been originally the followers of the ancient "prophet" Hermes (Ar. ʿAdhīmūn), a Hellenistic revelatory figure whom Muslims later identified with the Qurʾānic Idrīs (standing for Enoch). The Sabians then abandoned Idrīs' (ʿAdhīmūn's) prophetic teaching of the one God. They constituted a particular kind of deviation from true monotheism, besides the well-known deviations held by the Zoroastrians, Jews, and Christians. The Qurʾān mentions indeed the Sabians (2:59, 5:73, 22:17) in a positive sense besides the Christians, the Jews and also the Zoroastrians. By presenting Indian religion as a form of the more or less admissible Sabianism, al-Shahrastānī tries to 'rehabilitate' a great deal of Hindu thought and religion.

The information which al-Shahrastānī provides about the dualists (Zoroastrians and Manicheans) is especially interesting. The lively debate with the Sabians, who are portrayed according to the doctrines which used to be attributed to them, is also interesting. The author has a rather good knowledge of Christian doctrines.[23] He gives a fair treatment of Buddhism about which Muslim communities at the time could not have known much.

He also speaks about the existence of "leaves" of revelation which Ibrāhīm is supposed to have received and which would have been the common root of the religions of the Sabians and Zoroastrians. These leaves were then lost, which consequently necessitated the later revelation to Muhammad. On the other hand, al-Shahrastānī does not tell much about the Jews, and he is rather brief in his discussion of the Ismāʿīlīs in the section on the Islamic sects.

The organization of the book fulfills certain esthetic and literary criteria. The author, who wrote also several important theological treatises, was evidently concerned to provide basic information about non-Muslim religions and Muslim sects to his Muslim readers. The book has become a classic and is still considered by many Muslims as a basic source of information.

Abū ʾl-Maʿālī

Little is known about Abū ʾl-Maʿālī's[24] life. His family came from Balkh and he was a contemporary of Nāsir-i Khusraw (d. between 1072 and 1077). Abū ʾl-Maʿālī wrote his *Kitāb bayān al-adyān*[25] in the year 1092 in Ghazna during the reign of Sultan Masʿūd III (1089–1099), also called ʿAlāʾ al-Dawla.

The *Kitāb bayān al-adyān* is the earliest work in Persian about religions and sects. It is small, it has an abrupt literary style and it lacks a balanced structure. It was probably written for didactic purposes and meant for nonspecialized readers. In its short description of the major religions and sects it only offers their main lines. The occasion which gave rise to the writing of the book is not quite clear; there are only hints as to its origin and aim. In his introduction the author refers to a discussion, which supposedly took place in a prince's court, about various religions and sects and in which the well-known *hadīth* concerning the existence of 73 Islamic sects is referred to. The author alludes to the fact that in this world it is mandatory to obey those who are in power. He then mentions that an advantage of his book is that it informs the Sunnīs of the arguments of their adversaries and, hence, makes their refutation possible. The Sunnīs will then see that they themselves made the right choice so that their understanding and their self-assurance will increase.

The book itself consists of five chapters. The first chapter treats the idea of God and the universal belief in a Creator who bears different names. This chapter, which reads like a Muslim theological tract, throws light on the way in which Abū ʾl-Maʿālī treats his subject matter and which distinguishes him from al-Bīrūnī and al-Shahrastānī and, to a lesser extent, Ibn Hazm. It ends with the remark that most people believe in a Creator and that they all—each in his own language—recognize the almighty unique God under one special name which they call upon in times of misery. "This is the greatest proof of the existence of God," the author concludes, leaving aside the proofs given in Islamic theology.

The second chapter treats those religions which preceded Islam and which, characteristically, were in contradiction with one another. The ancient Arabs head the first list, followed by the Greek philosophers, the Jews, the Christians, the Zoroastrians, the Mazdakites, and the Manicheans. The idolaters are treated in the second place; a commentary on the origin of idolatry precedes discussions of the Hindus, who are highly praised for their refinement and wisdom; the Sabians; the Qarmatians and Zindīqs (Manicheans) who deny the existence of a Creator; and finally the Sophists, who put waking on a par with dreaming.

The last three chapters, which are of less interest here, successively treat the *hadīth* of the 73 Islamic sects, as well as certain extremist attitudes which consider man as God or as prophet.

Abū ʿl-Maʾalī uses available sources, but uncritically; there are in his book some incorrect quotations from al-Bīrūnī. One should therefore be cautious in assessing Abū ʿl-Maʿālī's remarks about non-Muslim religions. The best section of the book seems to be that which deals with the Shīʿa, in particular the Imāmīya or Twelvers. This suggests that Abū ʿl-Maʿālī may have been a Twelver Shīʿi himself for at least a part of his life.

Throughout the book the influence of Islamic norms and values can be felt in the way, for example, in which non-Islamic religions are classified. The author's openness can be seen in his readiness to offer information, without scholarly pretensions, about other religions and about Islamic sects to his contemporaries. What is unique about the work is that it was written in Persian, as early as the end of the eleventh century.

The Interest of These Four Scholars in Other Religions

Looking back on the four authors just described, we may conclude that with the exception of al-Bīrūnī they treated the non-Muslim religions in connection with the Islamic sects. For the most part these descriptions were followed by a theological discussion, whether it be in the form of a polemic or of a separate treatise of *kalām*.

It is fair to say that none of the books discussed were written exclusively for the sake of knowledge of the religion in question. The religion is put within an interpretative framework and the author draws his conclusions with the aim of somehow distinguishing good from bad. In view of this, he may either describe such religions as being fundamentally different from Islam and establish a barrier against their possible infiltration into Islam; for example, through sects advocating heretical doctrines. Or he may pay attention to previous revelations which are held to be at the basis of these religions. He may even give an interpretation of the fact that humanity is apparently always inclined to be religious. He may then justify his interpretation with accepted theological or philosophical doctrines.

It is important to notice the different ways in which these four authors use reason in their study and presentation: in order to systematize religious doctrines from a normative point of view, to compare that which is less known with that which is better known, or simply for purposes of classification. The use of reason as an instrument of inquiry prevents them from spiritualizing their study of other religions. It keeps them within the limits of reason and experience, eschewing mystical, gnostic, and speculative tendencies. This view of reason seems to me to be a firm point of departure in the study of other religions and comparative religion in general.

Questions

Several questions arise in connection with the work of the four scholars mentioned previously, and these are also relevant to the study of religion in general. One of these questions is whether or not a particular scholar appreciates the presence of more than one world-view positively. That is to say, whether he accepts the fact that there are several ways to interpret life, reality, and the world, and that other cultures and "worlds" exist apart from the one into which he was born.

As a matter of fact, in two of the four cases examined here, that is to say Ibn Hazm and al-Bīrūnī, the biographies show a life of reversals, under political and other pressures, as well as an involvement in broader intellectual and religious currents of thought. The societies in which these two scholars were working and writing were strongly influenced by political calamities, conflicting ideologies, or even foreign domination, which tried to eliminate the established order often in a radical way. During their lifetimes these scholars were exposed to other cultures and religions. This could be due to a number of factors: they may have lived in the border areas of a higher civilization; they may personally have met people of other religions and convictions; they may have lived near the remains of ancient pre-Islamic civilizations; and they may have been sent into exile or otherwise discovered the existence of other religious societies besides Islam.

I contend that in the case of Ibn Hazm and al-Bīrūnī we are not only dealing with a simple broadening of their mental and spiritual horizons. Their own life stories brought about a real break with the past for them, and perhaps even a separation from their own society. This break confronted them with different ways of life, as well as different worldviews and "life-worlds." It is precisely such a break or separation with a traditionally given world, with a more or less self-evident and even absolutized culture and religion, which was conducive to these thinkers' experiencing a new "real" world. This allowed for the discovery of the existence of a diversity of human ways of life, world-views and "life-worlds"—that is to say plurality—within the one given "real" world.

Such discoveries of course took place in the Muslim world as well as elsewhere, but further intellectual developments that could arise from them were hampered in the former case, unfortunately, and the discoveries apparently bore no intellectual or social fruits. One of the reasons may have been the idea that Islam was anyhow at the climax of the religious history of mankind. Why bother about other religions at all? Another reason may have been the presence of authoritarian regimes which did not encourage free inquiry in sensitive domains. Another reason again may have been the fact that Islam became identified with a particular Sunnī or Shīʿī orthodoxy which excluded a plurality of ways of life, world-views, and religions. It would seem fair to say that the establishment of institutionalized Sunnism or Shīʿism especially in education meant the end of a real interest in other religions. This was only to awaken again in the twentieth century.

Another question that arises from the analysis of the work of these and other Muslim scholars of the period, is that of the general extent of medieval Muslim interest in other religions. It seems that in the heyday of medieval Islamic civilization there was a definite interest in religions other than Islam and in religious history. This interest, however, seems to have remained extremely circumscribed. When Greek philosophy, medicine and sciences were studied, they were useful for the Muslim community. The study of religions in itself could not, however, be seen as something very useful for Islam and the Muslim community, except for apologetic or polemical purposes. The very existence of other religious communities which absolutized their truths and doctrines contradicted the claims of superiority of the Muslim community and the absolutization of its truth and its destiny in the world. Under such conditions the members of the community claiming superiority will not bother about other religions. And any universal interest which goes beyond their own community and world will remain confined to a few persons.

Deeper Questions

One may also look for deeper causes at the root of the more limited Muslim interest in other religions since the thirteenth century. Two lines of reasoning are possible. According to the first one, one can ask oneself whether there is something in Islam itself, as a *dernier venu* amongst the world religions, that could explain a certain insensitivity with regard to other religious orientations besides the Islamic one, and this particularly in regard to certain aspects of inner life. Could certain Islamic tenets be prohibitive of an interest in other religions? One can think of the defense of what is due to God, the notion of religion as a prescriptive system of divine origin, the conviction of the privileged role and mundane power of the Muslim community on earth, perhaps even the Islamic conception of "revelation" itself as contained forever in one single book. By looking at the way in which Islam is conceived as a religion, and how it it is seen to convey religious meanings, one may try to find at least a partial explanation of the decline of Muslim interest in other religions after having been ahead of Christianity in this respect.

According to the second line of reasoning, one can ask oneself whether an explanation for the limited Muslim interest in other religions besides Islam since the thirteenth century could not be found in the prevailing historical and social conditions. In fact, as a rule a lack of interest with regard to other religions is to be found in all religious traditions. In the case of Europe, we can refer to the extremely limited interest on the part of the Christians in other religions prior to the eighteenth century. Before the nineteenth century, Jewish interest in other religions was also minimal. For the Europeans, the historical and social conditions before the Enlightenment, including the Wars of Religion, blocked the discovery and the study of religions as a worthy subject of investigation. Due to a number of circumstances, the medieval and pre-Enlightenment period in the Muslim part of the world seems to have lasted for a longer period than in Europe and consequently the interest in an empirical study of other religions was delayed.

We shall now describe the way in which medieval Muslim authors perceived the main religions of the time, dealing first with their views of the so-called non-Biblical religions and later with their perceptions of Christiantity and Judaism. We must leave out a treatment of the way in which Muslims of the medieval period wrote about world history,[26] other great religions like the Chinese religions,[27] religions from the ancient past of which monuments remained,[28] the pre-Islamic religion of Arabia,[29] and literate or nonliterate religions known through travelers.[30]

Views on and Judgments of Specific Religions

Nonbiblical Religions

In addition to the biblical religions, Christianity and Judaism, that will be treated in the next section, Islam encountered some major nonbiblical religions in the Medieval period.[31]

Buddhism

It has become clear from recent studies[32] that only a few medieval Muslim authors knew about Buddhist doctrines, and then only fragmentarily. Buddhism as such on the whole remained outside the horizon of Islam, since there were only a few direct contacts.[33] Ibn al-Nadīm (wrote 377/987) deals with the person of the Buddha and some of his teachings,[34] al-Shahrastānī (d. 548/1153) is aware of a distinction between the Buddha (*al-Budd*),[35] whom he compares with the figure of *al-Khidr* in Islam, and a Bodhisattva (*Budhasf*). When treating the Buddhists (*ashāb al-bidāda*), he pays attention to their appearance in India and to their ethical doctrines.[36] Al-Irānshahrī (end 3rd/9th c.) must have given details of Buddhist cosmology which have been lost but which were used by al-Bīrūnī (d. after 442/1150),[37] and the author of the *Kitāb al-bad' wa'l-ta'rīkh* (written around 355/966) deals with the Buddhist doctrine of transmigration.[38] It is only Kamala Shri's account of Buddhism, which forms part of the end of the *Jāmiʿ at-tawārīkh* (World history of Rashīd al-Dīn) (d. 718/1318), that presents an overall view of Buddhism, and this was written by a Buddhist and shows many legendary features.[39] It is striking that al-Bīrūnī does not pay much attention to Buddhism in his extensive description of Indian religion and philosophy; it probably had largely disappeared from northern India by the end of the eleventh century.

Ibn al-Nadīm calls Budhasf the prophet of the Sumaniyya, a word derived from the Sanskrit *'sramana*, in the meaning of 'Buddhist monks'.[40] These Sumaniyya are described by Muslim authors as having constituted the ancient religion of Eastern Asia before the coming of the revealed prophetical religions here—that is to say, in Iran before Zarathustra's appearance, in ancient India, and in China. As a parallel to this, the religion of the Chaldeans was believed to have constituted the ancient religion of Western Asia, before the coming of the revealed prophetical religions there; the Harranians in northern Mesopotamia were thought to be the last descendants of these ancient Chaldeans. This is for instance reported by al-Khwārizmī (d. 387/997) and al-Bīrūnī (d. after 442/1050). In other words, the *Sumaniyyūn* and *Khaldāniyyūn* were held to have been the ancient idolaters in the East and the West, respectively, before the appearance of the prophets, and Buddhism as Sumaniyya was considered to have been the ancient idolatrous religion of the Eastern people.[41]

The main practice and doctrines of the Sumaniyya as reported by medieval Muslim authors were their worship of idols, their belief in the eternity of the world, their particular cosmology (implying, for instance, that the earth is falling into a void and that the world periodically goes under and is reborn), and the doctrine of the transmigration of souls (*tanāsukh al-arwāh*). Most interesting in this connection, however, is the idea that the Sumaniyya were skeptics, denying the validity of reasoning (*nazar*) and logical inference (*istidlāl*). In *kalām* those who deny reason, the *muʿattila*, are consequently called Sumaniyya.

Since the real Buddhists, as is well known, did not reject reasoning at all, we have an example here of a basic mechanism which we also meet in other cases. In scholastic theology (*kalām*), a particular metaphysical position that is refuted as being contrary to Islam is often projected upon a specific, lesser known group of non-Muslims. This was done not because they were known to hold this doctrine in reality (real knowledge was lacking) but *simply in order to ascribe a heretical doctrine to a particular group of outsiders*. In this way the *muʿattila* were called the Sumaniyya of Islam. This particular way of locating wrong doctrines implies a particular way of 'judging' non-Muslims without seeking to know them. After all, the real doctrine of the Sumaniyya was very different from that of the Muslim *muʿattila*.

Hinduism

Medieval Islam was better informed about Hinduism than about Buddhism, because of the gradual occupation of parts of northwest and north India first by Arab and then by Turkish conquests which led to the spread of Islam.[42] This becomes clear from the way in which India is regarded in historical works, travel accounts, and geographical and general encyclopedical works, as well as in works of *kalām* insofar as they have reached us.[43] The main issues discussed in connection with religion in India were the doctrine of transmigration of souls (*tanāsukh al-arwāh*), idol worship (e.g., several reports existed on a famous statue in Multān), the caste system, and some peculiar Indian doctrines and practices which struck the Muslims, such as the extreme asceticism of the yogis and, at the husband's cremation, the burning of widows and slaves. Only in a few cases, however, can we speak of an appreciation of Indian religion based on actual study and knowledge.

The celebrations of the millenary of al-Bīrūnī's birth in 362/973 have attracted new attention to his work, including his book on India. Apart from the valuable information contained in it, especially in view of the time at which it was written, it is a splendid case of what may be called a top-level Muslim perception of another religion and culture and has attracted attention from different sides.[44]

Another view and appreciation of Indian religions was given by al-Shahrastānī (d. 548/1153) a hundred years later. Al-Shahrastānī treats Hinduism in his *Kitāb al-milal wa'l-nihal* in the chapter of the *Ārā' al-Hind*, which deals in six successive sections with six groups. These are the Sabians, the *Barāhima*, the three groups of *ashāb al-rūhāniyyāt* (proponents of spiritual beings), *ʿabadat al-kawākib* (star worshippers) and *ʿabadat al-asnām* (idol worshippers), and finally the Indian philosophers. Where al-Bīrūnī divides the Hindus into the educated and the uneducated, al-Shahrastānī grades them according to degrees of idol-worship.

As mentioned earlier, Bruce B. Lawrence demonstrates convincingly that al-Shahrastānī uses the model of Sabianism in order to describe and legitimize different levels or grades of Hindu thought and worship.[45] This implies that al-Shahrastānī's judgment of the Hindus is differentiated in the same way as his judgment of the Sabians. The Vaishnavas and Shaivas are like the Sabian *ashāb ar-rūhāniyyāt*: they venerate Vishnu and Shiva as Spiritual Beings who were incarnated and brought laws, albeit without a scripture; as a consequence they cannot be called idolaters in the strict sense of the word. Those adoring Aditya and Chandra (sun and moon) are like the Sabian star-worshippers (*ʿabadat al-kawākib)*, which is a grade lower but still not idolatry. Only those who adore and prostrate themselves before man-made idols are real idolaters (*ʿabadat al-asnām)*, like the pagan Arabs of the *Jāhiliyya.*

In *kalām*, just as the Sumaniyya ('Buddhists') were described as those rejecting reason or as agnostics (*muʿattila*), the Barāhima ('Brahmins') were described as those accepting reason and believing in one God (*muwahhida*) but rejecting prophecy.[46] This too was a metaphysical position unacceptable in Islam, and, like the first position, this position was projected upon a specific, lesser-known group of non-Muslims. Little inquiry was made about the doctrines which the Buddhists or the Brahmins really held. The Sabians represent a third kind of metaphysical position which was judged to be contrary to Islam and projected on a certain obscure group of non-Muslims.[47]

Names like the Sumaniyya, the Barāhima, and the Sābiʾa are, consequently, categories of classification. They became technical terms designed within *kalām* as theological predicates and not as descriptions of empirical realities. As previously stated, this procedure implies a particular way of thinking about and then judging non-Muslims without seeking to know them. We shall see that the same holds true for the designation of people by means of their "constructed" religions, as Dualists, Jews, and Christians. They are not seen and studied for their own sake but as representing particular doctrines held to be contrary to Islam. The names simply serve to ascribe what are held to be wrong doctrines to particular groups of non-Muslims. They serve primarily to classify different beliefs held to be wrong.

These observations on al-Bīrūnī and al-Shahrastānī can be supplemented with similar observations on Rashīd-al-Dīn's (d. 718/1318) vision of India[48] which also shows a flexibility in interpreting Hinduism and a refusal to reject the whole religion outright. This trend to see the Indian religions in a more differentiated and positive light was to become even stronger when Muslims ruled great parts of India where Hindus constituted the majority of the population. The Hanafī and Mālikī schools of law, for instance, were willing to include Hindus within the category of *ahl al-dhimma* and give them protection accordingly.[49] Even when Hindus went on worshipping their gods they could enjoy the protection (*dhimma*) of the Muslim rulers on condition that they paid *jizya*. In other words, Hindus were not considered as polytheists *(mushrikūn)* in a strict sense. Consequently, they were not treated according to the *Sharīʿa*'s prescriptions for the treatment of *mushrikūn* in Muslim territory: conversion, departure, or death.

The three medieval authors mentioned here—al-Bīrūnī, al-Shahrastānī, and Rashīd al-Dīn—were not the only ones who saw India in a more positive light. There were some others whose views on Indian religion were not only negative.[50] Already the anonymous *Kitāb al-badʾ waʾl-taʾrīkh* (written ca. 966) suggests that the monotheistic Barāhima revere one God who sent an angel to them in human form. Al-Gardīzī (d. ca. 1060) describes two of the four basic divisions of the Hindu religion in purely monotheistic terms. Amīr Khusraw Dihlawī (1253–1325) even makes the statement that the Hindus are better than the adherents of the dualist religions and the Christians.[51] During the first century and a half of the Mughal period (1526–1857) positive Muslim views of Indian religions would develop further.

Mazdaism

Mazdaism,[52] also called Zoroastrianism, was founded by the prophet Zarathustra (Greek: Zoroaster) who may have lived in Transoxania, northeast present-day Iran as early as around 1000 B.C.E. Mazdaism became the state religion of the Iranian Sāsānid empire which was founded in 224 C.E. and it remained so until the Arab conquest of Iran was completed in 651.

During Muhammad's lifetime adherents of this religion were found in Arabia: in the northeast among members of the Tamīm tribe, in Hīra and Bahrein, in Oman and Yemen, and probably also among tradesmen in Mecca itself. Muhammad may have very well met them and S. 22:17 mentions the *majūs* (Zoroastrians) as a group whose beliefs fall somewhat between the People of the Book (*ahl al-kitāb*) and the polytheists (*mushrikūn*).

Starting out with a prophetic message which led to the formation of a community led by Zarathustra, Mazdaism developed into a strongly ritualistic, legalistic religion as attested to by the development of its Scriptures (the *Avesta*) and their commentaries (*zand*). Yet it retained an ethical impulse characterized by the belief proclaimed by Zarathustra that man has to continually choose between good and evil as two metaphysical principles. Besides the elaboration of ritual and legal prescriptions in much detail, there also developed various doctrinal currents. There was, for instance, a strong monotheistic tendency in Mazdean theological thought that concentrated on Zurvān as the eternal principle of time and on the primacy of Ohrmazd, the principle of the good, over Ahriman, the principle of evil. This tendency was particularly accentuated in apologetic literature addressed to Jews and Christians. There were also polytheistic tendencies as manifested in the importance given to the *Yazatas*, divine beings to whom a hymn is addressed in the Avesta and to whom a cult may be rendered. But there was also a rigidly dualistic theology, taking good and evil as two equally eternal principles; this strain of theology was developed in particular in ninth-century polemics against monotheistic Islam. At the end of the Sāsānid period, before the Arab conquest, the priestly class, closely linked to the aristocracy in a feudal, hierarchically structured society, exerted much power. Official rituals took place in fire temples where people could also undergo the prescribed rites of purification and where they could make food-offerings. There were no images in this religion and there was a positive, antiascetic attitude to life. Particular features included seasonal feasts, the avoidance of dead matter, the wearing of a sacred cord (*kustī*), and the exposure of the dead on "towers of silence" (*dakhmas*).

Most important perhaps for its later influence on political developments in Abbasid times (after 750) was the close link that existed in Sāsānid Iran between state and religion. This showed up in a religious glorification of Iran and the belief in a special charisma of its king, and especially in the fact that Mazdaism was considered to be the true religion of the Iranians. There were, however, religious minorities: in particular, Christians and Jews living in Mesopotamia, which constituted the western part of the empire, and Buddhists living in Afghanistan and Transoxania, which constituted the northeastern part. Up to the fifth century there had been persecutions of the Christians but those who belonged to the "Nestorian" Church of the East, which had been excommunicated from the Byzantine Empire, archenemy of Iran, enjoyed some degree of tolerance. At a later stage, certain religious minorities were given a kind of protected status in the empire, provided they did not become involved in politics; apostasy from Mazdeism was severely punished. Such rules may have been a model for the later *dhimma* rules in Islam.

Religious movements like those of Mani (216–276) and Mazdak (suppressed in 528) were in large part social protests against the hierarchical politicoreligious structure of Iranian society. Both communities were persecuted and Manicheism was to develop further outside Iran. It is interesting to note that Zoroastrians could also be found in western India, central Asia, and even China, probably among Iranians living there.

The Arab conquest in 651 meant the end of the Sāsānid empire. Muslims were confronted here with an important religion which was intimately linked to Iranian society and to which the Qur᾽ān made only one reference. Following a precedent according to which Muhammad is reported to have accepted *jizya* from the *Majūs* of Hajar, the Zoroastrians were treated relatively well by the Muslims, though not as well as the People of the Book, that is to say Jews and Christians. The Avesta was recognized by the Muslims as a kind of Scripture, a "semblance of the Book" (*shibhat al-kitāb*). Consequently, Zoroastrians were considered as *dhimmīs* and had to pay *jizya* for their protected status (*dhimma*). Their blood price, however, was only one-fifth of that of a Muslim and, unlike Jewish and Christian women, their women were forbidden to Muslims. They could keep their fire temples and celebrate their cult freely, at least at first, but they had no head of the community to represent them before the caliph. Precious information about Mazdaism, including Mazdean sects, is given by al-Baghdādī (d. 1037) and especially al-Shahrastānī (1076–1153).[53] Al-Khwārazmī in his *Mafātih al-ʿulūm* describes some eastern religions and religious groups, also in Iran.[54]

Although Mazdaism contained an important current of dualistic thought, Muslim polemics against the religion of Zarathustra were less vehement than, for instance, those against Manicheism.[55] This may be due in part to the fact that Mazdaism had many more adherents than Manicheism and represented, so to say, the national religion of Iran. Still, the Zoroastrians themselves lacked the missionary attitude of the Manicheans and, consequently, did not pose a direct threat to Islam. As mentioned earlier, Mazdaism was to be considered as a tolerable religion though not on the same level as the religions of the People of the Book. A certain spirituality in it was recognized.[56]

Interestingly enough, Mazdaism did not lend itself to the reproach of *forgery* (*tahrīf*) of its Scripture, perhaps since it was modest in its claim of having a prophet at its start and the Avesta as Scripture. It did not pass any judgment on prophets and revelations sent to other peoples in later times.

The main objection made against Mazdaism was that of *dualism*, a position which the Zoroastrians themselves in their replies defended tenaciously. Mazdean doctrines like the proper nature of evil, the existence of two eternal principles, and the idea of a continuous struggle between good and evil were subject to intense debate. Whereas for the Zoroastrians all suffering is inextricably linked with evil, for the Muslim polemicists this was not necessarily the case; in Islam, suffering and evil are not seen to be intrinsically related. Why should God not be the creator of evil? Why should evil have a creative force of its own? Evil is not determined in advance: Iblīs himself does not act out of determinism but out of his own free will.

Finally, certain religious practices of Mazdaism like the elaborate rites of purification, the New Year (*Nowrūz*) feast at spring, and the mythical stories of the creation of man and of the great kings of the past were considered by Muslims to be mere curiosities of a religion which was hardly thought to be harmful as long as it was subjected to Muslim authority. Indeed, *Nowrūz* was adopted in Abbasid court ritual, as was the autumn fest *Mihrijān*.

Although conversions were opposed by the priests and although they did not occur at the beginning on a mass scale, it was particularly the political and economic elite of Iranian society which converted to Islam, no doubt in order to retain their privileges.[57] There were sporadic destructions of fire temples and persecutions of Zoroastrians. The course of the eighth century witnessed a series of uprisings by Zoroastrian peasants, provoked by fiscal oppression, in particular in the eastern part of Iran. They crystallized in prophetical movements which became sometimes new Mazdean sects. Some changes in cult and customs took place in response to Islam such as, for instance, in the rituals of purification or in the exposure of the dead. When there came to be a shortage of priests, educated laymen seem to have played a more important role.

In the ninth and at the beginning of the tenth centuries, there was a noticeable recovery of Mazdaism. The old religious literature was collected for preservation, and a new apologetic and polemical literature against Islam emerged on a high intellectual level and in debate with Muslim Muʿtazilite thinkers. This was in particular in response to the problem of the origin of evil, to which the Zoroastrians claimed to have a more satisfactory solution with their dualist doctrine than the monotheistic Muslims could give. Yet this renaissance of Mazdaism did not last. This may have been due in part to the rise of the Samanid dynasty which promoted a renaissance of Iranian language and culture but under the banner of Islam. It led to the further development of the Iranian cultural heritage but not of Iranian religion. After the tenth century little is known about the apparently irreversible decline of Mazdaism in favor of Islam.

From the tenth century onward, groups of Zoroastrians migrated, when possible, to India where they settled as Parsis on the west coast. As far as Muslim attitudes toward Zoroastrians are concerned, Guy Monnot observes that they often have emotional resonances, in particular among Iranian authors. Whereas Arab authors and those Iranians who feel part of an "international" Islamic culture demonstrate a certain disdain of Mazdaism, many Iranian Muslims show some sensitivity and interest for the ancient religious traditions of their country.[58]

Manicheism

Manicheism[59] was a religion founded by Mani (216–276), a prophetical figure who, after the Sāsānid empire was established in 224, preached a synthesis of all preceding religions with a gnostic interpretation of the truths contained in them. Despite the hope of success in the beginning, Mani was accused of heresy by the Mazdean religious leaders and put to death. Part of the books, which he wrote himself, survived however, and his doctrine spread westward, around the Mediterranean where it was persecuted by the Christians, and eastward, where it penetrated from Iran into central Asia and China. In 762 it became the main religion of the Uygur Turks in present-day northwestern China, and remained so until the end of the Uygur state, a century later.

The encounter between Manicheism and Islam was particularly ominous. There are profound differences as to content, but Islam takes up some formal elements of Manicheism as far as the idea of a final revelation encompassing previous revelations is concerned. In both cases the prophet claims to be the seal of a series of earlier prophets, bringing the definitive revelation which had previously been given to the earlier prophets but which had been neglected by their followers and communities. In both cases revelation is conceived of as the literal dictation of sacred words by an angelic being and as written down in the form of Scripture, which was considered to be absolute truth in a literal sense and sacred reality in a mundane world. How would monotheistic Islam with its mundane interests in building a sociopolitically based *dīn* on earth respond to a religion that had an analogous concept of revelation but had developed along spiritual and dualistic-gnostic lines? Interestingly enough, the Qur'ān does not even mention Mani or Manicheism. Mani was never considered a prophet, and there is no recognition of Mani's writings as Scripture. Other religions which according to Islamic criteria were not strictly monotheistic were recognized. But Muslims did not consider Manicheism a religion at all, but rather a philosophical system or a sect only resembling Islam; it was thus a caricature of religion as it should be.

Muhammad himself may have heard of or even listened to Manicheans. Arabia had close commercial contacts with Egypt and Mesopotamia, where centers of Manicheism existed; there was a Manichean community in northeastern Arabia. Later Muslim authors wrote that among the Quraysh, which was the leading tribe of Mecca, there had been some *zindīqs* (i.e., Manicheans) who had learned the doctrine of *zandaqa* (Manicheism) from Christians in Hīra in northeastern Arabia at the border of present-day Iraq. It has been hypothesized that S. 6: 1–3 ("It is God who established darkness and light") implies a reference to the Manichean doctrine which held that light and darkness are two independent principles. The text in question proclaims God to be sovereign over them. Several *hadīths* give a severe condemnation of *zindīqs*.

At the conquest of Iran, Manicheism was more widespread in Khorasān and beyond than in Mesopotamia with the capital Ktesiphon where the central Sāsānid power was established and where Manicheism had been severely persecuted. After the conquest, the Umayyad dynasty (651–750) in Damascus and its governors in Mesopotamia seem not to have been unfavorable to the Manicheans, whose numbers, consequently, grew in Mesopotamia. The establishment of the Abbasid dynasty in 750 and its moving of the capital to Mesopotamia, however, led to a change in attitude toward Manicheism. Ideologically, the empire was now to become an "Islamic" state where religions without *dhimma* (protection) would not be permitted. Politically, the influence of Iranians who had been used to consider religion as the backbone of the state increased immensely under Abbasid rule. As Zoroastrian converts to Islam, who had been accustomed to the persecution of Manicheans, they probably did not look on Manicheism with much favor. Only in intellectual circles does Manicheism seem to have found a more positive response, and it is on this level that the encounter of the two religions took place.

Precious information about the Manicheans, often simply called "dualists," is given by Ibn al-Nadīm in his *Fihrist* (987) and also by al-Khwārizmi (d. 997) in his *Mafātīh al-ʿulūm*. Ibn al-Nadīm gives 15 names of important *zindīqs* and mentions that only five Manicheans still lived in Bagdad in his lifetime. ʿAbd al-Jabbār (d. 1025) mentions the names of nine Manichean leaders of the past.

It is in the eighth century that the terms *zindīq* and *zandaqa* appear in Arabic. In Sāsānid times the Pahlevi word *zandik* meant someone who has a *zand* (commentary) which is different from the orthodox, accepted *zand*. In a general sense this meant a heretic, an apostate, a free-thinker, but in a more specific sense it came to mean an adherent of Mani, a Manichean. In eighth-century Arabic the word *zindīq* also had the double meaning of an unbeliever in a general sense and of a Manichean, with a negative connotation.

It has been observed that, in Muslim thinking, just as the sin of the polytheists is idolatry (*shirk*), the sin of the Manicheans is that of agnosticism (*taʿṭīl*, literally, emptying, i.e., 'emptying' the concept of God). Manicheans with their mythical representations and their dualistic scheme of light and darkness are held to be agnostic. Moreover, in the Muslim view, with their spiritual church they do not represent a sociopolitical community in the ordinary sense of the word.

As soon as *zindīq* becomes a derogatory term, its application becomes more pervasive and extends to anyone suspected of heretical ideas. *Zandaqa* then means something akin to intellectual rebellion or pride which insults the honor of the prophet. There may have been the accompanying idea that *zandaqa* may be politically subversive. If the phenomenon of *zandaqa* was spreading in early Abbasid times, and if it was viewed as dangerous for the new Islamic state, Manicheism was supposed to constitute an important part of this abominable phenomenon and to be a potential danger for the state.[60]

The caliph al-Mahdī started a persecution of *zindīqs* in 780 and again from 782 on; his successor al-Hādī continued the persecutions until 786. It was the first state persecution of a non-Muslim religion in the history of Islam. At the same time, intense polemical activity was directed at the Manicheans. The first author to write a refutation of Manicheism was the founder of the Muʾtazila, Wāsil b. ʿAtāʿ; the text, written ca. 728, is unfortunately lost. The second author was the Imām Jaʿfar al-Sādiq (d. 765) himself; another Shīʿī author, Hishām b. al-Hakam (d. 795 or 815), also wrote a refutation of the *zindīqs* which is lost as well. During the eighth and ninth centuries no less than 18 refutations appeared, addressed specifically to the Manicheans.

Before the middle of the tenth century most Manicheans must have left Mesopotamia and sought refuge in Khorasān and beyond. Their headquarters were established in Samarkand where, showing prudence after persecution, they called themselves Sabeans (*Sābiʾūn*). The Sabeans are mentioned in the Qurʾān, in a list of religious groups (S. 2:62, 5:69, 22:17), as a community with a religion to be respected. Several groups, notably the people of Harrān in northern Iraq, claimed to be Sabeans so as to save themselves and their religion.

Manicheism spread both to the West and to the East, as far as China, thereby constituting a real world religion, adapting itself to various cultural and religious environments and proclaiming a gnostic truth which was contained in all former religions. Tragically, it has been persecuted by all monotheistic religions. Thanks to Ahmad Ashgār al-Shīrāzī we have a volume containing all Arabic and Persian texts on Mani and his religion as known in 1956, the year of publication.[61] These still existing materials make it possible to reconstitute to some extent the image of Mani and Manicheism which were developed by medieval Arab and Iranian authors.

Muslim medieval judgments of Manicheism were harsh. Next to Christianity, as the doctrine of the "tritheists," Manicheism, as the doctrine of the "dualists," was seen to be the main enemy of Islam. No original Manichean texts in Arabic have been preserved, and of the numerous polemical texts addressing the dualist doctrine only a few have survived.

The ways in which Manicheism represented a danger to Islam, and Islamic thought in general, was only realized some 50 years ago when scholarship established the extent to which Manicheism had been a "world religion" between the fifth and tenth centuries, before its gradual disappearance. We already drew attention to the state of Manicheism in Muhammad's lifetime and his possible relationship to it. Here we will confine ourselves to presenting the main arguments formulated by Muslim thinkers against Manicheism[62] and give some elements of the historical relationships between Muslims and Manicheans.

Since Islam does not recognize Mani's writings as revealed texts nor Mani as a prophet, the accusation of textual forgery levelled against the Hebrew Bible and the New Testament could not apply to the Manichean Scripture. Yet, the reproach of forgery could be made in a more general way, in the sense that Mani had falsified, for instance, the pure religion of Jesus and other prophets by putting it within a dualist framework and through the obscure myth of the struggle between the elements of light and the forces of darkness. The Manichean myth is judged by Muslim polemicists as being too fantastic to be equated with religion.

Errors of thought and doctrine In the view of Muslim polemicists, the Manichean doctrine of dualism (*thanawiyya*), the existence of two eternal principles, constitutes a fundamental attack on the truth of *tawhīd*, the oneness and uniqueness of God. As in the case of Buddhism and Brahmanism, Manicheism was probably identified with a particular form of heresy or unbelief formulated in Islamic *kalām*, namely *taʿtīl*, the "emptying" of the idea of God, which represented in Muslim eyes a kind of agnosticism. This doctrine was then ascribed to the Manicheans without, however, what Manichean theologians had thought themselves and what they meant with their system being really studied. The following errors were noted by Muslim theologians.

1. The doctrine of the *nature of evil*, which holds that evil constitutes a reality in itself and that it has an absolute origin, is rejected. An argument taken from the Qurʾān was that evil cannot detract from God's power and authority and that its force is not strong enough to dispense the human being with his or her basic responsibility to carry out what is good and to withhold from what is evil. Rational arguments were used to deny the absolute character of the force of evil.
2. The doctrine of the eternal nature of *two principles* is judged to be an error. This doctrine implies that good and evil have two absolutely different origins which are called their "authors" or principles. According to the Qurʾān, however, both light and darkness were created by God and do not constitute real or autonomous agents. It was also inferred from the Qurʾān that God possesses power over what is morally bad, and that God in his all-mightiness even has the power to commit evil himself, although in reality he does not do it. Furthermore, the idea of the eternal character of two principles was refuted by means of rational arguments: only one principle can be eternal.
3. The idea of a *mixing of good and evil* in a battle between the two forces was held to be impossible. The Qurʾān indeed defines good and evil, respectively, as obedience and disobedience to God's commandments, which excludes any intermingling of them.

Errors of religious practice Muslim polemicists presented serious objections to certain religious practices, especially among the Manichean elect, such as (a) disdain of the *body* and its needs, leading to a complete neglect of the basic needs of the human body by the elect; (b) contempt of *material* realities as belonging to the realm of darkness, and high esteem for *spiritual* realities as being part of the realm of light; and (c) certain practices and prohibitions as, for instance, the refusal to kill animals, even harmful ones. The Muslim religious vision seems to have been hurt particularly by certain elements of the Manichean view of life:

1. The absolute separation between good and evil disproves monotheism, that is to say the doctrine of *tawhīd*. The all-mightiness of God, and even the concept of one unique God, is questioned in this way.
2. The harmony between the creation and God, its creator, as well as the harmony given within creation itself find themselves disrupted because of the presence of an eternal enemy of God. The idea of a basic split in reality, and the idea that God would have to wage a permanent war against an enemy are contrary to the basic harmony of creation.
3. The idea of a mutual engagement or "mixture" of good and evil in fighting is absurd from a rational point of view and impossible as a reality.
4. The subordination of all oppositional concepts under the basic opposition of two contrary metaphysical principles undermines the primordial character of *tawhīd* both as the starting point of logical thinking and as the metaphysical principle of reality.
5. The relationship between the created human being with his individual responsibility, and God who is his creator is dislocated by the idea of two opposed ontological principles and by the idea that evil can constitute an autonomous reality.

The danger of Manicheism Earlier we gave some details about the history of Manicheism and its spread. We saw that under the Umayyads Manicheism acquired a new foothold in Mesopotamia. What then may have been the attraction of Manicheism and why was it seen as a danger by the new dynasty of rulers,[63] the Abbasids who moved the capital to Iraq in 750?

As a philosophical system Manicheism apparently appealed to the cultivated public, where its rational philosophical ideas and values rather than its mythological elements were stressed. It not only offered a rational solution for the problem of evil, but it also gave a coherent vision and a meaningful interpretation of human life and the world. As a philosophy, Manicheism could claim a particular rational universality, all the more so since Mani himself had made a conscious effort to bring the different religions of his time into a broad synthesis. Moreover, Manicheism stood for a long cultural tradition of philosophical religious thought which had long existed in the Near East and Iran before the Arab conquest and the arrival of an Islam which lacked philosophical inclination. This cultural tradition could not but resist Islam, by claiming to have a universal orientation with a gnostic kind of knowledge of God. It made a distinction between different kinds and degrees of knowledge and insight and applied a dualistic metaphysical scheme which was well-thought out. For a long time rational dualism had been part of Iranian culture and of an Iranian educated elite. The idea of a common hidden "gnostic" truth could effectively be used to minimize the differences and oppositions existing between different religions.

Besides its religious aspects Manicheism could also become the flag and symbol of the Iranian cultural heritage. In fact, it constituted a form of opposition to the Arabs and their Islam on the part of Iranians who suffered physically and culturally under the occupation of the culturally poor and religiously pretentious Arab Muslims. Thus Manicheism became part of the claim of Iranian cultural superiority over the Arabs—that is to say part of the movement of the *shuʿūbiyya*. It was able to mobilize pro-Iranian loyalties which were eventually to take dangerous political forms. As a consequence, the Abbasid leadership, after having used the Iranians to establish itself in 750, now made an effort to diminish Iranian influence and spiritual culture in favor of Islam regarded as a universal monotheistic religion and backbone of the empire.

On a religious level, Manicheism, as a vision of the world which was of gnostic origin, had a pessimistic view of the empirical reality of life and the world. It could not but oppose the more naive attitude of positive affirmation of life and the world as propounded in Islam. Indeed, Manicheism was well suited to become the religion and ideology of those who suffered under the domination of this Islam. As was pointed out earlier, on an intellectual level, the universally oriented view of Manicheism with its openness to humanism became a means of resisting the particularistic pressures of the Arab rulers. Last but not least, Manicheism was able to identify evil and to promise redemption after the present time of suffering. All of this explains why Manichean propaganda obtained positive results. From an Arab Muslim point of view, Manicheism represented both an ideological opposition to the religion of *tawḥīd* and a political, largely ethnic opposition to Arab domination. In short, Manicheism was, from the Abbasid rulers' point of view, a permanent potential source of agitation and revolt. It had to be suppressed.

The Biblical Religions

Christianity

Muslim writings about Christians and Christianity[64] during the medieval period were many and various. As far as the Christian religion is concerned, they were highly critical, in particular of those Christian doctrines referred to in the Qurʾān, insofar as they were perceived to be contrary to basic Islamic doctrines. These touched on, for instance, the unity and unicity of God (*tawḥīd*) and the fundamental difference and distance between man and God, his creator, lawgiver, and judge.

The knowledge of Christianity as a religion was largely confined to those doctrines to which the Qurʾān alludes and the main divisions between the Christian communities of the Middle East which had resulted from the doctrinal decisions of the Councils of Nicea (325) and Chalcedon (451). Muslims had little idea of the differences between the Eastern (Oriental and Orthodox) and Western (Catholic, later also Protestant) churches.

Muslims of the period identified Christianity as a religion opposed to Islam as a religion; the truths of these two religions were thought to be mutually exclusive. As in the case of the religions treated earlier, Muslim theologians projected what they considered to be false doctrines, according to the Qurʾān and *kalām*, on the Christians whom they generally perceived as unbelievers (*kuffār*). The term "Christians" was a term used to identify a group of unbelievers held to adhere to particular doctrines judged to be wrong in *kalām*. There was no further study of what Christians meant with their doctrines, and there was little interest in knowing more about the Christians' practical life or religious institutions. This was all the more so since Christianity was professed either by what would become minorities in Muslim territory who, like the Jews, had the secondary status of *dhimmīs*, or by political enemies outside Muslim territory, Byzantine and Latin Christians who were liable to attack Muslim lands.

From the Christians' point of view, Islam represented a fearful reality, and not only for doctrinal reasons. A large part of the lands which had been Christian under Byzantine rule in the sixth century were conquered by Arabs who had Islam as their religion (*dīn*). For the conquered Christians, Islam was the religion of a dominating power which imposed on them growing economic and political burdens even though they had been accustomed to the high demands of the Persians and the Greeks.

The Christians on the other, northern side of the Mediterranean, the Byzantines and Latins, saw Islam as the religion of an aggressive enemy. Muslim armies had taken the Near East including the Holy Land, North Africa, Spain, and most islands in the Mediterranean, as well as parts of Italy. They had encamped before the walls of Constantinople, at the beginning of the eighth century, and Rome, in the middle of the ninth century. In terms of military confrontation, the second half of the medieval period can be characterized as one great *reconquista* of Europe going as far as North Africa and the Volga. The liberation of the Balkans took another four centuries. In this "battle for Europe" the Christians employed both military and ideological means, and one can speak of ideological centers of anti-Islamic propaganda supported by interests of different kinds.

Much medieval Muslim and Christian writing about the other religion, to which the greater part of this section is devoted, remains incomprehensible if one does not take into account the conflictuous historical, social, and political context in which these texts were written. Equally, actions like the Crusades, the *reconquista* of Spain and Portugal, and the search for the legendary Prester John (the Christian king behind the Muslim ring around Europe) can only be understood in terms of the great conflict between two religiopolitical powers who saw each other as antagonists. In this conflict both Islam and Christianity were reduced to ideological instruments in the great contest of the two major power blocks of the Middle Ages. The following pages are meant to describe the polemics especially from the Muslim side and to see them in the context of the time.

Religious polemics in historical context It would seem logical that the violence and change of power in the Middle East, and the Arabization and Islamization of so many regions which followed, would lead to a serious confrontation in the spiritual realm, too.[65] An abundant polemical literature in Islam exists against Christianity, and many of the texts have not yet been edited.[66] After the more favorable judgments on Christians and Christianity expressed in the earlier sūras of the Qurʾān, the polemic starts at the end of the Medinan period, when Muhammad was confronted with Christian Arab tribes opposing his expansion in Northwestern Arabia. The main Qurʾānic accusations against Christians at the time are that they attribute a son to God, that they consider Jesus as God, and that they venerate priests and other beings besides God, so that they are not true monotheists. They commit *shirk* (associationism) and are to be considered as *kuffār* (unbelievers).

A first real confrontation with articulate Orthodox Christians who were theologically schooled took place in Damascus at the time of the Umayyad dynasty.[67] The initiative here seems to have been taken by the Christians who, partly spurred on by a superior culture and partly out of self-defense, put specific questions to the Muslims who had to develop resources to find answers to them. The debates dealt with subjects such as the Word of God, the nature of revelation and prophecy, the unity of God, and the destiny of man and his salvation. They constituted some of the themes which underlay the rise and further development of *kalām*.

This religious polemic between Muslims and Christians occurred in a context of continuous tensions and conflicts. Both within Muslim territory and in Byzantium, Christians viewed Islam in the first centuries as a heresy of the one great, true religion and as a heresy it was a threat to the true religion. The Christians' tactics were, as in the case of Christian heresies, to refute Islam on those points where it clashed with those elements of doctrine, law, and ethics which were the cornerstones of the firm construct of Christian theology. We can distinguish various periods in these mutual polemics.

1. In the *first period*, up until the middle of the ninth century and within Muslim territory, Christians could exert a certain sociopolitical, cultural, and religious pressure. The *sociopolitical* pressure consisted of a whole-hearted defense of the privileges given to the different Christian communities within Muslim territory, especially in the form of treaties negotiated between the Arab conquerors and the Christian towns and regions which surrendered. Christians also played an important role in administration and in trade. The *cultural* pressure consisted of the use of the full Hellenistic and Syriac cultural heritage, referring to a glorious past and deploying brilliant scholarship in philosophy, sciences, and medicine against invaders felt to be uneducated desert nomads.

Most important, however, was the *religious* pressure exerted. The Christians raised questions about Islam to which the Muslims were obliged to find answers. Thus they were forced to define their attitudes, not only on a sociopolitical level as Muslims in relation to Christians but also on a religious level as Islam's relationship to Christianity. The result was that already in the Umayyad period (661–750), the main issues of the Muslim-Christian debate had been formulated. From the very beginning, the Muslims maintained that God's will was the source of all human action. They explicitly rejected the Trinity, embraced Qurʾānic christology (that is, no crucifixion), and denied any divine nature in Christ—that is, the Incarnation. With regard to the doctrine of revelation, the Muslims proclaimed the doctrine of the literal identity of the Qurʾān with the Word of God and of the Qurʾān as final Revelation. They held to the doctrine of prophecy and of divine Law brought by prophets, with Muhammad as the "Seal of the Prophets." They maintained the accusation, based on Qurʾānic texts, that the Old and New Testament were falsifications of hypothetical Scriptures brought by Moses and Jesus. They interpreted the victories of the Arab Muslim armies as a sign of God's predilection toward Islam. On the Christian side, we possess from the Umayyad period a treatment of Islam by John of Damascus, in chapter 101 of his Book on the Heresies.[68] Other texts on Islam have been attributed to him, but their authenticity is questionable. For John, Islam was a forerunner of the Antichrist: *Prodromos tou Antichristou*. The encounter between Muslims and Christian theologians in Syria was a powerful incentive for the development of Islamic theological thought, with an apologetic tendency.[69]

There are reports of discussions, whether historical or fictitious, between Christians and Muslims during this first period. We have, for instance, in an early Syriac source a report of a debate held by a certain patriarch John, probably a Syrian Orthodox, with an "emir of the Agarenes."[70] There is the text of a letter which a certain Arethas, a Christian, is said to have sent to the governor of Damascus.[71] There was also a famous discussion between the Nestorian Catholicos (Patriarch) Timothy I (728–823) and the Abbasid caliph al-Mahdī (r. 755–785), probably in his later years.[72] Much later, a famous religious discussion between two friends, the Christian al-Kindī and the Muslim al-Hāshimī, was written, probably from within the territory acquired by the Byzantine conquest at the beginning of the tenth century. A literary work, the discussion takes place in the court of al-Maʾmūn and shows sophistication in terms of reasoning as well as frankness of expression.[73]

However, it was under the Abbasid dynasty (750–1258), and especially in the middle part of the ninth century, under caliphs such as al-Maʾmūn (813–833) and al-Mutawakkil (847–861), that polemical literature developed. This increase in Muslim polemics led to a *second period* of Muslim-Christian polemics. It was encouraged by the new rulers' policy of establishing an Islamic state, by their stressing of Islam as the religious ideology of the state, and by an increasing state interference in religious matters. This policy culiminated under al-Maʾmūn and al-Mutawakkil. The state interference concerned not only doctrinal expression but also a stricter definition of the rules according to which—and limits within which—non-Muslim minorities such as Jews and Christians could enjoy the protection (*dhimma*) of the state.[74] In the polemical writings of both sides we find the use of philosophy, in particular Aristotelian logic and metaphysics which not only philosophers but also Christian thinkers such as Theodor Abū Qurra (c. 740—c. 826)[75] had developed and already employed in their theological discourses. Abū Qurra alone wrote 17 polemical treatises against Islam and saw Muhammad as a false prophet working in the spirit of Arius (4th c.) who had been accused of heresy. Abū Qurra is one of the most important Christian theologians of the rich polemical literature written by Christian Arabs against Islam.[76] Muslims had learned Aristotelian logic through translations and, thanks to the effort of the Muʿtazilites, had adapted it for the formulation and reasoned defense of Islamic doctrines. Various schools of thought within Islam and Christianity used it for their debates and, equally, in refuting each other.

2. In this *second period* the initiative shifted to the Muslim side, once again on three levels. On the *sociopolitical* level, pressure was first exerted against the Manicheans and against Iranian social and political influence, which led to the downfall of the influential Iranian family of the Barmecids under Hārūn al-Rashīd in 803.

More than half a century later, a similar pressure was exerted against Christians who aroused hostility by their prosperity, social, and cultural influence. Under al-Mutawakkil (847–861) Christianity came under increasing attack. This found expression in the formulation and back-dating of the so-called Edict of ʿUmar which regulated the position of the religious minorities in a discriminatory way.[77] It also became visible in al-Jāhiz's (d. 869) vehement reply to a Christian tract in which he attempts to demonstrate the social vices of the Christians while using ambiguous invectives to incite his readers.[78] On a *cultural* level, the Christians within Muslim territory still dominated over the Muslims who remained the learners—and who were willing to learn—in the fields of philosophy, medicine, and the sciences. The Arab Muslims, however, prided themselves on their ethnic and linguistic superiority. Indeed, the ninth century saw a growth and flowering of Arabic literature together with a decisive development and formulation of the religious sciences of Islam in Arabic: *tafsīr* (Qur'ānic exegesis), *ʿilm al-hadīth* (science of tradition), *fiqh* (jurisprudence), and *kalām* (scholastic philosophy and theology).

Initiatives were also taken on a *religious* level. We have already mentioned al-Jāhiz who wrote at the request of the caliph al-Mutawakkil. Another well-known refutation was written in the same period, around 850, by the convert ʿAlī ibn Rabban al-Tabarī (d. 855).[79] The strength of Muslim polemical thought in the middle of the ninth century C.E. is, however, clearest in Abū-ʿĪsā al-Warrāq's refutation of Christian doctrines.[80]

The polemic was then carried out mainly with philosophical–dialectical arguments, in particular by Muʿtazilite *mutakallimūn*. There was a close connection between the intra-Muslim polemic against heresies and the polemic against other religions. Christians, for instance, were often compared with particular heretics within Islam like the Murjiʿites and Rāfidites, just as these Muslim groups could be attacked for having "Christianizing" tendencies. The Muʿtazilites themselves, however, who were leading this intellectual combat against the Christians as against the Manicheans, were in an ambivalent position. Having assimilated Greek logic, they could combat the Christians and refute with Aristotelian logic the doctrines of the trinitarian divine substance and the divine nature of Jesus. They had to pay the price, however, within their own community, for having arrived, by means of the same logic, at the formulation of doctrines denying the existence of the attributes of God as entities in themselves and the eternal character or "uncreatedness" of the Qur'ān. These doctrines were not accepted within the wider Muslim community, and Ashʿarī theology replaced Muʿtazilī theology.

From the middle of the ninth century onwards the Muslim attitude to the Bible also started to change. On the one hand, Biblical texts were now used in the debate with Christians; on the other hand, a kind of Bible criticism began to develop.[81] Muslim polemic combined the use of logical arguments of a philosophical nature with scriptural arguments based on the Old and New Testaments. This indicates a better knowledge of the Bible due to translations or information passed on by converts.[82] In the debate with the Christians about Scripture, the question of *naskh* (abrogation) arose; the Christians took a more lenient attitude toward this matter than did the Jews, since they themselves believed in the "abrogation" of the Old Covenant by the new one. Here the principal point of attack by Muslim polemicists, with regard to Scripture, consequently, is not *naskh* as in the case of Judaism, but the accusation of *tahrīf*, corruption of the text both of the Old and of the New Testament.[83] Different positions could be held with regard to the texts, corresponding with different interpretations of *tahrīf*. Was the text itself falsified, or were certain lines simply omitted? Or was the text itself reliable but wrongly interpreted by the Christians? Moreover, whereas the Qur'ān was supposed to have been transmitted faultlessly by Muhammad and those who had heard his recitations, it was held that this was not the case with the Christian Scripture. The argument of a wrong transmission (*tawātur*) of the *injīl* that God had supposedly given to Jesus was reinforced by the fact that contradictions exist between the four Gospels, something Muslim polemicists were glad to demonstrate.

Closely connected with the scriptural argument for the superiority of the Qur'ān (taken as a pure, revealed text) over the Bible (taken as a text that suffered from *taḥrīf*) are the arguments derived from the Islamic doctrine of prophethood. Just as the Qur'ān had been declared to be the uncreated and infallible Word of God, in the second half of the ninth century C.E., so Muhammad's status as the infallible seal of the prophets proclaiming definite truth was fixed. The three issues of *naskh*, *taḥrīf*, and *prophethood,* together with Aristotelian logic, formed the basis for the *mutakallimūn*'s polemics against Christianity, as they did for their polemics against Judaism. But there were considerable variations in Muslim views and interpretations.

Polemics against Christianity went further and further beyond the typical *kalām* works. The *tafsīrs* of the ninth and tenth centuries C.E. show increasing polemical tendencies against Christianity, and they now quoted texts from the New Testament and other Christian sources in support of certain verses of the Qur'ān or certain views of a particular commentator against Christianity.[84] It has been suggested by A. Abel that, on closer analysis, the stories of certain legendary figures, like Dhū-l-Qarnayn,[85] or stories like the *Qiṣaṣ al-anbiyā'* of al-Tha'ālibī (about prophets from the past) also show polemical tendencies directed against Christianity or the *ahl al-kitāb*. The same may be the case with more popular poetry and folk literature like the story of 'Antar, the *Dhāt al-himma*[86] or the *Alf layla wa-layla* ("1001 Nights") should also be investigated when studying the issue. The Muslim controversy with Christianity has found many different expressions and very probably also denotes a social controversy. Thus, the refutation of Christianity as a religion, with its particular doctrines and rites, implied a humiliation of the Christian community living in Muslim territory. Al-Jāhiz not only refuted Christian doctrines but also described the Christian people as a social evil.[87]

The literature of controversy hence becomes part of the social pressure exerted, for whatever reason, at a particular time and place on the non-Muslim minorities in Muslim societies. This holds true, whether it is directed against the Christians or against Jews, Manicheans, Zoroastrians, or Hindus. The many variations that can be found in this literature—which was read mainly by Muslims and hardly by the objects of the attack themselves—therefore represent different social and political profiles. Some major theological refutations in this period were those of the Zaidī Shī'ī al-Qāsim b. Ibrāhīm (785–860),[88] the Ash'arī Abū Bakr al-Bāqillānī (d. 1013),[89] and the Mu'tazilī 'Abd al-Jabbār (d. 1025).[90]

Apart from the exchanges and polemics between Muslims and Christians within Muslim territory, embassies and letters were also exchanged between Arab Muslims and the Byzantines, Christians outside Muslim territory. There were different kinds of relations between the Empire and the Caliphate.[91] Both parties had their views about each other,[92] and there were polemical writings between them as well.[93] The later patriarch Photios (ca. 820–891), for example, was part of a Byzantine embassy sent to the caliph al-Mutawakkkil in Baghdad in 855/856;[94] a correspondence was attributed to the caliph 'Umar II (717–720) and the emperor Leo III.[95] The quotation from the first letter which Nicholas I Mystikos, Patriarch of Constantinople (901–907 and 912–925) sent around 913 to the Abbasid caliph al-Muqtadir (908–932) in Baghdad is famous:

> 'Two sovereignties—that of the Arabs and that of the Byzantines—surpass all sovereignty on earth, like the two shining lights in the firmament. For this one reason, if for no other, they ought to be partners and brethren. We ought not, because we are separated in our ways of life, our customs and our worship, to be altogether divided; nor ought we to deprive ourselves of communication with one another by writing in default of meeting personally. This is the way we ought to think and act, even if no necessity of our affairs compelled us to it."[96]

The emperor Michael III (842–867) received at least one letter from a caliph inquiring about his faith and summoning him to accept Islam. He left the answer to Niketas Byzantios 'the Philosopher' who lived between 842 and 912 and who wrote two letters of response in the 860s. He also wrote a defense of the doctrine of the Trinity followed by a lengthy refutation of the Qur'ān.[97]

3. A new wave of Christian-Muslim polemics arose in the tenth century; one may speak of a new, *third period*. By that time Byzantine armies had reconquered Calabria, Crete, and Cyprus, and during the reign of Romanos I Lepapenos (914–944) they moved via Cilicia to Syria. In Byzantium and Syria some larger treatises in Greek were written against Islam, and in addition more popular Byzantine literature flourished on the subject, probably designed to bring the population of the reconquered territories back to Christianity. This must also have been an era of hope for the Christians, living deep in Muslim territory and awaiting a final Christian victory over the Muslims. Quite a number of polemical treatises were written by Christians within Muslim territory during this period, among which were the refutations by two Syrian Orthodox theologians of the polemical works of two Muslim theologians; these were written by Yahyā b. ʿAdī (893–974)[98] and Ibn Zurʿa (943–1008).[99]

History took another course, however. Not only was a collapse prevented, but also the Byzantines were pushed further and further back, and this took a serious turn with the arrival of the Seljuk Turks in the later eleventh century, and their subsequent penetration deep into Anatolia and the harrassment of pilgrims going to the Holy Land. The stream of Christian polemical pamphlets subsided.

Among the polemicists against Christianity, Ibn Hazm (994–1064)[100] in Spain sharply criticized the biblical text. In his *Fisal* (or *Fasl*) he writes about Christianity twice, first ranging the Christians in the category of the polytheists (*Fisal* I, pp. 48–65) and then, in the probably inserted *Izhār*, including them among the *ahl al-kitāb* (*Fisal* III, pp. 2–75). As with the Old Testament (*Fisal* I, pp. 98–224), he severely attacks the New Testament (*Fisal* II, pp. 2–75). He denounces contradictions between different texts and what he calls absurdities in the text itself; these he lays at the door of the Evangelists as far as the Gospels are concerned. The textual mistakes which he uncovers furnish as many arguments against the current Christian doctrine of the literal inspiration of the Bible. His conclusion is that the Bible cannot be considered to have been revealed.

Probably at the end of the eleventh century C.E. another text refuting Christian doctrines was written, *Al-radd al jamīl*.[101] It also takes the New Testament text as its departure and argues on the basis of this text against the doctrine of the divine nature of Jesus. There is an immense difference between the two refutations of Christianity on the basis of New Testament texts, as far as organization and execution is concerned.

During the eleventh century there were on the Christian side some well-known Nestorians who responsed to Muslim polemical writings. The names of Elias of Nisibis (975–1046)[102] and ʿAbdallāh b. al-Tayyib (d. 1043)[103] deserve to be mentioned.

The scene changed significantly with the arrival of the first Crusaders shortly before 1100, followed by others in successive waves; they finally disappeared a century and a half later. The Crusades were essentially a Latin affair, but their repercussions were also felt on the reemerging polemical literature in the Near East.[104] Christian Arabs such as Bartholomew of Edessa (12th c.?),[105] and Paul al-Rāhib ('the Monk') of Antioch (12th c.)[106] could afford to write lengthy treatises against Islam. They did not need to wait a long time for an answer.

4. The *fourth period* of Muslim-Christian polemics is that of the thirteenth and fourteenth centuries. In this period the classical refutations of Christianity were written which, together with that of Ibn Ḥazm have been current until the present day. They are largely compilations of six centuries of arguments against Christianity.

One may think of the *Kitāb al-ajwiba ʾl-fākhira* by al-Qarāfī (d. 684/1285),[107] who held that Christians are not *mushrikūn* (polytheists) but simply *kuffār* (unbelievers; that is, non-Muslims). The well-known Ibn Taymiyya (d. 728/1328)[108] wrote his large *Al-jawāb as-sahīh li-man baddala dīn al-masīh*,[109] arguing that the forgery of the biblical text is restricted to the historical parts only, whereas with regard to the legislative parts of the Bible, not the text itself but the Christian exegesis, is at fault. These two authors, together with the more Sufi-minded Muhammad Ibn Abi Tālib (d. 727/1327),[110] were responding to a polemic directed by the Christian author Paul ar-Rāhib (Paul of Antioch, 12th c.) against Islam.[111] Most of the polemical arguments against Christianity are assembled in al-Qarāfī's and Ibn Taymiyya's refutations, and one can find here nearly all the components of the previous polemics. Saʿīd b. Hasan al-Iskandarānī (d. 720/1320)[112] and Ibn-Qayyim al-Jawziyya (d. 751/1350)[113] wrote combined refutations of Judaism and Christianity.[114] Moreover, refutations of Christianity are to be found within the general works of *kalām*.

Spain produced some outstanding Muslim polemicists against Christianity,[115] the most famous being Ibn Hazm (933–1064).[116] Abūʾl-Walīd al-Bājī (d. 1081)[117] and Ibn Sabʿīn (d. 1271)[118] should also be mentioned. An important refutation of Christianity was the *Tuhfa* written in 1420 C.E. by the converted Spanish Franciscan ʿAbd-Allāh al-Tarjumān.[119]

Since we said something about Arab-Christian and Byzantine polemics against Islam, we may add also a few remarks about medieval Latin polemics which developed increasingly in the eleventh century, especially since the beginning of the Reconquista of Spain and the Crusades.[120] In Spain Peter of Alfonso (11th c.) wrote a treatise against Islam. Better knowledge of Islam was acquired by the initiative of Peter the Venerable (ca. 1092–1156), Abbott of Cluny, who visited Spain in 1142–1143 and commissioned some translations from Arabic into Latin, including a translation of the Qurʾān by Robert of Ketton. This translation project is known as the *Corpus Toletanum*. In the early thirteenth century Mark of Toledo translated a Christian attack in Arabic on the Qurʾān into Latin. This text, the *Contrarietas elpholica* had considerable influence on further Latin polemics. The Dominican Ramon Marti (ca. 1220–1285) is probably the author of the *Quadruplex reprobatio*, which is also addressed against Islam. Ramon Lull (1235–1315) on his part tried to prove the truth of Christian doctrines by rational means. He conceived the idea of a dialogue between the monotheistic religions and wrote several texts in this sense, but in the end he wrote a sharp attack on Islam himself. The Dominican Ricoldo da Monte Croce (ca. 1243–1320), who visited Baghdad around 1291, also polemicized against Islam. Theologians like Anselm (ca. 1033–1109), Guibert de Nogent (twelfth century) and Thomas Aquinas (ca. 1225–1274), when addressing Islam in their writings, tended to give a large place to reason. Muslims and Christians were supposed to agree on the level of natural theology. Nicolas of Cusa (1499–1464) and others had the same starting point and sought conciliation.[121]

The Muslim treatises show all the features which consistently pervade Islamic polemical literature against Christianity: the denial of the Trinity and of Jesus' divinity, proofs of the prophetic quality of Muhammad including those drawn from the Bible, contradictions and inconsistencies in the Old and New Testament, proofs of Muhammad's prophecies and miracles, evidence of the dignity and superiority of Islam, and the condemnation of the ethical and cult practices of Christians on the grounds that they are just as faulty as the Christian beliefs.

The "medieval" character of these Muslim-Christian perceptions A study of Muslims' and Christians' views of each other is largely a study of mutual misunderstanding. Many factors contributed to this, including emotions such as the fear of a superior power, with a foreign religion and ideology, exhibiting strength. Misunderstandings arose especially from the fact that both sides interpreted the other religion in light of their own. Medieval Islam saw Christians as believers gone astray but to be respected as People of the Book; medieval Christianity saw Muslims largely as believers in the wrong things, misled by ignorance. Neither party could adequately place the other's claim to absolute truth. Whereas Islam had its scholars and mystics to defend its case, Christianity had besides scholars and mystics its ecclesiastical organization, which, for better or worse, exercised a great deal of power.

On the level of apologetic technique, both Muslims and Christians had recourse to Scripture and reason in order to convince each other and especially themselves, although they did this in different ways. Each group used its Scripture to combat that of the opposing party's, and here the Muslims had a clear advantage since Muhammad had lived later than Jesus and since he, unlike Jesus, had left a written Scripture. Also, the idea of the Qurʾān as the revealed *words* of God was easier to grasp than the idea of Christ as the revealed *word* of God. Regarding reason, the Muslims recognized that things religious transcend reason, but they also held that religion should not contradict reason and that it should lend itself to analysis and logical inquiry. With this "rational" approach they fired devastating rational arguments against Christianity. The Christians, however, believed in salvation and religious mysteries leading to it, also in the realm of experience, which were not only inaccessible to reason but, in fact, contradicted any simplistic rationalization. Therefore, although they could certainly develop rational arguments against Islam, they could not press as hard rationally against Islam as the Muslims could do against Christianity. In fact, according to Christian doctrine, man's mind could not be forced by reason to see the truth of Christianity; rather, God's grace and man's free choice were needed for this.

Of course, there were nuances in this matter, and both Orthodox and Latin theology could be terribly rationalistic in their refutations of the Muslim faith. Among the different theological schools in Islam, the Muʿtazilites were in the vanguard of Muslim polemics with Christianity and Manicheism. We still need a careful investigation of the precise implications of the various schools of Muslim thought with regard to their interpretation and judgment of non-Muslim doctrines. The implications for this subject of Qurʾānic *tafsīr* and different strands in *ḥadīth* literature need to be better known as well. On the whole, it seems that Islam with its claim to be the "religion of the golden mean" tended to view other religions, Christianity included, basically as exaggerations of Islamic doctrines on certain given points. They were sects of the one Eternal Religion.

A supplementary problem in the relations between medieval Christianity and Islam was that Muslims held that the Qur'ān contained everything that needed to be known about Christianity, both descriptive and evaluative, so that a further study of Christianity was scarcely necessary. Moreover, Christianity was an out-of-date religion. The Christians, by contrast, could not consult their Scripture for descriptions and evaluations of Islam: insofar as they were aware of their ignorance, they were obliged to study it. On an intellectual level, thinkers of the stature of Ibn Sīnā (930–1037), al-Ghazālī (1058–1111), and Ibn Rushd (1126–1198) had no match among Byzantine theologians at the time. It took the Latins until the twelfth century, the "first Renaissance," inspired by Arab science and intellectual inquiry, to produce thinkers able to digest the Muslims' trends of thought and develop their own.

With regard to the religious minority groups existing on both sides in the medieval period, we may speak of a structural intolerance, measured according to present-day norms and criteria. We may acknowledge, however, a general religious tolerance combined with indifference on the part of the Muslims and a degree of toleration in certain circumstances and on the part of individual Christians as, for example, under some Norman kings of Sicily and some Christian kings in Spain. The prevailing attitude of the religious majority on both sides, however, was to feign not to see the minority and its religion and to avoid any intense contact. On the Muslim side there were no massacres of civilian Christians, no state persecutions, and no inquisition of Christians. There was never a systematic repression of the Christians within Muslim territory, except under the Fātimid caliph al-Hākim (985–1021) in Cairo, who was considered insane by his contemporaries. On the Christian side, on the other hand, from the eleventh century the Latin Church developed an aggressive attitude against Muslims and Islam both ideologically and politically. In the sixteenth century, after the Reconquista and against the treaty conditions, the Latin Church resorted to forced conversions and persecutions of Muslims in Spain. With regard to Islam the medieval Latin Church went berserk.

This kind of conflictuous tension and structural intolerance implied not only that no one tried to reformulate and rethink questions of truth in light of the other's existence or claims. It also implied that the Christians on the whole did not recognize a grain of truth in what Muslims considered as revelation, whereas the Muslims recognized the Christians' revelation at least in their own Islamic terms. On the whole, Muslims worked for the Islamization of the conquered areas within the limits of a tradition of religious toleration, yet applying strong pressures. Christians, when expanding their territories, did the same, but they adopted a rigid missionary approach to Muslims, individually and collectively. Particular pressures—economic, social, and psychological—could be and were exerted in the name of one religion on adherents of the other. This was considered to be necessary by the religious leaders of both religions and as just by those who had political power, provided the public order was not disturbed.

Such underlying structures are fundamental to understanding the relations and mutual views of Christians and Muslims—and also Jews—in the medieval period. The starting point for their study consists in identifying the problems of the three monotheistic religions. Medieval thought cannot be understood unless one takes into account the fundamental problems with which these three religions confronted people at the time and to which they tried to give answers. That there were common, deeper structures appears in the fact that thinkers on both sides, Christian and Muslim, recognized such problems and largely viewed the other party in terms of common, general problems. Moreover, both were confronted with the fact of the other's existence and had to find a solution for it. Islam did this by considering the Christians *ahl al-kitāb*, People of the Book, possessing a deficient revelation. The Christians vacillated, sometimes calling Islam a heresy and sometimes calling it a false religion, with no revelation at all.

Strikingly medieval, to our senses, is the centripetal and near solipsistic worldview, religiously fixed, of both civilizations. Strikingly medieval is also the idea that adherence to a faith other than one's own implies separation, while in fact there were common structures that allowed for deeper cultural contacts between members of these civilizations. Strikingly medieval, finally, was the wholesale identification of people at the time with the two entities of "Christianity" and "Islam" conceived of as outright antagonists as far as religion is concerned.

In their medieval polemical writings, the Christians (Arab, Byzantine, and Latin) and the Muslims

(Arab and Persian) saw each other as radical antagonists in the realm of religious truth. It was mainly theologians and jurists, however, who were at the forefront of this literature. They all moved against the background of a world of war and political tensions.

Perceptions beyond conflicts We ought not, however, be blinded by such widespread polemics to the fact that Muslims on the one hand, and Arab and Byzantine Christians on the other, had many areas of life and culture in common. They shared philosophy and science, commerce, and travel; and they also had (though each within their own society) similar ideas on authority, behavior, and social order.

There is even more than meets the eye. Gregory Palamas, a friend of John Cantacuzenos, wrote an account of his travels (probably as a prisoner) to Asia Minor in 1354 which included an encounter and discussions with Muslims.[122] An evergoing stream of pilgrims from Byzantium and from the Latin West made their way through Muslim territory to the Holy Land and back. Beliefs and practices of folk religion were often common to Muslims and Christians, as was the veneration of saints and adoration of the Virgin Mary.[123] Such practices could be borrowed by one community from the other, without any official authority being involved. It would seem that religious interaction and "dialogue" can occur much more easily on the popular level of people living together than on a more official level, whatever the authority and model function of the latter. Recently, some scholars have examined the image of Jesus in medieval Muslim writings, and they have shown that one can speak of an "Islamic Christology."[124] Medieval Muslim historians showed interest in the life of Jesus.[125] On closer consideration, the Islamic context has not simply been negative for meetings between Muslims and Christians.[126] There was the well-known transmission of Greek philosophy and science from Syriac and Greek into Arabic in the ninth and tenth centuries, and from Arabic to Hebrew and Latin in the twelfth and thirteenth centuries. In the domain of literature, art, architecture, and technology too, there have been sometimes surprising interactions.[127]

In addition, it must be said that, although cultural relations between Muslims and Christians were profoundly affected by political and religious antagonism, some Muslim authors wrote interesting descriptions of Franks and Byzantines, as well as their history.[128] First, various accounts of the Crusades, in particular those organized around the figure of Salāh al-Dīn (Saladin), portray the "Franks" with the vices and virtues proper to West European and in particular French knights.[129] Furthermore, some accounts tell of journeys by Muslims to visit Europe—either on a specific mission, for instance in an embassy or as traders as far as Scandinavia, or more freely venturing to explore the darker regions of the north. Two accounts are well known: that of Ibrāhīm ibn Yaʿqūb al-Turtūshī around 965, and that of Abū Hāmid al-Granadino (1081–1170).[130]

Slowly there developed a knowledge of the history of Western European Christians, which reached its apogee in the chapter on the Franks in Rashīd al-Dīn's world history at the beginning of the fourteenth century C.E.[131] In the historiography of Muslim countries or cities we find occasional references to the place of non-Muslim minorities. Al-Masʿūdī accorded Church history a place in his *Murūj al-dhahab.*

Whereas the Byzantines were seen as the successors of the ancient Greeks and admired for their civilization, equal during the ninth to eleventh centuries to that of the Abbasid caliphate, the Latin Christians were on the whole perceived as of a more barbarous nature. The superiority of the Arab-Muslim civilization over that of Western Europe up to—roughly speaking—the thirteenth century explains at least in part the lack of curiosity about what was happening on the other side of the Mediterranean, the Pyrenees, and the Alps. What could Muslims have learned from the northerners, who were rather on the receiving end of cultural exchanges?

Common structures On closer analysis, what was felt by the conflicting religious parties to be an absolute antagonism must be seen in a broader historical perspective of the meeting of cultures.[132] This very antagonism was in fact imbedded in certain assumptions and presuppositions which Muslims, Jews, and Eastern and Western Christians shared.[133] Thus we might speak of certain common structures underlying positions that seemed to be, to the people concerned, mutually exclusive.

Primarily, beyond the different elaborations, there was a common structure of faith in one God—a belief that this God manifests his will by means of precisely known revelations and by his acts in history. There was the notion of the one true religion rising above the many heresies, and of the existence of religious communities considering themselves to be living under God's more or less exclusive protection. The elements of this structure were articulated in different ways with different theological views, but these differentiations were only possible due to a common idea of revelation, a common framework of thought and the common acceptance of historical events as evidence of the truth of the faith.

The people concerned were sometimes conscious of these facts themselves. Christians tried to clarify and expound their idea of revelation by means of philosophical reason along the lines of Aristotle and Plotinus. Faith to them had its own *ratio*, so they were looking for the *ratio fidei*; in addition, they appealed to the tradition of the church and its power, visible like that of the Christian state, as an argument for their truth. Muslims, on the other hand, defended the oneness and uniqueness of God's being against any conceivable infringement. They carried out a rationalistic attack both on the text of the Bible and on the mysteries of faith in which the Christians believed. Their general stance was to take the Qur'ān as a starting point and to accept in addition only arguments based on reason. But whatever the differences between the positions upheld by Muslims and Christians with regard to the elements of such religious structures, and their meaning, both groups acknowledged as self-evident the existence, worth, and truth of these structures, as well as a number of their elements. From a philosophical point of view, it would be correct to say that it was their different views of truth which made them choose and interpret elements of common structures in different ways and consequently made them see each other in a different light as well.

The presence of such common structures does not alter the fact that there was, simultaneously, for their own consciousness a definite and "total" opposition between Muslims and Christians. The continuous military struggle, interrupted only by incidental truces, should not only be seen in light of the religious ideologies in question but also in terms of the political relationship of two giants. Similarly, many of the actual victories of one party over another can be interpreted in terms of the natural envy of military men from a nomadic background with regard to higher civilizations and their riches. Military history weighs heavily on the relationship between these two religions. One should keep in mind that Byzantine Christianity until the tenth century, and Latin Christianity until the eleventh century found themselves fighting on the defensive against Islam and that this was to be resumed in the eleventh and fifteenth century, respectively. The antagonism between Christian and Muslim countries was seen to be absolute since there was hardly ever a third party of any significance in the political field. The military and political opposition derived support from the different religious beliefs and practices, as well as the different social and ethical norms of the two civilizations. Such norms, practices, and beliefs had by then come to be not only the expression but also the legitimization of the social systems in question. Each society was organized within a religious framework; each religious community was a "nation" (*natio*) defined through its religion over and against the other. Psychologically speaking, each society projected the other religion as its ideological antagonist.

Main arguments against Christianity as a religion The Islamic theological arguments against Christianity can be grouped under three headings[134] —scripture, doctrines, and religious practices. Nearly all these arguments refer to Qur'ānic texts and are developed within the framework of Aristotelian logic.

1. *Forgery of Scripture.* Christian scripture is regarded as forged on two counts:

- There was a *historical* forgery because of a false transmission of the preaching and doctrine of Jesus, in particular before the writing and canonization of the New Testament. As a consequence, present-day beliefs and practices of the Christians do not parallel the original message of Jesus.
- There was a *literary* forgery for the following two reasons. First, the Christians canonized a text which was not the original text which Jesus, according to the Qur'ān, would have brought. Second, the Christians have given wrong interpretations of a number of Biblical texts while presuming that their interpretations were right. Thus the Christian scripture suffers from corruption (*fasād*) and *taḥrīf*: forgery of the text itself or else a wrong interpretation of the correct text.

This accusation of forgery rests on assumptions which are typically Islamic. The form of revelation as conceived of in Islam—that is, prophetical recitations brought together in a book, is held to be a model for any revelation. Qur'ānic verses on the existence of *taḥrīf* are applied without further ado to biblical texts, without paying attention to the meaning of these latter texts in their own literary and historical context and without inquiring about the kind of truth of such texts. It is assumed without questioning that anything that the Qur'ān says on a given subject is Truth, even in a literal sense.

2. *Errors of Thought and Doctrine.* Such errors are held to be fundamentally due to a neglect of the truth of *tawhīd*, the oneness and uniqueness of God. They concern three main doctrinal issues:

- The Christian doctrine of *incarnation*, that Jesus had a divine nature and was the son of God, is thoroughly rejected. The Qur'ān denies that Jesus was more than a prophet and the *mutakallimūn* tried to prove this by means of reason. They refused, on logical grounds, to distinguish between a human nature in Jesus (able to suffer) and a divine nature (unable to do so). They pointed to the differences between the christologies of different Christian churches and contended that the very unsoundness of the doctrine of a hypostatical union between God and man was proved already by the many confusions and contradictions resulting from it. They also refuted the doctrine of the incarnation by saying that this implied that God had been in need of a woman, whereas God is without need and creates out of his own will. Ibn Taymiyya and al-Qarāfī, as well as the author of *Al-radd al-jamīl*, noticed that Jesus' human weaknesses, as they are stressed in parts of the Gospels and certain words of Jesus and his disciples, imply that he was not of a divine nature. Moreover, in the Gospels Jesus never claimed to be God.
- The Christian doctrine of the *trinity*, that God consists of one substance and three persons, is rejected outright on the basis of the Qur'ān, which denies anything that might infringe on the oneness (*tawhīd*) of God. The *mutakallimūn* further refuted the doctrine by means of reason: a number of logical arguments were formulated against it, and Christian attempts to construct analogies of the trinity in defense of the doctrine were refuted. Arguments were also drawn from the New Testament itself, where the trinity is nowhere mentioned as such. The idea of a father–son relationship within God was particularly revolting to Muslim thought; logically God would become needy and contingent by the concept of *tawallud* (procreation).
- The Christian doctrine of *salvation* is also unambiguously rejected. The doctrine of original sin cannot be found in the Qur'ān and is held to be contrary to divine justice. The belief that the sins of individually responsible people could be remitted by someone else through atonement goes against the Qur'ānic ideas of law, justice, and human responsibility, and it also conflicts with reason. The Christian idea of the redemption of the faithful from their sufferings and sins, from the weight of the law, and from the demands of the world is clearly in conflict with the daily experience of Christians themselves.

Nearly all the doctrinal mistakes made by the Christians come down to one basic error: the frontal attack on the fundamental truth of *tawhīd* (the One God), through *shirk* (associating things that are not divine with God); moreover these formulations are felt to be logical impossibilities. Just as there can be no two eternal principles, so there can be no mingling of God and man, and there can be no three eternal principles within one. The consequence of these doctrinal errors is that the Christians hold beliefs that are in straightforward conflict with reason. This leads them into a maze of philosophical and theological confusion and to contradictions which they themselves abusively call "mysteries."

3. *Errors in Religious Practice.* Some of these include the following.

- In matters of cult, Christians are generally reproached with indulging in *idol worship* when adoring Jesus or venerating Mary and the saints, through images and other objects held to be sacred.
- In *ritual* practice they are reproached with laxity, for instance in abandoning of circumcision and neglecting ritual purity, as prescribed by Mosaic law.
- Inadmissible *novelties* have been introduced by the Christians since Jesus' lifetime. Al-Qarāfī and Ibn Taymiyya point out the various liturgical and popular religious celebrations and feasts, the sacraments (eucharist, baptism, confession), the veneration of Mary, certain church laws (marriage, celibacy, excommunication), and customs like the veneration of saints, which they consider as innovations, contrary to Jesus' teaching.

Other kinds of arguments were used, too. The demands of Christian ethics were judged to be extravagant and Christian asceticism was rejected. The freedom of man's will, as accepted in Christianity, was denied. Attention was drawn toward the divisions among the Christians themselves, the intellectual blindness and stupidity of their religion, the defeat of the Christian armies and concomitant victory of Islam as a sign of God's providence. New arguments were coined to counter Christian attacks on Islam and to work out a convincing apology for

Islam. Christian objections to the Qur'ān, for instance, had to be met, the rejection of Muhammad's prophethood had to be refuted, and the unity of prophetic revelation from Adam to Muhammad had to be proved. Of course, it also had to be proved both scripturally and by means of reasoning, that Muhammad was the seal of the prophets and Islam the final universal message for all mankind. Polemics against non-Muslims ended in an apology for Islam.

One of the results of these scriptural, doctrinal, and practical errors, according to the polemicists, has been that the Christians not only are alienated from the true message of Jesus but also do not listen to Muhammad's message and thus remain closed to the revelation brought by him and contained in the Qur'ān.

Further analysis reveals certain assumptions behind these arguments against Christianity. On one hand, the accusations of literary and historical forgery of divine revelation arose from the model of revelation as conceived of in Islam—that is, a text that corresponds literally with the Heavenly Book and was brought by a prophet. On the other hand, these accusations arose from the application of certain Qur'ānic texts about Christianity directly to the Christian Scriptures in order to search there for corroboration of what was said in the Qur'ān such as the claimed announcements of Muhammad. These Qur'ānic accusations, combined with a rather simple, commonsense idea of what is good literary and historical transmission, were then applied to the texts to be refuted. Assumptions underlying the accusations of doctrinal mistakes included the literal acceptance of statements found in the Qur'ān, the assumption that the Qur'ān provides not only a true but also a sufficient knowledge of God, the assumption that the Islamic model of revelation is the only possible one, and the assumption that the categories of Aristotelian philosophy are able to express religious truth adequately.

On closer consideration, these objections to Christianity show that the Muslim religious view was painfully touched by Christianity on several sensitive points:

1. Making a distinction between the different persons within God and the divine substance comes down to negating or denying God's unity. In the Muslim conception, God is one and unique and cannot be divided within himself.
2. The notions of the Fall and of original sin, and the concomitant notion of a subsequent self-sacrifice of the Creator, needed to restore his creation, disrupt the harmony given with creation as well as the harmonious relationship between creature and Creator. It also implies a diminution of the positive responsibilities assigned to man.
3. The idea of a mixture of what is human and what is divine in one person, held to be God's incarnation or the Son of God, is not only a logical impossibility and an affront to clear thinking, but is also blasphemous in that it attacks God's honor.
4. The historical trustworthiness of reports on factual events like the crucifixion of Jesus, as they are given in the Christian Scriptures, is simply denied as soon as they conflict with Qur'ānic statements. For medieval Muslim feeling any Qur'ānic statement has a normative and evaluative as well as empirical character; it can therefore serve to establish or deny historical or natural facts, taking precedence over all other sources of knowledge.

Just as in the refutation of Mazdaism and Manicheism *kalām* had to work out the implications of *tawhīd*, and as in the refutation of Judaism it worked out the implications of *naskh*, so it was led through the refutation of Christianity, to elaborate the doctrine of the Qur'ān considered as God's eternal word. Polemics against Christianity stimulated the assessing of the relationship between substance and attributes within God's oneness of being.

Judaism

The relations between Islam and Judaism have been complex from the very beginning.[135] However, although there was severe Muslim-Jewish strife in the early Medinan stage of Islam, to which the Qur'ān bears witness, classical Islam directed its polemics much more against Christianity. While the Christians in Muslim territory had a powerful Byzantine state behind them, and in the conquered lands actively defended their religion against the new faith, the Jewish communities, a smaller minority anyhow, kept to their own communal life and did not discuss their religion with outsiders. They rarely attacked Islam. So also the number of polemical treatises directed exclusively against Judaism is relatively small and dates from later times. Although after the Qur'ān critical statements and polemical utterances occur in *hadīth* literature,[136] proper information about Judaism as a religion and way of life was only later supplied by converts.

Muslim descriptions and refutations of Judaism until Ibn Hazm have been studied by Camilla Adang in her previously mentioned work. *Descriptions* of it were given in some historical works[137] and in encyclopedical works like the *Kitāb al-badʾ waʾl-taʾrīkh* attributed to al-Mutahhar al-Maqdisī (d. ca. 985). Its doctrines and sects are presented in *milal* literature, in particular in the books of Ibn Hazm (d. 1064) and, much more concisely, al-Shahrastānī (d. 548/1153).

Polemics Muslim-Judaic polemics go back to the Qurʾān.[138] Muhammad had already had intense debates with the Jews of Medina. Yet, these Qurʾānic texts have hardly ever led to the kind of religiously-based antisemitism that has developed in Christianity, although some of the arguments used in the first centuries C.E. by Christians against Judaism found their way, through converts in particular, into Muslim circles and were used then in the Muslim-Judaic polemic.

The best known polemical treatises of Muslim authors against Judaism are the following. Ibn Hazm (994–1064),[139] who is standing himself in a tradition of such writings wrote no less than three such treatises, one of them against the Jewish *wazīr* Ismaʿil b. Yūsuf ibn an-Naghrīla (993–1056). An analysis of Ibn Hazm's writings against Judaism was published by Camilla Adang.[140]

Several refutations of Judaism were written by Jewish converts to Islam. Samawʾal al-Maghribī (ca. 1125–1175),[141] for instance, wrote his *Ifhām al-Yahūd* ("Silencing the Jews") after his conversion in 1163, and Saʿīd b. Hasan (d. 1320)[142] who converted from Judaism in 1298, wrote a treatise against both Judaism and Christianity. Another convert and author, ʿAbd al-Haqq al-Islāmī,[143] is assumed to have lived in Morocco at the end of the fourteenth century. Well-known other polemicists were Al-Qarāfī (d. 1285);[144] Ibn Qayyim al-Jawziyya (d. 1350),[145] who also wrote a treatise against both Judaism and Christianity; and Abū Zakariyyā Yahyā ar-Rāqilī,[146] who in 761/1360 wrote a tract against Judaism while living in Christian Spain. Less known is the Moroccan al-Maghīlī (d. ca. 1504).[147] Moreover, there are refutations of Judaism within the general *kalām* works, as for instance in the *Kitāb at-tamhīd* of Al-Baqillānī, written around 369/980.[148]

The principal argument used specifically against Judaism concerned the doctrine of *naskh* (abrogation). Muslims adhered to this doctrine in a double sense: a revelation occurring later in time was supposed to abrogate an earlier one, and a revealed religious law of a later date was supposed to replace an earlier one. This implied that by means of a series of revelations, God could reveal his will successively in different ways. Jewish theologians, by contrast, held that it is impossible for God to change his mind, as God does not change his decree and dispensation. They therefore rejected *naskh* and did not recognize the Qurʾān any more than they had recognized the New Testament. Muslim thinkers such as Ibn Hazm declared it an error to think that God would not be able to change his mind or that there would be only one revelation given by God: the Torah. Much effort was expended by Muslim polemicists to convince the Jews of the necessity of *naskh* and to demonstrate that it was already present in the Torah itself, where the law of Jacob, for instance, had been superseded by the later and different law of Moses. The ideas which scholars like Ibn Hazm, Al-Juwaynī, and Fakhr ad-Dīn ar-Rāzī developed about the nature of a revealed text led to discussions on the subject of revelation and to a further questioning of what God had intended with his revelations. This was conducive to a further elaboration and refinement of the doctrine of *naskh* in Islam itself. Various positions were taken up with regard to the relationship between the Qurʾān and the earlier Scriptures, as well as between the *Sharīʿa* and preceding religious laws.

As early as 1878, Goldziher gave a general outline of the historical development of Muslim polemic against *ahl al-kitāb* and Judaism in particular.[149] He considers the oldest document for the polemic, the Qurʾān itself, which already contains the three main later themes of polemic. They are, first, the accusation that the *ahl al-kitāb* changed and corrupted their Scriptures (*tahrīf* 2:73; *tabdīl* 4:48, 5:16, 45, 52; *taghyīr* 3:72); second, the refutation of certain doctrines which they held; third, the rejection of certain of their rites and customs. It is worthwhile to recall the main points which Goldziher makes about the accusation of corruption of the Torah (*tabdīl*).[150]

The Qurʾān states in so many words that the Jews and the Christians had corrupted their Scriptures, and this was to remain the main accusation against the *ahl al-kitāb*. Different arguments could be used as proof of the corruption (*tabdīl*) claimed in the ostensibly heavenly, perfect texts which, according to the Qurʾān, were the original *Tawrāt* and *Injīl* brought respectively by Moses and Jesus. One of the arguments for the fact of corruption was based on *tajsīm* or "anthropomorphism" in the wider sense of the word. In the Bible there were unworthy passages about patriarchs, prophets, and political leaders and their lineage, their words and deeds, and their scandalous stories which should not occur in a sacred text and which indicated unworthy authorship. Another argument was based on obvious textual contradictions in the Bible. Furthermore, there were "mistakes" in the text, such as the substitution of the name of Isaac for Ishmael as the son whom Abraham was asked to sacrifice. Moreover, certain texts which, according to Muslim understanding, ought to figure within a revealed scripture, were lacking in the Old Testament; it was assumed that these had been suppressed. These texts included the tenet of the resurrection at the end of time, along with the following reward and punishment and the recognition of the existence of prophets outside Israel. Lastly, the presence in the Old Testament of prophets who were not mentioned in the Qur'ān, such as Isaiah and Jeremiah, was held to be altogether superfluous.

The biblical Torah was apparently not identical with the pure *Tawrāt* which was held to have been given as a revelation to Moses. There was, however, a considerable difference of opinion on the extent to which the Scriptures preceding the Qur'ān were corrupted.

On the one hand, Ibn Hazm, who was the first thinker to consider the problem of *tabdīl* systematically, contended, as did al-Qarāfī, Ibn Qayyim al-Jawziyya, and al-Tarjumān later on, that the text itself had been changed or forged (*taghyīr*). In support of this contention he drew attention to immoral stories which had found a place within the corpus, as well as to obvious contradictions within the text itself. By contrast, thinkers like al-Qāsim b. Ibrāhīm, al-Tabarī, Fakhr ad-Dīn ar-Rāzī, and Ibn Khaldūn held that the text itself had not been forged, but that the Scriptures had been misinterpreted (faulty *ta'wīl*) by the Jews and the Christians. This was especially true of texts that predicted or announced the mission of Muhammad and the coming of Islam: the so-called *a'lām* texts. Others again developed a theory about certain texts, in particular the *a'lām* texts, to which the Qur'ān referred, but which were not easy to find in the available Scriptures. The Jews and Christians would have simply removed these texts from their Scriptures, but they would not have added to or forged the scriptural text itself.

Whether a Muslim scholar showed greater or less respect for the Bible, and whether and how he could quote from it, depended very much on his particular interpretation of *tabdīl* (the doctrine of corruption). However, contradictions in the work of the polemicists themselves could also occur. Ibn Hazm, for instance, rejects nearly the entire Old Testament, branding it a forgery, but he cheerfully quotes the *tawrāt* when bad reports are given of the faith and the behavior of the *Banū Isrā'īl*, considering them to be evidence against the Jews and their religion!

The search for *a'lām* texts in the Hebrew and Christian Scriptures was in fact a search for proof of Muhammad's prophethood. Since the Qur'ān stated that the mission of Muhammad and the coming of Islam had been announced in the earlier Scriptures, Muslim polemicists started to read through the Bible looking for such texts and interpreting them according to what may be called a "Muhammadan" Bible exegesis. There were variations in the number of quoted Bible places, and not everyone agreed that the Jews and the Christians actually removed certain *a'lām* texts from their scriptures. In his article of 1878 Goldziher deals with the 51 Bible places to which al-Qarāfī refers.

Closely connected with the accusation of *tahrīf* or *tabdīl* of the earlier Scriptures is the reproach that the historical transmission (*tawātur*) of the text of the original *tawrāt* was not reliable, so that *tahrīf* could in fact have occurred in the span of time which had elapsed since the life of Moses. Against the claims of the Jews in this respect, Muslim polemicists held that the transmission of the Judaic tradition had not been any more reliable than that of other traditions. Biblical anecdotes about the unreliability, lack of faith, and changeability of the Israelites were used by some Muslim authors as arguments to this effect. They not only proved that the Jews could not be God's chosen people or children but also they gave plausability to the view that they could not have been able to transmit correctly the *tawrāt* given to Moses in its original form. Muslim polemicists held Ezra[151] in particular responsible for having made inadmissible innovations in the text of the original *tawrāt*. The issue of *tawātur* (transmission) has been an important one in Muslim polemic. Good *tawātur* not only guarantees the authenticity of a given text but can also serve, for instance, as a guarantee and proof for miracles if these were witnessed by several people who subsequently testified about the true happening of such a miracle. If the historical transmission (*tawātur*) shows defects, reports on miracles that happened in the past cannot be trusted. This issue, as well as that of *taḥrīf* and of *a'lām* texts, was also important in the polemic against Christianity.[152]

Other arguments were also used in the Muslim polemic against Judaism. For instance, Samaw'al al-Maghribī uses the nearly Christian argument that the Talmud makes life a burden which is impossible to bear, and he also uses the argument of the difference between Rabbanites and Karaites within Judaism to show the imperfection and weakness of the religion. The very fact of the dispersion and the institutionalized humiliation (*dhull*) of the Jews could also be employed to prove the truth of Islam, to which God had given victories on earth, and to provide an opening for conversions to Islam. Other authors added other arguments regarding Jewish rites and customs and other forms of Jewish particularism. It is interesting to observe how in these polemics between representatives of Islam and Judaism there gradually developed a common understanding about what should be considered as valid scriptural and rational arguments and proofs. Such proofs had to be based on scriptural revelation, prophethood, miracles, and sound historical transmission as constitutive elements of a valid religious tradition. Each author could stress one or more elements in particular.

As a general rule, Muslims—conditioned as they were by what they typically identified as divine revelation, sacred Scripture, and prophethood—showed great reservations about the analogous claims of revelation, Scripture, and prophetical qualities upheld in Judaism, which was considered an "out-of-date" religion. This was reinforced by the fact that the Jewish community for its part did not recognize Muhammad as a prophet, or the Qur'ān as revelation, and that it rejected *naskh*.

Main arguments against Judaism as a religion
As in the case of Christianity, the arguments against Judaism can be summarized under the heading of arguments against the Scripture, against doctrines, and against religious practices.

1. *Forgery of Scripture.* As with Christian Scripture (the New Testament), Jewish Scripture (the Hebrew Bible or "Old Testament") is accused of forgery on two counts:

- There was a *historical* forgery due to a wrong transmission of the preaching and Law of Moses, in particular during the uncertainities of the Israelites' battles when they arrived in Canaan and after the return from Babylon to Canaan, when the Law was proclaimed anew by Ezra. As a consequence, already before Jesus, the beliefs and practices of the Jews were not in agreement with Moses' original message.
- There was a *literary* forgery of the *Tawrāt* which Moses brought as a complete Scripture. Certain texts were added, others omitted. In general, Muslims did not consider the books of the Prophets and the Books of Wisdom of the Hebrew Bible to have been revealed. Historical catastrophes contributed to the fact that parts of the ancient *Tawrāt* were lost; the texts which were left were often falsely interpreted. The Jewish Scripture, accordingly, suffers from corruption (*fasād*) and *taḥrīf* (forgery of the text itself or incorrect interpretation of a correct text).

These accusations Muslim polemicists made against the Hebrew Bible correspond to the accusations they levelled at the Greek New Testament and are based on the same assumptions. One may add that Muslim authors hardly spoke about the Mishna; however, they held the Talmud to be almost as important for Jewish believers as the Torah.

2. *Errors of thought and doctrine.* The following errors of thought are particularly the object of Muslim polemics:

- The doctrine of *God* suffers on account of its lack of universality, although the Jewish recognition of his oneness and uniqueness is more in line with *tawḥīd* than the Christian doctrine of God. Being bound through his supposed alliance with the children of Israel and the Jews, God is not recognized in his full, universal dimension as being concerned with his creation and humanity as a whole. Also, the Jewish idea that God is unable to change his mind means that no further revelation other than that of the Torah is accepted and that Jesus and Muhammad are rejected as prophets. It also leaves out a rational solution for the apparent contradictions which can be found in the text of the Torah.
- The doctrine of the *children of Israel* and the Jewish people as the Chosen People has led to the wrong assumption that the Jewish people are apart from, and superior to, other peoples. This is why the children of Israel annexed Ibrāhīm as their own physical ancestor and why they disdain the prophets and revelations given to other peoples. Others should not be excluded from the particular revelation that the children of Israel once received.

3. *Errors of Religious Practice.* There are a number of differences in religious *Law* which cannot be treated here. Suffice it to draw attention to two typical reproaches directed at Jewish religious practice, on the basis of Islamic assumptions:

- Keeping the Sabbath as a day of rest could not have been among God's prescriptions. The whole idea of a God who needed a rest after having made his creation is an offense to his honor and dignity.
- The Jews introduced *isrā'īliyyāt*, certain elements of Jewish thought and tradition, into Islam. Similarly, the Christians were reproached for having introduced *rahbāniyya*, or monasticism, into Islam. Subsequent polemics were directed against such "borrowings" from Judaism which should be removed from Islam. Islam should purify itself of such Jewish and Christian novelties that found their way into the Muslim community through, for example, Jewish and Christian converts to Islam.

Historical relationships Muslim-Jewish relationships, until the mid-nineteenth century, were unique in the sense that the Jewish communities living in Muslim territory, unlike the Christian minorities, had no recourse to a foreign power which could offer refuge or intervene if necessary.[153] As a consequence, unlike the Christian minorities, Jewish communities were less suspected of being a fifth column for an enemy from abroad. One may assume that during the Medieval period and beyond, Muslim political leaders were not unaware of the fact that Jewish minorities in Christian lands had a much less favorable position than in Muslim lands. This was certainly the case with the Ottoman political leadership.

Apart from the Khazars, for a limited time from 740 onward, no Jewish political entity existed, and, as a result, Jews constituting small minorities had to survive as such, as peasants, as tradesmen, or as holders of free professions. Because of the strong links among the Jewish communities and their families, networks of communication developed, with possibilities of "free passage" which were not available to members of larger political entities. The study of the Geniza documents by S. D. Goitein, in particular, has opened new insight into Jewish life around the Mediterranean and in Muslim lands in the tenth and eleventh centuries, and into the relationships between the Jewish communities and the Muslim societies in which they lived. Roughly speaking, Jewish traders had a freedom to move, provided they could bring back valued goods to the countries in which they were living. And, of course, they should not disturb the public order.

The beginning of Muslim-Jewish relations after the elimination of three Jewish tribes from Medina, along with the accompanying invectives against the children of Israel and the Jews in the Qur'ān, was gloomy. Muhammad's treaty with the subjected Jewish community of Khaibar, however, established a precedent for later treaties with Jews, as well as Christians, in Muslim territory. Typically, the negative Qur'ānic judgments of the Jews did not lead to a form of Muslim "anti-Semitism" parallel to that found in Europe. Yet, like the Christians, the Jews had to leave Arabia, except for Yemen, and live under the rules and hardships of their status as *dhimmīs* in Muslim territory. Whenever rule and order declined, where there was hardship and people looked for a scapegoat, Jews, perhaps even more than Christians, were victims.

When the Jewish communities in the Near East were subjected to Arab Muslim rule in the seventh century (and their coreligionists, in Spain, somewhat later) they had their own traditions, which were well established in Mesopotamia and Egypt. The degree to which Muslim legal thought (*fiqh*) was influenced by—and influenced in its turn—Jewish orientations (in the same way as the development of *kalām* was influenced by debates with Manichean and Christian thinkers) is still an open field of research. The Muslim tradition at the time was still much more open than after the establishment of a Sunni "orthodoxy" in the second half of the twelfth century. The Jewish tradition, too, had differing branches not only on a popular level but also in religious thinking. The Karaites who have since nearly disappeared had a strong position in the medieval period.

During the medieval period, mutual interactions, influences, and parallelisms between "official" Islam and Judaism, as between their "unofficial" popular, philosophical, and mystical trends, must have occurred and should be explored further.[154] The nature of the encounter between Jews and Muslims, given the fact that the Jews lived in Islamic societies and shared a good deal of culture, including the Arabic language, with their Muslim neighbors, needs further study. In some cases, forms of "symbiosis" occurred; in other cases, oppression and conflict prevailed. Maimonides could not work in Spain, but he found enough freedom to work fruitfully in Cairo. Some of the arguments used in pre-Islamic times by Christians against Judaism found their way, through converts in particular, into Muslim circles and were then used in the Muslim polemic against Judaism.

Another question is the effect of the presence of Christians, inside or outside Muslim territory, on the situation of the Jews. Whereas the Christians in Spain were pitiless against Jews and Muslims alike, the Ottoman empire received both Jewish and Christian immigrants well. The common medieval history of Muslims, Christians, and Jews has yet to be written.

Conclusion: Medieval Judgments on Other Religions

Nature of Muslim Judgments and Images

It has become clear that the names under which religions other than Islam, largely unknown, were designated—like Sumaniyya, Sābi', Barāhima, Majūs, Thānawiyya, and to some extent also the Judaism of the *Tawrāt* and the Christianity of the *Injīl*—are not at all descriptive but evaluative and even normative concepts. They were applied to non-Muslims and served as predicates in *kalām* and *fiqh*. The same holds true for the basic concepts under which the adherents of these religions are classified, like *ahl al-kitāb*, *ahl al-dhimma*, *mushrikūn*, and *kuffār*. Some of the concepts were taken from the Qur'ān, and the normative character of these terms was clear. All of them served not to further empirical knowledge as in the present-day study of religions, but to appreciate, qualify, and judge the reality, strange to Muslim feeling, of non-Muslim religiosity and religions. Fundamentally, they reflect the basic Muslim view of other religions as deviations from the one primordial religion. The actual reality of other religious beliefs and practices is subordinated a priori to some primary concepts and categories: Buddhists are skeptics, Brahmins are rationalists who deny prophecy, the Jāhiliyya was pure idolatry, Christians are tritheists, and Zoroastrians and Manicheans are dualists. These names and concepts qualified reality; they did not serve to know it. Only when something more became known about these religions could the meaning of the names and concepts be expanded or narrowed down, and variations in judgment could arise. But they remained Muslim judgments, based on Islamic norms; they were not empirical knowledge in the modern sense.

Often parallels were drawn between groups of non-Muslims and Muslim heretics, and heresiography dealt with both. This implies that heretical opinions could be ascribed to influences from outside; in addition, there was a search for some basic structures behind all deviations from true Islam, whether inside or outside the common religion. The inference was that such parallel mistaken groups were at fault because they made the same "exaggeration" or doctrinal error, either within the Muslim community or outside it. Even idol-worshippers could be seen, basically, as Muslims by origin who later deviated, like the Sabians, Dualists, Christians, and Jews. Heretics and non-Muslims could be grouped according to the basic theological "sins"—*shirk*, *thānawiyya*, *taʿṭīl*, *dahriyya*, and *tanāsukh*—and in this framework the doctrine of incarnation could be viewed as a form of idolatry. All those not adhering to true Islam, however defined, shared the common name *kuffār*, unbelievers in the broad sense of the word.

In the course of history, when Muslims came into contact with people unknown before, there was a tendency to subsume more and more religions like Mazdeism, official Hinduism, and official Buddhism under the heading of the People of the Book or, rather, of a "semblance" of a book (*shibh kitāb*). Another tendency was to distinguish, among the adherents of other religions those people who are nearest to Islam—because of following their innate *fitra*—from the others. Later, on the whole, a somewhat less unfavorable judgment of nonmonotheistic religions developed than that which prevailed in the first period of Islam. Whereas on the level of practice people could be polytheists, on the level of thought and with education they became monotheists.

In the foregoing pages we tried to place the views and judgments that Muslim authors gave on other religions within the historical context of the sometimes strained relations that existed between the Muslim community and the community under consideration. In the course of time, the polemical literature which was meant to refute other religions developed into a genre in itself with its own tradition. When needed, people—including new authors—could draw on this tradition, and this, of course, presupposed that author and reader identified with the cause of Islam.

All sources point to the fact that contacts between Muslims and non-Muslims in the medieval period were limited in scope and size. Medieval society distinguished communities and groups according to their religious identity, and each religious community tried to be as self-sufficient as possible. Moreover, the society had rather formal and fixed social structures; prevailing concepts of life and the world, based on religious tradition, also had a rather static character. One of the functions of religion in this society was to provide a means of identification. It was a social fact, and apparently few people succeeded in surpassing this and reaching a more flexible concept of religion which would lend itself to free discussion and debate between people from different communities and traditions.

Another important fact was that the Christian and Jewish communities, for instance, living in Muslim territory, had to pay special taxes and were subject to rules which, imposed and applied, were humiliating. This simple fact must have eliminated any inclination these two groups may have felt to enter into discussion with Muslims who already felt themselves to be the masters over the *dhimmīs*. Christians and Iranians, moreover, possessed a collective memory of a past in which they had been great nations wielding power, which probably functioned much like a dream but strengthened identity.

Under such circumstances, the social climate did not favor the awakening of much interest in adherents of another religion. Moreover, the facts known about foreign religions were limited in number and subjected to rather severe value judgments and schematized interpretations. At the very most, people arrived at some general normative descriptions and classifications of foreign ideas, representations, and practices.

All of this explains why, in medieval and later premodern Muslim societies, rather fixed images prevailed of other religions. These images were part of traditions from the past which could go on for centuries without being corrected or even revised, especially where religion was concerned. Of course, in contrast, among those whom the Muslims had fought against or those who had calmly submitted, the same fixation of images of other religions and cultures took place. With the exception of a few individual cases, there were no revolutionaries in this domain. No one possessed an intrinsic interest in changing, correcting, or even breaking such images in order to arrive at more reliable knowledge, not to speak of making the acquaintance of the people behind the images.

Different Kinds of Muslim Judgments

Muslim judgments of other religions, which refer to Islam as a normative standard, are based on at least two fundamental claims. In the first place, it is claimed that a revelation of divine origin is readily available, offering mankind in all circumstances the knowledge they need about God, the right view of reality, man, and the world as well as the right values and norms for action. The revelation is held to be the Qurʾān, and the religion resulting from it is Islam. In the second place, it is claimed that this revelation and religion offer the framework, norms, and laws to organize a just human society.

Two Kinds of Muslim Judgments

Looking more closely at the different ways in which medieval Muslim authors judged non-Muslims, we can distinguish basically two kinds of judgment. The first type concerns the doctrines, rites, and laws of other religions, and the second is concerned with the way of life, culture, and society of other civilizations. The same distinction exists, incidentally, in present-day Muslim judgments of non-Muslim religions and societies.

1. *Judgments of other religions: doctrines, rites, and laws.* Such judgments may be properly called *theological* and *legal* judgments, expanded upon in *kalām* and *fiqh*. These judgments go back to the claim of the Qurʾān to be a revelation of divine origin, which was given once and for all. The Qurʾān remains the unchangeable judgmental norm, although correct interpretation is always needed. In this scheme, the different religions are classified in four main categories according to their doctrines, rites, and laws:

- Muslims of various persuasions who are part of the Islamic *umma*, with discussions on the status of the Muslim sects.
- The *ahl al-kitāb*, People of the Book as referred to regularly in the Qurʾān—that is, Jews and Christians, with discussions on their status as *dhimmīs* in Islamic territory.
- Additional communities which have a *semblance* of Scripture, like the Zoroastrians, and others, like the Sabians, who enjoy certain privileges of the *dhimmīs*.
- The *mushrikūn*, polytheists who offend the oneness and uniqueness of God (*tawhīd*), with the possible presence of monotheists in such polytheist communities.

These categories of classification represent a scale of evaluation; the very act of placing a given religion in a specific category implies a judgment. Such judgments are formulated in theological and legal terms, within the context of *kalām* and *fiqh*. Behind them, however, we find basic intentions and religious orientations which express fundamental views of humanity and the world.

In these theological and legal judgments, an important factor seems to have been the particular *kalām* or *fiqh* school which the writer followed and which logically leads to particular judgments of other religions, some schools being stricter than others. Qur'ānic texts, for instance, that express a negative judgment can still be interpreted in a narrower or a broader sense; texts that give a positive judgment can be interpreted to be more or less applicable to the case in question. Thus many nuances which are linked to the given interpretation of such key concepts as *dīn*, *umma*, *milla*, *aslama*, *islām*, *amāna*, and *imān* are possible. The discussion of the status of *dhimmīs*, for instance, is rather abstract and elusive as to empirical reality, and is conducted in legal terms.

Historical circumstances, including political and social factors, may condition all these judgments, but the way in which judgments are founded on texts and presented in *fatwās* and other writings, is rather technical and difficult to grasp for someone not trained in *tafsīr*, *ʿilm al-hadith*, *fiqh*, or *kalām*.

2. *Judgments of other ways of life: ideologies, cultures, and societies.* In these judgments the subject is not in itself of a religious nature but it is considered to be somehow linked to religion, and Islam is used as a norm and criterion of evaluation and judgment. Basically, this type of judgment rests on the claim that Islam offers the best social order.

These judgments are not theological or legal in the technical sense of the word, as the preceding group. We may call them *ideological* judgments in the broad sense of the word, to the extent that they all refer to Islam as a value and norm. In fact, the "Islamic" character of these judgments is rather fluid. Their interest is the way in which and the degree to which a given author interpreted and used Islam as a norm and as an ideal in order to pass judgment.

Such ideological judgments on other ways of life, ideologies, cultures, and societies may enjoy great popularity, but they evidently do not have the same authority as the strictly theological and juridical judgments which refer to the Qur'ān and other sources of true religious knowledge according to rules known to the specialists. Even more than the theological and legal judgments, ideological judgments are linked to the historical situation in which they were formulated. Very often such ideological judgments are difficult to understand if one neglects the contemporary situation with its underlying social structures and tensions.

Four Normative Levels of Muslim Judgments

It is useful to make a distinction between different normative levels on which Muslim judgments of other religions are based.

First of all, there are *universal* norms valid for all of humanity which are mentioned in the Qur'ān, especially of the Meccan period. Such norms often refer to pre-Islamic "patriarchal" times or even earlier and make reference to the order of creation. In a sense, these norms are timeless as the Ten Commandments are.

Second, there are more *particularistic* religious norms which may have their roots in the Qur'ān but which were further developed during the history of Islam. One instance concerns the relations established with other religious communities or with individual adherents of other religions. We may consider such norms to be more historical since they were formulated in the course of Islamic history, at least in part in response to outside challenges, often posed by the presence of other religions. Such particularistic norms superimpose themselves on the more universal norms already mentioned.

Third, besides such religious norms of a more universal or more particularistic nature, many other *social rules and customs* played a role in the Muslim judgments of adherents of other religions, expressed in specific situations and contexts. These rules and customs, however, were of a social nature and had little to do with the normative Islamic system as it was circumscribed and elaborated by theologians and jurists. In the course of time, such social rules and customs could, however, obtain an ideological relevance and a religious legitimacy and could be called "Islamic" on the level of "living" religion as, for instance, in popular Islam.

Fourth, besides such explicit norms applied in Muslim judgments of other believers, a great number of "implicit" perceptions and judgments are based less on rational criteria than on immediate *sensitivities and emotions*. It seems that precisely in situations of tension and crisis between Muslims and non-Muslims, hidden sensitivities came out into the open and gave rise to judgments based on particular experiences of human life rather than on Islamic norms or rational considerations.

Some Observations on Muslim Judgments

As a hypothesis, I would like to propose that the defensive position that Muslims were obliged to take at the outset of Islamic history regarding the religions and civilizations which they found in the territories they conquered—especially missionary religions such as Christianity and Manicheism—gave a particular apologetic tendency to Islamic thought. This defensive attitude, combined with the notion of religious superiority because of possessing the Qurʾān as revelation and Islam as heavenly religion, may help explain the relatively modest interest in other religions, except for the investigations of some exceptional Muslim scholars. These other religions had formulated and examined religious and cultural problems that were unknown in the Muslim way of life and thus evoked little interest. Muslim attitudes to other civilizations and religions remained ethnocentric for a very long time.

It would seem that the rather limited contacts that existed between Muslims and non-Muslims in Muslim territory at least in the medieval period, were affected by religious controversy only in periods of tension and conflict. At moments of crisis, Muslims appealed to what they felt to be the essential values of Islam in order to defend both themselves and Islam. Of course, such an appeal could only stress the differences between Muslims and non-Muslims. At a later stage, political and group interests could then use such communal differences to stimulate negative attitudes and behavior in particular situations even to the point of physical hostility toward certain groups of non-Muslims. In each case of conflict between a Muslim and a non-Muslim community, specific interests played a role on both sides; they should always be taken into account. The simple difference between Muslims and non-Muslims or the sheer idea of *jihād* is insufficient in itself as an explanation of factual conflicts as they occurred in history.

Muslim judgments of other religions were intimately linked to the way in which Islam itself was interpreted and the way in which the authors saw and identified themselves as Muslims. Many factors could play a role in identifying oneself as a Muslim. One could identify oneself, for instance, primarily by means of the *shahāda* and an *ʿaqīda* of faith as given in *kalām*. Or one could do this by means of a particular religious tradition to which one belonged or a school which one claimed to belong to, or simply by means of a particular religious community, like a *tarīqa*, or to a particular *shaykh* to whom one gave loyalty. What is important is that in practice a Muslim author always will tend to identify and judge non-Muslims on a religious and cultural level that parallels the level on which he identifies himself.

The function in society of Muslim judgments of other religions was to keep awake the sense of truth and of basic norms. Polemics and apologetics are part of a spiritual *jihād*, and whoever judges another religion takes on the function of a *mujāhid* for the cause of Islam. Especially in medieval times the task incumbent on the *mujāhid* was to defend the Muslim *umma* as well as its religious, ideological, and cultural foundations which were felt to be sacred. In so doing, he sought to maintain a basic truth and identity of society for which Islam stood and stands as a symbol.

NOTES

1. Guy Monnot, *Islam et religions*, Series Islam d'hier et d'aujourd'hui, vol. 27 (Paris: Maisonneuve et Larose, 1986). See especially the introductory chapter, "L'islam, religion parmi les religions" (pp. 9–23) and the bibliographical chapter 2, "Les écrits musulmans sur les religions non-bibliques" (pp. 39–82).

2. Compare the two contributions in this book: Ahmad Shboul, "Arab Islamic Perceptions of Byzantine Religion and Culture" (chapter 6) and Andrea Borruso, "Some Arab-Muslim Perceptions of Religion and Medieval Culture in Sicily" (chapter 7).

3. See the contribution by Hilary Kilpatrick, "Representations of Social Intercourse between Muslims and Non-Muslims in Some Medieval *Adab* Works" (chapter 13).

4. See the contribution by Charles Genequand, "Philosophical Schools as Viewed by Some Medieval Muslim Authors" (chapter 11).

5. For references to the Zoroastrians, see the contribution by J. Christoph Bürgel, "Zoroastrianism as Viewed in Medieval Islamic Sources" (chapter 12).

6. See the contributions by Camilla Adang, "Medieval Muslim Polemics against the Jewish Scriptures" (chapter 8), Steven Wasserstrom, "Heresiography of the Jews in Mamluk Times" (chapter 9), and Christine Schirrmacher, "The Influence of European Higher Bible Criticism on Muslim Apologetics in the Nineteenth Century" (chapter 18).

7. Especially the mystical texts are fascinating. See the contribution by Carl A. Keller, "Perceptions of Other Religions in Sufism" (chapter 10).

8. On Ibn Hazm's polemic against Judaism, see Camila Adang, *Islam frente a Judaísmo: La polémica de Ibn Hazm de Córdoba* (Madrid: Aben Ezra Ediciones, 1994). The same, *Muslim Writers on Judaism and the Hebrew Bible: From the Rabban to Ibn Hazm* (Leiden: E. J. Brill, 1996). Compare "Ibn Hazm" by Roger Arnaldez, *Encyclopaedia of Islam*, new ed., vol. 3 (Leiden: E. J. Brill, 1971), pp. 790–799. Abdelilah

Ljamai is carrying out a research project on Ibn Hazm and Muslim-Christian polemics. See also p. 45.

9. Edition, with al-Shahrastānīs' *Kitāb al-milal wa'l-nihal* in the margin, by Muhammad Amīn al-Khānjī and his brother, 5 books in 2 vols. (Cairo, 1317–1321 H./1899–1903 C.E.); 2nd ed. by ʿAbd al-Rahmān Khalīfa, in 1 vol. (Cairo, 1384 H./1964 C.E.). Reprints appeared in Baghdad (1964) and Beirut (Khayat: reprint of the 2nd Cairo ed., n.d.; later edition by M. S. Kilānī, Beirut, Dār al-Maʿrifa li'l-tibāʿa wa'l-nashr, in 3 vols., 1395 H./1975 C.E.). See the study of Ghulam Haider Aasi, "Muslim understanding of other religions: An analytical study of Ibn Hazm's *Kitāb al-fasl fī al-milal wa-al-ahwā' wa al-nihal.*" Ph.D. diss. (Philadelphia: Temple University, 1986). A succinct Spanish translation with an introductory study was made by Miguel Asín Palacios: *Abenházam de Córdoba y su historia crítica de las ideas religiosas*, 5 vols. (Madrid: Real Academia de la Historia, 1927–1932).

10. S. H. Nasr, *Al-Bīrūnī: An Annotated Bibliography* (Tehran, 1973). Compare D. J. Boilot, "L'oeuvre d'al-Bērūnī: Essai bibliographique," *Mélanges de l'Institut Dominicain d'Etudes Orientales du Caire*, vol. 2 (1955), pp. 161–256 and vol. 3 (1956), pp. 391–396. See *Al-Bīrūnī Commemoration Volume, A.H. 362–1362* (Calcutta: Iran Society, 1951); *Biruni Symposium*, ed. Ehsan Yarshater with Dale Bishop (New York: Iran Center, Columbia University, 1976); *Al-Bīrūnī Commemorative Volume*, ed. Hakim Mohammed Said (Karachi: Hamdard Academy, 1979). Compare "al-Bīrūnī" by D. J. Boilot in the *Encyclopaedia of Islam*, new ed., vol. 1 (Leiden: E. J. Brill, 1978), pp. 1236–1238.

11. Edition by C. Edward Sachau under the title of *Chronologie orientalischer Völker von Albērūnī* (Leipzig: Brockhaus, 1878; repr. 1923). An English translation with notes was made by the same, *The Chronology of Ancient Nations: An English Version of the Arabic Text of the Āthār-ul-Bākiya of Albiruni, or "Vestiges of the Past"* (London, 1879; repr. Frankfurt M.: Minerva, 1969).

12. Edition by C. Edward Sachau under the title of *Alberuni's India* (London, 1887). Another title of the same book is *Kitāb tahqīq mā li'l-Hind min maqūla maqbūla fī 'l-ʿaql aw mardhūla*. A more recent and here and there revised edition of the Arabic text appeared under the title of *Kitāb tahqīq mā lil-Hind or Al-Bīrūnī's India* (Osmania Oriental Publications Bureau at Osmania University, Hyderabad, Deccan, India, 1958; repr. Beirut: ʿĀlam al-kitāb, 1403 H./1983 C.E.). C. Edward Sachau also made an English translation with notes under the title of *Alberuni's India. An Account of the Religion, Philosophy, Literature, Geography, Chronology, Astronomy, Customs, Laws and Astrology of India about A.D. 1030*, 2 vols. (London, 1888; 2nd ed. 1910; repr. New Delhi: Chand, 1964).

13. The *Canon Masudicus*, Arabic text edition in 3 vols. (Hyderabad, Deccan, India, 1954–1956).

14. See Arvind Sharma, *Studies in Alberuni's India* (Wiesbaden: Otto Harrassowitz, 1983). See for instance ch. 3, "Albīrūnī on Hindu Xenophobia," pp. 115–132.

15. The question to what degree al-Bīrūnī knew Sanskrit has been much discussed. See, for instance, S. Pines and T. Gelblum, "Al-Bīrūnī's Arabic version of Patanjali's Yogasūtra," *Bulletin of the School of Oriental and African Studies*, Vol. 29 (1966), pp. 302–325.

16. Alessandro Bausani, "L'India vista da due grandi personalità musulmane: Bābar e Bīrūnī," in *Al-Bīrūnī Commemoration Volume, A.H. 362–A.H. 1362* (Calcutta: Iran Society, 1951), pp. 53–76.

17. Franz Rosenthal, "Al-Biruni between Greece and India," in *Biruni Symposium* (New York: Iran Center, Columbia University, 1976); Rosenthal, "On some epistemological and methodological presuppositions of al-Bīrūnī," *Beyruni'ye Armagan'dan ayibasim* (Ankara: Türk tarih kurumu basimevi, 1974), pp. 145–167 (English and Turkish). Compare Bruce B. Lawrence, "Al-Biruni's approach to the comparative study of Indian culture," in *Biruni Symposium* (New York, 1976), pp. 24–47; Lawrence, "Al-Bīrūnī and Islamic mysticism," in *Al-Bīrūnī Commemorative Volume* (Karachi, 1979), pp. 362–379.

18. Arthur Jeffery, "Al-Bīrūnī's contribution to comparative religion," in *Al-Bīrūnī Commemoration Volume*, A.H. 362–A.H. 1362 (Calcutta, 1951), pp. 125–161. W. Montgomery Watt, "Al-Bīrūnī and the study of non-Islamic religions," in *Al-Bīrūnī Commemorative Volume* (Karachi, 1979), pp. 414–419.

19. On al-Shahrastānī as a scholar of religions, see Bruce B. Lawrence, *Shahrastānī on the Indian Religions* (The Hague: Mouton, 1976).

20. Arabic text edition by William Cureton (London: Society for the Publication of Oriental Texts, 2 vols., 1842 and 1846). Larger critical edition by M. F. Badrān (Cairo: Matbaʿat al-Azhar, 2 vols., 1951 and 1955). Compare the edition by M. S. Kīlānī, 2 vols. (Beirut, 1975). The text of al-Shahrastānī's *Kitāb al-milal wa'l-nihal* is often printed in the margin of text editions of Ibn Hazm's *Kitāb al-fisal fī 'l-milal wa'l-ahwā' wa'l-nihal.* Under the auspices of UNESCO a complete French translation, with introduction, notes, and bibliography, was prepared by Daniel Gimaret, Guy Monnot, and Jean Jolivet: *Shahrastani, Livre des religions et des sectes* (Leuven: Peeters & Paris: Unesco), vol. 1, 1986 and vol. 2, 1993.

21. See the publications of B. B. Lawrence mentioned in notes 17 and 19.

22. On the Sabians, see Bayard Dodge, "The Sabians of Harrān," *American University of Beirut Fes-*

tival Book, ed. Fuād Sarrūf and Suha Tamin (Beirut: A.U.B. Centennial Publications, 1966), pp. 59–85; Jane Dammen McAuliffe, "Exegetical identification of the Sābiʾūn," *Muslim World*, vol. 72 (1982), pp. 95–106; Michel Tardieu, "Sābiens coraniques et 'Sābiens de Harrān," *Journal Asiatique*, 274, no. 1/2 (1986), pp. 1–44. Compare Jan Hjärpe, "Analyse critique des traditions arabes sur les sabéens harrāniens," Ph.D. dissertation (Uppsale: Skriv Service AB, 1972).

23. W. Montgomery Watt, "A Muslim account of Christian doctrine," *Hamdard Islamicus*, Vol. 6 (1983), no. 2, pp. 57–68.

24. "Abū'l-Maʿālī" by Henri Massé in the *Encyclopaedia of Islam*, new ed., vol. 1, p. 137.

25. Edition by Charles Schefer in his *Chrestomathie persane*, vol. 1 (Paris, 1883), pp. 132–171. New edition by ʿAbbas Iqbāl (Teheran 1312/1934). A completely new edition of the Persian text with extensive notes was prepared by Hāshem Rezā under the title of *Tārīkh-e kāmel-e adyān* (Tehran: Moʾassese-ye Farāhānī, 1342/1964). Compare *The Bayān al-Adyān by Abū'l-Maʿālī Muhammad ibn ʿUbayd Allāh*, translation, introduction, and notes by Mohamed Abdul Salam Kafafi (London, 1949). French translation by Henri Massé in *Revue de l'Histoire des Religions* (1926), pp. 17–75.

26. See for example the world history of Rashīd al-Dīn, in Karl Jahn's translations: *Die Geschichte der Oġuzen* (1969), *Die Chinageschichte* (1971), *Die Geschichte der Kinder Israels* (1973), *Die Frankengeschichte* (1977), *Die Indiengeschichte* (1980). All these volumes appeared under the auspices of the Österreichische Akademie der Wissenschaften in Vienna.

27. Here, though less than in the case of the Indian religions, imagination played a role. On Chinese history written by Rashīd al-Dīn, with some references to religion, see Karl Jahn with Herbert Franke, *Die Chinageschichte des Rašīd ad-Dīn: Übersetzung, Kommentar, Facsimiletafeln* (Wien: H. Böhlaus Nachf., 1971). See also, much earlier, *ʿAḫbār as-Sīn wa l-Hind: Relation de la Chine et de l'Inde, Rédigée en 851*, texte établi, traduit et commenté par Jean Sauvaget (Paris: Ed. Les Belles Lettres, 1948). Compare V. Minorsky (ed., trans., comm.), *Sharaf al-zamān. Tāhir Marvazī on China, the Turks and India (ca. 1120)* (London: Royal Asiatic Society, 1942).

28. See Ulrich Haarmann, *Das Pyramidenbuch des Abū Ǧaʿfar al-Idrīsī (st. 649/1251). Eingeleitet und kritisch herausgegeben* (Beirut and Wiesbaden, 1991); Haarmann, "Die Sphinx. Synkretistische Volksreligiosität im spätmittelalterlichen islamischen Ägypten," *Saeculum*, vol. 29 (1978), pp. 367–384; Haarmann, "Heilszeichen im Heidentum—Muhammad-Statuen aus vorislamischer Zeit," *Die Welt des Islams*, vol. 28 (1988), pp. 210–224. Compare Erich Graefe (ed. and trans.), *Das Pyramidenkapitel in al-Makrīzī's "Ḫitat" nach zwei Berliner und zwei Münchener Handschriften unter Berücksichtigung der Bulāker Druckausgabe* (Leipzig: Hinrichs, 1911).

29. A well-known text is Ibn al-Kalbī, Kitāb al-asnām. See, for instance, Wahib Atallah, *Les idoles de Hicham Ibn al-Kalbi*. (Paris: Klincksieck, 1969) (Arabic text with French translation). See the comprehensive study by Toufic Fahd, *Le panthéon de l'Arabie centrale à la veille de l'Hégire* (Paris: Geuthner, 1968).

30. On religious customs in the Volga region, see *Ibn Fadlān's Reisebericht*, ed. Ahmad Zaki Velidi Togan (Leipzig: Brockhaus, 1939; 2nd ed. 1966) (Arabic text with German translation). French translation by Marius Canard, *Ibn Fadlan, Voyage chez les Bulgares de la Volga*, with introduction and notes (Paris: Sindbad, 1988). One of the most famous travelers was Ibn Battūta. See *The Travels of Ibn Battuta*, translation with notes by H. A. R. Gibb, 3 vols. (Cambridge: Cambridge University Press, 1958–1971). Gibb, *Selections from the Travels of Ibn Battuta in Asia and Africa, 1325–1354* (London, 1929). Compare Said Hamdun and Noël King, *Ibn Battuta in Black Africa* (London: Rex Collings, 1975). See also Ivan Hrbek, "The chronology of Ibn Battuta's travels," *Archiv Orientalni* (Prague), vol. 30 (1962), pp. 409–486. On religious customs in Africa, see besides Ibn Battuta, Tadeusz Lewicki, *Arabic external sources for the history of Africa to the South of the Sahara* (Wroclaw: Polska Akademia Nauk, 1974). There are incidental remarks on nonliterate religions—as well as on other religions—in the works of authors like al-Masʿūdī, Ibn Qutayba, and others.

31. For a bibliography of Muslim writings on nonbiblical religions, see Guy Monnot, "Les écrits musulmans sur les religions non-bibliques," *Mélanges de l'Institut Dominicain d'Etudes Orientales du Caire*, no. 11 (1972), pp. 5–49 and no. 12 (1974), pp. 44–47. Reprinted in Monnot, *Islam et religions* (Paris: Maisonneuve et Larose, 1986), pp. 39–82.

32. Daniel Gimaret, "Bouddha et les Bouddhistes dans la tradition musulmane," *Journal Asiatique*, no. 207 (1969), pp. 273–316. Compare Bruce B. Lawrence, *Shahrastānī* (Note 19), pp. 100–114.

33. S. M. Yusuf, "The early contacts between Islam and Buddhism," in *Studies in Islamic History and Culture* (Lahore: Institute of Islamic Culture, 1970), ch. 2, pp. 42–78.

34. *Fihrist*, Ch. 9, section 2. See Bayard Dodge, trans., vol. 2, pp. 831–832.

35. See "Budd" by B. Carra de Vaux, in the *Encyclopaedia of Islam*, new ed., vol. 1 (1960), pp. 1283/4.

36. *K. al-milal wa'l-nihal*, ed. Cureton (London 1842) and ed. M. F. Badrān (Cairo: Matbaʿat al-Azhar 1366/1947).

37. *Tahqīq mā li'l-Hind min maqūla maqbūla fī 'l-ʿaql aw mardhūla*, ed. E. Sachau, pp. 4 and 166.

38. *Kitāb al-bad' wa 't-tarīkh*, ed. Cl. Huart, vol. 1, pp. 187–188.

39. Karl Jahn, "Kāmalashrī-Rashīd al Dīn's 'Life and teaching of Buddha': A source for the Buddhism of the Mongol period," in Karl Jahn, *Rashīd al-Dīn's History of India: Collected Essays with Facsimiles and Indices* (The Hague: Mouton 1965).

40. On the Sumaniyya, see D. Gimaret's article quoted in Note 32, pp. 288–306.

41. Buddhism plays an interesting role in Iranian literature. See A. S. Melikian-Chirvani, "L'évocation littéraire du bouddhisme dans l'Iran musulman," in *Le monde iranien et l'islam,* vol. 2 (Geneva, 1974), pp. 1–72.

42. On the arrival of Islam in India, see A. Wink, *Al-Hind: The Making of the Indo-Islamic World*, vol. 1: *Early Medieval India and the Expansion of Islam, 7th–11th centuries* (Leiden: E. J. Brill, 1991). The historical relations between Muslims and Hindus in India have become a subject of intense studies. For the medieval period in Bengal, see J. N. and J. Sarkar, *Hindu-Muslim Relations in Bengal (Medieval Period)* (Delhi: Idarah-i Adabiyat-i-Delli, 1985).

43. For a survey of the channels along which information on India reached the medieval Muslims, see Bruce B. Lawrence, *Shahrastānī on the Indian Religions*, Religion and Society 4 (The Hague: Mouton, 1976).

44. See pp. 27–29.

45. Lawrence (Note 43), Compare Lawrence, "Shahrastānī on Indian idol worship," *Studia Islamica*, no. 3 (1973), pp. 61–73.

46. On the Barāhima, see Bruce B. Lawrence, *Shahrastānī on the Indian Religions*, Religion and Society 4 (Paris: Mouton, 1976). Compare S. Stroumsa, "The Barāhima in early kalām," *Jerusalem Studies in Arabic and Islam*, vol. 6 (1985), pp. 229–241.

47. On some Muslim views of the Sabians, see Saad Grab, "Islam and non-scriptural spirituality," *Islamochristiana*, vol. 14 (1988), pp. 51–70.

48. Karl Jahn, *Rashīd al-Dīn's History of India: Collected Essays with Facsimiles and Indices* (The Hague: Mouton 1965).

49. Yohanan Friedmann, "The temple of Multan: A note on early Muslim attitudes to idolatry," *Israel Oriental Studies*, vol. 2 (1972), pp. 176–182.

50. See Yohanan Friedmann, "Medieval Muslim views of Indian religions," *Journal of the American Oriental Society*, vol. 95 (1975), pp. 214–221. Compare Friedmann, "Islamic thought in relation to the Indian context," *Purusārtha*, vol. 9 (1986), pp. 79–91.

51. On Amīr Khusrau's and others' poetical views of India, see Annemarie Schimmel, "Turk and Hindu . . . A poetical image and its application to historical fact," in *Islam and Cultural Change in the Middle Ages*, ed. Speros Vryonis Jr. (Wiesbaden: Harrassowitz, 1975), pp. 107–126.

52. "Madjūs" by M. Morony in the *Encyclopaedia of Islam*, new ed., vol. 5 (Leiden: E. J. Brill, 1986), pp. 1110–1118. Compare Guy Monnot, *Penseurs musulmans et religions iraniennes: ʿAbd al-Jabbār et ses devanciers* (Paris: J. Vrin, 1974).

53. H. S. Nyberg, "Sassanid Mazdaism according to Muslim sources," *Journal of the K. R. Cama Oriental Institute*, vol. 39 (Bombay, 1958), pp. 1–63.

54. C. E. Bosworth, "Al-Khwārazmī on various faiths and sects, chiefly Iranian," in *Iranica Varia: Papers in Honor of Professor Ehsan Yarshater* (Leiden: E. J. Brill, 1990), pp. 10–19.

55. Monnot, *Penseurs musulmans* (Note 52), pp. 137–142.

56. Compare Saad Grab, "Islam and non-scriptural spirituality," *Islamochristiana*, vol. 14 (1988), pp. 51–70.

57. Bertold Spuler, *Iran in frühislamischer Zeit* (Wiesbaden: Franz Steiner, 1952). See also Jamsheed K. Choksy, "Conflict, coexistence, and cooperation. Muslims and Zoroastrians in Eastern Iran during the medieval period," *Muslim World*, vol. 80 (1990), pp. 213–233.

58. See the contribution by J. Christoph Bürgel, "Zoroastrianism as viewed in Medieval Islamic sources" (Chapter 12).

59. Guy Monnot, *Penseurs musulmans* (1974) (Note 52), pp. 77–150. Compare "Mānī" by C. E. Bosworth in the *Encyclopaedia of Islam*, new ed., vol. 6 (Leiden: E. J. Brill, 1991), p. 421.

60. A. Abel, "Les sources arabes sur le manichéisme," *Annuaire de l'Institut de Philologie et d'Histoire Orientales et Slaves* (Brussels), vol. 16 (1961–62), pp. 31–73. C. Colpe, "Der Manichäismus in der arabischen Überlieferung," Ph.D. Diss. (Göttingen, 1954). F. Gabrieli, "La 'Zandaqa' au Ier siècle abbasside," in *L'élaboration de l'Islam*, Colloque de Strasbourg, 1959 (Paris: Presses Universitaires de France, 1961), pp. 23–38. I. Goldziher, "Sālih b. ʿAbd-al-Kuddus und das Zindīkthum während der Regierung des Chalifen al-Mahdi," (1892), repr. in *Gesammelte Schriften*, vol. 3 (Hildesheim: Georg Olms, 1969), pp. 1–26. H. S. Nyberg, "Zum Kampf zwischen Islam und Manichäismus," *Orientalische Literaturzeitung*, vol. 32 (1929), pp. 425–441. H. H. Schaeder, "Der Manichäismus und sein Weg nach Osten," in *Glaube und Geschichte: Festschrift für Friedrich Gogarten*, ed. Heinrich Runte (Giessen: Schmitz, 1948), pp. 236–254. G. Vajda, "Les zindiqs en pays d'Islam au début de la période abbasside," *Rivista degli Studi Orientali*, vol. 17 (1938), pp. 173–229.

61. S. H. Taqī-Zāde, *Mānī va dīn-e ū*, and Ahmad Ashgār al-Shīrāzī, *Motūn-e ʿarabī va farsī dar bāre-*

ye Mānī va mānaviyyat. Both in one volume (Tehran, 1335/1956).

62. Monnot, *Penseurs musulmans* (1974), pp. 128–136.

63. For relevant literature, see Note 60.

64. No comprehensive study has yet been made of Medieval Muslim writings about Christians and Christianity. Compare Jacques Waardenburg, *Islamisch-christliche Beziehungen. Geschichtliche Streifzüge* (Würzburg: Echter Verlag; Altenberge: Oros Verlag, 1992). For literature on Muslim-Christian relations, with special attention paid to mutual perceptions and encounters in the course of history, see the various bibliographies on Islamic-Christian dialogue. For the medieval sources see the "Bibliographie du dialogue islamo-chrétien" in the first 15 issues of *Islamochristiana* (Rome: Pontificio Instituto di Studi Arabi e d'Islamistica, 1975–1989). For other literature, see for instance two bibliographies prepared by G. C. Anawati. The first appeared under the title of "Polémique, apologie et dialogue islamo-chrétiens. Positions classiques et positions contemporaines," *Euntes docete* (Rome), vol. 22 (1969), pp. 375–452. The second appeared under the title of "Vers un dialogue islamo-chrétien" in *Revue Thomiste*, vol. 64 (1974), pp. 280–306 and 585–650. Other bibliographies have appeared during the last 20 years. See on the subject also specialized journals such as *Islam and Christian-Muslim Relations*, *Muslim World*, and *Islamochristiana.*

65. G. C. Anawati, "Factors and effects of Arabization and Islamization in medieval Egypt and Spain," in *Islam and Cultural Change in the Middle Ages*, ed. Speros Vryonis Jr. (Wiesbaden: O. Harrassowitz, 1975), pp. 17–41.

66. A bibliography of manuscript sources was already published by Moritz Steinschneider, *Polemische und apologetische Literatur in arabischer Sprache* (Leipzig, 1877; repr. Hildesheim: G. Olms, 1966). The best introduction to the subject is still Ignaz Goldziher, "Über muhammedanische Polemik gegen Ahl al-kitāb," (1878), repr. in Goldziher, *Gesammelte Schriften*, vol. 2, pp. 1–47. For a survey of the Muslim polemics until the thirteenth century C.E., see, for instance, Ali Bouamama, *La littérature polémique musulmane contre le christianisme, depuis les origines jusqu'au XIIIe siècle* (Alger: Entreprise Nationale du Livre, 1988). Compare J. Waardenburg, "Religionsgespräche II. Muslimisch-christlich," *Theologische Realenzyklopädie*, vol. 28 (Berlin: Walter de Gruyter, 1998), pp. 640–648.

67. For the complexity of the medieval Muslim polemics against Christianity, see Armand Abel, "Masques et visages dans la polémique islamo-chrétienne," in *Tavolo Rotonda sul tema Cristianesimo e Islamismo* (Roma: Accademia Nazionale dei Lincei, 1974), pp. 85–128 and 129–131. Compare Abel, Historische und dogmatische Charaktere der christlich-islamischen Polemik von den Anfängen bis zum 13. Jahrhundert (Typescript, Brussels, 1969).

68. This is part of his great work, *Pêgê tês gnôseôs*. See Patrologia *Graeca* (*PG*), ed. Migne, vol. 94, cols. 764–773 (*Peri haireseôn*). The *Dialexis Sarrakênou kai Christianou* attributed to John (*PG*, vol. 106, cols. 1335–1348; shorter version *PG*, vol. 104, cols. 1585–1596) was in fact written by Abū Qurra (*PG*, vol. 97, col. 1543).

69. C. H. Becker, "Christliche Polemik und islamische Dogmenbildung" (in his *Islamstudien*, vol. 1 [Leipzig: Quelle & Meyer, 1924], pp. 432–449) was one of the first scholars who drew attention to the fact that Islamic theology in its early development was very much conditioned by questions raised by Christian theologians. See also Armand Abel, "La polémique damascénienne et son influence sur les orgines de la théologie musulmane," in *L'Élaboration de l'Islam*, Colloque de Strasbourg (Paris: Presses Universitaires de France, 1960), pp. 61–86. This has led to numerous investigations as to the origin and early development of Islamic *kalām*, into which we cannot enter here. Compare Jacques Waardenburg, "Koranologie und Christologie: Ein formaler Vergleich," in *Gnosisforschung und Religionsgeschichte. Festschrift für Kurt Rudolph zum 65. Geburtstag*, ed. Holger Preissler, Herbert Seiwert, and Heinz Mürmel (Marburg: Diagonal Verlag, 1994), pp. 575–585.

70. See F. Nau, "Un colloque du patriarche Jean avec l'émir des Agaréens," *Journal Asiatique*, vol. 11, no. 5 (1915), pp. 226–279. Compare H. Lammens, "À propos d'un colloque entre le patriarche Jean et ʿAmr b. al-As," *Journal Asiatique*, vol. 13 (1919), pp. 97–110.

71. Armand Abel, "La lettre polémique 'd'Aréthas' à l'émir de Damas," *Byzantion*, vol. 24 (1954), pp. 343–370.

72. For the Syriac text with translation and introduction, see Alphonse Mingana, "Timothy's apology for Christinity," in *Woodbrooke Studies*, vol. 2 (Cambridge, 1928). Compare Mingana, "The apology of Timothy the Patriarch before the Caliph Mahdi," in *Bulletin of the John Rylands Library*, vol. 12 (1928), pp. 137–298. The Arabic text with translation was published by Robert Caspar in *Islamochristiana*, vol. 3 (1977), pp. 107–175. A definite study was published by Hans Putman, *L'Église et l'Islam sous Timothée I (780–823): Étude sur l'Église nestorienne au temps des premiers ʿAbbasides.* (Beirut: Dar el-Machreq, 1977).

73. This text was edited by Anton Tien, *Risālat ʿAbd Allāh b. Ismāʿīl ilā ʿAbd al-Masīh b. Ishāq al-Kindī wa-risālat al-Kindī ilā ʾl-Hāshimī* (London, 1880, 1885, 1912 and Cairo, 1895, 1912). See Georges Tartar, *Dialogue islamo-chrétien sous le calife Al-*

Ma'mūn (813–834): Les épîtres d'Al-Hāshimī et d'Al-Kindī (Paris: Nouvelles Editions Latines, 1985). A description and partial translation had been given already by William Muir, *The Apology of al Kindy, Written at the Court of al Māmūn (circa A.H. 215; A.D. 830), in Defense of Christianity against Islam* (London: SPCK, 1882; 2nd ed. 1887). Al-Kindī's answer to al-Hāshimī became one of the classical texts of Christian apologetic against Islam. See Armand Abel, "L'Apologie d'al-Kindī et sa place dans la polémique islamo-chrétienne," in *L'Oriente cristiano nelle storia della civilita* (Rome, 1964), pp. 501–523.

74. Two classical studies on the situation of religious protected minorities (*dhimmīs*) in Muslim territory are those written by Arthur S. Tritton, *The Caliphs and Their Non-Muslim subjects* (London: Humphrey Milford–Oxford University Press, 1930) and by Antoine Fattal, *Le statut légal des non-musulmans en pays d'Islam* (Beirut: Imprimerie Catholique, 1958).

75. *Contra haereticos, Judaeos et Saracenos varia* of Abū Qurra in *PG*, vol. 97, cols. 1461–1609. Arabic texts were edited by L. Cheikho and by P. Sbath. See G. Graf, *Die arabischen Schriften des Theodor Abu Qurra*, Forschungen zur chr. Literatur- und Dogmengeschichte, X, Heft 3/4 (Paderborn, 1910).

76. For Christian polemical literature in Arabic against Islam, see besides M. Steinschneider also E. Graf, *Geschichte der christlichen arabischen Literatur*, 5 vols. (Vatican City: Bibl. Apostolica Vaticana, Studi e Testi, 1944–1953).

77. On the 'Edict of ʿUmar,' see the study of A. S. Tritton mentioned in Note 74.

78. Al-Jāhiz' text, *Risāla fī 'l-radd ʿalā 'l-nasārā*, was edited by J. Finkel in his *Three Essays of Abū Othmān Amr ibn Bahr al-Jāhiz* (Cairo: Salafiyya Press, 1926), and translated by him into English in *Journal of the American Oriental Society*, vol. 48 (1927), pp. 311–334.

79. The polemical text of ʿAlī al-Tabarī, *Al-radd ʿalā 'l-nasārā*, was edited by I. A. Khalife and W. Kutsch in *Mélanges de l'Université Saint-Joseph*, vol. 36 (1959), pp. 115–148. A French translation was published by Jean-Marie Gaudeul under the title of *Riposte aux chrétiens par ʿAlī Al-Tabarī* (Rome: Pontificio Istituto di Studi Arabi e d'Islamistica, 1995). An apologetical text of the same author, *Kitāb al-dīn wa'l-dawla*, was edited by A. Mingana (Manchester: 1923; Cairo: Muqtataf, 1342), and translated by him as *The Book of Religion and Empire* (Manchester, 1922).

80. David Thomas, *Anti-Christian Polemic in Early Islam. Abū ʿĪsā al-Warrāq's 'Against the Trinity'* (Cambridge: Cambridge University Press, 1992). Compare Emilio Platti, "La doctrine des chrétiens d'après Abū ʿĪsā al-Warrāq dans son Traité sur la Trinité," *Mélanges de l'Institut Dominicain d'Etudes Orientales du Caire*, vol. 20 (1991), pp. 7–30.

81. Hava Lazarus-Yafeh, *Intertwined Worlds: Medieval Islam and Bible Criticism* (Princeton, NJ: Princeton University Press, 1992). Compare W. Montgomery Watt, "The early development of the Muslim attitude to the Bible," *Transactions of the Glasgow University Oriental Society*, vol. 16 (1955–1956), pp. 50–62.

82. For instance, ʿAlī at-Tabarī, a convert from Christianity (d. A.D. 855), cites many biblical passages which are supposed to announce the mission of Muhammad and the coming of Islam. Compare Note 79.

83. Jean-Marie Gaudeul and Robert Caspar, "Textes de la tradition musulmane concernant le *tahrīf* (falsification des Écritures)," *Islamochristiana*, vol. 6 (1980), pp. 61–104. Compare I. di Matteo, "Il tahrīf od alterazione della Biblia secondo i Musulmani," *Bessarione*, vol. 38 (1922), pp. 64–111 and 223–260; vol. 39 (1923), pp. 77–127. Compare also Notes 149 and 150.

84. Abdelmajid Charfi, "Christianity in the Qur'an Commentary of Tabarī," *Islamochristiana*, vol. 6 (1980), pp. 105–148. French text "Le christianisme dans le 'Tafsīr' de Tabarī" in *Mélanges de l'Institut Dominicain d'Etudes Orientales du Caire*, vol. 16 (1983), pp. 117–161.

85. Armand Abel, "D̲u'l Qarnayn, prophète de l'universalité," in *Mélanges Henri Grégoire*, vol. 3 (*Annuaire de l'Institut de philologie et d'histoire orientales et slaves*, vol. 11) (Brussels: 1951, pp. 5–18.

86. Udo Steinbach, *D̲āt al-himma. Kulturgeschichtliche Untersuchungen zu einem arabischen Volksroman* (Wiesbaden: Franz Steiner, 1972), esp. pp. 78–92.

87. See Note 78.

88. Al-Qāsim b. Ibrāhīm's refutation of Christianity, *Kitāb al-radd ʿalā 'l-nasārā,* was edited and translated by I. di Matteo, "Confutazione contre i cristiani dello Zaydita al-Qāsim b. Ibrāhīm," *Rivista degli Studi Orientali*, vol. 9 (1922), pp. 301–364.

89. For al-Bāqillānī's refutation of Christianity in his *Al-Tamhīd* ("The Introduction"), see Wadi Z. Haddad, "A tenth-century speculative theologian's refutation of the basic doctrines of Christianity: al-Bāqillānī (d. A.D. 1013)," in *Christian-Muslim Encounters*, ed. Yvonne Yazbeck Haddad and Wadi Z. Haddad (Gainesville: University Press of Florida, 1995), pp. 82–94. Compare Armand Abel, "Le chapitre sur le Christianisme dans le *Tamhīd* d'al-Bāqillānī," *Études d'Orientalisme dédiées à la mémoire de Lévi-Provençal*, vol. I (Paris, 1962), pp. 1–11.

90. For ʿAbd al-Jabbār's refutation of Christianity, see his *Al-mughnī fī abwāb al-tawhīd wa 'l-ʿadl*, vol. 5: *Al-firaq ghayr al-islāmiyya*, ed. M. M. al-Khodeiri (Cairo, 1965), pp. 80–151. See also his *Tathbīt dalā'il nubūwat sayyidna Muhammad*, edited by ʿAbd al-Karīm ʿUthmān, 2 vols. (Beirut: Dār al-ʿarabiyya, 1386/1966), pp. 198ff. On these texts see Shlomo Pines, *The Jewish Christians of the Early Centuries of Chris-*

tianity, According to a New Source (Jerusalem: Israel Academy of Science and Humanities, 1966). S. M. Stern contests the conclusions of S. Pines in his two articles "Quotations from the Apocryphal Gospel in ʿAbdeljabbār" and "ʿAbdeljabbār's account of how Christ's religion was falsified by the adoption of Roman customs," in the *Journal of Theological Studies* (Oxford), vol. 18 (1967), pp. 34–57 and vol. 19 (1968), pp. 128–185, respectively.

91. For Byzantine-Muslim relations during the first century of Islam, see Daniel J. Sahas, "The seventh century in Byzantine-Muslim relations: characteristics and forces," *Islam and Christian-Muslim Relations*, vol. 2 (1991), pp. 3–22.

92. For Muslim views of Byzantium, see Ahmad M. H. Shboul, "Arab attitudes towards Byzantium: official, learned, popular," in *Kathigitria: Essays presented to Joan Hussey* (Porphyrogenitus, 1988), pp. 111–128; Shboul, "Byzantium and the Arabs. The image of the Byzantines as mirrored in Arabic literature," in *Byzantine Papers*, ed. E. and M. Jeffreys and A. Moffat (Canberra, 1981), pp. 43–68.

93. A survey of Byzantine views of Islam is given by Erich Trapp in his *Manuel II. Palaiologos: Dialoge mit einem 'Perser'* (Vienna, 1966), pp. 13*–48*, and by John Meyendorff, "Byzantine views of Islam," *Dumberton Oak Papers*, vol. 18 (1964), pp. 115–132. A survey of Byzantine polemical literature is given by Adel-Théodore Khoury, *Les théologiens byzantins et l'Islam; textes et auteurs* (*VIIIe-XIIIe s.*) (Paris-Louvain: Nauwelaerts, 1969). Compare his *Polémique byzantine contre l'Islam, 2e tirage* (Leiden: E. J. Brill, 1972). See also Wolfgang Eichner, "Die Nachrichten über den Islam bei den Byzantinern," *Der Islam*, vol. 23 (1936), pp. 133–162 and 197–244. Carl Güterbock, *Der Islam im Lichte der byzantinischen Polemik* (Berlin, 1912) is now outdated.

94. The embassy has also been dated in 851. On such embassies, see Francis Dvornik, "The embassies of Constantine-Cyril and Photius to the Arabs," in *To Honor Roman Jakobson*. Essays on the occasion of his seventieth birthday, 11 October 1966. vol. I (The Hague: Mouton, 1967), pp. 569–576.

95. The letter to ʿUmar is supposed to be the answer by the emperor Leo III to the caliph ʿUmar II (717–720) inquiring about the Christian faith. An Armenian version of this letter has been preserved and was translated by A. Jeffery, "Ghevond's text of the correspondence between ʿUmar II and Leo III," *Harvard Theological Review*, vol. 37 (1944), pp. 269–332. A shorter Latin version of the letter is to be found in *PG*, vol. 107, cols. 315–324. The true authorship has not been established with absolute certainty. See Jean-Marie Gaudeul, *La correspondance de ʿUmar et Léon* (*vers 900*) (Rome: Pontificio Istituto di Studi Arabi e d'Islamistica, 1995).

96. *PG*, vol. 3, col. 28B.

97. For the letters see *PG*, vol. 105, cols. 807–821 and 821–841. The larger work, *Anatropê tês tou Arabos Môamet plastographêtheisês Biblou* (Nicetae Byzantini *Refutatio Mohamedis*), was written during the reign of Basil I (867–886). For this text, see *PG*, vol. 105, cols. 669–805; the refutation of the Qurʾān is to be found in cols. 701–805.

98. Yahyā b. ʿAdī refuted the *Kitāb al-maqālāt* of al-Warrāq (d. around 861). On this author see A. Périer, *Petits traités apologétiques de Yahyā Ben ʿAdi* (Paris, 1920) and *Yahyā Ben ʿAdī: Un philosophe chrétien du Xe siècle* (Paris, 1920). Compare Georg Graf, *Die Philosophie und Gotteslehre des Jahjā ibn ʿAdī und späterer Autoren* (Münster, 1910).

99. Ibn Zurʿa refuted the *Awāʾil al-adilla* of al-Balkhī (d. 931) who was dependent on al-Warrāq. On Ibn Zurʿa see Cyrille Haddad, *ʿĪsā Ibn Zurʿa, philosophe arabe et apologiste chrétien* (Beirut: Dār al-kalima, 1971).

100. See Ghulam Haider Aasi, "Muslim understanding of other religions: An analytical study of Ibn Hazm's *Kitāb al-Fasl Fi al-Milal wa al-ʿAhwāʾ waʾl-Nihal*. Ph.D. diss. (Temple University, Philadelphia, 1987). A summary of Ibn Hazm's arguments against Christianity was given by J. Windrow Sweetman in his *Islam and Christian Theology: A Study of the Interpretation of Theological Ideas in the Two Religions*, Part 2, vol. 1 (London: Lutterworth Press, 1955), pp. 178–262. See also the earlier section on Ibn Hazm (Notes 8 and 9).

101. The complete title is *Al-radd al-jamīl li-ilāhiyyat ʿĪsā bi-sarīh al-injīl*. The text was edited and translated into French by Robert Chidiac as Al Ghazālī, *Réfutation excellente de la divinité de Jésus-Christ d'après les Evangiles* (Paris: Ernest Leroux, 1939). An English summary of the contents was given by J. Windrow Sweetman in his *Islam and Christian Theology: A Study of the Interpretation of Theological Ideas in the two Religions*, part 2, vol. 1 (London: Lutterworth Press, 1955). A German translation with introduction and commentary was published by Franz-Elmar Wilms under the title of *Al-Ghazālīs Schrift wider die Gottheit Jesu* (Leiden, E. J. Brill, 1966). Hava Lazarus-Yafeh convincingly demonstrated that the text was wrongly attributed to al-Ghazālī. See her article "Étude sur la polémique islamo-chrétienne: Qui était l'auteur de *al-Radd al-jamīl li-Ilāhiyyat ʿĪsā bi-sarīh al-Injīl* attribué à al-Ghazzālī?," *Revue des Etudes Islamiques*, vol. 37, no. 2 (1969), pp. 219–238. The author was probably a converted Christian from Egypt who was familiar with the New Testament.

102. Elias of Nisibis was a Nestorian metropolitan. His main work was translated into German by L. Horst under the title of *Buch vom Beweis der Wahrheit des Glaubens* (Colmar, 1886).

103. ʿAbdallāh b. al-Tayyib was a well-known philosopher and physician. He was author of several theological treatises.

104. Hans Daiber, "Die Kreuzzüge im Lichte islamischer Theologie: Theologische Interpretamente bei Abū Sāma (gest. 665/1268)" in *Orientalische Kultur und Europäisches Mittelalter*, ed. Albert Zimmermann and Ingrid Craemer-Ruegenberg (Berlin: W. de Gruyter, 1985), pp. 77–85. For the relations between the Muslim and the Christian world at the time of the Crusades, see Claude Cahen, *Orient et Occident au temps des Croisades* (Paris: Aubier Montaigne, 1983). For a bibliography, see Aziz S. Atiya, *The Crusade: Historiography and Bibliography* (Bloomington: Indiana University Press, 1962). Compare Atiya, *Crusade, Commerce and Culture* (Bloomington: Indiana University Press, 1962). See also Steven Runciman, *A History of the Crusades*, 3 vols. (Cambridge: Cambridge University Press, 1952–1954). The Crusades not only stimulated polemics against Christianity but also brought about militant Muslim attitudes with regard to Islam. See Emmanuel Sivan, *L'Islam et al Croisade* (Paris: A. Maisonneuve, 1968). Compare Margaret E. Bertsch, "Counter-Crusade. A Study of Twelfth Century Jihād in Syria and Palestine," Ph.D. diss. (Ann Arbor, University of Michigan, 1950).

105. Bartholomaei Edesseni, *Elenchus aut Confutatio Agareni (Elenchos Agarênou)*, see *PG*, vol. 104, cols. 1383–1448. Although the author' s lifetime is not known, it has been submitted that this text was written between 1129 and 1146, when Edessa was in Frankish hands. See Armand Abel, "La 'Réfutation d'un Agarène' de Barthelémy d'Edesse," *Studia Islamica*, no. 37 (1973), pp. 5–26.

106. On Paul al-Rāhib, see Paul Khoury, *Paul d' Antioche, évêque melkite de Sidon (XIIe.s.): Texte établi, traduit et introduit (Recherches, XXIV)* (Beirut: Imprimerie Catholique, n.d., 1965?). Of special interest is his *Letter to the Muslims* (P. Khoury, text pp. 59–83, trans. pp. 169–187) to which Ibn Taymiyya answers in his well-known *Al-jawāb al-sahīh li-man baddala dīn al-masīh.* Compare Note 109.

107. Al-Qarāfī, *Kitāb al-ajwiba ʾl-fākhira* (Cairo, 1322/1904).

108. On Ibn Taimiyya, see Henri Laoust, *Essai sur les doctrines sociales et politiques d'Ibn Taymiyya* (Cairo: Institut Français d'Archéologie Orientale, 1939). See also Laoust, "Ibn Taymiyya," *Encyclopaedia of Islam*, new ed., vol. 3 (Leiden: E. J. Brill, 1971), pp. 951–955.

109. Text edition in four volumes, Cairo, 1322/1905. See the study of this book with partial English translation by Thomas F. Michel, *Ibn Taymiyya: A Muslim Theologian's Response to Christianity* (Delmar, NY: Caravan Books, 1984). Ibn Taymiyya is also the author of *Al-risāla al-qubrusiyya* (Text ed. Cairo 1319/1901). See about this *Letter to Cyprus* Jean R. Michot, *Ibn Taymiyya: Lettre à un roi croisé (al-Risālat al-Qubrusiyya)* (Louvain-la-Neuve and Lyon, 1995). An earlier study had been made in German by Thomas Raff, "*Das Sendschreiben nach Zypern, Ar-risāla al-qubrusīya, von Taqī Ad-Dīn Ahmad Ibn Taimīya (661–728 A.H./1263–1328 A.D.).*" Ph.D. diss., Bonn, 1971. A polemical tract is his *As-sarīm al-maslūl ʿalā shātim al-rasūl* (Hyderabad, 1322/1905). Ibn Taymiyya's *Takhjīl ahl al-injīl* (Ms. Bodl. 11 45, according to E. Fritsch, *Islam und Christentum im Mittelalter: Beiträge zur Geschichte der muslimischen Polemik gegen das Christentum in arabischer Sprache* (Breslau: Müller and Seiffert, 1930), p. 25) exists in manuscript. A comprehensive study of Ibn Taymiyya's arguments against Christianity in these writings and of their influence is needed.

110. Author of the *Jawāb risālat ahl jazīrat Qubrus,* Ms. Utrecht, Cod. ms. or. no. 40 (according to Fritsch, *Islam und Christentum im Mittelalter*, pp. 33–34).

111. See Note 106.

112. Saʿīd b. Hasan al-Iskandarānī, *Masālik al-nazar fī nubuwwat sayyid al-bashar*. Edited and translated with introduction and notes by Sidney Adams Weston, *JAOS*, vol. 24 (1903), no. 2, pp. 312–383.

113. Ibn Qayyim al-Jawziyya, *Hidāyat al-hayāra min al-yahūd wa'l-nasārā* (Cairo, 1322/1904).

114. See Note 66.

115. See Miguel de Epalza, "Notes pour une histoire des polémiques anti-chrétiennes dans l'Occident musulman," *Arabica*, vol. 18 (1971), pp. 99–106.

116. See Notes 8, 9, and 100.

117. See Abdelmajid Turki. "La lettre du 'moine de France' à al-Muqtadir billāh, roi de Saragosse et la réponse d'al-Bāǧī, le faqīh andalou," *Al-Andalus*, vol. 31 (1966), pp. 73–153. Compare D. M. Dunlop, "A Christian mission to Muslim Spain in the XIth century," *Al-Andalus*, vol. 17 (1952), pp. 259–310. See also Alan Cutler, "Who was the 'Monk of France' and when did he write?," *Al-Andalus*, vol. 28 (1963), pp. 249–269.

118. Ibn Sabʿīn may have had a philosophical correspondence with Frederick II. See M. A. F. Mehren, "Correspondance du philosophe soufi Ibn Sabʿīn Abd oul-Haqq avec l'empereur Frédéric II de Hohenstaufen . . . ," *Journal Asiatique*, Series 7, vol. 14 (1879), pp. 341–454.

119. *Tuhfat al-arīb fī ʾl-radd ʿalā ahl as-salīb* (Text ed. Cairo 1895). French translation by Jean Spiro, "'Le présent de l'homme lettré pour réfuter les partisans de la Croix,' par ʿAbd Allāh ibn ʿAbd Allāh, le Drogman. Traduction française inédite," *RHR*, vol. 12 (1885), pp. 68–69, 179–201, and 278–301. See the large study by Miguel de Epalza, *La Tuhfa, autobiografía y polémica islámica contra el Christianismo de ʿAbdallāh al-Taryūmān (fray Anselmo Turmedo)* (Rome: Accademia Nazionale dei Lincei, 1971).

120. On medieval polemical writings against Islam, sometimes of base quality, see Norman Daniel, *Islam and the West: The Making of an Image* (Edinburgh: Edinburgh University Press, 1961; 2nd rev. edition 1980; pb. Oxford: Oneworld). See also Daniel "Christian-Muslim Polemics," *Encyclopedia of Religion* (New York: Macmillan, 1987), vol. 11, pp. 402–404.

121. For later medieval Latin views of Islam, see Richard W. Southern, *Western Views of Islam in the Middle Ages* (Cambridge: Harvard University Press, 1962).

122. The account is followed by a refutation of Islam. The text was published in *Neos Hellênomnêmôn* (Athens), vol. 16 (1922), pp. 7–21.

123. Veneration of the "Seven Sleepers" and of Mary has been common among Muslims and Christians, e.g., in Ephese. See Louis Massignon, "Les VII Dormants, Apocalypse de l'Islam," *Opera Minora*, vol. 3 (Beirut: Dar al-Maaref, 1963).

124. Mahmoud M. Ayoub, "Towards an Islamic Christology: (I) An image of Jesus in early Shīʿī Muslim literature" (*Muslim World*, vol. 66 [1976], pp. 163–188) and "II: The death of Jesus, reality or delusion (A study of the death of Jesus in Tafsīr literature)" (*Muslim World*, vol. 70 [1980], pp. 91–121). Compare Jacques Jomier, "Jésus tel que Ghazālī le présente dans 'Al-Ihyā,'" *Mélanges de l'Institut Dominicain d'Etudes Orientales du Caire*, vol. 18 (1988), pp. 45–82. On the spiritual Jesus as perceived in Islam, see Javad Nurbakhsh, *Jesus in the Eyes of the Sufis* (London: Khaniqahi Nimatullah Publications, 1983). Compare Seyyed Hossein Nasr, "Jesus through the eyes of Islam," *Islamic Life and Thought* (London: Allen and Unwin, 1981), pp. 209–211.

125. See for instance the text by al-Tabarī, "The story of Jesus son of Mary and his mother," in *The History of al-Tabarī*, vol. IV: *The Ancient Kingdoms*. Trans. Moshe Perlmann (Albany, NY: SUNY Press, 1987), pp. 112–125. Compare André Ferré, "La vie de Jésus d'après les *Annales* de Tabarī," *Islamochristiana*, vol. 5 (1979), pp. 7–29, and Ferré, "L'historien al-Yaʿqūbī et les Evangiles," *Islamochristiana*, vol. 3 (1977), pp. 65–84.

126. Mahmoud M. Ayoub, "The Islamic context of Muslim-Christian relations," in *Conversion and Continuity: Indigenous Christian Communities in Islamic Lands, Eighth to Eighteenth Centuries*, ed. Michael Gervers and Ramzi Jibran Bikhazi (Toronto: Pontifical Institute of Mediaeval Studies, 1990), pp. 461–477.

127. See for instance Rudolf Sellheim's suggestion in his "Die Madonna mit der Schahāda," in *Festschrift für Werner Caskel*, ed. Erwin Gräf (Leiden: E. J. Brill, 1968), pp. 308–315. The suggestion, however, must be dismissed.

128. See Bernard Lewis, *The Muslim Discovery of Europe* (New York: W. W. Norton, 1982). The reader will find here the sources for our knowledge of the Arab and Turkish Muslim image of Europe throughout history. Apart from the brief chapter 6 (pp. 171–184), the Muslim image of European Christianity is not treated and would require a separate study.

129. Francesco Gabrieli, ed., *Arab Historians of the Crusades* (Berkeley: University of California Press, 1969). See also the Memoirs of Usāma translated by P. K. Hitti, *An Arab-Syrian Gentleman and Warrior in the Period of the Crusades* (New York, 1929). See esp. Hadia Dajani-Shakeel, "Natives and Franks in Palestine: Perceptions and Interaction," in *Conversion and Continuity: Indigenous Christian Communities in Islamic Lands, Eighth to Eighteenth Centuries*, ed. Michael Gervers and Ramzi Jibran Bikhazi (Toronto: Pontifical Institute of Mediaeval Studies, 1990), pp. 161–184.

130. André Miquel, "L'Europe occidentale dans la relation de Ibrāhīm b. Yaʿqūb," *Annales, Economies, Sociétés, Civilisations*, vol. 21 (1966), pp. 1048–1064.

131. Karl Jahn, *Die Frankengeschichte des Rašīd ad-Dīn* (Vienna: Verlag der Österreichischen Akademie der Wissenschaften, 1977).

132. As a first introduction, see George C. Anawati, "Islam et christianisme: La rencontre de deux cultures en Occident au Moyen Age," *Mélanges de l'Institut Dominicain d'Etudes Orientales du Caire*, vol. 20 (1991), pp. 23–299.

133. See, for instance, Gustav E. von Grunebaum, "Parallelism, convergence, and influence in the relations of Arab and Byzantine philosophy, literature, and piety," *Dumberton Oak Papers*, no. 18 (1964), pp. 89–112. Such an approach is fruitful to analyze certain common social and cultural patterns beyond obvious tensions and conflicts. It also opens research on parallel religious movements in different religions or religious traditions. See for instance Sidney H. Griffith, "Images, Islam and Christian icons: A moment in the Christian/Muslim encounter in early Islamic times," in *La Syrie de Byzance à l'islam, VIIe-VIIIe siècles*, Colloque international 1990 (Damascus: Institut Français de Damas, 1992), pp. 121–138. Social and cultural relations in medieval Spain and the West in general are a promising field of research. See, for example, Mohammed Hammam (Ed.), *L'Occident musulman et l'Occident chrétien au Moyen Age*. Rabat: Publications de la Faculté des Lettres, 1995.

134. For this scheme, compare E. Fritsch, *Islam und Christentum im Mittelalter: Beiträge zur Geschichte der muslimischen Polemik gegen das Christentum in arabischer Sprache* (Breslau: Müller and Seiffert, 1930), pp. 39–150, and F. E. Wilms, *Al-Ghazālīs Schrift wider die Gottheit Jesu* (Leiden: E. J. Brill, 1966), pp. 223–243. See Notes 109 and 101, respectively.

135. For basic literature on medieval Muslim views of Judaism, see Camilla Adang, *Muslim Writers on Judaism and the Hebrew Bible: From Ibn Rabban*

to Ibn Hazm (Leiden: E. J. Brill, 1996) and Steven Mark Wasserstrom, *Between Muslim and Jew: The Problem of Symbiosis under Early Islam* (Princeton: Princeton University Press, 1995). See also the contributions of these authors to this book: Camilla Adang, "Medieval polemics against the Jewish Scriptures" (chap. 8) and Steven Wasserstrom, "Heresiography of the Jews in Mamluk Times" (chap. 9).

136. G. Vajda, "Juifs et Musulmans selon le *Hadīṯ*," *Journal Asiatique*, no. 209 (1937), pp. 57–127.

137. See, for instance, Karl Jahn, *Die Geschichte der Kinder Israels des Rashīd ad-Dīn* (Vienna: Verlag der Österreichischen Akademie der Wissenschaften, 1973).

138. A bibliography of the Arabic sources of these polemics is given in Moritz Steinschneider, *Polemische und apologetische Literatur in arabischer Sprache, zwischen Muslimen, Christen und Juden* (1877; repr. Hildesheim: G. Olms, 1965). Important studies are Moshe Perlmann, "The medieval polemics between Islam and Judaism," in *Religion in a Religious Age*, ed. S. D. Goitein (Cambridge, Mass.: Association for Jewish Studies, 1974), pp. 103–138, and Perlmann, "Muslim-Jewish Polemics," *The Encyclopedia of Religion* (New York: Macmillan, 1987), vol. 11, pp. 396–402. Of an older date but still invaluable are Ignaz Goldziher, "Über muhammedanische Polemik gegen Ahl al-kitāb," *ZDMG*, vol. 32 (1878), pp. 341–387 (repr. in his *Gesammelte Schriften*, vol. 2, pp. 1–47); and Martin Schreiner, "Zur Geschichte der Polemik zwischen Juden und Muhammedanern," *ZDMG*, vol. 42 (1888), pp. 591–675.

139. *Kitāb al-fisal fī ʾl-milal wa -ʾl-ahwāʾ wa-ʾl-nihal*, five books ed. in 2 vols. (Cairo 1317–1321/1899–1903; and later editions). Compare M. Asín Palacios' succinct translation with introduction, *Abenházam de Córdoba y su Historia crítica de las ideas religiosas*, 5 vols. (Madrid: Academia de la Historia 1927–1932). On this book, see the study by Ghulam Haider Aasi, "Muslim understanding of other religions: An analytical study of Ibn Hazm's Kitāb al-Fasl fī al-milal wa-al-ahwāʾ wa al-nihal," Ph.D. diss., Temple University, Philadelphia, 1986. Into the *K. al-fisal* . . . (I, 216–II, 91) 130 pages have apparently been inserted which contain the polemical treatise *Izhār tabdīl al-Yahūd wa-ʾl-Nasārā li-ʾl-Tawrāt wa-ʾl-Injīl*, adding to Ibn Hazm's treatment of the Jews in I, 98–116 that in I, 116–224. This hypothesis was submitted by I. Friedländer, "Zur Komposition von Ibn Hazm's Milal wa-n-Nihal," in *Orientalische Studien Theodor Nöldeke gewidmet* . . . , vol.1 (Giessen, 1906), pp. 267–277. The third polemical treatise against Judaism is *Al-radd ʿalā Ibn al-Naghrīla al-yahūdī*. On this polemic, see M. Perlmann, "Eleventh century Andalusian authors on the Jews of Granada," *Proceedings of the American Academy for Jewish Research*, vol. 18 (1948/9), pp. 269–290. See also David S. Powers, "Reading and misreading one another's Scriptures: Ibn Hazm's refutation of Ibn Nagrella al-Yahudi," in *Studies in Islamic and Judaic Traditions*, ed. W. M. Brinner and S. D. Ricks (Atlanta, Georgia: Scholars Press, 1986), pp. 109–122. Compare E. García Gómez, "Polémica religiosa entre Ibn Hazm e Ibn al-Nagrīla," *Al-Andalus*, vol. 4 (1936), pp. 1–28. Compare Ignaz Goldziher, "Proben muhammedanischer Polemik gegen den Talmud, I: Ibn Hazm, Zeitgenosse Samuel Nagdêlā's (al-Barāmikī)," *Jeschurun*, vol. 8 (1872), pp. 76–104 (repr. in *Gesammelte Schriften* , vol. 1, pp. 136–64). On Ibn Hazm's logic see Moshe Perlmann, "Ibn Hazm on the equivalence of proofs," *Jewish Quarterly Review* , vol. 40 (1949/50), pp. 279–290. See also Notes 8, 9, and 100.

140. Camila Adang, *Islam frente a Judaïsmo. La polémica de Ibn Hazm de Córdoba* (Madrid: Aben Ezra Ediciones, 1994). For the place of Ibn Hazm within the tradition of Muslim-Jewish polemics, see also her broader study mentioned in Note 135.

141. Samau'al al-Maghribī, *Ifhām al-Yahūd* (Silencing the Jews), ed. and trans. M. Perlmann (New York: American Academy for Jewish Research, 1964).

142. Saʿīd b. Hasan al-Iskandarānī, *Masālik an-nazar fī nubuwwat sayyid al-bashar*, Ed. and trans. with introduction and notes by Sidney Adams Weston, *Journal of the American Oriental Society*, vol. 24, no. 2 (1903) 312–383. Compare Ignaz Goldziher, "Saʿīd b. Hasan d'Alexandrie," *Revue d'Etudes Juives* , vol. 30 (1895), pp. 1–23 (repr. in *Gesammelte Schriften* , vol. 3, pp. 397–419).

143. ʿAbd al-Haqq al-Islāmī, *Al-husām al-majrūd fī ʾl-radd ʿalā ʾl-Yahūd* (or alternatively: *Al-sayf al-mamdīd fī ʾl-radd ʿalā (akhbār) al-Yahūd*). See Moshe Perlmann, "ʿAbd al-Hakk al-Islāmī, a Jewish convert," *Jewish Quarterly Review*, vol. 31, no. 2 (Oct. 1940), pp. 171–191.

144. Ibn Idrīs al-Qarāfī as-Sanhājī, *Kitāb al-ajwiba ʾl-fākhira ʿan al-asʾila al-Fājira*, in the margin of ʿAbd al-Rahmān Bacegizāde, *Al-fāriq bayna ʾl-makhlūq wa-ʾl-khāliq*, vol. 1 (Cairo 1322/1904), pp. 2–265.

145. Ibn Qayyim al-Jawziyya, *Kitāb hidāyat al-hayārā min al-Yahūd wa-ʾl-Nasārā* (Cairo, 1323/1905). See Ignaz Goldziher, "Proben muhammedanischer Polemik gegen den Talmud, II: Ibn Kajjim al-Ǧauzija," *Jeschurun*, vol. 9 (1873), pp. 18–47 (repr. in *Gesammelte Schriften* , vol. 1, pp. 229–258).

146. Abū Zakariyyā Yahyā al-Rāqilī, *Taʾyīd al-milla*. See M. Asín Palacios, "Un tratado morisco de polémica contra los judios," in *Mélanges Hartwig Derenbourg* (Paris, 1909), pp. 343–366.

147. G. Vajda, "Un traité maghrébin 'Adversus Judaeos': 'Ahkām ahl al-dhimma' du shaykh Muhammad b. ʿAbd al-Karīm al-Maghīlī," in *Études d'Orientalisme dédiées à la mémoire de Lévi-Provençal*, vol. 2 (Paris: G.P. Maisonneuve et Larose, 1962), pp. 805–813.

148. Ed. R. J. McCarthy (Beirut: Librairie Orientale, 1957), pp. 122–131. See Robert Brunschvig, "L'argumentation d'un théologien musulman du Xe siècle contre le Judaisme," in *Homenaje a Millás-Vallicrosa*, vol. 1 (Barcelona, 1954), pp. 225–241. See also Note 89 on al-Bāqillānī's refutation of Christianity.

149. I. Goldziher, "Über muhammedanische Polemik gegen Ahl al-kitāb," *Zeitschrift der Deutschen Morgenländischen Gesellschaft*, vol. 32 (1878), pp. 341–387 (repr. in *Gesammelte Schriften*, vol. 2, pp. 1–47).

150. See Hava Lazarus-Yafeh, *Intertwined Worlds: Medieval Islam and Bible Criticism* (Princeton: Princeton University Press, 1992). Compare also earlier H. Hirschfeld, "Muhammedan criticism of the Bible," *Jewish Quarterly Review*, vol. 13 (1901), pp. 222–240.

151. Mahmoud Ayoub, "ʿUzayr in the Qurʾān and Muslim Tradition," in *Studies in Islamic and Judaic Traditions*, ed. W. M. Brinner and S. D. Ricks (Atlanta, Georgia: Scholars Press, 1986), pp. 3–18. Compare Hava Lazarus-Yafeh, "Ezra-ʿUzayr: The metamorphosis of a polemical motif," *Intertwined Worlds: Medieval Islam and Bible Criticism* (Princeton: Princeton University Press, 1992), pp. 50–74.

152. Compare Notes 81, 82, 83, and 100.

153. For Muslim-Jewish relationships in history, see Salo W. Baron, *A Social and Religious History of the Jews*, 2nd ed., esp. vol. 5 (New York, 1957); S. D. Goitein, *A Mediterranean Society: The Jewish Communities of the Arab World as Portrayed in the Documents of the Cairo Geniza*, 6 vols. (Berkeley: University of California Press, 1967–1993); Bernard Lewis, *The Jews of Islam* (Princeton, New Jersey: Princeton University Press, 1984); Ronald L. Nettler, ed., *Studies in Muslim-Jewish Relations*, vol. 1 (Chur: Harwood, 1993); Nettler, ed., *Medieval and Modern Perspectives on Muslim-Jewish Relations* (Luxembourg: Harwood, 1995); and Steven M. Wasserstrom, *Between Muslim and Jew: The Problem of Symbiosis under Early Islam* (Princeton, N.J.: Princeton University Press, 1995).

154. In due time, such research should extend to the three monotheistic religions, on both normative and empirical levels.

3

The Modern Period

1500–1950

JACQUES WAARDENBURG

Writings from the Muslim Empires 1500–1800 C.E.

The emergence of new, more extensive empires, such as the Ottoman empire in the fourteenth century and the Iranian and Moghul empires in the sixteenth, created a new situation in the Muslim world and may be regarded as the beginning of the modern period. The fact that these empires brought together different ethnic groups and religious communities under one central Muslim authority is of special interest for our study. Not only did a new kind of "togetherness" develop between Muslims, Christians, and Jews, or Muslims and Zoroastrians, or Muslims and Hindus, but also the state saw its interest in preventing conflicts between the religions within its territory and passed legislation to regulate the situation of non-Muslim inhabitants.

The most interesting writings on other religions in the period of the great Muslim empires were produced in India. India had already aroused the imagination of Muslims in the medieval period and, in addition to al-Bīrūnī's scholarly description around 1029, various medieval texts containing accounts of travels in which the imagination or at least the sense of the marvelous often predominate have survived. By the end of the medieval period a certain image of the religions of India had been established in Muslim writings.

The direct contact with Hindus within the Moghul empire, and in particular at and around the court, where interests of state were involved, signified a modification of the separateness previously established and the beginning of a new kind of interaction.[1] The emperor Akbar, who ruled for nearly half a century (1556–1605), was especially concerned to take initiatives in this domain.[2] He favored meetings and discussions between Muslims and Hindus, Jains, and Parsis, not only for political reasons but also out of personal interest.[3] He also founded a kind of politicoreligious fraternity, the *Dīn-i ilāhi* (literally, "Religion of God") which brought together Muslims and Hindus on a political, social, and religious level. Akbar also wanted to deepen knowledge of Hindu culture and religion among Muslims and encouraged the translation of Sanskrit works into Persian, which was the language of the court.

The study of Hindu religious thought was further promoted by Dārā Shukōh (1615–1659), the eldest son of Shah Jahān (r. 1628–1658) who, like his father Jahāngir (r. 1605–1627), had continued Akbar's policy of cooperation between Muslims and Hindus after the latter's death, although pressure from the *ʿulamāʾ* had put an end to the Dīn-i ilāhi. Dārā Shukōh, a spiritual man himself, was in close touch with Muslim Sufis and Hindu *sanyāsīs* and studied both Muslim and Hindu mysticism.[4] Looking for a rapprochement between Hinduism and Islam, Dārā Shukōh held that all holy books, including the Vedas, stem from one source and that they constitute a commentary on each other. He also contended that the advent of Islam did not necessarily abrogate the religious truths contained in the Vedas or supersede the religious achievements of the Hindus. He wrote several works in which he expounded ideas relativizing the supposed absolute opposition between Muslim monotheism and Hindu polytheism, arguing that Brahmins accept one divine principle behind the plurality of gods. His famous *Majmaʿ al-bahrayn* ("The coming together of the two seas," 1655) is a kind of comparative study of the technical terms used in Sufism and Vedānta philosophy.[5] With the help of learned Hindus he translated 52 Upanishads from Sanskrit into Persian under the title of *Sirr-i akbar* ("The greatest secret," 1657). He encouraged further translations of Sanskrit works into Persian, which Akbar had started, and some 25 translations were edited and printed in the course of the seventeenth century.[6] Dārā Shukōh may be seen as having carried furthest the meeting of Muslim and Hindu spirituality and most actively promoted Muslim studies of Hindu religious thought. Militarily defeated by his younger brother Aurangzēb, who seized the right of succession, Dārā Shukōh was accused of heresy and executed in 1659. His works survived, however.

Aurangzēb, who ruled under the name of ʿĀlamgīr I (r. 1658–1707), reversed the tolerant policies of his predecessors, treating Hindus as people who should convert to Islam and showing no interest in the tenets of their religion. The policy he inaugurated was to lead to growing antagonism between Muslims and Hindus in India. It also meant the end of a literature in which different Muslim views of Hinduism were expounded.[7]

Among the works on non-Muslim religions in India in this period, special mention should be made of the *Dabestān-e madhāheb* ("School of religions").[8] Written in Persian by a certain Muhsin Fānī, it gives a rather flowery account of the various religions that could be found in northern India at the time. It shows Zoroastrian leanings, has been ascribed to Mohsin-e Kashmīrī or Zuʾlfiqar Ardastānī, and has been dated around the middle of the seventeenth century. It testifies to the imaginative interest in religions that prevailed around the Moghul court before Dārā Shukōh's fall. It was to be two centuries later that a completely new kind of interreligious encounter in India took place, with the arrival of Christian missions.

Whereas the Moghul state in India had a majority of non-Muslims, the *Safawid* state in Iran had only a small minority of Zoroastrians, Christians, and Jews, who were treated as *dhimmīs*. ʿAbbās I (r. 1587–1629) had moved a number of Armenians to Isfahan to help in constructing the new capital. I am not aware of Persian Muslim texts written between the sixteenth and twentieth centuries, describing the religions of these minorities or other religions in general. It would have been interesting to compare Twelver Shīʿī descriptions and evaluations with Sunnī texts on the subject and also to trace the historical roots of the interest in ancient Iranian religion which was to become more prominent in the course of the twentieth century. In the published diaries written by Nāsir al-Dīn Shah (r. 1848– 1896) about his travels to Europe in 1873, 1878, and 1889, religion plays only a minor part.[9] As in India, the shock of encountering another world religion was to take place with the arrival of Christian missions in Iran in the second half of the nineteenth century.

The *Ottoman* empire was the most extensive of the three empires considered. It had numerous Christian and Jewish minorities, not only in Anatolia but also in many regions of its Balkan territories and its Arab lands. It was involved in a number of wars with European nations and its conflictuous relationships with Europe which lasted several centuries still loom in the European subconscious. Europeans seldom realize, however, that it may well be thanks to the Turkish danger that the Reformation in Germany could survive.[10]

One of the most interesting books of the seventeenth century is the ten-volume *Seyāhatnāme* ("Book of Travels") of Evliyā Celebi (1611–ca. 1684), a man of great culture who made extensive travels in and outside the empire. His "Travels" provide precious historical and contemporary accounts of the regions and cities he visited, including information about non-Muslim communities.[11] His contemporary Hājjī Khalīfa (Kātib Celebi, 1609–1657), an outstanding scholar and author of historical, geographical, and bibliographical works, wrote in 1655 a small work on the history of the Greeks, Romans, and (Byzantine) Christians.[12] The sixteenth and the first half of the seventeenth century was the great period of Ottoman culture which does not seem to have produced any new description of religions other than Islam. Besides the Qurʾān, the accounts of al-Shahrastānī and other medieval authors remained authoritative. The Ottoman world histories touched on the history of religions before Islam but, like medieval historical works, they treated the subject as the history of those religious communities that were founded by prophets mentioned in the Qur'ān.[13]

On a more popular level we have some interesting accounts written by an Ottoman interpreter, ʿOsmān Agha about his adventures in Austria and Germany around 1700.[14]

Historical studies have helped us become better informed about the situation of the Christian and Jewish *dhimmīs* living in the Ottoman empire, who were formally organized and administered according to the well-known *millet* system of autonomous communities according to their religion.[15] The conditions of these religious minorities varied considerably between the Balkans, Anatolia, and the Arab regions.[16] The rules of protection which had been applied during the sixteenth and seventeenth centuries unfortunately were less strictly enforced during the decline which had set in by the end of the seventeenth century. Although the European powers pressed for improvements in the situation of the religious minorities, in particular the Christians, this pressure turned out to be a two-edged sword. The European intervention in Ottoman internal affairs, together with the independence movements of the Balkan peoples, aroused bitterness among the Turks,[17] a bitterness to which the Armenians fell victim in 1895, 1908, and especially 1916. It was only through the Constitution of 1924 that, along with the *Sharīʿa*, the *millet* system was abolished in the new Republic not only formally but also in practice.

There was one province of the Ottoman empire, however, that distinguished itself through its rapid modernization in the course of the nineteenth century, and this was Egypt.[18] The account of the French occupation between 1798 and 1801 and other events in Egypt around these years written by al-Jabartī (1753–ca. 1825) is a precious document of the way in which an intelligent Egyptian historian and observer viewed the French occupation and French life and customs on Egyptian soil.[19] This experience and the following modernization policies of Muhammad ʿAlī (r. 1805–1848) would spark interest in Europe among a new generation of Egyptians. Some of them would go and study there and familiarize themselves with European culture. From the beginning of the nineteenth century, Egypt was a meeting place for Europe and the Arab world, as well as for different peoples from the Middle East. It was here and in northern India that Muslim intellectuals started movements of reform and modernization of Islam.

As far as Safawid *Iran* is concerned, the third of the three great Muslim empires of the modern period, the position of the non-Muslims was here even less favorable than that in the Moghul and the Ottoman empires. Both writings against the Jews and persecutions of them are known in the seventeenth century.[20]

From the sixteenth century onward, as European expansion began, Islam was also spreading outside the three great empires already mentioned, in Africa and South and Southeast Asia, an expansion which had started already in the medieval period. The late medieval traveler Ibn Battūta (1304–1377), a Muslim Marco Polo, wrote a description of his journeys to these non-Muslim regions, including China (which he may not have visited himself), in which he also deals with the inhabitants' religious customs.[21]

Indonesia presents a special interest as a meeting-place between Muslims and non-Muslims. The Indian Muslim scholar and mystic *shaykh* Nūruddīn al-Ranīrī (d. 1658) was *shaykh al-islām* in the Sultanate of Acheh in North Sumatra from 1637 until 1643. Among the many books he wrote is an interesting account of the religions known at the time as the *Tibyān fī maʿrifati 'l-adyān*,[22] written on the model of al-Shahrastānī's *Kitāb al-milal wa'l-nihal*.

Other Muslim writings from Asia and Africa dealing with non-Muslim beliefs and customs and dating from before the colonial period may still be discovered.

During the colonial period, however, roughly speaking from the middle of the nineteenth until the middle of the twentieth century, a new kind of Muslim literature about other religions, in particular Christianity, came into existence. This was largely in response to the rapid spread of Western domination and the growing influence of modern science and technology, European cultural self-confidence, and Christian missions from the West.

Europe and the West in general never had a high opinion of Islam, and this was particularly true for the colonial period. With a few exceptions, the soldiers, administrators, merchants, settlers, missionaries, and teachers coming from Europe, who established themselves in Muslim lands, tended to look down on Islam as a religion and civilization, and in many cases on religion in general. Colonial policy makers perceived Islam as a real or potential danger to be eliminated from the sphere of politics, rather than as a living social force sustaining Muslim societies or as a moral force sustaining human relations. Paradoxically, countries under colonial rule which had sizable communities of adherents of traditional religions as well as a Muslim population, as in Sub-Saharan Africa and Southeast Asia, witnessed a clear expansion of Islam at this time. This was made possible precisely by the new peace and order which the Europeans had established and the improvements they had made in communication. Islam also symbolized resistance to colonial intrusion.

Western rule not only facilitated a further expansion of Islam, it also opened up the colonies to Christian missions, with their manifold religious, educational, medical, and social activities. The history of these missions has been written mostly from a missionary Christian and sometimes from a broader historical or anthropological angle. But rarely have the missions been studied from the point of view of the people the missionaries worked among. How did Muslims at the time, in various regions and under various circumstances, perceive the missionaries and their work? What ideas did they develop about Christianity as they saw it entering Mulsim societies? We have the generally negative ideological response as expressed in polemics against Christianity, and a slightly less negative answer in the form of a growing apologetical literature contrasting Islam with Christianity. But there are also some more impartial accounts of what the missionaries did and how Muslims reacted to them. There have been expressions of esteem for and even friendship with Christians, testifying to a new kind of perception of Christianity that emerged from the direct interaction of Muslims with Western Christians.

We shall concentrate here on the period from the arrival of Western administration until its departure around the mid-twentieth century. This is the time when a number of new independent Muslim nation-states were established besides the few that had remained independent, like Turkey, Iran, Afghanistan, and Yemen. We shall look first at the context in which the encounter of Muslims with religions other than Islam took place during the period, a context that was conditioned by far-reaching social changes. Next, we shall pay attention to some Muslim texts about other religions, and in particular Christianity, dating from this period of Western military and political domination.

The Colonial Period

Characteristic of the colonial period was that several European states—Great Britain, France, Russia, the Netherlands, Germany until 1918, Spain and, toward the end, Italy—exerted political control of the government and administration of the majority of the Muslim regions of the world. Their policies were secular. If needed, they used Christian minorities for their own political interests.[23] They used military force to occupy these regions and to suppress rebellions. They penetrated these countries to serve both their economic and imperial interests, which also determined the policies they followed to modernize these societies. They introduced a modern school system at the primary and secondary levels, as the result of which new educated classes arose with direct links with the colonial power concerned.[24]

In Turkey and Iran, which remained politically independent, the same kind of "secular" policies were imposed by Kemal Atatürk and the Pahlevi shahs in the twentieth century. Besides the Western countries just mentioned, most other European countries as well as the United States increased their economic influence in Muslim countries and propagated Western cultural ideals and values among the new educated classes. In this sense, all Western countries somehow participated in the expansion of Western influence in the Muslim world and beyond.

As a consequence, European and American value systems and ideologies started to spread in the new intellectual centers of the Muslim world, with different emphases depending on the particular countries and the period concerned. The situations in Algeria, Egypt, Turkey, Lebanon, Iran, India, and the Soviet Union varied greatly, but the impact of the West made itself felt everywhere. Critical scholarship, science, and technology were presented as major achievements of Western civilization. The French consciously propagated a secularist ideology (*laïcité*) after 1870 and especially after the separation of state and church in France in 1905. Great Britain and the United States put forward an ideology of enlightened liberalism and open market economy. German cultural and political ideals were spread in the German colonies until 1914 and later as an alternative to the "colonial" ideologies after 1918.

The major alternative in the West to the various ideologies of colonialism was socialism, mostly represented by a minority in the parliaments of the colonial powers. Socialism was also acceptable for those intellectuals in the colonies who were no longer indebted to religious tradition, looking for justice and striving for independence. The great alternative to all Western "bourgeois" and "capitalist" ideologies, of course, was Communism; after 1917, Communism was politically centralized in the Soviet Union which, incidentally, had "colonized" its own Muslim territories in Central Asia and in and beyond the Caucasus.

The impact of these different ideas and ideologies on the educated and largely Westernized elites of Muslim countries has been tremendous and may be considered a kind of corollary of the economic and political colonization. As a reaction, Muslim authors started to underline in their writings what they saw as the fundamental differences between Islam and all ideologies with a Western origin. They had more reason to do so, since all these ideologies were critical of Islam, seeing it either as a source of resistance to Western rule, or as a socioreligious structure that resisted development.

As mentioned earlier, the expansion of the West's influence also led to an expansion of Western Christianity, in particular through the missions which, in their different variants, were no less critical of Islam than the various secular Western ideologies. In the way in which Christian missions were conducted, one must avoid easy generalizations. Not only must different situations, times, and places be distinguished, but also different ways in which the missions operated. The approaches of the various Roman Catholic Orders, the Church of England and its missionary societies, the numerous Protestant missionary societies (a number of which had no direct links with any particular Protestant Church), and the missionary work carried out by the Russian Orthodox Church until 1914, must be clearly differentiated.[25]

The implications of this growing Western influence in the ideological and religious domain, exerted as it was in the shadow of political and economic power, have been immense. Western influence not only called for different Muslim responses in the name of Islam but also changed existing relationships between Muslim and other local religious communities.[26] It led to the emergence of new religious communities with a Western type of organization and outlook. All of this also brought about a discussion among the *ʿulamāʾ* and other Muslim leaders about the attitude Muslims should take to non-Muslims and the status of non-Muslims generally.[27] A positive development in the colonial period was that the situation of the non-Muslim minorities in Muslim societies improved. The *dhimmī* status disappeared when all citizens became equal before the law; Muslims and non-Muslims enjoyed equal status and treatment at least in law.

It is also in this broader context that the revitalization of religions outside the West in general should be seen. The Christian churches of the Near East received support from Western churches but still were an object of missionary efforts until after World War II. New Christian communities and churches were established in most Muslim regions and countries, if only for the sake of Christian settlers and migrants.

Thanks to support from the West, many Jewish communities in the Near East came to new life. Most important, the establishment of Jewish colonies in Palestine and later of the state of Israel not only caused the departure of most Jews from Muslim lands but also led to religious estrangement insofar as Muslims generally viewed Zionism as the political expression of religious Judaism.

In India, the revitalization of *Hinduism*, partly as a response to Christian missions and partly as an effort to mobilize Hindus for the national struggle and for modernization, increased the existing communalism of Hindus and Muslims. The establishment of Pakistan led to a growing estrangement not only between Pakistan and India as states but also between Hindus and Muslims in India itself.

In Africa south of the Sahara, Western influences led to new relationships between Muslim and Christian communities sharing a common African heritage. The opening of Europe and North America to growing numbers of Muslim immigrants in the course of the twentieth century has exposed Muslims to situations of religious plurality in modern secular societies. Moreover, it has led to a certain proletarization of these immigrants at least in the industrial cities of Western Europe. Since the 1970s, social inequality between immigrants and local inhabitants has been running parallel in Europe with ethnic and religious differences. At the same time, the predominantly Muslim countries surrounding Europe have a much lower standard of living than the European ones. All of this implies a growing difference in well-being between Westerners and Muslims along the North-South divide, something that could not but affect their mutual perceptions even apart from religion and politics.

Looking back, one must admit that the growing influence of the West in Muslim regions and countries has led to a number of Muslims feeling themselves, their societies, and Islam to be threatened. The advent of non-Muslim secular ideologies, as well as religious movements, in the midst of a gradual disruption of traditional social structures could only strengthen the sense of an imminent ideological danger against which Muslims had to arm themselves.

This danger was first attributed to a Christian and then to a de-Christianized, secular West.

Some Writings from the Period 1800–1950

Islam and the West

The accounts by Egyptian students and travelers of their experiences in Paris, starting with Rifāʿa Rāfiʾ al-Tahtāwī's stay in Paris from 1826 until 1831,[28] and Muslim travelers in Europe in general[29] have been a subject of studies which we shall not deal with here. These accounts testify to the amazement and astonishment that Egyptian visitors felt when looking at the social and personal lifestyles of Europeans. Typically, they did not pay attention to the religious aspects of European societies; it was in the first place the social behavior that struck them as one of the most visible differences between Egyptian and European life—at least, life in the cities with which they came into contact. But there are travel accounts of other than Egyptian Muslims as well. Apart from some travel accounts of Turks visiting Central and Eastern Europe before the nineteenth century, discussed previously in this chapter, there are also some by Muslim travelers to Spain.[30] Al-Hajarī al-Andalusī from Spain (and later Marrakesh) visited France and the Low Countries from 1611 to 1613, leaving a fascinating account of his experiences.[31] The Moroccan Muhammad al-Saffār visited France in the 1820s and 1830s and reported about it.[32] From Iran, Pir Zadeh visited Paris in 1887 and wrote down the results of his observations.[33]

The fruits of the French Revolution, as presented by the French, made a great impression on all of them.[34] Discussions started on the relationship between the East and the West.[35] The ideals of freedom, equality, and brotherhood were taken up by younger intellectuals. Together with the confidence in reason and Western science,[36] these ideals were to challenge the existing structures and authorities of North African, Turkish, Middle Eastern, and other Muslim societies. Over and against traditional Islam (*al-qadīm*, literally "the old"), new views developed (*al-jadīd*, literally "the new"). During the period 1870–1930 new interpretations of Islam tended to stress the positive role of reason and modernity.[37] At that time, other values, where the West played only a minor role or which were opposed to the West, like a new recourse to Islam or national independence, started to impose themselves. In their turn, they were to obtain a nearly absolute character for those who were moved and mobilized by them.

Famous visitors from Egypt to Paris in the first decades of the twentieth century were Tāhā Husayn, Tawfīq al-Hakīm, and Muhammad Husayn Haykal.[38] All three of them studied in Paris and brought back to Egypt the confidence in reason and Western civilization that was so typical of the European intellectual elites before World War I and afterward. Each tried to transfer the critical use of reason in research and education, in literary writing and cultural ideals. But each of them, too, after having embraced the West for its liberal and intellectual virtues, was to become disenchanted with precisely that egoism of liberalism which does not care about other people's well-being. The end of this "liberal age" can be very well spotted in the work of these three prominent authors[39] who, after having been in the balance between "East and West," between "Islam and Europe," all finish just as most others of their and the following generations in choosing for the first term, either the East, Islam, or simply the roots of their own society.[40]

In fact, there always had been an undercurrent of hostility in Muslim societies to the West, first because of its encroachments on Muslim societies and second because of its negative attitude to Islam, when Westerners took a haughty attitude to Muslims and tended to despise Islam. European colonial conquests were answered by the call to *jihād*, mostly at a local level.[41] One of the first Muslim intellectuals to be aware of the global danger of Western domination over Islam was Jamāl al-Dīn al-Afghānī (1838–1897) who, like Marx with the workers some decades earlier, saw the need for Muslims to unite—not only against the West but also against their own regimes which were dependent on the West or simply corrupt.[42] Whereas the West gave liberal Muslims hope that their societies could be modernized, for al-Afghānī and his followers the West rather was the incarnation of evil and should be resisted, ideologically and otherwise. Many Muslims reacted with relief to Russia's defeat by Japan in 1905,[43] and World War I would show them that the colonial powers were neither as united nor as invincible as they had been thought to be.

Islam and Christianity

In this battle of the minds about how to take a stand to the West, and which one, the debate about the attitude to take toward the religion of the West, Christianity, played an important role. We should remember that, according to the Qur'ān and religious tradition, Jesus was a prophet bringing essentially the same monotheistic message as Muhammad did six centuries later. Accordingly, as to its origins Christianity was a heavenly, revealed religion, but very soon in the course of its history the Christians alienated themselves from the original "Islamic" message of Jesus and distorted the religion brought by him. As in the medieval period, Muslims in the modern period either stressed the heavenly message brought by Jesus or the distortions introduced into it by the Christians. In the former case their attitude tended to be more positive, in the latter case more negative. Here the conflict was only aggravated when Christian missionaries tried to persuade Muslims that Islam was not a good religion and that the Qur'ān could not be a revelation. Muslims retorted by saying that the text of the Bible cannot be a revelation since it has been wrongly interpreted or even falsified (*tahrīf*).

One of the most famous disputations was that held in 1854 in Agra (India) between the German missionary Karl Gottlieb Pfander (1803–1865) and the Indian Muslim Rahmatullah al-Kairanāwī, nicknamed 'al-Hindī' (1818–1890).[44] Besides his *Izhār al-haqq* (Demonstration of the Truth), treated separately in this volume, al-Kairanāwī wrote a number of other treatises, some of them of considerable length. The *Izhār al-haqq* itself was first published in Constantinople (not in India!) in 1867, with several new editions and translations in the following years. It became a model for subsequent Muslim refutations of Christianity and especially its Scriptures. Many other examples of controversial literature flourishing on both sides could be given.

Sayyid Ahmad Khan

The most important Muslim thinker of this period (1800–1950), as far as his attitude to Christianity was concerned, was probably Sayyid Ahmad Khan (1817–1898) in India.[45] Coming from an important Muslim family, he received a perfect education according to the Muslim standards of the time. He was fluent in Urdu, Persian, and Arabic, and then also in English. The Rebellion of 1857, the so-called Mutiny, meant the collapse of the world of Sayyid Ahmad's youth. For the rest of his life he made immense efforts to promote the education, cultural standards, and social life of the Muslim community in India in order to catch up with Western standards, as well as with the economic and intellectual developments in the Hindu community. He also defended the Muslim community against British reproaches of having instigated the "Mutiny" of 1857. As the Egyptians looked to the French, Sayyid Ahmad saw the British as the model for the development of the Indian Muslims. His experience of 1857 had taught him that British power, at least for the time being, could not be resisted and that Muslims ought to learn the secrets of the power of the Europeans, including their religion. For Sayyid Ahmad this meant in the first place an intellectual and even spiritual venture and, unique in his time, he started to make a scholarly study of the Old and New Testaments.

The result was published in his *Tabyīn al-kalām fī tafsīr al-tawrāt wa'l-injīl 'alā millat al-islām* (Theological clarification on the subject of the exegesis of the Old and New Testaments destined to the community of Islam), with the English subtitle, "The Mohamedan Commentary on the Holy Bible." Three parts of this work were published. Part one, an introduction to the subject, appeared in 1862. Part two, an introduction to the Old Testament in general and the Book of Genesis in particular, with a commentary on Genesis 1–11, appeared in 1864. These two parts appeared both in Urdu and in English. Part three, a short history of Christianity up to the arrival of Islam, with a commentary on Matthew 1–5, appeared only in Urdu in 1865 and was never translated. As far as I know, this has been the only Muslim effort ever undertaken to write a coherent commentary on the Bible, with due knowledge of critical Bible research in the West.[46] The purpose was to make the Bible known to the Muslim public without polemical or apologetic intentions. Even if the initial project to write a commentary on the whole Bible could not possibly be realized, we have to do here with a unique document which, by the way, is difficult to find in Western libraries. Most interesting for our purpose is to see how Sayyid Ahmad Khan, speaking as "we" and "we Muslims" in the name of the Muslim community, treats the key concept of Revelation (Arabic: *wahy*).

The author defines Revelation as "that by which God's will is disclosed (to us) in things unknown."[47] Such Revelation can be addressed to prophets and is then called *wahy*; this is the highest level of Revelation. But persons other than prophets can have revelation experiences as well, which Sayyid Ahmad indicates with terms such as *tahdīth* (revelation to persons who are not prophets), *ilhām* (immediate inspiration of the heart of a human being, specifically a mystic), and *mushāhada* or *mukāshafa* (what is communicated in a dream or a vision). Consequently, there is a gamut of communications that man can receive from "elsewhere," and Sayyid Ahmad gives examples of these different kinds of Revelation not only from the Qurʾān (on his own authority) but also from the Bible (on the authority of Christian theologians). It is important to note that Sayid Ahmad, when dealing with the Bible or typical Christian doctrines, always used Bible texts themselves with interpretations from prominent Christian theologians.

The author indicates two major differences between Revelation given to prophets and to persons other than prophets. First, the texts revealed to prophets are without error, whereas the texts revealed to others can contain errors—for instance, because something that was revealed is accompanied by an interpretation of the person concerned. Second, the texts revealed to prophets can contain a religious prescription (*hukm sharʿī*), whereas revelations received by others cannot contain any religious law.

It is interesting also to note the difference Sayyid Ahmad makes between the Revelation (*wahy*) given to Muhammad in the Qurʾān and that given to the prophets who lived before Muhammad. The Qurʾān is literally dictated (*wahy matlū*); God himself is at the origin of its words. That is, the Revelation received by Muhammad and present in the Qurʾān is a miracle of language (*muʿjizat al-fasāha*), a language that is immediately divine. The prophets before Muhammad, by contrast, received only the contents (*madmūn*) of the Revelation, which they then rendered into their own language; thus, not all words had a divine origin. In certain cases a "special text" was revealed (*matn khāss*), and in other cases a personal "elaboration" (*riwāya*) was made by the prophet concerned. As a consequence, Sayyid Ahmad takes all words of the Qurʾān as literally revealed, whereas he is free to differentiate texts of the Old and New Testament, interpreting them according to this distinction between "text" and "elaboration"—that is, between revealed divine text (*matn*) and human elaboration (*riwāya*).

As a result, the three "heavenly" Scriptures all have their origin in God, but the quality of their Revelation is different: in the Qurʾān everything is literally revealed; in the Old and New Testaments, certain texts are literally revealed (*matn khāss*) but there are also human elaborations (*riwāya*). We leave Sayyid Ahmad's further and more detailed treatment of the Bible and its cases of assumed "corruption" (*tahrīf*) aside. Most important for our purpose is to see that Sayyid Ahmad's acceptance of the presence of Revelation in the Old and New Testaments, as well as certain hermeneutical criteria which he derived from Islamic theology, made him investigate the Bible in an intellectually positive way no Muslim had done before. He clearly made use of the results of Western biblical critical scholarship as it was available in his time. His purpose, however, was not to destroy the Bible—as Rahmatullāh and long before him Ibn Hazm had wanted to do—but better to sort out what elements of Revelation it contained. His approach must be seen in the line of a long tradition of positive appreciation by Muslim thinkers of Scriptures earlier than the Qurʾān.

Other Muslim Indian thinkers like Amir Ali[48] and Khuda Bukhsh[49] also held more or less positive views of Christianity.

Muhammad ʿAbduh

The Egyptian reformer Muhammad ʿAbduh (1849–1905),[50] though culturally and intellectually of lesser stature than Sayyid Ahmad Khan, had an equally strong desire to modernize Muslim society and improve Muslim education and scholarship. Muhammad ʿAbduh, too, accepted the intellectual achievements of Europe in so far as they were not in contradiction with the basic principles of Islam such as could be derived from the Qurʾān and Sunna with the help of reason. Like Sayyid Ahmad, ʿAbduh studied Christianity but his attention was directed less toward the study of the Bible as Scripture than toward the history of Christianity. And as Sayyid Ahmad tried to distinguish critically the positive texts in the Bible, held to be "revealed" from other texts, ʿAbduh tried to discriminate critically between the negative trends and developments in the history of Christianity and the positive ones, which he held to be in accordance with the teachings of Jesus.[51]

From 20 August 1902 onward, ʿAbduh published in *al-Manār* six articles entitled *Al-islām waʾl nasrāniyya maʿa al-ʿilm waʾl-madaniyya* (Islam and Christianity with [reference to] science and civilization).[52] They were a response to an article that the Greek Catholic ("Melkite") Farah Antūn (1861–1922) had published elsewhere, in which he contended that in the course of history Christianity had been more tolerant than Islam toward science and culture. In his articles, which later appeared as a book, ʿAbduh defended the opposite position. It was not Islam but Christianity—in particular, the Church—that had been opposed to the free use of reason and that had shown intolerance, for instance, in the horrors of the Inquisition. Islam, on the contrary, had passed on philosophy and science to an ignorant medieval Europe; it was lastly thanks to Islam that the Renaissance and the Enlightenment had taken off in Europe. Contrary to Christianity, imbued as it is with mysteries and antirational doctrines, Islam is a religion that honors reason and research and thus promotes science and civilization. And in his sixth and last article, ʿAbduh appealed to Muslims in general, and Egyptians in particular, to use their intelligence in the search for knowledge. In this way they would at one and the same time revitalize science and religion in Muslim societies, true religion being for ʿAbduh intimately linked to reason. Science and religion should fraternize again, as in the beginning of Islamic history and as prescribed by the Qurʾān.

In his objections against Christianity's causing obstacles to the development of science, ʿAbduh could very well have been a nineteenth-century European humanist opposing science to religion. This becomes clear in the following six points which ʿAbduh considers as the essence of the Christian religion and of which he outlines the negative consequences and effects for the development of science.[53]

1. Christianity holds miracles to be a proof of truth, whereas science looks for laws instead of miracles.
2. In Christianity the religious leaders exercise an authority and power that opposes free thinking and research of the faithful.
3. Christianity has the innate tendency to turn away from this world and address itself to the hereafter, whereas science does not occupy itself with the hereafter but with this world.
4. Christianity views faith and belief as gifts that cannot be attained by means of reason. Consequently, it teaches the faithful that they can use reason, at most, in order to understand what they believe. Christianity obstructs anyone who wants to investigate something that is completely opposed to what he believes.
5. Christianity teaches that the Bible contains everything man should know and that all knowledge should be drawn from Scripture. This principle goes against scholarly research that wants to go beyond what Scripture says or to address Scripture itself.
6. Christianity makes an extremely sharp separation between Christians and other people, those who follow Jesus and those who do not (Mt 10: 34, 35). In this way it cuts across the fundamental ties of family and kinship, destroying society and culture.

Over and against these six negative aspects of Christianity's attitude to the development of science, ʿAbduh argued that Islam, in these six respects and others, favors the development of science.

What is strikingly modern in ʿAbduh's treatise is his comparative approach, applied to what he considers to be the "principles" held by the two religions about intellectual pursuits. He gave copious examples from Islamic and European history of the treatment meted out to science and thought in Muslim and Christian lands. Like Sayyid Ahmad, he establishes a direct connection between religion on the one hand and reason, science, and culture on the other; none of the latter treats religion as a separate domain or sphere. Both authors consequently arrive at a beginning of "comparative religion" or at least a comparative study of Christianity and Islam according to the possibilities at the time and their own commitments. Their presentation not only of Christianity but also of Islam differed considerably from earlier Muslim presentations. We must leave aside here their exegetical work on Qurʾānic texts dealing positively with other religions including Christianity.[54]

A different attitude from the harmonizing attitude of the modernist reformers, whose first care was to improve Muslim thinking and pedagogy with the help of reason and certain values of European culture, was held by those reformers who exerted themselves to defend Islam against attacks by Christian missionaries and in their turn went on to attack Christianity. This was the case, for instance, with ʿAbduh's younger collaborator, the Syrian-born Sayyid Muhammad Rashīd Riḍā (1865–1935).[55] He claimed to work in the spirit of ʿAbduh but had a less open—not to say less liberal—attitude, and he was much less familiar with Europe than was ʿAbduh, who had been there several times and knew English and French. He also had a much more political and critical view of the West than ʿAbduh had.[56] Rashīd Riḍā was a prolific writer on nearly all problems confronting Islam at the time, in particular in al-Manār, which he had inaugurated and which barely survived him. Various articles written by him on the subject of Christianity on different occasions were collected in his early book entitled *Shubuhāt al-Nasārā wa hujaj al-islām*

(Demonstration of the Criticisms by the Christians [sc. against Islam] and the Proofs of Islam).[57] The problem of the Scriptures occupies a large place in his debates with the Christians.[58] Christianity, like all other religions that were the outcome of prophetic preaching, including Eastern religions, was contaminated by polytheistic tendencies and thus its monotheistic fundaments were changed.[59] The same author also polemicizes with Christianity elsewhere, as in his *al-Wahy al-muhammadī* (The Revelation of Muhammad).[60] Rashīd Ridā was also the first to organize an institution to educate Muslim missionaries to be sent out; it was closed when World War I broke out.

We are here in the broad field of controversial literature. Useful summaries of Muslim polemical literature against Christianity that appeared in Egypt from the end of the nineteenth until about the middle of the twentieth century are given by Arthur Jeffery in the 1920s[61] and by Harry Gaylord Dorman Jr. soon after World War II.[62] Recently, Hugh Goddard published a more thorough study of this literature.[63] In missionary circles the rise of anti-Christian Muslim writings in the Near East and elsewhere after World War I was of course taken as a negative point, but in the sociopolitical context of the time its occurrence was understandable.[64]

A particularly aggressive brand of anti-Christian polemics came from the Ahmadiyya movement, especially the militant Qadiani[65] but also the Lahore[66] branch, in particular until World War II. The Ahmadiyya was active both in the Indian context where the movement arose and through missionary efforts in Europe and Africa. Other Muslim perceptions of the Ahmadiyya are here left out of consideration.

Muhammad Abū Zahrah and Others

In the framework of Islamic University teaching, in 1942 the Egyptian Azhar scholar Shaykh Muhammad Abū Zahrah published nonpolemical "Lectures on Christianity" (*Muhādarāt fī ʾl-nasrāniyya*) which he had delivered at the Azhar University for more advanced students. His point of departure was a traditional one: in order to know "true" Christianity, that is to say the teaching of Jesus, one cannot rely on the Scriptures and historical accounts of the Christians since they have been corrupted. True knowledge about original Christianity should therefore be derived from Qurʾānic data to be supplemented by those results of Western scholarship that conform to what the Qurʾān says about Jesus and the Christians.

The fundamental question in all Muslim writings of this kind is, Where can one find the true written *Injīl* (Gospel) that, according to the Qurʾān, Jesus brought himself and of which the four Gospels of the New Testament are only later witnesses? Perhaps more important than the existing poor state of knowledge, even compared with what Sayyid Ahmad wrote 80 years earlier, is the fact that at this time the Islamic al-Azhar university started to show interest in other religions and provide some kind of teaching about other religions.[67] Some liberal intellectuals, however, followed their own curiosity in a spirit of free inquiry. It would be important to trace the kind of interest they had in other religions, in Egypt and elsewhere.[68]

During the period under consideration (1800–1950), notwithstanding the considerable expansion of Islam in Asia and Africa, it was practically only Christianity which attracted attention from Muslim authors. This happened mainly as a response to Christian missionary activity and to the domination of Europe and the West in general where Christianity was the typical religion. As already suggested, there has been a great variety in Muslim responses to Christianity in the nineteenth and twentieth centuries which need to be studied academically.[69] In Iran a certain interest in the ancient Persian religion of Zarathustra and even in Manicheism developed. Before 1950, however, publications on religions other than Islam here mainly concerned Christianity.[70] As far as travel accounts during this period are concerned, there exists an interesting description of Tibet by Khwājā Ghulām Muhammad (1857–1928), who visited the region in 1881–1882 and 1886.[71]

Spiritual Orientations

During the period 1800–1950 there were also several spiritual movements among Muslims which addressed themselves to non-Muslims too and took a more universalistic attitude. Two of them, originating in Iran, must be considered to have crossed the borders of Islam. The first was the "messianic" Bābī movement in Shiraz around Sayyid ʿAlī Muhammad (1821–1850); this movement started in 1844 but was severely persecuted from 1852 onward. The other was the "messianic" Bahai movement around Bahāʾ Ullāh (1817–1892) which started in 1863, as a kind of fulfillment of the Bābī movement. Both communities were persecuted in Iran, but the adherents of Bahāʾ Ullāh succeeded in developing their communities in the Ottoman Empire and later elsewhere. The

Bahai movement became a religion of its own, independent of Islam, in much the same way as Christianity became a religion of its own after it had become independent of Judaism.

Another movement with a universalistic attitude, but without conflicts with Islam, was the Sufi Movement established by Ināyat Khan (1882–1927). Originating from the Čistī *tarīqa*, Ināyat Khan decided to open membership of his own *tarīqa* to adherents of other religions too; only Muslims, however, could be initiated. He founded the Sufi Movement in 1923 in Geneva, with summer courses being given in Suresnes, France. The Sufi Movement's spirituality attracted European adherents. A similar interreligious, spiritual orientation is characteristic of the spirituality of Idrīs Shah (b. 1924).

In Europe itself, some thinkers of a gnostic orientation who were looking for a wider Eternal Tradition than the traditions of the established religions discovered Islam. René Guénon (1869–1951), who had been initiated to the Shādhiliyya Order, and Fritjof Schuon, who had been initiated to a branch of the ʿAlāwiyya Order, deserve mention here. Both men had become Muslims, but their followers in the West came from different religious traditions and were not required to convert to Islam.

The few Europeans and Americans who formally converted to Islam before the middle of the twentieth century tried to create a better understanding of Islam in the West, in a period in which Islam had quite negative connotations. They made little effort, however, to make Christianity or any other religion understandable to their fellow Muslims. Often reacting as converts rather negatively to their former religion, or to any other religion than Islam, they fall outside our inquiry about Muslim perceptions of other religions. They scarcely perceived them at all.

NOTES

1. On this Muslim-Hindu interaction and its context, see Aziz Ahmad, *Studies in Islamic Culture in the Indian Environment* (Oxford: Clarendon Press, 1964).

2. See especially Saiyid Athar Abbas Rizvi, *Religious and Intellectual History of the Muslims in Akbar's Reign, 1556–1605, with Special Reference to Abu'l-Fazl* (New Delhi: Munahiram Manoharial Publishers, 1975). See also Sri Ram Sharma, *The Religious Policy of the Mughal Emperors*, 3rd rev. ed. (Bombay: Asia Publishing House, 1972).

3. A. B. M. Habibullah, "Religious debates in Akbar's court," in *Prof. Syed Hasan Askari Felicitation Volume*, ed. S. V. Sohoni. Special issue 1968 of *The Journal of the Bihar Research Society* (Patna), pp. 97–109.

4. See for instance Cl. Huart and L. Massignon, "Les entretiens de Lahore (entre le prince impérial Dārā Shikūh et l'ascète hindou Baba La'l Das). Persian text with translation. *Journal Asiatique*, 209 (1926), pp. 285–334.

5. Daryush Shayegan, *Les relations de l'hindouisme et du soufisme d'après le Majmaʿ al-bahrayn de Dārā Shukōh* (Paris: Ed. de la Différence, 1979). See also M. Mahfuz-ul-Haq, *Majmaʿ-ul-Bahrain or the Mingling of the Two Oceans by Prince Muhammad Dārā Shikūh* (Calcutta, 1929). Compare Tara Chand, "Dārā Shikoh and the Upanishads," *Islamic Culture*, vol. 17 (1923), pp. 397–413.

6. A listing of Persian translations made in India of Sanskrit works is given by A. B. M. Habibullah, "Medieval Indo-Persian Literatures relating to Hindu Science and Philosophy, 1000–1800 A.D.: A bibliographical survey," *Indian Historical Quarterly*, vol. 14 (1938), pp. 167–181.

7. See Yohanan Friedmann, "Islamic thought in relation to the Indian context," *Parusārtha*, vol. 9 (1986), pp. 79–91.

8. David Shea and Anthony Troyer, trans., *Oriental Literature or The Dabistan* (New York: Tudor Publishing, 1937). Aditya Behl, at the COMERS Congress on Pre-Modern Encyclopedic Texts held in Groningen in 1996, ascribed the work to the Zoroastrian Mubad Shah.

9. J. W. Redhouse, *The Diary of H.M., the Shah of Persia* (London, 1874). Compare A. Houtoum-Schindler and L. De Norman, *A Diary Kept by His Majesty, the Shah of Persia, during His Journey to Europe in 1878* (London, 1879).

10. See Stephen A. Fischer-Galati, *Ottoman Imperialism and German Protestantism, 1521–1555*. Cambridge, Mass.: Harvard University Press, 1959.

11. See for instance about Crete, Paul Hidiroglou, *Das religiöse Leben auf Kreta nach Ewlijā Čelebi* (Leiden: Brill, 1969). Ewlijā Čelebi spent two months and a half in Vienna in 1665; an account of this travel is to be found in volume 7 of the *Seyāhat-nāme* and was translated into German by R. F. Kreutel, *Im Reiche des Goldenen Apfels: Des türkischen Weltenbummlers Evliyā Čelebi denkwürdige Reise in das Giaurenland und in die Stadt und Festung Wien Anno 1665* (Graz: Verlag Syria, 1957). Compare also R. F. Kreutel, "Ewlijā Čelebīs Bericht über die türkische Grossbotschaft des Jahres 1665 in Wien: Ein Vergleich mit zeitgenösslichen türkischen und österreichischen Quellen," *Wiener Zeitschrift für die Kunde des Morgenlandes*, vol. 51 (1948/52), pp. 188–242. On other Ottoman travelers to Central and Eastern Europe, e.g., visiting "lost lands" in the eighteenth century, see Bernard

Lewis, *The Muslim Discovery of Europe* (New York: Norton, 1982), ch. 4. Compare Milan Adamovič, "Europa im Spiegel osmanischer Reiseberichte," in *Asien blickt auf Europa: Begegnungen und Irritationen*, ed. Tilman Nagel (Stuttgart: Steiner, 1990), pp. 61–71.

12. *Guide for the Perplexed on the History of the Greeks and the Romans and the Christians* (in Turkish). Another Ottoman historian offering interesting data of European history was Münejjimbashi (Ahmed ibn Lutfullah) who wrote in Arabic *Sahā'if al-akhbār*; he died in 1702. See B. Lewis, *Muslim Discovery*, pp. 135ff.

13. Karl Jahn, "Universalgeschichte im islamischen Raum," in *Mensch und Weltgeschichte* (Salzburg, 1969), pp. 145–170.

14. Richard F. Kreutel, "Die Schriften des Dolmetschers ʿOsmān Aġa aus Temeschwar," in *Der Orient in der Forschung: Festschrift für Otto Spies zum 5. April 1966*, ed. Wilhelm Hoenerbach (Wiesbaden: Harrassowitz, 1967), pp. 434–443.

15. See Benjamin Braude and Bernard Lewis (Eds.), *Christians and Jews in the Ottoman Empire: The Functioning of a Plural Society*. Vol. 1: *The Central Lands*; Vol. 2: *The Arabic-Speaking Lands* (New York: Holms & Meier, 1982). See also H. A. R. Gibb and Harold Bowen, *Islamic Society and the West: A study of the Impact of Western Civilization on Moslem Culture in the Near East*, esp. vol. 1, part 2 (London: Oxford University Press, 1957), ch. 14: "The Ḏimmīs" (pp. 207–261). Compare Gülnihal Bozkurt, "Die rechtliche Lage der nichtmuslimischen Untertanen im osmanischen Reich während der Reformzeit bis Ende des 1. Weltkrieges," Ph.D. diss., University of Cologne, 1937.

16. An interesting case was that of the Jews who had remained in Yemen where they mainly worked as peasants. If no Christians or Jews were allowed to live in the Arabian peninsula, should these Jews then be expelled? See Michela Fabbro, "Al-Husayn ibn Muhammad b. Saʿīd b. ʿĪsā al-Lā'ī al-Maghribī, *Risāla fī baqā' al-Yahūd fī ʿard al-Yaman*," *Islamochristiana*, vol. 16 (1990), pp. 67–90.

17. Salāhi R. Sonyel, *Minorities and the Destruction of the Ottoman Empire* (Ankara: Turkish Historical Society Printing House, 1993).

18. On the situation of non-Muslims in the second half of the eighteenth century in Egypt, see Harald Motzki, *Ḏimma und Égalité: Die nichtmuslimischen Minderheiten Ägyptens in der zweiten Hälfte des 18. Jahrhunderts und die Expedition Bonapartes (1798–1801)* (Bonn: Selbstverlag des Orientalischen Seminars, 1979). Compare an earlier *fatwā* on church-building in Cairo in 1653: Moshe Perlmann, "Shurunbulali militant," in *Studies in Islamic History and Civilization in Honour of Professor David Ayalon*, ed. M. Sharon (Jerusalem and Leiden, 1986), pp. 407–410. The situation of the Jews in Egypt would slowly improve. See Jacob M. Landau, *Jews in Nineteenth-Century Egypt* (New York: New York University Press & London: University of London Press, 1969); G. Kraemer, *The Jews in Modern Egypt, 1914–1952* (Seattle: University of Washington Press, 1989).

19. ʿAbd al-Rahmān al-Jabartī's, *History of Egypt* (*ʿAjā'ib al-athār fī 'l-tarājim wa'l-akhbār*). Text edited by Thomas Philipp and Moshe Perlmann, 2 vols. With *A Guide* (Register) by Thomas Philipp and Guido Schwald (Stuttgart: F. Steiner, 1994). See I. K. Poonawala, "The evolution of al-Ǧabartī's historical thinking as reflected in the *Muẓhir* and the *ʿAǧā'ib*," *Arabica*, vol. 15 (1968), pp. 270–288. See also Gilbert Delanoue, *Moralistes et politiques musulmans dans l'Égypte du XIXe siècle (1798–1882)*, esp. vol. 1 (Cairo: I.F.A.O., 1982), pp. 3–83. Compare Amin Sami Wassef, "Al-Ǧabarti, ses Chroniques et son temps," in *D'un Orient l'autre*. Vol. 2. *Identifications* (Paris: Editions du C.N.R.S., 1991), pp. 177–199.

20. For anti-Jewish writings, see Vera Basch Moreen, "*Risāla-yi sawāʿiq al-yahūd* (The treatise lightning bolts against the Jews) by Muhammad Bāqir b. Muhammad Taqī al-Majlisī (d. 1699)," *Die Welt des Islams*, vol. 32 (1992), pp. 177–195. For persecutions, see Amnon Netzer, "The fate of the Jewish community of Tabriz," in *Studies in Islamic History and Civilization in Honour of Professor David Ayalon*, ed. M. Sharon (Jerusalem, 1986), pp. 411–419.

21. *Voyages d'Ibn Battūta*. Texte arabe accompagné d'une traduction par C. Defremery et B.R. Anguinetti. Préface et notes de Vincent Monteil, 4 vols. (Paris: Ed. Anthropos, 1968). Part of Ibn Battūta's text was translated by H.A.R. Gibb, *The Travels of Ibn Battuta*, 2 vols. (Cambridge: Cambridge University Press, 1962).

22. The text was studied and translated into Dutch by S. van Ronkel. See Karel A. Steenbrink, "The study of comparative religion by Indonesian Muslims," *Numen*, vol. 27 (1991), pp. 141–167, esp. pp. 141–144. He also treats other texts by Indonesian Muslims on other religions and shows that Indonesia has its own tradition of studying religions.

23. See, for instance, Alfred Schlicht, *Frankreich und die syrischen Christen 1799–1861: Minoritäten und europäischer Imperialismus im Vorderen Orient* (Berlin: Klaus Schwarz, 1981). Other examples can easily be added.

24. The purely negative sides of the colonial encounter between Muslims and the West are stressed by a Soviet author like Grogori Bondarevski, *Muslims and the West* (New Delhi: Sterling Publishers, 1985). Needless to say, there have been positive sides as well.

25. See, for instance, Lyle L. Vanderwerff, *Christian Mission to Muslims: The Record—Anglican and Reformed Approaches in India and the Near East, 1800–1938* (South Pasadena: William Carey Library, 1977). Other and more detached studies on the missionary enterprise and Islam are needed.

26. John Joseph, *The Nestorians and Their Muslim Neighbors: A Study of Western Influence on Their Relations* (Princeton: Princeton University Press, 1961).

27. See, for instance in the case of India, Johannes M. S. Baljon, "Indian *muftīs* and the non-Muslims," *Islam and Christian-Muslim Relations*, vol. 2 (1991), pp. 227–241.

28. Al-Tahtāwī (1801–1873) wrote about his experiences in France *Takhlīs al-ibrīz ilā talkhīs Bārīz* (The extraction of gold in the summary of Paris), 3rd ed. (Cairo, 1905). He initiated an important translation movement of European books into Arabic, which continued into the twentieth century. About this movement and other Egyptian travelers to France, see Ibrahim Abu-Lughod, *Arab Rediscovery of Europe: A Study in Cultural Encounters* (Princeton: Princeton University Press, 1963). See also Anouar Louca, *Voyageurs et écrivains égyptiens en France au XIXe siècle* (Paris: Didier, 1970). Compare *Le miroir égyptien: Rencontres Méditerranéennes de Provence*, ed. Robert Ilbert and Philippe Joutard (Marseille: Ed. du Quai, 1984). About al-Tahtāwī, see especially Gilbert Delanoue, *Moralistes et politiques musulmans dans l'Egypte du XIXe siècle (1798–1882)*, vol. 2 (Cairo: Institut Français d'Archéologie Orientale, 1982), pp. 383–487.

29. Henri Pérès, "Les voyageurs musulmans en Europe: Notes bibliographiques," in *Mélanges Maspéro*, vol. 3 (Cairo: Institut Français d'Archéologie Orientale, 1940), pp. 185–195.

30. Henri Pérès, *L'Espagne vue par les voyageurs musulmans de 1610 à 1930* (Paris: Alcan, 1937).

31. *Nāsir al-dīn ʿalā ʾl-qawm al-kāfirīn*, ed. M. Razuq (Casablanca, 1987). See Gerard Wiegers, "A life between Europe and the Maghrib: The writings and travels of Ahmad b. Qāsim ibn Ahmad ibn al-faqīh Qāsim ibn al-shaykh al-Hajarī al-Andalusī (born c. 977/1569–70)," in *The Middle East and Europe: Encounters and Exchanges*, ed. Geert Jan van Gelder and Ed de Moor (Amsterdam: Rodopi, 1992), pp. 87–115.

32. Susan L. G. Miller, "A Voyage to the Land of Rum: The Rihlah of the Moroccan Muhammad al-Saffar to France, December 1845–March 1846," Ph.D. diss., University of Michigan, 1976.

33. Jean-Philippe Lachèse, "Le voyage d'un Iranien en Europe à la fin du XIXe siècle," *Mélanges de l'Institut Dominicain d'Etudes Orientales du Caire*, vol. 21 (1993), pp. 359–371.

34. Leon Zolondek, "The French Revolution in Arabic literature of the nineteenth century," *Muslim World*, vol. 57 (1967), pp. 202–211.

35. L. M. Kenny, "East versus West in *Al-Muqtataf*, 1875–1900: Image and Self-Image," in *Essays on Islamic Civilization, Presented to Niyazi Berkes*, ed. Donald P. Little (Leiden: Brill, 1976), pp. 140–154.

36. Western science meant a radical change in traditional worldviews. See for example Adel A. Ziadat, *Western Science in the Arab World: The impact of Darwinism, 1860–1930* (London: Macmillan, 1986).

37. See for India at the time, Wilfred Cantwell Smith, *Modern Islām in India. A Social Analysis* (1943) Lahore: Sh. Muhammad Ashraf, 1963. See also the contribution by Sheila McDonough, "The Muslims of South Asia (1857–1947)," chap. 16 in this volume.

38. On this new generation of Egyptian students in Paris, see Ed De Moor, "Egyptian love in a cold climate: Egyptian students in Paris at the beginning of the twentieth century," in *The Middle East and Europe: Encounters and Exchanges*, ed. Geert Jan van Gelder and Ed de Moor (Amsterdam: Rodopi, 1992), pp. 147–166.

39. See Albert Hourani's classic, *Arabic Thought in the Liberal Age, 1798–1939* (London: Oxford University Press, 1962).

40. On the special case of Haykal, see Baber Johansen, *Muhammad Husain Haikal: Europa und der Orient im Weltbild eines ägyptischen Liberalen* (Beirut: Steiner Verlag, 1967). Compare M. H. Haikal, "Les causes de l'incompréhension entre l'Europe et les musulmans et les moyens d'y remédier," in *L'Islam et l'Occident* (Paris: Les Cahiers du Sud, 1947), pp. 52–58.

41. Rudolph Peters, *Islam and Colonialism: The Doctrine of Jihād in Modern History* (The Hague: Mouton, 1979).

42. On al-Afghānī, see Nikki R. Keddie, *Sayyid Jamāl ad-Dīn ʿal-Afghānīʾ: A political biography* (Berkeley: University of California Press, 1972). A translation of writings by al-Afghānī is given in Nikki R. Keddie, *An Islamic Response to Imperialism: Political and Religious Writings of Sayyid Jamāl ad-Dīn ʿal-Afghānīʾ* (Berkeley: University of California Press, 1968).

43. Klaus Kreiser, "Der japanische Sieg über Russland (1905) und sein Echo unter den Muslimen," *Die Welt des Islams*, vol. 21 (1981), pp. 209–239.

44. In his dispute with Pfander, Rahmatullah proved his better knowledge of German critical Bible research. See Avril Ann Powell, *Muslims and Missionaries in Pre-Mutiny India* (London: Curzon Press, 1993). Compare Christine Schirrmacher, *Mit den Waffen des Gegners: Christlich-muslimische Kontroversen im 19. und 20. Jahrhundert* (Berlin: Klaus Schwarz, 1992). See also Schirrmacher's contribution, "The Influence of European Higher Criticism on Muslim Apologetics in the Nineteenth Century," chapter 18 in this volume.

45. Christian W. Troll, *Sayyid Ahmad Khan: A Reinterpretation of Muslim Theology* (New Delhi: Vikas, 1978). In what follows we gratefully refer to ch. 3, "Islam and the Scriptures of Jews and Christians" (pp. 58–99). Compare by the same author, "Sayyid Ahmad Khan on Matthew 5, 17–20," *Islamochristiana*, vol. 3 (1977), pp. 99–105.

46. See Raymond George Schaeffer, "Studies in Sir Sayyid Ahmed Khan's use of some Christian writ-

ers in his Biblical commentary," M.A. thesis, Hartford Seminary Foundation, 1966, 140 pp. Compare Note 45.

47. *Tabyīn*, Part I, p. 7. Quoted by Troll, *Sayyid Ahmad Khan*, p. 86.

48. See for instance Ameer Ali, "Christianity from the Islamic standpoint," *Hibbert Journal*, vol. 4 (1905–1906), no. 14, pp. 241–259. Elsewhere he gives favorable judgments about Christianity. See Ali, *The Spirit of Islam: A History of the Evolution and Ideals of Islam, with a Life of the Prophet* (London: Christophers, 1922; Repr. London: Methuen, 1965).

49. Khuda Bukhsh, "A Mohammedan view of Christendom." See J. W. Sweetman, "A Muslim's view of Christianity," *Muslim World*, vol. 34 (1944), pp. 278–284.

50. On Muhammad ʿAbduh as well as Muhammad Rashīd Riḍā, the "classical" study is still Charles C. Adams, *Islam and Modernism in Egypt* (London: Oxford University Press, 1933).

51. On ʿAbduh's view of Christianity compared to Islam, see Mahmoud Ayoub, "Islam and Christianity: A study of Muhammad ʿAbduh's view of the two religions," *Humaniora Islamica* (The Hague: Mouton), vol. 2 (1974), pp. 121–137.

52. A German translation is given in Gunnar Hasselblat, *Herkunft und Auswirkungen der Apologetik Muhammad Abduh's (1849–1905), Untersucht an seiner Schrift Islam und Christentum im Verhältnis zu Wissenschaft und Zivilisation*. (Göttingen, 1968).

53. On closer analysis, the six negative points attributed to Christianity also represent a criticism of certain empirical forms of Islam in Egypt at the time, which in ʿAbduh's view were obstacles to desired development.

54. See Maurice Borrmans, "Le Commentaire du *Manār* à propos du verset coranique sur l'amitié des Musulmans pour les Chrétiens (5, 82)," *Islamochristiana*, vol. 1 (1975), pp. 71–86. Similar remarks could be made about the Commentary of *al-Manār* on S. 2, 62 with its positive judgment of Jews, Christians, and Sabeans.

55. For a comparison between Rashīd Riḍā and ʿAbduh, see Charles C. Adams, *Islam and Modernism in Egypt* (London: Oxford University Press, 1933). See also Malcolm H. Kerr, *Islamic Reform: The Political and Legal Theories of Muhammad ʿAbduh and Rashīd Riḍā* (Berkeley: University of California Press, 1966). Compare Mahmoud Ayoub, "Muslim views of Christianity: Some modern examples," *Islamochristiana*, vol. 10 (1984), pp. 49–70.

56. See Emad Eldin Shahin, *Through Muslim Eyes: M. Rashīd Riḍā and the West* (Herndon, Virginia: International Institute of Islamic Thought, 1994).

57. Cairo, 1322/1905. We refer in the following to Mahmoud Ayoub's article mentioned in note 55. M. Ayoub uses a later edition of the *Shubuhāt* (Cairo: Nahdat Misr, 1375/1956). Two other books of Rashīd Riḍā on Christians and Christianity deserve mentioning: *al-Muslimūn waʾl-qibt waʾl-muʾtamar al-islāmī* (1329/1911) and *ʿAqīdat al-ṣalb waʾl-fidaʾ* (1353/1934 or 1935). All three books were published by the al-Manār Press in Cairo.

58. It is important to compare different views held by the Reformists about the nature and interpretation of the Scriptures. Some texts by ʿAbduh, Rashīd Riḍā, Kāmil Husayn, and Ahmad Khan are presented in English translation in Jean-Marie Gaudeul, *Encounters and Clashes: Islam and Christianity in History*. Vol. 2: *Texts* (Rome: Pontificio Istituto di Studi Arabi e Islamici, 1984), pp. 298–311.

59. "Christianity was originally a heavenly religion of divine unity but Christians later turned it into the worship of human beings such as Jesus and his mother" (*Shubuhāt*, p. 29, quoted by M. Ayoub, "Muslim views of Christianity," pp. 57–58).

60. 2nd ed. (Cairo, 1352). See "Orientalist [*sic*], The Moslem doctrine of revelation and Islamic propaganda," *The Muslim World*, vol. 25 (1935), pp. 67–72. For a study on Rashīd Riḍā as an apologist of Islam, see Henri Laoust, "Renouveau de l'apologétique missionnaire traditionnelle au XXe siècle dans l'oeuvre de Rashīd Riḍā," in *Prédication et propagande au Moyen Age: Islam, Byzance, Occident*. Penn-Paris-Dumbarton Oaks Colloquia III, 1980 (Paris: Presses Universitaires de France, 1983), pp. 271–279.

61. See Arthur Jeffery's articles in *Muslim World*, vol. 15 (1925), pp. 26–37 and vol. 17 (1927), pp. 216–219. See also Jeffery, "New trends in Moslem apologetic," in *The Moslem World of Today*, ed. John R. Mott (London: Hodder & Stoughton, 1925), pp. 305–321.

62. H. G. Dorman Jr., *Toward Understanding Islam: Contemporary Apologetic of Islam and Missionary Policy* (New York: Bureau of Publication, Teachers College, Columbia University, 1948).

63. Hugh Goddard, *Muslim Perceptions of Christianity* (London: Grey Seal, 1996).

64. As we saw in the case of India, the polemical literature against Christianity increased, as a reaction against Christian missions, in the second half of the nineteenth century. This was also the case elsewhere. See for instance about the Ottoman empire, "Corrispondenza da Costantinopoli: La polemica dell'Islam a Costantinopoli," *Bessarione*, vol. 8, no. 5 (1900), pp. 145–161. The same upsurge of Muslim polemics took place between the two world wars.

65. Ghulam Mohammed, "Islam versus Christianity," *Review of Religions* (Qadian), October 1919. Compare the extract of the article in *Muslim World*, vol. 10 (1920), pp. 76–81. The original text would have been written by the founder of the Ahmadiyya Movement, Mirzā Ghulām Ahmad (1835–1908), to whom the Qadianis attributed prophetical qualities.

66. John Warwick Montgomery, "The apologetic approach of Muhammad Ali and its implications for Christian apologetics," *Muslim World*, vol. 51 (1961), pp. 111–120. This Maulvi Muhammad ʿAlī was a spokesman of the Ahmadiyya of the Lahore branch. He became particularly known because of his Qurʾān translation into English (Woking 1917; 2nd edition, Lahore, Woking, and London 1920; 3rd edition 1935). This translation contains typically Ahmadiyya text interpretations and is not recognized by Muslim Sunnī and Shīʿī authorities.

67. Charles C. Adams, "Comparative religion in the Azhar University," *Muslim World*, vol. 35 (1945), pp. 111–125.

68. As an example, see the interesting article about Ahmad Amīn's attitude toward other religions during the first half of the twentieth century, by William E. Shepard, "A modernist view of Islam and other religions," *Muslim World*, vol. 65 (1975), pp. 79–92.

69. How different such responses could be appears in the two contributions about Iran and India—by Isabel Stümpel-Hatami, "Christianity as Described by Contemporary Persian Muslims" (chap. 14 in this volume) and Christine Schirrmacher, "The Influence of European Higher Criticism on Muslim Apologetics in the Nineteenth Century" (chap. 18 in this volume).

70. An excellent analysis of this literature is given by Isabel Stümpel-Hatami, *Das Christentum aus der Sicht zeitgenössischer iranischer Autoren: Eine Untersuchung religionskundlicher Publikationen in persischer Sprache* (Berlin: Klaus Schwarz Verlag, 1996).

71. Marc Gaboriau, *Récit d'un voyageur musulman au Tibet* (Paris: Klincksieck, 1973).

4

The Contemporary Period

1950–1995

JACQUES WAARDENBURG

The far-reaching historical changes caused by World War II and the establishment of a number of independent Muslim nation-states—that is, states with a Muslim majority population—could not but affect the relationships between Muslims and adherents of other religions. One only needs to think of the consequences of the establishment of the state of Pakistan in 1947 for Muslim-Hindu relations and of the effects of the establishment of the state of Israel in 1948 for Muslim-Jewish relations.

Most important for the Muslim countries was the end of the European powers' immediate military and political domination, although economic dependence on Europe and the United States would make itself ever more palpable, and Western political, social, and cultural ideals would continue to present themselves as universally valid. In most Muslim countries and regions, but also in other newly independent countries, direct Christian mission from the West was no longer allowed. Western Christians who wanted to serve in other, and specifically Muslim countries, could engage in health service, educational institutions, or social work—but not in religion for its own sake. At most, a few Christian theologians from the West could teach at local theological colleges or seminaries with Christian students. In a number of Muslim states Christian missions were forbidden outright, and in Saudi Arabia, for instance, Christianity cannot even manifest itself in public.

In most of these countries, revolutions by the military took place sooner or later after independence. These revolutions not only brought about a shift in power but also were accompanied by more or less profound social upheavals that put an end to the privileges of certain established classes. These could be big landowners, merchants assuring economic exchanges with Western markets, or the upper strata of the urban bourgeoisie, but they could also be creative artists, writers, and intellectuals who maintained cultural links with Western countries where they had studied or visited. Often smaller or larger groups of Christians belonged to these privileged groups, and when they were forced into the imposed molds of the new society, it was not so much because of their being Christians but because the groups they belonged to were dispersed and the country came under the sway of a new national ideology and a new regime. The results varied in the different countries. In Egypt, the better situated Copts lost most of their riches; in the Ba'thist regimes of Syria and Iraq, Christians could participate more easily in state organizations but they lost their fortunes.

There were other factors at work as well. All newly independent countries needed to develop in order to survive; technological modernization and economic development had to be carried out. This brought about the rise, in the armies, industries and elsewhere, of new classes of technicians, economists, managers, and skilled labor who developed a more rational view of things than was offered by tradition. These new classes were not, at least not in the beginning, especially concerned with religion in a particularistic sense.

On the international scene, the influence of the United States increased quickly, starting during World War II, and this influence gradually came to surpass that of the former colonial powers in Europe. Throughout the Muslim world, from the beginning of the 1950s, the political and economic power of America was ever more felt. "Modernization" became more and more identified with "Americanization." The alternative power was the Soviet Union, which boasted of opposing what remained of the old colonial relations of dependence. It helped at least certain new nation-states to resist the imposition on their economies of the capitalist market-system, which as a rule was to destroy much of the traditional economic and social structures in large measure. But the Soviet Union also made its power felt, through local Communist parties and pressures from outside. It revolutionized countries in its own way, binding them to itself.

The history of most Muslim states between 1950 and 1990 has been conditioned by the fact of the Cold War between the two superpowers. Even the state of Israel's impact on the Middle East scene has been much more linked to the Cold War, and its own interests in it, than was realized by most observers at the time. One may even surmise that the rise of Islamic consciousness and Islamic movements was more closely linked with Cold War interests than the current literature on the subject suggests. If it is true that, broadly speaking, the period from 1850 to 1950 was conditioned by colonial tensions, that from 1950 to 1990 was conditioned by Cold War tensions. These were sometimes accompanied by economic conflicts as in the Mossadegh crisis of 1953 in Iran, the Suez crisis of 1956 in Egypt, and the oil crisis of 1973–1974 in the Middle East. Often these and other tensions led to terrible wars. One should remember the savage war in Algeria (1954–1962), the Suez War (1956), the Yemen War (1962–70), the Arab-Israeli Wars (1948, 1956, 1967, 1973), the wars between Pakistan and India (1949, 1965, 1971), the Afghan wars starting in 1979, the Iraq-Iran War of 1980–1988, and the Gulf War of 1991. Outside the Muslim states, Muslim minorities in the former Soviet Union and in the People's Republic of China, as in Israel and the Occupied Territories, have endured oppressive situations. Moreover, Muslim nation-states have had their own internal problems and have occasionally conflicts. All of this has conditioned the framework within which relations between Muslim and other religious communities have developed in various directions.

It is in this world ridden with tensions that Islam has come to play a growing political role. Its increasing ideologization has had an impact on the relations between Muslims and non-Muslims which started to unfreeze in the climate of dialogue of the 1960s, 1970s, and early 1980s. During the last decade it has become quite clear that provocative actions against and oppression of Muslim populations—by Christians, Jews, Hindus, outright secularists, and even Muslim regimes—are leading to an increasing politization and ideologization of Islam.

Most countries on the eve of independence had already known movements advocating the establishment of an Islamic state—that is, a state based on the *Sharīʿa.* Sometimes, as in the *Dar ul Islam* movement in Indonesia in the 1940s and 1950s, such movements tried to impose their views by force. The national leaders, however, who had led the struggle for independence and came to power when the new states were founded, opposed the idea of an Islamic state. All of them advocated a modern state on the model of the Western democratic states, mostly that of the colonial power itself, and they had in general a more or less secular view of the state organization. With the exception of Saudi Arabia which had been created explicitly as an Islamic state in 1932, and some traditional Islamic states of ancient date like Yemen, Mauretania, and Afghanistan, or even Morocco, all new states with a Muslim majority were officially secular and recognized a separation of state and religion. Most of them, however, stressed their Muslim character by accepting the Sharīʿa as a major source of personal law and by requiring that the head of state be a Muslim.

By the end of the 1960s, however, the secular national ideologies that had prevailed since independence and were linked in a number of countries to ideologies advocating economic development according to the Western or the socialist model, no longer satisfied the needs of the population. Promises of economic development had not been kept; boasting of national honor and pride could no longer mobilize the people; regimes in many cases were compromised by injustices or even corruption, or by an excessive dependence on one of the superpowers engaged in the Cold War. A new generation did not let itself be seduced by the ideologies spread by the nationalist, often military leadership. In most countries this meant going into opposition either as a leftist or under the banner of Islam. When 20 years had passed, around 1985, it was the latter choice that had won. Among the many meanings which the notion of Islam conveyed, those of resistance to dependence on either the Western or Eastern block countries, and of organizing society according to socioreligious norms of justice to which most people were committed had a most powerful appeal.

Economic problems caused by petrodollars flowing to the few and bringing increased poverty to the many, and political tensions due to ever-increasing state control parallelled by growing infractions of justice and human rights by the government, to some extent explain the revolutionary forms which this politicized Islam took in some countries. The Iranian revolution of 1979, first anti-Shah and then Islamic in its orientation, worked to catalyze Islamic movements elsewhere, especially since revolutionary Iran had been able to humiliate the powerful United States upon which many Muslim states were dependent. States like Pakistan, Libya, and Sudan turned Islamic; Islamic movements gained support among the masses everywhere; in Egypt and some other countries "Islamists" showed their teeth to the regime in power. And while Iran exported Islamic revolution, Saudi Arabia exported Islamic order. It did this largely through money, through the newly founded international Islamic organizations with headquarters in Mecca and Jeddah, through encouraging the Islamization of society or simply through paying for mosques, Islamic instruction, local Islamic movements, and other Islamic purposes. In both cases Islam served the state interest, becoming an instrument of interior or foreign policy.

In this way, throughout the 1970s and 1980s Islam more and more became a means, or a cover, to legitimate other things. Political opposition against established regimes was obliged to speak and act in the name of Islam when other formulas of opposition were not allowed. Movements appealing to Islamic norms and ideals could be understood by people looking for justice, especially those who came from the countryside, where Islamic traditions were still solidly anchored in society. The populist character of so many Islamic movements at present does not necessarily prove that these movements have gained many more adherents. It may also indicate that tradition-bound country people, in their search to survive, have mobilized themselves; since these people were used to interpret the world in Islamic terms, they tend to see Islam as providing the solution. That this renewed stress on Islam has meant increasing pressures on non-Muslim minorities living in Muslim countries has been an unfortunate consequence for the relationships between Muslims and non-Muslims there. "Islamists" in particular tend rather to sharpen the difference between non-Muslims and Muslims than to look for common ground.

Another important factor that has conditioned and changed relationships between Muslims and Christians, in particular in the period since 1950, is the increasing Muslim presence in Western Europe and in the West in general.[1] We have seen that even before 1950 Muslim groups had established themselves in Europe: the Ahmadiyya mission, the Sufi Movement, adherents of the more esoteric teachings of Guénon and Schuon, some European converts. After World War II, however, international migration increased immensely, and Muslims moving to the West were part of it. In North America and Britain qualified migrants from Muslim countries could enter and enjoy the freedom to organize and express themselves. In continental Europe, Muslim immigrants were used as cheap labor, and although they suffered economic hardship, they could organize or participate in Islamic or other movements that were sometimes forbidden in their countries of origin.

Western societies confronted the next generations of these immigrants with a challenge to move toward either a more secular outlook and adaptation to Western society or toward a certain rediscovery of their Islamic roots. It is no accident that, parallel to the increasing role of Islam in the political discourse in Muslim countries, we can see an increasing affirmation of Islam in the Muslim discourse in Western countries. Mosques are put up or newly built; Islamic education is advocated and spread; Islamic ways of life are stressed in Muslim organizations in Europe. Incidents like the Salman Rushdie affair when Khomeiny declared Rushdie an apostate who could be killed with impunity or the problems caused by girls wearing headscarfs at school or at work not hiding their Muslim identity, are little tests. They allow Muslims in the West to assess how far they can go to affirm Islam in the societies in which they live and perhaps further it. When non-Muslims have Muslims as neighbors, and the other way round, this leads to more direct contacts between them, with positive but also with negative results, the latter in particular in a time of economic crisis.

Three other conditionings may be mentioned that have arisen over the last 20 years and exert a powerful effect on the attitudes of Muslims and non-Muslims to each other and their perceptions of each other. First, a great number of Muslim minority groups exist in non-Muslim countries, including India and the People's Republic of China. There is a kind of solidarity with them in Muslim countries, and attitudes of new self-awareness are developing among them such as are found among other socioreligious minority groups. Whereas in former times the number of Muslims living under non-Muslim political authority was small, this number has increased tremendously in the course of this century. Each country now has its Muslim majority or minority.

Second, there is the issue of violence. For a long time and in many quarters Muslims were held to be initiators of violence, according to a rather simple reading in the dominating West of the doctrine of *jihād*. The last 20 years, however, have shown Muslims to be victims of other peoples' violence: Palestinian Muslims suffered at the hands of Israelis, Lebanese Muslims at the hands of Maronite Christians, Bosnian Muslims at the hands of Serbian and Croatian Christians, and Chechen Muslims at the hands of Russians. To perceive Muslims as victims of other peoples' violence changes old views and stereotypes of relations between non-Muslims and Muslims.

The third conditioning factor of new attitudes and new perceptions which Muslims and non-Muslims have of each other is the close connection that evidently exists in many Muslim communities between ethnic and Muslim identity as two sides of the same coin. Just as Armenians are held to be Christians, within the community and by the outside world, so Turkic and Iranian peoples are held to be Muslims and want to be so. In many cases the stress laid on Islam is less a religious affirmation than an affirmation of a person's social identity, of his or her being part of a broader community and feeling solidarity with it in times of crisis when existence is at stake. It then becomes an expression of communal identity.

All of this must be seen as the new and critical background of Muslim perceptions of non-Muslims in the second half of this century. Without taking this bitter background into account, much of what Muslims have written critically about other religions during this period runs the risk of being misunderstood.

Some Writings from the Period 1950–1995

On Christianity

Most Muslim writings about other religions than Islam since World War II concern Christianity.[2] A great number of them are refutations of it in one form or another,[3] written for Muslim readers in the "Islamic" languages Arabic, Turkish, Persian, and Urdu. As in earlier periods, the arguments are based on Qur'ānic texts and common sense, and they are addressed specifically against such Christian doctrines as the sonship of Jesus, the Incarnation, the Trinity, and the Bible as Revelation. More recently, with the presence of Muslim *daʿwa* centers in the West and elsewhere, Muslim publications critical of Christianity are now also printed and sold in the West.[4] Besides such straightforward polemical literature, one also finds a more informative kind of literature that tries to compare Christianity and Islam, evidently concluding that Islam is superior.[5]

Throughout the period one finds specific attacks on all attempts to convert Muslims to Christianity. Christian missionaries, especially in the years immediately after independence, could be accused of having been agents of Western imperialism. Muslims were warned against the methods certain groups of missionaries used to obtain conversions.[6] Rules against any form of apostasy have existed since the beginning of Islam, when the Muslim community was constituted. This literature acquired a new relevance, however, when Christian missionaries appeared in Muslim lands in the nineteenth century and factual debates occurred between missionaries and Muslims. Over and against missionary efforts to bring about conversions, the rule that Muslims should not be allowed to leave Islam was maintained with various means, and not without success.

Besides much controversial literature emphasizing the superiority of Islam, often on a popular and even base level, and intellectually deplorable, other kinds of publications about Christianity have appeared especially since the "dialogue years" of the 1960s and 1970s.

A range of books and articles presents *Jesus* as a great prophet. Several authors have meticulously studied the four Gospels of the New Testament. They interpret the New Testament accounts within the general framework of Qur'ānic data—that is, without reference to the crucifixion and the resurrection stories. Best known is *Qarya zālima* (The city of wrongdoing) by Muhammad Kāmil Husayn,[7] which appeared in Arabic in Cairo in 1954 and has been translated into several languages. It is a novel describing the course of events leading to Good Friday, and it places special emphasis on the disciples' reactions to the victimization of the innocent Jesus, out of which the Christian community and the Christian faith and religion arose. Other texts respectfully describe Jesus's exemplary prophetic behavior and his universal significance not only for Christians but also for the whole of mankind.[8] Some authors stress the passion of Jesus as a symbol of the suffering of the innocent or, for instance, of the Palestinian people.

In the Muslim view, the *history of Christianity* is its fall. The Christian religion developed in ways that went against and beyond what Muslims hold to be the teachings of Jesus properly speaking. This would have consisted mainly of the preaching of monotheism, the warning of the Judgment with the announcement of the resurrection and man's eternal destiny, and the handing over of the religious Law of the Injīl. Mostly Paul but also other New Testament authors and of course the church are held responsible for these deviations.[9] Some Muslim scholars, familiar with the results of Western critical New Testament scholarship, have started to produce new texts about Christianity and the development both of its doctrine and of its community and church.[10]

Here and there, new assessments have been made of the intrinsic nature of the relationship between *Islam and Christianity*,[11] going beyond the traditional scheme of a complete opposition.[12] Besides existing lapidary presentations of Christianity in Muslim journals, schoolbooks, and other writings,[13] there are also assessments which quote sayings of certain prominent critical and self-critical Christian theologians. Some authors refer to what has been conveyed to them by Christians in a direct way, for instance in Muslim-Christian dialogues.[14]

One also may find signs of new research breaking through long-established patterns, of new questions being formulated, and new problems being treated. M. Ayoub insists on a more careful and precise reading of Qur'ānic texts concerning Christians, away from the oppositional scheme of traditional Qur'ān exegesis.[15] H. Hanafī raises hermeneutical questions. M. Arkoun applies modern semiotics in his reading of the Qur'ān, bypassing the purely literal meaning of the words.

At least three studies were published on the subject of the classical medieval Islamic polemical literature against Christianity.[16] They remind the reader of the unsurmountable doctrinal differences between the two religious systems, but they also show that this literature arose in a particular historical and social context and set out the conditions under which it developed and flourished. One scholar who carefully analyzed the nature and validity of the classical polemicists' arguments has appealed for further scholarly research on Christianity within the framework of the discipline of history of religions.[17] Another sign of reorientation is the introduction of the concept of "Societies" of the Book, rather than "Peoples" of the Book. Instead of stressing the doctrinal and legal differences between the contents of the three Scriptures accepted in the three major monotheistic religions, M. Arkoun wants to stress the importance of their sheer existence. Having a Scripture has particular implications and plays an important role in shaping Muslim, Christian, and Jewish societies and cultures.

Another way in which Muslim perceptions of Christianity express themselves is through art and literature. The example of *Qarya zālima* has already been mentioned. There exists a Turkish literary elaboration of the trial of Jesus in the form of a theater play.[18] Ali Merad wrote an account of the Christian hermit Charles de Foucauld.[19] Several novels and short stories portray Christians, some indigenous, some Western, in a Muslim context and suggest the significance of their being different from Muslim believers.[20]

On Judaism

Whereas, on the whole, Muslim presentations of Christianity have become more sympathetic and sometimes gained in precision since World War II—at least in writings coming from Arab Mediterranean countries—the presentations of Judaism, on the contrary, have developed in the direction of growing hostility. The reasons, of course, are political. On the one hand, the fact that nearly all Muslim countries acquired their independance before or during the 1950s weakened the negative associations which

Muslims had established between Christianity and Western imperialism, and freed the way for a better acquaintance with the Christian religion. On the other hand, the Zionist movement, the Jewish immigration in Palestine, and the establishment of Israel in 1948 together with the harsh confrontations between Israel and the surrounding Arab states, as well as the grim military regime in the occupied territories, could not but strengthen the negative associations that Muslims made between Judaism and the state of Israel as an agressive *Fremdkörper* in the region. Especially after Israel's victory in the June war of 1967, a number of publications in Arabic saw the light. Some of them were attacks on Judaism and what was seen as its political outgrowth, Zionism, whereas others were defamatory and must in part be qualified as anti-Semitic. The appearance of these publications may have functioned as a psychological compensation for the defeat and an ideological mobilization against the powerful enemy. However, this does not detract from the fact that a number of Egyptian and other intellectuals were mobilized for a campaign of hatred that was traumatic rather than intellectually honest.

In any case, the Muslim image of present-day Judaism has changed remarkably in the course of the last 50 years, from that of a "heavenly" religion promulgating divine law to that of a political project using this religion for its mundane ambitions.[21] Israeli views of contemporary Islamic movements seem to have little eye for their moral and religious aspects; they tend to consider them as sociopolitical movements or at most as a politization of religion. Such mutual views are definite proof of the rule that military and political conflicts have a profound and politicizing influence on the perceptions of each other's religion held by the conflicting parties. The same rule applies in the Pakistani-Indian, Azeri-Armenian, and Serbian-Bosnian conflicts. It also holds true for tensions between minorities and majorities in which the religions involved are depreciated by the other party. All of this points to the general rule of politization of perceptions; in the case of mutually exclusive monotheistic religions the effects are particularly devastating.

One of the tragic consequences of this state of affairs is that whereas a Muslim-Christian dialogue of several decades has been able to clear up a certain number of misunderstandings on both sides at least for an inner circle, the political conflicts around Israel have made any real Muslim-Jewish dialogue practically impossible even in religious matters. Provocative Israeli policies—unfortunately endorsed by the United States—in practice have meant that further misunderstandings have been able to develop freely. The way has then become open for anti-Jewish attitudes to arise even in Muslim countries which had kept an open relationship with Israel.[22]

On the West and Western Orientalism

Without going so far as to reduce specific relationships between religious communities and religions simply to a function of general cultural, economic, and political relations, there can be no doubt that twentieth-century Muslim images of Christianity have been strongly affected by the strained relations between certain Muslim and Western countries during this century. The same can be said of Western images of Islam. The problem of these relations is symbolized by the formula of the relationship between "Islam" and "the West."[23]

Up to World War I, and in many intellectual and business circles up to World War II and later, the West was widely regarded as the model of civilization for Muslim countries, which were at the time mostly politically dependent on the West. Since World War II this view has been maintained in what may be called "Westernized" circles who had adopted Western ways of life and thought. But even there, such a positive view of the West has not been without problems and tensions for those who had been brought up with their own cultural values, often observing them at home while identifying with Western values in public. Probably few Muslim authors have analyzed the traumatic effects of the shock of Western modernity on those brought up in Muslim societies better than Daryush Sharegan.[24] As he describes it, the impact first of the West and then of modernity as developed in the West has led to forms of what he calls a schizophrenia that affects not only outward patterns of behavior but also the domain of culture and religion. This analysis seems to hold good for most Muslim societies at least during part of the twentieth century. Notwithstanding heavy external pressures, people have simply refused to abandon norms and values with which they have grown up and which they summed up, or rather symbolized, by the word "Islam."

The visible Westernization of a certain elite in Muslim countries, in a time in which these countries were or had been fighting for independence from the West, could not but lead to resentment in the society at large. As a reaction to the Westernization process in which an intellectual and economic elite had become involved, or to which it fell victim, the second half of the twentieth century has seen a stream of publications which attacked the West not only for its political and economic but also its cultural imperialism.[25] The same West whose culture had been adulated at the end of last century is now decried as void of real culture and destroying other cultures. The idea that Western societies and Western civilization itself are in decline, moral and otherwise, has gained ground; at a somewhat later stage, the norms and values represented by Islam have come to be seen in some circles as the right alternative, and successor to the morally decadent and secular West.[26]

This negative view of the West has also been a response to Western "Orientalism," unmasked as a way of submitting the Muslim world to a Western vision with the aim of dominating it. In self-defense some Muslim authors have launched a devastating attack on existing Western studies of Muslim societies and Islam.[27] They have reproached Western Orientalists with reducing phenomena of life to dead facts and lifeless structures, neglecting the values of Muslim culture and feeling no ethical responsibility. Their approach contrasts sharply with that of Easterners "Westernizing" themselves, and sympathizing and even identifying with the culture or civilization they have studied. In fact, such Orientalists have been unable to see Easterners as free partners in the venture of knowledge. Furthermore, together with missionaries, Orientalists have been accused of wanting to annihilate the highest values, even the absolute norm of Muslim societies—that is to say, Islam. They have been seen as even more dangerous than the missionaries because they have obtained knowledge of the Islam they wanted to destroy. It should be pointed out that similar attacks on a certain Western Orientalist scholarship have been made by Indian, African, and other non-Western scholars both Muslim and non-Muslim.

This general accusation brings together reproaches on several questions which most Orientalists had never put to themselves. They had not felt obliged to explain to Muslims with what aims they carried out their studies, giving no other reason than the advancement of scientific knowledge or scholarship as a kind of absolute in itself. They had not cooperated with people from Muslim societies on a level of equality, but rather made use of their services as informants. They had not put the results of their research at the disposal or in the service of the people and societies they had studied. They had rarely given evidence of being aware of any moral problems pertaining either to this kind of research on other peoples' culture and religion or to their own attitude to the people and religion they were studying.[28]

Especially on a popular level, many Muslim publications have decried the moral decay of Western societies, the enslaving of people including women in an economic system in which communal society gives way to a social jungle in which each individual is forced to defend his or her own interests. In this view, Christianity had lost any real influence on Western societies, a fact which also proves the weakness of Christianity and thus points to the rightness of Islam. The atheism and materialism prevailing in Eastern-block socialist societies have similarly been criticized. Both communism and capitalism as economic, political, and ideological systems have been decisively rejected, and Islam has been presented as the right middle way, avoiding the extremes of the two ideologies which were till the end of the 1980s represented by the two superpowers.

On a less popular level, however, Western technology is approved of and European culture not completely rejected. In the West, but also in certain universities in Muslim countries, forms of cooperation have developed between Muslim and Western scholars where the difference of religious background does not play a role. In the field of the humanities including Islamic studies it can even be seen as a positive asset.[29] Moreover, the countries around the Mediterranean Sea have a common history and common interests, and throughout the second half of the twentieth century they have stressed the need for affirming, developing, and deepening their relations. The expressions "Islam" and "Europe" here stand for the southern and eastern, and the northern and western parts of the Mediterranean, respectively. Many colloquia and publications have been devoted to the need for Mediterranean cooperation and Euro-Arab dialogue, taking account of the economic and political interests, as well as the religions and cultures involved.[30] Cultural anthropologists have shown the presence of many cultural traits which the north and the south of the Mediterranean share, whatever the doctrinal and ideological oppositions. On an intellectual level, much discussion among Muslims has been devoted to the nature of the relationships between Muslim and European culture.[31] These cultures have a number of problems in common nowadays, and different solutions have been proposed. While

M. Arkoun, for example, sees a continuation of eighteenth-century Enlightenment thinking on both sides,[32] S. H. Nasr envisages an Islam, aware of its spiritual treasures, extending a hand to a continent suffering under increasing materialism.[33]

On Muslim Minorities

Like conflicts, minorities have played an important role in the mutual perceptions of Muslims and Christians.[34] Up to the twentieth century, the situation of Christian minorities in the Near East had an important—and often negative—influence on the general views of Islam current in Europe. In an unforeseen way, the reverse has also turned out to be true. The presence of several million Muslim migrant workers in Western Europe since the 1960s has considerably affected Muslim perceptions of European societies and Christianity in Western Europe. And here the picture has not been positive either.

The first care of the migrants, of course, was to survive economically and socially, and not to lose their Muslim identity. They were now in a position to observe Christians in their Western societies, just as a century ago European settlers had had the opportunity to observe Muslims in their own societies—in North Africa, the Near East, India, Indonesia, and elsewhere. The broad range of attitudes that Muslim migrants have taken toward European and American societies in general and Christians in particular would demand a study in itself and falls outside the scope of this essay. Between the extreme views that the pope and the Catholic Church exert the real power in Europe, or that Christianity is dying out, unable as it is to withstand the forces of secularism and materialism, the new contacts have also led to new perceptions of at least some forms of living Christianity, and, by extension, of living Islam.

These perceptions have been extremely diversified. The experiences of encounter in different countries and groups varied widely. Europe or the West in general has been perceived and judged according to diverging norms and values, often symbolized by "Islam" seen as that which constitutes the essential difference with Europe and the West. In Muslim circles numerous voices have been raised about the problems that Muslims have encountered in Europe, where Islam is not usually a recognized religion and the *Sharīʿa* not a recognized source of legislation, a fact that has to be admitted. Many Muslims in Europe feel themselves in a diaspora situation.[35] The number of serious studies about Muslim communities in Europe and North America which take into account the cultural and religious dimension is still restricted.[36]

Concern about the situation of Muslim minorities and their needs in the West has led Muslims here and there to look in new ways at non-Muslim minorities in Muslim countries. The usual attitude among Muslim authors was formerly to describe the situation of Christian and Jewish minorities as satisfactory. They hinted at the *dhimmī* regulations of former times and the foresight of the Muslim governments. That Christians[37] as well as Jews[38] could actually have suffered as minorities in Muslim states could hardly have been understood from the premises of this scheme.

As a consequence of the increase in Muslims living as minorities in a number of countries, some Muslim authors have started now to inquire about the situation of non-Muslim minorities in Muslim states where social control and political pressure play a role. Their situation and their actual rights and duties have begun to be discussed.[39] This is especially the case in countries where for a long time Muslim and non-Muslim communities have lived side by side, such as in Lebanon, Egypt, Jordan, Syria, and Iraq. Such coexistence also has a history in countries like Nigeria, Sudan, Pakistan, Malaysia, and Indonesia.

Speaking of Muslim minorities one must also refer to the Indian subcontinent, where a Muslim minority and a Hindu majority have been living side by side for centuries and under very different political regimes.

On India

Mutual perceptions of religious communities in India and Pakistan would require separate study. The problems of the Muslim minority situation took a new form after the partition of 1947. Those Muslims who had chosen to stay in India were committed to a secular state where they would occupy their due place, accepting cooperation with the large Hindu majority and the smaller Sikh, Christian, Jain, Buddhist, and Jewish communities. Such cooperation meant a revision of the classical scheme applied in the Moghul time, according to which Muslims had their own political organization and enjoyed a dominating position with regard to non-Muslims living in the same country. In present-day India, Muslims and Hindus as citizens are equal before the law.

The need for cooperation, which Hindu leaders like Nehru strongly urged, required Muslims to develop new attitudes. As in the case of other minorities, tolerance became a key to survival and as such it was hailed by Muslims. The need for harmonious relations was stressed, primarily by the government as in Middle Eastern states with significant Christian minorities. Several Muslim politicians have had important positions, most noticeably Abū ʾl-Kalām Azād (1888–1958) who was minister of education (1947–1958) and saw Islam and Hinduism as well as other religions as one in their essence.[40] But it was also demanded by Muslims under pressure themselves.[41] They constituted a vulnerable minority and often underwent the treatment to which in practice most minorities have been exposed throughout history. And, as elsewhere where minorities' rights are violated, since the 1970s Muslims have penned protests against the violation of their legitimate rights by Hindu extremists. In the meantime political tensions have increased. On a more reflective level, the new kind of Muslim minority situation in a number of countries has led several Muslim thinkers to revise traditional ideas of Muslim self-sufficiency.[42] They have made a number of studies about Muslim communities and Muslim-Hindu relations in the past. Here and there preparatory studies for a Muslim-Hindu dialogue have been started.[43]

On Israel

Already since World War I but certainly since the establishment of Israel in 1948 the situation of the Muslim community in Israel has been complex. Nearly all of them are Palestinian Arabs who could not enjoy the same rights as the Jewish citizens. From 1967 on, when Israel occupied East Jerusalem, the West Bank, and Gaza, all with a majority Muslim population, and encouraged Jewish settlements there, the situation of the Muslim communities as Palestinian Arabs has steadily deteriorated. The expectations awakened among Muslims by the so-called Peace Process have been turned into anger and bitter frustration, especially since the reversal of Israeli policies in 1996. The effects may turn out to be detrimental for Israel in the long run.

There is urgent need here for solid studies about Muslim-Jewish-Christian relations in past and present. Mutual perceptions between the three communities in their social and historical varieties should be taken into account.[44] Any analysis should take critical account of the political and other interests of all parties involved, including those of the USA.

Cultural and Religious Plurality

The reflection, also by Muslims, on the implications of religious plurality,[45] that is to say, the acceptance of other religious communities side-by-side with the Muslim one, has gained in acuteness during the last years.[46] This is not only due to the fact that many countries have a situation of religious plurality. It is also a kind of compensation for the growth of "Islamist" movements protesting what is called religious "pluralism." It expresses an ongoing concern with Islam's role in society in general. Muslim thinkers also enter into discussion with others on this subject.[47]

A first result of the situation of religious plurality is that several studies have been made on what the Qurʾān has to say about religious plurality.[48] In the special case of Christianity, but also on a more general level, attention is focused on the problem of the relation between the Qurʾānic message and the existing religions, including Christianity. In these studies new hermeneutics and other methods are used.[49] Thus, quite a few Muslim thinkers have arrived at a more positive appreciation of other religions than was the case formerly.[50] This led to more positive views about the relations between Muslims and non-Muslims,[51] but it also met with stiff resistance by people keeping to established tradition.

A second result of the situation of religious plurality has been that, after an interlude of more than seven centuries after al-Shahrastānī, some Muslim authors have published books of an informative and more descriptive nature about religions other than Islam.[52] Many surveys, however, fit into the category of apologetics rather than informative descriptive studies; one example is Ahmad Shalabī's four-volume work *Muqāranat al-adyān*, followed by other such surveys in the Islamic languages.[53] All of them start from the assumption that Islam is the final and most excellent religion of mankind and try to prove this while treating other religions. They are marked by an apologetic tone, some of them straightforwardly decrying certain "un-Islamic" views held in other religions.

Some of these books have a strong political bias—for instance, comparing the political and economic force of Muslim countries with that of non-Muslim ones. They often consider political Zionism a logical outgrowth of religious Judaism, just as Western imperialism is sometimes seen as a political outcome of organized Christianity. National, ethnic, and religious sentiments and loyalties can be important motivations distorting impartial research.[54]

Although an explicit affirmation of the independent status of science of religion is rarely found here, a number of careful investigations in the field of history of religions and sociology and anthropology of religion have been carried out by Muslim researchers, both in Western and in some Muslim countries.[55] Religions other than Islam are taught at certain universities in Muslim countries.[56] Here and there, discussion has started to what extent a science of religion could develop in specific Muslim countries or in the Muslim world in general, or how it could be developed by Muslims living in the West.[57] Such scholarship will of course take into account the existing approaches in this field.[58] Researchers have taken different positions, and it seems that the call for a scholarly study of religions is being heard, especially in countries of religious plurality and in those insisting on having academic standards in research and teaching. Naturally, more traditional or "Islamist" quarters put up resistance to such a scholarly study of religions.[59] Furthermore, the results of social scientific research on the role of religion in contemporary societies or in the social history of Muslim societies are published here and there. But since they deal with Islam, they fall outside the present survey.

A third result of the situation of religious plurality is that some prominent Muslim thinkers who are interested in this field of research have called for dialogue with adherents of other faiths, without renouncing Islamic positions and starting points.[60] In alphabetical order the names of Mohammed Arkoun,[61] Mahmoud Ayoub,[62] Ismail R. al-Faruqi,[63] Hassan Hanafi,[64] Seyyed Hossein Nasr,[65] and Mohamed Talbi[66] deserve to be mentioned here, but other names could easily be added.[67] A unique example of dialogue in the sense of common research is the Muslim-Christian Research Group (GRIC), a French language research group of Muslims and Christians. Several publications have resulted from their work.[68]

Recently, some Muslim institutions for interreligious dialogue have been established. The Āl al-Bayt foundation in Amman has organized a series of dialogues. In 1993 the Indonesian Institute for the Study of Religious Harmony was established in Yogyakarta; in 1995 the first issue appeared of *Religiosa: Indonesian Journal on Religious Harmony*, published by the State Institute of Islamic Studies in Yogyakarta. Relations between Islam and other religions in Indonesia with its *Pancasila* formula have a unique character and deserve to be studied closely.[69]

No doubt an opposition to interreligious dialogue also exists. It appeals to the absolute truth of Islam which cannot be discussed or reflects the feeling that any dialogue may weaken the forces of Islam in the long run.[70]

But what about the scholarly study of religions? There certainly have been interesting developments in Muslim countries. Fifty years ago (1948) the first chair of the history of religions was established in Ankara, and there are now seven of them in Turkey. In a number of countries scholars of religion have familiarized themselves with the tradition of the discipline and carry on teaching and research under such different names as history of religions, comparative religion, and philosophy of religion—or simply as anthropology, sociology, or psychology of religion. Before World War II such activities were virtually unknown in Muslim countries. Nowadays certain lines of interest can be distinguished, reflected in scholars' statements and publications, in libraries and scholarly institutions, and in the questions of students and a broader interested public. In countries like Turkey[71] and Indonesia[72] studies of religion already have their own identity, while Iran and Egypt have cultural traditions in which such studies fit perfectly. Interesting new initiatives have been taken in Tunisia and Morocco but also by Muslim researchers in countries like South Africa and Lebanon where they are directly exposed to the fact of religious plurality. There can be no doubt that Muslim perceptions of other religions will be influenced in the future by many factors, including better knowledge of and insight into these religions.[73]

NOTES

1. Jörgen Nielsen, *Islam in Western Europe* (Edinburgh: Edinburgh University Press, 1992). For a bibliography, see *Musulmans en Europe occidentale: Bibliographie commentée—Muslims in Western Europe: An Annotated Bibliography*, ed. Felice Dassetto and Yves Conrad (Paris: L'Harmattan, 1996). See also *L'Islam et les musulmans dans le monde*. Vol. 1: *L'Europe occidentale*, ed. Mohammed Arkoun, Rémy Leveau, and Bassem El-Jisr (Beirut: Centre Culturel Hariri, 1993).

2. A survey is given in Hugh Goddard, *Muslim Perceptions of Christianity* (London: Grey Seal Books, 1996). See also Goddard, "An annotated bibliography of works about Christianity by Egyptian Muslim authors (1940–1980)," *Muslim World*, vol. 80 (1990), pp. 251–277. Compare Goddard, "Contemporary Egyptian Mus-

lim views of Christianity" in *Renaissance and Modern Studies* (Nottingham University), vol. 31 (1987), pp. 74–86, and Goddard, "Modern Pakistani and Indian Muslim perceptions of Christianity," *Islam and Christian-Muslim Relations*, vol. 5 (1994), pp. 165–188.

3. For Egypt, see for instance the book reviews of Muslim books on Christianity published by Kenneth E. Nolin in *Muslim World*, vol. 55 (1965), pp. 237–245 (with an annotated bibliography of books on Christianity by Muslim writers, pp. 243–245), vol. 57 (1967), pp. 342–345, and vol. 58 (1968), pp. 74–75. Compare Hugh P. Goddard, "An annotated bibliography of works about Christianity by Egyptian Muslim authors (1940–1980), *Muslim World*, vol. 80 (1990), pp. 251–277.

4. They include books like Al-Rahim, *Jesus, Prophet of Islam* (Norfolk: Diwan Press, 1977) and *About "The Myth of God Incarnate": Being a Unique Collection of Theological Essays—An Impartial Survey of Its Main Topics*, ed. Abdus-Samad Sharafouddin (Jeddah: King Abdul-Aziz University Press, 1978). See also Abdul Hamid Qadri, *Dimensions of Christianity* (Islamabad: Daʾwah Academy, International Islamic University, 1989).

5. Ulfat Aziz-Us-Samad, *A Comparative Study of Christianity and Islam* (Lahore: Sh. Muh. Ashraf, 1976). Compare Aziz Samad and Mrs. Ulfat, *Islam and Christianity* (Karachi: Begum Aisha Bawany Waqf, 1970). Since Muhammad ʿAbduh, a recurrent theme of comparison is that of tolerance in both religions. See for instance Muhammad al-Ghazzali, *Al-taʿassub waʾl-tasāmuh bayna ʾl-masīhīya waʾl-islām* (Polemics and tolerance between Christianity and Islam) (Cairo, n.d. [ca. 1953?]). Its contents are summarized in Olaf Schumann, "Das Christentum im Lichte der heutigen arabisch-islamischen Literatur," *Zeitschrift für Religions- und Geistesgeschichte*, vol. 21 (1969), pp. 307–329, esp. pp. 315–325.

6. Mustafa Khalidy and Omar A. Farroukh, *Missionaries and Imperialism: Being an Account of Mission Work in the Arab World as a Medium of Cultural Expansion and a Preparation for Political Intervention*, 2nd ed. (Saida-Beirut: al-Maktaba al-ʿAsriyya liʾl-tabāʾa waʾl-nashr, 1957). Compare Ahmad ʿAbd al-Wahhāb, *Haqīqat al-tabshīr bayna al-mādī waʾl-hādir* (The truth on proselytism yesterday and today) (Cairo: Maktabat Wahba, 1981) and ʿAbd al-Jalīl Shalabi, *Maʿrakat al-tabshīr waʾl-islām: Harakat al-tabshīr waʾl-islām fī Asiyā wa-Ifrīqīyā wa-Ūrubbā* (The fight of proselytism against Islam: The movement of proselytism in Asia, Africa and Europe) (Kuwait: Muʾassasat al-khalīj al-ʿarabī, 1989). See also Ahmad ʿAbd al-Rahīm Nasr, *Al-idāra al-barītānīya waʾl-tabshīr al-islāmī waʾl-masīhī fī ʾl-Sūdān dirāsa awwaliyya* (Khartum: Ministry of Education and Guidance [*tawjīh*], 1979/1399). Warnings against existing Christian attempts to proselytize Turkish Muslim workers in Europe are contained in Eyub Sanay, *Gurbetcinin el kitabi* (Manuel of the Turks living abroad) (Ankara: Diyanet Isleri Baskanligi, 1984). (Translation of some 15 pages in *Se Comprendre*, No. 90/09, 29 June 1990 pp. 3–13.)

7. Muhammad Kāmil Husayn, *Qarya zālima*, 4th ed. (Cairo: Maktabat al-Nahda al-Misrīya, 1974). English translation with introduction by Kenneth Cragg, *The City of Wrong* (Amsterdam: Djambatan, 1959). On this book and other publications by the same author, see G. C. Anawati, "Jésus et ses juges d'après 'La cité inique' du Dr. Kamel Hussein," *Mélanges de l'Institut Dominicain d'Etudes Orientales du Caire* 2 (1955), pp. 71–134; J. Jomier, "Un regard moderne sur le Coran avec le Dr Kamel Husein," *Mélanges de l'Institut Dominicain d'Etudes Orientales du Caire* 12 (1974), pp. 49–64; Marc Chartier, "La pensée religieuse de Kāmil Husayn," *IBLA*, No 133, pp.1–44; Hélène Expert-Bezançon, "Notes biographiques sur le docteur Kāmil Husayn, médecin et humaniste égyptien (1901–1977)," *IBLA* 48 (1985), No. 155, pp. 19–43. See also Harold S. Vogelaar, "The religious and philosophical thought of M. Kāmil Hussein, an Egyptian humanist," Ph.D. Diss. Columbia University, New York, 1976, and Vogelaar, "Religious pluralism in the thought of Muhammad Kāmil Hussein," in *Christian-Muslim Encounters*, ed. Yvonne Yazbeck Haddad and Wadi Z. Haddad (Gainesville: University of Florida Press, 1995), pp. 411–425.

8. David Pinault, "Images of Christ in Arabic literature," *Die Welt des Islams*, vol. 27 (1987), pp. 104–125; Jonathan S. Addleton, "Images of Jesus in the literatures of Pakistan," *Muslim World*, vol. 80 (1990), pp. 96–106. Jacques Jomier, "Quatre ouvrages en arabe sur le Christ," *Mélanges de l'Institut Dominicain d'Etudes Orientales du Caire*, vol. 5 (1958), pp. 367–386; Fathi ʿUthmān, *Maʿa al-masīh fīʾl-anājil al-arbaʿa* (Cairo: Maktabat Wahba, 1961), reviewed by Kenneth E. Nolin, *Muslim World*, vol. 53 (1963), pp. 252–254; ʿAbd al-Karīm al-Khatibi, "Christ in the Qurʾān, the Taurāt, and the Injīl: A continuing dialogue," *Muslim World*, vol. 61 (1971), pp. 90–101. Compare Olaf H. Schumann, *Der Christus der Muslime: Christologische Aspekte in der arabisch-islamischen Literatur* (Gütersloh: Gerd Mohn, 1975).

9. Muhammad Abu Zahra presents the traditional Muslim position, with chosen materials added from Western scholarship before World War II. See his *Muhādarāt fī al-nasrāniyya* (Cairo: Dār al-kitāb al-ʿarabī, 1949) 5th ed., Cairo: Dār al-fikr al-ʿarabī, 1977.

10. Ismaʾil Raji al-Faruqi, *Christian Ethics: A Historical and Systematic Analysis of its Dominant Ideas* (Montreal: McGill University Press, 1967); al-Faruqi, "Judentum und Christentum im islamischen Verständnis," in *Weltmacht Islam* (Munich: Bayerische Landeszentrale für politische Bildungsarbeit, 1988), pp. 137–148. Compare Ahmad Hijāzī al-Saqqa, *Aqānīm*

al-nasārā (The Trinity of the Christians) (Cairo: Dār al-ansār, 1977), and al-Saqqā, *Allāh wa-sifātuhu fī al-yahūdīya wa'l-nasrānīya wa'l-islām* (God and his attributes in Judaism, Christianity, and Islam) (Cairo: Dār al-nahda al-ʿarabīya, 1978).

11. Hassan Hanafi, "Certainty and conjecture: A prototype of Islamo-Christian relations," in *Religious Dialogue and Revolution: Essays on Judaism, Christianity and Islam* (Cairo: Anglo-Egyptian Bookshop, 1977), pp. 56–68.

12. We must leave aside the question to what extent such new Muslim orientations are a response to dialogue initiatives on the Christian side. On the Council of Vatican 2 and Islam, see Robert Caspar, "Le Concile et l'Islam," *Etudes*, vol. 324 (Jan.–June 1966), pp. 114–126. See also *Déclarations communes islamo-chrétiennes de 1954 à 1992 (1373 à 1412 h.): Textes choisis*, ed. Augustin Dupré la Tour and Hisham Nashabé (Beirut: Dar el-Machreq, 1995).

13. See for instance Filippo Dore, "Cristianesimo e Cristiani in *Majallat al-Azhar* 1958–1978," Ph.D. Diss., Pontifical Institute of Arabic and Islamic Studies, Rome, 1991 (printed excerpt 85 pp.). About Turkish descriptions of Christianity in Turkish school books and official or semiofficial religious literature of the 1970s, see Xavier Jacob, *Christianity as Seen by the Turks*. Research Papers Muslims in Europe No. 22 (Birmingham: Center for the Study of Islam and Christian-Muslim Relations), June 1984. For the German original text, see Jacob, *Das Christentum in der religiösen Literatur der Türkei*. CIBEDO Texte, no. 28/29, 15 July 1984. In the last 20 years Turkish presentations of Christianity have improved.

14. See Mahmoud Ayoub, "Muslim views of Christianity: Some modern examples," *Islamochristiana*, Vol. 10 (1984), pp. 49–70. Compare Ayoub, "Islam and Christianity: A study of Muhammad ʿAbduh's view of the two religions," *Humaniora Islamica*, vol. 2 (The Hague: Mouton, 1974), pp. 121–137, and Muhammad Talbi, "Le christianisme vu par l'islam et les musulmans," in M. Talbi and O. Clément, *Un respect têtu* (Paris: Nouvelle Cité, 1989), pp. 67–108.

15. Mahmoud M. Ayoub, "The Islamic context of Muslim-Christian relations," in *Conversion and Continuity; Indigenous Christian Communities in Islamic Lands—Eighth to Eighteenth Centuries*, ed. Michael Gervers and Ramzi Jibran Bikhazi (Toronto: Pontifical Institute of Mediaeval Studies, 1990), pp. 461–477.

16. Ali Bouamama, *La littérature polémique musulmane contre le christianisme depuis ses origines jusqu'au XIIIe siècle* (Algiers: Entreprise nationale du livre, 1988). ʿAbd al-Majīd al-Charfi (al-Sharfī), *Al-fikr al-islāmī fī al-radd ʿalā al-nasārā ilā nihāyat al-qarn al-rābiʿ al-ʿasharī* (Islamic thought on the refutation of Christianity until the end of the fourteenth century) (Tunis: Al-dār al-tūnisīya li'l-nashr and Algiers: Al-muʾassasa al-watanīya li'l-kitāb, 1986). Compare in Turkish Mehmet Aydin, *Müslümanların Hıristyanliğa karşı yazdiği reddiyeler ve tartişma konuları* (Konya, 1989).

17. Abdelmajid Charfi, "Pour une nouvelle approche du christianisme par la pensée musulmane," *Islamochristiana*, vol. 13 (1987), pp. 61–77. This is a French translation by R. Caspar of pp. 515–528 of Charfi's large study mentioned in the preceding note.

18. Kemal Demiral, "The high judge," *Muslim World*, vol. 80 (1990), pp. 107–144.

19. Ali Merad, *Charles de Foucauld au regard de l'islam* (Paris: Chalet, 1976) with appendix.

20. Pierre Cachia, "Themes related to Christianity and Judaism in modern Egyptian drama and fiction," *Journal of Arabic Literature*, vol. 2 (1971), pp. 178–194. Compare Jean Dejeux, "L'image des chrétiens dans les romans et les recueils de nouvelles maghrébins de langue française de 1920 à 1978," *Islamochristiana*, vol. 5 (1979), pp. 193–220.

21. M. Y. S. Haddad, "Arab perspectives of Judaism: A study of image formation in the writings of Muslim Arab authors, 1948–1978," Doctoral Diss., University of Utrecht, 1984.

22. Jacob M. Landau, "Muslim Turkish attitudes towards Jews, Zionism and Israel," *Die Welt des Islams*, vol. 28 (1988), pp. 291–300. Other examples could easily be added.

23. On mutual perceptions and images of Europe and the Muslim world, in particular the Arab world, see *D'un Orient l'autre: Les métamorphoses successives des perceptions et connaissances*. Vol. 1: *Configurations*; Vol. 2: *Identifications* (Paris: Ed. du CNRS, 1991).

24. Daryush Shayegan, *Le regard mutilé: Schizophrénie culturelle—pays traditionnels face à la modernité* (Paris: Albin Michel, 1989).

25. See, for instance, two small books by Iranian authors: Jalal Al-I Ahmad, *Occidentosis: A Plague from the West*, trans. R. Campbell; Annotations and Introduction by Hamid Algar (Berkeley: Mizan Press, 1984); Ehsan Naraghi, *L'Orient et la crise de l'Occident*, trans. Brigitte Simon in collaboration with Thierry Lemaresquier (Paris: Ed. Entente, 1977).

26. See Paul Khoury, *L'Islam critique de l'Occident dans la pensée arabe actuelle: Islam et Sécularité*, 2 vols. (Altenberge: Oros Verlag and Würzburg: Echter Verlag, 1994 and 1995).

27. See, for instance, Willem A. Bijlefeld, "Controversies around the Qurʾānic Ibrāhīm narrative and its 'orientalist' interpretations," *Muslim World*, vol. 72 (1982), pp. 81–94. Such criticism mostly concerned Western Islamic studies in general. See Ekkehard Rudolph, *Westliche Islamwissenschaft im Spiegel muslimischer Kritik: Grundzüge und aktuelle Merkmale einer innerislamischen Diskussion* (Berlin: Klaus Schwarz, 1991). It could, however, also concern specific studies

by certain Western Islamicists which were criticized because of their lack of scholarly adequacy. See, for instance, Syed Muhammad Al-Naquib al-Attas, *Comments on the Re-Examination of al-Rānīrī's Hujjatu'l-Siddīq: A Refutation* (Kuala Lumpur: Muzium Negara, 1975). Whereas normally such reproaches should have led to a scholarly debate, in this case—in which two Dutch scholars happened to be involved—no response was forthcoming to Al-Attas's scholarly, but also spiritually committed, defense of his religion and culture, as symbolized by al-Rānīrī. C. Snouck Hurgronje would have done better! Certain forms of scholarship are felt to "kill" the religion and culture studied, or to treat it as being "dead" already. Normal communication was clearly lacking. A weakness of old-style orientalism?

28. To a large extent, Western scholars of Islam were not well aware of such problems and may be termed naive or amoral. On the whole, anthropologists through their fieldwork have given much more thought to the human problems connected with the study of other peoples, their cultures, and their religions. But too few scholars of Islam have taken account of their responsibilities as researchers.

A useful list of twentieth-century Western scholars of Islam, in particular Roman Catholic scholars, is given in the "Bibliografia" of Carlo Gasbarri, *Cattolicesimo e Islam oggi* (Rome: Città Nuova, 1972), pp. 315–344.

29. Mahmoud Zakzouk, "Cultural relations between the West and the world of Islam: Meeting points and possibilities of co-operation on the academic level," *Islam and Christian-Muslim Relations*, vol. 3 (1992), pp. 69–82

30. One of the more important meetings was that organized under the auspices of the European Community and the League of Arab States in Hamburg, in 1983. See *Euro-Arab Dialogue: The Relations between the Two Cultures—Acts of the Hamburg Symposium April 11th to 15th 1983*. English version edited by Derek Hopwood. (London: Croom Helm, 1985).

31. Hichem Djait, *L'Europe et l'Islam* (Paris: Ed. du Seuil, 1978). (English translation in 1985.) Compare at about the same time by the Sheikh al-Azhar ʿAbd al-Halīm Mahmūd, *Ūrūbbā wa'l-islām* (Europe and Islam) (Cairo: Dār al-Maʿārif, 1979). The discussion concerned in particular the negative influence of Western secularism on Muslim societies. This is a vast subject which has led to a number of publications by Muslim authors. See, for instance, Syed Muhammad Naquib al-Attas, *Islam, Secularism and Philosophy of the Future* (London: Mansell, 1985).

32. See, for instance, Mohamed Arkoun, "Response to Professor A. Vergote" in the book *Euro-Arab Dialogue* mentioned in note 30, pp. 163–175. Arkoun in his dialogue with the West calls for a recourse to reason.

33. Seyyed Hussein Nasr, *Islam and the Plight of Modern Man* (London: Longman, 1975). Nasr wants to awaken the West to true spirituality.

34. For Muslim perceptions of Muslim—and also Christian—minorities, see the *Journal of the Institute of Muslim Minority Affairs* (Jedda and London), since 1979.

35. F. El-Manssoury, "Muslims in Europe: The lost tribe of Islam," *Journal of the Institute of Muslim Minority Affairs*, vol. 10 (1989), no. 1, pp. 62–84. Compare Smail Balic, "Moving from Traditional to Modern Culture: Immigrant experience of Jews, Oriental Christians and Muslims," *Journal of the Institute of Muslim Minority Affairs*, vol. 10 (1989), no. 2, pp. 332–336.

36. For Europe, see, for instance, Jörgen Nielsen, *Muslims in Western Europe* (Edinburgh: Edinburgh University Press, 1992); T. Gerholm and Y. G. Lithman, eds., *The New Islamic Presence in Europe* (London: Mansell, 1988); and W. A. R. Shadid and P. S. Van Koningsveld, eds., *The Integration of Muslims and Hindus in Western Europe* (Kampen, Netherlands: Kok Pharos, 1991).

For North America, see for instance Yvonne Yazbeck Haddad, ed., *The Muslims of America* (New York: Oxford University Press, 1991). Compare *The Muslim Community in North America*, ed. Earle H. Waugh, Baha Abu-Laban, and Regula B. Qureschi (Edmonton: University of Alberta Press, 1983).

On Muslim minorities in the West in general, see, for instance, Crawford Young, "Muslims as minorities: An outsider's perspective," *Journal of the Institute of Muslim Minority Affairs*, vol. 12 (1991), no. 1, pp. 1–22; Larry Poston, "Becoming a Muslim in the Christian West: A profile of conversion to a minority religion," in idem, vol. 12 (1991), no. 1, pp. 159–169; Maurice Borrmans, "Future prospects for Muslim-Christian coexistence in non-Islamic countries in light of past experience," in idem, vol. 10 (1989), no. 1, pp. 50–62. See also, from a historian's point of view, Bernard Lewis, "Legal and historical reflections on the position of Muslim populations under non-Muslim rule," in idem, vol. 13 (1992), no. 1, pp. 1–16. Compare the review essay by M. Ali Kettani of Gilles Kepel, *Les Banlieues de l'Islam: Naissance d'une religion en France*, in idem, vol. 12 (1991), no. 2, pp. 504–519. The only larger Muslim study on the subject is that of A. Kettani, *Muslim Minorities in the World Today* (London: Mansell, 1986), but its data and analyses are not always reliable.

37. Sami Awad Aldeeb Abu-Sahlieh, *L'impact de la religion sur l'ordre juridique: Cas de l'Egypte—Non-musulmans en pays d'islam* (Fribourg: Ed. Universitaires, 1979).

38. One of the reasons for the migration of the majority of Jews living in Muslim countries to Israel was the desire of being freed from the minority status.

39. Fazlur Rahman, "Non-Muslim minorities in an Islamic state," *Journal of the Institute of Muslim Minority Affairs*, vol. 7 (1986), no. 2, pp. 13–24. Compare Hasan Askari, "Christian mission to Islam: A Muslim response," in *Journal of the Institute of Muslim Minority Affairs*, vol. 7 (1986), no. 2, pp. 314–329. We do not deal here with those voices who want to apply the *dhimmī* status to non-Muslim minorities again.

40. See Ian Henderson Douglas, *Abul Kalam Azad: An Intellectual and Religious Biography*, ed. Gail Minault and Christian W. Troll (New Delhi, 1988).

41. Asghar Ali Engineer, "Harmony in a multireligious society: An Islamic view," *New Blackfriars*, Special Issue "The World of Islam" (Feb. 1990), pp. 86–93. Engineer, "The Hindu-Muslim problem—a cooperative approach," *Islam and Christian-Muslim Relations*, vol. 1 (1990), pp. 89–105. There is much literature on the subject. Compare ch. 10, "What then of the future?," in Syed Mahmoud, *Hindu Muslim Cultural Accord* (Bombay: Vora, 1949), pp. 76–87.

42. See the contribution by Asghar Ali Engineer, "Muslim views of Hindus since 1950" (ch. 17 in this volume). See also the psychological study by Qamar Hasan, *Muslims in India: Attitudes, Adjustments and Reactions* (New Delhi: Northern Book Centre, 1988).

43. See K. S. Durrany, ed., *Inter-Religious Perceptions of Hindus and Muslims* (New Delhi: Indian Institute of Islamic Studies Hamdard Nagar, Department of Comparative Religion, 1982). In this situation, comparative studies of Hindu and Muslim thinkers, carried out by Muslim researchers, become relevant. See, for instance, M. Rafique, *Sri Aurobindo and Iqbal: A Comparative Study of Their Philosophy* (Aligarh: Aligarh Muslim University, 1974).

44. Studies on historical relations between Muslims and Jews, after S. D. Goitein and B. Lewis, have been carried out by William M. Brinner, Ronald Nettler, and Steven M. Wasserstrom. See notes 151 and 153 in Part 2. Compare Stefan Wild, "Judentum, Christentum and Islam in der palästinensischen Poesie," in *Der Islam im Spiegel zeitgenössischer Literatur der islamischen Welt*, ed. J. C. Bürgel (Leiden: E. J. Brill, 1985), pp. 259–297.

45. On societies with religious plurality several studies have been made. See, for instance, in particular about Lebanon but of wider validity, Georges G. Corm, *Contribution à l'étude des sociétés multi-confessionnelles: Effets socio-juridiques et politiques du pluralisme religieux* (Paris: Pichon & Durand-Auzias, 1971).

46. See, for instance, the positive attitude taken by the Pakistani author, Charles Amjad-Ali, "Not so much a threat as a challenge: Acknowledging the religio-cultural heritage of others," *New Blackfriars*, Special Issue "The World of Islam" (February 1990), pp. 94–103. In Pakistan, too, Dā'ud Rahbar's writings *Kalchar Ke Rūḥānī 'Anāṣir* ("The Spiritual Elements of Cultures"), drew attention. They were first published in the journal *Nayā Dawr* in Karachi (1993) and later as a book by Sang-i-Mīl Publications, Lahore.

47. See, for instance, Tarek Mitri, ed., *Religion, Law and Society: A Christian-Muslim Discussion* (Geneva: WCC Publications & Kampen: Kok Pharos, 1995). See also T. Mitri, ed. *Religion and Human Rights: A Christian-Muslim Discussion*. Geneva: WCC Office on Inter-Religious Relations, 1996.

48. See, for instance, Ghulam Haider Aasi, "The Qur'ān and other religious traditions," *Hamdard Islamicus*, vol. 9 (1986), pp. 65–91. Compare I. H. Azad Faruqi, "The Qur'ānic view of other religions," *Islam and the Modern Age*, vol. 18 (1987), pp. 39–50, and S. Vahiduddin, "Comment le Coran conçoit l'harmonie et la réconciliation entre les confessions religieuses," *Islamochristiana*, vol. 6 (1980), pp. 25–31. See also A. J. Powell, "The Qur'ānic view of other Scriptures: A translation of sections from writings by 'Afīf 'Abd al-Fattāh Tabbāra and al-Ustādh al-Haddād," *Muslim World*, vol. 59 (1969), pp. 95–105. Compare Christian W. Troll, "Der Blick des Koran auf andere Religionen: Gründe für eine gemeinsame Zukunft," in Walter Kerber, ed., *Wie tolerant ist der Islam?* (Munich: Kindt Verlag, 1991), pp. 47–69.

49. Hassan Hanafi, "Hermeneutics as axiomatics: An Islamic case," in *Religious Dialogue and Revolution: Essays on Judaism, Christianity and Islam* (Cairo: The Anglo-Egyptian Bookshop, 1977), pp. 1–17. See also the thoughtful study by Seyyed Hossein Nasr, "Islam and the encounter of religions." Text from 1965, revised and published as chapter 9 in the author's book *Sufi Essays* (London: Allen and Unwin, 1972), pp. 123–151.

50. Muhammad Abdullah Draz, "Islam's attitude towards and relations with other faiths," *Islamic Literature* (Lahore), vol. 10 (1958), pp. 69–76. This was one of no less than 13 papers on the subject read at Session 8, "Islam's attitude towards, and relations with, other faiths," with participation of both Muslims and non-Muslims, at an international Islamic Colloquium held in Lahore, Dec. 1957–Jan. 1958. See the publication *International Islamic Colloquium Papers, December 29, 1957–January 8, 1958* (Lahore: Panjab University Press, 1960), esp. pp. 184–236. The fact that the colloquium had a special session on this theme is significant. See also S. A. Akbarabadi, "Islam and other Religions," in *Islam*, ed. Abdul Haq Ansari and others (Patiala: Punjabi University, 1969), pp. 103–115; Syed Vahiduddin, "Islam and diversity of religions," *Islam and Christian-Muslim Relations*, vol. 1 (1990), pp. 3–11. Compare Christian W. Troll, "Salvation of non-Muslims: Views of some eminent Muslim religious thinkers," *Islam and the Modern Age*, vol. 14 (1983), pp. 104–114. New attention has been paid to such posi-

tive views held by Muslim thinkers of the past. See, for instance, Abdelmajid Charfi and Maurice Borrmans, "L'Islam et les religions non musulmanes: Quelques textes positifs," *Islamochristiana*, vol. 3 (1977), pp. 39–63. A standard work along established lines is Hasan Khālid, *Mawqif al-islām min al-wathaniyya wa'l-yahūdiyya wa'l-nasrāniyya* (Islam's attitude to paganism, Judaism and Christianity) (Beirut: Maʿhad al-inmāʾ al-ʿarabī, 1986). Compare Fawzi Bedoui, "Mulāhazāt hawla manzilat al-adyān ghayr al-islāmīya fī al-fikr al-islāmī al-muʿāsir" (Observations on the place of the non-Islamic religions in contemporary Islamic thinking), *Islamochristiana*, vol. 17 (1991), pp. 1–31.

51. Khalid Duran, "Die Muslime und die Andersgläubigen," in *Der Islam: Religion–Ethik–Politik*, ed. Peter Antes and others (Stuttgart: Kohlhammer, 1991), pp. 125–152. See also Hélène Expert-Bezançon, "Regard d'un humaniste égyptien, le Dr Kāmil Husayn, sur les religions non-musulmanes," *Islamochristiana*, vol. 14 (1988), pp. 17–49. Compare Ali Merad, "Un penseur musulman à l'heure de l'oecuménisme: Mahmūd Abū Rayya," *Islamochristiana*, vol. 4 (1978), pp. 151–163. Compare note 50.

52. See the contribution by Patrice Brodeur, "Contemporary Arabic Muslim Writings on Religions Other Than Islam" (chapter 15 in this volume). An interesting comparative study is that by S. Irtiza Husain, *Parallel Faiths and the Messianic Hope (A Comparative Study)* (Aligarh: Aligarh Muslim University, 1971). There are a few books in English written by Muslim authors and offering a survey of religions—for instance, Ahmad Abdullah al-Masdoosi, *Living Religions of the World: A Socio-political Study* (Karachi: Begum Aisha Bawany Wakf, 1962). This book is an English rendering and elaboration by Zafar Ishaq Ansari of the original Urdu edition of 1958. Of a much lesser standard is Mahmud Brelvi, *Islam and Its Contemporary Faiths* (Karachi, 1965). A number of books on other religions appeared in Arabic. Of a descriptive nature is also Muhammad Abū Zahra, *Al-diyānāt al-qadīma* (The religions of the past) (Cairo: Dār al-fikr al-ʿarabī, 1965). An older view of the history of religions is that of ʿAbbās Mahmūd al-ʿAqqād, *Allāh: Kitāb fī nashʿat al-ʿaqīda al-ilāhīya* (God: A book on the rise of the belief in God) (Cairo, 1947). 7th ed. Cairo: Dār al-Maʿārif, 1976. The study by Muhammad ʿAbdallāh Drāz, *Al-dīn: Buhūth mumahhida li-dirāsat taʾrīkh al-adyān* (Religion: Preparatory investigations for the study of the history of religions) (Cairo, 1952), opens new perspectives. New ed., Cairo: Matbaʿat al-saʿāda, 1969. Purely empirical studies are rare; the study of religions is nearly always linked to a philosophy of religion.

53. The four volumes were published in Cairo by the Maktabat al-nahda al-hadītha in successively enlarged editions. Vol. 1 *al-Masīhīya* (Christianity) (1960); Vol. 2 *al-Islām* (Islam) (1961); Vol. 3 *Adyān al-Hind al-kubrā: al-Hindawīya, al-Jaynīya, al-Budhīya* (The great religions of India: Hinduism, Jainism, Buddhism) (1964); Vol. 4 *al-Yahūdīya* (Judaism) (1965). These volumes have been translated into several Islamic languages. Other similar books in Arabic on comparative religion have appeared more recently, such as Ibrāhīm Khalīl Ahmad, *Muhādarāt fī muqāranat al-adyān* (Lectures on Comparative Religion) (Cairo: Dār al-Manār, 1989); Rāshid ʿAbdallāh al-Fahrān, *Al-Adyān al-muʿāsira* (Contemporary religions) (Kuwait: Matbaʿat al-Jādūr, 1985); Mustafā Hilmi, *Al-Islām w'al-adyān: dirāsa muqārana* (Islam and the religions: A comparative study) (Cairo: Dār al-Sahwa, 1990); Amīn al-Qudāt and others, *Adyān wa-firaq* (Religions and sects) (Amman, 1990); Laylā Hasan Saʿd Al-Din, *Adyān muqārana* (Religions compared) (Amman: Dār al-fikr li'l-nashr wa'l-tawzīʿ, 1985); Muhammad ʿAbdallāh al-Sharqawī, *Fī muqāranat al-adyān: buhūth wa-dirāsāt* (On comparative religion: Investigations and studies) (Cairo: Maktabat al-zahrāʾ, 1990); ʿAbd al-ʿAzīz al-Thaʿālibī, *Muhādarāt fī taʾrīkh al-madhāhib wa'l-adyān* (Lectures on the history of schools and religions), ed. Hammādī al-Sāhilī (Beirut: Dār al-gharb al-islāmī, 1985). On the publications of Abū Zahra, Drāz, and Ahmad Shalabī in this field, see the M. A. thesis of Patrice C. Brodeur, "Contemporary Muslim approaches to the study of religion: A comparative analysis of three Egyptian authors," Institute of Islamic Studies, McGill University, Montreal, 1989. In Turkish, see Günay Tümer and Abdurrahman Küçük, *Dinler tarihi* (The history of religions) (Ankara: Eylül, 1988). In Indonesian, see H. Abu Ahmadi, *Perbandingan agama* (The study of religions) (Jakarta: Rineka Cipta, 1970).

54. See for instance, on Turkish accounts of the ancient Turkic religion, Wolfgang-Ekkehard Scharlipp, "Die alttürkische Religion und ihre Darstellung bei einigen türkischen Historikern," *Die Welt des Islams*, vol. 31 (1991), pp. 168–192.

55. For instance, Harith Abdoussalam in Yogyakarta, a pupil of A. Mukti Ali, wrote introductions like *Pengantar phenomenologi agama* (Introduction to phenomenology of religion, 1981), *Kristologi* (Christology, 1982) and contributed to *Fenomenologi agama* (Phenomenology of religion, 1985), which are quite valuable, especially for teaching purposes. On Indonesian studies in this field, see Karel A. Steenbrink, "The study of comparative religion by Indonesian Muslims: A survey," *Numen*, vol. 37 (1990), pp. 141–167, and Steenbrink, "The Pancasila Ideology and an Indonesian Muslim Theology of Religions," chapter 19 in this volume.

56. It is not certain when and where the teaching of other religions started. See for instance for Egypt C. C. Adams, "Comparative religion in the Azhar University," *Muslim World*, vol. 35 (1945), pp. 111–125. In 1948 a chair of history of religions was established at the University of Ankara, in the Faculty of Theology.

Compare, most recently, Thomas Michel, "Enseignement de la foi chrétienne dans les facultés de théologie de Turquie," *Se Comprendre*, no. 90/07, 15 mai 1990, pp. 1–5.

57. Ibrahim H. Khan, "The academic study of religion with reference to Islam," *Scottish Journal of Religious Studies*, vol. 11 (1990), pp. 37–46. The author thinks such a Muslim "science of religion" will not develop. The late Isma'il Raji A. al-Faruqi, author of *Christian Ethics: A historical and systematic analysis of its dominant ideas* (Montreal: McGill University Press, 1967), in contrast, wanted to develop "science of religion" in an Islamic sense, also as an instrument of Muslim-Christian understanding. See his "History of religions: Its nature and significance for Christian education and the Muslim-Christian dialogue," *Numen*, vol. 12 (1965), pp. 35–95. Whatever the opinions, in fact the study of other religions is developing in various Muslim countries, and a clear need is felt for information on other religions. The main question is: What kind of information? Compare Jacques Waardenburg, "Twentieth-century Muslim writings on other religions: A proposed typology," *Proceedings of the Tenth Congress of the Union Européenne des Arabisants et des Islamisants*, ed. Robert Hillenbrand (Edinburgh, 1982), pp. 107–115. See also Waardenburg, "Muslimisches Interesse an anderen Religionen im sozio-politischen Kontext des 20. Jahrhunderts," in *Loyalitätskonflikte in der Religionsgeschichte: Festschrift für Carsten Colpe*, ed. C. Elsas and H. G. Kippenberg (Munich: Königshausen & Neumann, 1990), pp. 140–152.

58. A. Mukti Ali, *Ilmu perbandingan agama* (The scholarly study of religion) (Yogyakarta: Yayasan Nida, 1975). Here and there appear publications with the results of social scientific research on the role of religion in contemporary societies, or in the social history of Muslim societies. Since they deal with Islam, they fall outside the present survey. A book touching methodological questions is Muhammad Kamāl Ibrahīm Jaʿfar, *Al-islām bayna al-adyān: Dirāsa fī turuq dirāsāt al-dīn wa-ahamm qadāyāh* (Islam among the religions: A study on the approaches of religious studies and its most important problems) (Cairo: Maktabat dār al-ʿulūm, 1977).

59. Such resistance fundamentally condemns the fact that a Muslim would busy himself at all with other religions unless he wants to refute them. Similar positions are held in certain quarters in all religions. In Islam as in Christianity and Judaism this shows up, for instance, in condemnations of freemasonry. See Jacob M. Landau, "Muslim opposition to Freemasonry," *Die Welt des Islams*, vol. 36 (1996), pp. 186–203.

60. On Muslim dialogue efforts in general, see Leonard Swidler, ed., *Muslims in Dialogue: The Evolution of a Dialogue* (Lewiston, N.Y.: Edwin Mellen Press, 1992).

61. Mohammed Arkoun, "New perspectives for a Jewish-Christian-Muslim dialogue," *Journal of Ecumenical Studies*, vol. 26 (1989), pp. 523–529.

62. Mahmoud Ayoub, "Roots of Muslim-Christian conflict," *Muslim World*, vol. 79 (1989), pp. 25–45; Ayoub, "Islam and Christianity between tolerance and acceptance," *Islam and Christian-Muslim Relations*, vol. 2 (1991), pp. 171–181.

63. Ismaʾīl Rājī al-Faruqi, ed., *Trialogue of the Abrahamic Faiths: Papers presented to the Islamic Studies Group of American Academy of Religion* (Herndon, Virginia: International Institute of Islamic Thought, 1982; 2nd ed. 1986); al-Faruqi, "Islam and Christianity: Diatribe or Dialogue," *Journal of Ecumenical Studies*, vol. 5 (1968), pp. 45–77; al-Faruqi, "Islam and other Faiths," in *The Challenge of Islam*, ed. Altaf Gauhar (London: Islamic Council of Europe, 1978), pp. 82–111; al-Faruqi, "The Muslim-Christian dialogue: A constructionist view," *Islam and the Modern Age*, vol. 8 (1977), pp. 5–36; al-Faruqi, "The role of Islām in global interreligious dependence," in *Towards a Global Congress of the World's Religions*, ed. Warren Lewis (New York: Rose of Sharon Press, 1980), pp. 19–53.

64. Hassan Hanafi, *Religious Dialogue and Revolution: Essays on Judaism, Christianity and Islam* (Cairo: Anglo-Egyptian Bookshop, 1977). See, for instance, ch. 7, "Muslim and Christian—dialogue," pp. 110–114.

65. Seyyed Hossein Nasr, "Comments on a few theological issues in Islamic-Christian dialogue," in *Christian-Muslim Encounters*, ed. Yvonne Yazbeck Haddad and Wadi Z. Haddad (Gainesville: University of Florida Press, 1995), pp. 457–467, and Nasr, "Response to Hans Küng's paper on Christian-Muslim dialogue," *Muslim World*, vol. 77 (1987), pp. 96–105. See *The Complete Bibliography of the Works of Seyyed Hossein Nasr, from 1958 through April 1993*, compiled by Mehdi Aminrazavi and Zailan Moris (Kuala Lumpur: Islamic Academy of Science of Malaysia, 1994).

66. Mohamed Talbi, "Islam and Dialogue: Some reflections on a current topic," *Encounter: Documents for Muslim-Christian Understanding*, nos. 11–12 (January–February 1975). This article appeared as a brochure in French under the title *Islam et dialogue: Réflexions sur un thème d'actualité* (Tunis: Maison Tunisienne de l'Edition, 1972; 2nd ed. 1979). An Arabic translation appeared in *Islamochristiana*, no. 4 (1978), pp. 1–26. See also Talbi, "Possibilities and conditions for a better understanding between Islam and the West," *Journal of Ecumenical Studies*, vol. 25 (1988), pp. 161–193, and Talbi, "Islam et Occident au-delà des affrontements, des ambiguités et des complexes," *Islamochristiana*, vol. 7 (1981), pp. 57–77.

67. Abdelwahab Bouhdiba, "L'avenir du dialogue islamo-chrétien," *Islamochristiana*, vol. 15 (1989), pp. 87–93; Gino Cerbella, "Il dialogo tra Cristiani e Musulmani nel pensiero di Ahmed Taleb," *Africa*, vol. 26 (1971), pp. 219–223; and Saād Ghrab, "Islam and Christianity: From opposition to dialogue," *Islamochristiana*, vol. 13 (1987), pp. 99–111.

68. In English a translation appeared: Muslim-Christian Research Group, *The Challenge of the Scriptures* (Maryknoll, N.Y.: Orbis Books, 1989). Other publications are: GRIC, *Foi et justice: Un défi pour le christianisme et pour l'islam* (Paris: Centurion, 1993); GRIC, *Pluralisme et laïcité. Chrétiens et musulmans proposent*. Paris: Bayard/Centurion, 1996.

69. See the contribution by Karel A. Steenbrink, "The Pancasila Ideology and an Indonesian Muslim Theology of Religions"(chapter 19 in this volume). Thomas Mooren, "Einige Hinweise zum apologetischen Schrifttum des Islam in Indonesien," *Zeitschrift für Missionswissenschaft und Religionswissenschaft*, vol. 66 (1982), pp. 163–182. See in particular H. Tarmizi Taher, *Aspiring for the Middle Path. Religious Harmony in Indonesia*. Jakarta: Center for the Study of Islam and Society (CENSIS), 1997.

70. For different views among Muslims concerning dialogue with Christians, see the contribution of Ekkehard Rudolph, "The Debate on Muslim-Christian Dialogue as Reflected in Muslim Periodicals in Arabic (1970–1991)" (chapter 20 in this volume). Compare Rudolph, *Dialogues islamo-chrétiens 1950–1993: Introduction historique suivie d'une bibliographie étendue des sources arabes* (Cahier No. 1, Département interfacultaire d'histoire et de sciences des religions, Université de Lausanne, December 1993). This Cahier has a useful introduction (in German or in French) on the history of some 40 years of organized Muslim-Christian dialogues.

71. On the history of the rise of history of religions in Turkey, see Hikmet Tanyu, "Türkiye'de dinler tarihi'nin tarihçesi," in *Ankara Üniversitesi Ilāhiyat Fakültesi Dergisi*, vol. 8 (1961), pp. 109–124. For present-day work and publications, see Mustafa Erdem, "Türkiye'de dinler tarihi sahasında yapılmış lisansüstü tezler üzerine düşünceler," in *Türkiye I. Dinler Tarihi Arastırmaları Sempozyumu (24–25 Eylül 1992)* (Samsun, 1992), pp. 83–95.

72. Karel A. Steenbrink, "The study of comparative religion by Indonesian Muslims: A survey," *Numen*, vol. 37 (1990), pp. 141–167.

73. Jacques Waardenburg, "Observations on the scholarly study of religions as pursued in some Muslim countries," *Numen*, vol. 45 (1998), pp. 235–257. Compare Waardenburg, *Islam et sciences des religions: Huit leçons au Collège de France* (Paris: Les Belles Lettres, 1998).

II

MEDIEVAL TIMES

5

Christians in the Qur'ān and Tafsīr

JANE DAMMEN MCAULIFFE

From its inception Islam has lived with other religions. Its emergent self-definition evolved through a process of differentiation from other contemporary belief systems. As textual attestation to this process, Islam's foundational Scripture offers abundant evidence of varied interreligious concerns and connections. For example, a primary theological assessment created the fundamental categorization of believer/unbeliever, while further particularization recognized such groupings as Christians, Jews, Majūs, Ṣābi'ūn, idolators, and so on. Those generations of scholars who then explicated the Qur'ān sought and stabilized the referents for these terms as they elaborated the theological judgments to which they found textual allusion. From this interplay of the Qur'ān and its exegesis arose a fluctuating ethos of interreligious perspectives, prescriptions, and proscriptions. One aspect of this ethos captures the Muslim attitudes to Christians and Christianity as classically defined and transmitted. Certainly, the full scope of this can only be read out as countless Muslim sources which incorporate exegetical elements. The brief exemplification that follows can do no more than evoke some small sense of this vast and centuries-long process of exegetical amplification of the Qur'ānic text.

Collection and Classification

Qur'ānic statements that refer to Christianity may be provisionally put into two general categories.[1] The first category would include allusions to prominent Christian figures, especially Maryam and ʿĪsā b. Maryam, and to the theological assertions which have for so long preoccupied Muslim polemicists and Christian apologists. There is no need to rehearse the principal scenes of that debate and the long history of charges and countercharges which it has provoked. What Christians term the doctrines of the Incarnation and the Trinity, Muslims have frequently excoriated as the blasphemies of divine reproduction and tritheism. Study of the Qur'ānic Jesus has also received considerable attention, enough, in fact, to have generated a book-length bibliography about 20 years ago and, more recently, an English-language monograph on this topic has been published.[2] Although the Qur'ānic figure of Maryam has not attracted commensurate attention, interest in the topic continues unabated.[3]

The second category would be one which includes the references to Christians (through a variety of verbal designations) as a particular religious group. I refer to this as a general and provisional form of classification because taxonomic precision can only be consequent upon the interplay of text and interpretation. On first reading of the Qur'ānic text, what constitutes a Qur'ānic reference to Christians as a social group ranges from the unequivocal to the ambiguous. At one end of that spectrum stand those verses which contain the Arabic noun *al-naṣārā*, the common Qur'ānic term for Christians, and a word which is found seven times in *al-Baqarah* (S. 2), five times in *al-Mā'idah* (S. 5), and once each in *al-Tawbah* (S. 9) and *al-Ḥajj* (S. 22). Beyond such univocal designation lies a variety of Qur'ānic phrases. Some stress the scriptural heritage which Jews, Christians, and Muslims have in common and their mutual blessing as beneficiaries of divine revelation. These alternative modes of denotation include the title *ahl al-kitāb*, which occurs more than 30 times in the Qur'ān, and expressions such as "those who were given the book" (*alladhīna ūtū al-kitāb*), "those to whom We gave the book" (*alladhīna ātaynāhum al-kitāb*), "those who were given a portion of the book" (*alladhīna ūtū naṣīban min al-kitāb*), and "those who read the book before you" (*alladhīna yaqra'ūna al-kitāba min qablika*). Additional Qur'ānic referencing may be culled from passages which mention ʿĪsā and then speak of his apostles (*al-ḥawārīyūn*) or of "those who follow him" (*alladhīna ittabaʿūhu*). Moving yet further along the spectrum from clarity to ambiguity elicits inclusion of verses which make only associative reference to the Christians.[4] At this point and beyond, textual specification must be sought from exegesis, and text must be read from *tafsīr*.

Within the second provisional classification of Qur'ānic statements about Christians, further subdivision is apparent and appropriate. This category and its subclassifications, however, cannot include references to Christians alone. As the spectrum of denotation makes clear, reference to Christians is frequently made in tandem with reference to Jews. Apart from the term *al-naṣārā* and mention of ʿĪsā and his apostles or followers, Qur'ānic phraseology has been generally interpreted to carry at least dual applicability. Christians, Jews, and, occasionally, Ṣābi'ūn and Majūs are understood to fall within the scope of the phrases just mentioned. Bearing such multiple applicability in mind, it should now be useful to sketch the subdivisions within this category of nontheological references to Christians—that is, references to Christians as a particular religious group. The largest of these subdivisions contains direct or indirect criticism. Among the most persistent charges are the following: (1) Christians fight one another and divide into sects; (2) some do not follow Jesus' message; (3) they are tritheists and make a god of Jesus; (4) they make vainglorious statements; (5) they want Muslims to follow the Christian religion; and, most comprehensively, (6) they are transgressors and do evil. Additional charges condemn perceived aspects of scriptural transmission and of Christian monasticism.

A second grouping can be made of those verses that seek to guide Muslim behavior toward Christians, both socially and economically, such as reference to the collection of a special tax, the *jizyah*, levied on Christians (and others of the *ahl al-kitāb*) and provisions for the protection of existing churches and cloisters. Representative examples of this category include both cautionary strictures, such as those which urge Muslims not to make friends with Christians, and more positive calls for interreligious understanding and altruistic competition.

Verses that make ostensibly positive remarks about the Christians compose the final subcategory. As I have published a monograph on this group of verses, I include references to them here only among the representative case studies which I shall present.[5]

Concentrating on al-Naṣārā

To exemplify this preliminary taxonomy and to provide some sense of its range and diversity, I will draw specific verses from the three subdivisions just outlined. In an effort to mount a discussion which is as focused as the constraints of space permit, my choice is limited to those verses that make unequivocal reference to Christians—that is, those which use the term *al-naṣārā*. In addition to specifying particular verses, I also must select those voices from within the full exegetical tradition who can serve as representatives for some of the principal periods and perspectives. It may thus be helpful at this juncture to provide a very brief excursus on the genre of Islamic literature known as *ʿilm al-tafsīr* and a few of its major practitioners.

Surveys of the exegetical discipline, both Muslim and non-Muslim, generally divide the subject chronologically into two main periods, classical and modern/contemporary. While a great deal of recent attention in Western scholarship on the Qur'ān has concentrated on the preclassical period, the vast bulk of published material falls into the two categories just noted. It would be a mistake, however, to present these two periods of exegetical scholarship as discontinuous. Classical and modern *tafāsīr* represent, in the main, a fundamentally coherent and internally consistent body of literature. Having developed within the confines of a limited number of hermeneutical principles, Qur'ānic commentary is a remarkably uninterrupted craft, whose contemporary practitioners are fully conversant with their tenth-, twelfth-, and fourteenth-century counterparts. This very cohesiveness has led some contemporary scholars of the genre to question the usefulness of applying the adjective "modern," with its present epistemological and sociopolitical connotations, to most nineteenth- and twentieth-century commentaries.

In addition to this basic chronological categorization, the products of exegetical activity are usually classified according to their fundamental methodological orientation. Those which emphasize the interpretive statements enshrined in the Prophetic *ḥadīth* and its ancillary reports are assigned to the category of *al-tafsīr bi-al-maʾthūr*—that is, interpretation by the received tradition. Preservation and transmission of applicable *ḥadīth*s and verification of their trains of transmission (*isnād*s) constitute the essential responsibilities of this form of Qurʾānic exegesis. The complementary categorization, which is either lauded or disparaged, depending on one's theological assessment of it, is termed *al-tafsīr bi-al-raʾy*—that is, interpretation which expands the exegetical agenda to include doctrinal, philosophical, or mystical considerations.

Keeping in mind these fundamental forms of classification, both chronological and ideological, I have chosen three *mufassirūn* as the primary sources for this essay. The first of these is Abū Jaʿfar Muḥammad b. Jarīr al-Ṭabarī, the undisputed foundation upon which the edifice of classical *tafsīr* was erected. Born about 224/838 in the former Sāsānid province of Ṭabaristān, his youth encompassed the normal educational progression, beginning with studies in his native city of Āmul but moving well beyond that in his more mature years to major centers of learning in Iraq, Syria, and Egypt. The principal venue, however, for his years of scholarly productivity was the ʿAbbāsid city of Baghdād. It is here that he completed his two monumental contributions to Islamic literature, his notional history of the world, *Taʾrīkh al-rusul wa-al-mulūk* (The history of messengers and kings), and his commentary on the Qurʾān entitled *Jāmiʿ al-bayān ʿan taʾwīl āy al-Qurʾān* (The comprehensive clarification of the interpretation of the verses of the Qurʾān). It is here, too, that he died in 310/923.[6] *Jāmiʿ al-bayān*, with its compilation and methodical arrangement of the first two and a half centuries of Muslim exegesis, inaugurates the classical period of Islamic exegetical activity. In his recent remarks on this work John Burton judges that it "abruptly scaled heights not previously glimpsed and never subsequently approached."[7] It is usually judged to be a particularly important example of *al-tafsīr bi-al-maʾthūr* because of the enormous number of exegetical *ḥadīth*s which it incorporates.

To represent the category of *al-tafsīr bi-al-raʾy* and the achievement of developed classical exegesis, I have selected the medieval *mufassir*, Muḥammad b. ʿUmar Fakhr al-Dīn al-Rāzī. Born in 543/1149 or 544/1150 in the Persian city of Rayy, al-Rāzī ranks among the most significant intellects produced by the Islamic Middle Ages. He was educated initially by his father and then proceeded to study with prominent scholars of *fiqh*, *kalām*, and *falsafah*. In his adult years he traveled widely in the western part of Central Asia, securing supportive patronage at various courts. Eventually he settled in Herāt under the sponsorship of Ghiyāth al-Dīn, the Sulṭān of Ghaznah, who permitted him to open a madrasah within the precincts of the palace. Fakhr al-Dīn died in Herāt on the feast day following the fast of Ramaḍān (*ʿīd al-fiṭr*) in 606/1210.[8]

Al-Rāzī's *tafsīr*, entitled *Mafātīḥ al-ghayb* (The keys of the unseen—a phrase found in *al-Anʿām* [S. 6]:59), is a massive work of 32 volumes in the most widely available edition. It is commonly printed under the title *al-Tafsīr al-kabīr* (The great commentary), a titular evaluation of both its length and importance. Replete with philosophical and theological erudition, its relative paucity of transmitted exegetical material makes it quite different from the much traditional *al-tafsīr bi-al-maʾthūr*.[9] Yet such elements are not completely excluded. Rather, numerous earlier authorities, whom he engages in a wide-ranging exegetical discourse, are selectively used to offer subsidiary support to those arguments and interests upon which al-Rāzī has chosen to focus.

To present contemporary currents in *tafsīr*, I draw on the Shīʿī exegete, Muḥammad Ḥusayn Ṭabāṭabāʾī, an Iranian scholar who died a few years after the revolutionary events of 1979. Born in Tabrīz in 1321/1903, he was educated in that city before moving to Najaf for further study. There Ṭabāṭabāʾī pursued advanced studies in *uṣūl al-fiqh* and began work on such major sources as the *Shifāʾ* of Ibn Sīnā and the *Asfār* of Ṣadr al-Dīn Shīrāzī (Mullā Ṣadrā, d. 1050/1642). In 1353/1934 Ṭabāṭabāʾī returned to Tabrīz where he continued his work as a teacher and writer. After World War II he settled in the pilgrimage city of Qum, the intellectual center of Persian Shīʿism,[10] where he taught chiefly in the fields of *tafsīr* and philosophical mysticism. Ṭabāṭabāʾī, who died on 18 Muḥarram (5 November) 1403/1982, lived to be 80 years old. Almost half of those years were spent in

Qum, where he gained a reputation which spread far beyond its boundaries.

His *al-Mīzān fī tafsīr al-Qur'ān* (The measure of balance in the interpretation of the Qur'ān) testifies to his broad scholarly background and abiding interest in comparative religion and philosophy. In addition to etymological and grammatical discussions, it combines his own thoughts and elucidations of the passage under consideration with discourses on its moral implications or mystical-philosophical ramifications. Also included with some frequency are excerpts from *ḥadīth* collections and from previous commentaries, particularly those of al-ʿAyyāshī (d. 320/932), al-Qummī (d. 328/939), and al-Ṭabarsī (d. 548/1153).[11]

From the perspective of these three representative *tafāsīr*, I can now preface the investigation of my selected verses with some attention to the word *al-naṣārā* itself. The basic etymological study of this term, which was done by Josef Horovitz, provides a Syriac derivation for it and notes cognates in such other languages as Mandaic and Ethiopic.[12] In an early study Richard Bell remarked that *al-naṣārā* had "become the usual name for Christians in Arabic, and as such was in use amongst the Arabs before Muḥammad's time."[13] All but three references to *al-naṣārā* are to be found in *al-Baqarah* (S. 2) and *al-Mā'idah* (S. 5).[14] The very first of these qur'ānic mentions, one which makes an apparently positive association, appears in verse 62 of *al-Baqarah*:

> Truly those who believe and those who are Jews, the Christians and the Ṣābi'ūn, whoever believes in God and the Last Day and does right, for them is their reward near their Lord; they will have no fear, neither will they grieve.

Given the sequential nature of the exegetical task, for many commentators this verse quite naturally prompted the most extensive discussion of the term. In his own consideration, al-Ṭabarī first offers a brief presentation of alternative plurals for *al-naṣārā* and then advances three explanations for the name. The first is that this lexeme, one of whose notional root meanings in Arabic could be 'to help, offer assistance', was applied to this group "because of their support (*nuṣrah*) for each other and their offering mutual assistance (*tanāṣur*) among themselves."[15] The second is that these people were associated with a place called *Nāṣirah*, with ʿĪsā himself being called "the Nazarene" (*al-Nāṣirī*). The third is that its etymology is Qur'ānic, being based on ʿĪsā's question to his disciples as recorded in *al-Ṣaff* (S. 61):14: "Who will be my helpers (*anṣār*) for God?" (The word here translated as 'helpers' is yet another form of the Arabic radicals NṢR from which *al-naṣārā* was thought to be formed. Thus this third derivational hypothesis is really a variant on the first.) Clearly the preferred explanation in al-Ṭabarī's view is the second, as indicated by the number of *ḥadīth*s he records in support of it. In several of these *ḥadīth*s more precise identification is made and *Nāṣirah* is specifically identified as the village where ʿĪsā used to live (i.e., Nazareth).[16]

In *al-Tafsīr al-kabīr* Fakhr al-Dīn al-Rāzī pays relatively little attention to the etymology of this term. While he does include reference to the *ḥadīth*s usually associated with the customary etymologies, his treatment is concise and derivative.[17] It concludes with a direct quotation from the eleventh-century commentary of Maḥmūd b. ʿUmar al-Zamakhsharī, where that author insists that the Christians are so designated because they "helped" (*naṣarū*) the Messiah.[18] While Muḥammad Ḥusayn Ṭabāṭabā'ī opts for the geographical etymology first noted in al-Ṭabarī, his discussion indicates a closer familiarity with the Gospel narratives than that expressed by either of the other commentators: the word is associated "with a village called *Nāṣirah* in the land of Syria where ʿĪsā and Maryam lived after their return from Egypt."[19]

Three Case Studies from al-Mā'idah

In the chronology of Qur'ānic disclosure offered by Nöldeke, *al-Mā'idah*, the fifth *sūrah* of the Qur'ān, stands as substantially the last to be revealed.[20] (As an aside, I should observe that the schemata developed by both Muslim and non-Muslim scholars that place the *sūrahs*, or parts thereof, within different periods of Muḥammad's life have been called into question by recent revisionist historiography. Nevertheless, such chronological determinations remain an operative part of qur'ānic exegetical literature, the genre with which I am here concerned.[21]) From that *sūrah* may be drawn exemplars of each of the three categories into which I have classified the Qur'ānic references to Christians as a social group. I have chosen one verse which makes explicit reference to *al-naṣārā* as representative of each category.

al-Māʾidah (S. 5):14

The first verse selected for this sampling of exegetical material falls within the category of accusations made against the Christians. Structurally this verse combines a divine charge of religious inconstancy with a report of the divinely prompted consequences of that inconstancy. The concluding statement reinforces this declaration of past misconduct and its repercussions with a stern prediction of future accountability. Although any translation of the Arabic text inevitably begs some of the exegetical issues, a provisional rendering of *al-Māʾidah* (S. 5):14 is as follows:

> We made covenant (*al-mīthāq*) with those who say "We are Christians" but they forgot a portion of that of which they were reminded. So We provoked hatred (*al-ʿadāwah*) and enmity (*al-baghḍāʾ*) among them until the Day of Resurrection when God will announce to them what they were doing.

Three issues preoccupy al-Ṭabarī as he analyzes this passage, preoccupations which then become the basic agenda for subsequent commentators. The first issue constitutes a quasi-legal specification of the terms of the convenant or contract (*al-mīthāq*) which the Christians are accused of forgetting. Enumerating the particulars of covenanted behavior affords al-Ṭabarī an opportunity to list the specific demands: to obey God, to perform the mandated religious duties (*farāʾiḍ*), and to follow and give credence to God's messengers.[22] The contrasting accusations are phrased more generally, linking Christian conduct to the parallel malfeasance of the Jews and to a comprehensive infringement of covenantal commitment. A *ḥadīth* from Qatādah b. Diʿāmah (d. 177/735) makes somewhat more explicit reference to their forgetting "the book of God in their midst (*bayna aẓhurihim*)," an allegation which echoes the qurʾānic mention (*al-Baqarah* [S. 2]:101) of "a group of those who were brought the book" but who "toss the book of God behind their backs" (*warāʾa ẓuhūrihim*).[23]

Although he is concerned about lexical precision in the use of the terms enmity (*al-ʿadāwah*) and hatred (*al-baghḍāʾ*), al-Ṭabarī's second line of analysis allows him to concentrate on ascertaining what aspects of religious misbehavior were consequent to God's "provocation."[24] Dividing his exegetical attestations into two groups, he proposes alternative interpretations and then indicates his preference for one of them. The implicit logic of al-Ṭabarī's categorization creates a sequential rather than parallel ordering. In the first line of interpretation, all of whose attestations go back to the Successor Abū ʿImrān Ibrāhīm b. Yazīd al-Nakhaʿī (d. 96/715), the objects of divine provocation are the heretical views (*al-ahwāʾ*) and disputatious quarrels about religion to which these people incite each other.[25]

The alternative understanding, culled from a *ḥadīth* attributed to Qatādah, places the blame at the more fundamental level of neglecting the book of God and disobeying his prophets.[26] Religious division and reciprocal animosity are subsequent effects of the underlying enmity and hatred that God makes consequent to neglect and disobedience. Abū Jaʿfar, however, prefers al-Nakhaʿī's interpretation and notes that Christian antagonism in particular revolves chiefly around differing doctrines about the Messiah.[27]

In itself, this preference provides a clue to al-Ṭabarī's adjudication of the third, and final, exegetical concern prompted by this verse. The phrase "between/among them" has been understood in terms of either Jewish/Christian enmity or intra-Christian religious rivalry. Again al-Ṭabarī elects the second of these two options, the one transmitted from al-Rabīʿ b. Anas (d. 139/756). Here the justification used is a straightforward argument from Qurʾānic context and structure. The *ḥadīth* from al-Rabīʿ itself draws a parallel with the malediction made about the Jews, somewhat later in this *sūrah* (5:64), after their being charged with having declared the hand of God fettered. Al-Ṭabarī adds to this structural parallelism the contextual contention that God had completed his reference to the Jews in verses prior to this one and then begun a statement about the Christians.[28] It is interesting to note, however, that when basing his argument on Qurʾānic context al-Ṭabarī feels he must add a disclaimer relativizing his choice as simply somewhat closer to the mark.

Fakhr al-Dīn al-Rāzī introduces a new consideration by refusing to take the phrase "with those who say 'We are Christians'" at face value. He points out that God could simply have said "with the Christians." That He chose not do so indicates to al-Rāzī that the individuals thus designated are not really Christians but only false claimants to the name. Echoing the etymological exegesis of *al-naṣārā* previously given, this commentator connects the name to the apostles' statement to ʿĪsā in *al-Ṣaff* that "we are God's helpers"(*qāla al-ḥawārīyūna naḥnu anṣāru allāh*) and insists that it is a name expressing praise (*ism madḥ*). These people may call themselves Christians, concludes al-Rāzī, but that does not make them so in God's eyes.[29]

In addressing the issue of covenant, Fakhr al-Dīn quite specifically glosses the terms of God's covenant as "what is written in the Injīl about their believing in Muḥammad" and further asserts that the "forgotten portion" was precisely this, the most consequential and important part.[30] Although he lists the possibility that the verse may refer to animosity between Christians and Jews, the full thrust of his exegesis on this passage supports its significance as intra-Christian antagonism. Noting that Christians "will call each other infidels until the Day of Resurrection," al-Rāzī draws attention to a parallel prediction in *al-An'ām* (S. 6):65.[31]

With the contemporary exegesis of Muḥammad Ḥusayn Ṭabāṭabā'ī, contextual considerations achieve a prominence that is far less marked in his predecessors. Ṭabāṭabā'ī customarily groups verses within a *sūrah* into what he considers to be exegetically meaningful units and in this instance has collected verses 8–14 as unified by a common regard for matters both temporal and eternal in their individual and their collective aspects.[32] Absent from his exegesis is any equivocation about whether the verse connotes both Christians and Jews or any specification of the reference to covenant. Rather, Ṭabāṭabā'ī chooses to contrast the teaching of 'Īsā, which he characterizes as a call to compassion, peace, and reconciliation, with the historical realities of war, enmity, and hatred. "Forgetting a portion" thus means ignoring or neglecting the teaching of Jesus, an entirely intra-Christian condemnation.

Ṭabāṭabā'ī elaborates this charge in a manner that moves it far beyond the earlier exegetes' emphasis on intrareligious wrangles and accusations. Remarking how deeply rooted *enmity and hatred* have become among the Christians, he notes that over time doctrinal disagreement grew fixed and ever more divisive, "continuing to augment and increase until it changed to wars, battles, invasions and the various sorts of flight and attack."[33] The culminating horrors of such intrareligious enmity are, for him, this century's great world wars with their human annihilation and devastation of the earth.

al-Mā'idah (S. 5):51

Within the second category of Qur'ānic statements about Christians, the class of verses which seek to guide Muslim behavior toward Christians both socially and economically, stands another passage from *al-Mā'idah*. Addressed to the "believers," it replicates a common Qur'ānic rhetorical structure: a command with explication followed by injunctive declarations. Like many of the passages relevant to this essay, it also links Christians with Jews in a joint applicability. A preliminary translation of 5:51 is as follows:

> O you who believe, do not take Jews and Christians as friends/allies (*awliyā'*). They are friends of one another. Whoever of you makes friends with them is one of them. God does not guide the wrong-doing people (*al-qawm al-ẓālimīn*).

Al-Ṭabarī turns immediately to considerations of the *asbāb al-nuzūl* for this verse. What were the particular situations which prompted its revelation? The three incidents which he relates became the standard historical explanations in subsequent *tafāsīr*. Two of these episodes are attached to named individuals, while a third has less precise attribution. The first contrasts the behavior of 'Ubādah b. al-Ṣāmit with that of 'Abdallāh b. Ubayy.[34] Both were among the *Anṣār* of Medina who had long-standing affiliations with Jewish tribes of that city. Whereas 'Ubādah publicly renounced his confederacy with the Banū Qaynuqā', Ibn Ubayy did not.[35] Another of the *Anṣār*, Abū Lubābah b. 'Abd al-Mundhir was similarly chastised for treachery in his dealings with the Banū Qurayẓah at the time when Muḥammad was preparing to move against them. Sent to consult with their tribal elders, Abū Lubābah gesturally denied his spoken assurances by drawing his hand across his neck to indicate that a slaughter was being planned.[36] The third incident which al-Ṭabarī collects with the *asbāb al-nuzūl* of this verse names no individuals but recounts efforts at the time of the battle of Uhud to secure alliances with Jews and Christians should the engagement turn against the Muslims.[37]

Having systematically presented these three possible *asbāb al-nuzūl*, al-Ṭabarī promptly refuses precedence to any of them.[38] While all are possible, none predominates. The verse's imperative therefore should apply to all attempts "to take the Jews and Christians as supporters (*anṣār*) and allies (*ḥulafā'*) against the people who believe in God and His Messenger."[39] Consequently, al-Ṭabarī's understanding of the phrase "they are friends of one another" reiterates reference to these alliances which Christians and Jews make, both among themselves and with each other, against the Muslims.

The consequences of such confederations are further clarified with the declaration that "whoever of you makes friends with them is one of them." The fundamental argument here is a staple of social psychology: to forge an alliance is but the prelude to a change of allegiance. Political association becomes religious affiliation.[40] The *ḥadīths* presented on the authority of ʿAbdallāh b. ʿAbbās (d. 68/687–688) address the obvious social concerns of eating Christian slaughtered animals (*dhabāʾiḥ*) and marrying Christian women,[41] while the verse itself reaches culmination in a clear pronouncement of wrongdoing (*ẓulm*) against those who seek such connections with Christians and Jews.

While citing only one of the three *asbāb al-nuzūl* which al-Ṭabarī presented, Fakhr al-Dīn al-Rāzī ratifies al-Ṭabarī's nonrestrictive interpretation. According to Fakhr al-Dīn, the command not to take the Christians and Jews as friends means "do not depend upon seeking their assistance and do not show affection for them" (*lā taʿtamidū ʿalā al-istinṣārihim wa-lā tatawaddadū ilayhim*).[42] In explicating the assertion that "whoever of you makes friends with them is one of them," he draws a Qurʾānic parallel with the verse in *al-Baqarah* (S. 2):249 where Saul uses abstaining from the river's water as a test of his army's solidarity. Quoting from Ibn ʿAbbās, al-Rāzī asserts that such revelations as 5:51 and 2:249 are the necessary boundary markers of religious difference.

To illustrate the concluding phrase of this verse, Fakhr al-Dīn recounts an exchange between the governor of Baṣrah, Abū Mūsā al-Ashʿarī (d. 42/662), and ʿUmar b. al-Khaṭṭāb, the second Caliph. When Abū Mūsā attempted to justify his employment of a Christian secretary ʿUmar recited this verse to him. Abū Mūsā retorted with the remark, "To him is his religion and to me is his secretarial skill" (*lahu dīnuhu wa liya kitābatuhu*), an obvious play on the concluding verse of *al-Kāfirūn: lakum dīnukum wa liya dīni* (S. 109). But once again ʿUmar urged severance with the injunction: "Do not honor them [Christians] when God has debased them; do not exalt them when God has humbled them; and do not draw them near when God has distanced them."[43] As Abū Mūsā continued to insist on the man's indispensability, ʿUmar reasoned that were he to die he would have to be replaced and thus urged Abū Mūsā to act as if that were the case and to get rid of him now. With this dramatic little scenario Fakhr al-Dīn concludes his exegesis of this verse.

Moving from the tenth through the thirteenth to the twentieth century produces a profound change of interpretive orientation on this verse. While al-Ṭabarī had pressed beyond the limitations inherent in identifying the verse with a particular *sabab al-nuzūl* to a more comprehensive connotation, Ṭabāṭabāʾī rejects this move as still unacceptably restricted. He repeats the *asbāb al-nuzūl* presented by al-Ṭabarī but then finds contradiction in their very plurality and in the fact that none of them reflect specific connection with Christians.[44] A clue to the direction which Ṭabāṭabāʾī's own interpretation will take may be found in the gloss which al-Rāzī used to express the meaning of "do not take Jews and Christians as friends": "Do not depend upon seeking their assistance and do not show affection for them." While the first part of this repeats al-Ṭabarī's prohibition of contractual alliances, the second phrase points ahead to the interpretive turn taken by Ṭabāṭabāʾī.

This contemporary exegete centers his argument directly on the semantics of *walāyah* (or *wilāyah*), an Arabic *maṣdar* whose basic meanings include friendship/support and authority/power and which is the concept underlying this verse's reference to *awliyāʾ* (friends/allies).[45] Unlike his predecessors, Ṭabāṭabāʾī refuses to support an understanding of *walāyah* as only alliance, sworn allegiance, or supportive association. Rather, he argues, it must also include *walāyah* as love and affection—that is, the sentiments of close and enduring friendship. Recognizing that this is a less tolerant reading of the verse, Ṭabāṭabāʾī supports his contention with several lines of debate. As a rhetorical item of evidence, he points to the first two consecutive statements in this verse and contends that because *awliyāʾ* in the second of these means only affective relations it must convey the same significance in the first. Had God intended otherwise He would have said, "Do not make alliances (*lā tuḥālifū*) with the Jews and Christians; they are allies (*ḥulafāʾ*) of each other."[46]

Another approach adopted is intra-Qurʾānic attestation (*tafsīr al-Qurʾān bi-al-Qurʾān*). Ṭabāṭabāʾī immediately draws attention to the parallel verse in *al-Mumtaḥanah* (S. 60):1 which forbids friendship with God's enemies by employing a term, *al-mawaddah*, which unequivocally connotes affective relationships.[47] His second textual parallel, *Āl ʿImrān* (S. 3):28, forbids making friends (*awliyāʾ*) with *al-kāfirūn*, a term which Ṭabāṭabāʾī straightforwardly glosses as including Christians, Jews, and *mushrikūn*.[48] Arguing historically, he notes that at the time when *Āl ʿImrān* was revealed, the Prophet certainly had alliances (*al-muʿāhadāt*) and treaties (*al-muwādaʿat*) with both

Jews and *mushrikūn* and, therefore, the *walāyah* intended can only be that of love and affection.[49]

Yet another proof for his position is built on a distinction made between the phrase "Jews and Christians" and the phrase *ahl al-kitāb*, with the latter seen as a term of approbation for a group to whom the prohibition against friendship does not apply. Looking ahead to 5:57, which begins just as the present verse does, Ṭabāṭabā'ī notes the qualifying phrase—that is, those of this group "who take your religion in disdain and jest," which accompanies the designation "those who were given the book before you" (*min alladhīna ūtū al-kitāba min qablikum*)."[50] Thus circumscribed, the designation ceases to be a praiseworthy one and descends to the same level as the appellation 'Jews and Christians'.

Having so forcefully buttressed his claim that the *walāyah* proscribed by this verse is not limited to political, social, or economic alliances but extends to the realm of affective relationships, Ṭabāṭabā'ī applies this understanding to the subsequent phrases of the verse.[51] The phrase "they are friends of one another" assumes, for him, a contemporary politico-military connotation. Although cognizant of Christian denominationalism and Jewish sectarianism, Ṭabāṭabā'ī asserts that both are unified, among and between themselves, in their enmity to Islam. Speaking to his Muslim readers, the author warns that Christians and Jews, "despite their internal division and cleavages, are as one power against you and thus nothing is to be gained from drawing close to them in affection and love."[52] To engage in such behavior is to leave the path of guidance and to join those deemed "wrong-doers."

al-Mā'idah (S. 5):82

The most striking example of Qur'ānic praise of Christians occurs in *al-Mā'idah* (S. 5):82. This verse figures prominently in virtually all attempts to base Muslim-Christian rapprochement on specific Qur'ānic texts. The passage itself constitutes an exegetical challenge of considerable proportions. Within the verse one finds a configuration of five categories: Jews, idolaters (*mushrikūn*), "those who believe," Christians, and priests and monks (*qissīsūn wa-ruhbān*). Obviously issues of identification will occupy a considerable portion of the exegetical effort expended on this pericope, as will the desire to ascertain the circumstances surrounding this revelation (*asbāb al-nuzūl*). One possible translation of *al-Mā'idah* (S. 5):82 is as follows:

> You will find the people most intensely hostile to the believers are the Jews and the idolaters. You will surely find those closest in friendship to those who believe to be those who say "We are Christians." That is because among them are priests and monks and because they are not arrogant.

Al-Ṭabarī begins his discussion of this verse with a rapid survey of the principal groups mentioned and then proceeds to evaluate the various views proposed about the occasion for its revelation. The first of two competing theories advanced is that which associates this verse with the contact made between Muḥammad and the Najāshī, the Abyssinian king.[53] Different scenarios for this are sketched, but the first one presented by al-Ṭabarī on the authority of Sa'īd b. Jubayr (d. 95/714) runs as follows. The Najāshī sent a delegation of his Christian subjects to the Prophet who recited from the Qur'ān for them. As they listened, they were overcome and immediately declared themselves Muslims. Upon their return to the Najāshī, they told him all they had learned and he, too, entered Islam and remained a believer until his death.[54]

Subsequent *ḥadīth*s included in al-Ṭabarī's commentary flesh out this brief sketch. One such from Mujāhid b. Jabr adds the fact that this Christian delegation formed part of the group that returned with Ja'far b. Abī Ṭālib from Abyssinia. Another, more lengthy *ḥadīth* from Ibn 'Abbās fills in the background with an account of what occurred during the first Muslim emigration to Abyssinia.[55] Among the group that later returned to the Prophet, according to a *ḥadīth* from Ismā'īl b. 'Abd al-Raḥmān al-Suddī (d. 128/745), were a number of Abyssinian priests and monks. These were the ones who were so struck by the Qur'ānic verses recited by Muḥammad that they immediately converted. They then went back to the Najāshī and convinced him of the validity of this new religion so that he too converted and returned with them to Muḥammad. This *ḥadīth* closes with the statement that the king died on this trip and when the news reached Muḥammad, he prayed for him.

Quite different is the second major interpretive theory advanced to identify these Christians. This one is far less specific or colorful. Rather it views the phrase "those who say 'We are Christians'" as a general reference to those who in an earlier time believed in Jesus and followed his teaching. "However when

God sent His Prophet, Muḥammad, they acknowledged him as a true prophet and believed in him, recognizing that what he brought was the truth."[56]

Al-Ṭabarī balances these two theories with a third which acknowledges the insufficiency of available information, a recognition to be found not infrequently in his commentary. He grounds himself in a very literal reading of the text, from which he seems loath to extrapolate. All that can be asserted, according to the exegete, is that God described a people who say "We are Christians" and whom the Prophet would find friendliest to the believers. "But," al-Ṭabarī emphatically asserts, "He did not name them for us."[57] It may be that the Najāshī and those around him were meant or perhaps the pre-Islamic followers of Jesus were intended. This exegete maintains that the text offers no real support for either option.

Fakhr al-Dīn al-Rāzī begins his commentary on this verse by reinforcing the divine castigation of the Jews. He sees in the near juxtaposition of the words "the Jews" and "the idolaters" a measure of the degree of Jewish belligerence, a curious argument from lexical placement. He repeats the prophetic *ḥadīth* which brands all Jews as potential Muslim-killers and quotes those who speak of a generalized Jewish hostility. "Jewish teaching requires them to inflict evil (*īṣāl al-sharr*) by any means on those who oppose them in religion. If they can do so by killing, then they choose that way. Otherwise they act by forcible seizure of property or robbery or any sort of cheating, deception and trickery."[58]

The Christians, on the other hand, are characterized as more mildly mannered. Fakhr al-Dīn al-Rāzī contrasts their ethics with those of the Jews by saying that "in their religion causing harm is forbidden" (*al-īdhā' fī dīnihim ḥarām*)."[59] Yet he is certainly unwilling to view all Christians in so flattering a light. Fakhr al-Dīn al-Rāzī cites Ibn ʿAbbās, Saʿīd b. Jubayr, ʿAṭā' b. Abī Rabāḥ (d. 114/732) and al-Suddī as referents for the association of this verse with the Najāshī and his associates. It is the only specification he proposes. He immediately follows it with the caution that certainly the verse does not mean all Christians (*jamīʿ al-naṣārā*), given the visible evidence of their animosity toward Muslims (*ẓuhūr ʿadāwatihim lil-muslimīn*).

Ṭabāṭabā'ī takes the initial approach of contextual analysis and sees this verse as crowning the fifth *sūrah*'s treatment of the *ahl al-kitāb*. Earlier verses have detailed the errors of the *ahl al-kitāb*, both moral and doctrinal, so the revelation concludes with a more general statement about the various religious groups, relating them to the Muslims and their religion. The *mushrikūn* are included "so that the discussion of the impact of Islam on non-Muslims, relative to how near or far they are from accepting it, should be complete."[60]

In commenting on the matter of greater Christian amicability, this exegete takes issue with one stream of traditional exegesis on this verse. To think that the divine commendation is based on the response of a particular group of Christians does violence to the logic of the text.[61] "If the coming to believe of a group had authenticated it, then the Jews and *mushrikūn* would have to be reckoned like the Christians and credited with the same attributes, since a group of Jews became Muslims . . . and a number of *mushrikūn* from Arabia became Muslims; in fact, today they are the generality of Muslims."[62] The very specification of the Christians, then, is proof of their greater receptivity to Islam and more positive response to the Prophet.

Without actually using the term *dhimmah*, which is commonly used by Muslim authors to designate the legal status of the *ahl al-kitāb*, Ṭabāṭabā'ī describes the options available to the various groups of newly subject people at the dawn of Islamic history. The Christians could choose between staying in their religion and paying a tax, the *jizyah*, or accepting Islam and fighting in its name. For the *mushrikūn* there was no choice other than accepting the Islamic summons. (Ṭabāṭabā'ī does not explain that the obvious reason for this is that the *mushrikūn*, as their designation indicates, were not considered monotheists by the Muslims, as were the Jews and Christians.) The fact that they had no choice makes their numerically greater conversion rate to Islam no particular factor in their favor. That many Christians, who did have a choice, chose to become Muslims is a strong rationale for this divine commendation.

To complete his argument, Ṭabāṭabā'ī must then ask why another group of the *ahl al-kitāb*, the Jews, are not accorded equal praise. After all, they, too, have the option of remaining in their religion and paying the *jizyah* or converting to Islam. What, then, differentiates them from the Christians? Ṭabāṭabā'ī finds his answer in those perennial accusations of arrogance and racial solidarity. He adds to this the sins of treachery and scheming and claims that they "wait for disaster to befall the Muslims."[63]

Ṭabāṭabā'ī also posits historical confirmation of this greater Christian receptivity to the message of

Islam. The larger number of Jews and *mushrikūn* who became Muslims in the first years of Islam—due in large part to their geographical proximity—has given way to "Christian numerical superiority in acceptance of the Islamic summons (*daʿwah*) during past centuries."[64] So self-evident does this exegete deem the argument for Christian receptiveness that his commentary on "You will find the people most intensely hostile to the believers are the Jews" consists of nothing more than citing two qurʾānic passages (*al-Māʾidah* [S. 5]:62 and 80) which describe Jewish perfidy.

The exegetical tradition on this verse has also sought to clarify and develop the basis for its contrast of Jews and Christians. Such a concern moves beyond an interest in purely historical specification. Rather it seeks to understand the religiocultural structures that buttress the varying relations among religious groups. The focus for such an investigation is to be found in that pivotal phrase "that is because among them are priests (*qissīsīn*) and monks (*ruhbān*) and because they are not arrogant." While historical identification is not absent from the commentators' concerns, the larger interest, as evidenced by al-Ṭabarī, is the explanatory nature of this whole phrase. It is *because* of the very presence of such individuals within groups who call themselves Christians—whoever they may be—that there is such friendliness with the believers. This divinely commended amicability on the part of Christians is due to the presence among them of "a people diligent in worship (*ahl ijtihād fī al-ʿibādāt*), living monastically in cells and hermitages (*tarahhub fī al-diyārāt wa-al-ṣawāmiʿ*). They are not far from the believers due to the fact that they assent to the truth when they recognize it, and they are not too proud to accept it when they see it clearly."[65] Al-Ṭabarī then proceeds to refer to them as "people of a religion" (*ahl dīnin*), vastly different from "the Jews who habitually killed prophets and messengers, stubbornly opposed God's commands and prohibitions, and altered the revelation which He sent down in His books."[66] By implication, then, it is the very lack of a faithful remnant among the Jews which exacerbates their hostility to the Muslims and prevents the development of that concord which exists between Christians—at least a certain group of them—and Muslims.

Rather than immediately involving himself in a philological analysis of the terms *qissīsūn* and *ruhbān*, as other commentators have, Fakhr al-Dīn al-Rāzī uses the phrase as the basis for a continued analysis of Jewish-Christian differences. This time he finds a contrast not between Jewish belligerence and Christian tractability, but between Jewish greed for worldly things and Christian renunciation of them. It is this latter polarity between avidity and renunciation which generates the resultant belligerent or compliant behavior. Fakhr al-Dīn al-Rāzī locates proof for this accusation of Jewish greed in *al-Baqarah* (S. 2):96. Greed (*ḥirṣ*), says this exegete, is the root and source of discord, because "the man who is greedy for worldly things discards his religious duty in pursuit of worldly pleasures. He has the audacity to do any forbidden or abominable deed in the search for temporal goods. Naturally his hostility increases towards anyone who gains wealth and fame."[67]

The obverse of this stark picture of Jewish moral deformation is Fakhr al-Dīn al-Rāzī's idealistic depiction of Christian rectitude. He maintains that unlike the Jews (who are greedy for the world's goods), the Christians are a people who renounce temporal satisfactions (*muʿriḍūn ʿan al-dunyā*) and who turn to divine worship (*muqbilūn ʿalā al-ʿibādah*). As a result their behavior is devoid of self-aggrandizement, arrogance, and haughtiness; their inner virtue is reflected in outward action. Anyone whose eyes are diverted from worldly gain "does not envy people or hold grudges against them or quarrel with them; rather his is a nature open to the truth and prepared for compliant submission to it."[68]

Having said this, Fakhr al-Dīn al-Rāzī hastens to add a strong corrective to his complimentary portrayal of Christianity. The issue he raises is that of the nature of Christian unbelief: "The unbelief (*kufr*) of the Christians is cruder (*aghlaẓ*) than that of the Jews because the Christians dispute about matters theological and prophetical while the Jews debate only about the latter."[69] Yet the Christian lack of worldly greed and inclination toward the Hereafter partially redeems them in God's eyes, as the divine honor accorded them in this verse attests. Again, in contrast stands the divine denunciation of the Jews "whose belief is not as coarse as that of the Christians" but whose condemnation is occasioned by "their greed for worldly things."[70]

The question of how to reconcile this phrase with the Qurʾānic rejection of monasticism found in *al-Ḥadīd* (S. 57):27, as well as the Prophet's denunciation of it, is answered by Fakhr al-Dīn al-Rāzī again in terms of Christian-Jewish contrast. The point, he insists, is not that monasticism is praiseworthy in general. Rather it is something to be praised "in comparison with the Jewish way of harshness and ruthlessness" (*al-qasāwah wa-al-ghilẓah*)."[71]

Ṭabāṭabā'ī is consonant with most of the exegetical tradition in treating the concluding phrase of this verse as an explanation for Christian-Muslim friendship. Among the Christians there are three characteristics that both the Jews and the *mushrikūn* lack—that is, the presence of priests, the presence of monks, and the absence of arrogance.[72] The mention of "arrogance" provides Ṭabāṭabā'ī the opportunity for an exhortatory digression on the need for eliminating bad attitudes in order to move from knowledge of the good to right action. "Attaining the truth does not suffice to prepare one to act in accordance with it"; the individual must first "pluck from himself the attitude which is holding him back from it."[73] The obstructive attitude to which Ṭabāṭabā'ī refers is "imperiousness towards the truth because of racial pride and so forth."[74] He realizes that such attitudes do not develop in a vacuum but are greatly influenced by one's society and culture. Right thinking flourishes with societal reinforcement, as do right actions in an environment "in which it would be embarrassing for the individual to neglect them."[75] The prerequisite, then, for a society's reception of the truth is the presence in that society of learned men who know and teach it, along with men who act in accordance with it, so that people can see that it is both possible and right to do so. The people themselves must be accustomed to surrendering to the truth and must lack arrogance toward it.

These prerequisites have been met by the Christians, as the final phrase of this verse manifests. Ṭabāṭabā'ī paraphrases this section in a way that makes completely clear how the Christians have satisfied the conditions he sets: "Among them are learned men who keep reminding them of the importance of truth and the things that must be known about religion, by word; among them are ascetics (*zuhhād*) who keep reminding them of the greatness of their Lord and the significance of their earthly and heavenly fortune, by deed; and among them there is no sense of being too proud to accept the truth."[76] The exegete then catalogues the deficiencies of the Jews and *mushrikūn* which prevent them from fulfilling these divinely instituted requirements. The Jews, in spite of their learned rabbis (*aḥbār*), are disqualified because "the vice of obduracy and presumed superiority does not induce them to be ready to receive the truth."[77] The *mushrikūn* are found wanting on all three counts: not only are they bereft of learned men and of ascetics, but also they are guilty of the vice of arrogance.

Concluding Observations

While illustrative of the centuries-long process of exegetical amplification, these case studies should not be forced to yield more than the insights that can be offered by exemplification. They convey some sense of the range of Qur'ānic references to Christians and of how those references have been understood, but they are necessarily evocative rather than comprehensive. The commentators here presented represent major strands of Qur'ānic exegesis but cannot be deemed to speak for all Muslims in all periods of history.

Some contemporary Muslims may argue that even to present such material, replete with derogatory attitudes toward Christians and Jews, does a disservice to Islamic standards of tolerance. Its dissemination in Western languages might simply reinforce dangerously negative images of Islam and Muslim societies, damning the present with the past. These are important objections and ones which Christian and Jewish groups, among others, have also raised when faced with aspects of their respective intellectual and social histories that do not conform to present-day standards of human values and rights.

The only adequate response must acknowledge, once again, the inherent plurality of each religious tradition. No system of faith and practice is, or ever has been, monolithic. As products of human thought and behavior in varied historical and social contexts, they are invariably multiform. It is fair to note, therefore, that the exegetical tradition of which I have offered representative examples continues to flourish in Muslim academies and schools. The commentaries of al-Ṭabarī, Fakhr al-Dīn al-Rāzī, and Ṭabāṭabā'ī are regularly reprinted and sold in Muslim bookstores worldwide. It is also fair to note that theirs are not the only interpretive tones to which contemporary Muslim ears are attuned. Other strong, vibrant voices seek to recast the exegetical exercise, to ensure the continuing vitality of the Qur'ānic word by speaking that word within the varied forms of current intellectual discourse.

For example, in 1985 a professor at Al-Azhar published a harmonious interpretation of 5:51 as considered in relation with *al-Mumtaḥanah* (S. 60):1: "O you who believe, do not take My enemy and your enemy as friends/allies" (*awliyā'*). He remarks that "relationships have to be formed between people despite differences in religion, and all need to cooperate in various spheres" but also cautions that "these relationships have to issue from heartfelt affection and friendship, and that is not easy for anyone whose heart follows a creed differing from the others."[78] More recently, Muhammad Arkoun has urged a new Qur'ānic hermeneutic, one forged within the contemporary considerations of semantics and sociohistorical contextualization, one that will draw us back to "the long march towards meaning, a march sometimes too assured and at others thrown out of step by unexpected and overwhelming revivals of the most archaic form of religion."[79] Finally, mention can be made of a new initiative in Jordan, the creation of a Royal Institute for Inter-Faith Studies. In August 1995 this institute hosted its inaugural conference with sessions devoted to exploring the history of Muslim-Christian perceptions and reciprocal understandings. Such examples could be multiplied, providing additional attestation to the enduring vigor of Qur'ānic reflection and analysis and to the continuing attention which the textual references to Christians can be expected to receive.

NOTES

1. This preliminary bifurcation approximates that suggested by Jacques Waardenburg in "Types of judgment in Islam about other religions," *Middle East: 30th International Congress of Human Sciences in Asia and North Africa, Mexico City 1976*, ed. Graciela de la Lama (Mexico City, 1982), pp. 138–140.

2. Don Wismer, *The Islamic Jesus: An Annotated Bibliography of Sources in English and French* (New York, 1977); Neal Robinson, *Christ in Islam and Christianity* (Albany, 1991). See also the section on "The Jesus of the Gospels and the Jesus of the Qur'ān" in Kate Zebiri, *Muslims and Christians Face to Face* (Oxford: One World, 1997).

3. Barbara Stowasser, *Women in the Qur'ān, Traditions, and Interpretation* (New York, 1994), especially chapter 7. See also my "Chosen of all women: Mary and Fāṭima in Qur'ānic exegesis," *Islamochristiana* 7 (1981): 19–28 and Jane I. Smith and Yvonne Y. Haddad, "The Virgin Mary in Islamic tradition and commentary," *Muslim World* 79 (1989): 161–187.

4. An example is *Mā'idah* (5):66 where reference to the Torah and Gospel is associated with the approbatory label, "a balanced people (*ummah muqtaṣidah*)."

5. *Qur'ānic Christians: An Analysis of Classical and Modern Exegesis* (New York, 1991). I thank Cambridge University Press for permission to include here some material from this volume. The reader is referred to pp. 293–327 for bibliography pertinent to the present discussion.

6. The best recent biography of al-Ṭabarī is to be found in the introductory chapter which Franz Rosenthal has produced for the English translation of the *Ta'rīkh*. See *The History of al-Ṭabarī*, Vol. 1: *General Introduction and From the Creation to the Flood*, trans. and annotated Franz Rosenthal (Albany, 1989). An important monograph on al-Ṭabarī's *tafsīr* has been published by Claude Gilliot, *Exégèse, langue et théologie en Islam: l'exégèse coranique de Tabari* (Paris, 1990).

7. "Qur'ānic Exegesis," in *Religion, Learning and Science in the ʿAbbasid Period*, ed. M. J. L. Young, J. D. Latham, and R. B. Serjeant (Cambridge, 1990), p. 46.

8. Aḥmad b. al-Qāsim b. Abī ʿUṣaybiʿah, *ʿUyūn al-anbā' fī ṭabaqāt al-aṭibbā'*, ed. August Müller (1884; reprint, Farnborough, 1972), 2:27. For a brief English-language biography, see Fathalla Kholief, *A Study on Fakhr al-Dīn al-Rāzī and His Controversies in Transoxiana* (Beirut, 1966), pp. 7–22.

9. While there has been no systematic and comprehensive treatment of *al-Tafsīr al-kabīr*, a number of studies address parts of the work. Mohammed Arkoun, for example, draws extensively on this *tafsīr* in his semiotic analysis of the first *sūrah*. He justifies his choice with the assertion that Fakhr al-Dīn al-Rāzī "doué d'une étonnante puissance de synthèse et d'une rare sagacité a, en effet, recueilli dans son Commentaire l'essentiel du travail effectué durant six siècles." "Lecture de al-Fātiḥa," in his *Lectures du Coran* (Paris, 1982), p. 60. Reprinted from *Mélanges d'islamologie dédiés à la mémoire de Armand Abel*, ed. P. Salmon (Leiden, 1974), pp. 18–44. Giovanna Calasso, by contrast, has studied Fakhr al-Dīn's remarks on the last *sūrah*, *sūrat al-nās*. "La 'sura degli uomini' nel commento di Fakhr ad-Din ar-Razi," *Egitto e Vicino Oriente* 2 (1979): 231–252. (Both authors make careful note of al-Rāzī's response to a position attributed to the Companion Ibn Masʿūd which denies that the first and last two *sūrah*s are a legitimate part of the Qur'ānic text.) Recently, Norman Calder has published a critically insightful reading of al-Rāzī's exegesis, "Tafsīr from Ṭabarī to Ibn Kathīr," in *Approaches to the Qur'ān*, ed. G. R. Hawting and ʿAbdul-Kader A. Shareef (London, 1993).

10. For a glimpse of Qum as a center of religious learning and for a fascinating depiction of the religious and spiritual formation of a twentieth-century intellectual within that traditional milieu, see Roy Mottahedeh, *The Mantle of the Prophet: Religion and Politics in Iran* (New York, 1985).

11. Muḥammad Ḥusayn al-Ṭabāṭabā'ī, *al-Mīzān fī tafsīr al-Qur'ān* (Beirut, 1394/1974), 1:193. An En-

glish translation of this work was begun by Sayyid Saeed Akhtar Rizvi, with the first of several volumes published in Tehran in 1983. To my knowledge, only five volumes, those covering the exegesis of the first two or three sūrahs, have ever been published. An independent translation initiative, which has solicited the participation of North American scholars, is presently under way.

12. *Koranische Untersuchungen* (Berlin, 1926), pp. 144–146. See also A. S. Tritton, who draws upon this in his "Naṣārā," *Encyclopaedia of Islam* (Leiden: E. J. Brill, reprint 1987) 6:848–851.

13. *The Origin of Islam in Its Christian Environment* (London, 1926), p. 149.

14. The remaining three are in *Āl ʿImrān* (S. 3):67 as *naṣrānī*, *al-Tawbah* (S. 9):30, and *al-Ḥajj* (S. 22):17.

15. Abū Jaʿfar Muḥammad b. Jarīr al-Ṭabarī, *Jāmiʿ al-bayān fī tafsīr al-Qurʾān* (Cairo, n.d.), 2:144.

16. Ibid.

17. Muḥammad b. ʿUmar al-Fakhr al-Dīn al-Rāzī, *al-Tafsīr al-kabīr* (Cairo, n.d.), 3:104.

18. Maḥmūd b. ʿUmar al-Zamakhsharī, *al-Kashshāf ʿan ḥaqāʾiq ghawāmiḍ al-tanzīl wa-ʿuyūn al-aqāwīl fī wujūh al-taʾwīl* (Beirut, 1366/1947), 1:146.

19. Ṭabāṭabāʾī, *al-Mīzān* 1:193. Cf. Matthew 2:19–23.

20. Theodor Nöldeke et al., *Geschichte des Qorans*, 2nd rev. ed. (1909–1926; reprint, Hildesheim, 1961), 1:227–234. For the stages of Muḥammad's relations with Christians, see Rudi Paret, "Islam and Christianity," *Islamic Studies* 3 (1964): 83–95, translated by Rafiq Ahmed from *Die Welt des Islam und die Gegenwart* (Stuttgart, 1961) and Jacques Waardenburg, "Towards a periodization of earliest Islam according to its relations with other religions," *Proceedings of the Ninth Congress of the Union Européenne des Arabisants et Islamisants, Amsterdam 1978*, ed. Rudolph Peters (Leiden, 1981), pp. 305–326.

21. Among the commentators whose exegesis of these verses will be considered, Muḥammad Ḥusayn Ṭabāṭabāʾī is the only one to discuss explicitly the chronology of revelation. Verses dealing with the Christians he assigns generally to the second half of the period in Medina. For example, taking Q.5:51–54 as a unit he questions its ascription to the year of the Farewell Pilgrimage because the reference to a future *fatḥ* in Q.5:52 cannot then refer to the conquest of Mecca. *al-Mīzān* 5:367.

22. al-Ṭabarī, *Jāmiʿ al-bayān* 10:135.

23. Also *Āl ʿImrān* (S. 3):187 and see my "The Qurʾānic context of Muslim biblical scholarship," *Islam and Muslim-Christian Relations*, vol. 7, no. 2 (June 1996), pp. 141–158.

24. A parallel phrase in verse 67 of *al-Māʾidah, wa-alqaynā baynahum al-ʿadāwata wa-al-baghḍāʾa ilā yawmi al-qiyāmah*, follows the charge made against the Jews that they declared God's hand to be fettered.

25. al-Ṭabarī, *Jāmiʿ al-bayān* 10:137.

26. The primary effects of this are to be found, according to both Qatādah and Mujāhid b. Jabr (d. 104/711), in the enmity between Jews and Christians—that is, at the level of interreligious rather than intrareligious antagonism.

27. al-Ṭabarī, *Jāmiʿ al-bayān* 10:137–138. In his *tafsīr* on this verse, the early *mufassir* Muqātil b. Sulaymān (d. 150/767) provides these specifics: "The Nestorians said that ʿĪsā is the son of God while the Jacobites said that God is the Messiah [*al-masīḥ*], son of Mary. The Melchites said that God is the third of three: He is a god, and Jesus is a god and Mary is a god." *Tafsīr Muqātil* (Cairo, 1979), 1:462–463.

28. al-Ṭabarī, *Jāmiʿ al-bayān* 10:139. He then specifies the consequences of Christian enmity as the divisions that existed among Nestorians, Jacobites, and Melchites.

29. Fakhr al-Dīn al-Rāzī, *al-Tafsīr al-kabīr* 11:193. See Roger Arnaldez, "Les Chrétiens selon le commentaire coranique de Rāzī," *Mélanges d'islamologie dédiés à la mémoire de Armand Abel*, ed. P. Salmon (Leiden, 1974), p. 49. A similar argument about Christian pretension is made by Abū al-Faraj ʿAbd al-Raḥman b. al-Jawzī (d. 597/1201), *Zād al-masīr fī ʿilm al-tafsīr* (Beirut, 1384/1964–1388/1968), 2:315.

30. Fakhr al-Dīn al-Rāzī, *al-Tafsīr al-kabīr* 11:193. For recent work on the Muslim belief in biblical attestion of Muḥammad and other intrascriptural relations, see Hava Lazarus-Yafeh, *Intertwined Worlds: Medieval Islam and Bible Criticism* (Princeton, 1992); Andrew Rippin, "Interpreting the Bible through the Qurʾān," in *Approaches to the Qurʾān*, ed. G. R. Hawting and Abdul-Kader A. Shareef (London, 1993), pp. 249–259; and my "The Qurʾānic Context of Muslim Biblical Scholarship," *Islam and Muslim-Christian Relations*, vol. 7 no. 2 (July 1996), 141–158; "Ṭabarī's Prelude to the Prophet," forthcoming in *Al-Ṭabarī: A Medieval Muslim Historian and His Work*, ed. Hugh Kennedy (Princeton: Darwin Press); "Assessing the Isrāʾīliyyāt: An Exegetical Conundrum," forthcoming in *Fiction in Nonfictional Classical Arabic Literature*, ed. S. Leder (Wiesbaden: Harrassowitz Verlag).

31. Fakhr al-Dīn al-Rāzī, *al-Tafsīr al-kabīr* 11: 193. The phrase quoted from Q.6:65 is *aw yalbisakum shiyaʿan wa-yudhīqa baʿḍakum baʾsa baʿḍin*. Fakhr al-Dīn actually begins his treatment of this verse by noting the comparable contractual invalidation of the Jews.

32. Ṭabāṭabāʾī, *al-Mīzān* 5:235. For a study of Qurʾānic *naẓm* which includes reference to Ṭabāṭabāʾī, see Mustansir Mir, *Coherence in the Qurʾān* (Indianapolis, 1986).

33. Ṭabāṭabāʾī, *al-Mīzān* 5:242.

34. For a transmission on the authority of ʿUbādah b. al-Ṣāmit's grandson, see al-Ṭabarī, *Jāmiʿ al-bayān* 10:397. See also ʿAlī b. Aḥmadḥ al-Wāḥidī, *Asbāb al-nuzūl* (Beirut, 1983), pp. 136–137.

35. Muḥammad b. Isḥāq, *Sīrat rasūl Allāh* (recension of ʿAbd al-Malik b. Hishām), ed. Ferdinand Wüstenfeld (1858; reprint, Frankfurt-am-Main, 1961), 1:546–547; W. Montgomery Watt, *Muḥammad at Medina* (Oxford, 1956), pp. 181–183 and 209–210; Gordon Darnell Newby, *A History of the Jews of Arabia* (Columbia, S.C., 1988), p. 88.

36. al-Ṭabarī, *Jāmiʿ al-bayān* 10:398 with a transmission from ʿIkrimah (d. 105/723). See Ibn Isḥāq, *Sīrat*, 684–688; Watt, *Muhammad at Medina* 188–189; and M. J. Kister, "The massacre of the Banū Qurayẓa: A re-examination of a tradition," *Jerusalem Studies in Arabic and Islam* 8 (1986): 61–96, in response to W. N. Arafat, "New light on the story of Banū Qurayẓa and the Jews of Medina," *Journal of the Royal Asiatic Society* (1976): 100–107. Abū Lubābah was subsequently pardoned and later appears among those listed as *ahl al-ṣuffah*, individuals venerated for their ascetism and piety. W. Montgomery Watt, "Ahl al-ṣuffa," *Encyclopaedia of Islam*, New edition, vol. 1 (Leiden: E. J. Brill, 1960), pp. 266–267.

37. al-Ṭabarī, *Jāmiʿ al-bayān* 10:397–398 on the authority of Ismāʿīl b. "ʿAbd al-Raḥmān al-Suddī (d. 128/745).

38. The three *asbāb* are nicely summarized in Ibn al-Jawzī, *Zād al-masīr* 2:377–378.

39. al-Ṭabarī, *Jāmiʿ al-bayān* 10:398–399. Abdelmajid Charfi in his article "Christianity in the Qurʾān commentary of Ṭabarī" remarks on al-Ṭabarī's exegetical procedure from a psychological angle. The vast inclusivity of al-Ṭabarī's *ḥadīth* collection masks issues of discrepancy and contradiction with the result that "all these interpretations gathered together in his comprehensive work create an impression in the reader's mind, seeking to influence his feelings rather than to provide any intellectual conviction." *Islamochristiana* 6 (1980): 105–148, esp. p. 30; trans. Penelope C. Johnstone from *Revue Tunisienne des Sciences Sociales* 58/59 (1979): 53–96; French trans. Robert Caspar in *Mélanges de l'Institut Dominicain d'Études Orientales du Caire* 16 (1983): 117–161.

40. al-Ṭabarī also explicitly mentions the matter of apostasy (*irtidād*) at this juncture.

41. al-Ṭabarī, *Jāmiʿ al-bayān* 10:400–401, including reference to the Banū Taghlib, a largely monophysite Christian tribe in the northern part of the peninsula. Henry Charles, *Le Christianisme des Arabes nomades sur le Limes et dans le désert syro-mésopotamien aux alentours de l'Hégire* (Paris, 1936), p. 3.

42. Fakhr al-Dīn al-Rāzī, *al-Tafsīr al-kabīr* 12:16. For further to al-Rāzī's views of Muslim/non-Muslim interaction, see my "Fakhr al-Dīn al-Rāzī on *āyat al-jizyah* and *āyat al-sayf*," *Conversion and Continuity: Indigenous Christian Communities in Islamic Lands, Eighth to Eighteenth Centuries*, ed. Michael Gervers and Ramzi J. Bikhazi (Toronto, 1990), pp. 103–19.

43. Fakhr al-Dīn al-Rāzī, *al-Tafsīr al-kabīr* 12:16. Ibn al-ʿArabī (d. 543/1148), *Aḥkām al-Qurʾān* 2:138–139, relates an abbreviated version of this episode.

44. Ṭabāṭabāʾī, *al-Mīzān* 5:369–371 which includes a general admonition against using *asbāb al-nuzūl* to restrict the signification of a verse.

45. The term *walāyah* has well-delineated political and juridical significations in the corpus of classical *fiqh*. See Hermann Landolt, "Walāyah," *The Encyclopedia of Religion*, ed. Mircea Eliade (New York, 1987) 15:316–323, and Willi Heffening, "Wilāyah," *Encyclopedia of Islam*, first edition, vol. 8 (Leiden: E. J. Brill, reprint 1987), 1137–1138. For cognate Qurʾānic uses of *awliyāʾ* against which the interpretation of Ṭabāṭabāʾī and others can be read, see Q.3:28; 4:89, 139, and 144; 5:57; 8:72; 9:23; and 60:1.

46. Ṭabāṭabāʾī, *al-Mīzān* 5:371.

47. As additional support, Ṭabāṭabāʾī refers to *al-Mujādalah* (S. 58): 22 which begins *lā tajidu qawman yuʾminūna bi-allāhi wa-al-yawmi al-ākhiri yuwāddūna man ḥādda allāha wa-rasūlahu* and uses another form of the root WDD.

48. Ṭabāṭabāʾī, *al-Mīzān* 5:371. The inclusion of Jews and Christians in the term "infidel" is discussed by Yohanan Friedmann, "'Islam is Superior . . .'," *Jerusalem Quarterly* 11 (1979): 36–42.

49. Ṭabāṭabāʾī observes that when prohibiting a previously permissible action, the Qurʾān habitually gives indication of temporal closure. The examples he draws from *al-Tawbah* (S. 9):28, *al-Baqarah* (S. 2):187, and *al-Aḥzāb* (S. 33):52 lead one to expect a corresponding intimation of sequentiality were the Prophet and believers being forbidden treaties with the Christians, Jews, and *mushrikūn*.

50. *alladhīna ittakhadhū dīnakum huzuwan wa laʿiban*.

51. Ṭabāṭabāʾī links the actual ethico-legal status of this verse to such injunctions as *al-Baqarah* (S. 2): 184, "But if you fast, it is better for you," and *al-ʿAnkabūt* (S. 29):45, "*Salāt* restrains from abomination and iniquity but remembrance (*dhikr*) of God is greater."

52. Ṭabāṭabāʾī, *al-Mīzān* 5:373. He further maintains that were Muslims to help one faction of Christians (or Jews) against another, they should not expect reciprocal support, for neither group would align themselves with Muslims against their own coreligionists.

53. See Ibn Isḥāq, *Sīrat* 1:208–221; Ibn Saʿd, *al-Ṭabaqāt al-kubrā* 1:201–208; al-Ṭabarī, *Taʾrīkh* 1: 1180–1184. A narrative summary is offered in Mehmet Aydin, "Rapporti islamo-cristiani all'epoca di Muhammad," *Islam, storia e civiltà* 5 (1986): 12–15. The Shīʿī *mufassir* ʿAlī b. Ibrāhīm al-Qummī (d. 328/929) provides interesting additional detail. *Tafsīr al-Qummī* 1:176–179.

54. al-Ṭabarī, *Jāmiʿ al-bayān* 10:499.

55. The key scene of this scenario is the Najāshī's

questioning of the Muslim delegation. When asked about Muḥammad's thoughts on ʿĪsā and Maryam, the group's spokesman made this response: "He [Muḥammad] says that ʿĪsā is the servant (*ʿabd*) of God and the word (*kalimah*) of God, which God cast into Mary, and His spirit (*rūḥ*). About Maryam he says that she is the virgin (*al-ʿadhrā' al-batūl*)." The Najāshī responded to this statement with an illustrative command: "Pick up a twig from the ground: between what your leader said about ʿĪsā and Maryam and what I believe there is not more than a twig's worth of difference." *Jāmiʿ al-bayān* 10:500.

56. Ibid. 10:501. Ibn al-Jawzī poses the question about the phrase "those who say 'We are Christians' quite precisely: "Is this a generalization about all Christians or is it specific?" If the phrase means particular Christians, then one of two groups could be intended. On the authority of Ibn ʿAbbās and Ibn Jubayr the first possibility is, of course, the Christian king of Abyssinia and his followers who subsequently became Muslims. The second possible specification repeats an identification earlier proposed by Qatādah: "They are a group of Christians who were strict adherents of the law of Jesus" (*mutamassikīn bi-sharīʿati ʿĪsā*). *Zād al-masīr* 2:408.

57. al-Ṭabarī, *Jāmiʿ al-bayān* 10:501. Ahmad von Denffer presents only this episode (of the delegation sent by the Najāshī to Muḥammad) as the *sabab al-nuzūl* of the verse, adding that only such a carefully specified group of Christians is here intended and, therefore, "this verse, when seen in its historical context, does not seem to be meant as a general statement characterizing Christians as such as being nearest to Muslims." *Christians in the Qur'ān and the Sunna: An Assessment from the Sources to Help Define Our Relationship* (Leicester, 1979), p. 13.

58. Fakhr al-Dīn al-Rāzī, *al-Tafsīr al-kabīr* 12:66.

59. Ibid.

60. Ṭabāṭabā'ī, *al-Mīzān* 6:79.

61. Ṭabāṭabā'ī repeats this in his comments on the *ḥadīth* material to which he makes reference for this verse, insisting that "the evident meaning (*ẓāhir*) of the verse is general, not specific." Ibid. 6:85.

62. Ibid. 6:79–80. The author was apparently unaware of (or ignoring) the vast demographic shift that has taken place in the Muslim world with the largest Muslim populations now to be found in south and southeast Asia.

63. Ibid. 6:80.

64. Ibid.

65. al-Ṭabarī, *Jāmiʿ al-bayān* 10:505. The basic study of the Qur'ānic understanding of monasticism, which examines the three relevant loci (i.e., *al-Mā'idah* [S. 5]:82–86, *al-Tawbah* [S. 9]:29–35, and *al-Ḥadīd* [S. 57]:27), is that by Edmund Beck, *Das christliche Mönchtum im Koran* (Helsinki, 1946).

66. al-Ṭabarī, *Jāmiʿ al-bayān* 10:506.

67. Fakhr al-Dīn al-Rāzī, *al-Tafsīr al-kabīr* 12:66.

68. Ibid.

69. Ibid. 12:67. See Jacques Jomier, "Unité de Dieu, chrétiens et Coran selon Fakhr al-Dīn al-Rāzī," *Islamochristiana* 6 (1980): 149–177.

70. Fakhr al-Dīn al-Rāzī, *al-Tafsīr al-kabīr* 12:67. Rudi Paret highlights this reason for Jewish/Christian contrast in his remarks on 5:82. *Muhammed und der Koran: Geschichte und Verkündigung des arabischen Propheten*, 5th rev. ed. (Stuttgart, 1980), p. 141.

71. Fakhr al-Dīn al-Rāzī, *al-Tafsīr al-kabīr* 12:67.

72. Ṭabāṭabā'ī, *al-Mīzān* 6:80–81. For another contemporary reappropriation of this position, see Syed Vahiduddin, "Islam and Diversity of Religions," *Islam and Christian Muslim Relations* 1 (1990): 7.

73. Ṭabāṭabā'ī, *al-Mīzān* 6:81.

74. Ibid.

75. Ibid.

76. Ibid. 6:81–82.

77. Ibid. 6:82.

78. Translated by Penelope Johnstone from ʿAlī al-Sayyid ʿAlī Yūnus's article in *Minbar al-Islām* of September, 1985 in her "Articles from Islamic journals: An Islamic perspective on dialogue," *Islamochristiana* 13 (1987): 140. In her introduction to this collection of articles Johnstone (p. 132) notes, however, the generally negative tone of virtually all of the articles to be found in the Muslim press on the subject of interreligious dialogue. Recognizing the "ancient fears and suspicions which can lurk just below the surface," she concludes that even if "some of the views expressed by Muslims are discouraging, at least it is probably better that we should be reminded that they still exist." More recently, Hugh Goddard has collected additional bibliographical information on this subject. See his "An annotated bibliography of works about Christianity by Egyptian Muslim authors," *Muslim World* 80 (1990): 251–277 and "The persistence of medieval themes in modern Christian-Muslim discussion in Egypt," in *Christian Arabic Apologetics during the Abbasid Period (750–1258)*, ed. Samir Khalil Samir and Jørgen S. Nielsen (Leiden, 1994), pp. 225–237.

79. "Religion and Society: The example of Islam," in *Islam in a World of Diverse Faiths*, ed. Dan Cohn-Sherbok (New York, 1991), p. 176.

REFERENCES

Aydin, Mehmet. "Rapporti islamo-cristiani all'epoca di Muhammad." *Islam, storia e civiltà* 5 (1986): 11–23.

Arkoun, Mohammed. *Lectures du Coran*. Paris: Édition G.-P. Maisonneuve et Larose, 1982.

———. "Religion and society: The example of Islam." In *Islam in a World of Diverse Faiths*. Edited by

Dan Cohn-Sherbok, pp. 134–77. New York: St. Martin's, 1991.

Arnaldez, Roger. "Les Chrétiens selon le commentaire coranique de Rāzī." In *Mélanges d'islamologie dédiés à la mémoire de Armand Abel*. Edited by P. Salmon, pp. 45–57. Leiden: E. J. Brill, 1974.

Beck, Edmund. *Das christliche Mönchtum im Koran*. Helsinki: Societas Orientalis Fennica, 1946.

Bell, Richard. *The Origin of Islam in its Christian Environment*. London: Macmillan, 1926.

Burton, John. "Quranic exegesis." In *Religion, Learning and Science in the ʿAbbasid Period*. Edited by M. J. L. Young, J. D. Latham, and R. B. Serjeant, pp. 40–55. Cambridge: Cambridge University Press, 1990.

Calasso, G. "La 'sura degli uomini' nel commento di Fakhr ad-Din ar-Razi." *Egitto e Vicino Oriente* 2 (1979): 231–252.

Calder, Norman. "Tafsīr from Ṭabarī to Ibn Kathīr." In *Approaches to the Qur'ān*. Edited by G. R. Hawting and Abdul-Kader A. Shareef, pp. 101–140. London: Routledge, 1993.

Charfi, Abdel Majid. "Christianity in the Qur'an Commentary of Ṭabarī." *Islamochristiana* 6 (1980): 105–148. Translated by Penelope C. Johnstone from *Revue Tunisienne des Sciences Sociales* 58/59 (1979): 53–96; French translation by Robert Caspar in *Mélanges de l'Institut Dominicain d'Études Orientales du Caire* 16 (1983): 117–161.

Charles, Henry. *Le Christianisme des Arabes nomades sur le limes et dans le désert syro-mésopotamien aux alentours de l'hégire*. Paris: Bibliothèque des Hautes-Études, 1936.

Denffer, Ahmad von. *Christians in the Qur'an and Sunna: An Assessment from the Sources to Help Define Our Relationship*. Leicester: Islamic Foundation, 1979.

Friedmann, Yohanan. "'Islam is superior . . .'." In *Jerusalem Quarterly* 11 (1979): 36–42.

Gilliot, Claude. *Exégèse, langue et théologie en Islam: l'exégèse coranique de Tabari*. Paris: J. Vrin, 1990.

Goddard, Hugh. "An annotated bibliography of works about Christianity by Egyptian Muslim authors." *Muslim World* 80 (1990): 251–277.

———. "The persistence of medieval themes in modern Christian-Muslim discussion in Egypt." In *Christian Arabic Apologetics during the Abbasid Period (750–1258)*. Edited by Samir Khalil Samir and Jørgen S. Nielsen, 225–237. Leiden: E. J. Brill, 1994.

Heffening, Willi. "Wilāyah." *Encyclopaedia of Islam*, first edition. Reprint Leiden: E. J. Brill, 1987. 8:1137–1138.

Horovitz, Joseph. *Koranische Untersuchungen*. Berlin: Walter de Gruyter, 1926.

Ibn Abī ʿUṣaybiʿah, Aḥmad b. al-Qāsim. *ʿUyūn al-anbāʾ fī ṭabaqāt al-aṭibbāʾ*. Edited by August Müller. 2 vols. in 1. 1884. Reprint, Farnborough: Gregg International, 1972.

Ibn al-ʿArabī, Muḥammad b. ʿAbdallāh. *Aḥkām al-Qur'ān*. Edited by Muḥammad ʿAbd al-Qādir ʿAṭā. 4 vols. Beirut: Dār al-Kutub al-ʿIlmiyyah, 1408/1988.

Ibn Isḥāq, Muḥammad. *Sīrat rasūl Allāh* (recension of ʿAbd al-Malik b. Hishām) Edited by Ferdinand Wüstenfeld. 2 vols. 1858. Reprint, Frankfurt-am-Main: Minerva, 1961.

Ibn-al-Jawzī, Abū al-Faraj ʿAbd al-Raḥman. *Zād al-masīr fī ʿilm al-tafsīr*. 9 vols. Beirut: al-Maktab al-Islāmī lil-Ṭibāʿah wa-al-Nashr, 1384/1964–1388/1968.

Ibn Saʿd. *al-Ṭabaqāt al-kubrā*. Edited by Iḥsān ʿAbbās. 9 vols. Beirut: Dār al-Ṣādir, 1985.

Johnstone, Penelope, trans. "Articles from Islamic journals: An Islamic perspective on dialogue." *Islamochristiana* 13 (1987): 131–171.

Jomier, Jacques. "Unité de Dieu, chrétiens et Coran selon Fakhr al-Dīn al-Rāzī." *Islamochristiana* 6 (1980): 149–177.

Kholief, Fathalla. *A Study on Fakhr al-Dīn al-Rāzī and His Controversies in Transoxiana*. Beirut: Dar El-Machreq, 1966.

Landolt, Hermann. "Walāyah." In *The Encyclopedia of Religion*. Edited by Mircea Eliade, 15:316–23. 16 vols. New York: Macmillan, 1987.

Lazarus-Yafeh, Hava. *Intertwined Worlds: Medieval Islam and Bible Criticism*. Princeton: Princeton University Press, 1992.

McAuliffe, Jane Dammen. "Chosen of all women: Mary and Fāṭima in Qurʾānic exegesis." *Islamochristiana* 7 (1981): 19–28.

———. "Fakhr al-Dīn al-Rāzī on *āyat al-jizyah* and *āyat al-sayf*." In *Conversion and Continuity: Indigenous Christian Communities in Islamic Lands, Eighth to Eighteenth Centuries*. Edited by Michael Gervers and Ramzi J. Bikhazi, 103–119. Toronto: Pontifical Institute of Medieval Studies, 1990.

———. *Qurʾānic Christians: An Analysis of Classical and Modern Exegesis*. New York: Cambridge University Press, 1991.

———. "The Qurʾānic context of Muslim biblical scholarship." *Islam and Muslim-Christian Relations*, Vol. 7 No. 2 (1996), 141–158.

———. "Assessing the Isrāʾīliyyāt: An exegetical conundrum." Forthcoming in *Fiction in Nonfictional Classical Arabic Literature*, ed. S. Leder (Wiesbaden: Harrassowitz Verlag).

———. "Ṭabarī's Prelude to the Prophet." Forthcoming in *Al-Ṭabarī: A Medieval Muslim Historian and His Work*, ed. Hugh Kennedy (Princeton: Darwin Press).

Mir, Mustansir. *Coherence in the Qur'ān*. Indianapolis, 1986.

Mottahedeh, Roy. *The Mantle of the Prophet: Religion and Politics in Iran*. New York: Pantheon, 1985.

Muqātil b. Sulaymān. *Tafsīr Muqātil b. Sulaymān*. Edited by ʿAbdallāh Maḥmūd Shiḥātah. 5 vols. Cairo: al-Hay'ah al-Miṣriyyah al-ʿĀmmah lil-Kitāb, 1979.

Newby, Gordon. *A History of the Jews of Arabia*. Columbia: University of South Carolina Press, 1988.

Nöldeke, Theodor, et al. *Geschichte des Korans*. 2nd revised edition; vols. 1 and 2 revised by Friedrich Schwally; vol. 3 revised by G. Bergsträsser and O. Pretzl. Leipzig: Dieterich'sche Verlagsbuchhandlung, 1909–1926.

Paret, Rudi. "Islam and Christianity." Translated by Rafīq Ahmad. *Islamic Studies* 3 (1964): 83–95.

———. *Muhammed und der Koran: Geschichte und Verkündigung des arabischen Propheten*. 5th revised edition. Stuttgart: W. Kohlhammer, 1980.

al-Qummī, ʿAlī b. Ibrāhīm. *Tafsīr al-Qummī*. Edited by al-Sayyid Ṭayyib al-Jazā'irī. 2 vols. Qomm: Mu'assasah Dār al-Kitāb lil-Ṭibāʿah wa al-Nashr, 1404/1984.

al-Rāzī, [Muḥammad b. ʿUmar] al-Fakhr [al-Dīn]. *al-Tafsīr al-kabīr*. 32 vols. Cairo: al-Maṭbaʿah al-Bahīyah al-Miṣrīyah, n.d.

Rippin, Andrew. "Interpreting the Bible through the Qur'ān." In *Approaches to the Qur'ān*. Edited by G. R. Hawting and Abdul-Kader A. Shareef, pp. 249–259. London: Routledge, 1993.

Rizvi, Sayyid Saeed Akhtar, trans. *al-Mizan: An Exegesis of the Qur'an*. 5 vols. Teheran: WOFis, 1983– .

Robinson, Neal. *Christ in Islam and Christianity*. Albany: State University of New York Press, 1991.

Rosenthal, Franz, trans. *The History of al-Ṭabarī*, Vol. 1: *General Introduction and From the Creation to the Flood*. Albany: State University of New York Press, 1989.

Smith, Jane I., and Yvonne Y. Haddad. "The Virgin Mary in Islamic tradition and commentary." *Muslim World* 79 (1989): 161–187.

Stowasser, Barbara. *Women in the Qur'an, Traditions, and Interpretation*. New York: Oxford University Press, 1994.

al-Ṭabarī, Abū Jaʿfar Muḥammad b. Jarīr. *Jāmiʿ al-bayān fī tafsīr al-Qur'ān*. 30 vols. Cairo: Maṭbaʿat al-Yamīnīyah, n.d.

———. *Ta'rīkh al-rusul wa al-mulūk*. Edited by M. J. de Goeje et al. 15 vols. Leiden, E. J. Brill, 1879–1901.

al-Ṭabāṭabā'ī, Muḥammad Ḥusayn. *al-Mīzān fī tafsīr al-Qur'ān*. 20 vols. Beirut: Mu'assasat al-Aʿlāmī lil-Maṭbūʿat, 1394/1974. See also under Rizvi.

Tritton, A. S. "Naṣārā." *Encyclopaedia of Islam*, first edition 6:848–851.

al-Ṭūsī, Muḥammad b. al-Ḥasan. *al-Tibyān fī tafsīr al-Qur'ān*. Edited by Aḥmad Ḥabīb Qaṣīr al-ʿĀmilī. 10 vols. Beirut: Dār Iḥyā' al-Turāth al-ʿArabī, n.d.

Vahiduddin, Syed. "Islam and diversity of religions." *Islam and Christian Muslim Relations* 1 (1990): pp. 3–11.

Waardenburg, Jacques. "Towards a periodization of earliest Islam according to its relations with other religions." In *Proceedings of the Ninth Congress of Union Européenne des Arabisants et Islamisants, Amsterdam 1978*. Edited by Rudolph Peters, 305–326. Leiden: E. J. Brill, 1981.

———. "Types of judgment in Islam about other religions." In *Middle East: 30th International Congress of Human Sciences in Asia and North Africa, Mexico City 1976*. Edited by Graciela de la Lama, 138–140. Mexico City: El Colegio de Mexico, 1982.

al-Wāḥidī, ʿAlī b. Aḥmad. *Asbāb al-nuzūl*. Beirut: Dār wa-Maktabat al-Hilāl, 1983.

Watt, William Montgomery. "Ahl al-ṣuffa," *Encyclopaedia of Islam*. New edition 1:266–267.

———. *Muḥammad at Medina*. Oxford: Clarendon Press, 1956.

Wismer, Don. *The Islamic Jesus: An Annotated Bibliography of Sources in English and French*. New York: Garland, 1977.

al-Zamakhsarī, Maḥmūd b. ʿUmar. *al-Kashshāf ʿan ḥaqā'iq ghawāmiḍ al-tanzīl wa-ʿuyūn al-aqāwīl fī wujūh al-ta'wīl*. 4 vols. Beirut: Dār al-Kitāb al-ʿArabī, 1947.

Zebiri, Kate, *Muslims and Christians Face to Face*. Oxford: Oneworld, 1997.

6

Arab Islamic Perceptions of Byzantine Religion and Culture

AHMAD M. H. SHBOUL

From the rise of Islam in the early seventh century to the advent of the Western Crusades in the late eleventh century (A.D.), the Arab Islamic world and Byzantium were the two main rival powers in the Mediterranean region. Their mutual relations involved not only regular warfare and exchange of prisoners but also subtle diplomacy, religious dialogue and polemics, active commercial exchange, and cultural contacts.

Of course, Arab-Greek contacts go back at least to the times of Alexander of Macedon and the early Nabataeans. Such relations became more direct after the Roman conquest of the Orient and the establishment of the Roman *Provincia Arabia* in the old Nabataean Arab territories of southern Syria.[1] From the fourth century A.D., with the dissolution of the old Roman Province, the Arabs of Syria and Palestine, and to a lesser extent those of the Hijaz, found themselves within the sphere of influence of the Hellenized, and now Christianized, East Roman Empire of Constantinople.[2] At the time of Muhammad's Call, Byzantium, the most important Christian power in the East, was not entirely beyond the horizon of the Arabs of the Hijaz. With the rise of Islam, first as a religious community then as a political power, the very nature of Arab-Byzantine relations and mutual perceptions was bound to undergo drastic transformation.

This historical and cultural encounter between the Arabs and Byzantium has to be kept in mind in our discussion of Arab Islamic perceptions of Byzantine religion and culture. It is equally important to consider the interplay between the vicissitudes of the historical encounter and the normative Islamic attitudes toward the Byzantines as Christians that was inherent in Islamic teachings. There is no doubt that early Islamic attitudes toward the Byzantine Christians, particularly as reflected in the Qurʾān and in the practice and sayings of the Prophet Muhammad, continued to define later perceptions and attitudes which, in turn, evolved in response to changing political circumstances.

Above all, this study is concerned with exploring the nature of the Arab Islamic discourse regarding Byzantium and the place of the religious dimension in that discourse.[3] In this context, perceptions and attitudes are closely and dialectically related. Although this study is not concerned with religious polemics as such, it is important to reflect on the nature and motives of Arab Islamic polemics, apologetics, and dialogue with the Byzantines, against the background of political conflict and cultural contacts between these two worlds.

The Qurʾānic Premise and the Historical Context

In studying the religious dimension of Arab Islamic perceptions of Byzantium, it is natural to begin with the time of the Prophet Muhammad and to refer to the Qurʾānic text and to *Hadīth* traditions. Let us recall that the Prophet and his early community were familiar with contemporary Christian communities, both within Arabia and in neighboring lands, including some individual Christian Arabs in the Hijaz. The Arabs of the Hijaz had maintained commercial and tribal connections with Christian Arab centers and tribes under Byzantine hegemony or Byzantine influence such as the Christian Arabs of Syria and the Yemen. The position of Byzantium as the most influential Christian power was well known to the people of Mecca at that time.

It is true that the Byzantine-Persian war of the early seventh century, the last great war of antiquity, in which the Byzantines *(Rūm)* were initially vanquished, prevented direct contacts between the early Muslims and Byzantium, from circa A.D. 614 to 628. However, Muhammad's friendly disposition toward Christian Abyssinia, Byzantium's distant African ally, is shown by his choice of the Aksumite kingdom as a place of asylum for the first Muslim refugees, or migrants. The friendly reception accorded them by the Christian king of that country must have strengthened the sympathetic attitude of the early Muslims toward Christians in general. The fact that the Byzantines were going through the agony of military defeat, at the hands of the Zoroastrian Sasanians of Persia, seems to have increased the feeling of affinity which the nascent persecuted religious community of Islam felt toward the Christians in their hour of trial.

It is within such a historical context that the opening lines of *Sūrat al-Rūm* should be understood: "The Byzantines have been defeated in the nearby land and after their defeat they would be victorious in a few years; on that day the believers would rejoice in God's victory." Although I do not attempt any detailed historical commentary on these lines, it is important to highlight their significance for our present theme.[4] The promised victory of the Byzantines against their Sasanian enemy as foretold in these verses is coupled with the anticipated rejoicing of the Muslim believers. Apart from reflecting the politico-religious atmosphere of the time and the impact upon the Hijaz of events in Syria, these verses clearly show Muslim sympathy and affinity with the Christian Byzantines, as fellow "Believers." One may also perceive in these verses a certain consciousness and sharing of the loss of Jerusalem to the Persians in A.D. 618, particularly as Jerusalem was still the *qibla* for Muslim prayer, and since the Prophet's miraculous nocturnal journey *(isrāʾ)* from Mecca to Jerusalem is generally associated with this period, according to Muslim tradition.

Let us also recall that such Islamic affinity with the Christian believers, as reflected in *Sūrat al-Rūm*, *is* in line with an inherent Qurʾānic position that is demonstrated in several other verses. Thus the particular sympathy toward the Byzantines should be viewed within the wider context of the Qurʾānic positive attitude toward Christians as a religious community. For despite the few well-known polemical verses in the Qurʾān against certain aspects of Christian theology, and the criticism of some supposed practices among contemporary Christians, it could be argued that the overall attitude of the Qurʾān is one of sympathy and tolerance toward Christians. In particular, the Qurʾān often emphasizes the affinity between the nascent Islamic community and the early Christian community.[5]

At the same time, the Qurʾān invites Muslims and Christians (and Jews) to engage in religious dialogue. The Qurʾān is seen as confirming the Torah and the Gospel, and as such it allows, even admonishes, both Jews and Christians to follow the precepts of their own respective scriptures.[6] Thus the Qurʾān acknowledges the religious and juridical diversity among the three communities and also establishes the principle of social interaction, by allowing the food of *ahl al-Kitāb* as *halāl*, with certain exceptions, and by permitting Muslims to marry women of *ahl al-Kitāb*.[7]

In addition, the Qur'ānic attitude toward Christian piety and spirituality is essentially one of recognition and respect. The Christian qualities of compassion and humility are particularly praised. Among contemporary Christian priests and monks, the Qurʾān distinguishes between those sincere ones whose hearts are filled with mercy and compassion, who seek God's pleasure in their ascetic life, and those who are greedy, who devour people's wealth unjustly and use their own position for self glorification.[8]

It is also important to recall that the Qur'ān reflects the concern of the Prophet of Islam to be accepted by both Christians and Jews in Arabia. For Islam saw its own rise not in opposition to Jewish or Christian teachings, but rather in line with their original principles and in opposition to Arab polytheism. It is in this context that the Qurʾānic call for dialogue with the "People of the Book" should be perceived.

In a context which implies that certain Christians, apparently including Arabs and non-Arabs, were willing to listen favorably to Qurʾānic revelations,

Christians in general are positively depicted as inherently well disposed toward the Muslims and as most spiritually inclined. "You will surely find the nearest of them in love to the believers are those who say 'We are Christians,' for among them are pastors and monks and they wax not proud . . . You will find their eyes filled with tears due to what they know of the Truth, as they proclaim: 'Our Lord! we do believe, so inscribe us among those who bear witness.'"[9]

The preceding brief outline is only meant to provide a contextual background for an understanding of the early Arab Islamic attitude toward Christians, as exemplified in the Qur᾽ān. It should provide a starting point for the unfolding historical encounter between the two religious communities and specifically for the evolving Arab Muslim perceptions of Christian Byzantium as a power and a culture. Despite other factors and changing circumstances, this normative Qur᾽ānic attitude, characterized by dialogue, tolerance, and sympathy, remains most influential in the future orientation of the Arab Islamic discourse on and dialogue with Byzantium.

However, the fact that the Qur᾽ān (specifically *Sūrat al-Rūm* 30:2–6) reflects Muslim sympathy towards the Christian Byzantines did not preclude the latter from being viewed politically and militarily as the potential adversary in subsequent periods. Here, we have to consider the wider political, economic, and cultural dimensions of the position of both Byzantium and the Arabs in the world of late Antiquity. The verses of *Sūrat al-Rūm* speak of a time when the Byzantines were still the defeated side in their war with the Persians and the Muslims were still a tiny persecuted minority.

After regaining Syria, Palestine, and Egypt from the Sasanians, Byzantium reemerged as the most formidable Christian power known to the Arabs at that time. Meanwhile, the Islamic community itself had evolved from a weak religious minority to a considerable spiritual and political force in Arabia, with potential links with Arab clans and settlements in southern Syria.[10] Thus, the victorious and confident Muslim Arab community, under Muhammad's leadership, found itself face-to-face with the victorious Byzantine Christian empire.

At the same time, the Prophet was hopeful that the Byzantine Christians might acknowledge his religious and political position. The Islamic historical tradition contains reports of correspondence between Muhammad and Heraclius in which the Arab Prophet invites the Byzantine emperor (among other contemporary rulers) to accept Islam. Such correspondence was supposed to have taken place in the same year as the important peace treaty of Hudaybiya with Mecca in A.D. 628, and possibly (if we postulate two incidents of correspondence) also in 630, the year in which Muhammad and his companions finally entered Mecca victorious and in which most Arabian tribes paid homage to him as Prophet and political leader. It was also the time when Heraclius celebrated his final victory against the Persians, including the recovery of the Holy Rood, and received delegations from far and near, including some Arab representatives offering congratulations or homage.

From an early Islamic perspective, God's promise of victory for the believers (as in Qur᾽ān 30: 2–6 and elsewhere) was seen as vindicated. It may have appeared possible to the Muslims, at least for a moment, that "the king of the Rūm" might now accept Muhammad as a true Prophet. But it may be said, with no intended irony but without escaping an obvious paradox, that the greater confidence each party felt about God being on their side the less avoidable their confrontation became. It is important to realize that the contemporaneous Muslim and Byzantine victories against their respective former adversaries, in A.D. 628–630, and the uncertain political climate in Syria, produced some unexpected reorientation of loyalty among Christian Arab tribes in that region. Thus by the end of Muhammad's life it was clear that Byzantium had increasingly become the potential enemy in the eyes of the Muslim Arabs. It was understandable from the Arab perspective, but not necessarily from the Byzantine one, that the same intelligence report that brought the news of Muhammad's death to Heraclius's camp also informed him of an Arab expedition into southern Palestine. From the Byzantine perspective, Heraclius's recent lightning victory against Persia, and the old Roman imperialist attitude of condescension toward the Arabs, would have produced a sense of complacency that prevented any realistic assessment of the implications of the Islamic revolution in Arabia.

Early Islamic historical and religious traditions clearly indicate that the Islamic community during the last two or three years of the Prophet Muhammad's life were prepared for future conflict with Byzantium. Qur᾽ānic verses which generally anticipate conflict with "a formidable foe" whom the Muslims would have to face, are usually interpreted to include the Byzantines (among others). Other Qur᾽ānic verses from the same period (most probably around

630 A.D.) enjoin Muslims to "fight those who believe not in God, nor the Last Day, nor forbid what God and His messenger have forbidden, nor acknowledge the Religion of Truth, from among those who have been given Scripture, until they pay the *jizya* with willing submission, and are subdued."[11] Although it is difficult to ascribe nonbelief in God or in the Last Day to Christians, these verses, at least on the bases of the two other points, were deemed by some commentators to include the Byzantine masters of Syria.[12]

An important category of source material for this period, in addition to the Qur'ān and the extensive historical reports, is the *ḥadīth* genre, including in this context, apocalyptic traditions depicting the *Rūm* as the perpetual enemy. Skepticism concerning the authenticity of such traditions has long been expressed by certain scholars.[13] However, such apocalyptic traditions were apparently widespread, not only in Arabia but even more so perhaps among the Jewish and Christian communities in Syria and neighboring lands, including Constantinople.[14]

In any case, after the early Arab conquest of Syria and Egypt and the complete collapse of the Sasanian Empire, Byzantium's image as the external enemy par excellence crystallized in the Arab Islamic consciousness; it was to continue at least until the period of the Crusades. However, as a counterbalance to this hostile attitude, it is important to remember that the earlier positive Qur'ānic image of the Christian Byzantines persisted, albeit with some modification. This aspect of the Islamic perception is further enhanced by certain *ḥadīth* traditions attributed to Muhammad. For example, the Prophet's testimony that "compassion belongs to the Byzantines" (*al-shafaqatu fī-al-Rūm*) seems to have confirmed a normative Qur'ānic attitude that continued into later periods.[15] Such a perception of Byzantine compassion was later reflected in official letters from Muslim caliphs or their representatives to Byzantine emperors, particularly when discussing peace and the treatment and release of prisoners of war.[16]

From the period of the conquest of Syria and Egypt, we have the important statement elaborating on the theme of "Byzantine compassion." One of Muhammad's prominent companions, ʿAmr b. al-ʿĀs, conqueror and first Arab governor of Egypt, is credited with identifying compassion, as well as philanthropy, particularly toward the weak, as positive traits of the Rūm. At the same time the Byzantines are perceived, among other things, as a people for whom religiosity, asceticism, and spirituality were extremely important.[17]

Thus, two seemingly paradoxical premises seem to have continued to collectively define later Muslim perceptions of, and attitudes toward, Byzantium. There is no doubt that the early positive attitude toward Christians as reflected in the Qur'ān, including the injunctions to have friendly dialogue with the People of the Book, provided a counterbalance to other injunctions to fight against neighboring centers of power until they submit. Similarly, statements and actions attributed to the Prophet concerning the Rūm, including his friendly invitation to Heraclius to accept Islam, became models for such caliphs as ʿUmar I, ʿUmar II, Harūn al-Rashīd, and al-Ma'mūn, all of whom combined religious dialogue with discussion of practical political matters, and sometimes open confrontation, in their correspondence and dealings with contemporary Byzantine emperors. Thus a perception evolved of Byzantium as a compassionate Christian society on the one hand, and as a neighboring hostile power whose monarch and population were theoretically suitable candidates for conversion or subordination on the other hand.

The Religious Dimension of the Arab-Byzantine Encounter: Was the Conflict Essentially a Religious One?

Given the religio-political and military character of the rise of the Arab Islamic power, the sympathetic and tolerant attitude of Islam toward Christianity and Christians, and the actual history of the Arab-Byzantine military and political conflict, can one describe this conflict, during the period of the Arab conquest and after, as simply or even principally a religious conflict? It is my submission that such a description would be inaccurate and misleading. To quote Norman Daniel on a somewhat parallel situation: "It is already to beg the question to speak of a religious war, before we have established that that is what it was."[18] In fact, it is possible to go further than this in the case of the Arab Islamic conquest of Syria and Palestine. For here a number of Christian Arab tribes identified more with the advancing Muslim Arabs than with the Byzantines, while the Syriac-speaking Christian population felt no strong affinity with Byzantium, ethnically, politically, culturally, or ecclesiastically. Religious zeal, it is true, was a significant factor in both the motivation and the success of the Arab conquests. Such religious zeal had its counterpart among the Byzantines in their wars. It was certainly important in the Heraclian victory over Persia, and it was also reflected in the Byzantine emperor's desperate attempt to hold onto Syria and Egypt in the face of the unexpectedly well-disciplined and effective Arab military advance.

There is no doubt that the Arabic historical tradition concerning the conquest of Syria and Palestine highlights the role of the religious factor in both Arab and Byzantine camps. For example, Heraclius is often depicted, in Arabic historical and semi-historical traditions, exhorting his armies in "crusading" religious terms. In the same Arabic sources, the victory of the Arabs and the defeat of the *Rūm* is attributed, even by the Byzantines themselves, to the Arabs' supposed high religious principles and self-discipline, as contrasted with the Byzantines' alleged moral corruption and deviation from true Christian principles.

It is also true that Arabic and Byzantine sources speak of economic, political, and tribal factors in this conflict.[19] In a real sense, early Arab Islamic sources seem to depict the war more as a conflict between "Arabs and Byzantines" rather than between "Muslims and Christians"—a fact that is also confirmed by Syriac sources.[20] At the practical level, large numbers of Christian Arab warriors from Syria joined the Muslim armies against the Byzantines, while other Christians (and Samaritans) cooperated in several ways with the advancing Muslim Arabs.[21]

The sympathy of the Syrian Monophysite Christians, many of whom were tribal Arabs, toward the Muslim Arabs and against the Byzantines is clearly reflected in Syriac sources.[22] Arabic sources support this. At Pella in Jordan, for example, the civilian inhabitants, as distinct from the Byzantine garrison, are reported to have sent messages to the Arab Muslim general saying specifically that they preferred the Arabs to the Byzantines. What needs to be highlighted in this context is that, in seeking an alliance with the Muslim Arabs, these Christians have turned away from the Byzantines "although they are our co-religionists" (*wa-in kānū ʿalā dīninā*). Similarly, Christian Arab clans are described as having "enthusiastically rallied to the side of the Arabs, since an Arab victory was preferable in their eyes to a Byzantine one."[23] In asserting their Arab identity in ethnocultural rather than strictly religious terms, such Christian Arabs are reported as candidly admitting that "we dislike fighting against our co-religionists, but we hate to support foreigners against our own kinsmen."[24]

Tribal pride worked the other way too in this context, and Byzantium was directly or indirectly involved in this. When certain Arabs of the tribe of Iyād crossed into Byzantine territory in upper Mesopotamia, they seem to have done so less from religious loyalty than tribal pride. From the Arab Islamic perspective, however, what seems to have been emphasized was more the ethno-cultural than the religious dimension. This may be illustrated with reference to the reported correspondence between ʿUmar I and the contemporary Byzantine emperor concerning the aforementioned Christian Arabs from the tribe of Iyād. ʿUmar apparently considered them as political defectors who should be returned to the Arab fold, and he wrote to the Byzantine emperor demanding the immediate return of "a clan from among the clans of the Arabs [who] had left our country and arrived in yours."[25] Similarly, the episode of the conversion to Islam and reconversion to Christianity of the Ghassanid chief, Jabala, illustrates, among other things, the conflict for some Arab chiefs between tribal pride, political ambition, and religious allegiance.[26] The fact that abandoning the Arab Islamic community to join the Christian Byzantines was considered as "turning foreigner and giving up being Arab" (*asbahta aʿjamiyyan baʿda an kunta ʿArabiyyan*) is a particularly significant index of the delineation of identity in cultural rather than religious terms in early Islamic times.[27]

Subsequently, for example during the Umayyad period, such tribal ethos was to demonstrate itself both among Islamized and Christianized Arabs. For the Christian Arab tribes, this was manifested in various forms. On the one hand, a prominent Christian Arab poet such as al-Akhtal of Taghlib not only sang the praises of his Arab tribe and satirized other tribes but also was a recognized poet laureate in the Umayyad court, wearing a large gold cross round his neck, competing with Muslim poets, moving freely between Arab court and Christian church, mixing with Christian priests, apparently including the famous John of Damascus, and at the same time eulogizing the Muslim Arab caliph for waging war against the Christian Byzantines.[28]

The official Islamic attitude toward Byzantium during the Umayyad period was far from static or uniform, as can be seen from an examination of the policies of successive Umayyad caliphs. Reflecting a pragmatic blend of political expedience and search for legitimacy, it is clear that the Arab Islamic policies toward the Byzantines were not confined to warfare or truces. It can be seen that administrative measures, such as Arabization and Islamization of fiscal registers, coinage, official papyri, and milestones under ʿAbd al-Malik, as well as the monumental architectural and urban projects undertaken by this caliph and his sons in Syria-Palestine, were not entirely unrelated to the Byzantine factor. This is understandable for an Arab Islamic dynasty whose political center was the important former Byzantine province of Syria and Palestine—the birthplace of Christianity.[29] Still, it would be instructive in the present context to consider more closely certain aspects of the Umayyad religious policy insofar as it may reflect Arab Islamic attitudes toward Byzantine religion and culture.

The inherent Islamic tolerance toward Christians, as defined in the Qurʾān and in the example of the Prophet, may be seen generally during the Umayyad period. Despite regular warfare with Byzantium, including the two lengthy sieges of Constantinople (A.D. 674–678 and 717–718), this period was, on the whole, characterized by amicable relations with the indigenous Christians of Syria and Egypt. Despite a few cases of converting a church into a mosque, there are reports of the building of new churches and exempting monasteries from tax while providing them with new sources of water.

Many of the officials and functionaries of the Umayyads were indigenous Christians. One of the manifestations of amicable relations with Christians can be seen from an investigation of references to Christian monasteries in classical Arabic literature, reflecting the situation under Umayyad and ʿAbbasid rule. This indicates visits and gifts paid to such monasteries by caliphs and other prominent Muslims, sometimes on their way to or from an expedition against the Byzantines. However, it was not unheard of for some Muslim officials in the Umayyad period to build churches or chapels for their Arab or Greek Christian mothers.[30]

A particularly controversial issue of this period, in the context of the Arab-Byzantine encounter, is the question of attitude to images in the Byzantine Church and whether there was any Arab Islamic position concerning Christian icons. Certain contemporary Byzantine supporters attributed the rise of iconoclasm to Arab influences; and some modern scholars accept this without much questioning. It seems to me that the question of the so-called edict of Yazīd II against the display of images has often been viewed from the wrong perspective. The matter should perhaps be seen in terms of the Umayyad caliph's wish to reduce the manifestations of old Byzantine Christianity, rather than a desire by him to tell the local Christians how to worship. Yazīd was in effect banning the display of the remaining symbols of the old imperial ecclesiastical influence in his domains.[31]

Such a conclusion can be further supported, directly or indirectly, by reference to at least three Christian ecclesiastical authorities of Syrian provenance who flourished under Arab (Umayyyad, and in one case also early ʿAbbasid) rule. Such testimony also illustrates the type of religious issues discussed at the time, and the attitude of Muslim rulers toward indigenous Christians and, by implication, toward the historical Islamic encounter with Byzantium, the Eastern Christian Empire. The three were followers of the Melkite, Chalcedonian doctrine and therefore usually in line with the Byzantine ecclesiastical position, though officially they were under the jurisdiction of the Antiochean Church. This fact may lend even more credence to their testimony as they would have no interest in going out of their way to paint Arab rulers as better than they were.

One of these was the celebrated John of Damascus, who lived all his life in Arab Islamic Syria and Palestine and worked in the Umayyad court for a while, rubbing shoulders with caliphs, Muslim scholars, and Muslim and Christian Arab poets. He spoke both Syriac and Arabic but wrote mostly in Greek, and was one of the greatest defenders of the veneration of images. His orations in defense of icons have been considered perhaps the most influential, even by comparison to works written within Byzantium itself.[32] The fact that the Byzantine iconoclasts applied the pejorative nickname "saracen-minded" to John of Damascus, while the iconodule side applied the same epithet to the iconoclastic Emperor Leo III, shows graphically how anti-Arab phobia was utilized for ideological purposes by both sides of the conflict over icons within the Byzantine camp.

The second authority is Theodore Abū Qurra, Bishop of Harrān, a great theologian and controversialist, and the most important Syrian disciple of John of Damascus. Although he is known to have written some works in Greek and Syriac, Abū Qurra in fact wrote mostly in Arabic, a fact of great significance for the cultural identity and common language of his Christian congregation and wider audience, although his own bishopric was Melkite rather than Monophysite. In fact, his fame and popularity is attributed by his Christian biographers to this communicating of his ideas in Arabic at this comparatively early period, including his articulate defense of the veneration of images, reflecting some of the skills of his more illustrious hellenized master. It is significant that Bishop Theodore, in reporting the attitude of the Umayyads toward Christian churches, makes it clear that there was no question of the Umayyads wishing to impose a certain doctrine on the Christians concerning the veneration of images. The Umayyad authorities, according to him, continued to allow Christians to display crosses on their churches, presumably because this was a common symbol to all Christians, whereas only Melkites usually made a big issue of venerating images.[33] This official attitude of the caliphs toward the question of images within the Christian communities has a later parallel in the ʿAbbasid period in the episode of Hunayn b. Ishāq who was apparently even punished by the caliph al-Mutawakkil for failing to show respect for Christian images as enjoined by the church.[34]

The third Christian authority in this context is the anonymous biographer of St. Peter of Capitolias (Bait Ra's in Jordan), though not directly connected with the controversy over images. Written in Greek, this hagiography shows Peter of Capitolias, a contemporary of the Umayyad Caliph Walīd I (705–715), as having been well known for his invective verbal attacks against Islam which he freely flaunted in public places, and in the presence of Arab Muslim notables of his town. The Caliph's attempt to dissuade him illustrates the practical dilemma concerning the limits of religious tolerance: "You have the freedom to consider as God Jesus who is a man and a servant of the Creator. But why should you blaspheme against our religion and call our . . . Prophet master of error and father of falsehood?"[35] While ostensibly demonstrating the steadfast fanaticism of the Christian martyr, and providing an early example of a familiar theme in the Christian anti-Islamic polemic, this Greek hagiographic text indirectly illustrates the official Muslim attitude toward Christians in the Umayyad period.

Religious Apologetics and Politicocultural Polemic

In Arabic literature, there are probably fewer, certainly far less vehement, examples of specifically anti-Christian polemics than there are anti-Islamic polemics emanating from Byzantine circles. Two important points, however, should be made concerning Christian-Muslim polemics, apologetics, and dialogue. First, Christian anti-Islamic writings in Syriac and Arabic are far more restrained than those written in Greek. Syriac, and particularly Arabic, Christian theologians were of course duly conscious of their wider Islamic environment. Having easier direct access to the Arabic text of the Qur'ān and other Islamic writings, as well as frequent contacts and dialogues with Muslims, their writings are more of the mild, apologetic type. They seem more concerned with assuring their own co-religionists of the validity of their faith rather than proving the invalidity of the other religion.

Second, Muslim writers who were engaged in dialogue, or often parallel monologues, with Christians usually kept to the original Qur'ānic premise concerning Christ and were mostly apologists in their approach. In this, they reflect similar methods to those of Arabic Christian apologists. The main concern of most Muslim apologetics is to demonstrate from biblical texts that Muhammad was anticipated and foretold in the Bible, to assert the humanity rather than the divinity of Christ and to reproach, or sometimes attack, in Qur'ānic terms, what they saw as the Trinitarian puzzle.

Islamic writings of this type include polemical tracts in the form of replies essentially aimed at the local Christian communities (e.g., Ibn Rabban, a convert to Islam, and Jāhiz). They also include official epistles specifically addressed to a Byzantine emperor on behalf of a Muslim ruler (e.g., Hārūn al-Rashīd to Constantine VI), and versified retorts to Byzantine anti-Islamic diatribes (e.g., responses by al-Qaffāl and Ibn Hazm to the poem composed on behalf of Nikephorus Phokas in the tenth century A.D.)

Furthermore, Arabic apologetics written for local consumption within the lands of the caliphate, whether by Muslims or Christians, do not usually take into consideration the Byzantine factor. When there is some awareness of this factor, and this is particularly so in the case of al-Jāhiz for example, the criticism centers on cultural aspects of Byzantium rather than on the teachings of Christianity. Thus when the Byzantines are criticized in this type of writing, it is not primarily in their capacity as Christians. Conversely, when indigenous Christians are criticized, it is not essentially because of any real or assumed association with the Byzantines. In such

Islamic writings the main concern is to defend Islam and the realm of the caliph rather than attack Christians, let alone Christianity.

The Arab-Byzantine encounter was therefore an encounter between two religions at one level and between two neighboring political cultural powers at another level. The two levels of conflict no doubt overlap, and for some they probably seem so closely related as to be one and the same. This is not the case, however; the geopolitical and cultural factors often seem more significant in the final analysis. This may find some confirmation in the official Byzantine policy toward Muslim and Christian subjects of the Caliphate. In their attacks against Egyptian ports or Syrian and Mesopotamian frontier towns, Byzantine raiders apparently did not discriminate between Muslim mosques and Coptic or Syrian churches, or between Muslim and Christian women and children whom they habitually abducted in large numbers, according to Arabic sources.[36]

Al-Rashīd's Epistle to Constantine VI

One of the most interesting examples of official Arab-Byzantine dialogue, from the Islamic side, is a lengthy epistle sent on behalf of the ʿAbbasid Caliph, Hārūn al-Rashīd (786–809) to the Byzantine Emperor, Constantine VI (780–797).

Reflecting a familiar pattern of mixed messages, this long letter reveals a great deal about Arab Islamic perceptions of and attitudes toward Byzantium as a rival empire and culture. It includes an invitation to accept Islam or conclude (rather, renew) a truce and pay tribute. I have already discussed the political and cultural aspects of this epistle elsewhere.[37] Here I turn my attention to it. The epistle was composed by Abu al-Rabīʿ Muhammad b. al-Layth, described as the "Preacher" (*Khatīb*, *Wāʿiz*), but about whom not much else is known.[38] A number of important points need to be highlighted here.

1. The caliph is presented as following Qurʾānic injunctions and the Prophet's *sunna* in opening a dialogue and calling upon the emperor to follow the way of God. The emperor is addressed as *ʿAzīm al-Rūm*, a title first used by the Prophet Muhammad in addressing Heraclius. In view of the emperor's familiarity with God's revealed Books and the large number of his people, the caliph expresses his hope that the emperor would heed exhortation (*mawʿiza*) and benefit from dialogue and debate (*mujādala*).

2. The epistle addresses familiar issues in Islamic apologetics: the oneness and uniqueness of God; that Christ was merely "the Messenger, Word and Spirit of God given to Mary"; that the People of the Book should not persist in their extremism concerning the Trinity. Also the truth of Muhammad's message was based not only on rational grounds and its own vindication through resounding success but also on specific predictions of Muhammad's coming, in Jewish and Christian Scriptures, which the People of the Book have deliberately obfuscated and misinterpreted. However, the well-known Muslim accusation of *tahrīf* against Jews and Christians is understood in this epistle not as "alteration" of the text as some scholars seem to assume, but rather as "misorientation of the meaning of the speech and misdirection of the interpretation of the Books" (*tahrīf taʾwīl al-kalām wa tahrīf tafsīr al-kutub*)."[39] The epistle quotes, usually accurately, from the Old and New Testament in order to identify supposed allusions to Muhammad's prophethood.[40]

3. Significantly, the caliph implies that the real battle is between belief on the one side and unbelief or destructive doubt on the other. Thus the emperor is warned against "lending your ear to some misguided person who probably doubted our Book as an excuse to doubt your Book and thus undermine your faith and weaken your religion."

4. A particularly instructive feature of the epistle in this context is that, as a rule, it employs the "language of inclusive discourse," if one may use this expression. The religion of the Byzantine emperor is acknowledged as authentic; the premises of both universal reason and revelation are presumed as common ground between the two sides. Both the Christian Scriptures and the Qurʾān are equally God's preserved Books, and His treasured proofs: addition or deletion has affected them with the passage of time. This has been "established by Jesus himself, peace be upon him, when he said to the gathered disciples: 'with revelation I speak unto you and parables I make for you' . . . His parables are thus speech and his splendid speech is revelation." On the basis of this, the caliph wonders why the emperor and his people should deny the authenticity of the Qurʾān while accepting that of the Gospels: Why should "your own consensus," be accepted but not "ours," although both Books are similar in the circumstances of their transmission?

5. The epistle reflects certain assumptions concerning the influence of ecclesiastical authorities in Byzantium, particularly upon the emperor. Thus the emperor is warned against being prevailed upon by bishops and religious leaders *(ruʾasāʾ)* whose rationality should be suspected. He is urged to "ask those bishops" (*asāqif* or *asāqifa*) and "deacons" (*shamāmisa*) to "seek, search and find out," just as "Jesus, peace be upon him, says: 'Every one that asks receives; and he that seeks finds; and to whom that knocks it shall be opened.'"[41] The writer admits, at several points, that the emperor and his people did not acknowledge the Qurʾān as Scripture, nor Muhammad as Messenger of God, but that the criterion of reason should be acceptable to the Byzantines. The emperor is then asked to "gather the scholars, knowledgeable people, bishops and monks" and to ask them regarding specific scriptural allusions to the coming of Muhammad.[42]

6. The epistle equally warns the emperor against following the interpretation of earlier authorities or the claims of contemporaries from his people. For they doubt the authenticity of the transmission of the Qurʾān while accepting the transmission of the Gospels. However, the writer assures the emperor that the caliph did not write to him regarding this point "to suggest that he had any doubt or argument" concerning the authenticity of Christ's Gospel. However, the epistle gently introduces arguments attributed to "our scholars . . . vehicles of knowledge and understanding, jurists and wise men."[43]

7. Recourse to reason as the only arbiter is claimed by the writer, and the caliph pleads with the emperor to be reasonable and open-minded and to let his heart guide him. The consistent appeal to reason and intelligence as true arbiters of truth and certainty indicates not only the extent to which rational methods had taken hold within Muslim theological discourse by al-Rashīd's times but also that the Muslims expected Byzantine culture to be quite familiar with such methods of argumentation.

8. The rest of the epistle is more concerned with expected practical results of making peace and paying tribute.[44] It is important, however, that the place of religion in Byzantine society is acknowledged. For while the caliph shows deep understanding of the economic, social, and human aspects of the Arab-Byzantine conflict and the role of agriculture, commerce, and the crafts in securing people's prosperity, he also points out that without such activities "their religion cannot survive" (*la baqāʾ li-dīnihim illā maʿah*).[45] He reminds the emperor how, during the previous truce, extensive commercial activity, by Byzantine traders as well as Muslim and *Dhimmī* (i.e., Christian and possibly Jewish) merchants from the Arab side, had led to mutual benefit and prosperity.[46]

9. A very significant allusion to aspects of Byzantine political concerns and cultural attitudes is seen in quite pragmatic and realistic terms. The emperor is told that "both the aristocratic *(khawāss)* patricians and the general public (*ʿawāmm*) in your religious community (*milla*), would acknowledge your compassion and mercy towards them [if the peace treaty was extended] . . . the blessing of your reign and the benefits of your policy would result in greater love . . . obedience . . . and loyalty from your subjects, as well as prestige, honour and greatness . . . in the eyes of both friend and foe among foreign nations."[47]

10. The Byzantines were always seen as a religious people in Arab eyes. The perception of religiosity and the role of monks and monasticism among the Byzantines goes back to early Islamic times, and this is clearly reflected in this epistle. However, the point is exploited for political purposes; moral pressure is applied to get the emperor to accept peaceful terms: "You and those among your people who are interested in worship, asceticism, holiness, religious retreat and sincerity . . . would not only ensure your safety from the burdens of war, but would . . . be spared having to otherwise disobey Christ in this world." The inherent Christian pacifist attitude, as preached in the Gospel, is similarly used: "For Christ teaches you that 'whoever shall smite thee on thy right cheek, turn to him the other also.'"[48]

11. Since fulfilling the terms of an agreement or covenant is emphasized in both the Qurʾān and *Hadīth*, and is therefore a constant theme in Islamic jurisprudence,[49] it is understandable that al-Rashīd is critical of the Byzantine emperor's decision to terminate the current treaty. But the matter is also expressed in terms of international relations. Thus the importance of Byzantium's prestige among its neighbors is equally invoked. "You must know that covenants and oaths, which God has made sacrosanct among his creatures, are to be kept by his worshippers so that their hearts and souls might feel tranquil, and they might engage in ordinary business and establish their religious and worldly affairs . . . Your covenant was given . . . with God as witness, people around your country had heard about this and your patricians as well as your bishops had confirmed it."[50]

12. As a last warning, the caliph demands that if Constantine did not "pay the *jizya* . . . which would guarantee compassion for the weak . . . and the poor . . . and spare them captivity, killing, and imprisonment," it would be his responsibility. In refusing this arrangement, "you have shown neither fear of God nor shame from mortals . . . so prepare for retribution. . . ." There is a conscious play on the theme of perceived social conflict within Byzantium and the power of the military aristocracy. "Your harshness of heart and selfishness would only serve the interests of the aristocracy (*khawāss*), and would cause the weak and poor to become refugees, since you would not be able to protect them . . . It would be a blatant disregard for the principles of mercy and compassion which Christ has taught you, when he said in the Book: 'Blessed are the merciful: for they are the chosen of God and the light of the children of Adam.'"[51]

13. The epistle makes it clear that the conflict with Byzantium was not essentially about wishing to convert the Byzantine subjects from Christianity to Islam nor to destroy them. The epistle expresses concern, in no uncertain terms, for their prosperity as well as their freedom of religion. There is obviously an interesting, perhaps even cynical, aspect of propaganda in the epistle's claim that "had the poor, the peasants and manual labourers in the land of Byzantium been apprised of the prevailing favourable conditions in the realm of the Commander of the Faithful they would have flocked thither." For, apart from promises of economic prosperity, including housing, land, and irrigation water, they would have superior justice to that of the emperor's. Above all, "they would be free to practice their own religion, and no one would force them to convert.[52]

Thus the perception of the other, indeed of the enemy, reflects the self-image at the same time. This, and a belief on both sides that God stood with them against the other, should be kept in mind in interpreting the discourse on Arab-Byzantine warfare, diplomatic correspondence, propaganda, and other self-defining literature.

Historical and Cultural Polemic in Verse

Turning to the two versified Muslim replies to the diatribe addressed to the ʿAbbasid caliph by emperor Nikephorus II Phokas (963–969) we find confirmation of a number of familiar themes in Islamic polemics against the Byzantines. The original Byzantine verbal attack was in the form of a poem in Arabic composed on behalf of Nikephorus, probably by a renegade. The first Muslim rebuttal was composed by a contemporary, the Shāfiʿī jurist and theologian al-Qaffāl al-Shāshī (A.H. 291–366) and this seems to have found its way to Byzantium almost immediately.[53] What is of relevance for our purpose is that the Muslim jurist not only refuses the emperor's claim to be a pure Christian monarch but also asserts that Nikephorus did not deserve to be counted as a Christian at all. This was on account of the emperor's notorious cruelty and lack of compassion, his treacherous and criminal acts, and his un-Christian oppressive policies, as seen in his treatment of Muslims near the frontiers. The allusion here must be to Nikephorus' destruction of the important Cilician towns of Tarsus, Adana, and Missisa and their countrysides.

Apart from usual themes of Islamic apologetics concerning Christ and the position of Muhammad in the Gospels, al-Qaffāl's poem also shows the role of Muhammad's early sympathy toward the Christian Byzantines, and how this has been the only factor that saved them from complete annihilation by early Islamic arms: "Had it not been for the commendations (*Wasāyā*) of our Prophet concerning you, your people would never have been spared at the time of the early Islamic conquests."[54]

Ibn Hazm (384/994–456/1064), the celebrated Andalusian Zāhirī jurist, theologian, philosopher, historian, man of letters, and poet, felt compelled to compose an impromptu rebuttal upon hearing the original Byzantine Arabic poem in the court of the last Umayyad caliph at Cordova. It is curious that this took place over a century after the event; the matter was no longer one of communication, but rather a literary ideological response for the edification of Andalusian and other Muslim audiences. Ibn Hazm is able to put the Christianity of Byzantium in its historical and contemporary context and to link it with the churches of Antioch, Jerusalem, Alexandria, and Rome. His poem takes up a number of familiar political and religious issues of contention between the two sides. Ibn Hazm hints at a favorite theme in Arabic cultural polemics against Byzantium. While he claims that the Arabs had mastery of all branches of knowledge "both ancient and modern," he accuses the Byzantines of being no more than laden donkeys led by their bleeding noses. This seems a subtle reference to the Arab perception that the Byzantines after the rise of Christianity were no longer interested in philosophy and that they merely kept loads of ancient books which they could not use.[55]

This perception of Byzantium as intellectually inferior is a persistent theme in the Arabic literature of the period. It seems to compensate for the uncomfortable realization by the Arabs that, by the tenth century A.D., Byzantium had become the superior military power in the age-old conflict between the two sides. An interesting example from the mid-tenth century A.D. is the conversation between Nikephorus Phokas himself and the celebrated Hamdanid prince and poet, Abu Firas, while the latter was a prisoner of war in Constantinople. The emperor claims that the Arabs were only good as "writers, men of the pen, but not men of the sword"; Abu Firas had to argue at length that his people were good both as men of learning and as warriors.[56]

Scholarly Interest and Intellectual Curiosity

I have dealt elsewhere with perceptions of Byzantium as reflected in the works of Arab Islamic geographers, historians, jurists, and men of letters.[57] Here I should like to highlight a few points related to the theme of Byzantine religion and culture, to provide a broader perspective.

Al-Jāhiz's perception of Byzantium can be gauged in several incisive statements in a number of his epistles (*Rasā'il*). The celebrated Muʿtazilī master controversialist and polymath, whose active career spanned the reigns from al-Maʾmūn to al-Mutawakkil, was of course never away from political and ideological polemic. In his *Reply to the Christians*, al-Jāhiz demonstrates his acute historical sense and analytical skills. He is fully aware of the place of Byzantium as a rival power and a dangerous adversary, and of the role of Christianity. What is of particular significance, in the light of the inherent Qurʾānic and early Islamic sympathy with Byzantium, is al-Jāhiz's impatience with the way in which the Qurʾānic premise of tolerance and sympathy with the Christians has, in his view, worked against the interests of Muslims, culturally and economically, if not necessarily in purely religious terms. Al-Jāhiz has a few negative pronouncements to make on Byzantine culture, including the accusation that Byzantium invented and perpetuated the terrible practice of castration of young slaves, as well as bad manners and miserliness.

For the historians, it is important to point out the remarkable position of al-Masʿūdī. Apart from taking an interest in Christian communities in the Islamic world, he was interested in the historical relationship between Christianity and Byzantium. He was keen to report the first six Oecumenical councils of the church held under Byzantine auspices (although neither he nor other Arabic historians, such as al-Yaʿqūbī and the Melkite Patriarch of Alexandria, Eutychius, mention the seventh Oecumenical council which took place after the Arab conquest). Al-Masʿūdī seems particularly aware of the way in which Church and state in Byzantium were two parallel institutions, although he was obviously not so well informed about the complex nature of the relationship. Thus he describes the patriarch of Constantinople as "the king of religious affairs just as the emperor is the master of the sword."[58] It must be remembered that this is a somewhat unfamiliar situation that has no equivalent in the classical Islamic polity and that al-Masʿūdī's reference to it in this way is, therefore, quite remarkable.

Through his contacts with Arab and Byzantine ambassadors, and his interest in Christianity, al-Masʿūdī was also able to comment on the position of Hellenic learning under Byzantium. As already indicated, the Islamic tradition in general saw the Byzantine period as one of decline in this respect, and al-Masʿūdī himself subscribes to this notion when writing generally about Byzantium. Nevertheless, human contacts across the cultural barrier can considerably modify negative perceptions. Thus al-Masʿūdī was able to describe, in positive and sympathetic terms, a distinguished and learned Byzantine ambassador, John Mysticus, whom he probably met in Damascus in 946. John Mysticus, a monk by training, is described by al-Masʿūdī as a man "of understanding and discernment, versed in the history of the kings of the Greeks and Romans and the philosophers who were their contemporaries and rather familiar with their [philosophical] systems."[59] It is the same context of direct contacts, as well as an inherent intellectual curiosity and fairmindedness, that enabled al-Masʿūdī not only to write in great detail about contemporary Byzantium but also to assess its place in world history positively as an empire "with well-established institutions and a highly organized administration." Presumably this included Byzantine church and monastic institutions which al-Masʿūdī singles out elsewhere in his works.[60]

One important genre of Arabic writing relevant to Byzantine religious life are the reports of Muslim visitors to Constantinople and Anatolia as reported in works of geography, history, belles lettres, and in personal travelogues. These include reports of compulsory visitors, if one may call those who were taken captive or prisoners by Byzantine raiders or in battle.

Among these the names of Muslim al-Jarmī (ninth century) and Hārūn b. Yahyā (tenth century) are well known to anyone familiar with Arab-Byzantine relations in that period.

Al-Bīrūnī preserves valuable information not only on Muslim knowledge of the calendar and hierarchy of the Byzantine Church but also on Byzantine pressures on Muslim prisoners to convert, and on procedures for baptism, based on the account of a returned prisoner, Abū al-Husayn al-Ahwāzī. Similar information is also incidentally recorded by earlier historians, including Tabarī.[61]

ʿAlī al-Harawī (twelfth century) and the celebrated Ibn Battūta (fourteenth) were two private or perhaps semi-private, travelers who reached Constantinople and succeeded in meeting Byzantine dignitaries including the Byzantine emperor of the time. Their accounts and the sense of mutual sympathy which they reflect offer a fascinating aspect of the Islamic Byzantine encounter at different points in its history. Thus, al-Harawī speaks of the "goodness and beneficence" (*al-Ghayr wa-l-ihsān*)" which the emperor Manuel showed toward him.[62]

Ibn Battūta, in particular, is quite positive about the religious and spiritual life in Constantinople which he visited for about five weeks after his insistence that he accompany a returning Byzantine princess from the court of her husband, the Khan of the Muslim Uzbeks of the Crimea to the Byzantine capital. His reception by the emperor, the retired emperor turned monk, as well as by scholars and ascetics, left a very strong impression on this intrepid Maghribi traveler who had a keen interest in asceticism. He was particularly impressed with the humility of the monks and was moved by their veneration for anybody or anything connected with Jerusalem and the Holy Land.[63]

Finally, there is sufficient evidence to demonstrate the inherently sympathetic attitude of the Qur'ān toward Christians, the example of the Prophet's treatment of them, the existence of covenants between Muslim rulers and the Christian communities in the lands of the caliphate, and the fact that most of these Christians did not identify with Byzantium, culturally, politically, or ecclesiastically. Consequently, the Arab-Byzantine conflict cannot be viewed simply as a religious conflict. Indeed, some Byzantine authorities—for example, the Patriarch Nicholas I Mysticus of Constantinople (901–907, 915–927)—specifically refers to the covenants established with the Christians by the Prophet and his immediate successors.[64]

It is true that the religious factor did play its part. But in the final analysis, the student of the history of Arab-Byzantine relations can see these relations mainly in political, cultural terms, even if sometimes expressed in religious vocabulary. It can be seen from Arabic literature (and also from Byzantine sources) that direct human contacts between the two sides usually produced more realistic and mutually positive perceptions.

The representatives of Byzantine Christianity never came to terms with accepting the Arabs as an equal power, nor Islam as a true religion. The Muslim Arabs accepted Christianity as a true religion within the terms of reference of the Qur'ān and tolerated Christians in compliance with these terms and the example of the Prophet. They accepted Arab and other indigenous Christians as subjects with certain restrictions in an Islamic political context, but also as partners in a common culture and a common intellectual enterprise. They accepted Byzantium as a rival, if inferior, power, both culturally and politically, but continued to anticipate its downfall at their hands, sometimes in apocalyptic terms. They believed that ultimately the anti-Christ who would only appear after they had captured Constantinople, would be defeated by the true Christ, son of Mary, and they as Muslims would be among his supporters when Muslims and true Christians would be on the same side.

It is hoped that the foregoing discussion illustrates the complexity of the Arab-Byzantine encounter, and helps to remind us that the more we examine this encounter in its true historical perspective, the less it appears as a "Muslim versus Christian" conflict and the more it presents itself as a geopolitical, economic, and cultural conflict.

NOTES

1. See in particular, G. W. Bowersock, *Roman Arabia* (Cambridge, Mass.: Harvard University Press, 1983).

2. See in particular, I. Shahid, *Byzantium and the Arabs*, 2 vols. (Washington, 1987 and 1991).

3. For other dimensions, see my earlier studies, A. Shboul, "Byzantium and the Arabs: The image of the Byzantines as mirrored in Arabic literature," *Byzantine Papers*, ed. E. & M. Jeffreys and A. Moffatt (Canberra, 1981), pp. 43–68; Shboul, "Arab attitudes towards Byzantium: Official, learned, popular," *Rathegetria, Essays presented to Joan Hussey* (Camberley, Porphyrogenitus, 1988), pp. 11–128.

4. Qur'ān 30:1–6.

5. For example, Qur'ān 61: 6, 14; see M. Hayek, *al-Masih fī l-Qur'ān* (Beirut, 1962); G. Parrinder, *Jesus in the Qur'ān* (London, 1965).

6. Qur'ān, 5: 47, 66.

7. Qur'ān, 5: 5.

8. Qur'ān, 57: 27; 9: 34.

9. Qur'ān, 5: 82–83 (after Arberry, *the Qur'ān Interpreted).*

10. See A. Shboul, "ʿAlāāt al-Umma al-Islamiyya fi al-ʿAsr al-Nabawi maʿa Bilād al-Shām wa-Bīzanta (Relations of the Islamic community at the time of the Prophet with Syria and Byzantium), *Dirāsat Tārīkh al-Jazīra al-ʿArabiyya*, Series 3: *al-Jazīra al-ʿArabiyya fī ʿAsr al-Rasūl wa-l-Khulafā' al-Rāshidīn*, Vol. 1 (Riyadh, King Saud University, 1989), pp. 157–182.

11. Qur'ān, 9: 29.

12. See, for example, Ibn ʿAsākir, *Tārīkh Dimashq, I*, ed. Munajjid (Damascus, 1951), 383–384 (quoting al-Hasan al-Basrī and Mujāhid).

13. See especially Ibn Khaldun, *Muqaddima* (Bulaq, 1867), p. 260ff.

14. See Paul Alexander, *The Byzantine Apocalyptic Tradition* (Berkeley: University of California Press, 1985); S. Brock, "Syriac views of emergent Islam," in *Studies on the First Century of Islamic Society*, ed. G. H. A. Juynboll (Carbondale: Southern Illinois University Press, 1982), pp. 22; I deal with Islamic apocalyptic tradition elsewhere.

15. For documentation, see Shboul, "Arab attitudes towards Byzantium," pp. 111–128.

16. See ibid., pp. 117, 119; cf. al-Rashīd's letter to the Byzantine emperor.

17. For details, see ibid.

18. N. Daniel, *Heroes and Saracens: An Interpretation of the Chansons de Geste* (Edinburgh, 1984), p. 3.

19. See, for example, Tabarī, *Tārīkh*, passim; Abū Mikhnaf Azdī, *Futūh al-Shām*, ed. A. M. ʿĀmir (Cairo, 1970).

20. See, for example, Tabarī's accounts of the battles of Yarmuk, Pella, and others; for Syriac sources, see S. Brock, "Syriac views of emergent Islam," in Juynboll, *Studies on the First Century of Islamic History*, p. 14.

21. Azdi, *Futūh al-Sham*, pp. 111, 130.

22. S. Brock, "Syriac views of emergent Islam," pp. 10–13.

23. Azdi, *Futūh al-Sham*, p. 44.

24. Ibid., pp. 168–169.

25. Tabarī, *Tārīkh*, vol. 4, pp. 543–555.

26. Isfahānī, *Aghānī* (Bulaq, 1868), vol. 14, pp. 4–9.

27. Ibn Habīb, *al-Munammaq* (Hyderabad, 1964), p. 496; cf. I. Kawar, "Djabala b. al-Ayham," *Encyclopaedia of Islam*, vol. 2, p. 354.

28. Isfahānī, *Aghānī*, vol. 6, pp. 169–188, esp. p. 176.

29. See Shboul, "Arab attitudes toward Byzantium," pp. 114–115.

30. For example, Balādhurī, *Futūh*, ed. M. de Goeje (Leiden, 1866), p. 286; Ibn ʿAsākir, *Tārīkh Dimashq*, ed. A. R. Badrān (Damascus, 2nd. ed. 1979), p. 42.

31. See Shboul, "Arab attitudes toward Byzantium," p. 115.

32. G. Ostrogorsky, *History of the Byzantine State*, trans. J. M. Hussey, 2nd ed. (Oxford, Blackwell, 1968), p. 163; J. M. Hussey, "Byzantine theological speculation and spirituality," *Cambridge Medieval History*, vol. 4, 2 (Cambridge, 1967), pp. 187–188; see also "John of Damascus" in the *Oxford Dictionary of Byzantium* (New York, 1991).

33. See S. Griffith, "Theodore Abū Qurra's Arabic tract on the Christian practice of venerating images," *Journal of the American Oriental Society* 105 (1985), pp. 53–73.

34. Ibn al-ʿIbrī, *Mukhtasar*, ed. A. Sālihānī (Beirut, 1890), p. 145. See P. Peeters, ed., *Passion de Saint Pierre de Capitolias*, in *Anal. Bollandistes*, 57 (1939), pp. 299–333, esp. 304–313; quoted by A.-Th. Khoury, *Les théologiens byzantins et l'Islam: textes et auteurs* (ViiJe–XiiJe S,), 2nd ed. (Louvain-Paris, 1969), p. 67.

35. See Peeters, *Passion de Saint Pierre de Capitolas*, pp. 299–333, esp. 304–313; quoted by Khoury, *Les théologiens byzantins et l'Islam*, p. 67.

36. Tabarī, *Tārikh*, vol. 9, p. 194: attack against Damietta in Egypt when 450 Coptic Christian women and 200 Muslim women were abducted, and some Coptic churches burnt; see also ibid, vol. 10, p. 85: many Christians were abducted and a number of mosques and churches were burned.

37. Shboul, "Arab attitudes toward Byzantium," pp. 116–117.

38. Tabarī, *Tārikh*, vol. 8, p. 288; al-Nadīm, *Fihrist* (Tehran, 1971), p. 134; trans. B. Dodge (Columbia University Press, 1970), 1: 264–265, 274; 2: 739; for the complete text of the epistle, see A. Z. Safwat, *Jamharat Rasā'il al-ʿArab* (Cairo, 2nd. ed., 1971), 3: 217–274.

39. Safwat, *Jamharat Rasā'il*, vol. 3, p. 262.

40. See ibid, pp. 266ff; cf. particularly, John 14: 26; 16: 13; Isaiah 21: 96; Psalms 9: 20; Habakkuk 3: 3; 6, 15; Psalms 149: 1–9; Isaiah 42: 1–4; 10–12; Psalms 45: 2–5; Deuteronomy 33: 1; 18: 15; Matthew 6: 9; 5: 7–9, 39–41.

41. Safwat, *Jamarat Rasā'il*, vol. 3, pp. 260–261; cf. Luke 11:10.

42. Safwat, *Jamarat Rasā'il*, vol. 3, p. 262.

43. Ibid., pp. 231, 233, 234, 240.

44. See Shboul, "Byzantium and the Arabs."

45. Safwat, *Jamarat Rasā'il*, vol. 3, p. 269.

46. Ibid., p. 270.

47. Ibid., p. 271.

48. Ibid., p. 270; Matthew 5: 39–41; on earlier Islamic perception of Byzantine religiosity, see Shboul, "Arab attitudes toward Byzantium," p. 125.

49. See Shboul, "Arab attitudes toward Byzantium," p. 121.

50. Safwat, *Jamharat Rasā'il*, vol. 3, p. 272.

51. Ibid., p. 273: a paraphrase of Matthew 5: 7–9.

52. Safwat, *Jamharat Rasā'il*, vol. 3, p. 273.

53. See S. Munajjid, ed., *Qasīdat Imbarātūr al-Rūm Nigfūr* . . . (Beirut, 1982), containing the original diatribe in 70 lines; al-Qaffāl's reply in 74 lines and Ibn Hazm's independent reply, about a century later, in 137 lines; on al-Qaffāl's reply, see also G. E. von Grunebaum, "Eine poetische Polemik zwischen Byzanz und Bagdad im 10. Jahrhundert," *Analecta Orientalia* (Rome, 1937), pp. 43–64; repr. in his *Islam and Medieval Hellenism* (London, Variorum, 1976), no. 19.

54. See ibid., lines 4, 5, 6, 25, 37, 40, 68, 74.

55. Ibid., pp. 41–58: lines 22–28, 135.

56. See *Dīwān Abī Firās*, ed. S. Dahhāan (Beirut, 1944), vol. 1, p. 36.

57. See A. Shboul, *al-Mas'udi and His World: A Muslim Humanist and His Interest in Non-Muslims* (London: Ithaca Press, 1979), esp. chapters 6 and 7; and my articles "Byzantium and the Arabs" (1981) and "Arab attitudes towards Byzantium" (1988); see note 3.

58. al-Mas'ūdī, *Tanbīh*, ed. M. de Goeje (Leiden, 1894), pp. 172–173; see Shboul, *al-Mas'udi*, p. 260.

59. al-Mas'ūdī, *Tanbīh*, p. 193; Shboul, *al-Mas'udi*, pp. 261–262.

60. *Tanbīh*, pp. 7; Shboul, *al-Masw'udi*, p. 260.

61. al-Bīrūnī, *Athar* (*Chronologie orientalischer Völker*), ed. E. Sachau (Leipzig, 1923), p. 289.

62. al-Harawi, *Isharat* (*Guide des lieux de pèlegrinage*), ed. J. Sourdel-Thomine (Damascus, 1953), pp. 56–57.

63. Ibn Battuta, *Travels*, Cairo, Tijariyya ed. (1958), p. 379ff.

64. Nicholas I Patriarch of Constantinople, *Letters*, Greek text & English trans., by R. J. H. Jenkins and L. G. Westerink (Dumbarton Oaks, Washington, 1973), nos. 1–2.

7

Some Arab-Muslim Perceptions of Religion and Medieval Culture in Sicily

ANDREA BORRUSO

The subject that will be treated here is of great amplitude and I have had to limit myself to a consideration of the fundamental aspects, selecting the most significant travel accounts, poetry, and sources in the fields of geography and history and concentrating above all on Sicily. There are, however, numerous other sources that deserve to be consulted in order to have more extensive and complete data on the topic, for example, fiscal, administrative, juridical, diplomatic and chancellery sources, and others.

I wish to make a few preliminary considerations. First, the Arab sources we possess pertaining to the reconstruction of the Arab-Islamic domination of Sicily were, for the most part, collected, edited, and translated by the Italian scholars Michele Amari (d. 1889) and Celestino Schiaparelli (d. 1919), to which must be added the names of Umberto Rizzitano and Francesco Gabrieli, of the Tunisian Ḥasan Ḥusnī ʿAbd al-Wahhāb, of Edmond Fagnan, Roger Idris, and Evariste Lévi-Provençal.

These are sources that, up until the present, have been used to trace the history of the Arab venture in Sicily, in all of its varied aspects. This reconstruction was made possible due to the Arab authors of these sources who showed a keen interest in their compatriots and their coreligionists but not (or at least to a lesser extent) in the culture, religion and customs of the indigenous populations. This is a certain aspect of the Arab impact on the island of Sicily in the Middle Ages. Furthermore, when Sicily no longer gravitated into the orbit of Islam, the interest of the travelers, historians, and geographers continued to be directed toward the Arab populations still surviving in Sicily and southern Italy.

These same sources must therefore be considered in order to unveil the progressive stages of the Muslim conception of Christian Italy and Sicily. This involves an effort and implies a study which may lead to unsatisfactory results, although such an approach is certainly attractive and stimulating. It obliges us to look at these texts and documents in order to read between the lines, to find in them observations and opinions expressed by Arabs and Muslims about the Christians. Such an approach will enable us to progress more solidly toward a common history of both the East and the West.

From the eighth century onward, the Mediterranean was what we might call an Arab lake. At that time, the Arabs already possessed all of North Africa and Spain: these territories were thus part of the *dār al-Islām*. France, Italy, and the Balkan peninsula remained outside the Muslim *oikumene*, even if they were marginally affected by some more or less extensive infiltrations. Northern Italy remained on the border of Arab expansion which briefly occupied Sardinia and some parts of Apulia and the Naples area. The Arabs arrived, carrying on both truce and war, but never succeeded in founding any permanent settlements, apart from the Emirate of Bari and the Muslim colonies in Garigliano. The first writer to visit the "Long Land" (the oriental geographic term for Italy) was apparently Hārūn ibn Yaḥyā: the account of his adventures has come down to us thanks to Ibn Ruṣta, a tenth-century geographer. This journey probably took place around 880 or 890. After the description of Constantinople—which for historical, topographical, and other reasons is the most important section—we should make reference to the description of Rome, which Hārūn ibn Yaḥyā reached after visiting Venice and crossing the Po Valley. As we may observe from the reading of a short passage, the description of Rome is replete with legends which are confusing and incomplete. It only occasionally contains a personal reflection. Common to other medieval Arab writers whose sources can be sought out in the Syro-Byzantine book of wonders, it describes Rome as an eternal city with the Tiber and its bronze bed, St. Peter's and the birds flying toward it bearing olives in their beaks, the countless gold crosses, the precious habits and chalices of the Christian faith, the swarms of priests and deacons.

The personal element which reveals the author's direct contact with the places described is seen in his allusion to the Romans' custom of shaving their beards and heads. In my opinion, this is an allusion to the ecclesiastic tonsure, even if his account is puerile and fantastic:

> Rome is a city ruled by a king called the Pope. It is about forty square miles in area. The western part is crossed by a river, which also crosses the streets; its bed and its banks, as well as the bridges spanning it, are all of bronze. In the middle of the city stands a great church, about two parasangs long, with three hundred and sixty doors; in the middle of this church there is a tower one hundred cubits high, surmounted by a bronze dome. At the top of the dome there is a bronze starling; at olive-picking time, the wind blows into the sculpture of this starling, making crying sounds, and all the starlings of the city gather together. Each one carries an olive in its beak, which it drops inside the tower. These olives are gathered and pressed, and sufficient oil is obtained to light the churchlamps until the following season.

Here is another short passage about the Pope which will enable us to see how this tale is imbued with strange and fantastic elements. However, the fables told in the Middle Ages in the Christian West about Mohammad were no less grotesque.

> In the church there is the golden tomb of two apostles: one called Peter and the other called Paul. Every year, at Easter, the King, that is to say the Pope, comes and opens the door of the sepulchre; he descends into the tomb with a razor in his hand. There he shaves the head and the beard of the dead Peter, and also cuts his nails; when he returns he gives a hair to every person present. This rite has been celebrated every year for nine centuries.

In conclusion, here is the dialogue which Hārūn ibn Yaḥyā claims to have had with the inhabitants of Rome:

> The Romans of humble condition shave off their beard entirely, leaving not a single hair on their chin; they also shave the top of their head. I asked them why, saying, 'Man's greatest ornament is his beard: why do you do this?' And they replied: "He who does not shave is not a good Christian: for Peter and the other apostles came to us with neither stick nor bag, as poor and humble men, when we were richly dressed kings and rich men, and they urged us to take up the Christian faith. We did not obey, on the contrary we arrested them and martyred them, and we cut off their hair and their beard. And now that the truth of their preaching has shown itself to us [to] be manifestly true, we behave like this in order to atone for our sin."

The most comprehensive but also most unreliable description by Arab geographers and travelers, between the ninth and the fifteenth centuries, thus concerns the city of Rome and its inhabitants; other less complete accounts refer to other towns such as Genoa, Venice, Pisa, Naples, and, further south, Reggio, Taranto, Otranto, and Brindisi; an allusion to Lucera (Luğārā or Lushīrā in Arabic spelling), where the Emperor Frederick II relegated the last of the Sicilian Muslims, is to be found in the writings of certain geographers, such as al-Ḥimyarī, Ibn Saʿīd al-Andalusī, Abū'l-Fidā', and a few others.

The data provided by the geographers and travelers regarding peninsular and insular Italy are not all equally extensive. It scarcely needs mentioning that their writings give priority to Sicily, considering that for two and a half centuries the island was part of the *dār al-Islām*. Among this remarkable Arab geographic production, particular mention should be made of ash-Sharīf al-Idrīsī's work in which four sections are devoted to Italy (three to the continental territory and one to the islands).

In the years 1140–1154 the Muslim scholar al-Idrīsī was working in Palermo, at the Norman court, on the composition of the celebrated *Kitāb Ruǧār*, better known by the title *Nuzhat al-mushtāq fī ikhtirāq al-āfāq* (Book of pleasure of him who has a passion for travel through the countries). Apart from the inherent value of this work, we can reflect on the fact that it represents a paradigm, a unique model of collaboration and, one might say, intellectual and spiritual syntony between a celebrated Muslim scholar and a medieval Christian milieu. Among the "infidel" monarchs, none received in Arabic the praise that we can read in the preface to the Book. Religious fanaticism did not prevent ash-Sharīf al-Idrīsī from putting his scientific knowledge at the service of a civilization and culture which, at that time, regarded Islam as an imposture that had to be fought against by all available means. If we consider Spain in the same historical period, it should be remembered that in the year 1143—when Roger II was on the throne—an initiative of capital importance occurred, that is, the translation of the Qur'ān from Arabic into Latin. Peter the Venerable gathered together a group of scholars with a knowledge of Arabic and entrusted them with the task of translating the Qur'ān. The prime aim was certainly the defense of the Christian faith against heresy: Islam was to be studied in order to better refute it, as Abbot Peter of Cluny declared in a letter to St. Bernard of Clairvaux.

In the Norman Palace in Sicily, the climate in which the *Kitāb Ruǧār* was begun and quickly developed was, on the contrary, much more peaceable. Idrīsī, as mentioned earlier, showed us in the preface to his text the prodigious range of Norman King Roger II's knowledge; what he says of him does not, moreover, seem to be dictated by flattery:

> It would be impossible [he says] to describe all his knowledge of mathematics and politics or to mark the limit of his acquaintance with these sciences, which he has studied with intelligence and assiduity in each and every aspect. He has brought to them singular innovations and marvellous inventions, such as no other prince ever achieved.

In addition to geographers, we have also mentioned the travelers. Among the writings of the Arab travelers who visited Sicily in the Middle Ages, a particularly important place is occupied by the account—in Arabic, *Riḥla,* the "Travel Journal"—of the Hispano-Arab pilgrim Ibn Jubayr, who, between the end of 1184 and the beginning of 1185, spent nearly three months in Sicily. This text is unique in its verve and the liveliness of its account. Its discovery more than a century and a half ago constituted one of the first fruits of the Arabic studies of Michele Amari, the celebrated author of the *History of the Muslims of Sicily.* Ibn Jubayr's account is, therefore, a precious source for our knowledge of how a non-Sicilian Muslim perceived and judged Sicilian Islam, together with the religion and culture of the Christians in the island. This highly personal and passionate narrative is limited to a short historical period—that is, the end of the reign of William II the Good—but it enables us, to some extent, to reconstruct the existence of the Muslim subjects of the Normans. Ample evidence of the enthusiasm and persistent vitality of Islam in the lands, and even in the court of the infidel monarchs, for the culture and the Arab surroundings of William II, and for the proselytism of his crypto-Muslim courtiers, is evident in the following passage:

> The attitude of the king is really extraordinary. His conduct toward the Muslims is exemplary; he entrusts them with official tasks, he chooses his officers from their members, and all, or nearly all, keep their faith secret and remain faithful to Islam. The king trusts the Muslims entirely and relies upon them in his affairs and in his most essential preoccupations to such a degree that the intendant of his kitchen is a Muslim.

But the most interesting image is that of the Norman King William II's religious tolerance:

> It was related to us that the island was shaken by a great earthquake, which severely frightened this polytheist king. He passed swiftly through his palace, where he heard naught but invocations to God and his prophet, pronounced by his wives and eunuchs. If any of the latter showed dismay before him, he told them reassuringly: "Let each of you invoke God he worships and whose faith he observes."

Nor can we forget his description of Palermo, once a Muslim city named al-Madīna, the capital:

> The king's palaces are ranged on the breast of the city, like necklaces on the neck of a young woman with rounded breasts; pleasures and games succeed each other in its gardens and hippodromes. How many private gardens and ornamental lakes, pleasure domes and belvederes this king possesses, without dwelling in them! How many convents he possesses, most generous estates and churches with crosses plated in gold and silver! May God in his power soon redeem the lot of this island, reestablish it as a dwelling-place of faith, and lead it back to fear [of God] and security.

> The Muslims still keep in the city some vestiges of their faith; they attend most of their mosques, wither they are summoned by a clearly heard call to celebrate their ritual prayers. They have their own quarters where only they live, to the exclusion of all Christians. The *suqs* are thronged by them, and they are the merchants here. They have no collective prayer on Fridays, for the *khutba* would be impossible for them. But they say the prayers of the festivities with a *khutba* with an invocation to the Abbassid caliph. They have a *cadi* before whom they conduct their trials; they have a main mosque where they assemble, and which they take great care to illuminate in this blessed month.
>
> The ordinary mosques are numerous, indeed countless. Most of them serve as classrooms for the teachers of the Qur'ān. All in all, these people are isolated, separated from their brothers, they are subject to the authority of the infidels, they have no security either for their goods or for their women or for their sons. May God by a favourable act of intervention restore them to their previous state!

To examine Ibn Jubayr's impression of Norman Sicily, one must imagine his basic attitude. We have seen that the traveler begins by making a show of his enthusiasm for the Arab culture and environment of William II; but he then proceeds, when dealing with Palermo, to the overall judgment that his coreligionists lived without any security, within the power of the infidels, cut off from their brothers in the Muslim world (as in the passage quoted above). Finally, in his last and longest Sicilian sojourn in Trapani, he is happy that the Christians allowed the Muslims to celebrate the end of *Ramadān* with public processions to the sound of trumpets and drums, but he is moved to pity for the agony of Sicilian Islam, which he says exposed them to the most painful harassment by the Christian authorities, and whose total extinction the better informed observers already foresaw in the very near future. Today we can acknowledge the accuracy of these observers' predictions, for the real collapse of Islam in Sicily was to begin within just a few years, with the death of William II. But, apart from these pessimistic observations, it is Ibn Jubayr who has left us with the most memorable records of the survival and the prosperity of the Muslim faith and Arab culture on the island in this period. One need only recall his celebrated pages on King William's tolerance, his entourage and oriental way of life, his description of Palermo, in particular, of the Muslim quarters, and his detailed information about the Muslim rural population in the Val di Mazara.

To reconcile all these remarks and contradictory impressions, we must reflect on his passionate attachment to his faith and his culture. He is always ready to exalt their glories and no less ready to criticize the failures and losses they have undergone. For him, King William's Arabophilia and Islamophilia, which he knew through the high officials of the Royal Palace, are not proof of the sovereign's breadth of mind and tolerance but rather of the prestige and the superiority of Islam, both as religious faith and as Arab culture. The freedom of the Islamic cult in the capital and throughout the island is no more than the exercise of a Muslim right. Where the cult is practiced and where it is threatened is due to the diabolical wickedness of the infidels. There is no denying that Ibn Jubayr's conclusion is clearly pessimistic: the account of his personal experiences in the island, now Christian, ends with the moving episode of the Muslim girl whose father tries to marry her to one of the travelers so that she may be taken away to the land of Islam and thus be saved from the trials and temptations of apostasy. However, it is thanks to the "things seen" by this cultured pilgrim and writer that the image of Arab-Norman Sicily has been handed down to us, with its languages, religions, and various ethnic groups, among which Islam stood out on account of its ancient civilization, not unlike the mosques which raised their minarets alongside the streaming gold mosaics of the Christian cathedrals.

To return to the age of Roger II, King Roger, driven by the intellectual curiosity that in Sicily was to be transmitted to Frederick II and his son, appears to have been truly seduced by Arab culture. It is certain that of all his subjects the Muslims were those who, at that time, could present to him the most brilliant civilization. In the second half of the twelfth century the historian Ibn al-Athīr wrote as follows: "Roger also adopted the custom of the Muslim kings by instituting in his court aide-de-camps, chamberlains, equerries, bodyguards, and other officers. He thus abandoned the practice of the Franks who did not know these categories of officers."

The favor with which Roger surrounded the Arab and Muslim scholars naturally extended to the poets. At the time of the Norman conquest, a certain number of Muslims had abandoned Sicily, probably hoping that their coreligionists would avenge them. But it seemed that the majority remained on the island, because they either would not or could not expatriate. Many very quickly rallied round the new state, which brought them not only religious tolerance but also true peace and the end of dissension. An elite class emerging from the Arab-Sicilian milieu appeared to have encircled the throne that protected it. From its ranks emerged some admirable poets: Abū'd-Dawʿ who lived on familiar terms with Roger II and seems to have sincerely loved him. The elegy this poet composed on the occasion of the death of a young prince (possibly the eldest son of Roger II, who died in 1146) is full of an emotion that honors both protector and protégé. Here is the elegy:

> Alas! When he was in the prime of his beauty and his majesty, when the great ones and all the country prided themselves on him.
> Destiny, always fickle, carried him away like a thief, this young prince whose glory is betrayed!
> Burn, breasts! Souls, be dumbfounded! Sorrows, multiply! And weeping, be without measure!
> Burst forth, afflications! Eyes, overflow with tears so that their flow may meet the fire that devours the hearts . . .
> For whom do they cry, if not for him, the wild beasts in the woods? If they could but understand, the very boughs would weep with the doves.

This elegy is clearly imbued with the excesses of Arab lyricism. It is not a vain declamation, however. Can we imagine, four centuries later, an Arab poet in Grenada celebrating in impeccably metric verse Ferdinand the Catholic or Charles V?

It is therefore possible to glean in the Arab poetry of Sicily some data about the theme that concerns us. The most interesting source, in this respect, is certainly Ibn Ḥamdīs (b. 1055, d. 1133), due to the quantity of his output (about 6,000 verses) and his intrinsic poetic qualities. He is remembered for the wandering life he led far from his homeland, Sicily; for the nostalgia of his language; and for the vehemence of his attacks against the Christian usurpers. The short poems on the millstone, the lustre of the mosque, the night and the dawn, the stars, the storm at sea, and so on certainly bring the poet close to the Arabic-Andalusian milieu, to which he was closely linked, as the Arab anthologists of the Middle Ages already perceived. But the distinguishing feature of his poetry is the touching nostalgia of his verse, as, for example, in the last part of the poem, where the poet addresses his native island:

> But Sicily. A hopeless sorrow
> Is born anew for you in my memory.
> Youth. I see again happy
> Lost follies and splendid friends.
> O the paradise I was driven from!
> Why remember your splendour?
> My tears. If your taste were not so bitter
> You would now form rivers.
> O Sicily!

In the *diwān* of Ibn Hamdīs, more than 4,000 lines are laudatory. They are addressed to princes or patrons of Andalusia and North Africa, or to friends and coreligionists who had remained in Sicily. Setting aside the possibility of a real characterization of the persons mentioned, which the poet sometimes permits us to attempt, there are among these poems some that lend themselves to historical usage, as they throw light on events in the Mediterranean area between the eleventh and twelfth centuries: events ranging from the struggle of the Andalusian *reyes de taifas* (the *mulūk at-tawā'if*) against Alfonso VI of Castille to the victories—or defeats—of the Zīrid princes in battles against the Normans.

In this regard, a precious source is the long poem in which Ibn Hamdīs speaks of the Battle of Cap Dimas in Tunisia (1123), which was a setback for the Norman sovereign Roger II. The poem seems to be almost a chronicle of the happenings: we find in it the names of the tribes taking part in the struggle, the deployment of the enemy forces, allusions to the Muslim raids in Calabria, scores for the Christians and praise for the Zirid Emir Ḥasan Ibn ʿAlī Mahdiyya, during whose reign the victory occurred. This Muslim success encouraged the poet to hope that the beloved island of Sicily might return to the *dār al-lslām,* but this hope was soon dashed. Roger is portrayed as an infidel hungry for booty. The Arabs and the Muslims were presented as the bearers of the true faith, and the crushing victory is seen as a grace from God. It should be mentioned, incidentally, that this Arab poet from Sicily is our most complete source of information about this historical event.

The writings of this poet thus inform us, sometimes in a previously unprecedental manner, of the events of the time and techniques of war: for example, the use of *naphta* (Greek fire) in naval battles (never described by other poets); and they also inform us of the war galleys which contained men and horses, about "doe's foot" crossbows, and so on. Here is an excerpt:

> The Christian infidels have seen the war galleys that hurl *naphta*: *naphta* that burns and extinguishes lives.

The molten lead of hell seems to be enclosed in
this pipe, and it spurts into men's faces.
When the breasts of the Barbarians are torn open
by it, they die at once, groaning.
In the pipe of *naphta* is the mouth of a volcano,
which calls to mind the tortures of hell.
A scorning blaze flashes through the pipe, a
mortal blaze for the lives of the infidels.
Water has no power to quench it, when it blazes
and bursts.

The island, which the poet had to abandon at the time of the Norman conquest, is thus seen as a land of *jihād,* the war that the Muslims who remained in Sicily fought against the foreign invader. A short passage from a long poem by Ibn Ḥamdīs describes his brave coreligionists, whom he urges moreover to lay down their lives to defend their homeland and their families, choosing death rather than the bitterness of exile:

The hands of the Christians have transformed the
mosques of my land into churches.
In them the monks ring the bells as loud as they
can, from morning to nightfall.
A cruel destiny has betrayed the land of Sicily,
which before was sheltered from the whims of
fate.
I see my country abased, humiliated by the Rūm,
while with the Muslims it was honored.

With this poet (and, in general, with the Arab poetry of Sicily) we still remain in the Arab-Norman period. It is, in my opinion, necessary to go on a little further, at least until the time of Frederick II, whose philo-Islamic character is attested by several Arab sources. However, Frederick II's Arabo-Islamic perception deserves special attention, in order to overcome the contradiction between the philo-Islamic, philo-Arabic sovereign, on the one hand, and the emperor on the other, who uprooted Sicilian Islam with a cruelty whose echo was to be heard as far as the Orient. One source, for example, tells us of the arrival in the court of al-Malik al-Kāmil in Egypt, of a Muslim fleeing from Sicily, who implores the Sultan to intervene against the policy pursued by the emperor in Italy and directed against the Muslims still surviving in Sicily. This is in the year 1230, just after Frederick's Crusade, when he was in an idyllic, interconfessional state with al-Malik al-Kāmil, who then wrote to him, asking him to leave the Muslims in peace or at least to allow them to emigrate to Egypt. But this move seems to have had no effect whatsoever. Furthermore, the overall impression which Islam received of the great Swabian monarch was above all linked to the Crusade: his passage across the oriental political scene was meteoric, but the Arab sources immediately noted the singular personality of this new friend-enemy, so different from other crusader sovereigns previously known. This man who spoke Arabic, who was surrounded by an almost entirely Muslim retinue, who was so familiar with Islamic culture, who passed successively from diplomatic negotiations to questions of logic and mathematics, physics, and metaphysics, this man was bound to excite the curiosity and imagination of the Muslims.

In summary, we may conclude that a bond of personal friendship and mutual esteem developed between the emperor and his Ayyubid hosts which was much more solid than the compromise of Jerusalem, a bond that was destined to survive the oriental adventure. The friendly relations with al-Malik al-Kāmil continued until the Sultan's death in 1238, and they carried on with his son and successor. These emirs and vizirs must have observed and appreciated in Frederick not only the materialist (*ad-dahrī*) who mocked Christianity but above all the man of culture, the scholar, the knight and the sovereign who knew and admired oriental civilization.

I would like to make some concluding remarks. I am interested in sources for the study of Arabo-Islamic Sicily, and until now I have not found a complete Muslim document or monograph dealing specifically with Christianity in Sicily and the way in which it was considered by the Muslims both within and outside the island. I have, therefore, not had the good fortune, for example, to find a work parallel to the letter by the "monk of France" and to the reply by the Andalusian Abū'l-Walīd al-Bājī, edited by Dunlop and later by at-Turkī.

The absence of any such controversial texts, in harmony with the artistic syncretism and cultural symbiosis in Sicily during the Arabic-Norman period, has enabled scholars to speak of Sicily as a "land without crusaders," alluding to a peaceful tolerance and cohabitation between the Christian and the Muslim faith and culture. This existed, to be sure, but above all, it seems that contrary to those Muslims who were close to the Normans and then to the Swabian court, there were those who, from a juridical and social point of view, lived in a state of inferiority. What was their perception of the world around them? This is not clear. But it is clear that those for whom the gates of exile were opened continued to regard the island as their lost homeland, torn from the *dār al-Islām* by the barbaric hands of the infidels.

BIBLIOGRAPHY

Abulfia, D. *The End of Muslim Sicily*. Princeton: Princeton University Press, 1990.

Amari, M. *Storia dei Musulmani di Sicilia*. 2nd ed. by C. A. Nallino. 3 vols. Catania: Prampolini, 1933–1939.

———. *al-Maktaba al-ʿarabiyya as-siqilliyya*. 2nd ed. by U. Rizzitano. 2 vols. Palermo: Accademia Nazionale di Scienze Lettere e Arti, 1988.

Borruso, A. *Islām e Occidente*. Mazara: Liceo Ginnasio "G. C. Adria," 1984.

———. *L 'Imām al-Māzarī*. Naples: Istituto Universitario Orientale, 1986.

———. *Poesia araba in Sicilia*. Rome: Accademia Nazionale dei Lincei, 1988.

Cusa, S. *I diplomi greci ed arabi di Sicilia*. 2 vols. Palermo, Pedone, 1868.

Gabrieli, F. *Storici arabi delle Crociate*, 4th ed. Turin: Einaudi, 1973.

———. *Viaggi e viaggiatori arabi*. Florence: Sansoni, 1975.

———. *Pagine arabo-siciliane*, by A. Borruso. Mazara: Liceo Ginnasio "G. C. Adria," 1987.

Ibn Hamdīs, *Poesie*, Selection, translation and notes by A. Borruso, Mazara: Liceo Ginnasio "G. C. Adria," 1987.

Ibn Jubayr, *Viaggio*, Italian translation by C. Schiaparelli. Rome: Casa Editrice Italiana, 1906. English translation by R. J. C. Broadhurst, London, 1952. French translation by M. Gaudefroy-Demombynes, Paris, 1949.

Moritz, B. "Ibn Saʿīds Beschreibung von Sicilien." In *Centenario Amari*. Palermo: Virzi, 1910. Vol. 1, pp. 292–305.

Rizzitano, U. *Storia e cultura nella Sicilia saracena*. Palermo: Flaccovio, 1975.

8

Medieval Muslim Polemics against the Jewish Scriptures

CAMILLA ADANG

Islamic polemics against Judaism and its adherents is a phenomenon as old as Islam itself, and the Qur'ān is its very first source. In it, we find, among others, the following arguments: the Jews are hostile toward the Muslims; the cumbersome Jewish laws are a punishment from God; the Jews are extremely attached to earthly life, and they display an excessive reverence for their leaders, thus compromising their monotheism.[1]

More numerous and important, however, are the arguments that concern the very foundation of the Jewish faith, namely the Torah.[2] According to the Qur'ān, this earlier scripture, which must be considered abrogated,[3] contains references to the mission of the Prophet Muhammad.[4] At the same time, the Torah is said to have been tampered with by the Jews (*tahrīf*).[5]

We do not possess any polemical works from the first four centuries of the Islamic era that are specifically directed against Judaism; the Muslims seem to have been more preoccupied with the defense of their faith against attacks coming from Christians.[6] None of the refutations of the Jewish religion mentioned by the bibliographer Ibn al-Nadīm (d. ca. 385/995) in his *Fihrist* have come down to us.[7] Occasionally, tracts against Christianity, such as al-Jāhiz' *Radd ʿala ʾl-Nasārā* (Refutation of the Christians),[8] include arguments against the Jews, but apart from that, we must turn to a variety of sources whose primary goal is not polemical. Criticisms of the Jews and their religion may be encountered in works of history, *kalām* (speculative theology), *tafsīr* (Qur'ānic commentary), and apologetics, as well as writings from other categories. Here I propose to discuss some Scripture-related arguments that appear in texts belonging to different genres. The authors under review here are ʿAlī b. Rabban al-Tabarī, Ibn Qutayba, Muhammad b. Jarīr al-Tabarī, al-Maqdisī, and Ibn Hazm. They will be discussed in chronological order, starting with Ibn Rabban.[9]

ʿAlī b. Rabban al-Tabarī

ʿAlī b. Rabban al-Tabarī[10] was a Nestorian physician, born, as his *nisba* indicates, in the province of Tabaristān in eastern Iran. During the reign of the ʿAbbasid caliph al-Mutawakkil (*regn.* 232/847–247/861), he converted to Islam. This step is usually attributed to ulterior motives; it is suggested that Ibn Rabban simply wished to avoid the restrictions imposed by the caliph on non-Muslims as part of his campaign to restore orthodox Sunnī Islam after years of heterodox, Muʿtazilī domination.[11] The former Nestorian defended his new religion in two apologetical tracts, which may have been commissioned by the caliph himself. For the present discussion, we shall limit ourselves to the tract entitled *Kitāb al-dīn waʾl-dawla fī ithbāt nubuwwat al-nabī*

Muhammad (The book of religion and empire on the confirmation of the prophethood of the Prophet Muhammad).[12]

The declared object of this book is to remove the doubts and skepticism with which the history of the Prophet Muhammad and the divine origin of the Islamic message were viewed by the adherents of other religions, and especially by the Christians. Ibn Rabban mentions that similar projects had been undertaken by authors before him, but that they had been unsuccessful, largely because they had failed to take account of the Jewish and Christian scriptures.[13] Ibn Rabban, on the other hand, knew Syriac—plus perhaps a smattering of Greek and Hebrew—and thus had access to the Bible.

The author explains on which grounds Muhammad should be accepted as a true prophet: like his precursors, he preached monotheism; he was pious and sincere, and his laws worthy of praise; he wrought miracles; he prophesized about events unknown to him, which occurred in his lifetime; he foretold events that took place after his death; he produced a book which testifies to the truth of his office; his military victories and those of his followers over the nations are a clear sign; the missionaries who transmitted his history were honest and righteous; he is the last of the prophets, and without him, the biblical prophecies would have been in vain; the earlier prophets annunciated his coming, described his mission, his country, his time, his victories, his followers.

These or very similar criteria had already been adduced by Jewish and Christian theologians as proof of the veracity of Moses and Jesus, respectively.[14] Ibn Rabban sought to demonstrate that the Muslims' acceptance of Muhammad's mission was based on the same criteria as those which have led the Jews and the Christians to lend credence to their prophets, and, this being the case, that there is no reason why these People of the Book should reject Muhammad, for what applies to one must necessarily apply to the other as well.

To each of the previously mentioned criteria, Ibn Rabban devotes a chapter of his *Kitāb al-Dīn waʾl-Dawla*. The longest one, taking up almost half of the book, deals with the alleged references to Muhammad in the earlier scriptures.[15] In this chapter, Ibn Rabban scans the Bible (in its wider sense, including the New Testament) for passages taken to refer to Muhammad and events related to the advent of Islam. As far as we know, he was the first Muslim author to do so *on this scale*; a smaller number of biblical testimonies in support of Muhammad's mission had earlier been adduced by Abūʾl-Rabīʿ Muhammad ibn al-Layth in an epistle addressed to the Byzantine emperor, Constantine VI (*regn.* 780–797 CE), on behalf of caliph Hārūn al-Rashīd (*regn.* 170/786–193/809), in which he called on the emperor to convert to Islam,[16] and even Ibn al-Layth probably made use of an already existing collection of testimonies in Arabic.[17]

Apart from a few quotations from the New Testament, the testimonies in Ibn Rabban's work are all taken from books belonging to the Hebrew Bible, such as Genesis, Exodus, Numbers, Deuteronomy, Psalms, Isaiah, Hosea, Micah, Habakkuk, Zephaniah, Zechariah, Jeremiah, Ezekiel, and Daniel.[18] An examination of Isaiah proved especially rewarding. To a large extent, of course, these passages had already been claimed by the Christians as references to Jesus, as Ibn Rabban, with his Nestorian background, knew very well. In many cases, all he had to do was to explain why it was more plausible that they referred to Muhammad. Moreover, he was able to add to the already considerable arsenal by translating every word connected with the meaning 'praise' (the root *sh-b-h* in Syriac) with a word derived from the Arabic root *h-m-d*. Thus Psalm 48:1–2 is paraphrased: *inna rabbana ʿazīmun mahmūdun jiddan*, which translates to "Mighty is our Lord, and greatly praised." The word used to translate the participle "praised" (*mahmūd*) has, according to Ibn Rabban, the same meaning as the word *muhammad*, and thus constitutes a reference to the very name of the Prophet.[19] This trick could, of course, only be employed against the Christians who read the Scriptures in Syriac. Ibn Rabban makes no attempts to trace the Prophet's name in the Hebrew text as well.

The principle of translating Syriac *sh-b-h* to Arabic *h-m-d* does not seem to have been invented by Ibn Rabban himself; already in Ibn al-Layth's testimonies, the root *h-m-d* occurs too frequently to be a coincidence. However, Ibn Rabban may have expanded the list of such references to the name of the Prophet.

Ibn Rabban not only finds that the Prophet's name is mentioned in the Bible; his physical appearance, too, is allegedly described: Isaiah's famous verse "Unto us a child is born, and unto us a child is given, whose government is on his shoulder" is interpreted as a description of the moles on Muhammad's shoulder that are the sign or the seal of prophethood.[20]

In yet another way Ibn Rabban seeks to trace Muhammad in the earlier Scriptures: through numerology. As is well known, the letters of the Arabic alphabet each have a numerical value. In Ibn Rabban's view, now, the mysterious figure 1,335 in Dan. 12:12 is a reference to the Prophet. The numerical value of the words *Muhammad khātim al-anbiyā' mahdī majīd* (Muhammad, the Seal of the Prophets, is an illustrious Mahdi) is 1,335.[21] Ibn Rabban is aware that the explanation is rather thin; theoretically, he agrees, it would be possible to apply this figure to other persons, but the fact that it is backed by so many testimonies from other prophets clearly indicates it as a reference to Muhammad.[22]

Islam's emergence from the desert, its spread over the world, the spread of the Arabic language, the rituals of the pilgrimage to Mecca, and the subjugation of nations and kings to Muslim rule are all found described in the Bible.[23] Ibn Rabban invites his readers to accept this decisive evidence, and expresses his hope that God will make them turn to Islam.[24] Those who persist in denying these clear signs are deaf and blind, and on the way to perdition.[25] Everlasting shame, eternal regret, and torment will be their share.[26]

Ibn Rabban explains why the world was in need of a new revelation. For one thing, the Torah is replete with curses and injustices,[27] the likes of which are not encountered in the Qur'ān, which stresses God's forgiveness and mercy instead.[28] Moreover, the Torah is mainly a historical chronicle about the Israelites and cannot lay claim to universal validity.[29] The Gospel is praised by Ibn Rabban for its high morality and sublime wisdom, but it does not contain much in the way of laws. As for the Psalter, its hymns are of great beauty, but again it is not very useful when it comes to laws and prescriptions. The books of Isaiah and Jeremiah, like the Torah, are full of curses.[30] According to Ibn Rabban, the Qur'ān qualifies the laws and prescriptions contained in the Torah, making them more just and humane. As such, the Qur'ān abrogates the earlier revelation and makes way for the religion that is "easy and free from restraint."[31] Man can only obey God by obeying Muhammad.[32]

Since the "Book of Religion and Empire" mainly addresses itself to Christians, we find few explicit arguments against the Jewish religion. Ibn Rabban raises some collective objections against both communities of the Book, who, after all, share the Hebrew Bible. Specifically directed against the Jews, however, is the objection that their religion lacked universality: "it had appeared only in one section of mankind."[33] Moreover, it wielded no power, and worldly power and military victories are among the signs of God's grace. In the book of Ezekiel it is told that the vine representing the Jewish people was uprooted and consumed by fire. This means that the power of the Jews has disappeared from the surface of the earth, and was substituted by another administration, namely that of the Muslims.[34]

Yet the Jews refuse to see: "How great is my amazement at the Jews, who avow all these things and do not go beyond contemplating them, and burden themselves with claims through which they become full of illusion and deception."[35]

Whether the author was in touch with Jews at all cannot be established with certainty; the only thing that would seem to point in that direction is that he displays some rudimentary knowledge of Hebrew. However, he may have obtained this information from Jewish converts to Islam.

Although Ibn Rabban was aware that there were discrepancies between the Septuagint and the Syriac and Hebrew versions of the Torah, this does not seem to have made him question the authenticity of the Jewish Scripture. The accusation of deliberate distortion of the Torah, which we find for example in the works of Ibn Hazm (to be discussed here), is nowhere voiced in *Kitāb al-Dīn wa'l-Dawla*. If at the beginning of the work Ibn Rabban accuses the possessors of an inspired book, of having hidden Muhammad's name, and changed his description contained in the books of their prophets, he refers to a distortion of the *interpretation* of the scriptures, and not of the text itself. According to D. S. Margoliouth, Ibn Rabban's failure to take a firm stand on this issue may have rendered the work unpopular—a possible explanation for the fact that it has come down to us in one manuscript only.[36] However, a more likely explanation for this fact seems to be that *Kitāb al-Dīn wa'l-Dawla* was simply eclipsed by a tract of a similar nature by Ibn Qutayba who, rather than to a non-Muslim readership, addressed himself to his fellow Muslims.

Ibn Qutayba

Abū Muhammad 'Abd Allāh b. Muslim ibn Qutayba[37] was born in 213/838, probably in Kufa, of a family of Persian descent. The scholars by whom he came to be influenced most were theologians, traditionists, and philologists who held views similar to those of their contemporary, the staunchly orthodox Ibn

Hanbal (d. 241/855). Ibn Qutayba's first works were philological commentaries on the revealed sources of Islam (Qur'ān and *hadīth*), that were well received by those responsible for implementing the religious reforms decreed by the Caliph al-Mutawakkil. In appreciation of his contribution to the restoration of orthodox Islam, Ibn Qutayba was appointed *qādī* in Dinawar around 236/851, an office which he seems to have held until 256/870. After falling from grace, Ibn Qutayba returned to Baghdad where he devoted most of his time and energy to the teaching of his works. He died in 276/889, leaving a rich and varied oeuvre.

Even though his first modern biographer, I. M. Huseini, portrays Ibn Qutayba as a religious fanatic,[38] and his severest critic, Charles Pellat, brands him as a narrow-minded reactionary,[39] his approach to non-Islamic sources was in fact quite open-minded, and we encounter references to biblical and postbiblical Jewish books in several of his works. He was apparently the first Muslim-born author to compare and supplement the legendary accounts of creation and the lives of the Israelite prophets with genuine passages from the Torah, mostly from the book of Genesis. His quotations, preceded by phrases like "I have read in the Torah," "I have found in the Torah," and "It is said in the Torah," are surprisingly accurate.[40] We encounter them especially in Ibn Qutayba's best-known work, *Kitāb al-Ma'ārif* (The book of noteworthy information),[41] which has been described as an encyclopedia of general culture, a kind of "Who's who in pre-Islamic and Islamic history." Considering the nature of this book, it is not surprising that it contains no explicit polemical arguments. However, at one point Ibn Qutayba states that the Torah was burned: "As regards Ezra, he restored the Torah for the Jews after it had been burned [for they did not] know it at the time he returned to Syria. Now a group of Jews say that Ezra is the son of God."[42] The first statement, about the restoration of the lost Torah, probably goes back indirectly to the apocryphal book of *IV Ezra* (or *II Esdras*), which gained widespread popularity among Muslims.[43] Ibn Qutayba sees a connection between Ezra's role in the restoration of the Torah and the allegation in the Qur'ān that the Jews venerate Ezra as the son of God (S. 9:30). The motif of Ezra as the inspired restorer of the holy scriptures recurs in the works of other Muslim writers, among them al-Tabarī (see the following discussion).

The fact that the Torah was at one point lost does not seem to invalidate it in Ibn Qutayba's eyes as a revealed Scripture and a historical source. Apparently *tahrīf* was not an issue for him. He believes that Muhammad is annunciated in the Jewish Scriptures, notably in the book of Isaiah. The latter is described as "the one who annunciated the Prophet, peace be with him, and described him."[44]

These biblical annunciations are discussed by Ibn Qutayba in a tract entitled *Dalā'il al-Nubuwwa* (The proofs of the prophethood). The work as such has not come down to us, but substantial fragments of it have been preserved in works by later authors such as Ibn Qayyim al-Jawziyya, Ibn al-Jawzī, and Ibn Hazm.[45]

Even on the basis of these limited fragments, we can conclude that Ibn Qutayba's *Dalā'il al-Nubuwwa* was very similar in style and content to Ibn Rabban's *Kitāb al-Dīn wa'l-Dawla*. A comparison of Ibn Qutayba's list of biblical testimonies with that of Ibn Rabban reveals a considerable overlap. But even if Ibn Qutayba used Ibn Rabban's work as a source (he does not mention it), he did not content himself with merely copying the latter's prooftexts; sometimes, he gives entirely different renditions of biblical passages also occurring in *Kitāb al-Dīn wa'l-Dawla*. Apparently, he consulted other sources as well, both oral and written ones, which enabled him to add new testimonies.

On three occasions in the extant fragments of *Dalā'il al-nubuwwa*, Ibn Qutayba refers to the *abrogation* of the Torah. The first one is a comment on two biblical passages—Gen. 17:20 and Gen. 16:9–12—in which it is announced that Ishmael shall be a great nation: "When the apostle of God was sent," says Ibn Qutayba, "the prophethood was passed on to Ismā'īl's offspring. Kings owed him allegiance, and nations submitted themselves to him. God abrogated every law through him, sealed the succession of prophets with him, and made the caliphate and the kingship reside among the people of his house until the end of time."[46]

The second reference to abrogation appears in a comment on Isa. 42, a popular testimony among Muslim writers. Ibn Qutayba quotes: "[Muhammad] is the light of God that shall not be extinguished, and he shall not be defeated, so that he may establish My proof on earth; with him, every excuse shall cease [to be valid] and the *jinn* will submit to his Torah." He adds: "Now this is a clear reference to his name and his characteristics. If they say, 'Which Torah does he have?,' we shall reply that it means that he shall bring a book that is to take the place of your Torah for you."[47]

Finally, Ibn Qutayba quotes a story attributed to Ka'b al-Ahbār, a contemporary of Muhammad who is said to have been one of the first Jews to convert to Islam: "When Jerusalem (or: the temple, *bayt al-maqdis*) complained to God about its ruin, it was told, 'We shall give you, in exchange a new Torah and new rulers who shall spread their eagles' wings over the House and shall watch over it affectionately like a dove watching its eggs, and they will fill you with soldiers who will prostrate themselves in worship.'"[48]

For all the respect that Ibn Qutayba apparently had for the Jewish Scriptures, he does not hesitate to polemicize between the lines against their possessors. This is especially the case in his *Taʾwīl Mukhtalif al-Hadīth*, which deals with apparently contradictory *hadīth*s. In this work, Ibn Qutayba expresses the Qurʾān-based view that the elaborate laws of Judaism constitute a burden and are a proof of this religion's inferiority to Islam. Islam has come to relieve the burden by abrogating onerous laws.[49] He quotes a tradition to the effect that it is good to dance and be merry, so that the Jews may know that "our religion is ample"—that is, that there is room in Islam for such things.[50] In the same context, Ibn Qutayba expresses his gratitude to God that His religion is easy and without constraint.[51] Given the context, this is probably to be taken as a dig at the Jews.

Ibn Qutayba never explicitly mentions any contacts with practicing Jews, although he once refers to a discussion he had with a member of the People of the Book, who may have been a Jew, but then again may have been a Christian.[52] He also mentions a Jewish renegade who informed him about the pronunciation of a biblical passage believed to contain a reference to the Prophet,[53] though this is possibly no more than a *topos*.[54] However, because Ibn Qutayba was apparently much less bigoted and narrow-minded than critics like Pellat and Huseini care to admit, the possibility that he also interacted with practicing Jews is not to be rejected out of hand.[55] That he did not boast of these contacts at a time when such relations were no doubt viewed with suspicion—it should be recalled that Ibu Qutayba flourished in a period of orthodox restoration—is not surprising.[56]

Al-Tabarī

Abū Jaʿfar Muhammad b. Jarīr al-Tabarī[57] (d. 310/923) is the author of two of the fundamental works of Islamic scholarship,[58] namely the *Jāmiʿ al-Bayān fī Taʾwīl Āy al-Qurʾān* (The complete clarification of the interpretation of the verses of the Qurʾān), in short *Tafsīr* (Explanation), and the *Taʾrīkh al-Rusul waʾl-Mulūk* (History of the messengers and the kings), also known as *Annales*. I shall limit my observations mainly to the first work.

Al-Tabarī's *Tafsīr* is extremely valuable (and voluminous) because it records the opinions of many earlier commentators, among them companions of the Prophet, such as Ibn ʿAbbās, and religious scholars of the generation following that of Muhammad. Al-Tabarī certainly did not include *all* current exegetical *hadīth*s in his collection: those that had not been reliably transmitted through an uninterrupted chain of authorities and those that reflected certain sectarian biases were excluded. However, the materials that are included by al-Tabarī are set forth as equally plausible, and alternatives are rarely discounted.[59] Nevertheless, al-Tabarī usually clearly indicates which interpretation has his preference. Thus, it is possible to distill the commentator's personal views on the issues connected with the Jewish Scriptures from the mass of material presented by him. A study of al-Tabarī's explanations of the verses in which the accusation of *tahrīf* occurs, as well as those in which similar allegations are leveled at the Jews, allows us to summarize his views on the issue as follows.

God made a covenant with the Israelites and their descendants, the Jews, which obliged some of them to divulge the annunciations of Muhammad contained in their Scripture, and to believe in his prophethood. However, not only did they fail to do so but also they even called Muhammad a liar. Thus they broke their covenant and forfeited God's mercy—and hence their chances of ever entering Paradise.[60]

Because the Israelites of Moses' days had broken their covenant, God made their hearts impure, so they went about misrepresenting the words that their Lord had revealed to Moses and altered them.[61] When Moses ordered the Israelites to express their repentance, they changed the phrase they had been told to use.[62] Al-Tabarī makes it clear that this was an *oral* distortion and that the written text of God's word was not affected. The same applies in the case of the 70 elders who accompanied Moses to Mount Sinai and were allowed to hear God's speech. Once they returned to their people, some of them gave a false report of what they had heard, distorting God's spoken words, but not the written Torah, as is explicitly stated by al-Tabarī.[63]

Tahrīf thus took place already in Moses' days and it continued to be practiced by Muhammad's contemporaries. With their own hands, they wrote something which they then passed on to the ignorant people among them as part of God's revelation.[64] According to al-Tabarī's interpretation, the Qur'ān issues a warning to the Muslims of Medina not to expect their Jewish townsmen to have faith; their ancestors did not shirk from misrepresenting the very word of God that they themselves had heard, so it should not surprise anyone that the modern-day Jews distort the descriptions of Muhammad that are in their book and denounce him as a liar.[65]

Al-Tabarī sees a parallel between the enmity of the Israelites toward God and His prophet, Moses, and the animosity of their descendants, the Jews, toward God and Muhammad.[66] Most of all to blame in al-Tabarī's eyes, however, are the rabbis (*ahbār*) who are said to have misled even their own ignorant coreligionists who could not themselves consult the Torah and who therefore ended up uttering lies, all the time thinking they were in fact part of Scripture. Meanwhile, they failed to accept that which undeniably comes from God, namely Muhammad's message.[67] The rabbis of Muhammad's days were better than anyone qualified to inform people about the descriptions of the Prophet as found in the Torah. They should know better, therefore, than to denounce the Prophet as a liar, for in denouncing him, they denounce their own Scripture, which explicitly refers to him.[68]

The rabbis are admonished in the Qur'ān not to hide this knowledge in their desire for power and worldly gain. Yet some of them write a book according to their own interpretations, alongside the Torah,[69] and twist their tongues, so that the Muslims might think that what they misrepresent is from the book of God and part of His revelation, while in actual fact, God never revealed any such thing to any of His prophets.[70] In so doing, they add to God's book what does not belong to it. (The context suggests that al-Tabarī understands these additions as oral, not textual ones). When these Jews twist their tongues, they distort the real meaning of the words into something objectionable, scorning Muhammad and his religion.[71] Al-Tabarī explicitly states what he understands by distorting the word of God: changing its meaning and interpretation, deliberately bending its original meaning to something else.[72]

A clear case of such misrepresentation occurred when the Jews of Medina brought an adulterous Jewish couple before the Prophet, wanting him to pass a verdict on them. The Prophet wished to judge them according to their own law, the Torah, and asked them what penalty it prescribed. Instead of telling him truthfully that it prescribed stoning, they informed him that the Torah orders the offenders to be flogged and their faces to be blackened. When Muhammad found out the truth, he had the couple stoned. Again, the rabbis were held responsible for this *tahrīf*: they changed the judgment of God concerning adultery.[73] However, when the Qur'ān says that the Jews reveal much of what is in their parchments, but also keep much hidden from the public view, the reference, according to al-Tabarī, is usually to the allusions to Muhammad and his prophethood in their Scripture, which they prefer to keep hidden.[74]

There is no suggestion in al-Tabarī's *Tafsīr* that he believed the Torah was lost or perished at some point in history. In his *Annales*, however, the author does state that it was burned and lost, but that Ezra miraculously restored it:

> When [the Israelites] returned to Palestine, they had no divine Scripture, for the Torah had been seized and burned, and it perished. Ezra, one of the captives in Babylon who returned to Palestine, spent day and night grieving over it, in solitude. While he was in waterless valleys and in the wilderness, grieving over the Torah and weeping, lo and behold, a man approached him as he sat, and [the man] said, "O Ezra, what grieves you?" Ezra said, "I grieve over God's Scripture and covenant which was among us, but our transgressions and the Lord's wrath against us came to such a pass that He made our enemy prevail. They slew our men, destroyed our country and burned our divine book, without which our worldly existence and our life to come has no meaning. What shall I weep over if not this?" The man said, "Would you like it to be returned to you?" Ezra asked, "Is that possible?" "Yes," the man replied. "Go back, fast, cleanse yourself, and cleanse your garments. Then be at this place tomorrow."
>
> Ezra went back, cleansed himself and his garments, and went to the appointed place. He sat there, and the man came carrying a vessel filled with water—he was an angel sent by God—and gave Ezra to drink from that vessel. The Torah then presented itself in Ezra's consciousness. Ezra returned to the Children of Israel and set down the Torah for them, so that they might know what it permits and what it prohibits, its patterns, precepts and statutes. They loved it as they had never loved anything before. The Torah was established among them, and with it their cause fared well. Ezra stayed among them to carry out the divine truth. Then he died. In the course of time, the Israelites considered Ezra to be the son of

God. God again sent them a prophet, as He did in the past, to direct and teach them, and to command them to follow the Torah.[75]

It would seem that in the view of the commentator, there simply existed a second text alongside the Torah, which was written by some rabbis and mistaken by ignorant Jews for the word of God. It is possible that al-Tabarī suspected the Jews of his own generation of using this text instead of the genuine books of Moses, for in his historical work, he refers to the Jewish Scriptures as "the Torah that they possess today."[76] This would help explain why he chooses not to use the Torah as a historical source, unlike authors like Ibn Qutayba and al-Yaʿqūbī, who had made extensive use of genuine biblical materials in their accounts of the earliest history.[77] Al-Tabarī, on the other hand, only uses reports that had been handed down to him via reliable channels of Muslim authorities. Thus it is on the authority of a Muslim informant that he includes his one biblical reference to the Prophet. It is a combination of elements from the book of Isaiah and the Qurʾān, and it goes back to ʿAtāʾ b. Yasār, who says:

> I met ʿAbd Allāh b. ʿAmr [b. al-ʿĀs], and asked him concerning the description of the Messenger of God in the Torah. He said, "Yes, by God, he is described in the Torah in the same way that he is described in the Qurʾān: 'O Prophet, We have sent thee as a witness, and good things to bear, and warning' [S. 33:45]; a refuge to the nations. Thou art My messenger, I have named thee the trusting. He is neither harsh nor rough, nor crying in the streets. He does not reward evil with evil, but pardons and forgives. We shall not take him until through him We have caused the crooked nation to say, There is no god but God, and through him We shall open uncircumcised hearts, deaf ears, and blind eyes."[78]

Al-Maqdisī

So far, we have only encountered authors who subscribed to the view that the misrepresentation of the Torah, referred to in the Qurʾān, only concerns the *meaning* of the Torah and not its *text*. One author who disagrees is al-Maqdisī.

Abū Nasr Mutahhar b. Tāhir al-Maqdisī,[79] who was in all likelihood a Shīʿite, is the author of a work of encyclopedic dimensions, entitled *Kitāb al-badʾ waʾl-taʾrīkh* (The book of creation and history).[80] It was written around the year 355/966 in Bust, in the province of Sijistān, at the behest of a minister of the Samanid dynasty. The *nisba* al-Maqdisī indicates that the author hailed from Jerusalem, but apart from that, we know next to nothing about him. His work contains a few chance references to various cities and regions he visited, such as Bethlehem, Cairo, Upper Egypt, Takrit, and Basra—where he had discussions with a learned Jew. He also made the pilgrimage to Mecca and traveled widely in the Iranian provinces. It is not known in what capacity al-Maqdisī made these journeys nor what his position at the Samanid court was.

His sole surviving work, *Kitāb al-badʾ*, cannot be called a traditional history, in the sense of a chronological presentation of events of the past, for it has a strong theological component. Before dealing with creation and what came after, al-Maqdisī devotes several chapters to what already was before, namely God; these are followed by descriptions of what was created before Adam, and in this context several theological issues are tackled. On many important points he compares Muslim dogma with that of other religions, among which Judaism figures prominently. Thus, he can truly be considered a student of comparative religion. On the Messianic age and the afterlife, for example, the author gives the views of Jewish groups and individuals, unfortunately without identifying them.[81] In his discussions, he usually includes the biblical passages that are adduced by the Jewish parties in support of their own views. Jewish informants—orthodox as well as sectarian—must have been the main source for the substantial section on Jewish sects, beliefs, and customs in his book.[82] Al- Maqdisī seems to have supplemented this oral information with written sources; he refers to an enigmatic book entitled *Sharāʾiʿ al-Yahūd* (The laws of the Jews) and repeatedly claims to have read certain things "in the translation of the Torah," although the passages adduced are not always accurate. The author defends his consultation of non-Muslim sources and informants by stating that as long as their information does not patently contradict the Qurʾān and the teachings of Islam, it is acceptable. Texts and opinions, however, which cannot be reconciled with the teachings of Islam are to be rejected outright.

Al-Maqdisī's attitude to the Torah is ambivalent: on the one hand, he warns that it should be used with caution since it was tampered with by the Jews. On the other hand, he interprets certain passages from this very same Torah as annunciations of Muhammad.

As for the allegation that the Torah was tampered with by the Jews, al-Maqdisī claims that the text of the Torah was subjected to alteration and corruption right from the beginning. During the very lifetime of Moses, the 70 elders who had joined him on Mount Sinai distorted the divine revelation. Following the death of Ezra the scribe, who had restored the Torah for the Israelites after it had been burned by Nebuchadnezzar, the text was even further corrupted. This is what happened according to al-Maqdisī:

> When Nebuchadnezzar destroyed Jerusalem, burned the Torah and exiled the Israelites to the land of Babylon, the Torah disappeared from among the Jews until the time when Ezra renewed it for them, according to what they say. It has been learned from those knowledgeable about history and legends that Ezra dictated the Torah at the end of his life, and died soon after having completed his task. He had handed the book over to one of his disciples, and ordered him to read it before the people after his death. It is from this disciple that [the Jews] have taken their Torah and subsequently copied it. They claim that it was this disciple who corrupted [the text], adding to it and distorting it. This is why distortions and corrupted passages occur and why certain words of the Torah have been replaced by others, because it is the work of a man living after Moses, for in it is related what happened to Moses such as how he died, how he gave his last instructions to Joshua, son of Nun; how the Israelites grieved and wept over him, and other things of which it is obvious to anyone endowed with reason that they are not the word of God, nor the word of Moses.[83]

In al-Maqdisī's view, the fact that there are certain discrepancies between the Jewish Torah, the Samaritan one, and the Greek Septuagint constitutes another argument in support of the falsification theory:

> All this points to distortions and alterations effected by them, since it is inconceivable that [the Torah] should contain contradictions coming from God. I have explained all this to you, so that you will not be discouraged when they say that Muhammad is not mentioned in the Torah.[84]

For despite the Jewish denials,[85] al-Maqdisī is convinced that the Prophet is indeed mentioned in the Torah; after all, it is explicitly stated in the Qur'ān and is therefore beyond any doubt. Besides, "the scholars have extracted from the Torah, the Gospel and the other books revealed by God the characteristic signs and proofs of his prophethood."[86] From one of these compilations of testimonies, al-Maqdisī quotes two quasi-biblical passages:

> "O David, say to Solomon, who will succeed you, that the world belongs to Me; I shall give it as an inheritance to a praiseworthy (*muhammad*) one and to his nation, whose prayers are not accompanied by lutes, and who do not worship me with string instruments." The confirmation of this passage is given by the Qur'ān, which has: "For We have written in the Psalms, after the Remembrance, 'The earth shall be the inheritance of My righteous servants'" [S. 21:105]. And in the same [work] we find: "God will show from Zion a praiseworthy (*mahmūd*) crown." They say that the crown is a metaphor of the leadership and the imamate, and that the praiseworthy one (*al-mahmūd*) is Muhammad.[87]

Al-Maqdisī adds that the Torah does not contain many allusions to Muhammad and his nation, the reason for this being the corrupted state of its text. Yet he proceeds to adduce two accurate quotations, namely Gen. 17:20 and Deut. 33:2.[88] The interesting thing about these two quotations is not so much that al-Maqdisī interpreted them as references to Muhammad or Islam; as he himself admits, he simply took them from a list of such passages, prepared by earlier Muslim scholars. Indeed, the examples he chooses are far from original; we come across them in the works of Ibn Rabban and Ibn Qutayba. What is original, though, is that al-Maqdisī gives these verses in the original Hebrew, with an Arabic transcription, some directions as to the pronunciation of the Hebrew, and finally an Arabic translation, which is subsequently compared with the versions given in the "extracts by the Muslim scholars."[89] The reason he gives for citing these passages in their original language is that he has found that many among the People of the Book are quick to deny their true interpretation, in imitation of their ancestors.[90] While he probably learned the Hebrew phrases from a convert from Judaism—for a renegade would be more inclined than a practicing Jew to provide such potentially sensitive information—one gets the impression that al-Maqdisī was prompted to seek this knowledge after an unsatisfactory discussion with a Jew.

As for the source of the testimonies he cites, I have argued elsewhere that al-Maqdisī may have used Ibn Qutayba's *Dalā'il al-nubuwwa*.[91] However, he appears to have consulted other collections of testimonies as well. He writes that the Muslims had composed a great many treatises on the subject of the signs of Muhammad's prophethood, some from the traditionalist point of view, others from a more rationalist one. Al-Maqdisī does not mention any titles, but merely states that it would be no exaggeration to say that they exceed the number of the chapters in his own work—which is 22.[92] Ibn al-Nadīm mentions several works entitled *Aʿlām al-nubuwwa*, *Dalāʾil al-nubuwwa*, *Ithbāt al-risāla*, and others that may have been available to al-Maqdisī,[93] and several other titles might be added to this list. Yet, he did not fully exploit the *dalāʾil* genre, not only because he may have felt that the ground had been sufficiently covered by specialized works like the ones mentioned here, but probably also because of his own ambivalent feelings toward the Hebrew Bible.

These ambivalent feelings notwithstanding, al-Maqdisī's interest in contemporary Judaism seems genuine, and he succeeds in giving a generally fair and largely accurate description of the beliefs and practices of the Jews, in a courteous tone. It is this latter quality which is often lacking in the works of the Spaniard Ibn Hazm (d. 456/1064), the only one among our authors to write tracts whose express purpose was to refute Judaism.

Ibn Hazm

The son of an important official at the court of al-Mansūr, the ruler of al-Andalus, Ibn Hazm[94] seemed destined to make a political career. However, his ambitions were frustrated by the final collapse of the Spanish Umayyad caliphate, in 1031, and its subsequent division into numerous petty kingdoms. These events, which led Ibn Hazm to withdraw from the political scene and to dedicate himself entirely to learning, engendered new opportunities for non-Muslim minorities. So far, they had had to content themselves with a subordinate position, in accordance with the *dhimma*-system, and could never aspire to the highest positions in the Muslim administration. However, especially in the kingdom of Granada, the Jews now reaped the benefits of the new state of affairs under the leadership of Ibn Hazm's Jewish counterpart, Ismāʿīl ibn al-Naghrīla, also known as Shemuel ha-Nagid, with whom Ibn Hazm had held disputations when both men were 20 years old.[95]

Ibn al-Naghrīla was only one of many Jews with whom Ibn Hazm was in contact; apart from orthodox Rabbanite Jews, he also associated with skeptics and sympathizers of the little-known ʿIsāwiyya sect.[96] Moreover, although he does not say so explicitly, he seems to have maintained close relations with members of the Karaite sect; we can discern a notable Karaite influence in his polemics against mainstream Judaism, and one gets the impression that the Karaites helped shape Ibn Hazm's views. This is not to say that these sectarians themselves were spared in his polemics; Ibn Hazm sometimes appears to have turned anti-Rabbanite arguments of apparently Karaite origin into arguments against the Jews in general, including the Karaites.[97]

References to Jews and Judaism—almost invariably of a polemical nature—may be found in several works of Ibn Hazm's,[98] the main ones being *Al-Radd ʿalā ibn al-Nagrīla al-Yahūdī* (Refutation of Ibn al-Naghrīla the Jew—possibly but not certainly directed against the above-mentioned vizier of Granada[99]—and *Kitāb al-Fisal fīʾl-Milal waʾl-Ahwāʾ waʾl-Nihal* (Book of opinions on religions, sects, and heresies).[100] This latter work includes an originally separate tract,[101] entitled *Izhār Tabdīl al-Yahūd waʾl-Nasārā liʾl-Tawrāt waʾl-Injīl* (Exposition of the alterations that Jews and Christians have effected in the Torah and the Gospel). Discussions of Ibn Hazm's knowledge of the Hebrew Bible and Judaism are usually based on these works only; the fact that some of his other works also contain important data on these topics is often overlooked.

The main arguments raised against Judaism are the following. Jewish law has been abrogated by Islam. For this reason, Muslims would do well not to use the Torah as a legal source, since they are not bound by its precepts.[102] Its value as a historical source must also be considered limited, since it dates from a much later period than is claimed by the Jews. Several of the arguments cited by Ibn Hazm as proof for the abrogation of the Torah had been current for at least a century; they had been refuted by Jewish authors such as Saʿadya Gaōn and al-Qirqisānī (who worked in the first half of the tenth century CE), and also crop up in works by Muslim theologians such as al-Baqillānī (d. 403/1013).[103]

In Ibn Hazm's view, the main reason Muslims should steer clear of the Torah is that it has been tampered with by the Jews in the course of history and was destroyed and ultimately substituted by a forgery. The people he seeks to convince of this are those fellow Muslims who still respected the Jewish Scripture as a divine book, as may be inferred from the following passage:

> Word has reached us about certain Muslims who, in their ignorance, refuse to accept the teaching that the Torah and the Gospel that are in the hands of the Jews and the Christians have been distorted. What makes them reject this teaching is their negligible insight into the texts of the Qur'ān and the Sunna. I wonder if they have ever heard these words of God: "People of the Book! Why do you confound the truth with vanity and that wittingly?" And "a party of them conceal the truth and that wittingly," and "a sect of them twist their tongues with the Book, that you may suppose it part of the Book, yet it is not part of the Book, etc." and "they pervert words from their meanings," and there are in the Qur'ān many similar things.[104] . . . We do not see how any Muslim could justifiably dispute the distortion of the Torah and the Gospel while hearing the following words of God: "Muhammad is the Messenger of God, and those who are with him are hard against the unbelievers, merciful one to another. Thou seest them bowing, prostrating, seeking bounty from God and good pleasure. Their mark is on their faces, the trace of prostration. That is their likeness in the Torah, and their likeness in the Gospel: as a seed that puts forth its shoot, and strengthens it, and it grows stout and rises straight upon its stalk, pleasing the sowers, that through them they may enrage the unbelievers."[105] Now, we do not find any of this in [the books] that the Jews and the Christians possess and which they claim to be the Torah and the Gospel. Therefore, it is inevitable that these ignorant men should accept from their Lord the fact that the Jews and the Christians have altered their Torah and Gospel.[106]

It is clear, then, that these remarks are addressed to a Muslim readership and are not aimed at convincing Jews. However, in his public disputations with them, he did try to persuade them to acknowledge the superiority of Islam,[107] but whether these attempts at converting Jews were at all successful is uncertain. I am inclined to think they were not, for Ibn Hazm would no doubt have mentioned his successes, just as he triumphantly records the times when he was able to silence a Jewish opponent.[108]

In two ways, Ibn Hazm seeks to show his readers that the Torah was corrupted beyond recognition. First, he gives an analysis of over 50 passages from the Five Books of Moses, drawing attention to errors in computation, historical and geographical inaccuracies, blasphemous assertions (like anthropomorphisms), and statements that contradict each other or, even more damning, contradict the Qur'ān.[109] Second, he traces the fate of the Torah in the remaining books of the Bible, of which his knowledge was somewhat more superficial.[110] Both analyses lead him to conclude that the Torah as it was known in his days was not to be equated with the text originally revealed to Moses, which must now be presumed lost.

Like al-Maqdisī, Ibn Hazm gives an account of what happened to the Torah following Moses' death. His version of events is much more detailed and gives a rather less sympathetic description of Ezra's role in the genesis of "the Jewish Torah." According to Ibn Hazm, the Israelites turned to foreign gods soon after Moses had died. He was succeeded by a series of rulers, the judges, quite a few of whom were idolators. Under their rule, the Israelites began to hold the Torah in contempt, subjecting it to distortion. After a brief discussion of David and Solomon, Ibn Hazm deals at length with their successors on the throne of Judah and describes their attitude to religion.

Following the biblical books of Kings and Chronicles, he finds that of the 20 successors to King Solomon, no fewer than 15 worshipped idols. The kings of Israel were even more depraved. All the while, there was only one single copy of the Torah in existence, and this was kept in the Temple, where the only ones to have access to it were the High Priests. They had ample opportunity to tamper with the Torah at will; the common people had no way of noticing the difference.[111]

And as if all this were not enough to guarantee the destruction of the unique copy of the Torah, the Temple was sacked and pillaged several times. Moreover, one king of the house of David deleted the name of God from the text, while his successor surpassed him in impiety by committing the Torah to the flames.[112] With the invasion of Jerusalem by Nebuchadnezzar, who razed the Temple to the ground, every remaining doubt concerning the fate of the Torah was removed. The inhabitants of Judah were deported to Babylon where they developed a new religion, Judaism, which, with its newly invented prayers and rituals, was totally different from the original Mosaic faith. When they were allowed to return to Jerusalem, they not only rebuilt their Temple but also rewrote their Torah, and it is plain to see that it does not represent the divine revelation.

But if God was not the author of this Law, who, then, was? Ibn Hazm has no clear answer. Sometimes, *the* Israelites or *the* Jews are collectively held responsible, or the accusing finger is pointed at an anonymous Jew, who is described in turn as an ignoramus who did not have the faintest notion of, say, geography and mathematics and as a very cunning individual, who maliciously passed off this blasphemous nonsense as the word of God with the object of making fun of religion in general, or of discrediting his fellow Jews, for whatever reason.[113] However, on several occasions, Ibn Hazm identifies the forger as Ezra, the biblical scribe, who, as we have seen, had been credited by Ibn Qutayba, al-Tabarī, and al-Maqdisī with restoring the Torah.[114] According to Ibn Hazm, Ezra dictated a new Torah, allegedly from his memory but in reality changing it so dramatically that the result no longer resembles the divine original. It is on this false "revelation" that the Jewish religion is based.

The true Torah was once more revealed to Jesus, the Messiah, along with the Gospel, but with Jesus' ascension to heaven, both holy Scriptures were taken up also and mankind was left with corrupted scriptures until Muhammad came to restore these books in their original glory. The only way in which Jews and Christians can fulfill the precepts of their Scriptures is by embracing Islam and fulfilling the laws of the Qur'ān.[115]

Like al-Maqdisī, Ibn Hazm adduces discrepancies between the Jewish, Samaritan, and Greek versions of the Torah as additional proof of the unreliability of the former Scripture.[116] But however unreliable Ibn Hazm thinks the Jewish Scriptures are, he does not hesitate to quote passages from it that he believes refer to Muhammad. He has a simple explanation for this paradox: God preserved these particular passages and a few others from distortion. They thus constitute the only genuine elements in "Ezra's Torah."[117]

According to Ibn Hazm, it was not only the Jewish Scriptures that were falsified; the very religion of the Jews in no way resembles the original Mosaic faith. The rabbis are held responsible for the creation of Judaism as it was known in Ibn Hazm's day, an argument which seems to echo Karaite views.[118]

Throughout his polemic, Ibn Hazm shows a rare familiarity with the text of the Hebrew Bible, albeit in an Arabic translation. He does not seem to have had a complete copy of the Torah at his disposal. As for the remaining books of the Jewish canon, he presumably relied on a set of excerpts. This is true also for the rabbinical sources he attacks.

While Ibn Hazm's familiarity with the biblical text was exceptional and had no parallels among his predecessors, his knowledge of Jewish beliefs and practices was less of an exception, as a comparison with the works of authors like al-Maqdisī and al-Bīrūnī (d. ca. 442/1050) reveals. It should also be pointed out that Ibn Hazm's motives for inquiring into Jewish matters differed from those of the other two authors; while the latter sought to inform their readers, Ibn Hazm's criterion for the inclusion of information on Judaism seems to have been the degree to which the material served his polemical purposes.

Finally, mention should be made of the author's attitude toward the Jews. His polemical writings are characterized by vituperative language, which has led some scholars to consider him a virtual anti-Semite.[119] However, his polemics denounce both Christians and Muslim sectarians in similar terms as well, so his wrath is by no means limited to the Jews. Furthermore, when one looks beyond Ibn Hazm's polemical writings to include his legal writings, it is found that his rulings concerning social interaction between Muslims and Jews (as well as Christians), are often milder than those of jurists belonging to other legal rites, a fact which has so far received little attention. Nevertheless, it should be kept in mind that this reflects Ibn Hazm's strict adherence to the principles of the Zāhirī or literalist school of law, rather than a liberal spirit.[120]

Conclusions

In this essay we have examined some polemical arguments used by Muslim writers from the classical period against the Jewish Scriptures. Apart from the biblical references to the Prophet Muhammad, the issue that dominates in the works of the authors under review (as well as in the Qur'ān) is that of the authenticity or spuriousness of the Torah, which in its wider sense includes the remaining books of the Hebrew Bible. Each author in his own way reveals an ambivalent attitude to the Jewish Scriptures. This is not surprising, since already the Qur'ān displays a tension between the statement that the Torah is a divine Scripture which refers to Muhammad on the one hand, and the allegation of scriptural misrepresentation on the other. Ibn Rabban and Ibn Qutayba feel justified to use the Jewish Scriptures for their own apologetical purposes by subscribing to the view that it was only the interpretation, not the text, of the Torah that was distorted; al-Tabarī agrees and yet chooses to steer clear of the Jewish Scriptures, while both al-Maqdisī and Ibn Hazm reject them as a forgery. Yet even these two authors will accept some passages as genuine, namely those supposedly referring to the Prophet. Both interpretations of *taḥrīf*, the mild one and the radical one, have their partisans among modern Muslim authors.[121]

NOTES

1. Cf. S. 5:82; 2:96; 4:160; 6:146; 16:118; 9:31. On these and other Qur'ānic arguments against the Jews and their religion, see Heribert Busse, *Die theologischen Beziehungen des Islams zu Judentum und Christentum: Grundlagen des Dialogs im Koran und die gegenwärtige Situation*, Grundzüge, 72 (Darmstadt: Wissenschaftliche Buchgesellschaft, 1988), pp. 43–51, 58–61; Johan Bouman, *Der Qur'ān und die Juden: Die Geschichte einer Tragödie* (Darmstadt: Wissenschaftliche Buchgesellschaft, 1990); G. Vajda, "Ahl al-Kitāb," *Encyclopaedia of Islam*, New edition, Vol. 1 (Leiden, E. J. Brill, 1960), pp. 264–266.

2. On the scripture-related arguments to be discussed in this article, see Moritz Steinschneider, *Polemische und apologetische Literatur in arabischer Sprache zwischen Muslimen, Christen und Juden, nebst Anhängen verwandten Inhalts* (Leipzig, 1877; reprint, Hildesheim: Georg Olms, 1966), esp. pp. 320–329; I. Goldziher, "Über muhammedanische Polemik gegen Ahl al-kitab," *Zeitschrift der Deutschen Morgenländischen Gesellschaft* 32 (1878): 341–387 (*Gesammelte Schriften*, vol. 2, 1–48); Martin Schreiner, "Zur Geschichte der Polemik zwischen Juden und Mohammedanern," *Zeitschrift der Deutschen Morgenländischen Gesellschaft* 43 (1888), 591–675; Hartwig Hirschfeld, "Mohammedan criticism of the Bible," *Jewish Quarterly Review* 13 (1901): 222–240; Ignazio di Matteo, "Il 'tahrif' od alterazione della Bibbia secondo i musulmani," *Bessarione* 38 (1922): 64–111, 223–260. An abridged translation of this article, by M. H. Ananikian, was published in *The Moslem World* 14 (1924): 61–84, under the title "Tahrif or alteration of the Bible according to the Moslems." See also Ignazio di Matteo, "Le pretese contraddizioni della S. Scrittura secondo Ibn Hazm," *Bessarione* 27 (1923): 77–127; Erdmann Fritsch, *Islam und Christentum im Mittelalter: Beiträge zur Geschichte der muslimischen Polemik gegen das Christentum in arabischer Sprache* (Breslau: Müller and Seiffert, 1930); Herman Stieglecker, "Die Muhammedanische Pentateuchkritik zu Beginn des 2. Jahrtausends," *Theologisch-praktische Quartalschrift* 88 (1935): 72–87, 282–302, 472–486; E. Strauss (Ashtor), "Darkhe ha-pulmus ha-Islami," in *Sefer ha-Zikkaron le-Veth ha-Midrash le-Rabbanim be-Vina*, ed. Aryeh Schwartz (Jerusalem: Ruben Mas, 1946), pp. 182–197; W. Montgomery Watt, "The early development of the Muslim attitude to the Bible," *Transactions of the Glasgow University Oriental Society* 16 (1955–'56): 50–62; Michel Allard, trans. and ed.,*Textes apologétiques de Ǧuwaini* (*m. 478/ 1085*): *Textes arabes traduits et annotés*, Recherches, Serie I: Pensée arabe et musulmane, 43 (Beirut: Dar el-Machreq, 1968); M. Perlmann, "The Medieval Polemics between Islam and Judaism," in *Religion in a Religious Age*, ed. S. D. Goitein (Cambridge, Mass.: Association for Jewish Studies, 1974), pp. 103–138; Perlmann, "Eleventh-century Andalusian authors on the Jews of Granada," in *Medieval Jewish Life: Studies from the Proceedings of the American Academy of Jewish Research*, ed. Robert Chazan (New York: Ktav, 1976), pp. 147–168. [= *Proceedings of the American Academy of Jewish Research* 18 (1948–1949): 269–290]; Perlmann, "Polemics, Muslim-Jewish," in *The Encyclopedia of Religion*, ed. Mircea Eliade et al. (New York: Macmillan, 1987), 11:396–402; Perlmann, "Polemics, Islamic-Jewish," in *Dictionary of the Middle Ages*, ed. Joseph R. Strayer (New York: Scribner, 1988), 10:7–9; Jacques Waardenburg, "World religions as seen in the light of Islam," in *Islam: Past Influence and Present Challenge—In Honour of William Montgomery Watt*, ed. Alford T. Welch and Pierre Cachia (Albany: SUNY Press, 1979), pp. 255–258; Robert Caspar and Jean-Marie Gaudeul, "Textes de la tradition musulmane concernant le *taḥrīf* (falsification) des Ecritures," *Islamochristiana* 6 (1980): 61–104; Ali Bouamama, *La polémique musulmane contre le christianisme depuis ses origines jusqu'au XIIIe siècle* (Algiers: Entreprise Nationale du Livre, 1988); Norman Roth, "Forgery and abrogation of the Torah: A theme in Muslim and Christian polemic in Spain," *Proceedings of the American Academy of Jewish Research* 54 (1987): 203–236; Hava Lazarus-Yafeh, *Intertwined Worlds: Medieval Islam and Bible Criticism* (Princeton, N.J.: Princeton University Press, 1992); Camilla Adang, *Muslim Writers on Judaism and the Hebrew Bible: From Ibn Rabban to Ibn Hazm* (Islamic Philosophy, Theology and Science 22) Leiden: E. J. Brill, 1996. This essay is based on the latter publication.

3. The idea that the earlier revelations have been superseded, or at least qualified, can be found in S. 7:157, where God promises to show his mercy to those Jews and Christians who follow Muhammad, the prophet described in the Torah and the Gospel, who is "bidding them to honour, and forbidding them to dishonour, making lawful for them the good things and making unlawful for them the corrupt things, and relieving them of their loads, and the fetters that were upon them." The translation cited here and throughout the essay is that of Arthur J. Arberry, *The Koran Interpreted* (Oxford: Oxford University Press, 1964 and various reprints).

4. Cf. n. 3.

5. The *tahrīf*-verses are S. 2:75–79; 4:46; 5:13; 5:41. In other verses, the Israelites and/or the Jews are accused of confounding the truth with vanity (S. 2:42; 3:71) or concealing the truth (e.g., S. 3:187); hiding part of the Book (S. 6:91); substituting words (S. 2:59; 7:162); twisting their tongues when reciting the Book (S. 3:78); in some verses, we find a combination of accusations, e.g., S. 2:42; 3:71; 4:46. On the interpretation of these verses by commentators and apologists from both the classical and the modern periods, see Caspar and Gaudeul, "Textes de la tradition musulmane." On contemporary literature in which the accusation of *tahrīf* is leveled against the Jews, see Mohanna Y. S. Haddad, "Arab perspectives of Judaism: A study of image formation in the writings of Muslim Arab authors 1948–1978," Ph.D. thesis, Rijksuniversiteit Utrecht, 1984, esp. pp. 89–122.

6. On Christian polemical and apologetical writings in Greek, see Adel-Théodore Khoury, *Les théologiens byzantins et l'Islam: Textes et auteurs* (*VIIIe–XIIIe s.*), 2nd ed. (Paris: Beatrice-Nauwelaerts, 1969); Khoury, *Polémique byzantine contre l'Islam* (*VIIIe–XIIIe s.*) (Leiden: E. J. Brill, 1972); Daniel J. Sahas, *John of Damascus on Islam: The "Heresy of the Ishmaelites"* (Leiden: E. J. Brill, 1972); Raymond Le Coz, *Jean Damascène: Ecrits sur l'Islam—Présentation, Commentaires et Traduction*, Sources chrétiennes, 383 (Paris: Editions du Cerf, 1992). On Christian authors writing in Syriac and Arabic, see Sidney H. Griffith, "The Prophet Muhammad, his scripture and his message according to the Christian apologies in Arabic and Syriac from the first Abbasid Century," in *La vie du prophète Mahomet: Colloque de Strasbourg 1980*, ed. Toufic Fahd (Paris: Presses Universitaires de France, 1983), pp. 99–146.

7. (Ibn) al-Nadīm, *Fihrist*, ed. Reza Tajaddud (Beirut: Dār al-Masīra, 1988), pp. 185 (Bishr b. al-Muʿtamir), 204 (Abū'l-Hudhayl), 211 (al-Jāhiz), 214 (al-Asamm), 216 (Abu ʿĪsā al-Warrāq); see pp. 357, 388, 406, 415, 419 in vol. 1 of *The Fihrist of al-Nadim: A Tenth-century Survey of Muslim Culture*, ed. and transl. Bayard Dodge, 2 vols. (New York: Columbia University Press, 1970).

8. *Al-Radd ʿalāʾl-Nasārā*, in *Three Essays of Abu Othmān Amr ibn Bahr al-Jāhiz*, ed. Joshua Finkel (Cairo: Salafiyya Press, 1926), pp. 9–38. A partial translation of the tract was published by Joshua Finkel: "A Risāla of al-Jāhiz," *Journal of the American Oriental Society* 47 (1927): 311–334 at pp. 322–334; a full translation by I. S. Allouche appeared in *Hespéris* 26 (1939): 123–155 at pp. 129–153 ("Un traité de polémique christiano-musulmane au IXe siècle").

9. Short biographical notices of each of the authors under review in this article are given in Adang, *Muslim Writers*, chapter 2. In the following pages, only some general works will be referred to.

10. On Ibn Rabban, see Max Meyerhof, "ʿAlī ibn Rabban at-Tabarī, ein persischer Arzt des 9. Jahrhunderts n. Chr.," *Zeitschrift der Deutschen Morgenländischen Gesellschaft* 85 [Neue Folge 10] (1931): 38–68; M. Bouyges, "Nos informations sur ʿAliy . . . at-Tabariy," *Mélanges de l'Université St. Joseph* 28 (1949–1950), 83–91.

11. See Adang, *Muslim Writers*, 25f. On al-Mutawakkil's crackdown on the *dhimmīs*, see Bernard Lewis, *The Jews of Islam* (Princeton, N.J.: Princeton University Press, 1984), 47–49.

12. Ibn Rabban ʿAli Tabari, *Kitāb al-Dīn waʾl-Dawla*, ed. A. Mingana (Manchester: University Press, 1923). English translation: *The Book of Religion and Empire: A Semi-Official Defence and Exposition of Islam Written by Order at the Court and with the Assistance of the Caliph Mutawakkil (A.D. 847–861)*, edited with a critical apparatus from an apparently unique MS. in the John Rylands Library by A. Mingana (Manchester: University Press, 1922). On the question of the authenticity of the tract, see Adang, *Muslim Writers*, 27–29. The other apologetic tract by Ibn Rabban is entitled *Al-Radd ʿalāʾl-Nasārā* (Refutation of the Christians). It was edited by I. A. Khalife and W. Kutsch in *Mélanges de l'Université St. Joseph* 36 (1959): 113–148.

13. Ibn Rabban, *Dīn wa-Dawla*, p. 20; *Religion and Empire*, p. 18.

14. The Jewish *mutakallim* al-Muqammis (wrote first half of the ninth century CE) has a similar list of prerequisites for the veracity of a prophet. As has been shown by Sarah Stroumsa, the Jewish author took his arguments from an as yet unidentified Christian source. Even though the aim of this source was no doubt to prove the truth of Jesus' mission, al-Muqammis seeks to demonstrate the applicability of the same criteria to Moses and to Judaism. See *Dawūd ibn Marwān al-Muqammis's Twenty Chapters* (*ʿIshrūn Maqāla*), edited, translated, and annotated by Sarah Stroumsa (Etudes sur le Judaïsme médieval, XIII. (Leiden, New York: E. J. Brill, 1989), 31f., 262–271 (the odd page numbers refer to the Judaeo-Arabic text; the even ones to the translation). See also Sarah Stroumsa, "The signs of prophecy—The emergence and early development of a theme in Arabic Theological Literature," *Harvard Theological Review*, 78 (1985): 101–114.

15. Ibn Rabban, *Dīn wa-Dawla*, pp. 66–119; *Religion and Empire*, pp. 77–152.

16. *Risālat Abi Rabiʿ Muhammad b. al-Layth allatī katabaha liʾl-Rashīd ilā Qustantīn malik al-Rūm*, in *Jamharat rasāʾil al-ʿArab*, ed. Ahmad Zaki Safwat, vol. 3: *Al-ʿasr al-ʿAbbāsi al-awwal* (Cairo: M. al-Halabi, 1356–1937), pp. 309–314. The Old Testament passages mentioned by the author are Isa. 21:6–9; Ps. 9:20; Hab. 3:3–6; Ps. 149; Isa. 42:10–12; Isa. 42:1–4;

Ps. 45:2–5; Deut. 33:2; Deut. 18:18. On Ibn al-Layth, see D. M. Dunlop, "A letter of Harun ar-Rashid to the Emperor Constantine VI," in *In Memoriam Paul Kahle*, ed. Matthew Black and Georg Fohrer (Berlin: Alfred Töpelmann, 1968), pp. 106–115; cf. the contribution by A. Shboul in this volume.

17. On the use of biblical testimonies in early Islam, see Uri Rubin, *The Eye of the Beholder: The Life of Muhammad as Viewed by the Early Muslims—A Textual Analysis* (Studies in Late Antiquity and Early Islam, 5) (Princeton, N.J.: Darwin Press, 1995), pp. 21–43.

18. For a list of biblical passages invoked by Ibn Rabban and others as testimonies to Muhammad, see Adang, *Muslim Writers*, pp. 264–266.

19. Ibn Rabban, *Dīn wa-Dawla*, pp. 76, 77, 88, 90, 93f.; *Religion and Empire*, pp. 89, 90, 103, 105, 108.

20. Ibn Rabban, *Dīn wa-Dawla*, p. 81; *Religion and Empire*, p. 95.

21. Ibn Rabban, *Dīn wa-Dawla*, pp. 117f.; *Religion and Empire*, p. 138.

22. Ibn Rabban, *Dīn wa-Dawla*, p. 118; *Religion and Empire*, pp. 138f.

23. Examples of references to Islam's emergence from the desert (in the south, at the ends of the earth): Gen. 21:20f.; Deut. 33:2f.; Isa. 42:11–13; Isa. 21:1–10; Isa. 24:16–18; Isa. 35:1f.; Isa. 41:17–20; Isa. 43:20f.; Isa. 46:9–11; Isa. 54:11–15; Isa. 49:16–21; Hos. 13:5; Mic. 4:1f.; Hab. 3:3–13; Ezek. 19:10–14. The spread of Arabic: Zeph. 3:8–10; Jer. 5:15f.; Isa. 49:1–5; Muhammad's victories and leadership: Ps. 45:2–5; Ps. 50:2f.; Ps. 72:8–12; Ps. 140:4–9; Isa. 2:12–19. See also the categories in Bouamama, *Polémique*, pp. 201–213, and Lazarus-Yafeh, *Intertwined Worlds*, pp. 83–110.

24. Ibn Rabban, *Dīn wa-Dawla*, p. 106; *Religion and Empire*, p. 124.

25. Ibn Rabban, *Dīn wa-Dawla*, p. 85; *Religion and Empire*, p. 104.

26. Ibn Rabban, *Dīn wa-Dawla*, p. 129; *Religion and Empire*, p. 152.

27. Ibn Rabban, *Dīn wa-Dawla*, pp. 27f., 46f.; *Religion and Empire*, pp. 28f., 52f.

28. Ibn Rabban, *Dīn wa-Dawla*, p. 47; *Religion and Empire*, p. 53.

29. Ibn Rabban, *Dīn wa-Dawla*, p. 45; *Religion and Empire*, p. 51.

30. Ibn Rabban, *Dīn wa-Dawla*, pp. 45f.; *Religion and Empire*, p. 51.

31. Ibn Rabban, *Dīn wa-Dawla*, pp. 27f., 47; *Religion and Empire*, pp. 28, 53.

32. Ibn Rabban, *Dīn wa-Dawla*, pp. 134f.; *Religion and Empire*, pp. 158f.

33. Ibn Rabban, *Dīn wa-Dawla*, p. 71; *Religion and Empire*, p. 82.

34. Ibn Rabban, *Dīn wa-Dawla*, p. 110; *Religion and Empire*, p. 129.

35. Ibn Rabban, *Dīn wa-Dawla*, p. 123; *Religion and Empire*, p. 145.

36. D. S. Margoliouth, "On 'The Book of Religion and Empire' by ʿAlī b. Rabban al-Tabarī," *Proceedings of the British Academy* 14 (1930): 168f.

37. General works on Ibn Qutayba: Ishāq Mūsā Huseini, *The Life and Works of Ibn Qutayba* (Oriental Series 21) Beirut: American University of Beirut, 1950; Gérard Lecomte, *Ibn Qutayba (mort en 276/889), l'homme, son oeuvre, ses idées* (Damascus: Institut Français de Damas, 1965); Lecomte, "Ibn Kutayba," *Encyclopaedia of Islam.* New edition, Vol. 3 (Leiden: E. J. Brill, 1971), pp. 844–847.

38. Huseini, *Life and Works of Ibn Qutayba*, pp. 19, 83, 89.

39. Ch. Pellat, "Ibn Qutayba waʾl-thaqāfa al-ʿarabiyya," in *Mélanges Taha Husain*, ed. A. Badawi (Cairo, 1962), pp. 33, 35; Pellat, "Les encyclopédies dans le monde arabe," *Journal of World History* 9 (1966): 637ff. Pellat compares Ibn Qutayba with al-Jāhiz, al-Yaʿqūbī, and others.

40. On Ibn Qutayba's quotations from an Arabic translation of the Bible, see Georges Vajda, "Observations sur quelques citations bibliques chez Ibn Qotayba," *Revue des études juives* 99 (1935): 68–91; Gérard Lecomte, "Les citations de l'Ancien et du Nouveau Testament dans l'oeuvre d'Ibn Qutayba," *Arabica* 5 (1958): 34–46.

41. Ibn Qutayba, *Al-Maʿārif*, 2nd ed., ed. Tharwat ʿUkasha (Cairo: Dar al-Maʿarif, 1969).

42. Ibid., 50; cf. Adriana Drint, "The Mount Sinai Arabic version of IV Ezra," Ph.D. thesis, Rijksuniversiteit Groningen, 1995), p. 65.

43. On the echoes of *IV Ezra* in works by Muslim authors, see Mahmoud Ayoub, "ʿUzayr in the Qurʾān and Muslim tradition," in *Studies in Islamic and Judaic Traditions*, ed. William M. Brinner and Stephen D. Ricks (Atlanta: Scholars Press, 1986), pp. 3–18; Lazarus-Yafeh, *Intertwined Worlds*, chapter 3; Drint, *The Mount Sinai Arabic Version*, 51–85.

44. Ibn Qutayba, *al-Maʿārif*, 50.

45. See my article "Some hitherto neglected biblical material in the work of Ibn Hazm," *Al-Masaq: Studia Arabo-Islamica Mediterranea* 5 (1992): 17–28, and Appendix 3 of my *Muslim Writers* for a translation of these fragments.

46. Ibn Qutayba, *Dalāʾil al-nubuwwa* in C. Brockelmann, "Ibn al-Jawzī's Kitāb al-wafāʾ fī fadāʾil al-Mustafā nach der Leidener Handschrift untersucht," in *Beiträge zur Assyriologie und semitischen Sprachwissenschaft*, vol. 3, ed. Friedrich Delitzsch and Paul Haupt (Leipzig: Hinrichs, 1898), p. 46.

47. Brockelmann, "Ibn al-Jawzī's Kitāb al-wafā," 48.

48. Ibid., 48.

49. Ibn Qutayba, *Taʾwīl Mukhtalif al-Hadīth*, ed.

Muhammad Zuhri al-Najjār (Cairo: Maktabat al-Kulliyat al-Azhariyya, 1966/1386), p. 195; French translation by Gérard Lecomte, *Le traité des divergences du hadīt d'Ibn Qutayba (mort en 276/889): Traduction annotée du Kitāb Ta'wīl Muhtalif al-Hadīt* (Damascus: Institut français de Damas, 1962), 216f.; cf. Lecomte, *Ibn Qutayba*, 270.

50. Ibn Qutayba, *Ta'wīl Mukhtalif al-Hadīth*, p. 293; Lecomte, *Traité des divergences*, p. 324. Perhaps Ibn Qutayba is thinking of some austere Jewish sect which disapproved of joy and dancing.

51. Ibn Qutayba, *Ta'wīl Mukhtalif al-Hadīth*, p. 293; Lecomte, *Traité des divergences*, 325.

52. See Brockelmann, "Ibn al-Jawzī's Kitāb al-wafā," 48.

53. This reference is given in a polemical tract by Ibn Qayyim al-Jawziyya: *Kitāb hidāyat al-hayārā min al-Yahūd wa'l-Nasārā* (Cairo, 1323/1905), 76.

54. The 4th C.E./10th H.–century Imāmī Shīʿite al-Nuʿmānī cites the same passage, allegedly on the authority of a Jewish scholar; see Etan Kohlberg, "From Imāmiyya to Ithnā-ʿashariyya," *Bulletin of the School for Oriential and African Studies* 39 (1976): 526f.

55. Cf. Lecomte, *Ibn Qutayba*, pp. 336, 429.

56. Ibid., p. 430.

57. See on al-Tabarī: *The History of al-Tabarī*, vol. 1: *General Introduction and From the Creation to the Flood*, transl. and annotated by Franz Rosenthal (Albany: State University of New York Press, 1989, pp. 5–134; Claude Gilliot, *Exégèse, langue et théologie en islam: L'exégèse coranique de Tabarī* (Paris: Librairie philosophique J. Vrin, 1990), pp. 19–70; Jane Dammen McAuliffe, *Qur'ānic Christians: An Analysis of Classical and Modern Exegesis* (Cambridge: Cambridge University Press, 1991), pp. 38–45.

58. Jane Dammen McAuliffe, "Quranic hermeneutics: The views of al-Tabarī and Ibn Kathīr," in *Approaches to the History of the Interpretation of the Qur'an*, ed. Andrew Rippin (Oxford: Clarendon Press, 1988), p. 48.

59. Peter Heath, "Creative hermeneutics: A comparative analysis of three Islamic approaches," *Arabica* 36 (1989): 185. On al-Tabarī's method, see also McAuliffe, "Quranic hermeneutics," pp. 47–54. For a more elaborate discussion of al-Tabarī's hermeneutical principles, see Gilliot, *Exégèse, langue et théologie*.

60. Al-Tabarī, *Tafsīr al-Tabarī: Jāmiʿ al-bayān ʿan ta'wīl al-Qur'ān*, ed. M. M. Shakir and A. M. Shakir (Cairo: Dar al-Maʿārif, 1961– , vol. 1, pp. 412f., 557, 559, 560, 563; vol. 2, pp. 254ff.; vol. 4, p. 272; vol. 10, pp. 124ff.

61. Ibid., vol. 10, pp. 126–129.

62. Ibid., vol. 2, pp. 112, 116; vol. 13, p. 178.

63. Ibid., vol. 2, pp. 247ff.

64. Ibid., vol. 2, pp. 259f., 262f., 264, 265f. 269ff, 273f.; vol. 10, p. 129.

65. Ibid., vol. 2, pp. 111, 244f.

66. Ibid., vol. 2, pp. 111, 249; vol. 10, p. 125, 133.

67. Ibid., vol. 1, pp. 410ff., 554, 572, 575.

68. Ibid., vol. 1, p. 554; vol. 3, pp. 327, 335.

69. Ibid., vol. 2, pp. 270ff.

70. Ibid., vol. 6, p. 535.

71. Ibid., vol. 8, pp. 433ff.

72. Ibid., vol. 2, pp. 248f.; vol. 8, pp. 432, 435.

73. Ibid., vol. 10, pp. 309, 311ff. Cf. *Kitāb Sīrat Rasūl Allāh: Das Leben Muhammed's nach Muhammed Ibn Ishak bearbeitet von Abd el-Malik ibn Hischam*, ed. F. Wüstenfeld, vol. 1 (Göttingen, 1858; reprint Frankfurt a/M.: Minerva, 1961). Translated in *The Life of Muhammad:* A Translation of Ibn Ishaq's *Sīrat Rasūl Allāh*, with introduction and notes by A. Guillaume (Karachi, Oxford University Press, 1990). On Muhammad's sentence on the Jewish couple and its consequences for Muslim practice, see John Burton, *The Collection of the Qur'ān* (Cambridge: Cambridge University Press, 1977), pp. 68–86; and Burton, *The Sources of Islamic Law: Islamic Theories of Abrogation* (Edinburgh: Edinburgh University Press, 1990), pp. 129–156.

74. Al-Tabarī, *Tafsīr*, vol. 11, pp. 526ff.

75. Al-Tabarī, *Ta'rīkh al-rusul wa'l-mulūk, Annales*, ed. M. J. De Goeje et al. (Leiden: E. J. Brill, 1879–1901, reprint 1964); cf. *The History of al-Tabarī*. Vol. 4: *The Ancient Kingdoms*, trans. and annotated by Moshe Perlmann (Albany: State University of New York Press, 1987), pp. 64f. For a different translation, see Lazarus-Yafeh, *Intertwined Worlds*, pp. 54f.; Drint, *The Mount Sinai Arabic Version*, p. 55.

76. Al-Tabarī, *Annales*, p. 16; *The History of al-Tabarī*, vol. I, p. 184.

77. Ibn Qutayba, *Maʿārif*, pp. 9–52; al-Yaʿqūbī, *Ta'rīkh*, vol. 1 (Beirut: Dār Sādir/Dār Bayrūt, 1960), pp. 5–67. On the use of biblical materials by these authors, see Vajda, "Observations"; Lecomte, "Les citations"; G. Smit, *"Bijbel en Legende" bij den Arabischen schrijver Jaʿqubi, 9e eeuw na Christus: Vertaling en onderzoek naar de bronnen van Ibn-Wadhih qui dicitur Al-Jaʿqubi, Historiae, Pars prior 1–89, ed. M. Th. Houtsma, 1883* (Leiden: E. J. Brill, 1907); R. Y. Ebied and L. R. Wickham, "Al-Yaʿkūbī's account of the Israelite prophets and kings," *Journal of Near Eastern Studies* 29 (1970): pp. 80–98. See also my *Muslim Writers*, pp. 112–120.

78. This same testimony had earlier been adduced by Ibn Saʿd (d. 230/845); see *Al-Tabaqāt al-kubrā*, vol. 1 (Beirut: Dār Sādir/Dār Bayrūt, 1957/1377); see also Ibn Qutayba as quoted by Ibn Hazm, *Al-Usūl wa'l-Furūʿ*, vol. 1, p. 193. On the early use of this testimony, see Rubin, *The Eye of the Beholder*, 30ff.

79. On al-Maqdisī and his work, see Tarif Khalidi, "Muʿtazilite historiography: Maqdisī's *Kitāb al-Bad' wa'l-Ta'rīkh*," *Journal of Near Eastern Studies*, 35

(1976), 1–12; "Al-Mutahhar b. Tāhir," *Encyclopaedia of Islam*, New edition vol. 7 (Leiden: E. J. Brill, 1992), p. 762.

80. Al-Maqdisī, *Kitāb al-Bad' wa'l-Ta'rīkh: Le livre de la création et de l'histoire de Motahhar ben Tahir el-Maqdisi attribué à Abou-Zeid Ahmed ben Sahl el-Balkhi*. Publié et traduit d'après le manuscrit de Constantinople par M. Cl. Huart. 6 vols. (Paris: Ernest Leroux, 1899–1919).

81. For some examples, see my *Muslim Writers*, pp. 84ff., 126ff.

82. See al-Maqdisī, *Bad'*, vol. 4, pp. 34–41 (32–40 in the French translation). The section on Jewish sects has been studied and translated by Steven M. Wasserstrom, "Species of Misbelief: A History of Muslim Heresiography of the Jews" (Ph.D. thesis, University of Toronto, 1985), pp. 89–94, 354–356. The Jewish practices described by al-Maqdisī are discussed in my *Muslim Writers*, pp. 84–87, 257–263.

83. Al-Maqdisī, *Bad'*, vol. 5, pp. 29f. (Tr. 32).

84. Ibid., p. 30 (Tr. 33).

85. Some Jewish authors, however, were prepared to acknowledge that Muhammad and his nation were referred to in the Scriptures, but always in a negative sense; none of them accepted the Muslim claim that Muhammad's prophethood or his mission were corroborated by the Tanach. If anything, it was the falsity of these claims that could be demonstrated on the basis of the biblical text. See Haggai Ben-Shammai, "The attitude of some early Karaites towards Islam," in *Studies in Medieval Jewish History and Literature*, vol. 2, ed. Isadore Twersky (Cambridge, Mass.: Harvard University Press), pp. 3–40.

86. Al-Maqdisī, *Bad'*, vol. 5, p. 27 (Tr. 30).

87. Ibid., p. 28 (Tr. 30f).

88. Ibid., pp. 30–32 (Tr. 33f.).

89. Ibid., p. 33 (Tr. 35).

90. Ibid., p. 29 (Tr. 32).

91. Adang, *Muslim Writers*, p. 156.

92. Al-Maqdisī, *Bad'*, vol. 5, pp. 25f. (Tr. 28).

93. Ibn al-Nadīm, *Fihrist*, pp. 36, 185, 214, 229, 252, 272. For a list of *Dalā'il al-Nubuwwa* works, see Adang, *Muslim Writers*, p. 157. I am currently preparing a separate study on this type of literature.

94. Some general literature on Ibn Hazm includes the following. Miguel Asín Palacios, *Abenházam de Córdoba y su historia crítica de las ideas religiosas*, vol. 1 (Madrid: Real Academia de la Historia, 1927); A. G. Chejne, *Ibn Hazm* (Chicago: Kazi Publications, 1982); Muhammad Abu Laila, "An introduction to the life and work of Ibn Hazm," *Islamic Quarterly* 29 (1985): 75–100, 165–171; Roger Arnaldez, "Ibn Hazm," *Encyclopaedia of Islam*, new ed., vol. 3 (Leiden: E. J. Brill, 1985), pp. 790–799. Ibrahīm al-Hardallo, *Al-Tawrāt wa'l-Yahūd fī Fikr Ibn Hazm* (Kartum: Dār Jāmiʿat al-Kartum, 1984) deals more specifically with Ibn Hazm's writings on Judaism, as does my *Islam frente a Judaísmo: La polemica de Ibn Hazm de Cordoba* (Madrid: Aben Ezra Ediciones, 1994).

95. On the Jews of al-Andalus in this period, and in particular on Ibn al-Naghrīla, see David Wasserstein, *The Rise and Fall of the Party-Kings: Politics and Society in Islamic Spain, 1002–1086* (Princeton, N.J.: Princeton University Press, 1985), pp. 190–223.

96. On Ibn Hazm's Jewish interlocutors, see my *Muslim Writers*, pp. 94ff. On the ʿIsāwiyya sect, see Steven M. Wasserstrom, "The ʿIsāwiyya revisited," *Studia Islamica* 75 (1992): 57–80, and Wasserstrom, *Between Muslim and Jew: The Problem of Symbiosis under early Islam* (Princeton, N.J.: Princeton University Press, 1995), pp. 69–89.

97. On Ibn Hazm's use of Karaite arguments, see Adang, "Eléments karaïtes dans la polémique anti-judaïque d'Ibn Hazm," in *Diálogo filosófico-religioso entre cristianismo, judaismo e islamisco durante la edad media en la Península Ibérica*, ed. Horacio Santiago-Otero (Turnhout: Brepols, 1994), pp. 419–441.

98. In fact, most of Ibn Hazm's works, not only his polemical monographs, contain some criticism or other of the Jews; see, for example, *Jamharat Ansāb al-ʿArab*, ed. ʿAbd al-Salām Muhammad Hārūn (Cairo: Dār al-Maʿārif, 1982), pp. 8, 505ff.; *Kitāb al-Akhlāq wa'l-Siyar*, ed. Eva Riad (Acta Universitatis Upsaliensis, Studia Semitica Upsaliensia, 4) (Uppsala, 1990), pp. 48f.; *Al-Ihkām fī Usūl al-Ahkām* (Cairo, n.d.), pp. 445ff., 722f.

99. Ibn Hazm, *Al-Radd ʿalā Ibn al-Naghrīla al-Yahūdi warasā'il ukhrā*, ed. Ihsān ʿAbbās (Cairo: Dār al-ʿUrūba, 1960), pp. 45–81. Rev. ed. in *Rasā'il Ibn Hazm al-Andalūsī*, ed. Ihsān ʿAbbās, vol. 3 (Beirut: Al-Mu'assasa al-ʿArabiyya li'l-Dirāsāt wa'l-Nashr, 1987), pp. 41–70. See on this tract and the question of the identity of its addressee Emilio García Gómez, "Polémica religiosa entre Ibn Hazm e Ibn al-Nagrīla," *Al-Andalus* 4 (1936–1939): 1–28; Roger Arnaldez, "Controverse d'Ibn Hazm contre Ibn Nagrila le juif," *Revue de l'Occident musulman et de la Méditerranée*, 13–14 (1973): 41–48; David S. Powers, "Reading/misreading one another's Scriptures: Ibn Hazm's refutation of Ibn Nagrella al-Yahudi," in *Studies in Islamic and Judaic Traditions*, ed. Brinner and Ricks, 109–121; Wasserstein, *The Rise and Fall*, 199–205; Sarah Stroumsa, "From Muslim heresy to Jewish-Muslim polemics: Ibn al-Rāwandī's *Kitāb al-Dāmigh*," *Journal of the American Oriental Society*, 107 (1987): 767–772; Maribel Fierro, "Ibn Hazm et le *Zindīq* juif," *Revue du Monde Musulman et de la Méditerranée*, 63–64 (1992): 81–89.

100. Ibn Hazm, *Al-Fisal fī'l-Milal wa'l-Ahwā' wa'l-Nihal*, 5 vols. (Beirut: Dar al-Maʿrifa, 1395/1975). The work has been translated almost in its entirety by Miguel Asín Palacios in vols. 2–5 of his *Abenhazam*

de Cordoba y su historia crítica de las ideas religiosas (Madrid: Real Academia de la Historia, 1928–1932).

101. See I. Friedlaender, "Zur Komposition von Ibn Hazm's Milal waʾn-Nihal," in *Orientalische Studien Theodor Nöldeke gewidmet*, vol. 1, ed. Carl Bezold (Giessen, 1906), pp. 267–277. For a different view, see Ghulam Haider Aasi, "Muslim understanding of other religions: An analytical study of Ibn Hazm's Kitab al-Fasl Fi al-Milal wa al Ahwa wa al-Nihal," Ph.D. Diss., Temple University, 1987, p. 77.

102. See on this topic my article "Ibn Hazm's criticism of some 'Judaizing' tendencies among the Malikites," in *Medieval and Modern Perspectives on Muslim-Jewish Relations* (Chur: Harwood Academic Publishers, 1995), pp. 1–15.

103. On the issue of abrogation, see Adang, *Muslim Writers*, chapter 6.

104. The passages quotes are from S. 3:71; 2:146; 3:78, and 4:46; cf. also S. 5:13 and 5:41.

105. S. 48:29.

106. Ibn Hazm, *Kitāb al-Fisal*, vol. 1, pp. 215f.

107. Cf. ibid., p. 116; vol. 5, p. 120.

108. Cf. for example ibid., vol. 1, p. 135.

109. Ibid., pp. 116–186.

110. Ibid., pp. 187–203. He does reveal a substantial knowledge of the genealogy of the Israelites and their kings, both in this tract and in his *Jamharat Ansāb al-ʿArab*, pp. 503–511.

111. Ibn Hazm's allegation that there was only one copy of the Torah, and that its contents were unknown to the people, was to be denied vigorously by the great Jewish thinker Maimonides (d. 1204 CE); see Hava Lazarus-Yafeh, "*Tahrīf* and thirteen Torah scrolls," *Jerusalem Studies in Arabic and Islam* 19 (1995): 81–88.

112. See on the possible origins of this accusation (the Talmud; the book of Jeremiah; the apocryphal book of *IV Ezra*) Adang, *Muslim Writers*, pp. 244f.

113. Ibn Hazm, *Kitāb al-Fisal*, vol. 1, pp. 123, 128, 129, 134, 135, 138, 140, 150.

114. Ibid., pp. 117, 178, 187, 197, 198, 210.

115. Ibid., pp. 212f.

116. Ibid., pp. 99, 117; vol. 2, pp. 6–10.

117. For a translation of these passages, see Adang, "Some Hitherto Neglected Biblical Material," and Adang, *Muslim Writers*, pp. 160f.

118. See Adang, "Eléments karaéments karaïtes" and Adang, *Muslim Writers*, pp. 102ff.

119. Ibn Hazm's vile language (see Perlmann, "Eleventh-century Andalusian authors," p. 157, for some examples) has led some scholars to employ the terms "anti-Semitic" or "almost anti-Semitic"; see Emilio García Gómez's introduction to Ibn Hazm de Cordoba, *El collar de la paloma: Tratado sobre el amor y los amantes* (Madrid, Alianza Editorial, 1971), p. 48, and Lazarus-Yafeh, *Intertwined Worlds*, p. 66.

120. On the Zāhirī school and Ibn Hazm's contribution to it, see Ignaz Goldziher, *The Zāhirīs: Their Doctrine and Their History—A Contribution to the History of Islamic Theology*, ed. and trans. Wolfgang Behn (Leiden: E. J. Brill, 1971).

121. The paper read at the conference in December 1991 was based on my doctoral thesis, then in progress. The thesis was submitted in 1993, and a revised version was published in 1996 under the title *Muslim Writers on Judaism and the Hebrew Bible: From Ibn Rabban to Ibn Hazm* (Leiden, E. J. Brill, 1996).

9

Heresiography of the Jews in Mamluk Times

STEVEN M. WASSERSTROM

From the end of the sixth/twelfth century the various currents of Muslim heresiography begin to diverge markedly. The history and polemic fused in the presentation of an Ibn Ḥazm or a Baghdādī during the fifth/twelfth century, now separates out into Shahrastānī's admirably detached history of religions and Samauʾal al-Maghribī's purely polemical tract. By that century, then, the subgenres of Muslim heresiography of the Jews had become refined. Specialization, it would appear, began to break apart the comprehensive breadth of the Islamicate intellectual.

An equally impressive response to this loss of close coherence in the sixth/twelfth century was the assertion of a more explicitly anthological encyclopedism at the end of the eighth/fourteenth and the early ninth/fifteenth centuries. While the comprehensivist inclinations of most of the authors heretofore discussed were pronounced, these were usually well relegated to a distinctive style or confined to a particular avenue of inquiry. Subsumed and successfully domesticated by the literary and/or theological aims of the author in this way, comprehensivism could remain the tacit aspiration of the truly cultivated writer, guised in whatever ostensible genre was undertaken.

The masters of comprehensivism could write astonishingly long—and often correspondingly dense—productions. ʿAbd al-Jabbār's *Mughnī* and Fakhr al-Dīn's *Mafātīḥ al-Ghayb* are obvious examples. And yet, this was no mere hypertrophy: for whatever repetition, and sheer stringing-out, there may be in such books, they could retain their focus through whatever immense digressions might temporarily tempt them.

All these observations also apply to the great anthologists of the eighth/fourteenth–ninth/fifteenth centuries, but with a difference. Now, a new kind of "listing" fleshes out the all-inclusive tomes. Now, the author lists *lists*. One might suggest that the "lateness of the hour," the "cultural belatedness" of Qalqashandī, or Maqrīzī, led to the kind of anxious doubling-up of sources which distinguishes their work. That is to say, insofar as they practiced heresiography of the Jews, these authors energetically include more than did their predecessors, themselves hardly indolent, to make much the same point.

Indeed, the point of their concern here is the heresiographical naming and categorization of sects of Judaism. It is interesting to note that the first two authors to be discussed in this article, ʿUmarī and Ibn Qayyim al-Jauziyya, dealt with the Jewish groups in apologetic and jurisprudential contexts. The second triad to be discussed in this article, Ibn Khaldūn, Qalqashandī, and Maqrīzī, classify Jewish groups from a more complex variety of perspectives. With all of these contributions in mind, one is tempted to suggest that the early ninth/fifteenth century nearly equalled the great era of the mid-fifth/eleventh to mid-sixth/twelfth centuries—which included Bīrūnī,

Ibn Ḥazm, and Shahrastānī—in a kind of renascence for Islamicate history of religions.

This article will focus, then, on a two-century chain of North African scholars, most of whom, at one time or another, lived and worked in Mamluk Egypt.

ʿUmarī

Shihāb al-Dīn ibn Faḍl Allāh al-ʿUmarī (d. 748/1349) wrote the manual of administration known as the *Taʿrīf bi-al-Muṣṭalaḥ al-Sharīf*.[1] Its importance for our purposes lies in its presentation of the texts of the "charge of office" to the leaders of the various Jewish communities—Rabbanite, Karaite, and Samaritan—resident in Egypt. While a few other such documents prior to ʿUmarī have survived, the point here is simply to demonstrate that his work, like Qalqashandī's later *Ṣubḥ*, which copied from it, explicitly sets forth the oaths sworn by the leaders of these various communities. In so doing, these administrators express the "official" Mamluk classification of Jews.

Gottheil, at the turn of the century, devoted a series of studies to these oaths and charges.[2] Björkman, in 1928, investigated them in even greater detail.[3] More recently, Bosworth, Stillman, and B. Lewis have translated and discussed some of this material.[4] Goitein and Stern have done the most valuable recent research into such documents found in the Cairo Geniza.[5]

The concern of the study here, that of the naming and the categorization of Jewish sects, finds these oaths significant as the most explicit jurisprudential statements on the variety of Jewish communities. Earlier bureaucrats, like Khwārizmī, had compiled lists of Jewish groups. Legists like Isfarāʾinī, mentioned the kinds of Jews in terms of *fiqh*. They were also mentioned in the fourth/tenth-century recensions of the so-called Covenant of ʿUmar. But with the text of ʿUmarī, we possess an official document addressing the actual position of these communities at the time of the writer.

It should be kept in mind that ʿUmarī's oath refers to the Egyptian Jewish community. Correspondingly detailed materials on the Jewish communities under the ʿAbbāsids, for example, have not survived. In the period until the seventh/thirteenth century or so, under the ʿAbbāsids and other eastern Islamic dynasties, there existed some small Jewish communities besides the Rabbanites, Karaites, and Samaritans. The ʿIsāwiyya, at least, were almost invariably added by the bulk of the earlier authors. Moreover, this group certainly survived into the fourth/tenth or fifth/eleventh centuries, and perhaps beyond. But no trace of this latter group, or of the other sects, survives either in the Geniza documents or in the Faṭimid or Mamluk official documents of Egypt. These latter Egyptian materials are only concerned with the "big three"—the Rabbanites, Karaites, and Samaritans. It is unclear—and in any event beyond the purview of this study—whether this fact means that these sectarians had disappeared or were only confined to the eastern communities.

ʿUmarī, it should be noted here, gives two separate charters of office to the Jewish notables, one to the "Head of the Jews," and one to "the Leader of the Samaritans."[6] It seems clear, as Gottheil already noticed, that only Rabbanites are in fact considered "Yahūd" and that the Samaritans comprised a separate category, even though they are ultimately subsumed under the rubric of "Jews."[7] It has already been noted here that the Jewishness of the Samaritans was debated by Muslim jurisprudents and that the general conclusion was that they were a peculiar case of Jews, and thus were treated as a special case.[8] Nevertheless, they appear to have been treated more or less as were the Jews.

The contents of these oaths are less apposite to the present study than is the sheer fact of the differentiation of Jewish groups in legal documents. Heretofore, the listing of "Jewish" groups has had a tenuous relationship—in many cases, a historically uncorroborated connection—with actual Jewish groups. Be that as it may, the preponderance of lawyers and bureaucrats among the heresiographers has also left little doubt that their classifying of these non-Muslims reflected a concretely practical concern.

Muslim historians of religion, it should be remembered, dealt less with "foreign" religions than with non-Muslims resident in the *Dār al-Islām*. These historians of religion were almost all legist-theologians. Much of the Muslim heresiography of the Jews, like the wider phenomenon of Muslim "religious studies," then, may be understood as a function of the practical necessity of defining the position, theological, legal, and official, of non-Muslim communities existing under Muslim political domination.

In this regard it should be remembered as well that the official known as the *muḥtasib*, as part of his duties, supervised the public activities of the *ahl al-*

dhimma.[9] The practical decision as to whether the ʿIsāwiyya were Muslims, discussed by Baghdādī, therefore, is not so remote from the implications of ʿUmarī's distinguishing Samaritans from Jews: in both cases, the law must delimit the group in order to specify the ordinances pertinent to that group. These could then be implemented by the *muḥtasib.*

The significance of ʿUmarī for the history of Muslim heresiography of the Jews, therefore, lies with his recording these bureaucratic texts. His secondary importance also lies in his influence, for he is an important source for Qalqashandī. The details of his lists will therefore be discussed more fully in the section devoted to Qalqashandī.

Ibn Qayyim al-Jauziyya

Shams al-Dīn Abu Bakr Muḥammad Abī Bakr al-Zarʿī Ibn Qayyim al-Jauziyya (691/1292–751/1350) is remembered as a theologian and mystic closely associated with his more-celebrated mentor, Taqī al-Dīn Ibn Taymiyya (661/1263–728/1328).[10] Like Ibn Taymiyya and Ibn al-Jauzī, Ibn Qayyim was a Hanbalite, who has long been characterized in modern scholarship, as were his precursors, by a literalistic adherence to that school of jurisprudence. But in recent years George Makdisi has shown that Ibn Qayyim must be viewed not as a literalist-legist, but more accurately as a "Sufi-Hanbalite."[11]

Sufism, like Shīʿism, was not wont to address the heresiography of non-Muslim religions. Thus, for example, aside from some ʿAlid-leaning figures like Masʿūdī, almost no Shīʿī theologian, major or minor, took up the heresiography of Jews and Judaism.[12] Only Ḥaydar Āmulī even touched on these lists, and then only to copy Shahrastānī's lists as spokes on the wheel of his graphic depiction of world faiths emanating from one "axis."[13] Similarly, it seems that the closer a figure approached Sufism, the less concern there was for these scholarly questions: one finds this strikingly shown in the sharp dropping off of interest in these matters in Kalām circles, after Ghazalī shifted toward Sufism.[14]

Ibn Qayyim is therefore a somewhat anomalous figure in the history of Muslim heresiography of the Jews, for, while we now know that he was fully involved in Sufism, he was also actively involved in the heresiographic categorization of Judaism. In this connection he contrasts with his predecessors Ibn Taymiyya and Ibn al-Jauzī, neither of whom had anything to contribute to this question, though they did have much to say on the heresiography of Islam.[15] By contrast, Ibn Qayyim classified Jews in at least two distinct ways.

The first of these is found in his *Ighāthāt al-Lahfān Min Maṣāʾid al-Shayṭān.*[16] Drawing heavily if not plagiaristically upon the work of Samauʾal al-Maghribī, this heresiographic treatise was an attempt to show, in the phrase of Perlmann, that the *firqa nājiyya* (the saved sect) "can offer salvation . . . if impurities, imperfections and aberrations of religious experience be eliminated."[17] The several pages in it concerning "the two sects of the Jews" (*firqatā al-Yahūd*) are copied directly from the treatment of the Rabbanites and Karaites in Samauʾal's *Ifḥām.*[18]

The second passage in Ibn Qayyim's writings in which he discusses the classification of Jews is similarly derivative. In his *Aḥkām Ahl al-Dhimma*, he devotes two pages to a long-unresolved question of Muslim jurisprudence.[19] This question, in his words, relates to the Samaritans, and "the disagreement of the *fuqahāʾ* concerning them: Should the *jizya* be imposed on them or not?"[20] In this short section, Ibn Qayyim summarizes what he apparently perceived as the *status quaestionis* regarding the Samaritans, as it stood both in Muslim heresiography and in *fiqh.*

Ibn Qayyim begins this discussion by quoting Shāfiʿī's well-known temporizing on the extracting of *jizya* from Samaritans.[21] Ibn Qayyim adds examples of subsequent *fuqahāʾ* who supported both positions taken by the great Shāfiʿī. Ibn Qayyim himself sides with a certain Marwazī's opinion, that the apparent contradiction of the master was due to his having been corrected in the course of his original argument, at which point he consequently switched to the correct position, that the Samaritans were indeed fully *ahl al-kitāb.*[22]

However, Ibn Qayyim strongly dissents from those jurisprudents who say that the Samaritans are not liable to pay *jizya* while the Majūs are. "And this is extraordinary!" exclaims Ibn Qayyim. He then lists a number of blatantly non-Scriptuary traits of the Majūs—fire-worship, metaphysical dualism, want of divine revelation, mother–son marriage, and lack of apostolic proscriptions—as counterpoints to the characterization of the Samaritans as fully *ahl al-kitāb.*[23]

To drive home his point, Ibn Qayyim reiterates the facts about the Samaritan theology and praxis as they were well-known in Muslim scholarly circles. This material—concerning Samaritan doctrines on fasts, Torah, prophets, and their *qibla* at Nāblūs—comprised a familiar *topos* by the seventh/thirteenth century.[24] To round out the picture, Ibn Qayyim copies miscellaneous material, without attribution, from Shahrastānī, a scholar who enjoyed particular popularity in these years.[25] Having adduced the relevant facts of the matter, Ibn Qayyim concludes that, since it is possible to enumerate some points of family relationship between the Samaritans and the Jews, the former group should be made to pay *jizya*. True, they are not fully Jewish—"they are to the Jews as the Rāfiḍa are to the Muslims"—but they are sufficiently Jewish for the early Muslim leadership to have been correct to impose the *jizya* upon them: "And not to impose it on them is merely to allow them to persist in error: this is something that cannot be.[26]

As was the case with the oath for the leaders of the Scriptuary communities discussed previously in connection with ʿUmarī, the heresiographic distinctions made by Ibn Qayyim bear directly on the legal position of the groups under discussion. All of their restrictions and rights were directly derived from those clarifying classifications. It should therefore not be surprising to find that Ibn Qayyim's conclusions would seem to agree with those found in the oaths and secretaries' manuals. Thus, in both cases, as expressed in the summary of these materials by Gottheil, "the Raʾīs of the Rabbanite Jews had jurisprudence over Rabbanites, Karaites, and Samaritans, though a special form of commission to the Raʾīs of the Samaritans is also given."[27]

This situation held true also in later centuries, when the Samaritans were listed as Jews in the Ottoman registraries, and where they were consequently held liable for the *jizya*. Although they could occasionally attain high office, even the vizierate, in the Egypt of the centuries under discussion here, the Samaritans were not entirely inaccurately described by Ibn Qayyim as being "one of the smallest communities on earth."[28] It is therefore interesting to note just how the "long arm" of the Sharīʿa could embrace such a tiny sect, even taking care to distinguish them from Jews. It would seem that, in the case of the Samaritans, the jurisprudential concern for appropriate collection of taxes, fully summarized by Ibn Qayyim, was at least one, and perhaps a major, motivating factor in the collection of heresiographic materials concerning them.

Ibn Qayyim Al-Jauziyya
Aḥkām Ahl al-Dhimma
Ed. Ṣubḥi Ṣāliḥ (Damascus, 1381/1961)

Vol. 2, pp. 90–92:
"On the Sāmira and the disagreement of the *fuqahaʾ* concerning them: Should the *jizya* be imposed on them or not?"

Most hold that the *jizya* is incumbent on them. Shāfīʿī hesitated about them, and once said: "*Jizya* should not be collected from them." In another place he said: "It should be collected from them." In the *Umm* he said, "One should look into their matter. If they are in agreement with the Jews on the basic principles of religion, but disagree with them over the minor details, then their disagreement does not matter, for they agree on the same religion, so collect *jizya* from them. But if they disagree on the basic principles of religion, then they should not be held to the Jews' religion in the payment of *jizya*." This was transmitted about him on the authority of Rabīʿ.

As for al-Muzanī, it is reported of him that he said "They are a class of the Jews, and so the *jizya* should be taken from them." His companions differed in their ruling, some of them saying "They should be held to pay the *jizya*," others saying "They should not be so held."

Abū Isḥāq al-Marwazī said: "Shāfīʿī did not know the true facts of their religion, so he hesitated in that matter. Then it became clear to him that they are to be considered as among the *ahl al-kitāb*. So he returned to that position and subsequently included the Samaritans as *ahl al-kitāb*."

This is what al-Marwazī said, and it is indeed sound and decisive. Those, however, are incorrect who say: "*Jizya* should not be taken from them, but it should be taken from the Majūs, for they possess a pseudo-Scripture." And this is preposterous! To take it from a people who worship fire, and who believe that the universe has two gods, Light and Dark, and who believe neither in revelation nor that God resurrects those who are in their graves, and who allow copulation with mothers and daughters, and who do not believe in apostles and who do not forbid anything which the prophets forbad!

And on the other hand, not to take *jizya* from the Sāmira, even though they believe in Mūsā and Torah; and bind themselves to it; believe in the resurrection, heaven and hell; and pray the [fixed daily] prayers of the Jews; and fast their fasts and follow their general path; and recite the Torah; and proscribe what is proscribed to the Jews in the Torah and do not disagree with the Jews about the Torah nor about Moses, even if they do diverge [from the rest of the Jews] concerning belief in the prophets, for the Sāmira do not believe at all in any prophets except Moses, Aaron, Joshua and Abraham. They [also] disagree over the *qibla*, for the Jews pray towards the Holy Temple, while the Sāmira pray towards Mt. ʿAzūn in the district of Nāblūs. They assert that this is the *qibla* towards which God commanded Moses to pray (and that they are correct in their location of this and the Jews are wrong); and that God ordered David to build the Holy Temple at Nāblūs, which, according to them, was the mountain on which God spoke to Moses. David defied Him, and he built it at Īliyā: but he transgressed and sinned in that.

Their language is close to the language of the Jews, but is not exactly the same. They have many groups which branched off from two groups: Dūstāniyya and Kūstāniyya. The Kūstāniyya affirm the final reckoning and the resurrection of bodies, and Paradise and the Fire: the Dūstāniyya assert that reward and punishment occur in this world. There is much disagreement amongst them on statutory injunctions.

This community is one of the smallest communities in the world and one of the most foolish, and most opposed to other communities, and most burdened with encumbrances and fetters.

And if I wished to denote their relationship to the Jews, it is as the Rāfiḍa are to the Muslims. This community did not arise in Islamic times, rather it is a community to be found before Islam and before Jesus. Then the Companions conquered the great metropolises and agreed to impose it [*jizya*] on them [the Samaritans], as did the imāms and caliphs after them, and not to impose it on them is merely to allow them to persist in error: this is something that cannot be.

Ibn Khaldūn

Abu Zayd ʿAbd al-Rahmān b. Muḥammad b. Khaldūn (732/1332–808/1406) is widely recognized today to have been one of the first truly informed and systematic theorists of comparative civilizations.[29] This celebrity rests less on his mammoth world history, *Kitāb al-ʿIbar*, than it does on the *Muqaddima* (Introduction) to that work, in which prolegomenon the terms of reference and the theoretical overview are provided.[30] It is clear that, as he states in that introduction, his is not indeed a universal history, though he states at one point that his is "an exhaustive history of the world."[31] Rather, as he elsewhere clarifies, he intended by this to refer only to the lands of the West (as he understood the term), and to forgo an "exhaustive" report on the Indians, Chinese, and others.[32]

Similarly, Ibn Khaldūn's history of the various nations with which he was familiar, such as the Byzantines, Copts, Persians, and the ancient Israelites, deals with these respective histories "exhaustively" only in a special and restricted sense of that term. His was both a gift for and an apparent predisposition toward synthesis, and that concern for the overview seems to have somewhat swamped the details of the individual histories. To some extent, of course, this perspective was culturally determined. In the case of Ibn Khaldūn, though he does seem to try to accurately chart the arc of a nation's "trajectory," he is less concerned with the inner dynamics of that nation as such. One consequence of this is the relative slightness of his heresiography, which makes him of limited use for our purposes.

One of the marks of the greatness of Ibn Khaldūn as a historian is that he relied on a substantial and variegated corpus of sources. It would be unfair to suggest, therefore, that he was unconcerned with the details of Jewish history.[33] Indeed, to his credit, he is one of the first Muslim historians to address postbiblical Jewish history at some length.[34] His version of Jewish sectarianism is fundamentally (mis)shaped by his (mis)use of his sources, however. These same basic "mistakes" were to skew the "accuracy" of other Muslim heresiographies, such as that of Maqrīzī.

An especial irony of this error is that it is the ultimate result of a virtue. In being conscientious, Ibn Khaldūn gratefully utilized the Arabic translation of *Josippon* which came into his possession.[35] To his credit, he used it heavily in formulating his postbiblical Jewish history. It is not particularly important here that he assumed that Yūsuf b. Karīyūn was Flavius Josephus, and not in fact the medieval chronicler who himself relied on Josephus. More relevant to the purposes at hand, this intrinsically admirable reliance on Ibn Karīyūn, using a Jewish source for a study of postbiblical Judaism, nevertheless resulted in (mis)shaping Ibn Khaldūn's report in two important ways.

First, the use of Ibn Karīyūn seems to have reinforced a pronounced historiographic pattern of Muslim historians, a pattern already set by the earliest of these historians. This was the tendency to write extensively of the biblical periods, both of the Old and the New Testaments, while the post–Second Temple period, the Diaspora, is more or less passed over in silence. The major exceptions to this historiographic rule were the pre-Islamic Jewish communities of Arabia and the Jewish communities with whom Muḥammad came into contact.[36] By and large, the numerous minor mentions and discussions of Diaspora Jews and Judaism only highlight the disparity with the many long volume-length treatments of the Banū Isrāʾīl.[37] Ibn Khaldūn's extensive use of Ibn Karīyūn therefore amplified the section of his work dealing with the end of the biblical period, thereby further accentuating this disparity.

The second way in which Ibn Khaldūn erred in his use of Ibn Karīyūn was more directly the result of his concern with crafting a synthesis. In what appears to be his only heresiographic list of the Jews, Ibn Khaldūn does something interesting in his apparently going beyond the report of Ibn Karīyūn. He lists the three groups given by Josephus, whom we know as the Pharisees, Sadducees, and Essenes, but goes beyond the brief naming and characterization provided by the "ancient" chronicler.[38] Following the practice evident in such Christian sources as those of Agapius and Bar Hebraeus, Ibn Khaldūn uses well-known Arabic theological terms in identifying these characterizations: the Pharisees, he says, were "Fuqahāʾ and ahl al-qiyās"; the Sadducees were "Ẓāhiriyya"; and the Essenes were "ʿubbād" and "zuhhād."[39] While more or less valid as analogies, these identifications did probably distort the true dimensions of these groups in the minds of his readers.

In addition to this associating of the unfamiliar with the familiar, Ibn Khaldūn went further to identify the ancient groups with extant ones. Thus, he says more than once that the Pharisees are the Rabbanites and the Sadducees are the Karaites.[40] In this characterization he may have relied on medieval Rabbanites and Karaites, who themselves addressed the problematic of this equation.[41]

In his study "Ibn Khaldūn: On the Bible, Judaism and the Jews," Fischel observes that "compared with al-Bīrūnī, Shahrastānī or Maqrīzī, Ibn Khaldūn's knowledge of Jewish sects and Jewish institutions is most meagre."[42] This judgment is certainly correct. Ibn Khaldūn made general use of the works of such heresiographers as Masʿūdī, Ibn Ḥazm, and Abū al-Fidāʾ, but he seems never to have availed himself of, much less critically improved upon, their heresiographies of the Jews.[43] Willing to use a wide variety of source materials, broad-minded enough to include Jewish and Christian sources among them, and therefore working from a vantage point of almost unparalleled salience, Ibn Khaldūn (at least as a heresiographer of Judaism) missed his opportunity.

Ibn Khaldūn
Taʾrīkh al-ʿallāma Ibn Khaldūn
ed. Y. A. Dāghir (Beirut, 1956)

Vol. 2, p. 235:
Ibn Karīyūn said, "The Jews were divided in their religion at that time into three sects: (1) The sect of *Fuqahāʾ* and *Ahl al-Qiyāfa* [perhaps to be read: Qiyās] who are called the *Farūshīm*, and they are the *Rabbānīyūn*; (2) the sect of the *Ẓāhiriyya*, who adhere to the exoteric language of their scripture, and they are called *Ṣadūqiyya* and they are the *Qarrāʾūn*; (3) and the sect of the *ʿUbbād*, who are exclusively devoted to worship, glorification of God and ascetic practices in other matters, and they are called the *Ḥīsīd*.

Vol. 2, p. 393:
There were three Jewish sects among them: The Rabbānīyūn, next the Qarrāʾūn, who are known as the "Zanādiqa" in the Gospels, and then the [lacuna: but on the basis of vol. 2, p. 393, read: Ḥīsīd] who are known as the "Kataba" in the Gospels.

Qalqashandī

Abū al-ʿAbbās Aḥmad b. ʿAlī al-Shāfiʿī al-Qalqashandī (1355/756–1418/821) was, along with his approximate contemporary Maqrīzī, the fruition of the scholarly potential for excellence in heresiography of the Jews on the part of scholars in this period.[44] This potential was prominent in Ibn Khaldūn, who set high standards, was ambitious, and was in possession of good sources. Qalqashandī also had these features, which he employed with a quite different agenda from that of his predecessor. The result of this difference was a heresiography of the Jews unique in structure, rich in detail, and, indeed, unrivaled in length with the exception of that of Maqrīzī.

The difference in orientation is in part a reflection of the fact that Qalqashandī wrote as a bureaucratic secretary, and not strictly as a historian. His 14-volume magnum opus, the *Ṣubḥ al-Aʿshā fī Ṣināʿat al-Inshāʾ*, is not a history, but a bureaucratic secretary's manual.[45] But it is not devoid of historical materials. Indeed, as the major students of the work, Björkman and Bosworth, show, it is rich in materials concerning the various religions which came under the jurisdiction of the Mamluks.[46]

It was only appropriate that these heresiographic materials should appear in the chapter devoted to the various oaths by which the *dhimmī* community-leaders were required to swear.[47] As we have discussed in connection with ʿUmarī, the charges to office found in the administrative manuals of ʿUmarī and Qalqashandī have behind them the slow development of the office of *Raʾīs al-Yahūd*, which was closely examined by Mark Cohen in his fine study of the origins of the office of the Head of the Jews.[48] Also lying behind Qalqashandī's versions of the oaths are the centuries in which such oaths evolved. Little is known of the contents of the earlier oaths with any reliability: elsewhere in the *Ṣubḥ* he provides an example, probably apocryphal, of what he claimed was the first such oath, which he attributes to a vizier of Hārūn al-Rashīd.[49]

The heresiography of Qalqashandī, then, is the culmination of a long historical and literary development. On first looking over its general structure, one immediately observes that, as is the case with the evidence from ʿUmarī, the Geniza, and other surviving Mamluk documents, Qalqashandī subsumes the Samaritans under the general rubric "Jews" but in a separate category from the Rabbanites and Karaites.[50] Such classification tacitly expresses the perception that the latter two groups, despite their well-known enmity, belonged for all practical purposes to the same category. Qalqashandī states directly that "even though they are two groups, they are, as it were, one."[51] This treating of them together may also be a reflection of the unusual closeness which they were enjoying in Egypt. Stillman notes that the Karaite-Rabbanite "*esprit de corps*, which ignored sectarian lines, was typical of Egypt but all too rare in other countries of Jewish settlement."[52]

Beyond the broad strokes of general organization, Qalqashandī's chapter, in its details, is revealing of several points of interest for the history of the Muslim heresiography of the Jews. It appears, at first blush, to be one of the best-organized treatments of Jews and Judaism in all of Muslim heresiography. Indeed, on closer examination, Qalqashandī's organization holds up well enough, but for one ironic twist: in his effort to present a well-wrought outline, he becomes tangled in his own schema. A glance at the outline of his presentation makes this clear:

On the Oaths by which the Ahl al-Kufr swear, at least for one who may need that swearing

In two categories (*ḍarb*):

(*ḍarb*) I. Those professing belief in the Law of one of the Revealed Prophets, in three religions (*milla*):

(*milla*) A. *Yahūd*, in two sects (*ṭāʾifa*):

(*ṭāʾifa*) 1. Qarrāʾūn

(*ṭāʾifa*) 2. Rabbāniyūn

(*ṭāʾifa*) B. Samaritan Jews (al-Yahūd al-Samira)

(*firqa*) C. Christians

(*ḍarb*) II. Majūs (?)[53]

With some reflection, the intention behind the schema employed by Qalqashandī becomes more or less clear. But even after several readings it seems so inconsistent as to confuse the reader. Although he subsumes Jews, Samaritans, and Christians under the rubric of *milal* (sing. *milla*, an organized, recognized religious community), he also refers to the Samaritans as a *ṭāʾifa* (disorganized, unimportant subgroup) and the Christians as a *firqa* (usually, the sect of a *milla*). There may be some method in this apparently over-organized array, however: it could be suggested that Qalqashandī is using these various terms rigorously. On this hypothesis, it could be argued that he denominated the three major Scriptuary groupings so as to indicate the relative closeness of the Samaritans to the Jews—which he also stresses by calling them "Samaritan Jews"—as opposed to the clearly drawn distinction between these former two groupings and the Christians.

Qalqashandī thus categorizes Jews as Karaite/Rabbanite Jews and as Samaritan Jews. Chronologically speaking, he asserts that the Karaites were first, that the Samaritans were a schism from them, and that the Rabbanites were the result of a final schism and came from the ranks of the Karaites.[54] The bulk of his entire chapter on the Jews comprises a recitation of their differences (*ikhtilāf*). These are prefaced by two major differences, over the issues of *taʾwīl* and *qadar*.[55] He also mentions the particular revulsion of the Jews against worshipping Pharaoh and Haman, and against accepting the Virgin Birth.[56]

At this point Qalqashandī displays his research acumen. Prefacing his remarks by stating that the Jews "revere as important the occurrence of certain events," he proceeds to list 27 such hiero-historical moments.[57] Comprising a full six printed pages, this list amounts to a mini-compendium of Isrāʾīlīyāt and polemical motifs. Up to this point, it would still seem as if Qalqashandī were simply dispassionately relating interesting tidbits of historical information.

At the conclusion of this list, however, Qalqashandī produces the culminating text of the chapter, the "Jews' Oath."[58] This is to be distinguished from the aforementioned charge to office for the leaders of the community, which Qalqashandī reproduces from ʿUmarī and publishes elsewhere in the *Ṣubḥ*.[59] The centerpiece of the oath given here is a summarizing reiteration of the 27 aforementioned tenets, which aspects of Jewish belief and practice the oath-taker swears will be transgressed should he break the oath. With the oath, Qalqashandī's object in going to such lengths in his categorization of Jews and in his presentation of their many beliefs and practices becomes clear. He had no choice but to do it this way if he was to provide the oath, which is the consummating point of the chapter, with context and content.

The chapter, in retrospect, leads up to this, inasmuch as all the preliminary information, all the long listing of differences, was provided to clarify two essential questions: Who is legally considered a Jew, and by what oath should a Jew swear? Here is the fusion par excellence of the theory and the practical application of Muslim categorizations of Jews and Judaism.

Qalqashandī
Ṣubḥ al-Aʿshā (Cairo, 1963)

Vol. 13, p. 256:
Know that the Jews have broken up into many sects, two of which are well known:

The first group: There is general agreement concerning their Judaism: they are the Qarrāʾūn. They are two groups, who are, as it were, one, since their Torah is one, and they do not disagree over the essentials of Judaism. All agree on deducing 613 commandments from the Torah, by which they worship. Furthermore, they all agree on the prophethood of Moses, Aaron, Joshua and Abraham, Isaac and Jacob. The latter is "Israel," and the "Tribes" are his twelve children, to be mentioned in conclusion.

And they are to be distinguished from the second sect who will be mentioned, namely the Sāmira, over the issue of the prophethood of prophets other than Moses, Aaron and Joshua. And they transmit from Joshua nineteen books in addition to the Torah which they designate as being "the prophecies," known as "al-Uwal [the primordial (documents)]."

The Rabbānīyūn diverge from the Qarrāʾūn over the issue of commentaries set down concerning the obligatory duties in the Torah (mentioned above), and established by their learned men, and also over [the question of] secondary matters in the Torah, which they claim to have as transmitted from Moses.

The Rabbānīyūn and the Qarrāʾūn agree that they should face towards the Rock in Jerusalem in their prayers, and face their dead towards it also. [They also agree] that God spoke to Moses on Mt. Sinai, which is a mountain at the head of the Red Sea on the North side, with the tip of the island at its end, whose entrance is between two arms which surround it on both sides.

They disagree on two matters. One is the profession of a literalist position as against an inclination towards [arbitrary] interpretation. For the Qarrāʾūn rest with the literal texts of the Torah, and they construe their content in reference to God, [including such references as those to God's] form, speech, settling down on the throne, and coming down to Mt. Sinai in their exterior meanings, as do the Ẓāhiriyya among the Muslims. They go on from there to espouse the doctrine of *tashbīh*, and the doctrine that God has the attribute of direction. But the Rabbānīyūn proceed to "interpret" all that as it occurs in the Torah, as do the Ashʿariyya of the Muslims.

The second [difference between them] is the doctrine of *qadar* ["predestination," free will limited to God alone]. The Rabbāniyūn say that there is no *qadar* and that each thing happens as it happens, as say the Qadariyya [those who profess a doctrine of free will] of the Muslims. The Qarrāʾūn believe in predestination as do the Ashʿariyya. Apart from that, both groups say that God is Eternal, Sempiternal, One and Powerful, and that He inspired the Truth to Moses, and reinforced the truth to his brother Aaron. And they exalt to the utmost the Torah, which is their Holy Book, to such an extent that they even swear on the Torah, as the Muslims do on the Qurʾān.

p. 268:
The Second Group of Jews are the Sāmira:

. . . There is disagreement about the Sāmira: Are they Jews or not? The Qarrāʾūn and Rabbānīyūn deny that the Sāmira are Jews. Our colleagues the Shāfiʿiyya have said: They whose basic religious principles agree with those of the Jews are to be considered as being Jews, and thus are liable to pay the *jizya*: if not, then they are not [so liable.]

The Sāmira have a Torah special to them, different from that possessed by the Rabbānīyūn and the Qarrāʾūn, nor is it like that of the Christians. They part company with the Rabbānīyūn and Qarrāʾūn in denying the prophethood of anyone after Moses, with the exception of Aaron and Joshua. They also disagree [with the others] in facing the Rock in Jerusalem, and instead face a mountain in Nābulus, and they place the faces of their dead in their graves [facing in that direction], claiming that it was upon that mountain that God spoke to Moses. They claim that God commanded David to build the Temple on that mountain, but he disobeyed the injunction and built it instead in Jerusalem. May God fight against those who lie!

They also say: God is the Creator of Mankind, the Originator of them, and that he is Powerful,

Overwhelming, Infinite and Eternal. They agree on the prophethood of Moses (and Aaron), and that God sent him the Torah, but they have a special Torah of their own differing from the Torah of the Qarrāʾūn and Rabbānīyūn (which was discussed above). [They also believe] that He sent him likewise the Essential [i.e. original] Tablets, which include the Decalogue (which were also discussed above). They also affirm that God is the one who delivered the Children of Israel from Pharoah, and Who saved them from drowning. They believe that God designated Mt. Nābulus (discussed above) as the *qibla* for the worshipper.

They attach great gravity to unbelief in the version of the Torah which they recognize, as well as to the rejection of Moses, and this above any other of the Children of Israel. They exalt their mountain, Mt. Nābulus (discussed above). They regard as outrageous the levelling of it and the extirpation of all traces of the temple, which was built there; and they regard as a serious matter the desecration of the Sabbath, as do the rest of the Jews; they agree with the Qarrāʾūn in conforming with the exterior meaning of the texts of the Torah; and they reject the doctrine of exegesis as espoused by the Rabbanite Jews; and they deny the authenticity of the Torah of both the Qarrāʾūn and Rabbānīyūn, and place their reliance in their own Torah. They say "lā misās," which means that none should touch or be touched. He [unidentified] says in the *Kashshāf*: If anyone touched or was touched, both got a fever. God has given word of this in telling of Moses speaking to the Sāmiri: "Begone! it shall be thine all thy life to cry 'Untouchable!'"

They forbid [lacuna] as sacrifices, and [also forbid] eating meat mixed with milk, asserting that in their Torah is found the prohibition of eating the meat of a kid in its mother's milk; and they regard as a grave matter any attempt to go out into the land whose habitation is forbidden them, this being the city of Jericho.

Among the worst sins in their estimation is having sexual intercourse with a menstruant, and sleeping with her in the same bed, especially when this is done in the conviction that it is permissible. One of the greatest abominations in their eyes is the denial of the deputization of Aaron, and the disdaining of its status.

Maqrīzī

Abū al-ʿAbbās Aḥmad Ibn ʿAbd al-Qādir al-Ḥusaini Taqī al-Dīn al-Maqrīzī (765/1364–846/1442) not only wrote the longest of all Muslim heresiographies of the Jews, but also became the heresiographer with the most influence on modern scholarship of this subject.[60] This was due initially to Sylvestre de Sacy, who edited, translated, and annotated the entirety of Maqrīzī's lengthy treatment in 1826, bringing several Jewish sects to the attention of European scholars for the first time.[61] Along with Haarbrücker's translation of Shahrastānī, de Sacy's Maqrīzī dominated the Western study of Islamicate-era Jewish sectarianism well into the twentieth century.

Maqrīzī's chapter on the Jews comes near the end of his mammoth *Al-Mawāʿiẓ wa al-Iʿtibār fī Dhikr al-Khiṭaṭ wa al-Āthār*.[62] The great value of Maqrīzī's report derives from what might otherwise seem a weakness: its lack of integration. Maqrīzī's method of categorization, or lack thereof, consists of collecting the lists of others, without synthesizing these disparate reports. His heresiography is a list of lists, lacking a unifying point of view. It is therefore ironically to the advantage of the modern researcher that this collection of unmodified lists should contain so much of value and interest.

Maqrīzī utilizes Jewish, Christian, and Muslim sources. Most of these were at least several centuries old in his day, notwithstanding the rubric of his chapter: "An Account of the Groups of the Jews Today." Although he does provide a rudimentary, if confused, historical framework for understanding the various divisions he presents, it is inadequate for reconciling the unmistakably conflicting contents of those lists. The overall impression presented by Maqrīzī's chapter on the Jewish sects is that of an erudite, but frustratingly eclectic collection of texts uncritically assembled. Its faults notwithstanding, Maqrīzī's impressive effort resulted in a report which may be considered the consummation of Muslim heresiographical research on Jews and Judaism. His genius in this respect lies not in synthesis but in juxtaposition. In the *Khiṭaṭ* we find old reports taking on new aspects, as a consequence of Maqrīzī's illuminating positioning of them. To be fair, Maqrīzī does contribute several important and unparalleled bits of information to Muslim heresiography of the Jews, as we will show in what follows. This, however, may only reflect his use of different, if not better, versions of those texts we have already examined. It seems likely that his brilliance was inadvertent, for he excelled in finding texts, not in assessing them.

One example can be adduced to show that Maqrīzī did not bother to assess but tended merely to copy. Without ever indicating their relevance to each other, he provides six names for Karaites: Qarrāʾūn, ʿĀnāniyya, Qurrāʾ, Banū Miqrā, Mabādiyya, and Ismaʿiyya.[63] For these he primarily relies on the reports of Bīrūnī and Shahrastānī, which he simply copies more or less verbatim.

One can perceive here a telling difference of personality between Maqrīzī and the other major Mamluk-period heresiographer, Qalqashandī. The thrust of Qalqashandī's literary labors clearly went into crafting his presentation, whereas Maqrīzī concerned himself with the discovery of, rather than the felicitous shaping of, Judaica. To be sure, this was due to more than a merely characterological divergence. Maqrīzī's work is a kind of antiquarian survey, while Qalqashandī's served a practical purpose.

For the purposes of the historian of Muslim heresiography of the Jews, Maqrīzī's contribution can be satisfactorily indicated by outlining his chapter and indicating his sources. Such a procedure can reveal the unique breadth of his research, as well as his manner of presentation which is more or less that of an anthology. In so doing, we will also indicate points of particular interest as we come to them, thereby pointing out his special contributions to this literature.

Maqrīzī begins by stating that there were four groups deriving from the time of the destruction of the First Temple by Nebuchadnezzar.[64] These, he says, were the Rabbānīyyūn, the Qarrāʾūn, the ʿAnāniyya, and the Samara. This report appears to be based on one of the continuators of Shahrastānī, Abū al-Fidāʾ, al-Baṣrī, or Ibn al-Wardī—all of whom provide the same listing.[65] The ʿAnāniyya, who had died out as a discrete subsection of the Karaites by the tenth century, were still listed beside the Karaites in these late reports. Similarly, "ʿAnāniyya" was the common denomination for the Karaites in the Kalām texts. It was therefore not untoward for Maqrīzī to employ that same metonym.

In an apparent attempt to devise a chronological sequence, Maqrīzī next cites a passage from *Josippon*, without citing this source by name.[66] Here we are told that the Jews at the time of Hyrcanus ("Hūrqānūs") were divided into "Farūshīm," "Ṣadūfiyya," and "Jisidīm." Transparently evident behind this list of names is the medieval Hebrew translation of Josephus, as they were transliterated into Arabic, with the Hebrew names still recognizable (as Pharisees, Sadducees, and Essenes). Later in his chapter, Maqrīzī repeats this report, and explicitly cites "Ibn Karīyūn's" *Taʾrīkh* as his source.[67]

Reverting to the source with which he began, Maqrīzī again quotes, without identifying the source, from the Shahrastānī material (i.e., Shahrastānī himself, or one of his continuators).[68] He now omits the ʿAnāniyya, which may indicate that he relied on one version for his introductory list of four groups, and at this point relies on some other variant of that same literary tradition. Interestingly, he strongly criticizes the Rabbanites here—"they have become, in their principles of religion and in their incidental religious duties, the most remote of men from what the Prophets brought in the way of divinely revealed Laws"—and criticizes Maimonides, whom he accurately identifies by name and date.[69] Continuing with these same sources, he then relates reports on the Karaites, primarily from Biruni and the Shahrastānī source.[70]

At this point Maqrīzī relates a lengthy narrative concerning the Samaritans, which occupies fully one-third the space of his entire account of the Jewish sects.[71] This is clearly based on a variety of sources, though he specifies only Masʿūdī and Bīrūnī by name. The bulk of this report on the Samaritans comprises a long narrative of their historical origins, which would seem to be based on a Samaritan (or possibly centrally Jewish) source, though it is no doubt at several hands removed from that original source.[72] That this narrative was possibly of Samaritan origination is indicated by a comment Maqrīzī makes concerning the alphabet of the Samaritans. This remark closely resembles a report made by Benjamin of Tudela concerning the use of the Hebrew letters by the Samaritans.[73]

As he progresses to the next segment in his anthology, it is possible to perceive the motivation for his placing the "seam" between this last quoted text and the next. In his last sentences concerning the Samaritans, Maqrīzī (or his source) observes that Samaritans "have not set foot in Jerusalem since the days of the prophet David."[74] The next text he cites is prefaced thus: "In the Gospel Commentary (*sharḥ al-injīl*, with no further identification), it says that the Jews broke up after the days of David into seven sects . . ."[75] This text, like the citation from Ibn Karīyūn following it, would seem to be an addendum, one of several glosses on the chapter, the chronological sequence of which seems to end with the narrative concerning the Samaritans. The quotation from "the Gospel Commentary" is particularly significant. Deriving from the popularly reproduced list of seven Jewish sects originally given by Epiphanius, Maqrīzī's version provides one telling variant on the Epiphanian list.[76] Under the group known as the Nasoreans, whom Maqrīzī calls "mutaqashshifūn" (ascetics), Maqrīzī's source says that "they assert that the Torah is not entirely Mosaic: they cling to scrolls (or scriptures: *ṣuḥuf*) *ascribed to Enoch and Abraham.*"[77] Under the report on the same group in the identical list provided by the eighth-century Bishop of Kashgar, Theodore bar Khonai, we read, "They say that the law does not belong to Moses, and *they have revelations attributed to Enoch and Abraham.*"[78] Brock's observation on this sentence is that "it is without parallel elsewhere, and the new testimonium to the *Apocalypse of Abraham* is of interest."[79] The hitherto unnoticed parallel in Maqrīzī, with its additional testimonium to the Scripture of Abraham, is therefore of particular interest.

Maqrīzī may quote this "Gospel Commentary" at this point because it glosses the preceding comment concerning the division of the Jews at the time of David. If this supposition is correct, then it may be that the next text he quotes follows the "Gospel Commentary" quotation because it marks the next chronological step in Jewish sectarian history. Thus, he now repeats the same list of Jews and their characteristics as dating from the time of Hyrcanus, with which he began his chapter.[80] Here, however, he explicitly names his source as Ibn Karīyūn's *Tārīkh*. In this report, Maqrīzī identifies the ancient Jewish sects with Arabic names, as had Agapius, Bar Hebraeus, and Ibn Khaldūn before him.[81] Some of these identifications, such as the Muʿtazila, were also appellations for groups in the Muslim community. Such identifications may well not have been possible without the assumption of an essential homology between Judaism and Islam.

The chapter concludes with a list of 13 Jewish sects, which Maqrīzī copies, without attribution, from Maqdisī.[82] Maqrīzī's report was particularly influential through de Sacy's translation, though his source was not recognized for some time. In the absence of an investigation of the relevant manuscripts, I cannot certainly discern the basis for the one significant divergence between the report of Maqrīzī and that of Maqdisī. At the point where Maqdisī cites "Ashmaʿath," Maqrīzī's text, tantalizingly, reports instead on the "Shamʿūniyya, named after Shamʿūn al-Ṣiddīq, ruler of Jerusalem at the advent (*qudūm*) of Alexander's father."[83]

This variation on the "Ashmaʿath complex" provides the sole etymology for this term in all of the history of Muslim heresiography of the Jews. If this were to be entertained as a possibly accurate explanation of the origin of the term "Ashmaʿath," one could support that explanation by arguing that medieval Rabbanite historiography, what little of it there was, did emphasize the role of the High Priest Simon the Pure.[84] One could further argue that this Simon the Pure, in some Jewish traditions, was said to have met Alexander at his advent into Jerusalem, traditions which Shaye Cohen has recently analyzed.[85]

In addition to its conceivable concordance with the facts of Jewish tradition, several other arguments could be adduced for the derivation of "Ashmaʿath" from "Shamʿūn." First, in the formula for the abjuration of Judaism cited by Rāghib al-Iṣfahānī, the Jewish oath-taker is to abjure "Shamʿūn and SHMʿI (Shammai?)," which document may indicate a Muslim perception of this name as being centrally Jewish.[86] Second, if one were to suggest that the version in Maqrīzī in fact represents a more accurate version than that found in Huart's edition of Maqdisī, such a case could be supported by the fact that in Huart's version, "Ashmaʿath" does refer to a person, which would make sense if this were a corruption of "Shamʿūn."[87] Finally, the identification of the majority party of Jews as "Shamʿūniyya" did eventually gain prominence, as can be seen in the Qurʾān studies authored by several twentieth-century scholars at the al-Azhar University, where this term is used in reference to Rabbinical Judaism.[88]

However, the case for the derivation of "Ashmaʿath" from "Shamʿūn" cannot be ultimately sustained, for several reasons. First, we possess a number of early Christian and Muslim Arabic heresiographies which use explicitly the term "Ashmaʿath," including at least one (the Nestorian discussion of canon) which also links it to another permutation of the Aramaic word-root SHMʿ.[89] More significantly, it is possible to trace the path by which the term "Ashmaʿath" (itself possibly a corruption of something else) was still further corrupted.

Established by the fourth/tenth century, in the fifth/eleventh century "Ashmaʿathiyya" was corrupted as "Shamʿatiyya," whose orthography was then further corrupted, through a slight scribal slip, into "Shamʿaniyya."[90] Since it was commonplace for heresiographers to attach eponymous founder-figures to religious groups, it was not untoward at some point for a scholar, in the absence of any other explanation, to gloss this "Shamʿaniyya" as referring to some "Shamʿūn." In the absence of corroborating evidence we cannot be sure that this was Maqrīzī's own guess, but to whomever it should be credited, it must be seen as an inspired, albeit incorrect, conjecture. This, at any rate, would seem to be a plausible reconstruction of the way in which he may have arrived at this "fact."

It seems likely that Maqrīzī's own voice never in fact enters into his chapter on the Jews. There is no evidence in the chapter that he himself added to or modified the substance of any of his reports. In the case of all the reports whose sources can be identified, Maqrīzī quotes them virtually verbatim. He never even inserts pious or polemical anti-Jewish remarks, as was common in Muslim heresiography of the Jews. To be sure, his lack of criticism of the Jews betrays Maqrīzī's tacit but otherwise unacknowledged recognition of a kindred relationship between these two Abrahamic traditions. Guest, quoted approvingly by Nicholson, was indeed correct when he opines that Maqrīzī "writes without bias and apparently with distinguished impartiality."[91]

Maqrīzī
Khiṭaṭ
(Cairo, 1270/1892)

Vol. 2, pp. 476–479:
Know that the Jews, whom God dispersed in the world as nations, are four groups, each group accusing the others of error. They are the *Rabbānīyūn*, the group of *Qarrā'ūn*, the group of *'Ānāniyya*, and the group of *Sāmara* [our vocalization]. This division happened to them after the destruction of the Temple by Bukht Naṣr and their returning from the land of Babylon, after the Exile, to Jerusalem and the building of the Temple a second time. That is to say, [during] their dwelling in Jerusalem in the days when the Second Temple was being built, they diverged in their faith and became sects.

When the Greeks ruled them after Alexander b. Phīlibush [*sic*], Hūrqānūs b. Shamʿūn b. Mashīshā looked after their affairs in Jerusalem, and consolidated his power, and he was called a king. Previous to that time, he and all those who had preceded him among those who ruled the Jews in Jerusalem after their return from Exile, were simply called *Al-Kōhen al-Akbar*, so Hūrqānūs combined the status of king with the priestly status. The Jews were at peace in his days, and felt secure against all their enemies among the nations. [But,] they became discontented with their way of life, and disagreed over their religion, and grew mutually hostile because of their disagreement. So, of all their divisions, there emerged at that time:

> A group called the *Farūshīm* [Perushim, Pharisees], which means the same as Muʿtazila [i.e. "those who separate themselves off"]. Among their doctrines is the belief in the Torah according to the interpretation of the *hukamā'* among their forebears.
>
> And a group called the *Ṣadūfiyya (with a fā')* [Zadokim, Sadducees] named for a great man among them called Ṣadūf. They profess a belief in the text of the Torah [as it stands], and in further implications of the Divine Utterance concerning it, to the exclusion of all additional utterances.
>
> The third group is called *Jisidīm* [Ḥasidim: corruption of Ḥa' to Jīm] which means the "Righteous Ones." Their practice is concerned with asceticism and service of God, and the adoption of the most virtuous and most sound in religious life.

The *Ṣadūfiyya* used to hate the Muʿtazila with a great enmity, and King Hūrqānūs at first held the view of the Muʿtazila, which was the school of his fathers. Then he reverted to the school of Ṣadūf, and he departed from the Muʿtazila and worked up a hatred for them. [So, he] called upon the rest of his kingdom to restrain all men at large from learning the ideas of the Muʿtazila, and from studying under any of them and following them. And he killed many of them. The masses were, all of them, with the Muʿtazila, and so calamities erupted among the Jews, resulting in constant wars between them, and in the killing of one another. [This state of affairs continued] till the time when the Temple was destroyed by Ṭiṭush [Titus], the Second Destroyer, after the ascent of ʿIsā [Jesus]. From that time on, the Jews were dispersed to the far corners of the earth, and became subject populations, with the Christians killing them wherever they had the upper hand, until God brought the Muslim order.

In their diaspora the Jews are three groups: the *Rabbānīyūn*, the *Qurrā'* and the *Samara*.

As for the *Rabbāniyya*, they are called "Banū Mishnū," "Mishnū" meaning "Second." This is said of them because they revere the Temple, which was rebuilt after their return from Exile (the one which Ṭiṭush destroyed), and they treat it with as great sanctity and veneration as the First Temple, whose construction was initiated by David, completed by his son Solomon, and destroyed by Bukht Naṣr. And so it happened that they came to be called as if they were "Fellows of the Second Daʿwa [Call]." This group is the one which used to practice according to what is in the Mishnā, which was written in Tiberias after Ṭiṭush's destruction of Jerusalem, but they have come to rely upon what is in the Talmud for their ordinances of law, up to the present time.

The Rabbāniyūn are far from acting according to the divine texts, following [instead] the opinions of those learned men preceding them. Those who are well informed about the truth of their religion will clearly perceive that what God castigates them for in the Qurʾān is incontestably right, and that they do not deserve the name of Judaism, except by mere affiliation only. Not that they are in allegiance followers of the Mosaic dispensation, especially since the appearance among them of Mūsā b. Maimūn al-Qurṭubī, more than 500 years after the Hijra, for when he did he caused them to revert to the denying of God's attributes. They have become, in their principles of religion and their incidental duties, the most remote of men from what the Prophets of God brought in the way of divinely revealed Laws.

As for the *Qurrāʾ*, they are [known as] "Banū Miqrā," which means "Daʿwā." They do not all place their trust in the Second Temple, their *daʿwā* being only to that which was in force at the time of the First Temple. They used to be called the "Aṣḥāb Al-Daʿwā al-Ūlā." They rule on the texts of the Torah, and do not take into account the doctrine of those who dispute them: they conform to the text itself, and not to the absolute authority of their forebears. They are enemies of the Rabbāniyya, going so far as to not intermarry with them, nor to be their neighbors, nor to enter each others' synagogues.

As well as *al-Qarrāʾūn*, they are called *al-Mabādiyya*, for they used to define the beginnings of the months by way of conjunction of the sun and the moon. They are also called *al-Ismaʿiyya*, for they are careful to comply with the texts of the Torah to the exclusion of using *qiyās* and *taqlīd*.

As for the *ʿAnāniyya*, they are named after ʿĀnān, Raʾs Jālūt, who came from the East in the days of the Caliph Abū Jaʿfar al-Manṣūr. [ʿĀnān] brought with him manuscripts of the Mishnā written in the handwriting copied from the Prophet Moses. He believed that what the Jews, both Rabbānīyūn and Qarrāʾiyūn, were doing differed from what he had with him, and he devoted himself exclusively to opposing them. He attacked them concerning their religion, and derided them. He was a great man in the eyes [of the ʿĀnāniyya?], for they believed that he was descended from David, and that he was following a virtuous path of ascesis in accordance with the requirements of their religion. [So strong was this conviction that] they believe that, had he appeared in the days of the building of the Temple, he would have been a prophet. So they could not have disputed with him, on account of what he was given, taking into consideration also what we have said about the favor and honor shown him by the Caliph.

Mensal calendration was part of what he disputed with the Jews, [teaching that it was to be accomplished] by direct sight of the new moons, something like what was laid down in the Islamic religion. He did not care on which day of the week [the new moon fell], and he abandoned the Rabbinical calendration and intercalation of months, accusing them of erring in acting thus. He [also] relied on scrutiny of the barley-seed. He also spoke favorably about the Messiah Jesus b. Maryam, and acknowledged the prophethood of our Prophet Muḥammad. He said that [Muḥammad] was a Prophet sent to the Arabs, but that the Torah was not abrogated (and the truth is that he was sent to all peoples generally!).

Know that the group of *Samara* are definitely not of the Children of Israel, but are only a community who came from the Eastern lands, settled in the land of Shām, and were Judaized. It is said that they are of the "Banū Sāmirak b. Kufrak b. Ramī," they being a branch of the Persians who emigrated to Syria, taking with them horses, sheep and goats, camels, bows, arrows, swords and beasts of burden; and from these came the Samara who dispersed throughout those lands. It is said that when Solomon b. David died, the kingship of the Children of Israel was divided after him, and Reḥoboʿam b. Solomon became king of the tribe of Judah in Jerusalem, and Jeroboʿam Ibn Niyat ruled over the Ten Tribes of the Children of Israel. He settled outside of Jerusalem, and took two calves which he called upon the Ten Tribes to worship, instead of worshipping God, till he died.

There succeeded to the kingship of the Children of Israel after him many kings who followed a similar path in rejecting God and worshipping graven images, until ʿUmara b. Nūdhib of the tribe of Munshā b. Yūsuf ruled over them. He bought a place from a man named Shāmir for a *qinṭār* of silver, and built a castle on it. He named it by a derivation from that of the man who sold it to him, Shāmir. A city was built around this castle, which was named the city of Shomrūn, and he established his seat of authority there, till he died.

The kings of the Children of Israel took it after him, for their royal city, until the reign of Hūshāʿ b. Īlā. They were in a state of *kufr* toward God, being idolators of Baal and of other idols. As well, they killed the prophets, until God set up over them Senajārib [Sennacherib] king of Mauṣil, who besieged them in the city of Shomrūn for three years. He took Hūshāʿ captive and banished him and all of the Children of Israel in Shomrūn, resettling them in Herāt and Balkh and Nihāwand and Helwān. Henceforth, the king of the Children of Israel was cut off from the city of Shomrūn, which they had ruled after Solomon for 251 years. Then Senajārib moved many of the people of Kūshā and Bābil and Ḥamā to Shomrūn and settled them in it, to rebuild it. They sent to him complaining that they were frequently assailed by lack of culture in Shomrūn, so he sent them one who taught them the Torah. But they learned it defectively and began to read it omitting the four letters *alif*, *hāʾ*, *khā* and *ʿain*, not pronouncing these letters at all in their reading of the Torah.

They became known among the nations as the "Sāmira" because they dwell in the city of Shomrūn. This Shomrūn is the city of Nābulus, and it was [also] called "Somrōn" with an unpointed *sīn*. Its inhabitants were called Sāmira, which means "al-Samara," "watchmen" or "guardians." The Samara continued to stay in Nābulus until Bukht Naṣr invaded Jerusalem and banished the Jews there to Babylon.

Eventually, they returned after seventy years. They rebuilt the Second Temple, till Alexander came from the lands of the Greeks. He went forth intending to invade Persia, and passed Jerusalem on the way. He left there for the Persian gulf, and so he passed through Nābulus. A leader of the Samara came out to him. This was Sanballāṭ al-Sāmiri. The latter entertained him, treating him and his commanders and the great ones of his followers graciously. He brought forth abundant wealth and great gifts, and asked permission for the buiding of a temple to God on the mountain which they called Ṭūr Barīk. Alexander granted them this permission, then went off to fight Darius, King of the Persians.

Sanballāṭ built the Temple to resemble the Temple in Jerusalem, in order to incline the Jews towards him. Sanballāṭ falsified facts to the Jews in asserting that Ṭūr Barīk is the place God chose, mentioned in the Torah in the phrase "Place the blessing on Ṭūr Barīk." Sanballāṭ had had his daughter marry a Jerusalem Temple Priest called Munshā. The Jews hated Munshā for this. They banished him, and demoted him from his position, to punish him for marrying into the Sanaballāṭ family. Sanballāṭ then installed Munshā, his son-in-law, as priest of the sanctuary on Ṭūr Barīk. Groups of Jews came to him and were led astray by him and they began making pilgrimages to his sanctuary on their feast-days. They offered sacrifices there, and carried their votive offerings and tithes to it. They neglected God's Holy Place and turned away from it.

Wealth increased in this sanctuary, which became the rival to the Jerusalem sanctuary. Its priests grew rich, as did its lesser personnel. Munshā's power swelled and his position grew. This group continued to make pilgrimage to Ṭūr Barīk till the time of Hūrqānūs b. Shamʿūn, the priest from Banū Hithmatā in Jerusalem. He went to the Samaritan lands and settled in the city of Nābulus. After he was there for a while, he took it by force. He wrecked the Ṭūr Barīk sanctuary to its foundations and killed the *kāhins* resident there. It had flourished for 200 years.

The Samaritans continued, from then till now, to bow in their prayers, from wherever they are, towards Ṭūr Barīk on Mt. Nābulus. They have devotional obligations differing from those observed by the Jews. They have synagogues in every land, peculiar to themselves. They deny the prophethood of David and the prophets succeeding him, and deny there was any prophet after Moses. They pick their leaders from the progeny of Aaron. Most of them live in the city of Nābulus, but they are numerous in the cities of Shām. It is said that they are the ones who said "La misas." They claim that Nābulus is *the* Holy City, city of Jacob, and there are its grazing lands.

Masʿūdī says that the Samara are two distinct groups. One of these is the *al-Kūshān* and the other *al-Rūshān*. One of these two groups believes in the eternity of the universe.

The Sāmira assert that the Torah which the Jews possess is not the Torah which Moses produced and they say that the Mosaic Torah has been distorted and altered and substituted. They say that *the Torah* is the one in *their* possession, to the exclusion of the Torah-text belonging to any others.

Abū Rayḥān Muḥammad Ibn Aḥmad al-Bīrūnī said that the Sāmira were known as "Lamisāsiyya." He said that they are the replacements (*abdāl*) whom Bukht Naṣr sent to replace [the Jews] in Shām at the time he took the latter captive and sent them into exile. The Sāmira used to help him and guide him to the weaknesses of the Children of Israel, so he did not make war on them or kill them or take them prisoner [i.e., in war]. Rather, he settled them in Palestine under his aegis.

Their rituals and beliefs are a mixture of Judaism and Majūsiyya [Zoroastrianism]. The bulk of them are resident in a place in Palestine called Nābulus, which contains their synagogues. They have not even set foot in Jerusalem since the days of the Prophet David, for they claim that he acted unjustly and outrageously [against God when he] switched the Temple from Nābulus to Īlīa, which is Jerusalem.

They do not touch people: if they do [inadvertently], they wash. They do not recognize the prophethood of anyone after Moses from among the prophets of the Children of Israel.

In the Gospel Commentary it says that the Jews broke up after the days of David into seven sects:

1. *Kuttāb* They used to preserve the customs which their elders agreed upon but which did not derive from the Torah.
2. *Muʿtazila* They are the *Farīsīyūn*. They used to make a show of pious simplicity and fast twice a week. They gave a tithe of their wealth. They hung scarlet threads at the head of their clothes. They washed all their vessels. They

went to extreme lengths in manifesting their cleanliness.

3. *Zanādiqa* They are generically of the Sāmira people, but they also belong to the *Ṣadūfiyya*. They deny the existence of angels, and the resurrection after death and [they deny the existence of] all the prophets except Moses, for they acknowledge his prophethood.
4. *Mutaṭahhirūn* They used to thoroughly wash daily, holding that none is worthy of eternal life but the one who is baptized daily.
5. *Asābīyūn* Which means "hard" in character. They mandated all divine commands and denied all prophets except Moses. They revered certain nonprophetic books.
6. *Mutaqashshifūn* They used to reject most foodstuffs, especially meat. They rejected marriage to the best of their ability. They assert that the Torah is not entirely Mosaic. They cling to scrolls ascribed to Enoch and Abraham. They study astrology and act according to it.
7. *Hīrudhūsiyūn* They call themselves that because of their close relation to Hīrudhūs, their king. They follow the Torah and act upon what is in it. (The End [of the Gospel Commentary citation]).

Yūsuf b. Karīyūn mentioned in his *History* that the Jews in the days of their king Hūrqānūs, that is, in the time of the building of the Temple after their return from Exile, were three sects:

1. *Farūshīm*, which means [the same as] "Muʿtazila." Their school believes in the contents of the Torah and what the learned men of their forebears interpreted it to be.
2. *Ṣadūfiyya* are followers of a learned man named Ṣadūf, and their sect holds to the text of the Torah and what it implies, without the help of any other interpretation.
3. *Jisīdīm*, which means the "Righteous Ones" and they are the ones who occupy themselves with service of God and asceticism, and they adopt what is most virtuous and most sound in religious [practice]. The End [of this particular extract]. This sect is the origin of two others, the Rabbānīyūn and the Qurrā'.

A certain author [Maqdisī] asserts that the Jews comprise ʿAnāniyya, Shamʿūniyya, named after Shamʿūn al-Ṣiddīq, ruler of Jerusalem at the advent of Alexander's father, and Jālūtiyya, Fayyūmiyya, Sāmiriyya, ʿUkbariyya, Iṣbahāniyya, ʿIrāqiyya, Maghāriba, Sharshtāniyya, Filisṭīniyya, Mālikiyya, and Rabbāniyya:

The ʿAnāniyya hold for *tauḥīd* and *ʿadl* and reject *tashbih*.

The Shamʿūniyya anthropomorphize.

The Jālūtiyya go to extreme lengths in anthropomorphizing.

The Fayyūmiyya are named after Abū Saʿīd al-Fayyūmī. They interpret the Torah by individual letters.

The Sāmiriyya deny many of the laws of the Jews and reject the prophethood of anyone after Joshua.

The ʿUkbariyya are followers of Mūsa al-Baghdādī al-ʿUkbarī and Ismā'īl al-ʿUkbarī, who dissent from certain things in the matters of Sabbath observance and Torah interpretation.

The Iṣbahāniyya are followers of Abū ʿIsā al-Iṣbahānī, who claimed prophethood and [who claimed] that he had been taken up to heaven, where the Lord had stroked his head, and that he had seen Muḥammad and had come to believe in him. The Jews of Iṣbahān claim that he is the Dajjāl and that he will emerge from their district.

The ʿIrāqiyya dispute with the Khurāsāniyya on setting the times of their festivals and the lengths of their days.

The Sharshtāniyya are followers of Sharshtān, who claimed that eighty *sūqa*, that is, verses, were dropped from the text of the Torah, and that the Torah has an esoteric interpretation conflicting with its exoteric sense.

The Jews of Palestine believe that ʿUzair was the Son of God, but most Jews deny this doctrine.

The Mālikiyya claim that God will not raise the dead on Resurrection Day, except for those vindicated by prophets and holy books. This Mālik was a pupil of ʿĀnān.

The Rabbāniyya claim that if a menstruant touches one of a number of garments, all the garments must be laundered.

The ʿĪrāqiyya base the beginning of the months on new moons, but others work by means of a calendar.

NOTES

This article comprises the sixth chapter of my unpublished dissertation, "Species of misbelief: A history of Muslim heresiography of the Jews," directed by G. Michael Wickens at the University of Toronto, 1985. Given that large parts of my original contribution at the Lausanne conference of 1991 were published in my book *Between Muslim and Jew: The Problem of Symbiosis Under Early Islam* (Princeton, 1995) Professor Waardenburg asked if I would submit these annotated translations in the place of that lecture. They have been only slightly modified. I thank Floyd Mann for his help in preparing this piece for publication.

1. Cairo, 1312. Cf. Fattal, *Statuts*, pp. 216–218. For the work of C. E. Bosworth concerning administrative documents, see n. 44.

2. See, for example, R. J. H. Gottheil, "Dhimmis and Moslems in Egypt," in *Old Testament and Semitic Studies in Memory of William Rainey Harper*, vol. 2 (Chicago, 1908), pp. 353–414, and Gottheil, "A Cairo synagogue eleventh-century document," *Jewish Quarterly Review* o.s. 19 (1907), where, on p. 499 n. 1, Gottheil observes the peculiarity of the circumstance that, even though the Karaite community was larger and more influential than the Samaritan community, the Karaites were subsumed under the Rabbanites, while the Samaritans had their own titular leader to serve as official liaison with the government.

3. W. Björkman, *Beiträge zur Geschichte der Staatskanzlei im islamischen Ägypten* (Hamburg, 1928).

4. Bosworth, n. 44; N. A. Stillman, *The Jews of Arab Lands* (Philadelphia, 1979), pp. 267–268; B. Lewis, "Politics and war," *The Legacy of Islam*, 2nd ed., ed. J. Schacht and C. E. Bosworth (Oxford, 1979), pp. 180–181, n. 2.

5. S. D. Goitein, "A caliph's decree in favour of the Rabbinite Jews of Palestine," *Journal for Jewish Studies* 5 (1954): 118–125; S. M.Stern, *Fatimid Decrees* (London, 1964). For more on the subject of oaths required of the Jews, consult Juster, *Juifs*, vol. I, pp. 115–119. I would emphasize that the Jew's Oath is to be distinguished from the charges to office. The Jew's Oath given by ʿUmarī does not mention Jewish sects. However, it does shed light on the oaths of office given by ʿUmarī (and copied by Qalqashandī), which specify the leaders of the various communities. In this regard it should be noted that the Jew's Oath presumably was designed for Jews of all sectarian persuasions, while the charges to office are two: for the Head of the Jews (Rabbanite and Karaite) and for the Head of the Samaritans.

6. "Head of the Jews," pp. 142–143; "Head of Samaritans," p. 144.

7. "Dhimmis and Moslems," p. 373 n. 100.

8. See the following discussion concerning Ibn Qayyim's treatment of the "Samaritan question."

9. See von Grunebaum's *Medieval Islam*, p. 218 n. 122, and additional note, p. 355, for important comparisons with the parallel Byzantine institution of *agoronomos*. See also Ibn al-Ukhuwwa's *Maʿālim al-Qurba*, ed. R. Levy (London, 1938), pp. 38–43 of which are translated into English on pp. 271–272 of Stillman's *Jews of Arab Lands*.

10. "Ibn Kayyim al-Djawziyya," *Encyclopedia of Islam*, new ed. vol. 3 (Leiden: E. J. Brill, 1971), pp. 821–822 (H. Laoust); *Geschichte der Arabischen Literatur*, vol. 2, pp. 127–129; *Geschichte der Arabischen Schrifttums*, vol. 2, pp. 126–128. As far as our research can determine, Ibn Taymiyya never categorized Jewish groups. For a study of his attitudes toward the Jews, see A. Morabia's "Ibn Taymiyya, les Juifs et la Torah," *Studia Islamica* 49 (1979): 91–123; 50 (1979): 77–109. See, more generally, "Ibn Taymiyya," *Encyclopedia of Islam*, new ed. vol. 3, pp. 951–955 (H. Laoust).

11. "L'Islam hanbalisant," *Revue des Études Islamiques* 42 (1974): 211–244 and 43 (1975): 45–76. This has been translated into English by M. Swartz in the volume which he edited as *Studies on Islam* (Oxford University Press, 1981) pp. 216–275. For the characterization of Ibn Qayyim, see ibid., pp. 247–250.

12. The only exceptions are Ḥaydar Āmulī and the Zaydī Murtaḍā. For Ḥaydar Āmulī, see the following works of Henry Corbin: "Sayyed Ḥaydar Āmoli (VIIIe/XIVe siecle)," *Mélanges Henri Massé* (Teheran, 1963), pp. 72–103; Corbin, *En Iran Iranien*, vol. 3 (4 vols., Paris, 1971–1972), pp. 149–213; Corbin and O. Yahya, eds., *Le Texte des Textes* (*Nāṣṣ al-Nuṣṣūṣ*): *Prolegomenon au commentaire des Fuṣuṣ al-Ḥikam d'Ibn ʿArabī* (Paris, 1975); Corbin, *Paradoxe du monothéisme* (Paris, 1981), pp. 9–87.

Murtaḍā's section on the Muʿtazila from the "kitāb al-milal wal-niḥal" of the *Bahr al-Zakhkhār* has been edited twice independently of the work itself. Once as *The Muʿtazilah*, ed. T. W. Arnold (Leipzig, 1902), and again as *Ṭabaqāt al-Muʿtazilah* (*Die Klassen der Muʿtazilah*) ed. S. Diwald-Wilzer (Wiesbaden, 1961). The text itself has been edited in *al-Baḥr al-Zakhkhār al-Jāmiʿ li-Madhāhib ʿUlamāʾ al-Amṣār*, 6 vols. (Ṣanʿa-, 1394/1975). According to S. M. Stern, the introduction to the latter work includes a section on *al-milal wa al-nihal* based, Stern believed, on Bayhaqi's *Sharḥ ʿUyūn al-Masāʾil*. See *Studies*, p. 300.

13. The chart is found in Corbin, *Paradoxe*, p. 41 (diagram 22) and *Texte*, p. 24.

14. See my *Species of Misbelief*, "Kalām heresiography of the Jews," pp. 153–178.

15. See Ibn Taymiyya's large-scale attack on Christianity, *al-Jawāb al-Ṣaḥīḥ lī-man Baddala Dīn al-Masīḥ* (Cairo 1322/1905), 4 vols. Ibn Qayyim's *Hidāya al-Ḥiyāra fī Ajwibāt al-Yahūd wa-al-Naṣārā*, edited in the margins of Bachizade's *Al-Farq Bayn al-Khalq wa-al-Khāliq* (Cairo, 1904) [*non vidi*], is said to have been a plagiarism of *al-Jawāb al-Ṣaḥīḥ*: see Sharfī, "Bibliographie," *Islamochristiana* 4 (1978): 259. Goldziher gave the Arabic text and accompanying German translation of a passage in the *Hidāya* in which Ibn Qayyim discusses the relativity of the Muḥammad revelation with a Jew: "Proben muhammedanischer Polemik gegen den Talmud (II) (Ibn Kajjim al-Gauzijja), *Kobak's Jeschurun*, vol. 9, pp. 18–47.

For Ibn al-Jauzī (510/116–597/1200) as heresiographer, see *Talbīs Iblīs* (Cairo, 1928) and the useful discussion by Laoust, "L'hérésiographie musulmane sous les Abbassides," *Cahiers de civilisation médiévale* 10 (1967): 157–178, at pp. 174–176.

16. 2 vols. (Cairo, 1357/1939); vol. 2, pp. 332 ff. For a summary of this work, see M. Perlmann's "Ibn Qayyim and the devil," *Studi Orientalistici in onore di G. Levi Della Vida*, vol. 2 (Rome, 1956), pp. 330–337.

17. Perlmann, "Ibn Qayyim and the devil," p. 336.

18. This was already pointed out by Perlmann in "Ibn Qayyim and Samauʾal al-Maghribi," *Journal of Jewish Bibliography* 3 (1942): 71–74.

19. 2 Vols., ed. Subḥī Ṣāliḥ (Damascus, 1381/1961). Sharfī has called this "l'ouvrage le plus complet, à l'époque classique, sur les statuts des *dhimmis* en terre d'Islam" ("Bibliographie," *Islamochristiana* 4 (1978): 259).

20. Vol. 2, pp. 90–92.

21. P. 90.

22. P. 91.

23. P. 91.

24. P. 91. See above, *passim*, on these motifs.

25. See *Species of Misbelief*, pp. 260–264, for Abū al-Fidāʾ (who was a contemporary of Ibn Qayyim's) and other continuators of Shāhrastāni.

26. P. 92.

27. "Dhimmis and Moslems," p. 373 n. 100.

28. P. 92. For the vicissitudes of the status of Samaritans under various early medieval Muslim governments, especially the ʿAbbāsids, see the important study of original sources gathered by H. Zayyāt in "Al-Yahūd fī Khilāfat al-ʿAbbāsiyya," *Al-Mashriq* 36 (1938): 149–173, esp. 168 ff., on the Samaritans.

For a slightly later period, the tenth/sixteenth century, under the Ottomans, see U. Heyd, *Ottoman Documents of Palestine 1552–1615* (Oxford, 1960), pp. 163–174; M. A. Epstein, *The Ottoman Jewish Communities and Their Role in the Fifteenth and Sixteenth Centuries* (Freiburg, 1980); B. Braude and B. Lewis, eds., *Christians and Jews under the Ottomans*, 2 vols. (New York, 1982); A. Cohen, *Jewish Life under Islam* (Cambridge, Mass., 1984). See also W.-D. Hutteroth and K. Abdulfattah, *Historical Geography of Palestine, Transjordan and Southern Syria in the Late Sixteenth Century* (Erlangen, 1977); A. Cohen and B. Lewis, *Population and Revenue in the Towns of Palestine in the Sixteenth Century* (Princeton, 1978).

For the seventeenth century, see E. Mittwoch, "Muslimische Fetwās über die Samaritaner," *Orientalistische Literaturzeitung* 29 (1926): cols. 845–849. On these documents Baron has observed that "although written in 1670 and later, these responsa of Muslim jurists reflect the well-established policy of treating Samaritans as Jews." *A Social and Religious History of the Jews*, vol. 5, p. 368 n. 32.

29. "Ibn Khaldūn," *Encyclopedia of Islam*, new ed., vol. 3 (Leiden: E. J. Brill, 1971), pp. 825–831 (M. Talbi); *Geschichte der arabischen Literatur*, vol. 2, pp. 314–317; *Geschichte des Arabischen Schrifttums*, vol. 2, pp. 342–344. See also the magisterial translation of the *Muqaddima* by F. Rosenthal (3 vols., New York, 1958), with a bibliography compiled by W. J. Fischel.

30. For a recent collection of papers which address the significance of the *Muqaddima* from various perspectives, see the special issue of *Journal of Asian and African Studies* vol. 18 (1983) entitled "Ibn Khaldūn and Islamic ideology," ed. B. Lawrence. Most of the literature written on Ibn Khaldūn since Fischel's bibliography of 1958 can be found discussed therein.

31. *Muqaddima*, trans. Rosenthal, vol. I, p. 12.

32. On this, see W. J. Fischel "Ibn Khaldūn: On the Bible, Judaism and the Jews," *Ignace Goldziher Memorial Volume* 2 (Jerusalem, 1956), pp. 147–171, at p. 149.

33. For the details of Ibn Khaldūn's discussion of Jewish history, see ibid. For a synthesis of Ibn Khaldūn's conceptualization of that history, see K. Bland's "An Islamic theory of Jewish history: The case of Ibn Khaldūn," *Journal of Asian and African Studies* 18 (1983): 189–197. For a more general overview, see J. Cuoq, "La religion et les religions (judaisme et christianisme) selon Ibn Khaldūn," *Islamochristiana* 8 (1982): 107–128.

34. Bland aptly quotes Fischel in this connection: "Ibn Khaldūn is one of the few Islamic historians, if not the only one, who was not satisfied to present merely the biblical history. He made every effort to outline also the post-biblical history from the restoration of the first Temple on until the destruction of the second Temple by Titus." *Ibn Khaldūn in Egypt* (Berkeley, 1967), p. 139 (cited by Bland, p. 189).

It is well known that medieval Christians and Muslims largely confined their historiographic interest in Judaism to the biblical period. For an acute critique of this approach and its modern ramifications, see G. I. Langmuir's "Majority history and post-biblical Jews," *Journal of the History of Ideas* 27 (1966): 343–364. To be sure, even Ibn Khaldūn does not bring that history beyond the Second Temple period. See A. Al-Azmeh, *Ibn Khaldūn: An Essay in Reinterpretation* (Totowa, New Jersey, 1982), p. 13.

35. See Fischel, "Ibn Khaldūn and Josippon," *Homenaje a Millas-Vallicrosa*, vol. 1 (Barcelona, 1954), pp. 587–598. A proper edition and full study of the Arabic versions of *Josippon* have yet to be undertaken. As L. Feldman, in his comprehensive survey of Josephan scholarship, remarks, "In view of the tremendous interest in Josippon, it is surprising that the version in Arabic . . . which should be of considerable interest for reconstructing the text of the original Josippon, has still not been scientifically edited." *Josephus and Modern Scholarship (1937–1980)* (New York, 1984), p. 74. Of what has been done, see, for example, Wellhausen "Der

arabische Josippus," *Abhandlungen der Königlichen Gesellschaft der Wissenschaften zu Göttingen*, vol. 4 (Berlin, 1897), pp. 1–50.

It should be pointed out that Ibn Khaldūn not only used this Jewish written source, but he was also friendly with a Jewish scholar, one Ibrāhīm Ibn Zarzar. See Fischel, "On the Bible, Jews and Judaism," pp. 166–170.

36. For an important collection of studies discussing, among other issues, the Jews of Arabia, see the papers delivered at the 1980 colloquium held at the Hebrew University, "From Jāhiliyya to Islam," now published in two volumes in *Jerusalem Studies in Arabic and Islam*, vols. 4–5. See also Gordon Newby, *History of the Jews of Arabia*.

37. See Goitein, "Isrāʾīliyyāt," *Encyclopedia of Islam*, new ed., vol. 4 (Leiden: E. J. Brill, 1978), pp. 211–212.

38. The Christian heresiographers were also wont to make such identifications. Cf. Bar Hebraeus, *Tārīkh Mukhtaṣar al-Duwal* (Beirut, 1958), pp. 68–69; Agapius of Menbij, *Kitāb al-ʿUnwān* (*Patrologia Orientalis*, vol. 7) (1911), p. 490.

39. Vol. 2, p. 122.

40. P. 122.

41. G. Cohen, ed. and trans., *The Book of Tradition* (*Sefer ha-Qabbalah*) by Abraham Ibn Daud (Philadelphia, 1967), Introduction, p. xxxviii, nn. 108–111.

42. P. 155 n. 35.

43. W. J. Fischel, "Ibn Khaldūn and al-Masʿūdī," *Al-Masʿūdī Millenary Commemoration Volume*, ed. S. Maqbul Ahmad and A. Rahman (Calcutta, 1960), pp. 51–60.

44. "Kalkashandi," *Encyclopaedia of Islam*, New edition, vol. 4, pp. 509–511 (C. E. Bosworth); Björkman, *Beiträge*; G. Wiet, "Les classiques du scribe égyptien," *Studia Islamica* 18 (1963): 41–80; Pellat, "Les encyclopédies arabes," pp. 654–655; *Geschichte der arabischen Literatur*, vol. 2, pp. 166–167; *Geschichte des Arabischen Schrifttums*, vol. 2, pp. 164–165.

In the collection *Medieval Arabic Culture and Administration* (London, 1982) three of the important studies that C. E. Bosworth has devoted to this subject have been reprinted: no. 13, "The section on codes and their decipherment in Qalqashandī's *Ṣubḥ al-Aʿshā*, *Journal of Semitic Studies* 8 (1963): 17–33; no. 14, "A *Maqāma* on secretaryship: Al-Qalqashandī's *al-Kawākib ad-durriyya fī ʾl-manāqib al-Badriyya*," *Bulletin of the School of Oriental and African Studies* 27 (1964): 291–298; no. 16 "Christian and Jewish religious dignitaries in Mamlūk Egypt and Syria: Qalqashandī's information on their hierarchy, titulature and appointment," *International Journal of Middle Eastern Studies* 3 (1972): 59–74, 199–216.

45. Edited in 14 volumes, Cairo, 1963.

46. See n. 44.

47. See n. 5.

48. M. R. Cohen, *Jewish Self-Government in Medieval Egypt: The Origins of the Office of the Head of the Jews, ca. 1065–1126* (Princeton, 1980). Cohen suggests that the accepted classification of Karaites alongside Rabbanites in this earlier period may have been a function of economic power: "[Marriage] matches between Rabbanites and Karaites during this period were quite common in Egypt, where the Karaites, by virtue of their high socioeconomic position, still enjoyed the status of a denomination within Judaism rather than that of an ostracized heresy" (pp. 188–189).

49. Vol. 13, pp. 266–267. An English translation can be found in Stillman's *Jews of Arab Lands*, pp. 165–166. Goldziher collected what few scraps are available in his "Serments." On p. 8 of that study he quotes a line from an oath for the abjuration of Judaism in Rāghib al-Iṣfahānī's *Muḥādharāt al-Udabāʾ*; the full text of of this oath can be found on pp. 488–489 of Vol. 3–4 of the *Ṣubḥ*.

50. See n. 30.

51. P. 256.

52. *Jews of Arab Lands*, p. 52.

53. P. 253.

54. P. 257.

55. P. 257–258.

56. P. 258.

57. Pp. 257–264.

58. See n. 5 for the background to this oath, copied here from ʿUmarī.

59. See n. 5.

60. *Geschichte der arabischen Literatur*, vol. 2, pp. 47–50.

61. *Chrestomathie Arabe*, vol. 1 (Paris, 1826): text, pp. 88–117; translation, pp. 284–308, notes pp. 309–369.

62. The edition used here is the Cairo 1270/1892 edition in two volumes, vol. 2, pp. 476–480. The incomplete six-volume French translation by U. Bourriout and P. Casanova (1893–1920) never reached the section on the Jews. Nor did the seven-volume partial edition and translation by G. Wiet (Cairo, 1911–1928). The later Cairene edition (1959) simply copies the Cairo 1270/1892 edition.

63. The variations of these reports were long misleading to scholars who were unaware of Maqrīzī's sources.

64. P. 476.

65. *Mukhtaṣar Taʾrīkh al-Bashar*. See Dunlop, *Arab Civilization*, p. 131. See also B. Lewis, "Gibbon on Muhammad," *Daedalus* (Summer 1976): 89–103, at p. 93. *Abulfedae historia anteislamica* (Leipzig, 1831), which is used herein. The section on the Jews is found on pp. 157–162. *Geschichte der arabischen Literatur*, vol. 2, pp. 55–57; *Geschichte des Arabischen Schrifttums*, vol. 2, p. 44. *Tārīkh Ibn al-Wardī*, 2 vols. (Baghdad, 1389/1969), vol. I, pp. 100–103.

66. P. 476.
67. P. 478.
68. Pp. 476–477.
69. P. 476.
70. Pp. 476–477.
71. Pp. 477–478.
72. P. 477.
73. Benjamin of Tudela, who recorded his travels through the Middle East in the middle of the twelfth century, reported that the Samaritan alphabet lacked the letters *He*, *Ḥet*, and *ʿAyin*, in which place they used the *Aleph* (Baron, *A Social and Religious History of the Jews*, vol. 5, p. 176). Maqrīzī says of the Samaritans that they "imperfectly read four letters, *Alif*, *Hāʾ*, *Khāʾ* and *ʿAyn*, and they did not pronounce these letters in their reading of the Torah" (p. 477).
74. P. 478.
75. P. 478.
76. Brock, "Some Syriac Accounts," provides details of all the known variants in the Syriac tradition.
77. P. 478.
78. "Some Syriac Accounts," p. 276.
79. "Some Syriac Accounts," p. 276 n. 34.
80. P. 478.
81. See n. 40.
82. Muṭahhar Ibn Ṭāhir al-Maqdisī, *al-Badʾ wa'l-taʾ-rīkh (Le Livre de la création et de l'histoire)*, 6 vols., ed. and trans. Cl. Huart (Paris, 1899–1919). T. Khalidi "Muʿtazilite Historiography: Maqdisī's *Kitāb al-Badʾ wal-Taʾrīkh*," *Journal of Near Eastern Studies* 35 (1976): 1–12; *Geschichte des Arabischen Schrifttums*, vol. 1, p. 222; *Geschichte der arabischen Literatur*, vol. 1, p. 337, no. 40.
83. P. 478.
84. For example, Abraham Ibn Daud, in Cohen's translation of the *Book of Tradition*, pp. 16–17.
85. "Alexander the Great and Jaddus the High Priest According to Josephus," *Association for Jewish Studies Review* 7–8 (1982–1983): 41–69. Cohen points out a rabbinic parallel to the Josephus account, in which the High Priest is Simon the Righteous: p. 58, n. 51 (citing Leviticus Rabbah 13.5, p. 293, ed. Margolioth).
86. See n. 51.
87. See my contribution "A Muslim designation for Rabbanite Jews and its significance," to the Princeton meeting of the Society of Judeo-Arabic Studies, forthcoming in *Studies in Muslim-Jewish Relations* (Oxford University Press).
88. ʿAlī Ḥasan al-ʿArīḍ, *Fatḥ al-Mannān fī Naskh al-Qurʾān* (Cairo, 1973), pp. 143 ff.; Muṣṭafā Zayd, *Al-Naskh fī al-Qurʾān al-Karīm*, 2 vols. (Cairo, 1383/1963), vol. I, pp. 1–30; Muḥammad ʿAbd al-ʿAẓīm al-Zurqānī, *Manāhil al-ʿIrfān fī ʿUlūm al-Qurʾān*, 2 vols. (Cairo, 1943), vol. 2, pp. 98–105.
89. See n. 87.
90. See n. 87.
91. A. R. Guest, "A List of Writers, Books and other Authorities mentioned by El-Maqrizi in his *Khiṭaṭ*," *Journal of the Royal Asiatic Society* (1902): 103–125, at p. 106; cited by Nicholson, *A Literary History*, p. 453.

BIBLIOGRAPHY

ʿArid, ʿAli Ḥasan al-. *Fatḥ al-Mannān fī Naskh al-Qurʾān*. Cairo, 1973.

Azmeh, Aziz al-. *Ibn Khaldūn: An Essay in Reinterpretation*. Totowa, N.J., 1992.

Baron, Salo W. *A Social and Religious History of the Jews*. 18 vols. to date. New York, 1958–1985.

Björkman, Walter. *Beiträge zur Geschichte der Staatskanzlei im islamischen Ägypten*. Hamburgische Universität Abhandlungen aus dem Gebiet der Auslandskunde, vol. 28, ser. B. Völkerkunde, Kulturgeschichte und Sprachen. Vol. 16. Hamburg, 1928.

Bland, Kalman. "An Islamic theory of Jewish history: The case of Ibn Khaldūn." *Journal of Asian and African Studies* 18 (1983): 129–197.

Bosworth, C. E. "Christian and Jewish religious dignitaries in Mamlūk Egypt and Syria: Qalqashandī's information on their hierarchy, titulature and appointment." *International Journal of Middle Eastern Studies* 3 (1972): 59–74, 199–216. Repr. as ch. no. 16, in *Medieval Arabic Culture and Administration*, London, 1982.

———. "Ḳalḳashandī," *Encyclopaedia of Islam*, new ed., vol. 4 (Leiden: E. J. Brill, 1978), pp. 509–511.

———. "A Maqāma on secretaryship: al-Qalqashandī's *al-Kawākib ad-durrīya fī 'l-manāqib al-Badrīyya*." *Bulletin of the School of Oriental and African Studies* 27 (1964): 291–298. Repr. as ch. no. 14, in *Medieval Arabic Culture and Administration*, London, 1982.

———. "The section on codes and their decipherment in Qalqashandī's *Ṣubḥ al-Aʿshā*." *Journal of Semitic Studies* 8 (1963): 17–33. Repr. as ch. no. 13, in *Medieval Arabic Culture and Administration*, London, 1982.

Braude, B., and Lewis, B., eds. *Christians and Jews in the Ottoman Empire*. 2 vols. New York, 1982.

Brock, S. P. "Some Syriac accounts of the Jewish sects." In *A Tribute to Arthur Vööbus*, ed. R. H. Fischer. Chicago, 1977, pp. 265–276.

Brockelmann, C. *Geschichte der arabischen Literatur*, 2nd ed., 2 vols. Leiden, 1943. Supplement I, Leiden, 1937; Supplement II, Leiden, 1938; Supplement III, Leiden, 1942.

Cohen, A. *Jewish Life under Islam*. Cambridge, Mass., 1984.

———, and Bernard Lewis. *Population and Revenue in the Towns of Palestine in the Sixteenth Century*. Princeton, 1978.

Cohen, Gerson, ed. and trans. *Sefer ha-Qabbalah: Ibn Daud*. Philadelphia, 1967.

Cohen, Mark. *Jewish Self-Government in Medieval Egypt: The Origins of the Office of the Head of the Jews ca. 1065–1126*. Princeton, 1980.

Corbin, Henry. "Sayyed Ḥaydor Āmolī (VIIIe/XIVe siècle)." *Mélanges Henri Massé*. Teheran, 1963, pp. 72–103.

Cuoq, Joseph. "La religion et les religions (judaisme et christianisme) selon Ibn Khaldūn." *Islamochristiana* 8 (1982): 107–128.

De Sacy, Silvestre. *Chrestomathie Arabe*. 2 vols. Paris, 1806.

Dunlop, D. M. *Arab Civilization to 1500 A.D.* Beirut, 1971.

Epstein, M. A. *The Ottoman Jewish Communities and Their Role in the Fifteenth and Sixteenth Centuries*. Freiburg, 1980.

Feldman, Louis. *Josephus and Modern Scholarship (1937–1980)*. New York, 1984.

Fishel, W. J. "Ibn Khaldūn and al-Masʿūdī." In *Al-Masʿūdī Millenary Commemoration Volume*, ed. S. Maqbul Ahmad and A. Rahman. Calcutta, 1960, pp. 51–60.

———. "Ibn Khaldūn and Josippon," *Homenaje a Millas-Vallicrosa*, vol. 1. Barcelona, 1954, pp. 587–598.

———. "Ibn Khaldūn on the Bible, Judaism and the Jews." In *Ignace Goldziher Memorial Memorial Volume*, vol. 1, ed. S. Lowinger and J. de Somogyi. Budapest, 1948, pp. 145–171.

———. *Ibn Khaldūn in Egypt*. Berkeley, 1967.

Goitein, S. D. "Isrāʾīliyyāt," *Encyclopedia of Islam*, new ed. vol. 4 (Leiden, E. J. Brill, 1978), pp. 211–212.

Gottheil, R. H. "Dhimmis and Moslems in Egypt." *Old Testament and Semitic Studies in Memory of William Rainey Harper*, vol. 2. Chicago, 1908, pp. 353–414.

Guest, A. R. "A list of writers, books and other authorities mentioned by El-Maqrīzī in his *Khiṭaṭ*." *Journal of the Royal Asiatic Society* (1902): 103–125.

Heyd, Uriel. *Ottoman Documents on Palestine, 1552–1615*. Oxford, 1960.

Hutteroth, Wolf-Dieter, and Abdulfattah, Kamal. *Historical Geography of Palestine, Transjordan and Southern Syria in the Late Sixteenth Century*. Erlangen, 1977.

Ibn al-Wardī, Zayn al-Dīn ʿUmar ibn al-Muẓaffar. *Tārīkh ibn al-Wardī*. 2 vols. Baghdad, 1389/1969.

Ibn Khaldūn, ʿAbd al-Raḥmān Abū Zayd ibn Muḥammad. *The Muqaddimah*, 3 vols. Trans. Franz Rosenthal. New York, 1958.

Ibn Qayyim al-Jauziyya, Shams al-Dīn Abū Bakr Muḥammad ibn Abū Bakr al-Zarʿī. *Aḥkām Ahl al-Dhimma*, 2 vols., ed. Ṣubḥī Ṣāliḥ. Damascus, 1381/1961.

———. *Ighāthāt al-Lahfān Min Maṣāʾid al-Shayṭān*. 2 vols. Cairo, 1357/1939.

Juster, Jean. *Les juifs dans l'empire Romain*. 2 vols. Paris, 1914.

Khalidi, Tarif. "Muʿtazilite historiography: Maqdisī's Kitāb al-Badʾ Waʾl-Taʾrīkh," *Journal of Near Eastern Studies* 35 (1976): 1–12.

Langmuir, Gavin. "Majority history and post-biblical Jews," *Journal of the History of Ideas* 27 (1966): 343–364.

Laoust, Henri. "Ibn Kayyim al-Djawziyya," *Encyclopedia of Islam*, new ed., vol. 3 (Leiden: E. J. Brill, 1971), pp. 821–822.

———. "Ibn Taymiyya," *Encyclopedia of Islam*, new ed., vol. 3 (Leiden, E. J. Brill, 1971), pp. 951–955.

———. "L'hérésiographie musulmane sous les Abbassides," *Cahiers de Civilisation Médiévale* 10 (1967): 157–178.

Lewis, Bernard. "Gibbon on Muḥammad," *Daedalus* (Summer, 1976): 89–103.

Maqdisī, Muṭahhar ibn Ṭāhir al-. *Kitāb al-Badʾ wa al-Taʾrīkh (Livre de la Creation et de l'Histoire)*, 6 vols. Ed. and trans. C. Huart. Paris, 1899–1919.

Maqrīzī, Abū al-ʿAbbās Aḥmad b. ʿAbd al-Qādir al-Ḥusainī Taqī al-Dīn al-. *Al-Mawāʿiẓ wa al-Iʿtibār fī Dhikr al-Khiṭaṭ wa al-Athār*. 2 vols. Cairo, 1270/1892.

Mittwoch, Eugen. "Muslimische Fetwās über die Samaritaner." *Orientalistische Literaturzeitung 29* (1926): col. 845–849.

Morabia, A. "Ibn Taymiyya, les Juifs et la Tora," *Studia Islamica* 49 (1979): 91–123; 50: 77–109.

Pellat, Charles. "Les encyclopédies dans le monde arabe," *Journal of World History* 9 (1966): 631–658.

Perlmann, Moshe. "Ibn Qayyim and Samauʾal al-Maghribī." *Journal of Jewish Bibliography* 3 (1942): 71–74.

———. "Ibn Qayyim and the devil." *Studi Orientalistici in onore di G. Levi Della Vida*, vol. 2. Rome, 1956, pp. 330–337.

Qalqashandī, Abū al-ʿAbbās Aḥmad ibn ʿAlī al-Shāfiʿī al-. *Ṣubḥ al-Aʿshā fī Ṣināʿat al-Inshāʾ*. 14 vols. Cairo, 1963.

Sharfī, ʿAbd al-Majīd (Abdelmajid Charfi). "Bibliographie du dialogue islamo-chrétien; Auteurs musulmans, XIe–XIIe siècles," *Islamochristiana 2* (1976): 196–201.

Swartz, Merlin, ed. and trans. *Studies on Islam*. Oxford University Press, 1981.

Talbi, M. "Ibn Khaldūn," *Encyclopedia of Islam*, New edition, vol. 3, pp. 825–831.

ʿUmarī, Shihāb al-dīn ibn Faḍl Allāh al-. *Al-Taʿrīf bi-al-Muṣṭalaḥ al-Sharīf*. Cairo, 1312.

von Grunebaum, Gustav E. *Medieval Islam*. Chicago, 1946; 7th printing, Chicago, 1969.

Wiet, G. "Les classiques du scribe Egyptien." *Studia Islamica* 18 (1963): 41–80.

Zayd, Muṣṭafā. *Al-Naskh fī al-Qurʾān al-Karīm*. 2 vols. Cairo, 1383/1963.

Zayyāt, Ḥabīb. "Al-Yahūd fī Khilāfat al-ʿAbbāsiyya," *Al-Machriq* 36 (1938): 149–173.

Zurqānī, Muḥammad ʿAbd al-ʿAẓīm al-. *Manāhil al-ʿIrfān fī ʿUlūm al-Qurʾān*. Cairo, 1943.

10

Perceptions of Other Religions in Sufism

CARL-A. KELLER

Dealing with the very diverse perceptions of other religions by the Sufis and their predecessors in early Islam, I shall follow more or less the historical development. It must be remembered at the outset that the Sufi movement was anything but a homogeneous unity. There are differences with regard to specific techniques and ritual, and even as far as the general outlook and the theological underpinnings of mystical techniques are concerned. Sufism does not go back to a single founder, although most Sufis are convinced that the Sufi movement was inaugurated either by the Prophet himself or by ʿAlī, his cousin and son-in-law. Sufism has indeed grown out of a general climate of profound religious awareness and striving which was stimulated by the sayings and doings of Muḥammad and his first companions. It is clear that the strong desire of many Muslims of the first generation to maintain an intimate relationship with the God of Qurʾānic Revelation—a God who wanted to be remembered, obeyed, adored, known, and even loved—triggered an attitude toward life which developed into the vast stream of Sufi activities and experience.

In its essence, Sufism is one of the fruits on the tree of Qurʾānic piety. Many verses in the Qurʾān, let alone certain *ḥadīth*, suggest experiential interiorization of the message. Such interiorization can easily lead to a living and intimate relationship with God. Nevertheless, there is no particular follower of the Prophet who could be identified as the very first representative of that particular type of Islamic religiousness which finally produced the Sufi movement. There were many pious people. Tradition names hundreds of them, including the group called *ahl al-ṣuffa*, the "people of the bench," who are said to have gathered regularly at the mosque of Medina, having chosen to live in poverty and discussing matters of piety. We also know of men who took to fierce asceticism in order to be nearer to God. A very famous one is Abū ʾl-Dardāʾ who was rebuked by the Prophet himself for his tendency to push asceticism to limits that were not compatible with the social obligations of a Muslim. But asceticism was practiced earnestly, and the works of piety varied in quality with different people, so that the roots of Sufism are manifold, yet going back to the time of the Prophet, his companions, and their immediate successors.

Post-Qurʾānic Pietism

The Muslims who were attracted to an interiorized type of Qurʾānic and post-Qurʾānic piety soon met pious people and ascetics from other religions, particularly from Christianity. Christian monks and ascetics were a common sight in the countries that had been conquered by the Muslims. In a book which has become a classic on the subject, Margaret Smith described in much detail the world of Near Eastern piety and mysticism as it occurred before the appearance of Islam and during the first century of the Hijrah.[1] She analyzes the many items that link Qurʾānic piety with pre-Qurʾānic Christian piety and monasticism, and stresses the importance of even post-Qurʾānic contacts between the emerging Islamic and the living Christian traditions. Later on, the Swedish scholar Tor Andrae took up the same theme, quoting many examples of contact between the communities and especially between Muslim and Christian ascetics.[2] One of these examples is attributed by Abū Nuʿaim al-Isbahānī to Mālik ibn Dīnār (d. 744?), a man who had read the Torah and was familiar with Gospel stories:

> I saw a monk sitting on a hill. I addressed him saying: "Monk! Teach me something by which you may make me a stranger to the world!" He answered: "Are you not in possession of the Qurʾān and the Revelation (*furqān*)?" I said: "Yes, but I want you to teach me something from your experience so that I may become a stranger to the world." He replied: "If you are able to put an iron curtain between yourself and your desires, then do it!"[3]

We note that the Muslim narrator suggests implicitly that even a Christian monk is aware of the decisive importance of the Qurʾānic Revelation. There is no need for a Muslim to be taught by someone who does not submit to it. Yet the Muslim seeker is keen on learning something from the Christian's personal knowledge and experience (*min ʿindika*). If the Christian complies, it will be easier for him to practice *zuhd*, restraint in the world. The counsel which the monk gives him is an elementary one but it resumes the essential principle of monastic ethics: the fight against the *epithumiai*, *šahawāt*, a principle which is taken up by the Muslim ascetics in the form of the fight against the "*ego* which asks to do evil" (*al-nafs al-ammāra bi-ʾl-sūʾ*; Qurʾān 12:53).

If this purely moral advice appears as rather clumsy, it must not be forgotten that Sufism is by no means only "religious" practice and experience but first of all, and to a very high degree, *adab*, noble behavior and moral perfection. *Al-taṣawwuf kulluhu adab*, "Sufism is nothing but *adab*," as the saying goes.

Other examples might be quoted to illustrate the attitude of Muslim pious men and ascetics toward Christian hermits and monks. Although our sources admit that Muslims did not abhor social intercourse with Christian ascetics, they always insist on the superiority of Islam, proven regularly at the end of the event. This is what happens in the story of Muḥammad ibn Yaʿqūb, a contemporary and companion of Ḥārith ibn Asad al-Muḥāsibī (d. 857):

> Having left Damascus, I went into the desert. Suddenly I found myself in a pathless wilderness in which I went astray until I was almost dead. When I was in that state, I saw two monks coming along. I thought that they had started from some near-by place and that they were going to some monastery, surely not far away. I approached them, saying: "Where are you going?"—"We do not know!"—"Do you know where you are?"—"Yes! We are in His Reign, in His Kingdom and in His Presence!" Hearing this, I chided my ego (*nafs*) severely, telling myself: "Both of these realize *tawakkul*, unconditional trust in God, and you don't!"—Then I asked them; "May I stay with you?" They said: "Do as you like!" So I went with them.
>
> When the night was about to fall, they stopped for their prayers. Seeing them praying, I did my own evening prayer after having purified myself with sand. When they saw me handling sand, they smiled at my doings.
>
> When they had finished their prayers, one of them scratched the earth with his fingers and, lo! there appeared water and well-prepared food. I stood wondering, but they said: "What is the matter with you? Come, eat and drink!" We ate and drank. When I was ready for the next prayer, the water subsided and disappeared. Then they continued to pray and so did I beside them, till morning broke. Then we did the morning prayers and then set out for the journey, marching the whole day, till evening.
>
> When the night fell, the second monk came forward, prayed with his friend, asked God for help, scratched the earth with his fingers—and immediately water gushed forth and the meal was ready.
>
> The third evening they said: "Muslim! It's up to you tonight! Ask God for something!" I followed suit, for I was ashamed and rather upset. So I prayed: "O God! I know that my faults do not give me any merit in your sight. But I pray, do not dishonor me in their presence and do not let them triumph over our Prophet Muḥammad and over the *umma* of your Prophet!" And, lo! there appeared a rushing source and plenty of food.

This succession of three evenings happens several times. In the end, the Muslim hears a voice saying: "Muḥammad ibn Yaʿqūb! We want to manifest through you the superiority we have granted the Prophet Muḥammad over all the other prophets and apostles. And this is the sign, in order to honor you and the *umma* of my Prophet!" Thus the divine voice announces the final triumph of the Muslims over the Christians and vindicates the superiority of Islam. It is clear that the two monks do not withstand such a demonstration and that they accept Islam on the spot.[4]

We have quoted the story at some length for it is, in its naive simplicity, a very profound one. The two monks realize, as Christians, the model of life which is going to be the one of later Sufism. It is also the ideal of the mystical quest in all religions: total freedom in the Presence of the Ultimate. They know only one thing; that wherever they go they are living "in God's Reign, in His Kingdom, in His Presence." They know nothing else. The circumstances of their earthly life do not bother them. Wherever they roam, they remain under God's protection. As the Qur'ān puts it: "Wherever you look, everywhere is God's Presence" (2:115). They enjoy divine freedom. The assurance that God provides for all their needs is part of this freedom. So they take things as they are, thanking and adoring God. Popular language expresses the certitude of total freedom by imagining the miraculous appearance of food and drink. This legendary detail is a most significant feature of the story. Total freedom in God places religious men above all problems of sustenance. That is the fruit of *tawakkul*, the religious attitude which had been taught by Jesus Himself (Matt 6:25ff).

The Muslim recognizes immediately the high status of the monks. But he has to answer a challenge: Is the Christian religion the final truth? Where is ultimate Revelation to be found? With the Christians or with the Prophet Muḥammad? The Muslim's answer is significantly different from that of the monks. The monks are somewhat unearthly people: they just enjoy their enviable status, whereas the Muslim practices Islam, submission. He acknowledges his faults, asks for forgiveness, and appeals to the honor of the Prophet and of his *umma*. So God Himself makes it clear that it is indeed His divine will to make sure that the privileges of the Muslim people are safe. For if the Christians' religious achievements are extraordinary, Islam is still superior, for it establishes God's reign on earth as a politically structured order.

Among the early "Sufis" (who were not yet given this term), a special place must be reserved for Dhū ʾl-Nūn Miṣrī (796–856), one of the most charming among them. The study of the traditions about this fascinating personality is most rewarding and opens up several new perspectives. He is one of the foremost witnesses to the remarkable open-mindedness of post-Qurʾānic pietism.

During his numerous journeys "on the border of the Nile" and "on the mountains of Jerusalem and Damascus," Dhū ʾl-Nūn met many hermits and ascetics whom one is tempted to regard either as Christians or as followers of some gnostic doctrine. Here is one of his stories:

> When I was traveling in the country of Damascus, I sighted a man fearing God (*ʿābid*) who emerged from one of the caves. When he saw me, he hid immediately in the thicket. Then I heard him saying: "O my Lord, I take refuge in you to protect me from those who keep away from you, O Refuge of the gnostics, Friend of those who turn to you, Helper of the sincere, and Hope of the lovers!" Then he cried aloud and his tears made him swoon. The long time he had to remain in the world was distress for him. Then he said again: "Glory to the one who allows the hearts of the gnostics to taste the sweetness of retiring unto Him by cutting off from the world (*ʾinqitāʾ ilaihi*). Nothing is more delicious for them than uttering His Name and seeking the solitude of familiar discourse." Then he walked on, shouting "*Quddūs! Quddūs! Quddūs!*" I invited him to come near. He did so and said, praying: "I put out of my heart all impediments and deal with none of your creatures except with you alone!" I wished him peace and asked him to pray to God on my behalf. He said. "My God, according to His good pleasure, may ease your pains and troubles on your journey toward Him, so that there may be no impediment between you and Him." Then he ran away, out of my sight, like someone fleeing from a lion.[5]

What kind of man was this "servant of God" (*ʿābid*)? His strange behavior—he lives in a cave, shies off from all people, avoids contact with travelers, thinks only of God, and invokes his Lord with a triple *Quddūs*—suggests strongly a Christian hermit. It is interesting to note that Dhū ʾl-Nūn, the Muslim, asked him to pray for him and that he was granted a benediction.

Very often we come across the formula "God has servants or worshippers (*ʿābidūn*)" who lead a life of unusual piety and have profound religious experiences. Why are they referred to as "worshippers" or as "men fearing God," not as Muslims? The most ready explanation is that they are pious people who do not belong to the Islamic fold. The Muslim pietists do not reject them but consider them as models for their own practice. In his numerous prayers, Dhū ʾl-Nūn generally asks God to "put him on a footing with those who have (these experiences)." One such experience consists in ascending to the heavenly palaces, and the description of such an ascent closely parallels similar accounts in Jewish and Christian apocalypses and mystical writings.[6] Dhū ʾl-Nūn knows the various stages of the ascent—confessing one's sins, asking for forgiveness, demanding help, ascending through the heavens, entering the Palace—, but it is hardly admissible to suppose that this knowledge has exclusively and specifically Islamic origins. Moreover, Dhū ʾl-Nūn is said to have been familiar with hermetic and magic lore. In spite of this, he must be considered a truly Islamic lover of God, although he was immersed in the spiritual climate of his time—a climate heavily laden with Hellenistic, Christian, and gnostic asceticism and spiritual ambitions.

Early Muslim ascetics are known as *zuhhād* or, more specifically, as *nussāk.* The latter term is the proper equivalent for "hermit" or "ascetic." *Nussāk* are often mentioned in the religious literature of ancient Islam, and the documents have retained many of their characteristics. Al-Ašʿarī, in his *Maqālāt al-islāmiyyīn*, lists eight items that throw much light on the wide range of their convictions and habits:

1. *Nussāk* say that God can incarnate (*ḥulūl*) in bodies. If they see something beautiful, they say: One never knows, perhaps it is our Lord.
2. It is possible to see God already in this world, as the fruit of pious activities. The more one's works are beautiful, the more beautiful also is the appearance of God.
3. It is possible while living in the world to embrace God, to touch Him, and to be seated with Him.
4. God has a human form, with members and particles of flesh and blood.
5. God is joyful when His friends obey Him and sad when they disobey.
6. True worship of God liberates the worshipper from the obligation to do good works and makes room for moral freedom.
7. True worship of God allows people to see God already in this world, to eat the fruits of Paradise, to embrace the *Ḥūr al-ʿain*, and to fight the *šayāṭīn.*
8. True worship puts the worshipper above prophets and angels which are near to God.[7]

Most of the items on this list attest a very strong and overwhelming experience of nearness to God. Several points (2, 3, and 7) remind one of the visualizing techniques of Christian monks, particularly in Egypt, whose aim has been to live concretely, through visualization, the heavenly realities. The allusion to moral freedom (point 6) is a parallel to certain consequences of gnostic perceptions of being in the world. God's feelings as to the worshippers' obedience or otherwise have become quite understandable as popular interpretations of Christianity. Point 1 may be a reminiscence of stories like that of the Burning Bush in Exodus 3. The last point reminds one of the Christian message that the believers will be "judges over angels" (1 Cor 6:8).

Whatever the exact origin of the various items, it is evident that the *nussāk* borrowed many things from sources that are not strictly Qurʾānic, but partly popular and pertaining to folklore, partly esoteric, and partly hailing from ascetic practices. We may add that Sufism has all along and until modern times incorporated and absorbed many such elements. It has freely entered into close relationships with folklore and spontaneous religiousness. Sufi hagiographical literature abounds in traditions of that sort. On the popular level, Sufi religious life and experience do not always yield to strict juristic and theological demands. That is one of the reasons it has been opposed by many *ʿulamāʾ.*

When speaking of non-Islamic elements in early Sufism, we may in passing mention the theory of Indian influences expounded by several authors, particularly by Max Horten[8] and R. C. Zaehner.[9] Such elements are undoubtedly present in later Sufism—the very popular parable of the blind men who tried to describe an elephant has crept into Sufism as a loan from Buddhist texts—but such contacts are more doubtful in early Sufism. Zaehner maintained that Abū Yazīd Basṭāmī (d. 848 or 874) had learned from an Indian convert to Islam the most essential elements of his spirituality of searching for unity in God. He founds this theory on a sentence in Sarrāj's *Kitāb al-lumaʿ fī al-taṣawwuf* where Abū Yazīd says: "I used to keep company with Abū ʿĀlī al-Sindhī. I used to teach him how to execute his religious duties, and in exchange for this he would teach me the way of divine Unity and the true nature of things."[10] Zaehner concludes that the experience of unity with God which is prominent in Abū Yazīd's sayings is the fruit of Abū ʿĀlī's teaching, and he tries to support this interpretation by quoting four illustrations which suggest the Indian origin of some of Abū Yazīd's statements.

Apart from the problem of the identity of the place where Abū ʿĀlī came from (was it the Indian province Sindh or a village in Iran?), it is possible to interpret the saying in question in a strictly Sufi way.

Abū Yazīd was probably teaching the *inner meaning* of Islamic religious duties, and in exchange he received instruction, by a fellow Sufi, about details of the mystical path to God. Nevertheless, some of the parallels adduced by Zaehner are rather puzzling.

The Formation of Systematic Sufi Thought

During the ninth and tenth centuries, Islamic thinkers—jurists and theologians—gave the Islamic tradition its final shape and profile. At the same time, Sufism underwent a similar process of systematization and purification. Leading Sufis started interpreting the Qurʾān, including the traditional life of the Prophet Muḥammad, and they insisted that true Sufism consisted in emulating the Prophet's lifestyle. There had always been many ascetics and early Sufis who were not in the least interested in foreign religious traditions, being content with deepening the Qurʾānic roots of interiorized *tawḥīd*. Total experience of *tawḥīd* was conceived of as a path to be followed (*ṭarīqa*), and the various steps on that path were described and elaborated upon with reference to inner-Islamic discussions, convictions, and experiences.

That is why the great masters of early and classical Sufism hardly mention other religions and their adherents. The classical authorities on systematic *taṣawwuf*, such as Shaqīq Balkhī (d. 810),[11] Ḥārith ibn Asad al-Muḥāsibi (d. 857), Sarī al-Saqatī (d. 867), Sahl ibn ʿAbdallah al-Tustarī (d. 896), and especially Abū ʾl-Qāsim al-Junaid (d. 910) and Ibn ʿAtā (d. 921)[12] do not find it necessary to talk about other religions, their Islamic references being a clear and sufficient basis for their practices. In the course of time, Islamic references became more and more abundant and manifold in content.

That does not mean that Sufis would never meet members of other faiths. But it seems that such encounters were not always very friendly. It is said that al-Ḥallāj (d. 922) once entered a Zoroastrian fire-temple, opening miraculously the closed door. Inside, he quenched the sacred fire, plunging the guardian into dire despair. Although he lighted the fire again by his miraculous powers, the damage was done—the guardian had to pay a handsome fine—but the superiority of Islam was convincingly demonstrated.[13] Even if this tale is probably a legend, it is witness to the reputation of this type of Sufi: they were supposed to be staunch defenders of Islam.

The Perception of Other Religions in Postclassical Sufism

Once the Sufi movement had fixed its technical vocabulary (mainly on the basis of the Qurʾān and the Sunna), its main practices finding wide acceptance (admitting numerous and sometimes important differences among the various branches), and when it had organized itself in schools each of which hailed from its particular master, Sufis became more and more conscious of their Islamic identity. As it happened with most of their masters, so it did with the disciples: meeting members of other religious traditions was an occasion of showing off with the superiority of Islam. Many anecdotes whose message is revealing though there is reason to question their historical accuracy, attest an aggressively haughty attitude. Abū Saʿīd ibn Abī ʾl-Khair (967–1049), a Sufi master from Khurasan, once entered a Church and saw the pious pay obeisance to the statues of the Virgin and of Jesus. In anger, he addressed the latter: "Is it not you who have told people to worship yourself and your Mother? Now, if the Prophet Muḥammad's words are true, prostrate yourself before the true God!" At the very moment, the statues fell to the ground, facing the Kaʿba, and 40 Christians converted to Islam.[14]

Fortunately, there is another incident which may have a more legitimate claim for historicity and which throws a different light on the same personality:

> Abū Saʿīd once entered a Church where the Christians were assembled for worship. Seeing the shaykh, they treated him with great respect. The shaykh allowed a reader of the Qurʾān to recite some verses from the Book. The Christians were listening in amazement, with tears in their eyes. Having left the Church, the attendants of the shaykh regretted that their master had not invited the Christians to tear off their girdle (*zunnār*) in token of their conversion to Islam. The shaykh replied: "I have not given them the *zunnār*, thus it is not up to me to loosen it."[15]

The Holy Book, properly recited, ought to provoke approval by itself; on such an occasion it is not the shaykh's duty to push people to conversion.

The hesitation and ambiguity in the appraisal of other religions—allowing them to exist and simultaneously forcing their adherents to embrace Islam—is also found in later masters of the Sufi path. Jalāl al-Dīn Rūmī (1207–1273) is not an exception to the rule. When studying his case, we are in a particularly favorable position: we possess his authentic words, taken down and collected by his disciples.[16] In one of his talks, Rūmī states that

> the love for the Creator is latent in all the world and in all men, be they Magians, Jews or Christians, indeed in all things that have being. How indeed should any man not love Him that gave him being? Love indeed is latent in every man, but impediments veil that love; when those impediments are removed that love becomes manifest.[17]

A little later on, Rūmī quotes a verse from the Persian poet Sanāʾī (*Ḥadīqat al-ḥaqīqa, 60*) which we shall come across again toward the end of this essay:

> *Kufr* and *dīn* are running on the path towards you
> (God),
> Saying: He is one and has no companion
> (*waḥdahu lā šarīka lahu*).

There is a sort of gradation in these statements. Having admitted that love of God is virtually present in other religions, only veiled by some impediments, he goes on to declare that *kufr* is practically identical with Islam. Sanāʾī, the authority he quotes, puts indeed into the mouth of *kufr* the sacred formulas of the Qurʾān!

In another talk Rūmī says that the worship of stones and idols which are unable to respond to their worshippers' wishes has been established by God. It is true that the idols are dead and do not have any sensibility. But the fact that they are worshipped is willed by God:

> Those who worship stones, venerate and magnify them, and to them direct their hopes and longings, their petitions and needs and tears. The stone neither knows nor feels anything of this. Yet God most High has made stones and idols to be a means to his devotion in them, of which the stones and idols are entirely unaware.[18]

Non-Islamic religions which worship images are thus considered legitimate because they are willed by God most High. A very significant uttering in this respect is Rūmī's report of an incident he shared with some non-Muslims:

> I was speaking one day amongst a group of people, and a party of non-Muslims was present. In the middle of my address they began to weep and to register emotion and ecstasy.
>
> Someone asked: What do they understand and what do they know? Only one Muslim in thousand understands this kind of talk. What did they understand that they should weep?
>
> The Master answered: It is not necessary that they should understand the inner meaning of these words. The root of the matter is the words themselves, and that they do understand. After all, every one acknowledges the Oneness of God, that He is Creator and Provider, that He controls everything, that to Him all things shall return, and that it is He who punishes and forgives. When anyone hears these words, which are a description and commemoration of God, a universal commotion and passion supervenes, since out of these words comes the scent of their Beloved and their Quest.

Since the knowledge of God is present in all human beings—that is, in all religions!—words speaking of God kindle love and ecstasy through the scent which is in them, although their mystical inner meaning may not be intellectually grasped. Scent and sound in themselves convey a deeper truth and release feelings of commotion among those who understand and among those who are just "touched." Rūmī goes on to explain that there are many ways to reach the Kaʿba. Many different ones: from Syria, from Persia, from China, from India, from Yemen. The variety of the roads is stupendous. So pilgrims travel many and diverse roads. But when they arrive at the Kaʿba, they are all united in the same feelings of sanctity and love. So one should avoid stressing the differences of the paths and rather rejoice in the communion of the goal:

> When believer and infidel (*muʾmin* and *kāfir*) sit together and say nothing by way of expression, they are one and the same. There is no sequestration of thoughts, the heart is a free world. For the thoughts are subtle things, and cannot be judged. . . . Thoughts, then, so long as they are in the heart, are without name and token; they cannot be judged either for unbelief or for Islam. . . . There is a world of bodies, a world of ideas, a world of fantasies, a world of suppositions. God most High is beyond all worlds, neither within them nor without them.[19]

Thus Rūmī arrives at the conclusion that silent communion between Muslims and adherents of other religions is real communion in God, God's true essence being beyond all words and ideas, "neither within those words nor beyond them"—entirely different. In that silence, in the silence of apophatic infiniteness, there is no more any "perception of other religions," as all religions are found to be only ways to God who is none of these ways. So all ways are legitimate, perhaps even necessary, but the target is beyond the ways, it is silent abstraction in the ineffable ONE.

In one of his poems Rūmī expresses the same reality in the language of intoxication with love:

> What is to be done, O Moslems? for I do not recognize myself.
> I am neither Christian, nor Jew, nor Gabr, nor Moslem.
> I am not of the East, nor of the West, nor of the land, nor of the sea . . .
> My place is the Placeless, my trace is the Traceless:
> 'Tis neither body nor soul, for I belong to the soul of the Beloved . . .
> I am intoxicated with Love's cup, the two worlds have passed out of my ken . . .
> O Shamsi Tabriz, I am so drunken in this world,
> That except of drunkenness and revelry I have no tale to tell.[20]

But this is only one side of the story. Even if it is true, according to Rūmī, that in the drunkenness of divine Love or in the total silence beyond thoughts and concepts, that is in the ineffable essence of God, all religions vanish and do no more have any pertinency. Islam is nevertheless the only path which Rūmī would accept as truly willed by God. The following incident makes this clear.

Once a Christian told Rūmī that a number of disciples of a certain shaykh had drunk wine with him, the Christian, and that the shaykh had said: "Jesus is God, as you assert. We confess that to be the truth; but we conceal and deny it, intending thereby to preserve the Community." Rūmī became angry and engaged with the Christian in a theological discussion, using arguments of shrewd Islamic theology. Finally, the Christian justified himself by saying that he had inherited his religion from his father and his ancestors. Thereupon Rūmī invited the Christian to change his religion:

> You inherited from your father a paralyzed hand; and you found a physic and a physician to mend that paralyzed hand. You do not accept, saying, "I found my hand so, paralyzed, and I desire not to change it." Or you found saline water on a farm wherein your father died and you were brought up, then you were directed to another farm whose water is sweet, whose herbs are wholesome, whose people are healthy; you do not desire to move to that other farm and drink the sweet water that would rid you of all your diseases and ailments. No; you say "We found that farm with its saline water bequeathing ailments, and we hold on to what we found." God forbid! That is not the action or the words of an intelligent man possessed of sound senses.[21]

Christianity is here perceived as a sick and crippled body or as a farm with bitter, unhealthy water which brings only diseases and death. An intelligent man would quickly abandon ailments and bitter, deadly water, as soon as better living conditions would be offered. And such conditions are in fact offered:

> Inasmuch as God has sent a prophet superior to Jesus, manifesting by his hand all that he manifested by Jesus' hand and more, it behooves him to follow that Prophet, for God's sake, not for the sake of the Prophet himself.[22]

Transcendent Union in God, beyond all words and worlds, is one thing. But hard facts of the world are another thing, and in daily life it is the latter that prevail. In talking with Christians, the superiority or the uniqueness of Islam has to be maintained. We are reminded of the story of Muḥammad ibn Yaʿqūb and the two monks in whose company he walked in the desert: the monks enjoyed perfect union with God, but the hard facts of the world require, such was the conviction of the Sufis, a firm grounding in the truths of Islam.

A sad case of total disregard of another religion by a Sufi occurred in India, in 1384. Its questionable hero was a great shaykh of the Suhrawardīya, Makhdūm Jahāniān, a Sayyid:

> A Hindu, Nawahun, a revenue official, visited the shaykh Makhdūm Jahāniān on his death-bed and while praying for his recovery stated that the sick man, a Sayyid, was the seal of the saints, just as the Prophet Muhammad was the seal of the prophets. Disregarding the fact that in a previous discourse he had expressed the theory that the formal recitation of the *kalima* did not make the speaker a Muslim, the Sayyid concluded that Nawahun's statement amounted to a protestation of faith. As the Hindu was not willing to accept Islam, he fled to Delhi and sought refuge with the Sultan of whom he was a favorite . . .

But at the instigation of the dying shaykh, his brother intrigued at the court of the Sultan, and Nawahun was put to death on the charge of apostasy.[23] The Hindu understood apparently his friend's, the Muslim's, faith very well, but such was not the case with the Sayyid-shaykh. The Sufi's unrelenting Islam announces the memorable invectives of Simnānī and Shāh Walī Allāh against Hinduism.

Ibn ʿArabī

Given Ibn ʿArabī's (1165–1240) role in the history of Sufi thought and practice, and given also the celebrity of some of his statements, it is necessary to present his stance in a special chapter.

Some verses from the Diwan *Tarjumān al-ʿashwāq* are well known and are quoted in any treatise on the attitude of Islam towards other religions:

> (13) My heart has become capable of every form: it is a pasture for the gazelles and a convent for Christian monks,
> (14) And a temple for idols and the pilgrim's Kaʿba and the tables of the Tora and the book of the Koran.
> (15) I follow the religion of Love: whatever Love's camels take, that is my religion and my faith.[24]

Is this poetry the expression of generous perception of other religions—animism, Christianity, Judaism, and others—and of appreciative knowledge about them? There are reasons for serious doubt.

The verses must be approached from two sides. First, they must be read in the light of the whole body of the poem of which they are the conclusion. Second, they must be interpreted in the light of Ibn ʿArabī's own commentary.

First, the verses must be understood as a sort of positive formulation of Rūmī's negative description of intoxication with Love. Drunk with Love, Rūmī is neither a Christian, nor a Jew, nor a Muslim. Drunk with Love, Ibn ʿArabī is all of that: Christian, Jew, Muslim, Zoroastrian. Love-drunkenness wipes out all distinctions. And total abandonment to the "religion of Love" (*adīnu bi-dīn al-ḥubb*) does the same. These celebrated verses are indeed the conclusion of a heartrending poem on Love. Ibn ʿArabī has become the victim of hopeless Love and he is unable to bear the strain. That is at least what he says:

> (3) I respond to her, at eve and morn, with the plaintive cry of a longing man and the moan of an impassionate lover.

Ibn ʿArabī sighs under the tyranny of Love. His love is overwhelming, totally absorbing. There is no more room for anything else. His heart, deprived of a clear line of thought and action, falls prey to any image, to any thought, to any religion: "My heart has become a pasture-ground for gazelles, a temple for idols and whatever you like. . . . Because my religion is Love and nothing else." Thus these verses are anything but the expression of a genuinely sympathetic perception and appreciation of other religions.

Second, in his own commentary to the verses under discussion, Ibn ʿArabī reminds us that in Arabic the heart is called *qalb* because it is constantly exposed to *taqallub*, to "fluctuation" and change. The heart "fluctuates" on account of changing "inrushes" (*wāridāt*) and "states" (*aḥwāl*), and these in turn fluctuate following the modifications of "divine manifestations" or "self-disclosures" (*tajalliyāt ilāhīya*) which are granted to the "innermost consciousness," the "secret" (*sirr*) of the heart. The divine disclosures are the driving factor; they release inrushes and psychic states which manifest themselves in the heart which is constantly changing. Thus, the heart which is the place of divine self-disclosures cannot but become everything the divine self-disclosure wants it to become.

If we try to interpret this brief commentary in the light of Ibn ʿArabī's theological system, we must start from the central structure of that system: the divine Names. According to our author, the divine Names—which are innumerable—must be understood as "relations and polarizations" (*nisab* and *ʾiḍāfāt*) which determine the true unchanging essences of things (*aʿyān thābita*) in their relation to God, or rather within God. These unchanging essences (the essence of each thing being contained in a certain Name of God) manifest themselves in images and forms (*ṣuwar*) which are subject to constant change in accordance with the variations of divine self-disclosure. Beliefs and religious practices are part of these images and forms. All beliefs are forms of the divine essences—that is, expressions of divine Names. Ibn ʿArabī indeed insists in many places that every belief (*muʿtaqad, iʿtiqād*) is true and unquestionable because it is determined by a divine Name. The various religions are nothing but images and forms of divine self-disclosure.

In the poem under discussion, the place of divine self-disclosure, its *maẓhar*, is, according to the author's own commentary, the "innermost consciousness" (*sirr*) of the heart. It is for this reason that the heart can become filled with any self-disclosure of God, be it a non-Islamic one or Islam. Again, we come to the conclusion that our verses attest in no way a benevolent perception of other religions. With Ibn ʿArabī the apparent acceptance of all religions is not the result of sympathetic observation, knowledge and approval of foreign creeds but it is a statement a priori, an element of the fundamental structure of his theological system.

Each thing in the universe is at its right place, and so is every religion, a manifestation of a divine Name.

That does not mean that everything has equal value. Ibn ʿArabī insists time and again that the phenomena are ranking in value and dignity (*tafāḍul*), that certain things are better than others and that there is a hierarchy of manifestations and productions. Consequently there is a hierarchy, *tafāḍul*, of Revelations and religions, the Prophet Muḥammad and Islam ranking of course at the top. Says he:

> All the revealed religions are lights. Among these religions, the revealed religion of Muḥammad is like the light of the sun among the lights of the stars. When the sun appears, the lights of the stars are hidden, and their lights are included in the light of the sun. Their being hidden is like the abrogation of the other revealed religions that takes place through Muḥammad's revealed religion.[25]

There is an unresolved tension in Ibn ʿArabī's thought. As manifestations of divine Names, all religions have a right to exist and to be practiced. But they are included in and overwhelmed by Islam, and so they are in fact abrogated. Their existence is a very precarious one, at once lawful and in contradiction with the true and final Law of God. We shall see that our author draws harsh conclusions from this very ambiguous judgment.

In the final chapter of the *Fuṣūṣ al-ḥikam*, the most condensed presentation of his thought, Ibn ʿArabī restates the matter in the form of a commentary on the well-known saying of al-Junaid: "The color of the water is the same as that of its container." The container is the "inherent predisposition" (*istiʿdād*) of the believer which is "colored" according to the self-disclosure of a particular Name and the "permanent essence" (*ʿain thābita*) which is his transcendent mode of being. The colored container is thus a "form" or "image" (*ṣūra*) of God. But the color of the container, understood as a form of God, colors the "water"—that is, the believer's image of God. In accordance with the particular self-disclosure and its image, the believer's image of God might be animist, Jewish, Christian, Zoroastrian, or Islamic. This image conditions the modes of adoration and the rules of religious practice, so that the worshipper worships only the God of his "inherent predisposition" which is an image of God. This coloring is subject to fluctuation (*taqallub*), so that the heart (*qalb*) is not sure to worship always the same divine image.

The ranking of religions according to lower or higher dignity has, with Ibn ʿArabī, very important practical consequences. Our author is an undisturbed Muslim—his "inherent predisposition" allows him in fact no other stance, and that notwithstanding the "fluctuation" which, overcome with love, he is talking about in the *Tarjumān*.

So when discussing Ibn ʿArabī's perception of other religions, we should not forget the letter he sent to Kaikāʾūs I, Sultan of Konia, in which he urged the addressee to stick strictly to the *dhimmī* laws, especially with regard to Christians.[26]

Ibn ʿArabī thought that this letter was important enough to be included in the last chapter of his *Futūḥāt* as one of the directives with which he concluded his *magnum opus*. It is to be regretted that William C. Chittick, one of the most knowledgeable specialists of Ibn ʿArabī's theology and spiritual practice, does not even mention this text in his recent study of our author's theories about the origins of religious diversity, *Imaginal Worlds*.[27] Owing to this omission, the picture that emerges from Chittick's otherwise very penetrating observations is rather one-sided.

After having forcefully reminded the sultan of his religious duties and impressed on him the necessity to apply with vigor all the rules of Islamic social life, the writer deplores the fact that Islamic existence is marred by the sound of church bells, the manifestations of Christian *kufr*, the proclamation of Christian polytheism and the nonrespect of laws concerning *dhimmī*s. He commands the sultan to reinforce those laws and not to allow the Christians to ring their bells, to build churches, monasteries, or hermitages, be it in the town or in the neighborhood, nor to repair churches and other buildings threatened with decay. Neither could Christians be allowed to talk to Muslims about their "polytheism." On the other hand, they ought to be obliged to entertain Muslims during three days in their churches. The purpose of this seems clear: in the course of time, Christianity must be strangled or at least be forced underground.

Even if it may be conceded that Ibn ʿArabī is simply asking the Sultan to apply *Sharīʿa* laws, this letter is proof that its author was not in the least prone to acquire true knowledge about Christianity nor to recommend universal tolerance. His position as a legal *ẓāhirī* and as a theologian who never forgot to stress the absolute complementarity of "outer" and "inner" aspects of Islam precluded every attempt in the direction of sympathy for other religions. His remarks about the relative value of all beliefs are nothing but the theoretical implications of his fundamental theological options. It is the tragedy of his faithfulness toward Islam that he was unable to work out different practical consequences of his spiritual insight.

Ibn Sabʿīn

In contrast to Ibn ʿArabī who propounds a theology of divine manifestations (*tajalliyāt*), Ibn Sabʿīn (1216/7–1270) is, within the broad stream of Sufi thought and practice, the leading representative of absolute monism.[28] In his writings, the exclamation "God alone!" (*Allāhu faqaṭ!*) is an ever-recurring refrain. God alone *is*, He alone, the ONE in His uniqueness, and everything else is but the product of imagination and a mental construct (*wahm*). Nevertheless, this uncompromising monist also defends the necessity of true Revelation, in particular of the Revelation which was accorded to Muhammad. In the *Risālat anwār al-Nabī* (Badawi, pp. 201–211), he embarks on a most enthusiastic description of the "lights" that distinguish the Prophet. Already his birth announced the downfall of foreign religions: cosmic cataclysms surrounded the event; moreover, the sacred fire of the Zoroastrians was quenched and the palace of the Persian Emperor torn asunder, whereas the idols of the Hindus trembled (p. 206). After having adduced numerous proofs for the outstanding and incomparable greatness of Muhammad, Ibn Sabʿīn exhorts the Jews and the Christians to acknowledge this compelling evidence for Muhammad's uniqueness (p. 210).

In another context, though, he admits that ancient religions prepared the way for the ultimate Revelation granted to Muhammad, explaining that all religions are but paths leading up to Islam:

> None of the outstanding qualities of this our religion has been heard of as accorded to more ancient religions, and nothing of the sort has been reported about them. The sciences of ancient religions have traced the ways toward our religion. As to their distant and near-by causes, including all the sciences of the nations, the sects and the religions, time and divine providence have handed them over to them. (p. 292)

There is, then, a positive link between God and all religions, but solely as announcements of the full Revelation to come. In his great study of the glories and wonders of making memory of God (*dhikr*): *Risālat al-naṣīha wa-ʾl-nūriyya* (Badawī, pp. 151–189), Ibn Sabʿīn exploits this idea in several passages and in various ways. Stating that God has "tied" the practice of *dhikr* to all religions, he expounds this point by quoting in turn, "one of the books that are descended from heaven," Christian monks, and the author of *Dalālat al-ḥāʾirīn* (The guide of the perplexed)—that is, Moses Maimonides (1135–1204), and "a Rabbi" (p. 157). Later, he mentions Hindus, Black people, Christians, and astrologers (p. 161), and again, examining the symbolism of light, he offers comments about philosophers, Zoroastrians, Brahmins, Jews, and Christians. Overviews of this kind where various religions are alluded to in a certain order are rather typical of this treatise on *dhikr*.

Although it seems, then, that our monist had some knowledge of non-Islamic religions, nothing is farther from the truth. It is true that Ibn Sabʿīn quotes some evidence, but such evidence is mostly apocryphal or even fanciful. It is nothing more than what was certainly current talk among Muslims about religions other than Islam. Take, for instance, what he says about the religious practice, that is the *dhikr*, of Black people:

> When the Black people want to take on a beautiful appearance, they write the names of God on their faces, the names which they have inherited from their forebears. Here they are altogether: "Yāshī, Fāshī, Yāryārjik, Shaʿshaʾ," which means "all enemies flee before the one who makes memory (*dhikr*) of God. The anger of God becomes powerful and shall not be overcome." (p. 161)

His information about the *dhikr* of the Hindus does not strike the reader with greater plausibility, although it betrays some acquaintance with Hindu theology, especially with the problem of the relationship between God and the "soul" or the "Self" (*ātman*):

> When the Hindus decide to build a temple, they must recite the names which I shall quote, and place them on the site of the building: "*Wāhin*, Idol of eternity, *Awḥadān*, *Harshān*, *Awraḥsān*," which means: "O Thou because of whom the obedient one has burnt his skin and is heading towards some of his creatures! Grant us your favor by a breath from you which circulates in us and decides about the states of our spirits! O Thou, Origin of everything that has origin! O idol of its meaning by whom things exist and who by his being is in everything!" (p. 161)

Our author mentions several times the Hindu priestly caste, the Brahmins:

> Whenever light is mentioned among them, the Brahmins prostrate themselves immediately. They utter words whose meaning would be, after "In the Name of God the Merciful, the All-Merciful, and may God pray over our Master and Teacher Muhammad and his family": "You! You! You! You are exalted, Lord of Lords!" (p. 187)

If the religions of India are not, for Ibn Sabʿīn, the object of much research, he can speak with more authority about the Zoroastrians. He mentions them only once, but he is aware of the essence of their theology: "They apply the symbol of light to God and to pure Goodness" (p. 187).

As to Ibn Sabʿīn's information about the Jews, we have already mentioned the remarkable fact that he quotes the author of *Dalālat al-ḥāʾirīn*, that is, Maimonides, whom he has perhaps read. However, the statement which purports to be authored by this Jewish authority is rather astonishing: "God has revealed His Wisdom on Tuesday to Moses, and His Word on Thursday" (p. 157). I appeal to specialists in Maimonidean studies to trace this saying to Maimonides' work. Ibn Sabʿīn is aware of the existence of the Jews' "Ten Words":

> Concerning the *dhikr* of God, the most exalted thing which comes from the Jews is this: the Ten Words whose contents do not contradict the meaning of the *Verse of the Throne* (Qurʾān 2: 255), nor the conclusion of the Sūrat al-Hašr (S. 59) concerning disagreements among them. (p. 182)

In contrast, he is not very far from the target when he interprets the symbolism of light in the Jewish Scriptures: "With the Jews, the light is, whenever it is mentioned in the Torah, the World of angels, the Presence of God and His attributes" (p. 187). He is also fond of stories about Rabbis:

> A Rabbi was told to adore his Master. He said: "That is the very thing I have done just now!" Later on, he was given the same order. He replied: "I have done that just now!" People wondered: "How is that possible? You are a liar!" The Rabbi explained: "I make memory of Him. He behaves with me in such a way that it is possible for me to attain under all circumstances the state of making memory of Him!" (p. 157)

Christianity is a religion which Ibn Sabʿīn mentions rather often in his treatise on *dhikr*. The reader cannot escape the impression that in his time, stories about monks, very popular in the early stages of Sufi piety, were still handed on in Sufi circles:

> A monk cried out for help. Somebody wanted to know why. He said: "I have been practicing *dhikr*, but time and again I have stopped uttering the formula, being unable to do it without interruption. But negligence in pronouncing the Name of God entails frightful separation from God (*ḥurma*), so I suffer from being excluded (*maḥrūm*) from communion with God. Now I take refuge in God from what happened today." (p. 157)

> Somebody asked a monk: "Do you observe fasting?" He replied: "My fast is nothing else but making memory of God. As soon as I make memory of something else, I am breaking the fast." (p. 159)

This "permanent *dhikr*" ascribed to the monks betrays perhaps some knowledge of the Christian "prayer in the heart," often practiced by the monks, a prayer which aims at permanent invocation of the Name of Jesus. Some information about that practice may also transpire in one of the "quotations" from the Gospels with which Ibn Sabʿīn props up his theory of universal *dhikr*: "In the Gospel it is said: The breath of the believer is the place of *dhikr*, and the place of *dhikr* is my Presence" (p. 165). This saying reminds one of the well-known use of respiration in the practice of the prayer of Jesus in the heart. That prayer, the specific invocation of the Name of Jesus developed by Christian monks, can indeed be thought of as a kind of *dhikr*: "The Gospel says: There is no good in a servant who does not make memory (*dhikr*) of me!" (p. 164).

If these "quotations" can hardly be discovered in the Gospels (at any rate not in the canonical ones), some other items reveal more adequate information about Christianity. Take this exhortation which God is said to have addressed to Jesus: "O Jesus, make memory of me as a child makes memory of his father!" (p. 164). Here, the Christian message of the fatherhood of God seems to be echoed. Moreover, while describing the religion of the companions of Christ as "*dhikr*, traveling, living a lonely life, fasting, paying attention to divine voices, to associations and divine illuminations" (p. 165), our author adds: "this is nowadays the habit (the *sunna*) of the monks." He also has some vague knowledge about Christ's last supper and the Christian eucharist:

> In the Gospel is found the praise of John, and the Word of Christ which he said in the night. The gist of what was understood is summed up in some words which I am going to quote. I only hint at them, without suggesting that the one who utters them can benefit from them . . .

What follows is a long range of letters which are totally unintelligible although they are supposedly a reflection of the Syriac liturgy (and although, according to our author, Abū Ṭālib al-Makkī offers somewhere a similar list). Fearing perhaps that an obscure formula like the one he has given might be used for magical purposes, Ibn Sabʿīn opines:

> The best attitude in these matters is, I think, to be wary of what one hears from Jews and Christians, as we are taught in our tradition. An exception might be allowed for pious men (*rijāl*) who transmit things about other pious men and their experiences (*aḥwāl*). (p. 182) [That seems to mean: if there exists a kind of Jewish and Christian science of *ḥadīth*.]

Our author is of course aware of the fact that most Christians are governed by the Pope. But he has strange things to say about the *dhikr* of that man whom he describes as a kind of adept of Pentecostalism:

> As to the Christians, their Pope has not his position assured as long as he does not make memory of his Lord, first in human language, then in divine language (i.e., speaking in tongues?). The Pope makes memory of the Lord in his human language until he becomes absent in God (*ghaiba*). Then he employs divine language until he is overcome with something like madness. He makes memory of God by mentioning Persons, which is an attribute of God. (p. 161ff)

"Persons" (*uqnūmiyya*) as an attribute of God is of course a correct reminiscence of Christian trinitarian theology, quite surprising as a statement coming from a Muslim. But there is only one other passage where Ibn Sabʿīn offers some more detailed information about Christian theology:

> With the Christians, the light is used as metonymy for the Godhead, and most particularly for Jesus. He is the light which God has sent down on earth [we are reminded of the Gospel of St. John, ch. 1, v. 4–13]. He [God] is one in substance and diverse in speech and shape. The contrary is true when His much honoured appearance manifests itself [i.e., perhaps: the incarnate Jesus is one in speech and shape, but diverse—God and man—in substance?]. One can say in a general way that there are five schools of Christian theology (*madhhab*), the outstanding among them being close to philosophy. All of them talk about the light and magnify it. Others besides these five are worth nothing and to talk about them serves neither the learned nor the Muslims. (p. 187)

In this passage Ibn Sabʿīn indeed betrays some concrete knowledge of Christianity, although it is not easy to identify his "five schools" of Christian theology.

Our author, founder of a Sufi school of thought, is interesting in that he allows some glimpses of the views educated Muslims of his time entertained about religions outside the fold of Islam. He is also quite praiseworthy in that he tried to illustrate the themes of "light" and *dhikr* with examples from other religious traditions, but he has never made an effort to understand those traditions properly and to offer an interpretation which would give them more than the status of provisional and queer arrangements, destined to be abandoned in favor of Islam. In his mind, religions are nothing more than bizarre fantasies, although they are in some mysterious way related to God.

We may add that an unknown disciple of his, commenting on the Agreement (*ʿahd*) the master made with his followers (p. 43f; commentary pp. 45–129), develops a brilliant demonstration to the effect that religions are but "mental constructs" (*wahm*) or "quaint conceits" (*nukat*) whose function it is to lead people on the way to God, away from vanity. The final purpose is, of course, experience of the one God, beyond even the construct of the religion of Islam (compare p. 117ff). For outside the absolute unity of the one God, everything is but the product of imagination.

A Friend of Hinduism: Dārā Shukūh

Dārā Shukūh (1615–1659) can be deemed the very opposite of the Sufi theologians Ibn ʿArabī and Ibn Sabʿīn, although he accepts many of the former's theological ideas. These ideas had come down to him through men like Rūmī and several Indo-Persian Sufi authors. Dārā, a learned and rather advanced Sufi of the Qādiriyya order, carried Akbar's, his great-grandfather's, interest for other religions to its logical conclusions. Whereas Akbar intended to create his own *dīn ilāhī*, his great-grandson Dārā upheld the Sufi tradition but tried to penetrate as deeply as possible into the secrets of Hindu religious lore.

The outcome of his efforts is a most fascinating booklet: *Majmaʿ al-baḥrain*, the "Confluent of the two rivers": Islam and *kufr*, that is, Hinduism. It is possible that the title has been chosen in remembrance of the *samgama* of Hindu religious life, the point of meeting of two sacred rivers which is a most holy and hallowed place. The outstanding example is Prayāg, near modern Allahabad, where the ultra-sacred Gangā and Yamunā unite. *Majmaʿ al-baḥrain*, the confluent of two sacred religious rivers, is thus a very holy phenomenon.[29]

Right at the beginning of his work, Dārā quotes the verses of the poet Sanāʾī which we have already met with, but in a slightly different wording:

> *Kufr* and Islam are running on the way towards Him,
> Shouting: He alone! He has no companion!

"He alone!" One is reminded of Ibn Sabʿīn's *Allāhu faqaṭ!*

Dārā then states his intention. Having mastered the Sufi tradition, he "thirsted to know the tenets of the religion of the Indian monotheists." He considers indeed the Indian sages whom he had known well for having lived among them, as *muwaḥḥidān*, "people who proclaim and practice the Unity of God"; as *muḥaqqiqān*, "people who realize the Truth/God"; and as *kāmilān*, "perfect ones." Above all, he asserts that they have attained the aims of *taṣawwuf*. They are accomplished Sufis. So Dārā informs the reader that he has kept companionship with them, employing the hallowed Sufi term for true religious fellowship: *ṣuḥba*. He is clearly inclined to receive the Hindu sages into the Sufi fold.

Having mastered the tenets of Hinduism, Dārā arrives at the conclusion that *Kufr*—Hinduism—and Islam are identical. After much thinking, and thanks to his own experience of the highest Truth, he is able to declare that he "did not find any difference, except verbal, in the way in which they sought and comprehended Truth (*ḥaqq*)."

Dārā has not the slightest desire to abandon Islam and to follow the tradition of his Hindu friends. Rather than adapting the Sufi tradition to Hinduism, he would prefer to retrieve Hinduism for Islam. His little work is indeed a very impressive attempt to understand thoroughly the Hindu theistic tradition and worldview, in order to wipe out every trace of difference with Islam.

It is not possible to analyze here in detail the contents of the 22 chapters in which the author tries to equate Hindu and Sufi concepts.[30] It would of course be easy to raise serious criticisms. But that would be a futile enterprise which does not do justice to the author's achievements. It should rather be noted that—among other things— Dārā's explanations throw much light on his own understanding of Islamic and Sufi thought and practice. We take one example: chapter 7 where he equates the Hindu notion of the four *avasthā* or states of consciousness (of the *ātman*), first propounded in the *Māṇḍūkya-Upanishad*, with the Islamic and Sufi concept of the four "worlds." The state of waking, *jāgrat*, is equated with the "world of men," *nāsūt*; the state of "dream," *svapna*, is equated with the "world of dreams and spirits," *malakūt*; the state of "dreamless sleep," *sušupti*, stands for "the world where I and you vanish along with the perception of two worlds," *jabarūt*; whereas the "fourth" state, *turya*, is equated with "pure essence," *dhāt-i-maḥḍ*. It is to be remembered that already in the Upanishad the four states of consciousness appear as four kinds or layers of worlds. But we can see that Dārā has tried to understand the four "worlds" of Islamic lore as four states of consciousness—an interpretation which has some antecedents in the Sufi tradition but which, to my knowledge, Dārā is the first to develop systematically. Many similar perspectives, often surprising ones, open up in this pioneering work.

Conclusion

Islamic early "pietists" and ascetics took to the habit of putting questions to Christian monks in order to gain higher insight into the mysteries of a truly religious way of life. At the end of our rapid survey we find Dārā adopting a similar procedure with regard to Hindu sages: he too was aware of the feasibility of meeting consecrated people from other religions.

But inbetween—early curiosity having been satisfied and final new inquiry not yet found helpful—we have discovered very different attitudes. We are led to the conclusion that very few in number are the Sufis who sincerely tried to "perceive," to "apprehend," and sympathetically to understand other religions. Most of them were hardly bothered about them and did not care to encounter their adherents and their beliefs in a friendly and constructive way. Their point of view was at the outset and to the end conditioned by their Islamic convictions—and we cannot blame them for that. To them, Islam was absolutely sufficient. If they talked about religions other than Islam, they seldom reached a stage beyond the reproduction of popular rumors or even gossip.

It may be, however, that there were unnamed Sufis who, like Dārā Shukūh, lived on such a high—or profound—level of experience of the One Truth that they were able to meet as their equals seekers after Ultimate Reality who followed non-Islamic ways. But, unfortunately, we are not aware of them. For experience of Ultimate Truth ends often in silence, as Jalāl al-Dīn Rūmī once reminded his disciples, and nothing can be heard about silent union in the ineffable ONE.

NOTES

1. Margaret Smith, *Studies in Early Mysticism* (London, 1931). Reprints: Amsterdam, 1973, and London, 1976 (with new title: *The Way of the Mystics*).

2. Tor Andrae, *Islamische Mystiker* (Stockholm: Bonnier, 1947) (German translation, Stuttgart, 1960).

3. Abū Nuʿaim al-Isbahānī, *Ḥilyat al-ʾawliyāʾ*, vol. 2, 356, 10ff.

4. *Ḥilya* vol. 10, p. 288, ll. 18ff.

5. *Ḥilya* vol. 9, p. 356, ll. 10ff.

6. Compare for instance *Ḥilya* vol. 9, pp. 383, 5ff; 367, 9ff.

7. Al-Ašʿarī, *Maqālāt al-islāmiyyīn*, 2nd ed., ed. Hellmut Ritter (Wiesbaden, 1963), p. 367, 9ff.

8. Max Horten, *Indische Strömungen in der islamischen Mystik* (Heidelberg, 1927).

9. R. C. Zaehner, *Hindu and Muslim Mysticism* (London, 1960), pp. 86–109.

10. Abū Naṣr al-Sarrāj, *Kitāb al-lumaʿ fī al-taṣawwuf*, ed. Nicholson, p.177; ed. ʿAbd al-Ḥalīm, p. 235.

11. Compare Paul Nwyia, *Trois oeuvres inédites de mystiques musulmans* (Beyrouth, 1973), pp. 11–22.

12. Compare *Nwyia* (n. 10), pp. 26–275.

13. L. Massignon, *La passion d'al-Ḥallāj* (Paris, 1922), pp. 92f.

14. Mohammad Ebn Monawwar, *Les étapes mystiques du shaykh Abū Saʿīd*, trans. Mohammad Achena (Paris, 1974), p. 111.

15. Ibid., p. 215.

16. *Kitāb fīhi mā fīhi*, ed. Furūzānfār (Teheran, 1952). I quote from the English translation by A. J. Arberry, *Discourses of Rūmī* (London, 1961).

17. Ibid., pp. 214f. Persian text p. 206 (ch. 56).

18. Ibid., pp. 168f. Text p. 160 (ch. 43).

19. Ibid., pp. 108f. Text pp. 97f (ch. 23).

20. R. A. Nicholson, *Selected Poems from Divani Shamsi Tabriz* (Cambridge, 1898; repr. 1952), no. 21, pp. 124ff.

21. Arberry, *Discourses of Rūmī*, pp. 134f. Text pp. 124f (ch. 29).

22. Ibid., p. 136. Text pp. 125 (ch. 29).

23. Sayid Athar Abbas Rizvi, *A History of Sufism in India*, New (Delhi, 1975), vol. 1, pp. 279f; Khaliq Ahmad Nizami, *Some Aspects of Religion and Politics in India during the Thirteenth Century* (Delhi, 1961, 1974), p. 179.

24. R. A. Nicholson: *The Tarjumān al-ʿashwāq*, (1911) 1978, pp. 19 and 67f. Arabic Text: Beyrouth, 1961, pp. 43f. Quoted: verses 13–15 of the poem no. XI.

25. Ibn ʿArabī, *Al-Fūtuḥāt al-makkiyya*, vol. 3, p. 153. Translation of the quotation by William C. Chittick, *Imaginal Worlds: Ibn al-ʿArabī and the Problem of Religious Diversity* (Albany, NY: State University of New York Press, 1994), p. 125.

26. *Futūḥāt*, vol. 4, p. 547; also *Muḥāḍarāt*, vol. 2, pp. 260f. Claude Addas, *Ibn ʿArabī ou La quête du Soufre Rouge* (Paris, 1989), pp. 278ff.

27. William C. Chittick, *Imaginal Worlds: Ibn al-ʿArabī and the Problem of Religious Diversity* (Albany: State University of New York Press, 1994).

28. My references in the text are to the edition of the *rasāʾil* by Abdarrahmān Badawī, *Rasāʾil Ibn Sabʿīn* (Cairo, 1965). About Ibn Sabʿīn, compare the introduction and the notes to Michel Chodkiewicz's translation of Awḥad al-dīn Balyānī's *Epître sur l'Unité Absolue* (Paris, 1982). I am indebted to a member of the symposium to have suggested the inclusion of Ibn Sabʿīn in my study.

29. Edition, translation, and commentary by Mahfuz-ul-Haq, *Majmaʿ-ul-baḥrain* (Calcutta, 1929; 1982). Dārā's quotation of Sanāʾī (*Ḥadīqat al-Haqīqa*, 60) is on page 79. See also the study of both the Hindu and the Islamic concepts adduced by Dārā, by Daryush Shayegan, *Hindouisme et soufisme* (Paris, 1979).

30. Compare Shayegan, *Hindouisme et soufisme*.

11

Philosophical Schools as Viewed by Some Medieval Muslim Authors

Doctrines and Classifications

CHARLES GENEQUAND

In *al-Munqidh min al-ḍalāl* al-Ghazālī (450–505/1058–1111) relates how he set about studying philosophy (*falsafa*) and the dissatisfaction he felt about what had been said on the subject by his predecessors: "So far as I could see, none of the doctors of Islam had devoted thought and attention to philosophy. In their writings, none of the theologians engaged in polemic against the philosophers, apart from obscure and scattered utterances so plainly erroneous and inconsistent that no person of ordinary intelligence would be likely to be deceived, far less one versed in the sciences."[1] He then proceeded to make his own study of the subject and discovered that there are three main philosophical sects (*madhāhib*):

1. The *dahriyyūn* or *zanādiqa* is the earliest school. They deny God and assert the eternity of the world.
2. The *tabīʿiyyūn*, having seen the wonders of nature, acknowledge a wise Creator, but they also ascribe a major influence to the equal balance of the temperaments (*mizāj*) on the intellectual constitution of man, so much so that when the body dissolves, the soul also ceases to exist. Thus they deny the last day and must accordingly be reckoned as *zanādiqa* as well.
3. The *ilāhiyyūn*, the latest group (*mutaʾakhkhirūn*), includes Socrates, Plato, Aristotle, al-Fārābī, and Ibn Sīnā. They must also be reckoned as unbelievers, although some of their doctrines are true.

Al-Ghazālī then goes on to describe the main branches of philosophy: logic, physics, and metaphysics.

It is clear that this classification, which purports to be objective, is wrong from both the historical and the doctrinal points of view. Such purely materialistic or naturalistic schools have never existed. Aristotle, placed in the third category, upheld theories belonging to the first (eternity of the world) and to the second (the four elements or four primary qualities as basic constituents of matter and animal bodies), and so on. Although al-Ghazālī's presentation and criticism of philosophical ideas in his *Tahāfut al-falāsifa* goes much deeper than anything done before or since in Islam, he still cannot escape from certain traditional forms inherited from the very *mutakallimūn* he criticizes. I shall return to al-Ghazālī later, but in the first place I will examine some of the characteristics of these surveys of philosophical schools which we encounter in the Arabic theological and historical literature of the Middle Ages.

Doctrines

al-Māturīdī

The first author to be considered is al-Māturīdī (d. 333/944), Ḥanafī jurist and founder of a school of *kalām*. In his *Kitāb al-Tawḥīd*, he mentions the *dahriyya* in several places, with a more or less systematic exposition and refutation of their views on pages 141–152. Unlike most authors, he identifies them with the Naturalists (*aṣḥāb al-ṭabāʾiʿ*): all agree that the matter of the world is eternal, but are at variance as to whether the creation (*ṣanʿa*) itself is eternal or not.

The natures are four: hot and cold, moist and dry. The diversity (*ikhtilāf*) of the world depends on their different mixtures; it has always been as it is now, without beginning.[2] They compare the natures to the colors (white, red, black, green): by being mixed in different proportions they give rise to all colors without there being creation of color (*ḥādith lawn*).[3] But this view, replies al-Māturīdī, actually corroborates what the *ahl al-tawḥīd* say, for colors do not mix spontaneously, or when they do, they produce ugly colors; it is only when a wise and skilled (*ḥakīm ʿalīm*) being, knowing the consequences of what he does, mixes them that the mixture results in something beautiful. As the world is well fashioned, it is clear that it was made by a skilled and wise being who knew the consequences of things and produced them accordingly. This shows the error of those who say that matter, or the natures, or whatever, became what it is spontaneously. He who produced them was wise and caused them to arise from nothing (*lā min shayʾ*).

Another argument against the natures runs as follows: these natures are opposites, and opposites are mutually repellent and destructive; therefore they cannot coexist unless there is an agent who compels them (*qāhir*), and this implies beginning in time (*ḥudūth*). It is more rational to admit creation from nothing than the coexistence of opposites.[4]

This is followed by a short refutation of the belief in astrology and by a reference to the rebuttal of the doctrine of the eternity of the heavenly motions at the beginning of the treatise.[5]

Al-Māturīdī then adds a further argument against the theory of the natures; we can observe that motion produces heat, not the reverse; therefore, the natures are not primary, but result from what happens in the world, and the world cannot be generated (*mutawallid*) by them.[6]

Another group among the *dahriyya* claims that the matter of the world is eternal, without length, breadth or depth, without weight or surface, color, taste or smell, neither soft nor rough, neither hot, nor cold nor moist—in short, totally undifferentiated. A power present in it transformed it by nature, not by choice. The accidents (*aʿrad*) came into being and then the essence of the world. Separation (*iftirāq*) and conjunction (*ittifāq*) result from the accidents, and these cannot be defined in terms of separation and conjunction. The accident inheres in the essence which becomes different or similar through it.[7] But if this power were in matter and had this effect (of uniting and separating its parts), how is it that it did not have it in the preeternity (*qidam*)? Either the accidents were already in matter, or they were created from nothing.

The next philosophical school examined by al-Māturīdī is that of the Sophists (*al-Sūfisṭāʾiyya*). Their doctrine is this: we found that man knows something, and then that thing disappears; enjoys something, and then this pleasure vanishes. Bats see by night, but are blinded by daylight. It follows from this that no knowledge is true, that there are merely beliefs and that some peoples' beliefs differ from those of others.[8]

This was refuted by Ibn Shabīb[9] as follows: this doctrine of yours that there is no knowledge—either you affirm it according to a knowledge (*bi-ʿilm*) and therefore you affirm its existence, or you affirm it without knowledge and therefore you cannot affirm it. One cannot argue with these people since their speech is merely belief, not knowledge, and that whatever somebody says is this (i.e., belief). One can argue with somebody who denies realities by disproving his claim, but somebody who says, "There is only belief" can only be refuted by saying to him: "I believe your denial to be an affirmation" so as to compel him to assert what he was denying.[10]

Another argument of the Sophists is as follows: our senses deceive us. If somebody sees double because of a squint, he believes that there are actually two objects, but somebody else sees only one. Who is right? If he who sees two objects shuts one eye, he sees only one object, which shows that it was merely an illusion of the senses.[11] Also, the man suffering from hepatitis finds honey bitter, but it is possible to account for this phenomenon on medical grounds.[12] We dream impossible things, for example, that we are dead, and we believe it as long as we are asleep. The reply of al-Māturīdī to that is that sleep is a kind of disease (*āfa*) of the senses.[13]

In conclusion, al-Māturīdī summarizes these two chapters by saying that nature, the stars, and foodstuffs are incapable by themselves of producing or necessitating any of the physical phenomena. His position amounts to a denial of natural causality, or of what will be later called secondary causes, a thesis defended at great length by al-Ghazālī in his *Tahāfut*.

Ibn al-Jawzī

The second author whose presentation of philosophical schools I propose to examine is the famous Ḥanbalī jurist and historian Ibn al-Jawzī (510–597/1126–1200). Although his *Talbīs Iblīs* is primarily designed as a general onslaught against all Islamic trends other than his own strict ḥanbalī obedience, it also contains sections on non-Muslim religions and philosophies. He begins with the Sophists: they derive their name from a man called Sūfisṭā [*sic*]. Their doctrine is that there is no truth (*ḥaqīqa*). What we deem remote may be near, but small, and vice versa. This view may be refuted by asking them, "Is what you assert true or not? If you say: 'it is not true,' you give it up implicitly." Al-Nawbakhtī[14] says that it is useless to argue with people who claim not to know whether or not one is talking to them, whether or not they exist. Their denial of sensible realities may be illustrated by the story of the man whose son squinted: he saw two moons in the sky and was convinced that there actually were two moons, until his father told him to shut one eye, and then the son realized that the defect was in his eyesight. The absurdity of this doctrine is further demonstrated by two anecdotes.

Ṣāliḥ b. ʿAbd al-Quddūs was distressed because his son had died before he himself had completed his book *On Doubts* (*al-Shukūk*), in which he proved that what is can be thought of as not being and what is not as being, and his son had died before he could read that book. Whereupon al-Naẓẓām retorted that all Ṣāliḥ had to do was to think of his son as still alive and having read *al-Shukūk*.

A Sophist, upholder of the same doctrine, had a discussion with a *mutakallim* during which the latter arranged for the Sophist's mount to be whisked away. When he wanted to depart, the Sophist began to shout that his mount had been stolen, to which his interlocutor replied, "how can you affirm that you came on a mount if nothing has any reality and if waking is the same as sleeping?"[15]

A variant of this doctrine consists in saying that there is not one truth, but truth is for each people or group (*qawm*) what they believe. The man who suffers from hepatitis finds that honey tastes bitter. The world is eternal for those who believe it to be eternal.[16]

A third group of Sophists say the world is in a state of permanent flux (*dhawb wa sayalān*); one cannot think twice the same thought because everything changes continually.[17]

Ibn al-Jawzī then goes on to deal with the *dahriyyūn*: they hold that there is no God or Creator (*ṣāniʿ*). Things came to be without producer or maker (*mukawwin*). To counter this doctrine Ibn al-Jawzī again uses a concrete analogy: if somebody walking past a certain place sees that it is empty, and later on sees there a building, he concludes from this that there is a builder. Likewise this world, this sky, and so on prove the existence of a Creator. Ibn al-Jawzī also adduces teleological arguments—for example, that canine teeth are made to cut and molars to grind, that fingers can fold and seize things. All these facts bear witness to the existence of the Creator who created everything ex *nihilo* (*lā min shayʾ*), whereas the *dahriyyūn* say that matter is uncreated.[18]

The Naturalists (*al-Ṭabāʾiʿyyūn*) constitute for Ibn al-Jawzī a distinct category. They say that all created things are the work of nature (*fiʿl al-tabīʿa*); everything is created by the conjunction of the four active natures. Ibn al-Jawzī objects saying that the natures do exist but are not active, or efficient (*fāʿila*); their conjunction and mixing (*imtizāj*) is contrary to their natures, which shows that they do it under compulsion (*maqhūra*). The naturalists granted that the natures are neither knowing (*ʿālima*) nor powerful (*qādira*); but regular and ordered action like theirs can only be produced by a knowing and wise being (*ʿālim ḥakīm*).

That nature is not efficient by itself is further shown by the fact that the same natural phenomenon may have different effects. In the spring the sun causes the fruits to become moist and corn dry. Likewise, corn does not fall from its stem but the individual fruits do. Watering causes some flowers to become white and others red.[19]

On the Falāsifa

After a section on the Dualists to which I shall return later, Ibn al-Jawzī broaches the topic of the philosophers proper (*falāsifa*). Their error is to trust in reason alone and to discard prophecy. Some of them share the ideas of the Dahrites (i.e., they deny the Creator). Aristotle held that each star is a world like ours complete with rivers, trees, and other facts of nature. The world is eternal, and its cause is eternal as well. Socrates' philosophy rests on three principles: an efficient cause, matter, and form. The cause is God or, according to others, intelligence or nature.[20] Finally, Ibn al-Jawzī reports on the authority of al-Nihāwandī[21]: the strange views of three sects, presumably gnostic but difficult to identify with precision, according to which God created the world but then ceased to exist (*maʿdūm*). To sum up, the *falāsifa* have made important discoveries in mathematics, logic, and physics, but they contradicted themselves in questions of theology, in particular on the three points on which al-Ghazālī taxed them with *kufr* and which are adopted at this point.[22]

The opinions of those who believed in the eternity of the world and denied the possibility of creation from nothing are examined and refuted by al-Māturīdī at the beginning of his treatise. The same problem is taken up later in a chapter of a more doxographical nature which distinguishes different sects (*firaq*) among the upholders of this doctrine.[23] Having observed that the objects of sense-perception change from one state to another and are engendered from one another, and since furthermore creation from nothing cannot be *observed*, they concluded that the world has always been as it is (*fī ʾl-azal*). But they are divided into several groups:

1. The partisans of the natures (*aṣḥāb al-ṭabāʾiʿ*) who think that the differences in the physical world arise from the fact that the natures are mixed in different proportions so as to form all kinds of things in the same way as the basic colors can produce all shades and varieties of colors by being mixed together in different proportions. Thus the essence of man is dependent on the balance of the natures (*iʿtidāl al-ṭabāʾiʿ*).
2. Others think that the root (*aṣl*) of the world is composed of the four natures, but each essence has a root and the four natures belong to those.[24]
3. Others admit only one such root which is the cause of the world[25] and argue for the existence of a Creator (*ṣāniʿ*) who organized (*ittisāq*) and united (*ittifāq*) things on the grounds that the order of the world necessitates a knowing organizer (*mudabbir ʿalīm*) and nature is incapable of that. On this view, both the Creator and the world are eternal (*azal*).
4. Others consider that the Creator (*bāriʾ*)[26] produced the world from preexisting matter (*ṭīna*).
5. Another category derives the world's existence from the motions of the stars and the sun and their influence on matter (*hayūlā*).[27]
6. Finally there are those who posit two principles, light and darkness.

On the Dualists

Both al-Māturīdī and Ibn al-Jawzī included in their surveys of philosophical sects sections concerning the Dualists, a procedure which tends to show that they regarded them as a school of philosophy rather than as a religion (or religions).[28] This is further confirmed by the manner in which these sects are presented. I do not intend to analyze these pages in detail, as this has already been excellently done by several scholars.[29] My purpose here is not to extract new data concerning these sects from the refutations of their Muslim opponents, but to define the latter's position toward philosophical schools and ideas.

Al-Māturīdī returns once more to the topic of the dualists immediately after his section on the Sophists examined previously. This last discussion, together with that of the Zoroastrians (*Majūs*), concludes the non-Muslim part of his treatise, and the author then goes on to the demonstration of the prophecy (*risāla*) and to the specific problems of Muslim *kalām*.[30]

The Dualists are divided according to a very common scheme into the three branches of the Manichaeans (*Manāniyya*), Bardesanites (*Dayṣāniyya*), and Marcionites (*Marqiyūniyya*).[31] Not only do the Dualists with their mistaken doctrine of the two gods or two principles (good and evil; light and darkness) provide a transition between the philosophers who deny the existence of God, or at any rate deprive Him of any meaningful role in their systems, and true monotheism; they also constitute a kind of mirror image of the Naturalists. These, as we have seen, identified by al-Māturīdī with the *dahriyya*, considered matter to have existed eternally in an undifferentiated state until its parts began to separate and form individual composite entities. In other words, it was one and then became diverse (*tafarraqa*). On the contrary, according to the well-known cosmological myth of the Manichaeans and other Gnostics, the two opposite principles were separated in the preeternity, and our world was formed by their blending (*kānā mutabāyinayn fa-ʾmtazajā*).[32] The reason al-Māturīdī deals with the Dualists in several places is that his perspective is not historical, but follows the order of the "questions" (*masāʾil*).[33] Insofar as they believe in the eternity of the world, they are refuted in the chapter concerned with that specific question; from another point of view, however, they are related to the Naturalists. The short section devoted to them by Ibn al-Jawzī takes place between the Naturalists and the philosophers and does not call for special comment.

Principles of Classification

These classifications of philosophical schools or sects, although quite different in their details, are nonetheless clearly built on the same principles. The main divisions, as well as the stock examples and the main counterarguments reappear with striking regularity; the manner in which they are worked out and the ends which they are made to serve are different, however. The lengthy rebuttal of the *Aṣḥāb al-Ṭabāʾiʿ* by al-Māturīdī, for instance, makes clear allusions to some theories put forward by people like Ḍirār b. ʿAmr or al-Naẓẓām. But these people, like al-Māturīdī himself, believed in nature(s) as instrument of God, not as autonomous or secondary causes. It is questionable whether the kind of materialistic theory attacked by al-Māturīdī was ever seriously considered in the Islamic world.[34] Rather, it seems as if a preexisting frame with conventional subdivisions (Sophists, Materialists, Naturalists, Dualists, etc.)—that is, all doctrines conflicting with some aspects of Islam or monotheism in general—had been more or less arbitrarily filled with contents drawn from different doxographical sources. It is significant that we find in these texts distinct echoes of pre-Socratic theories mingled with very common medical notions and not very easily identifiable Muʿtazili speculation. The personalities of the different authors also come through: al-Māturīdī is a *mutakallim* who pursues very arduous arguments in purely abstract terms, whereas Ibn al-Jawzī who was in his day an extremely successful *khaṭīb* illustrates his demonstration with lively and concrete anecdotes. But on the whole, one may agree with al-Ghazālī and share his disappointment: if we had to rely exclusively on these texts for our knowledge of philosophical and theological thought, we should not be much enlightened.

If we now turn back to al-Ghazālī, it will be noticed that the Sophists are missing in his enumeration of the philosophical schools, but appear in another guise in the preceding chapter in which the author relates how he himself went through a stage of complete skepticism from which he was only saved by a direct divine intervention. In other words, the classification of the schools has become here an element of the author's life, which casts doubt on the reliability of the supposed "autobiography." But this is another matter.

The Greek Heritage: al-Yaʿqūbī

Why then did the *mutakallimūn* accept a scheme whose relevance and topicality are far from obvious? The answer must lie at least partly in the fact that this classification was inherited in one way or another from late antiquity. It already occurs in a passage of the historian al-Yaʿqūbī (about 870) with all the characteristics which we find in the later authorities. According to his text the kings of the Greeks and the Romans professed different doctrines:

1. The Sabaeans, also called *ḥanīf*, recognize the existence of a creator and claim to have prophets of their own: Urānī,[35] Abīdīmūn,[36] and Hermes (thrice-great). God is the cause of causes (*ʿillat al-ʿilal*); he created the world.
2. The disciples of Zeno who are the Sophists, a name that means "those who mislead" or "those who contradict each other." They observed that philosophers contradict and oppose each other and that every one of them claims to possess the truth, which must be one, whereas error is manifold. From this, they concluded that truth does not exist. Another of their arguments runs as follows. It is not enough to know; one must also know that one knows.[37] But then one must know that one knows that one knows and so on ad infinitum, which implies that one will never have definite knowledge. Alternatively, there is an end in something that is known—that is, ignorance—which also entails lack of knowledge, for how could anything be known through something which is not known?
3. The *dahriyya* deny religion, the existence of God and of the prophets, holy books, resurrection, and reward or punishment after death. Everything is without beginning and without end (hence their name). Coming to be (*ḥudūth*) is merely composition (*tarkīb*) after separation (*iftirāq*), and perishing is separation after conjunction.
4. An unnamed group combine a mythical cosmogony with a skeptical epistemology. The world sprang from a grain which split up and from which all sensible realities arose. But these things are not really differentiated; they merely appear to be different to different persons. This is why people suffering from hepatitis find honey bitter, bats see by night but not by daylight, a large object seen from afar appears small, and so on.
5. One group says that all things arose from four eternal roots (*uṣūl*)—hot, cold, moist, and dry—which produce everything without reflection or will. Alternatively, these four elementary principles are governed (*yudabbiru-hā*) by a fifth according to its will and wisdom: it is knowledge (*ʿilm*).

There follows a short paragraph on Aristotle mentioning principally the doctrine of the categories and of the four elements.[38]

Al-Yaʿqūbī ascribes these doctrines expressly to the ancient Greeks and Romans, not to contemporary *mutakallimūn or falāsifa.* That his claim is substantially correct is shown by the fact that the ideas, examples, and arguments he quotes have precise parallels in Greek sources,[39] and also by the purely doxographical character of his text, exempt of refutation or criticism. It seems thus that this classification was taken over by the *mutakallimūn* who found in it a convenient framework for their own presentation and refutation of doctrines they disapproved of. The properly critical element is an addition of the Muslim authors. This later stage in the development of the Muslims' reflection on non-Muslim religious and philosophical sects is best illustrated in the works of the two most famous Arab heresiographers, Ibn Ḥazm and al-Shahrastānī.

Ibn Ḥazm

At the beginning of his *kitāb al-Fiṣal*, Ibn Ḥazm declares that there are six groups opposed to Islam which he arranged according to their remoteness from the true religion:

1. Those who deny realities (the objective reality of things, *al-ḥaqāʾiq*), the Sophists.
2. Those who recognize the *ḥaqāʾiq* but assert that the world is eternal and has no creator (*muḥdith*) or organizer (*mudabbir*).
3. Those who recognize realities and assert that the world is eternal, but that it has an eternal organizer.
4. Those who recognize the *ḥaqāʾiq*, some of them saying that the world is eternal, others that it had a beginning in time, but all agreeing that it has more than one *mudabbir*, though they are at variance as to their number.
5. Those who say that the world had a beginning in time and one eternal Creator, but deny prophecy.
6. Those who profess the same ideas as 5) but accept some prophets and refuse others (clearly the Jews and the Christians).[40]

al-Shahrastānī

The culmination of this rational system of the philosophical sects is found in al-Shahrastānī at the beginning of the second part of his *Kitāb al-Milal wa-ʾl-Niḥal.* The exact classification, *al-taqsīm al-ḍābiṭ*, according to him, is as follows:

1. Those who acknowledge neither sensible nor intelligible realities; they are the Sophists.
2. Those who acknowledge sensible, but not intelligible realities; they are the Naturalists.
3. Those who acknowledge both sensible and intelligible realities but neither rules nor laws (*ḥudūd wa aḥkām*); they are the *Dahriyyūn.*
4. Those who acknowledge sensible and intelligible realities, rules, and laws, but neither *sharīʿa* nor Islam; they are the Sabaeans with their prophets Hermes and Adhīmūn.
5. Those who acknowledge the same as (4) plus a *sharīʿa* and a submission (*islām*); but not the *sharīʿa* of our prophet Muhammad; they are the Magians, the Jews, and the Christians.
6. Those who acknowledge all this—that is, the Muslims.[41]

This theoretical and so to speak mathematical classification of the sects remains without any practical effect on the actual practice of al-Shahrastānī. In what follows, he presents, as is well-known, a considerable amount of fascinating material on philosophers and philosophical schools, both Greek and Arab, in a roughly chronological order, but the scheme set forth at the beginning is altogether forgotten. We find there the juxtaposition of two distinct strands of the Muslim mind: a purely *pragmatic* approach which is content to hoard up items of knowledge without much regard for their practical value or their relation to Islam, and a *theoretical* attitude which evaluates everything and assigns it its proper place from the standpoint of Islam. In the second case, we have an almost pre-Hegelian system of all possible (if not actual) philosophical and religious systems leading up to the accomplishment of Islam in which all else is eventually absorbed.

NOTES

1. *Munqidh* 18; transl. Watt 29.
2. *Tawḥīd* 141.
3. Frank (*Notes and Remarks* 146 and n. 46) suggests to emend *ḥādith* in *ḥadath*, but the emendation is unnecessary and the passage had in any case been misunderstood by Frank who did not realize that colors are a mere analogy (*ḍarabū mathalan*). Cf. also *Tawḥīd* 112:3.
4. *Tawḥīd* 143.
5. Ibid., 143–144.
6. Ibid., 145.
7. Ibid., 147.
8. Ibid., 153.
9. Muḥammad b. Shabīb, Muʿtazilite author of a *K. al-Tawḥīd*, quoted more than once by al-Māturīdī; see Ibn al-Murtaḍā, *Ṭabaqāt al-Muʿtazila* 71.

10. *Tawḥīd* 153.

11. Ibid., 154.

12. Ibid.; the medical explanation which follows is also borrowed from Ibn Shabīb.

13. *Tawḥīd* 156.

14. Abū Muḥammad al-Ḥasan b. Mūsā al-Nawbakhtī. His lost *K. al-Arāʾ wa-ʾl-Diyānāt* appears to be Ibn al-Jawzī's main source in this passage.

15. *Talbīs* 39–40; on Ṣāliḥ b. ʿAbd al-Quddūs, see Ibn al-Murtaḍā, *Ṭabaqāt* 46–47 with the same anecdote; he was a Dualist.

16. *Talbīs* 41.

17. Ibid.; an interesting variation on Heraclitus's famous saying (fr. 91), on the authority of al-Nawbakhtī.

18. *Talbīs* 41–2.

19. Ibid., 43.

20. Ibid., 45–46.

21. Yaḥyā b. Bashīr b. ʿAmīr (or: ʿUmayr) al-Nihāwandī seems to be completely unknown. Ibn al-Jawzī says that he copied this passage from a manuscript in the Niẓāmiyya in Baghdad which had been written 220 years previously; this provides a *terminus ante quem* about 960 for al-Nihāwandī.

22. *Talbīs* 47.

23. *Tawḥīd* 11 ff.; 110 ff.

24. The meaning of this sentence is unclear.

25. Perhaps this alludes to philosophers like Thales or Anaximenes who posited one of four elements as the principle of the world.

26. No semantic distinction seems to be intended between the terms *bāriʾ* and *ṣāniʿ* in this passage.

27. Again, the terms *hayūlā* and *ṭīna* seem to be used indifferently.

28. Al-Māturīdī says explicitly that Dualism is a subdivision of the *dahriyya* (*Tawḥīd* 121:5).

29. G. Vajda and G. Monnot (see bibliography).

30. *Tawḥīd* 176 ff.

31. Ibid., 157, 163, 171. See also Van Ess, *Theologie und Gesellschaft*, pp. 416–456.

32. *Tawḥīd* 113:2.

33. See on this D. Sourdel, *La classification.*

34. For the difficulties attending a precise identification of the *Aṣḥāb al-Ṭabāʾiʿ*, see M. Bernand, *La critique.* The closest parallels are found in medical texts and in the Jabirian corpus; see P. Kraus, *Jābir*, vol. 2, pp. 98, 165 n. 7.

35. This name remains so far unexplained.

36. I.e., the Greek Agathodaimôn.

37. Literally "one knows by a knowledge" (*bi-ʿilm*); the same expression occurs in al-Māturīdī 153:12.

38. Al-Yaʿqūbī, *Taʾrīkh* 166–171.

39. The stock-example of honey tasting bitter to people suffering from hepatitis is found in Sextus Empiricus, *Outlines of Pyrrhoism*, vol. 1, p. 101.

40. Ibn Ḥazm, *K. al-Fiṣal*, vol. 1, p. 3.

41. Al-Shahrastānī, *Milal*, vol. 2, pp. 3–5.

BIBLIOGRAPHY

Arabic Texts

al-Ghazālī. *al-Munqidh min al-Ḍalāl*, ed. F. Jabr. Beirut, 1959. English trans. see Watt.

Ibn Ḥazm. *Kitāb al-Fiṣal fi-ʾl-Milal wa-ʾl-Ahwāʾ wa-ʾl-Niḥal*, 5 vols. n.d., n.p.

Ibn al-Jawzī. *Talbīs Iblīs*. Beirut, n.d.

Ibn al-Murtaḍā. *Kitāb Ṭabaqāt al-Muʿtazila*, ed. S. Diwald-Wilzer. Bibliotheca Islamica 21. Wiesbaden, 1961.

al-Māturīdī. *Kitāb al-Ṭawḥīd*, ed. F. Kholeif. Recherches publiées par l'Université Saint-Joseph, Pensée arabe et islamique, 50. Beirut, 1982.

al-Shahrastānī. *al-Milal wa-ʾl-Niḥal*, ed. M. S. Kīlānī, 2 vols. Beirut, 1975.

al-Yaʿqūbī. *Taʾrīkh*, ed. M. Th. Houtsma, 2 vols. Leiden, 1883.

Books and Articles

Bernand, M. "La critique de la notion de nature dans le Kalām." *Studia Islamica* 51 (1980): 59–105.

Frank, R. M. "Notes and remarks on the *ṭabāʾiʿ* in the teaching of al-Māturīdī." *Mémoires d'Islamologie dédiés à la mémoire d'Armand Abel*, ed. P. Salmon. Leiden, 1974, pp. 137–149.

Kraus, P. *Jābir ibn Ḥayyān: Contribution à l'histoire des idées scientifiques dans l'Islam*, 2 vols. Mémoires de I'Institut d'Egypte 44–45 (Le Caire 1942–1943).

Monnot, G. "Māturīdī et le manichéisme." *Mélanges de l'Institut Dominicain d'Etudes Orientales au Caire* 13 (1977): 39–66 = *Islam et Religions*. Paris, 1986, pp. 129–156.

Sourdel, D. "La classification des sectes islamiques dans le *Kitāb al-Milal* d'al-Shahrastānī." *Studia Islamica* 31 (1970): 239–247.

Vajda, G. "Le témoignage d'al-Māturīdī sur la doctrine des Manichéens, des Daysanites et des Marcionites." *Arabica* 13 (1966): 1–38 and 113–128 = *Etudes de Théologie et de Philosophie arabo-islamique*, vol. 14. (London, 1986).

van Ess, J. *Theologie und Gesellschaft im 2. und 3. Jahrhundert Hidschras*, vol. 1. Berlin, 1990.

Watt, W. M. *The Faith and Practice of al-Ghazālī*. London, 1953.

12

Zoroastrianism as Viewed in Medieval Islamic Sources

J. CHRISTOPH BÜRGEL

Some Glimpses from History

Islamic Times

In Arabic sources, the adherents of Zoroastrianism are called Madjūs, from Old Persian Magush, Akkadian Magushu, Greek Magos, originally meaning a priestly caste. At the end of the Sasanid period, Zoroastrians were to be found as administrators, landlords, and soldiers in non-Persian parts of the Sasanid Empire such as al-ʿIṛāq, Bahrayn, ʿUmān, and Yaman.[1]

The Lakhmids, an Arabic dynasty in Syria and Iraq playing the role of a buffer state between Iran and Byzantium, were culturally influenced by, and politically dependent on, Sasanian Iran.

Typical features of Zoroastrianism at the beginning of Islam were fire cults, animal sacrifices, consanguineous marriage, and ritual purity achieved by ablution with water or bull's urine.

Morony remarks on Sasanian society: "An élitist social ethic, honoring establishmentarian virtues, provided ideological justification for the hierarchic society of the Madjūs. High values were placed on order, stability, legality and harmony among the functionally-determined divisions of society (priests, soldiers, bureaucrats, and workers, or else priests, soldiers, farmers, and artisans) so each would perform its specific duty towards the others."[2]

Reflections in the Qurʾān

The only mention of the Madjūs in the Qurʾān is to be found in Sura 22:17: "Surely they that believe, and those of Jewry, the Sabaeans, the Christians, the Magians and the idolators—God shall distinguish between them on the Day of Resurrection; assuredly God is witness over everything."[3]

Arberry's translation as quoted here does not take into consideration a detail of the phrase structure—the second relative pronoun before *ashrakū*; there is a clear caesura between "they that believe" with the following specification and "they that commit idolatry." According to this verse, the Madjūs clearly belong to the believers, as do the Christians, the Jews, and the Sabaeans. However, as Morony remarks, "it was eventually decided in Muslim theory that the Madjūs were intermediate between the *ahl al-kitāb* and *mushrikūn*, since they had no real prophet or revealed scripture."

As for Mazdean influences in the Qurʾān, a comprehensive study is still lacking. A few points may be mentioned here, however. As shown by Père Jean de Menasce, the names of the two angels, who, according to a dark passage in the Qurʾān (2:102), taught men sorcery, Hārūt and Mārūt, stem from Pahlevi Haurvatat and Ameretat "integrity" and "immortality." This would mean that the original significance of these names had been perverted into their opposite, when Muhammad inserted them into the Qur'ān.[4] Parallels between Zoroastrian and Qur'ānic conceptions have also been noticed—for example, the idea that God was not tired after the six days of creation (Qur'ān 50:38) is to be found in the Avesta.[5] Furthermore, the role of the sea and sea images might be due to Persian mariners (who would have been Zoroastrians at the time in question), according to a recent study.[6] Even the strong emphasis on light and darkness in the Qur'ān suggests Zoroastrian influence.

Later Times

Whereas in the beginning, the Madjūs in Iran kept their fire temples and suffered little interference in their cult, they nevertheless gradually lost power and influence.[7] Very often, members of the Sasanid establishment became converts in order to keep their property and position, and children were taken captive and raised as Muslims. Persecutions happened time and again, for example, already under Ziyād ibn Abihi, who was governor of Iraq in the years 662–675.

Impoverishment led to tolerance and emphasis on spiritual values. On the other hand, social problems could also lead to violent religion-based reactions: "A series of risings by Zoroastrian peasants provoked by fiscal oppression in Eastern Iran in the 2d/8th century served as the occasion for the emergence of new antinomian, anti-establishment Zoroastrian sects" (Morony, p. 1111a).

"What remained of the old religious literature was collected and preserved" in the early ninth century. "A new didactic, apologetic and polemic literature was produced" in the second half of the 3rd/9th c. "The testimony of Muslim geographers indicates that Madjūs were still widespread and fairly numerous in Iran and the east as late as the 4th/10th c" (all three: Morony, p. 1112a).

After the tenth century, the history of the Zoroastrians is little known. Among the main features is the emigration of large groups to India, whereas Yazd and Kirman continue being the main centers in Iran. A new heyday was reached in the sixteenth century. The estimated number of Zoroastrians in Iran at the beginning of the eighteenth century was between 100,000 and one million. Then, however, rapid decay ensued: "Their numbers declined disastrously through the combined effect of massacre, forced conversion and emigration" (Morony, p. 1115a).

Still, several thousand Zoroastrians survived, and their numbers increased in the decades before the Khumaini revolution to about 25,000 by the seventies (Morony, p. 1116b).

Meanwhile, due to the mutual influences in the course of so many centuries, Persian Zoroastrianism and Islam show a number of common features.

Mazdeans in Muslim Theology

In Muslim theological treatises, Zoroastrians are dealt with under the heading of Dualists (*thanawīya*) along with the adherents of Bardesanes, Marcion, Mani, and Mazdak. Sometimes the dualism of light and darkness is mentioned; among the problems discussed is the question whether or not they are created or eternal, whether they are living beings, and so on.

The outstanding theologian al-Māturīdī (d. 944) reports an alleged Zoroastrian doctrine about God's covenant with Iblīs and criticizes it:

> The Magians say that God admired the beauty of his creation and did not want that anything should be opposed to it. So he formed a thought from which sprang Iblīs. According to certain Magians God was struck by the eye of Iblīs, so he turned around and beheld him. God made peace with Iblīs, and gave him a delay on the condition that after that he would make him perish. Every evil comes from Iblīs, every good from God.

This doctrine, even though it sounds very similar to the Islamic ideas about Iblīs as outlined in the Qur'ān, is severely criticized by Māturīdī, who says that either this God must have been unknowing of what would come from Iblīs or he must wittingly have let him wreak evil, both of which are incompatible with God's nature. So the Magians, instead of seeing in God the agent of both good and evil, made him the origin of evil.[8]

Ash-Shahrastānī (d. 1153), the author of a well-known history of religions praised for its objectivity, ascribes the covenant between God and Iblīs (Ahriman) to the Zurvānīya.[9]

According to Shahrastānī, the Madjūs fall into three groups—the Kāyumarthīya, the Zurvānīya, and the Zardushtīya. The Dualists are treated by him in a separate chapter. The common feature of the three groups of Madjūs is their belief in the existence of the two principles of light and darkness, but they differ as to their origin. One of their common beliefs is that the evil originated from a thought or a doubt of God who is either Yazdān or Zurvān, whereas the evil spirit is called Ahriman.

Shahrastānī makes no negative remarks about, nor launches any attacks against, the doctrines of Zoroaster: that is, that the world consists of and persists through the intermingling of the two principles of light and darkness, and that the struggle will not cease until the end of time and history. In the doctrine of Zoroaster as sketched by Shahrastānī, God is One and the originator of both light and darkness. So this representation provides no evidence for anathematizing the Madjūs or calling them heretics.

As a last example, let me refer to passages in a work by the famous Ismāʿīlī propagandist al-Muʾayyad from Shīrāz (d. 1077), who is considered to be among the greatest thinkers of Islam. Speaking of the Zoroastrians, he compares the veneration of fire with the Muslim veneration of the Kaʿba and makes the point that both fire and Kaʿba are symbols for the light of guidance, but that the Zoroastrians, as well as the Muslims of later days retained only the symbol without the reality it represents.[10]

Zoroastrianism in Works of Historians and Philologists

Al-Djāhiz, the great bel-esprit of the ninth century and a caustic commentator on his society, speaks very contemptuously of the Magians, but his argument is not very convincing. Zoroaster, says Djāhiz, threatened his opponents with a punishment of snow and cold. From this it clearly emerges that he was only sent to the people of that mountainous region in Afghanistan and Northern Iran where he made his appearance. It is true, he continues, that the Zoroastrians could use the same argument against Muhammad by saying that his punishment was fire because of the great heat of Arabia. But this, Djāhiz says, would not only be wrong but absurd, since the desert is hot only in summer, whereas in winter it is very cold. The obvious fact that Iran and Afghanistan are also warm in summer is passed over in silence by Djāhiz.[11] Furthermore, he emphasizes that Zoroaster's success was due only to the great corruption of the people to whom he had been sent. Had they been on a higher level of culture and civilization, he would not have succeeded. In the words of Djāhiz: "Had he not happened to appear in an epoch that was at the peak of corruption, and in a nation that was so remote from noble conduct, sense of honour and solidarity, from care for cleanliness, his affair would have failed."[12]

Moreover, Djahiz rejects the idea that Zoroaster started his career by persuading the king. He must rather have succeeded in winning over the troops who then forced the king to introduce the new religion. For kings never engage in any activity that could shake the foundations of their rule, except on the basis of a true prophetic mission.

> So it has to be considered that that time was the corruptest of all times and that people the worst of all peoples. This is why there has never been seen any adherent of any religion converting from his religion to Zoroastrianism. Furthermore this doctrine is spread only in Fars, Media, and Khorasan, which are all Persian. (Pellat, p. 269)

At this point, Djāhiz makes a remarkable reservation: The reader should not take this negative judgment to include every later Zoroastrian born into this religion. It does not include Khusraw Parvez, his friends, his physicians, his scribes, his sages and knights, whose intelligence Djāhiz will not question. The intellectual capacities of nations, Djāhiz states, is normally higher than the level of their religious beliefs.

> We know that the intelligence of the Greeks is above the belief of the materialists and the cult of stars and zodiacal signs, the intelligence of the Indians surpasses the obedience to Buddha and their idolatry, and the intelligence of the Arabs exceeds their cult of idols, carved pieces of wood, erected stones and chiselled blocks. (Pellat, p. 270)

The text sounds almost subversive!

A much more positive picture is presented by the great historian al-Masʿūdī (d. 956), who describes Zoroaster as the prophet of the Madjūs, who performed miracles and had the ability of foreseeing future events, both general and specific.[13] Zoroaster composed a tome in 12,000 volumes which contains promise and threat, prescriptions and prohibitions, laws and rituals. No one has been able to imitate it. The kings lived in accordance with this work until the time of Alexander who destroyed part of it. Zoroaster's book is entitled *Avesta*. He also wrote a commentary on his book, entitled *Zand*, and a commentary on the commentary, entitled *Bāzand*. Later scholars wrote a commentary on the secondary commentary which they designated *Yarda*.[14] Given that no one can possibly memorize the tome, it was either divided into four or seven parts. Zoroaster's mission lasted 35 years, his successor was the wise Djāmasp, who was the first Mobad.[15]

At another point in his work, al-Masʿūdī explains the origin of the term *zandīq*, meaning heretic, which dates back to Zoroastrian history and the rise of Manicheism. Zoroaster received the revelation of the Avesta, which was later explained by the commentary called *Zand*. Now, everyone who added something opposed to the revealed book was called a *zandīq*,[16] an etymology which has recently been confirmed by H. H. Schaeder and later scholars and is now generally accepted.[17]

Another interesting passage to be found in the historian al-Maqdisī's work *al-Bad' wat-Ta'rīkh* (vol. 1, p. 62) reads as follows:

> Persians call the Creator Hormoz, but also Izad or Yazdān. They pretend that the adoration of the fire reconciles them with the Creator, because it is the most powerful and sublime of the elements. The polytheists explained their adoration of idols in the same manner: "We only serve them that they may bring us nigh in the nearness to God" (Qur'ān 3:39). And this is indeed the only attitude possible for one adoring anything besides God. For he knows well that what he adores of wood or of stone or of brass or of gold or any other substance is not his Creator who has made him nor the One who decrees his existence and decides its states.
>
> Once, I entered a fire-temple in Khūz, a very old district town in Persia, and asked them (the Magians) about what is written about the Creator in their book. They showed me some leaves affirming that it was the *Avesta*, i.e. the Book brought by Zoroaster, and they read for me in their language and explained to me what they understood from the Persian text.

Monnot who quotes this passage in one of his articles, underscores the openmindedness manifested in it.[18]

A similar neutral view is presented by the eminent scholar al-Bīrūnī (d. after 1050), one of the most independent and ingenious spirits of the Islamic middle ages.[19] According to his *Chronology of Ancient Nations*, a book dealing with territories, calendar systems, and annual feasts in various cultures and religions, the Persians before Zoroaster were also called Madjūs, but these Madjūs were in fact the Sabaeans, who are mentioned in the Qur'ān and who are now known as Harrānians because they have their center in the town of Harrān. The rest of al-Bīrūnī's information is mainly about the feasts of the Zoroastrians and their handling of the problem of leap year.[20]

The negative view of al-Djāhiz reappears in the work of another historian of the tenth century, ath-Thaʿālibī, author of a fine anthology of Arabic poetry, and a valuable history of the pre-Islamic Persian kings, *al-Ghurar fī Siyar Mulūk al-ʿAdjam*. This author relates a number of compromising details from Zoroaster's life: He was a disciple of the prophet Jeremiah, whom, however, he betrayed by falsifying his words. Jeremiah punished him with a curse, which made him fall ill with leprosy. Zoroaster went to Adharbaidjān and succeeded in persuading King Vishtasp that he was a prophet. It was by the help of this king that he rose to power and influence, for the king forced his people, who had been adherents of the star-adoring Sabaean cult, to adopt the new religion, and he killed those who resisted. Thaʿālibī states that in his doctrines and ethical prescriptions there are many errors, but in his ensuing description he not only avoids any further deprecatory remarks but also leaves the impression that the Zoroastrian doctrines and prescriptions are in fact very similar to those of Islam. After 35 years of his pretended prophetic activity, Zoroaster was killed at the age of 77, whereupon Vishtasp killed not only his murderer but thousands of other people whom he suspected of fostering sympathy for the assassin.[21] Traces of this attitude are to be found in later sources.

Zoroastrianism in Literary Sources

The Thousand and One Nights

A completely negative picture of the Magians is offered in the "Tale of the Oldest Lady," the First of the Three Ladies of Baghdad, in the *Thousand and One Nights*. Here, the hero comes to an eerie town peopled by statues of black stone. Finally, he meets one living being, the prince, who explains the enigma to his perplexed visitor. The inhabitants of the town "were all Magians, worshipping fire in the place of God." The prince, however, had been happy enough to be brought up by a Muslim woman, "believing in God and his apostle, though she conformed with my family in outward observances." Notwithstanding a triple warning by a Heavenly voice to "abstain from the worship of fire and worship the Almighty God," they "persisted in their evil ways, until, drawing down upon themselves the abhorrence and indignation of Heaven, one morning, shortly after daybreak, they were converted into black stones, together with their beasts and all their cattle. Not one of the inhabitants of the city escaped excepting me."[22] Another totally negative Zoroastrian is the Persian alchemist in the story of Hasan the Jeweller of Basra.[23]

Firdawsī and Nizāmī

Coming now to Persian poetry, let us first glance at Firdawsī's *Shāhnāmeh*. In this national epos, comprising between 50,000 and 60,000 verses according to varying manuscripts, Zoroaster appears in a completely favorable light. He is the founder of a monotheistic religion with doctrines similar to Islam.[24] But what is more, its effect on the state of human society, the situation in Iran achieved after its propagation by King Isfandiyār is that of a utopic kingdom of peace and welfare, similar to the one envisaged by Alexander the Great in his official speech after the conquest of Iran, as phrased by Nizāmī.[25] Some more material from the Shāhnāmeh appears in the following discussion.

Nizāmī (1141–1209), the great Persian master of epic romance, three of whose epics are situated in pre-Islamic Persia, betrays a modified view. In his last epic, the *Iskandarnāmeh*, which portrays Alexander the Great as successful conqueror, philosopher, and prophet, Alexander's main activity after the conquest of Persia consists of the destruction of fire-temples.

Here are a few lines from the chapter in question, entitled "How Alexander destroyed the fire-temples of the Magians."

> The king of good intention gave order that nobody should perform the Magian rites any longer.
>
> He cleansed the world of impure religions and guarded the true religion for the people.
>
> Due to his firmness, there remained no Zoroastrian fire in Iran.
>
> He ordered that all the people living in that epoch should not adore anything except God.
>
> They should take refuge to the religion of Abraham (*dīn-i Hanīfī*) and turn away from (the veneration of) sun and moon.[26]

This combat continues also in later chapters culminating in the destruction of Adhargushasp, "Fire of Vishtasp," a famous fire-temple known from the Shāhnāmeh.

From such lines one gets the impression that Nizāmī's religious ardor increased in the later part of his life when he wrote the Alexander epic. Yet, as the poem proceeds, Alexander's attitude becomes less rigid and ends up being a philosophical tolerance totally opposed to his previous zeal.[27] At any rate, Nizāmī is free of anti-Zoroastrian sentiment in his second epos, entitled "Khosraw and Shīrīn." This poem, a romance of enthralling beauty, deals with the last great Sasanian emperor before the downfall of the dynasty, Khusraw Parvez, who ruled from 590 to 628 and thus witnessed the beginnings of Islam. According to Islamic tradition, Khusraw was one of those kings to whom Muhammad is reported to have sent a letter inviting them to embrace Islam. Nizāmī does not mention this fact in his narrative, which ends with the assassination of Khusraw by one of his sons from a former marriage. His marriage with his beloved Shīrīn, which could have closed the poem had the poet envisaged a happy ending, is consecrated by Zoroastrian priests with the poet using the following words: "Khusraw took Shīrīn's hand and ordered the priest to sit down next to him and the priest spoke the time-honored words and consecrated their marriage in accordance with the rites of the (Zoroastrian) priests."[28]

It is only in the appendix that the poet relates the incidents of a dream, in which the Prophet Muhammad appeared to the emperor, and of a letter, which he sent him, both in order to invite him to embrace Islam. Khusraw refused, however, and his ensuing downfall is here ascribed to this reticence.[29]

Nizāmī thus presents two images of Khusraw Parvez. In the narrative, he shows us a king who develops from an unbridled youth to an insightful emperor and tender husband; in the appendix, he offers an official Islamic version, as if on higher command. Thus Nizāmī deviates from a tradition of veneration for Zoroaster first perceived in some early pre-Firdausian Persian poets, then, as we saw, manifest in the Shāhnāmeh, and later, in a more and more emblemized form, like verses of many Persian poets, particularly those with a mystic strand.

Renaissance of Old-Persian and Zoroastrian Ideas

As I already stated, in the Shāhnāmeh, Zoroastrianism is presented as a monotheistic cult. I shall give a brief summary of Zoroaster's appearance as described by Firdawsī.[30] Firdawsī integrates the intentions and activities of Zoroaster into the constant struggle between Iran and Turan, which, in the Shāhnāmeh, means the struggle between light and darkness, good and evil.

When Zoroaster appears and wins over King Gushtasp (= vishtaspa), Gushtasp propagates the new faith and builds fire temples. Zoroaster persuades the king to retain the tribute owed to the Turanians. Therupon Arjasp, the king of Turan, sends a furious letter to Gushtasp in which he reproaches him for having listened to an old magician, embraced his doctrine, and destroyed their old common religion. He implores him to separate himself from that impostor, promising him every treasure he could possibly wish to possess, provided that he follows his advice, and threatening him with devastation of Iran, if he refuses to do so. Gushtasp invites the nobility of the state together with Zoroaster and asks for their advice. They encourage him not to give in. Gushtasp sends Isfandiyār to all the countries to convert people to the religion of Zoroaster. The kings of the world inform Gushtasp that they have embraced the true religion and request the *Zand Avesta*, which is thereupon sent to them. (The good effects of the spread of Zoroastrianism on society have already been mentioned.)

Al-Masʿūdī and Ibn Khurdādhbih state that the Persian kings of the Sasanian dynasty, after having been crowned in Ctesiphon, went on foot to Adhargushasp as if on a pilgrimage.[31] The erection of this sanctuary, known as Takht-i Sulaymān and located at Shīz in Adharbaidjān, is mentioned in the *Shāhnāmeh* and by medieval Arabic geographers, and the pilgrimage is described by Firdawsī. At one place, it is mentioned how Kaikhusrau, after having conquered and freed the place from demons, gave an order to erect a building with a cupola touching the black cloud, which was to contain the fire of Adhargushasp, and how the Mobads established themselves together with the astrologers and the sages.[32]

In a later chapter, the poet describes the pilgrimage made by Kaikāʾūs and Kaikhusraw after the victory over Afrāsiyāb:

He said to him: Now, with our two horses,
let us part and gallop until we arrive at
Adhargushasp!
Let us wash our heads and the body, the hands
and the feet,
as the true worshippers of God do,
and let us pay our tribute to the creator of the
world,
elevating his praise in secret!
Let us stand before the fire,
so that God may guide us!
At the place, where He has a sanctuary,
He who reveals (the law of) justice, will show the
path.[33]

Firdawsī then describes how they made the journey "in their white garments" and arrived at Adhargushasp:

On beholding the fire, they
Implored the Creator
Strewing jewels (= weeping) over the fire.[34]

Melikian-Shirvani, the great historian of Islamic art, who investigated the ruins of Takht-i Sulaymān, emphasizes that this description has to be regarded as an archetypal prefiguration of Muslim prayer and pilgrimage (white garments, ablution); but he also highlights the theological parallels: God as guide, creator of the world, lord of justice, and so on.[35]

The same holds true in a further passage about Kaikhusraw giving offerings to the temple of Adhargushasp, as well as presents to the priests and those destitute of the town after the definite victory over Afrāsiyāb. "Ici encore, le parallélisme avec les institutions et les usages de l'Iran islamique est manifeste."[36]

Strangely enough, the Zoroastrian religion became an emblem of moral integrity mainly in Persian poetry, a tradition culminating in the lyrics of Hāfiz, but foreshadowed in a story told by the Arabic writer at-Tawhīdī in the tenth century.

The Tale of the Zoroastrian and the Jew in at-Tawhīdī's "Regaling and Mutual Trust"

Two men were traveling together, one a Parsi from Rayy, and the other a Jew from Jayy. The Parsi was riding on a mule, provided with a bag of victuals and money, so that he could travel leisurely and at ease. The Jew, however, was walking devoid of victuals and travel money. While they were talking together, the Parsi asked the Jew: "What is your religion and your belief?"

The Jew answered: "I believe that there is a God in Heaven who is the God of the children of Israel and I serve him and respect his holiness and submit to him and ask him to give me what he may give me, such as rich supplies, long life, health and protection from all evil, support against the enemy; and I ask him to bestow welfare on myself and everybody who shares my belief and my religion, not caring for those who do not share my conviction. For I believe, that whoever does not share my conviction, I have the right to kill him, while I am forbidden to help him, support him and take pity on him."

Then he said to the Parsi: "Now, that I have explained to you my religion and my belief and my convictions, explain to me your religion and your manner of serving your Lord!"

The Parsi said: "My belief and my conviction is to do good to myself, as well as to every member of my species (i.e., human beings—*abnā' djinsī*) and to not cause evil or wish evil to any servant of God, neither those who share my convictions nor those who do not."

Thereupon the Jew said: "Even if he does you wrong and deploys hostile activities against you?"

The Parsi said: "Certainly, because I know that there is only one God in Heaven, who is wise and knowing and aware of the hidden things. And He recompenses the well-doer for his good deed and punishes the evil-doer for his wrong."

The Jew remarked: "Sir, It does not seem to me that you translate your religion into action and follow your belief!"

"What do you mean?" asked the Parsi.

"Because," said the Jew, "I am a member of your species, a human being like yourself and you see me hungry, tired, walking with labor, while you are riding leisurely and at ease and without hunger."

"You are right," said the Parsi, "so what do you want?"

"Give me some food from your supplies and let me ride a little bit, I am exhausted!" he said.

"Well, be your wish fulfilled!" And he dismounted, walking himself and talking to him for a while. The Jew, however, now in possession of the mule and realizing that the Parsi was without power, drove on the mule and rode ahead. The Parsi started to run, unable to catch up with him and shouting: "O man, stop and descend! I cannot follow and am out of breath!"

The Jew replied: "Did I not explain to you my religion, as you did yours to me and you carried it out and translated it into action. Now I shall carry out my religion and translate it into action." And he urged on the mule, whereas the Parsi ran after him, hobbling and shouting: "Stop, o man, and don't leave me at this spot, where I shall be devoured by some wild beast or at any rate die and perish! Take pity on me as I have taken upon you!" The Jew, however, did not care about his shouting and rode on until he vanished from his view.

When the Parsi despaired, facing perdition, he remembered his faith and how he had described his God (to the Jew). So he then raised his eyes to Heaven and prayed: "O God! You know, that I translated my belief into action and that I explained to him your power. You have heard it and know it. So prove to this evil-doer the truth of my praise of you!"

Hardly had the Parsi made a few more steps, when he beheld the Jew lying on the ground, with his neck broken, while the mule that had thrown him off was standing at a distance awaiting his master.

The Parsi went to the mule, mounted it and rode away leaving the Jew in his agony. But now, the Jew shouted: "O sir, take pity on me! Load me on the mule and don't leave me in this desert, where I shall die of hunger and thirst! Translate your religion into action and carry out your belief!"

The Parsi replied: "I've done it already twice! You, however, did not understand what I told you, nor grasp what I described to you." The Jew said: "What do you mean?"

He said: "I described to you my belief and you doubted it, until I confirmed it by my action. I said: There is only one God in Heaven, who is wise and knowing and aware of the hidden things. And he recompenses the well-doer for his good deed and punishes the evil-doer for his wrong."

The Jew said: "I understood it quite well."

"What then," asked the Parsi, "was the reason that you did not take a warning from it?"

"A belief," said the Jew, "in which I grew up, and a religion in which I've been brought up, so that it became my habit like a natural disposition through the length of exercise and the application of principles in emulation of my fathers and ancestors and the teachers of my religion. This became for me like an unshakable fundament and the root of a plant. It is very difficult to shake off such a thing and abandon it."

Thereupon, the Parsi took pity on him and carried him along, until they arrived in the town, where he delivered him to his relatives, in a deplorable state. He told people his adventure and they kept wondering about the two for quite a while.

Somebody asked the Parsi: "How could you take pity on him, after he had requited your kindness by treachery?"

He answered: "The Jew apologized to me referring to the condition in which he grew up, the religion for which to campaign he had accustomed. I realized that it would have been hard for him to abandon it, and I believed him and took pity on him. I did this out of gratitude for God's acting with me, when I implored him in the plight that came over me through that man. First God shew me his mercy by helping me, then I, in return, took pity on the Jew, thus showing my thanks to God."[37]

In all likelihood, the tale is modeled after the parable of the good Samaritan in Luke 10, but the educated Muslim reader must rather have been reminded of a passage in the *Rasā'il Ikhwān al-Safā'*, where two similar prototypes confront one another, both of them apparently Muslims, the one representing the religious fanatic, the other the tolerant humanistic believer in God. Even though their discussion takes place after they have died, the former being in Hell, the latter in Heaven, the way they describe their religious duties and views is very similar to the discussions in at-Tawhīdī's tale.[38]

Traces of Zoroastrianism in Islamic Hedonism, Mysticism, Humanism

For a correct understanding of what follows, it must be remembered that wine in Islamic lands was available in Christian, Jewish, and Zoroastrian communal places, wineshops as well as cloisters or monasteries. Very often the cupbearer was a beautiful coquettish young boy or girl, so one could indulge in two vices at the same time: drinking wine and flirting with a boy or a girl.

Abū Nuwās, the great Arabic poet of the ninth century known for his debaucherous lyrics opens his love poems addressed to Christian, Jewish, and Zoroastrian boys with oaths sworn with symbols or with the fundamentals of the respective religion. In the case of Zoroastrianism, these are mainly feasts, but fire-temples and certain ceremonies are also sometimes mentioned. The longest and most detailed of these oaths as cited in Wagner follows:

> By the fire of Khūrā', (which is) a light from paradise (*mīnū*), the delicious uppermost heaven (*karuzmān*),
> and by the sanctity of the bundle of twigs (*barsam*), used for the liturgy that is murmured by the priests (*harābidh*) of Astanūs . . . ![39]

About a century later, the Persian minstrel Daqīqī confesses, at the end of a bacchic poem, having chosen four things of the world: ruby lips, the harp's sound, purple-colored wine, and the religion of Zoroaster.[40] This is probably still a confession to real Zoroastrianism. Later on, however, this religion seems to function as an emblem for something rather different. Some early indications of this change are to be found in the poetry of Sanā'ī (d. 1141), one of the forerunners of Djalāluddīn Rūmī. Here, Zoroastrianism is proposed as an alternative to the rigid way of the Islamic sharī'a, along with wine-drinking and other such lofty escapism that in Persian poetry came to be called *rindī* or *qalandarī*.[41] "The religion of Zoroaster and the rule of qalandardom sould now and then be made the provisions of the lover's journey."[42]

Similar verses are to be found in the Mukhtār-nāmeh by the mystic poet ʿAttār, who declares himself ready to "change my religion" and to adopt either Christendom or Zoroastrianism for the sake of love.[43] ʿUmar Khayyām exclaims in one of his quatrains:

> I shall bind the Magian's girdle around my waist!
> Do you know, why? Because of my Islamdom![44]

Meanwhile mysticism was about to color every poetic expression in Persian with its iridescent light.

One important step was undertaken by as-Suhrawardī, the famous founder of the "Wisdom of Illumination" (*hikmat al-ishrāq*), a mixture of Greek, Persian, and Islamic traditions, philosophy, mysticism, and gnosticism. In the preface of his main work, *Hikmat al-Ishrāq*, he described his program as follows:

> In the science of light and all that is founded upon it, I was helped by all those who trod in the path of God. I drew on the experience of the guide and head of wisdom, Plato, the mighty enlightened one, and likewise the great sages, who lived before him since the time of the Father of all sages, Hermes, and until his time, such as Empedocles, Pythagoras, etc.
>
> The words of the ancients are expressed in symbols, they cannot be refuted. If one attacks their outward sense, one does not hit their intention and the symbolic meaning remains intact.
>
> It is on this principle that the Eastern concept (*qāʿidat ash-sharq*) of light and darkness is based, which was supported by Djamasp, Frashaoshtra, and Buzurgmihr, as well as their predecessors. This is not the doctrine of the pagan Magians nor the heresy of Mani and not anything resulting in polytheism.
>
> Don't believe that wisdom existed only in that short period. No, the world has never been void of wisdom and never without a man who supported it by arguments and proofs, such a one is the representative of God on earth, and so it will remain as long as Heaven and Earth will exist.
>
> The difference between the earlier and the later (sages) rests only in the terms (*alfāz*) and the various habits of using either direct or allusive language. All believe in the three worlds (this world, yonder world, and the Barzakh or world in-between) and are in agreement as to monotheism, without quarreling about the essentials.[45]

All the various traditions of positive attitudes toward Zoroastrianism merge in the poetry of Hāfiz, with whom I shall conclude. Hāfiz of Shīrāz, of whom Goethe was so fond that he called him his "twin" and addressed him as "Holy Hāfiz,"[46] may be called the propagator of a religion of love whose central figure is the "prior of the (convent) of the Magians," that is, Zoroaster, who initiates the adepts into the mysteries of the world. Hāfiz calls him his "spiritual guide,"[47] affirms that "the temple of the Prior of the Magians suffices as shelter"[48] and admonishes himself: "Hāfiz, the court of the Prior of the Magians is a safe place of fidelity."[49]

"Read the lessons of love before him and hear them from him!"[50]

Conclusion

It has been shown that the Zoroastrians did not only persist in a concrete manner but continued to form an important ferment in the development of Islamic thinking. Notwithstanding many attacks, calumniations, and condemnations, the Zoroastrian religion remained a symbol of high ethical values such as purity and sincerity, and it apparently takes this role even today among certain intellectual circles in Iran. To investigate these contemporary issues would, however, go beyond the limits of this essay.

NOTES

1. This passage is based on M. G. Morony: "al-Madjūs," in *Encyclopaedia of Islam*, new ed., vol. 5 (Leiden: E. J. Brill, 1986), 1110a–1118a. Quotations on Zoroastrianism in Islamic times are from this article.

2. Ibid., 1110b.

3. *inna lladhīna āmanū wa-lladhīna hādū was-Sābiʾīna wan-Nasārā wal-Madjūsa wa-lladhīna ashrakū inna Llāha yafsilu bainahum yawma l- qiyāma.*

4. Cf. G. Vajda: "Hārūt wa-Mārūt" in *Encyclopaedia of Islam*, new ed., vol. 3 (Leiden: E. J. Brill, 1971), 236b–237a.

5. Goldziher, "Islam et Parsisme" (1900), in *Gesammelte Schriften*, vol. 4 (Hildesheim: Olms, 1970), p. 259.

6. Cf. Monnot, *Penseurs Musulmans et religions iraniennes* (Paris: Vrin, 1974), p. 90.

7. *Encyclopaedia of Islam*, new ed., vol. 5 (Leiden: E. J. Brill, 1986), 1111a.

8. Monnot, *Penseurs*, pp. 305f.

9. Shahrastānī, *Livre des religions et des sectes*, vol. 1 (Paris: Peters/UNESCO, 1986), p. 639.

10. G. Monnot, "L'écho musulman aux religions d'Iran," *Islamochristiana*, vol. 3 (1977), pp. 88f.

11. Monnot, *Penseurs*, p. 295.

12. Ch. Pellat, *Arabische Geisteswelt* (Zurich: Artemis, 1967), p. 268.

13. For al-Masʿūdī's sources concerning pre-Islamic Persia and Zoroastrianism, see A. M. H. Shboul, *al-Masʿudi and His World* (London: Ithaca Press, 1979), pp. 102–113; for Zoroastrian religious traditions, see ibid., pp. 107–108.

14. The Pahlavi Zand Avesta (ca. 9th c. C.E.) offers a commentary of ancient Avestan texts.

15. al-Masʿūdī, *Murūdj adh-dhahab*, ed. Ch. Pellat, vol. 1 (Beirut: Université libanaise, 1965), pp. 270f.

16. Monnot: *Penseurs*, pp. 309f.

17. Cf. L. Massignon: "Zindīq," *Shorter Encyclopaedia of Islam*, ed. H. A. R. Gibb and J. H. Kramers (Leiden: E. J. Brill and London: Luzac, 1961).

18. Monnot: "L'écho musulman," pp. 86f.

19. See al-Biruni, *In den Gärten der Wissenschaft*, ed. G. Strohmaier. Texte aus den Werken des muslimischen Universalgelehrten (Leipzig: Redam, 1988).

20. al-Bīrūnī, *Chronologie orientalischer Völker*, ed. E. Sachau (Leipzig: Harrassowitz, 1878), p. xx.

21. Thaʿālibī, *Histoire des rois de Perse* (Paris: Imprimerie Nationale, 1900), pp. 256ff.

22. Edward William Lane, trans., *The Thousand and One Nights*, vol. 1 (London: Chatro and Windus, 1883), p. 178; E. Littmann, trans., *Die Erzählungen aus den Tausendundein Nächten*, vol. 1 (Wiesbaden: Insel-Verlag, 1977), pp. 193f. In the Story of the Petrified Prince, the adherents of the four religions—Jews, Zoroastrians, Christians, and Muslims—are all turned into fish of four different colors. Littman, *Erzählungen*, vol. 1, p. 90.

23. Lane, *Thousand*, vol. 3, pp. 352–483; Littmann, *Erzählungen*, vol. 5, pp. 315–503.

24. Firdawsī, *Le livre des rois par Abouʾlkasim Firdousi*, vol. 5, trans. M. Jules Mohl (Paris: Maisonneuve, 1855), pp. 552f.

25. Ibid., 864–868; for Nizāmī, see J. C. Bürgel, "Krieg und Frieden im Alexander-Epos Nizāmīs," in *The Problematics of Power*, ed. M. Bridges and J. C. Bürgel (Bern: P. Lang, 1996).

26. Nizāmī, *Sharafnāmeh*, ed. V. Dastgirdī (Teheran: Kitābpūrushīi Ibn Sīnā, 1335/1957), pp. 240, 8, 11, 12, 16, 17.

27. Bürgel, "Krieg und Frieden," pp. 99ff.

28. Nizāmī, *Khusraw u Shīrīn*, ed. V. Dastgirdī (Teheran: Kitābfūrushī-i Ibn Sīnā, 1333/1955), p. 387.

29. Ibid., pp. 430–438.

30. Firdawsī, *Shahnāme*, vol. 4, pp. 363f.

31. Ibn Khurdādhbih, *Kitāb al-Masālik wal-mamālik*, ed. J. de Goeje (Leiden: E. J. Brill, 1889), pp. 119–120; al-Masʿūdī, *Kitāb at-Tanbīh wal-Ishrāf*, ed. J. de Goeje (Leiden: E. J. Brill, 1893), p. 95; see also A. S. Melikian-Chirvani: "Le livre des rois, miroir du destin: Part 2. Takht-e Soleyman et la symbolique du Shāh-nāme," *Studia Iranica* vol. 20 (1991), pp. 37f.

32. Firdawsī, *Shāhnāme*, vol. 2, p. 552.

33. Ibid., vol. 4, p. 195, verses 2239–2243.

34. Ibid., verses 2247, 2250–2252.

35. Melikian-Chirvani "Le livre des rois," p. 46.

36. Ibid., p. 47.

37. al-Tawhīdī, *al-Imtāʿ wal-muʾānasa*, trans. H.

Zotenberg, vol. 2 (Paris: Imprimerie Nationale, 1900), p. 157.

38. S. Diwald, *Arabische Philosophie und Wissenschaft in der Enzyklopädie* (Wiesbaden: Steiner, 1975), pp. 358f.

39. E. Wagner, *Abū Nuwās* (Wiesbaden: Steiner, 1965), p. 192.

40. Z. Safā, *Tārīkh-i adabīyāt dar Irān* vol. 1 (Teheran, 1363/1985), p. 409.

41. Cf. J. C. Bürgel, "The pious rogue: A study in the meaning of *qalandar* and *rend* in the poetry of Muhammad Iqbal," *Edebiyat* 4 (1979): 43–64.

42. Sanā'ī, *Diwan*, ed. M. Razawi (Teheran: Kitabkhāne-i Ibn Sīnā, 1343/1963), no. 6.

43. H. Ritter, *Das Meer der Seele* (Leiden: E. J. Brill, 1978), p. 490.

44. Omar Khéyam, *Quatrains*, ed. J. B. Nicolas (Paris: Maisonneuve, 1981), no. 241.

45. Shihābuddīn as-Suhrawardī, *Ḥikmat al-ishrāq*, ed. H. Corbin, Opera metaphysica et mystica II, Bibliotheca Iranica 2 (Teheran, 1952), p. xxxx.

46. Cf. J. C. Bürgel, "Goethe et Hafis, quelques réflexions," *Luqman* 5 (1989): 87–104.

47. *Dīwān-i Ḥāfiz*, ed. P. N. Khānlarī (Teheran, 1980–1983), no. 70,9.

48. Ibid., no. 263,4.

49. Ibid., no. 398,7.

50. The Zoroastrian dimension in the poetry of Hāfiz is further elucidated in my article, J. C. Bürgel, "Ambiguity: A study in the use of religious terminology in the poetry of Hafiz," in *Intoxication Earthly and Heavenly*, ed. M. Glünz and J. C. Bürgel (Bern: P. Lang, 1991).

REFERENCES

al-Bīrūnī. *Chronologie orientalischer Völker: Al-Athār al-bāqiya ʿan al-qurūn al-khāliya*, ed. E. Sachau. Leipzig: Harrassowitz, 1878.

———. *In den Gärten der Wissenschaft*. Ausgewählte Texte aus den Werken des muslimischen Universalgelehrten, übersetzt und erläutert von G. Strohmaier. Leipzig: Reclam, 1988.

Bürgel, J. C. "The pious rogue: A study in the meaning of *qalandar* and *rend* in the poetry of Muhammad Iqbal." *Edebiyat* 4(1979): 43–64.

———. "Goethe et Hafis, quelques réflexions." *Luqman* 5(1989): 87–104.

———. "Ambiguity: A study in the use of religious terminology in the poetry of Hafiz." In *Intoxication Earthly and Heavenly: Seven Studies on the Poet Hafiz of Shiraz*, ed. M. Glünz and J. C.Bürgel. (Schweizerische Asiatische Studien, Studienheft 12). Bern: P. Lang, 1991, pp. 7–39.

———. "Krieg und Frieden im Alexander-Epos Nizamis." In *The Problematics of Power: Eastern and Western Representations of Alexander the Great*, ed. M. Bridges and J. C. Bürgel. (Schweiz. Asiengesellschaft. Monographie 22). Bern: P. Lang, 1996.

Diwald, S., *Arabische Philosophie und Wissenschaft in der Enzyklopädie: Kitāb Iḫwān as-Safāʾ (III). Die Lehre von Seele und Intellekt*. Wiesbaden: Steiner, 1975.

Firdawsī. *Le livre des rois* par Abou'lkasim Firdousi publié, traduit et commenté par M. Jules Mohl. Paris: Maisonneuve, 1855.

Goldziher, Ignaz. "Islam et Parsisme" (1900), in *Gesammelte Schriften*, vol. 4 (Hildesheim: Olms, 1970), pp. 232–260.

Hāfiz, *Dīwān*. Ed. P. N. Khānlarī. Teheran 1980–1983.

[Khayyām, ʿUmar] Khéyam, Omar. *Quatrains*. Texte, traduction par J. B. Nicolas. Paris: Maisonneuve, 1981.

Ibn Khurdādhbih, *Kitāb al-Masālik wal-mamālik*, ed. J. de Goeje. Leiden: E. J. Brill, 1889.

Lane, Edward William, Trans. *The Thousand and One Nights*, commonly called in England "The Arabian Nights' Entertainments," a new translation from the Arabic, with copious notes, 3 vols. London: Chatto and Windus, 1883.

Littmann, E., Trans. *Die Erzählungen aus den Tausendundein Nächten*, 6 vols. Wiesbaden: Insel-Verlag, 1977.

Massignon, L. "Zindīq." *Shorter Encyclopaedia of Islam*, ed. H. A. R. Gibb and J. H. Kramers. Leiden: E. J. Brill and London: Luzac, 1961.

al-Masʿūdī. *Murūdj adh-dhahab wa-ma ʿādin al-djawhar*. Manshūsrāt al-Djāmiʿa al-Lubnānīya—Qism al-dirāsāt al-tārīkhīya, ed. Ch. Pellat. Beirut: Université libanaise, 1965.

———. *Kitāb at-Tanbīh wal-Ishrāf*, ed. J. de Goeje. Leiden: E. J. Brill, 1893.

Melikian-Chirvani, A. S. "Le livre des rois, miroir du destin: Part 2: Takht-e Soleyman et la symbolique du Shāh-nāme." *Studia Iranica* 20 (1991): 33–148.

Monnot, G. *Penseurs Musulmans et religions iraniennes: ʿAbd al-Jabbār et ses devanciers*. (Etudes Musulmanes 16). Paris: Vrin, 1974.

———. "L'écho musulman aux religions d'Iran." *Islamochristiana*, vol. 3 (1977), pp. 85–98.

Morony, M. G. "al-Madjūs." *Encyclopaedia of Islam*, new ed., vol. 5 (Leiden: E. J. Brill, 1986), pp. 1110–1118.

Nizāmī. *Khusraw u Shīrīn*, ed. V. Dastgirdī. Teheran: Kitābfurūshī-i Ibn Sīnā, 1333/1955.

Nizāmī. *Sharafnāmeh*, ed. V. Dastgirdī. Teheran: Kitābfurūshī-i Ibn Sīnā, 1335/1957.

Pellat, Ch. *Arabische Geisteswelt*. Ausgewählte und übersetzte Texte von al-Ǧāhiz (777–869). Zurich: Artemis, 1967.

Sanā'ī, *Dīwān*, ed. M. Razawi. Teheran: Kitābkhāne-i Ibn Sīnā, 1341/1963.

Ritter, H. *Das Meer der Seele. Mensch, Welt und Gott in den Geschichten des Farīduddīn ʿAttār*. Leiden: E. J. Brill, 1978.

Z. Safā. *Tārīkh-i adabīyāt dar Irān*. Teheran, 1363/1985, vol. 1, p. 409.

Shahrastānī: *Livre des religions et des sectes*, vol. 1. Traduction avec introduction et notes par Daniel Gimaret et Guy Monnot. 2 vols. Paris: Peeters/UNESCO 1986 and 1993.

Shboul, A. M. H. *al-Masʿudi and His World: A Muslim Humanist and His Interest in Non-Muslims*. London: Ithaca Press, 1979.

Suhrawardī, *Hikmat al-ishrāq*, ed. Henry Corbin, Opera metaphysica et mystica II, Bibliotheca Iranica 2. Teheran, 1952.

al-Tawhīdī: *al-Imtāʿ wal-muʾānasa*. 3 vols., ed. A. Amin and A. al-Zain. Beirut: Dār Maktabat al-hayāt 1953.

Thaʿālibī. *Histoire des rois de Perse*. Texte arabe publié et traduit par H. Zotenberg. Paris: Imprimerie Nationale, 1900.

Vajda,G., "Hārūt wa-Mārūt" in *Encyclopaedia of Islam*, new ed., vol. 3 (Leiden: E. J. Brill, 1971), pp. 236b–237a.

Wagner,E. *Abū Nuwās: Eine Studie zur arabischen Literaturgeschichte der frühen ʿAbbasidenzeit*. Wiesbaden: Steiner, 1965.

13

Representations of Social Intercourse between Muslims and Non-Muslims in Some Medieval *Adab* Works

HILARY KILPATRICK

All texts have their limitations. These may be of two kinds: those given with the written tradition of a specific culture, and those related to the aims and subject matter of a particular genre or the interests of a particular writer. In the case of medieval Arabic texts, the references to peasant life and culture, for instance, in no way reflect the economic and social significance of the countryside. As far as kinds of texts are concerned, works of *fiqh*, for instance, represent an essentially normative approach to discussion of human behavior, while writings on other religious systems, whether polemical or not, tend to approach these systems as phenomena isolated from their wider social context.

In order to correct the distortions present in Muslim authors' writings devoted to perceptions of non-Muslims, it may be useful to turn to texts that hint at the relations existing between Muslims and non-Muslims in society, without showing any intention to discuss matters of faith and belief. One such category of texts are *adab* works, in which non-Muslims occur simply because they are part of the society reflected in the material these works contain. These texts have their disadvantages, too. The references to non-Muslims are incidental and do not allow a clear or complete description of relations between communities to emerge. Moreover, the information dates from different periods, which fragments the picture even further. These are not the only drawbacks of *adab* texts, as will emerge from the following discussion. What they offer, however, are some isolated informal insights into how individuals actually behaved, or at least might have behaved, and as such they contrast with the "official" statements and generalizations purveyed in specialist writings.

The range of *adab* texts is large, and my acquaintance with them is limited. The choice of material I will present here does not reflect an informed judgment about which *adab* books yield most insights in this connection; it is simply the result of reading undertaken with other aims in mind.

One source that yields some very interesting glimpses of interaction between Muslims and non-Muslims is the *Kitāb al-aghānī* of Abū l-Faraj al-Iṣfahānī (d. 363/972).[1] It is perhaps no accident that Abū l-Faraj is a more or less exact contemporary of al-Masʿūdī, and they shared a number of traits. Both were men of learning with wide interests and a critical spirit; both had a sense of the variety of human experience; and both accorded particular importance to history. But whereas al-Masʿūdī explores the connections between history and geography, drawing on his own extensive travels,[2] for Abū l-Faraj history is linked to literature, Arabic literature.[3] The *Kitāb al-aghānī*, consequently, seldom moves out of the confines of the Fertile Crescent, Iran and the Arabian Peninsula, though it takes its reader well back into pre-Islamic times. Another important difference between the two authors is that unlike al-Masʿūdī, Abū l-Faraj was not interested in theological disputes for their own sake. The controversies which are aired in the *Aghānī* have to do with musical schools[4] and poetic movements.[5] (This is not to say that all bias is absent from the presentation of characters in the *Aghānī*—on the contrary. But there is no discussion in such cases.)[6]

Because of Abū l-Faraj's lack of polemical spirit and his sense of the infinite variety of human behavior, he includes some unusual examples of interaction between Muslims and non-Muslims. They are subordinate to his main purpose, which is to provide the correct texts and melodies of the best songs of the Golden Age of classical Arabic music, together with information about their authors and composers.[7] A good example of the incidental nature of the insights he provides comes in the article on the great singer Ibrāhīm al-Mawṣilī (d. 188/804).[8] As a boy, Ibrāhīm had no formal musical education, but he discovered in himself a natural gift for singing. After spending some time in Rayy studying Persian and Arabic music, he heard of a skilled musician in Ubulla,[9] Jawānūya, and set off to see what he could learn from him. He later recalled their meeting: "When I went to see Jawānūya, I did not find him at home. So I waited until he came back. When he saw me he felt nervous toward me (*iḥtashamanī*), for he was a Zoroastrian. But I told him of my artistic activity and the circumstances in which I had come to see him. So he welcomed me."[10] What is noteworthy in the present connection is that Ibrāhīm reports the shock his presence caused his host and his own success in overcoming the strain caused by the difference in the two men's religious affiliations. He does not explain the reason for Jawānūya's *iḥtishām*, unfortunately, although as the son of a converted Zoroastrian himself,[11] he must have known what it was. The modern reader can only speculate: Was it the reaction of a member of a minority to someone of the dominant community, or was it perhaps connected with Zoroastrian prescriptions on purity and impurity?

That Ibrāhīm did not allow differences in religion to affect his contacts with other musicians is movingly illustrated in the account of how the flute-player Barṣūmā mourned him. Barṣūmā, whom Ibrāhīm had discovered in Kufa,[12] had accompanied the master for years. When Ibrāhīm died, Barṣūmā asked his son Isḥāq to accord him one day when he would carry out all his wishes. On the appointed day Barṣūmā arrived. In Isḥāq's account of what happened:

> "Send for robes of honour," Barṣūmā said. I did so, including among them a brocade mantle. He put them on as his outer garments and said: "Now let's go to the room where I used to meet your father." We both went there; I had perfumed it with fragrant scents beforehand. When we reached the door he threw himself down, writhing on the ground (*tamarragha fī l-turāb*), and wept. Then he got out his flute and started to play a dirge on it, walking round the room, kissing the places where Abū Isḥāq used to sit, crying and playing until he had relieved some of his grief. Grasping his clothes he rent them, and I began to calm him, weeping as I did so. It took him some time to regain his composure, but then he called for his own clothes and put them on, explaining: "I only asked for robes of honour so that people would not say Barṣūmā had torn his clothes in order to be given better ones." He went on: "Now let's go to your house. I've relieved my feelings as I wanted."[13]

The name Barṣūmā is Christian,[14] and the flute-player, who came of humble stock in Kufa, had a faulty pronunciation of Arabic.[15] The evidence points to him being a Christian of Aramean origin. But the difference in confession pales into insignificance beside the professional collaboration of a lifetime and the gratitude and affection it engendered. And the same sense that a professional tie overrides religious differences, at least among singers, is conveyed by the account of the invitation the three Hijazi (Muslim) singers, Ibn Surayj, Maʿbad, and al-Gharīḍ, issued to the Kufan (Christian) Ḥunayn al-Hīrī. "We have a brother in Iraq," it starts off.[16] However apocryphal the story is,[17] it reflects what its inventor thought the three singers would have said.

Another, smaller book by Abū l-Faraj, the *Kitāb adab al-ghurabāʾ*, provides an example of disinterested friendship between a Muslim and a Christian. The title of this book plays on the different senses of the word *adab*, for it includes examples of strangers' literary work, generally poetry, but also indications of how to contend with the predicament of being alone in a strange land.[18] In one *khabar* a Muslim traveling through the Byzantine marches stops at a pleasant walled city in the region of Kharshana.[19] He falls into conversation with one of the inhabitants, a fluent Arabic speaker. This man had been friends with a young, cultured Iraqi who had spent years in the city. He finally fell ill and died and the Byzantine, grieving, buried him in a domed tomb with his face turned towards Mecca (*ʿalā qiblat al-islām*).[20]

Not all Abū l-Faraj's *akhbār* where Muslims and non-Muslims interact reflect this kind of interfaith understanding. On the contrary, religious differences can have the most painful consequences. When al-ʿAbbās ibn Mirdās sets off to join the Prophet, he leaves a message telling his wife of his intention. She packs up her tent and goes back to her own tribe, reproaching him in poetry for the political consequences of his becoming a Muslim.[21] Qays ibn Āṣim's wife also leaves him when he converts, though it is her family, of the Banū Ḥanīfa, who refuse to accept Islam and force her to return to her tribe of origin. The *Aghānī* includes a moving passage where husband and wife evoke their happy life together and lament the circumstances which have caused them to part.[22] Even if the passage has been worked up for its rhetorical qualities (it serves as an example of *balāghat al-nisāʾ*), and the incident may have been embroidered to enhance Qays's reputation[23] or detract from the Banū Hanīfa's standing, the situation of a conflict of loyalties, in which individual feeling is subordinated to allegiance to the group, rings true, as does the fact that such a conflict could arise from a religious conversion.[24]

But conversion to the beloved's religion might take place, too. The ʿAbbāsid poet Dīk al-Jinn al-Ḥimṣī fell passionately in love with a Christian girl from his native city and asked her to convert so that they could marry. She complied, "because she knew how great his desire for her was," which implies that conviction played at best a subordinate part.[25] It may be that the incident of the conversion is included to give greater poignancy to the poet's romance, which ended tragically when, acting on false information, he killed his wife for having been unfaithful to him. But it could also imply that mixed marriages were not considered acceptable by the early third/ninth century.[26]

A rare reference to conversion from Islam to Christianity is to be found in the reports about al-Wābiṣī. This man, a member of the aristocratic Meccan clan of Banū Makhzūm,[27] found his way to Byzantine territory under circumstances about which the sources disagree. Either he fled to Byzantium when ʿUmar ibn ʿAbd al-ʿAzīz, then governor of Mecca, inflicted the prescribed punishment on him for wine-drinking,[28] or he fell in love with a beautiful Byzantine woman he glimpsed while besieging a citadel and went over to her side,[29] or he was captured and ill-treated until he agreed to convert.[30] This last version continues with him being discovered by an envoy from Damascus sent to ransom prisoners of war; it was his singing of an Arabic song that led the envoy to him.[31] On being offered the chance of a ransom if he had not abandoned Islam, he admitted this was the case. The envoy reported back to ʿUmar ibn ʿAbd al-ʿAzīz, now caliph, how the conversation had gone.

> "I beg you in God's name, accept Islam." "Shall I accept Islam when I have these two children and I have married a [Byzantine] woman who is their mother? When I arrive in Medina people, when they speak to me, will say: 'Christian!', and they will do the same to my children and their mother. No, by God, I shall not accept Islam." "You were able to recite the Qurʾān. What do you still remember of it?" "Nothing but this verse: 'It may be that those who disbelieve wish ardently that they were Muslims.'" (S. 15, v. 2; Pickthall's translation)
>
> I went back to him and said: "You will not be reproached because of this." "But what about venerating the Cross, drinking wine and eating pork?" "Good heavens! Don't you still recite: '. . . save him who is forced thereto and whose heart is still content with the Faith . . .' (S. 16, v.106). But al-Wābiṣī repeated: "What about what I have done? He did not agree to return with me." On hearing this, ʿUmar raised his hands with the words, "O God, let me not die till you have delivered him into my power."[32]

A shorter version of the encounter, which follows the romantic explanation of al-Wābiṣī's presence among the Byzantines, has a Muslim soldier propose the arrangement of a ransom after al-Wābiṣī had recited the first of the two Qurʾān verses. The renegade simply reflected for a moment and then said: "Go away, may God go with you."[33] These two versions are obviously incompatible. But it is not inconceivable that they both, in part at least, reflect actual happenings involving different protagonists. The figure of the prisoner-of-war who settles down in the country of his captors and builds a life there is credible. Less so is the soldier who, under the impulse of a *coup de foudre*, changes sides and marries his beautiful beloved. But the brevity of the dialogue between renegade and soldier and the indirect refusal of the offer could reflect a historical exchange.

It is noteworthy that in the longer version al-Wābiṣī used two arguments for not returning to his original faith: the external signs of Christianity which are incompatible with Islam and the social consideration that his and his family's position in Medina would be impossible. These were arguments likely to be understood, if not approved, by the envoy. Whether al-Wābiṣī had other reasons for keeping to Christianity is impossible to guess from this report, itself worked over by Muslim scholars.

Another famous case of Islam being abandoned for Christianity concerns Jabala ibn al-Ayham, the last Ghassanid ruler. He is said to have accepted Islam, but on a formal visit to ʿUmar he clashed with a Muslim of humble origins and, prevented from avenging himself on an inferior in a way he considered appropriate, he decided to abandon Islam for the less egalitarian Christianity. When Muʿāwiya became governor of Syria he tried to persuade Jabala to return to Islam, offering him land as an incentive, but the negotiations came to nothing, according to one version because of Jabala's untimely death.[34] These *akhbār* are even more apocryphal than those about al-Wābiṣī,[35] but it is not inconceivable that they contain a memory of a time, at the dawn of Islam, when the punishment for apostasy was not yet automatically execution, at least if the offender was sufficiently important.

Some *adab* texts reflect the fact that religious differences could exist within families without conversion or separation ensuing. The mother of the famous poet ʿUmar[36] ibn Abī Rabīʿa's brother al-Ḥārith was an Abyssinian Christian. She kept it from her son that she had not converted to Islam, but when she died her women attendants prepared her for burial with a cross round her neck. Her son sent away the Meccan aristocrats who had come to attend the funeral and allowed the Christian burial to go ahead.[37] Hishām ibn ʿAbd al-Malik's governor of Iraq, Khālid al-Qasrī, was also the son of a Christian mother, a woman from Byzantium.[38] In the third/ninth and fourth/tenth centuries accession to the vizirate was open only to Muslims, but vizirs included some converts. Among them was Ṣāʿid ibn Makhlad,[39] whose brother ʿAbdūn remained a Christian. ʿAbdūn benefited from his brother's position, despite his own limited capacities,[40] but also shared in his disgrace. After Ṣāʿid's death in prison, ʿAbdūn was released and spent the last 15 years of his life in a monastery.[41]

In the instances discussed so far, apart from the last one, either the relation between Muslim and non-Muslim forms only a detail in the presentation of the principal character or the character himself is insignificant. (Or, in Jabala's case, an aura of legend hangs over the events.) The life of the poet al-Akhṭal,[42] by contrast, offers an example of a prominent personality at the Umayyad court who made no secret of his Christianity, indeed even flaunted it. Here, however, the sources betray a certain embarrassment. Before they are discussed, it is worth recalling that al-Akhṭal, who was born around 20/640 and died in about 92/710, spent the greater part of his life in a state whose administration, in the former Byzantine provinces, was still carried on in Greek, and where his coreligionists predominated at court,[43] and that the Great Mosque of Damascus, that first visible symbol in the capital of Islam's self-confidence, was completed only around the time he died. Another piquant aspect of his character is that whereas his drinking habits contrasted sharply with the sobriety of the Umayyad court, they would have occasioned no great surprise at the court of any of the caliphs from Hārūn al-Rashīd on.

A member of the Christian tribe of Banū Taghlib, al-Akhṭal first attracted the notice of Yazīd ibn Muʿāwiya when he was looking for a poet to answer ʿAbd al-Rahmān ibn Hassān ibn Thābit, who had attacked the Umayyads in his poetry.[44] Yazīd first approached ibn Juʿayl,[45] but as a convert to Islam he was loath to lampoon the Anṣār and proposed his younger fellow-tribesman, al-Akhṭal, who had no such hesitations. From then on al-Akhṭal supported the Umayyads through thick and thin, and they rewarded him with official recognition. His poetry has the same epic grandeur as that of the pre-Islamic masters, in particular al-Nābigha, with whom he is often compared; he and his younger contemporaries Jarīr and al-Farazdaq dominated the genres of eulogy and satire in a period in which poetry still retained an important political purpose.

The reports of al-Akhṭal and his poetry mention his religious affiliation in two contexts. First, he is portrayed as ostentatiously wearing a cross, even in the Caliph's presence, drinking wine, and swearing by Christian symbols or, even more provocatively, by pre-Islamic divinities.[46] His flamboyant behavior when among Muslims is contrasted with his meekness toward the members of his own religious hierarchy when they force him to do penance for his far from exemplary life.[47] He uses the typically Christian term *ḥanīf* for Muslims when trying to find out what an unknown Muslim visitor wants to drink;[48] this tactful inquiry strikes an unexpected note in view of his generally overbearing behavior in public. He seems to have been a loyal, if wayward, son of his Church, resisting ʿAbd al-Malik's offer, probably made in jest, to shower wealth upon him if only he would convert.[49]

Together with his behavior, al-Akhṭal's achievement in being a great poet and a Christian calls forth comment in the sources. He himself is reported to have said that any connoisseur of poetry, when he encounters a good line, is not going to worry about whether its author was a Christian or a Muslim,[50] and the acceptance of his poetry side by side with that of Jarīr and al-Farazdaq bears this out. But among the many exchanges which attempt to evaluate the trio's relative merits are several where his Christianity is referred to. Jarīr is said to have considered that al-Akhṭal's unbelief (*kufr*) together with his age put him at a certain disadvantage in their poetic contests;[51] despite this, however, Jarīr was afraid of him. ʿUmar ibn ʿAbd al-ʿAzīz, when asked who was the better, al-Akhṭal or Jarīr, judged that unbelief cramped al-Akhṭal's style (*ḍayyaqa ʿalayhi kufruhu l-qawl*), yet he had clearly outclassed his rival (*balagha minhu ḥaythu raʾayt*).[52] If the philologist Ḥammād al-Rāwiya (d. c. 155/771) felt kindly disposed toward Christianity, it was thanks to al-Akhṭal's poetry.[53]

Apart from the speculation about the influence of a poet's convictions on his talent, another reason that al-Akhṭal's Christianity aroused interest among critics was because of literary-historical terminology. For al-Akhṭal is one of the leading "Islamic" poets. "Islamic," here, is a literary-historical designation; it is preceded by "*jāhilī*," pre-Islamic, and "*mukhaḍram*," spanning the pre-Islamic and early Islamic periods, and followed by "*mukhaḍram al-dawlatayn*," spanning the late Umayyad and early "ʿAbbāsid periods, "*muḥdath*," modern and so on. Hence the statement attributed to Abū ʿUbayda (d. c. 204/819), *shuʿarāʾ al-islām al-Akhṭal wa-Jarīr wa-l-Farazdaq* (the Islamic poets are al-Akhṭal, Jarīr, and al-Farazdaq),[54] and the consecration of this status in Ibn Sallām al-Jumaḥī's (d. c. 232/847) *Ṭabaqāt fuḥūl al-shuʿarāʾ*, where the first class of Islamic poets comprises al-Farazdaq, Jarīr, al-Akhṭal and the make-weight al-Rāʿī. The paradox that lurks in all this is brought out in an exchange reputed to have taken place between ʿAbd al-Malik and al-Farazdaq. The caliph asked, "Who is the most gifted poet in the Islamic period?" The poet answered, "You don't have to look further than the Christian woman's son when he composes a panagyric."[55]

The standing of the Christian al-Akhṭal at the Umayyad court and the freedom he allowed himself in his lifestyle and poetry evidently puzzled the Iraqi scholars of a later period in which the position of the Christians was very different. This is echoed in the comment made in the presence of the philologist Abū ʿAmr ibn al-ʿAlāʾ (d. c. 154/771): "How extraordinary al-Akhṭal was! An infidel Christian lampooning Muslims."[56] A figure like al-Akhṭal was unthinkable subsequently; already in the later Umayyad period a refusal to abandon Christianity at the caliph's behest might bring down a savage punishment.[57]

Although Christians occupied an increasingly subordinate status, Muslims for several centuries to come showed interest in their buildings and customs. Visiting churches is a pastime not merely attested to by the professional traveler but also by Abū l-Faraj in the *Kitāb adab al-ghurabāʾ*. He notes a number of incidents where Muslim wayfarers sought out well-known churches to visit in the cities they were passing through;[58] frescoes or icons seem to have been a particular attraction.[59]

The interest in ecclesiastical buildings gave rise to a distinct genre, the *kutub al-diyārāt*. Of the several titles listed, including one by Abū l-Faraj,[60] only the *Kitāb al-diyārāt* of al-Shābushtī (d. c. 390/999) has survived. It throws considerable light on the Muslim curiosity about churches and monasteries, although lost works on the subject might well have approached it in a different spirit.[61] Al-Shābushtī's book has been neatly, but somewhat inaccurately, characterized as "not so much a work of church history, more a guide to night-life in Iraq and Egypt."[62] In fact al-Shābushtī, who gives the impression of writing from firsthand knowledge,[63] combines in each chapter of his book a short description of a monastery and its surroundings with poetry which refers to it and information about one or more personalities who visited it. Although some of these celebrities were poets, libertines, or buffoons, others held important offices in the ʿAbbāsid state; there is, for instance, an extensive section on Ṭāhir Dhū l-Yamīnayn and his descendants.[64] A few sections, moreover, are set in much earlier times, when the night-life had not yet evolved. The use of the monasteries as pegs on which to hang the poetry and anecdotes is somewhat reminiscent of the function of the songs in the *Aghānī*, although the whole conception of the Diyārāt is much more modest. The fact that monasteries could fulfill such a function is in itself interesting.

Al-Shābushtī regularly notes the monastery's location, its size, and state of repair; when its particular feast days fell; when it was visited, and by whom. It is obvious that part of a monastery's attraction for him lies in the garden, vineyards, and well-tended land which surround it; it is a place of natural beauty, with something of the paradisiac about it.[65] But monasteries could offer more than this. In the first place, the vineyards were not for show but provided the wine so necessary to many an ʿAbbāsid poet's mental and psychological health. In the second place, the church services were attended by Christians of all ages and both sexes.[66] And third, the monasteries attracted pleasure-lovers from both communities. The cultured upper class of the ʿAbbāsid empire found the combination of beautiful natural surroundings, freely available wine, and at least the prospect of amorous adventures irresistible; this image of the monastery as a pleasure garden might come to many Christians as a surprise, but it is the one al-Shābushtī propagates in his book.[67]

How much contact was there between the Christian visitors to the monasteries and the Muslims? Al-Shābushtī notes that on feast days the Christians went to celebrate the festival, the Muslims to walk about and enjoy the surroundings (*fa-yuʿayyidu hā'ulāʾi wa-yatanazzahu hāʾulāʾi*).[68] But some ceremonies attracted members of both communities, for instance the festival of Qubbat al-Shatīq at al-Ḥīra, where the Christians went in procession, priests and deacons chanting and bearing incense-burners, with a crowd of merry-making Muslims and idle pleasure-seekers in their wake, until they reached the shrine. There they celebrated the liturgy and received communion, and baptisms were performed. Then they all returned in the same fashion to the Shakūra monastery. "It is a nice sight," he observes.[69] Although he does not say so, it may be assumed that the monasteries he mentions where healing miracles occurred or where there were medicinal springs[70] attracted people of all religious persuasions.[71] And in Dayr al-Fīq, which contained a stone on which Christ was reputed to have sat, "everyone who entered the place" chipped off a piece and took it home with him, as a means of acquiring blessing.[72]

When evaluating al-Shābushtī's account of the attitudes of the Muslims who attended Christian festivals, two points may be made. First, like other *adab* writers, he shows no interest in popular forms of Islam—precisely because they are associated with a section of society marginal to his vision.[73] Second, some of the Muslims who attended these festivals were descendants of Christians who had celebrated them; if the Muslims were converts they may have participated in the festivals before themselves. It is possible that such Muslims may have retained some Christian traditions, in particular those connected with the veneration of saints and pilgrimages, typically areas of religious activity which escape the control of the religious authorities.[74] Al-Masʿūdī, a much more systematic and careful observer, notes that in Egypt Christians and Muslims alike celebrated Epiphany, both not only merrymaking but plunging into the Nile, which they claimed had prophylactic qualities.[75] In other words, the distinction which al-Shābushtī carefully draws between the activities of Christians and Muslims at monasteries reflects his own practice and that of his circle, but it may not do justice to the behavior of all the Muslim visitors.

Al-Shābushtī also recounts meetings between individual Muslims and Christians at monasteries. These are of two kinds. First, a Muslim, generally occupying a prominent position, might visit a monastery and spend a few days there; the hospitality offered him and his suite was at least partly in fulfillment of a monastery's traditional obligation to receive and entertain travelers. As an example, al-Maʾmūn, when on his way to Syria, stopped at Dayr al-Aʿlā near Mosul for a few days around Palm Sunday. The caliph watched the worshippers going into church and the procession, and after the service young people came over to him, holding freshly plucked branches of basil in their hands and offering him various kinds of drink. His own women attendants then came forward, dressed in brocade, wearing gold crosses and carrying palm and olive branches.[76] Finally he summoned his singing-girl to perform appropriate songs. The correct way for the notable to round off such a visit was to give the monastery money.[77]

Al-Maʾmūn evidently enjoyed the sight of the Christian ceremonies (*istaḥsanahu*), as the text notes. His visit has the formal character of that of a head of state, however. A less formal occasion was when al-Muʿtazz felt thirsty while out hunting. The prince al-Faḍl, who was accompanying him, suggested they should visit a good friend of his, a monk in the nearby Dayr Mār Mārī, to which the caliph agreed. When al-Faḍl, al-Muʿtazz and his favorite Yūnus ibn Bughā arrived, the monk brought them cool water and offered to prepare a meal. Taking al-Faḍl aside, he asked who his two companions were, and received the answer: "Two young men from the army." "No, two husbands of houris who have escaped." "That isn't part of your religion or what you believe in." "Oh yes it is, now!"

After they had eaten the food they were offered, simple monastic fare but fresh and tasty, al-Muʿtazz urged al-Faḍl to ask his friend which of the two, al-Muʿtazz or Yūnus, he would like to keep with him. "Both of them, and then some."[78] Al-Muʿtazz, much amused, asked al-Faḍl to repeat the question, but the monk again neatly avoided it. Then their companions caught up with them, to the monk's alarm, but al-Muʿtazz reassured him, and they continued talking for a while. When the visitors left, al-Muʿtazz offered the monk a large sum of money, but he only accepted it on condition they visit him again, bringing with them whom they liked. They agreed on a day, and the monk entertained them royally. Al-Muʿtazz took such a liking to him that he visited him regularly after that.[79]

These notables' attitude to monks and monasteries expresses an appreciation and a measure of respect evidently unaffected by considerations of the rightness or wrongness of Christianity.[80] In the second kind of meeting theological considerations also play no part, but respect is hardly present either. Here the monastery is essentially a pleasure garden, a setting for amorous adventures. Such is the encounter between Abū l-Fatḥ Aḥmad ibn Ibrāhīm and a beautiful Christian girl in Dayr al-Thaʿālib; the girl here made the first advances, and the casual meeting led to a liaison.[81]

Al-Mutawakkil's visit to the monasteries near Homs offers traits of both types of visit. The sightseeing and appreciation of the beauty of churches and the young people in them was followed by a meeting with one of the senior monks. The caliph asked him about the people he had seen, and then a strikingly beautiful girl walked by. In answer to the caliph's inquiry, the monk said she was his daughter.[82] The caliph asked her to bring him water, and she obeyed. Taken with her good manners as well as her beauty, al-Mutawakkil asked her to spend the rest of the day with them, and when it turned out she could sing he was completely captivated. Finally, he asked her to convert to Islam and then he married her.[83]

In anecdotes like this the absence of any indication of the other side's point of view makes itself felt very keenly. What were the father's emotions, as he saw the caliph's eye fall on his daughter and sensed him fixing all his attention on her? When did he foresee what her fate would be? There is no reference to the caliph's power, but it is there in the background, influencing the behavior of all the actors.[84]

For monks could react violently to attempts by Muslims to lead astray their fellows. When the dissolute ʿAbbāda was banished by al-Mutawakkil to Mosul, he took to visiting Day al-Shayāṭīn, where he became infatuated with a young monk. He employed all his wiles to seduce him and finally succeeded. The enraged monks planned to throw the aggressor from the top of the monastery into the valley below, but he got wind of their plan and fled, never to return.[85]

One final insight which *adab* works offer into the contacts between Muslims and non-Muslims has already been illustrated in the account of Muʿtazz's meeting al-Faḍl's friend the monk. This is the friendly teasing which could occur among adherents of different religions alluding to each other's beliefs. And the same lightheartedness could inspire a Muslim poet in love with a Christian to sing the praises of Christianity[86] or suggest that the beloved could cause a mass conversion from Islam to Christianity.[87] ʿAbdallāh ibn al-ʿAbbās al-Rabīʿī, whose love for a Christian girl he expressed in a number of poems, complained in one of them that the meeting she had promised had not taken place, and now Christmas, Epiphany[88] and Ascension had all passed. When this poem was sung before al-Wāthiq he exclaimed: "Stop this man before he becomes a Christian!," evidently disconcerted by his familiarity with the Christian calendar of feasts.[89]

The examples of social relations between Muslims and non-Muslims I have mentioned range from friendship and professional cooperation to separation caused by a difference of religion. They include both conversion and refusal to convert to Islam. They show Muslims being present at Christian celebrations—though not non-Muslims attending any Muslim festivities.[90] The tone varies from serious, even ferocious, to light-hearted, and there are some moments of pathos. Although most of the incidents take place in an urban, detribalized milieu, the bedouin ethos is reflected in some of the older material.

But apart from variety, what can these *adab* texts contribute to understanding of Muslim perceptions of non-Muslims? First, their very limitations are instructive. Apart from their fragmentary nature, referred to at the beginning of this essay, they suffer from concentration on limited sections of society, essentially those to which the authors and audience of *adab* literature belonged. They have evident difficulty in approaching situations which, because of historical developments, differ significantly from those familiar to ʿAbbāsid literary circles, as the treatment of al-Akhṭal shows. And they rarely provide any insight into how the non-Muslims felt.

It is noteworthy that the information I have presented chiefly concerns relations between Muslims and Christians. As far as adherents of the pre-Islamic cults of Arabia are concerned, the sources must be treated with great caution. And in any case the Arab tribes soon adhered to Islam, at least officially. The absence of Zoroastrians can be ascribed at least partly to the fact that very few of the anecdotes which reflect informal social contacts are set in Iran; at best there may be a reference to an attractive *dihqāna*.[91] As for the Jews, there are some scattered allusions to them,[92] but nothing to compare with the material about Christians. Christians were, after all, far more numerous; indeed, at the beginning of the ʿAbbāsid period they were still the majority in Syria and Iraq.[93] They had institutions and customs which caught the Muslim fancy, and their coreligionists in Byzantium occupied a special place in the Muslim world view.[94] But perhaps, in connection with *adab* texts and writers, there is a simpler explanation: in the ʿAbbāsid period the Iraqi Christian communities provided many clerks,[95] and the Muslim *adab* writers were often civil servants, too. Working side by side with Christians and sharing the same literary culture, Muslims would be more familiar with them and their way of life than with those of the other religious communities.

To put things in perspective, it should be added that even the anecdotes in which Christians appear are a tiny proportion of belles-lettres texts. Arabic literature after the Islamic conquests was the literature of the Arab ruling elite, and this elite felt closer affinities to fellow[96] Arab Muslims than to the non-Muslim communities over which it ruled. By the time non-Arabs began to participate in Arabic literary culture, its predominantly Muslim character was established. Even when drawing on a book as large and various as the *Aghānī*, one has to search carefully to find much information on non-Muslims (apart from semi-legendary pre-Islamic Arabs) and contacts between them and Muslims.

It must be admitted, however, that the non-Muslims are not always identified as such in the texts. Apart from the example of Barṣūmā, referred to previously, whose typically Christian name gives him away, there are other minor characters who must have been non-Muslims, such as the wine-merchant Ḥunayn in al-Ḥira, the regular supplier of the poet al-Uqayshir[97] or a number of bearers of neutral names like Yaʿqūb, Yaḥyā or ʿAdī. But the difference in religion was not considered significant enough to mention; at most the indication of a profession or a tribal origin[98] might hint at the individual's belonging to one of the non-Muslim communities. And sometimes it is only the behavior of a character in an incident which gives him away, as in the anecdote told of Abū ʿAbbād, which incidentally provides a vivid glimpse of the frictions of civil service life in the time of al-Maʾmūn. One day Abū ʿAbbād, who was al-Maʾmūn's secretary,[99] got so annoyed with one of the clerks working under him that he threw an inkwell at him. This drew blood, and Abū ʿAbbād, regretting his behavior, said: "God, exalted be he, spoke truly indeed [when he said] 'And those who, when they are angry, go too far (*wa-lladhīna idhā mā ghaḍibū hum yatajāwazūna*)'." Al-Maʾmūn came to hear of the matter and took Abū ʿAbbād to task for not being able to recite a verse from the Qurʾān properly, even though he occupied an important position in the state. Thereupon the secretary claimed to be able to recite at least a thousand verses of any sūra. Al-Maʾmūn, laughing, asked which sūra he was thinking of, and Abū ʿAbbād replied: "Any sūra you like." Al-Maʾmūn laughed harder and asked him to recite from the sūra al-Kawthar. But he had him dismissed from his position;[100] evidently anyone in such a responsible post had to have a basic knowledge of the Qurʾān. The caliph's leniency points to Abū ʿAbbād's belonging to the *ahl al-dhimma*, for a Muslim who displayed such ignorance of the Revelation would have been a social outcast.

When all the above shortcomings are admitted, the fact remains that these *adab* texts present individual reactions to the situation of religious pluralism existing in the Middle East between the rise of Islam and the fourth/tenth century. Sometimes the reader senses clearly in the non-Muslim's behavior the awareness that he belongs to a subordinate community; sometimes there are glimpses of situations where Muslims and non-Muslims could laugh together about the religious differences that separated them. It is the variety of these reactions, which the *adab* authors have not sought to systematize, together with the vividness of their literary presentation, which gives the *adab* anecdotes a small, but not negligible, place among the surviving evidence about social intercourse between Muslims and non-Muslims as Arab Muslim authors of the ʿAbbāsid period perceived it.

NOTES

1. On the author, see *Encyclopaedia of Islam*, new ed. (Leiden: E. J. Brill). See also *Encyclopedia Iranica*. References are to the Dār al-kutub edition of the *Aghānī*, 24 vols. (Cairo, 1927–1974).

2. See Ahmad Shboul, *Al-Masʿūdī and his World* (London, 1979), pp. 77–79.

3. This can be explained in two ways. Much Arabic poetry and prose, particularly older poetry and the narratives of the *ayyām al-ʿarab*, are the product of historical events, as the preface to the *Aghānī* indicates (*Agh.* I, pp. 1–2). At the same time, literature, especially poetry, preserves history. There are several references to the immortality of literary works in the *Aghānī* itself (for example, vol. 10, p. 304; vol. 14, pp. 92, 99). I believe it is one of the fundamental ideas behind the *Aghānī* as Abū l-Faraj conceived it.

4. Notably the controversy between Iṣhāq ibn Ibrāhīm al-Mawṣilī and Ibrāhīm ibn al-Mahdī (*Agh.* vol. 10, pp. 141–148), which is reflected in the biographies of other musicians too, such as Shāriya (vol. 16, p. 14).

5. In his introduction to the article on Ibn al-Muʿtazz, Abū l-Faraj defends this poet's *badīʿ* style (*Agh.* vol. 10, pp. 274–276).

6. The treatment of Khālid al-Qasrī is a case in point; see Stefan Leder, *Das Korpus al-Haiṭam ibn ʿAdī (st. 207/822): Herkunft, Überlieferung, Gestalt früher Texte der aḥbār Literatur* (Frankfurt/Main, 1991), p. 170. Another form of bias can be observed in the suppression of material; there is no exposition, for instance, of the death of al-Ḥusayn ibn ʿAlī, even though an elegy on him is quoted (*Agh.* vol. 16, p. 142).

7. *Agh.* vol. 1, pp. 4–6.

8. See the *Encyclopaedia of Islam*, new ed. (Leiden: E. J. Brill).

9. A port city of southern Iraq, whose site is now occupied by the modern city of Basra.

10. *Agh.* vol. 5, p. 159.

11. Ibid., p. 154.

12. Ibid., p. 227.

13. Ibid., p. 255.

14. Cf. Georg Graf, *Geschichte der christlichen arabischen Literatur*, 5 vols. (Vatican City, 1944–1953), vol. 5, p. 23, which lists saints and clerics bearing this name, transcribed however as Barsawmā. For the musician himself, see Eckhard Neubauer, *Musiker am Hof der frühen ʿAbbāsiden* (Frankfurt am Main, 1965), pp. 126, 175. Here, too, the name is transcribed as Barṣawmā.

15. *Agh.* vol. 6, pp. 164–165.

16. *Agh.* vol. 2, p. 355.

17. According to this tradition, which goes back to Ḥunayn's grandson, Ḥunayn was one of the "four great singers." But other accounts name only Hijazis, Ibn Surayj, Ibn Muḥriz, Maʿbad, and either al-Gharīḍ or Mālik, as the four masters. Henry George Farmer, *A History of Arabian music* (repr. London, 1973), p. 80, n. 1.

18. Abū l-Faraj al-Iṣbahānī, *Kitāb adab al-ghurabāʾ*, ed. Ṣalāḥ al-dīn al-Munajjid (Beirut, 1972). For a discussion of the content, see my "The *Kitāb adab al-ghurabāʾ* of Abū l-Farağ al-Iṣfahānī" in *Actes du 8me Congrès de l'Union Européenne des Arabisants et Islamisants* (Aix-en-Provence, 1978), pp. 127–135.

19. Kharshana was the principal fortress of one of the themes. See André Miquel, *La géographie humaine du monde musulman jusqu'au milieu du 11e siècle*, 4 vols., vol. 2 (Paris, 1975), pp. 392, 398. Cf. Shboul, *Masʿūdī*, pp. 239, 241.

20. *Ghurabāʾ*, p. 43. Friendship as the remedy for *ghurba* is one of the book's main themes. It is interesting that such a *khabar* should be encountered in a book compiled during a time when the ʿAbbāsid empire was on the defensive and the Byzantines were recapturing some of their lost provinces. Cf. Shboul, *Masʿūdī*, p. 262.

21. *Agh.* vol. 14, pp. 304, 306–307. Al-ʿAbbās ibn Mirdās was a tribal *sayyid* renowned for his bravery. He died in ʿUthmān's caliphate. See Fuat Sezgin, *Geschichte des arabischen Schrifttums* (= GAS). Vol. 2: *Poesie* (Leiden, 1975), pp. 242–243.

22. *Agh.* vol. 14, p. 86. Qays ibn ʿĀṣim was a chief of one of the subtribes of the Banū Tamīm; he is said to have died in 47/667.

23. *Agh.*, vol. 14, p. 86.

24. A similar conflict between personal inclination and the laws of tribal social organization is to be found in the article on ʿUrwa ibn al-Ward (*Agh.* vol. 3, pp. 76–77). Here, however, religion plays no part. What finally drives ʿUrwa's wife to return to her own tribe is the contempt her husband's fellow-tribeswomen show her as a prisoner of war.

25. *Agh.* vol. 14, p. 55.

26. See p. 219 (in this volume), where al-Mutawakkil encourages a Christian girl to convert before he marries her.

27. Ironically in the later Umayyad and early ʿAbbāsid periods "individual Makhzūmīs crop up in the sources mainly in the context of religious learning and the application of Islamic law." *Encyclopaedia of Islam*, new edition (Leiden: E. J. Brill), vol. 6, p. 140.

28. *Agh.* vol. 6, p. 116 (an anonymous report, not elaborated in subsequent narratives). This bears a distinct resemblance to the account of Rabīʿa ibn Umayya ibn Khalaf (*Agh.* vol. 15, p. 21), who was punished by ʿUmar ibn al-Khaṭṭāb with exile for drinking in Ramaḍān. He found this so humiliating that he left for Byzantium, converted, and was well treated by the emperor.

29. *Agh.* vol. 6, p. 118.

30. Ibid. (a report purporting to go back to the caliph's envoy, who reproduces al-Wābiṣī's words).

31. This song forms the connecting link between al-Wābiṣī's *akhbār* and the *Aghānī* article which precedes them; al-Wābiṣī composed one of the settings for it.

32. *Agh.* vol. 6, pp. 117–118. Al-Masʿūdī, in this *Kitāb al-tanbīh wa-l-ishrāf*, ed. de Goeje, Bibliotheca Geographorum arabicorum 8) (Leiden, 1894), p. 189,

observes that captives were ransomed at the frontiers in the Umayyad period. He does not mention any large-scale exchange of prisoners.

33. *Agh.* vol. 6, pp. 118–119. The motif of an Arabic song sung by a "Byzantine" under siege catching the attention of a besieger recurs in the *khabar* about Rabīʿa ibn Umayya (see n. 28); his presence is thus revealed to the Umayyad troops. But there is no report of him conversing with them, as al-Wābiṣī does in this anecdote.

34. *Agh.* vol. 15, pp. 162–167.

35. Cf. *Encyclopaedia of Islam*, new ed. (Leiden: E. J. Brill), art. "Djabala b. al-Ayham," which hints at the legendary character of these anecdotes.

36. One of the great Umayyad love poets, and a member of the Meccan merchant aristocracy.

37. *Agh.* vol. 1, p. 67. Her death occurred during ʿUmar ibn al-Khaṭṭāb's caliphate.

38. *Agh.* vol. 22, pp. 14, 25. On Khālid al-Qasrī see *Encyclopaedia of Islam*, new ed. (Leiden: E. J. Brill). The presentation of Khālid's life and especially death, and the tendentious nature of some reports concerning him, are discussed in Leder, *Korpus*, pp. 146–195.

39. D. 276/889. Cf. *Encyclopaedia of Islam*, new ed. (Leiden: E. J. Brill), art. "Ibn Makhlad." He converted in al-Muwaffaq's presence. Yāqūt, *Muʿjam al-buldān*, vol. 2, ed. F. Wüstenfeld (Leipzig, 1866–1873), p. 678.

40. Abū l-Ḥasan ʿAlī ibn Muḥammad al-Shābushtī, *Kitāb al-diyārāt*, ed. Kūrkīs ʿAwwād, 2nd. ed. (Baghdad, 1966), p. 270. This may be a biased judgment, but he was certainly a dreadful poet, going by the lines of his quoted here. For further discussion of the *Kitāb al-diyārāt*, see n. 41.

41. *Diyārāt*, pp. 270, 273. A monastery near Samarra was named after him because he was such a frequent visitor to it. Yāqūt, *Muʿjam*, vol. 2, p. 678.

42. *Encyclopaedia of Islam*, new ed. (Leiden: E. J. Brill). See also the introduction to Īlīya Salīm al-Ḥāwī, *Sharḥ dīwān al-Akhṭal al-Taghlibī* (Beirut, n.d. [1968]), pp. 11–60.

43. See *Encyclopaedia of Islam*, new ed. (Leiden: E. J. Brill), art. "Dimashḳ."

44. ʿAbd al-Rahmān was the son of the Prophet's panegyrist. He came into conflict with the Umayyad ʿAbd al-Raḥmān ibn al-Ḥakam, whom he got the better of in poetry; see *Encyclopaedia of Islam*, new ed. (Leiden: E. J. Brill), Supplement *s.v.*

45. He had supported Muʿāwiya in his conflict with ʿAlī; *GAS* vol. 2, pp. 162–163.

46. *Agh.* vol. 8, pp. 299, 294, 288, 289. This last could be explained by a streak of intractability and lawlessness which al-Ḥāwī discerns in this character: al-Ḥāwī, *Sharḥ*, p. 20.

47. *Agh.* vol. 8, pp. 303, 309–310.

48. *Agh.* vol. 8, p. 300. For this use of "*ḥanīf*," see *Encyclopaedia of Islam*, new ed. (Leiden: E. J. Brill).

49. *Agh.* vol. 8, p. 290. There is a teasing note running through the whole anecdote.

50. Ibid., p. 289.

51. Ibid., p. 299, a variant on p. 285.

52. Ibid., p. 306.

53. Ibid., pp. 285, 305.

54. Ibid., p. 286.

55. Ibid., p. 306.

56. Ibid., p. 299.

57. *Agh.* vol. 11, p. 282 quotes a couplet by Aʿshā Banī Taghlib (d. c. 100/718) complimenting Shamʿala ibn ʿĀmir of the Banī Fā'id for refusing to convert; the caliph in question (unnamed) had fed him a piece of his own flesh, roasted, as a punishment for this recalcitrance. But cf. al-Mubarrad, *Al-kāmil*, ed. M. Abū l-Faḍl Ibrāhīm, 4 vols. (Cairo, n.d.), vol. 3, p. 158, for a quite different, nonreligious context of these lines.

58. *Ghurabā'*, pp. 64, 78.

59. Ibid. pp. 23, 36, 65.

60. Abū l-Faraj al-Iṣbahānī, *al-diyārāt*, ed. Jalīl al-ʿAṭīya (London, 1991), does not contain the text of this book but only a collection of passages from other works which may have been included in it. The editor lists a number of titles of books on monasteries in his introduction, pp. 27–31.

61. The role played by the individual author's intellectual training and *Weltanschanung* in such cases becomes clear when one compares, for instance, Ibn Abī Dunyā's (208–281/823–894) *Kitāb al-faraj baʿd al-shidda* with al-Tanūkhī's (327–384/938–994) book of the same name.

62. Ewald Wagner, *Grundzüge der klassischen arabischen Dichtung*, Vol. 2: *Die arabische Dichtung in islamischer Zeit* (Darmstadt, 1988), p. 43. Cf. Miquel, *Géographie*, vol. 4 (Paris, 1988), pp. 86–90, who stresses the marvels which al-Shābushtī relates in connection with the monasteries. But this special section only occupies a dozen odd pages of the 300-page edition. Miquel's earlier discussion of this book (see note 61, vol. 1 (Paris, 1967], pp. 149–150) gives a more accurate impression of it.

63. About al-Shābushtī's life very little is known, beyond the fact that he was the librarian of the Fatimid caliph al-ʿAzīz (reg. 365–386/975–996) and died c. 399/1008 (C. Brockelmann, *Geschichte der arabischen Literatur* [= *GAL*] [Leiden, 1937–1949], *Supplement* 1, p. 411). As the editor observes in his introduction, a passing reference shows that al-Shābushtī visited Basra (*Diyārāt*, p. 26*), and the author elsewhere names as a source "a Christian of the Jazira" (p. 309), which might mean that he visited the region. Certainly many of the detailed descriptions of the monasteries and their surroundings give the impression of coming from an eye-

witness. And there was a regular influx of Iraqi *kuttāb* into Egypt in this period; it is quite possible that al-Shābushtī was one of them.

64. *Diyārāt*, pp. 110–148.

65. Cf. Miquel, *Géographie*, vol. 4, p. 87. The monasteries outside Homs were situated in an area known as al-Farādīs (*Ghurabā'*, p. 64). Yāqūt mentions that the Syrians called vineyards and orchards *farādīs*, and refers to places near Damascus and Aleppo (but not Homs) which bore the name (*Mu'jam*, vol. 3, pp. 862–863).

66. The article on ʿAbdallāh ibn al-ʿAbbās al-Rabīʿi in the *Agh.* shows the poet-musician frequenting churches assiduously in order to catch sight of his beloved (*Agh.* vol. 19, pp. 234, 249).

67. Cf. Miquel, *Géographie*, vol. 1, p. 150.

68. *Diyārāt*, p. 93.

69. Ibid., p. 241.

70. Ibid., pp. 301, 303.

71. Cf. the observation made about later periods, for the region from Bosnia to Trebizond and Egypt: "Practically any of the religions of Turkey may share the use of a sanctuary administered by another, if this sanctuary has a sufficient reputation for beneficient miracles, among which miracles of healing play a dominant part." F. W. Hasluck, *Christianity and Islam under the Sultans* (Oxford, 1929), pp. 68–69.

72. *Diyārāt*, p. 204.

73. The characters of the *Diyārāt* represent social groups with most people of medieval Arabic belles-lettres: rulers and their relatives, generals, governors, secretaries, courtiers, poets, and singers.

74. Cf. Ger Duijzings, "Van het rechte pad geraakt: Gezamelijke pelgrimages van moslims en christenen in Joegoslavië en Albanië," in *Islamitische Pelgrimstochten*, ed. Willy Jansen and Huub de Jonge (Muiderberg, 1991), p. 114. Hasluck (*Christianity* p. 25, n. 5) mentions Muslims making pilgrimages to the church of St. Simeon Stylites near Antioch.

75. Al-Masʿūdī, *Murūj al-dhahab wa-maʿādin al-jawhar*, ed. Barbier de Meynard and Pavet de Courteille, rev. Charles Pellat, 7 vols., vol. 2 (Beirut, 1966), p. 70.

76. The text does not specify whether they were Muslims or Christians. Cf. Hasluck, *Christianity*, pp. 30–31, 34, for later examples of crosses being used by Muslims.

77. *Diyārāt*, p. 179. Cf. *Agh.* vol. 5, p. 428, where it was al-Wāthiq who distributed largesse. An example of more regular patronage is mentioned by Yāqūt (*Mu'jam*, vol. 2, p. 692), who reports that Sayf al-Dawla used to regularly interrupt his journeys at Dayr Mār Marūthā and give it money, because his mother had asked him to take care of it.

78. "*Kilāhumā* (var. *kilayhimā*) *wa-tamran*," a proverbial expression, meaning literally "both of them, and some dates as well"; cf. al-Zamakhsharī, *Al-mustaqṣā fī amthāl al-ʿarab*, 2 vols. (Beirut, 1397/1977), vol. 2, p. 231 (n. 780).

79. *Diyārāt*, pp. 164–165.

80. It is akin to al-Masʿūdī's attitude (except when he is writing of the Byzantine foe), which is characterized by "sympathy, fairmindedness and courtesy" (Shboul, *Masʿūdī*, pp. 294–295).

81. *Ghurabā'*, pp. 34–36.

82. In most Eastern churches a priest is not allowed to marry after ordination, and if his wife dies he may take monastic vows. For a monk to have a daughter need not be anything unusual.

83. *Ghurabā'*, pp. 64–68.

84. The fact that the caliph involved was al-Mutawakkil may be relevant, too. Al-Mutawakkil is well known for having introduced discriminatory measures against Christians and Jews. However, caliphs who adopted such measures did not necessarily eschew all contact with the *ahl al-kitāb*. Al-Muqtadir had to re-introduce similar measures—which suggests that they were not well observed. He also had a vizir, four of whose nine councillors were Christians. A. Mez, *Die Renaissance des Islams* (Heidelberg, 1922), p. 48.

85. *Diyārāt*, p. 185.

86. *Agh.* vol. 23, p. 189; the poet is the early ʿAbbāsid Bakr ibn Khārija.

87. *Diyārāt*, p. 206; the poet is Abū Nuwās.

88. "*dhabḥ*" in the *Agh.* amended to "*dinḥ*," for which see Georg Graf, *Verzeichnis arabischer kirchlicher Termini*, 2nd. expanded ed. (Louvain, 1954), p. 47. I am grateful to Professor Shboul for suggesting this correction.

89. *Agh.* vol. 18, p. 244. Cf. Yāqūt, *Mu'jam*, vol. 2, p. 689, for another poem where ʿAbdallāh claims to have made his home in a monastery and adopted the appropriate dress.

90. Mez (*Renaissance*, p. 49) quotes a case from Fatimid Egypt where a Christian local administrator had a Muslim deputy who performed the Friday prayer for him. The *adab* sources do not cast any light on whether Christian dignitaries of state were expected to make a formal appearance at any Muslim ceremonies.

91. E.g., *Agh.* vol. 13, pp. 331–332.

92. *Agh.* vol. 14, pp. 197–198; the same anecdote in the *Diyārāt* (p. 51) depicts the wine merchant as a Jew who had converted to Islam, which makes better sense. It also omits the puerile ending of the *Agh.* version.

93. Hugh Kennedy, *The Prophet and the Age of the Caliphates: The Islamic Near East from the Sixth to the Eleventh Century* (London, 1986), pp. 201–202.

94. Shboul, *Masʿūdī*, p. 227.

95. See *Encyclopaedia of Islam*, new ed. (Leiden: E. J. Brill), art. "Dayr"; Dominique Sourdel, *Le vizirat*

abbâside de 749 à 936 (132 à 324 de l'Hégire) (Damascus 1959), pp. 304, 313–317, 337–338, 512–513.

96. Kennedy, *Prophet*, p. 202.

97. *Agh.* vol. 11, pp. 261–262. Al-Uqayshir died around 80/699 (*GAS* vol. 2, pp. 326–327).

98. The woman who tricked al-Uqayshir out of the dirhams he intended for his daily ration was an ʿIbādī, and thus implicitly a Christian.

99. Abū ʿAbbād Thābit ibn Yaḥyā, a native of Rayy (Sourdel, *Vizirat*, pp. 231–232, 733).

100. Yāqūt, *Muʿjam*, vol. 2, p. 706, quoting the early fourth/tenth century Abū Bakr al-Ṣūlī.

III

MODERN TIMES

14

Christianity as Described by Persian Muslims

ISABEL STÜMPEL-HATAMI

Publications on "Jesus in the Qur'ān" or "Jesus in Islam" are numerous. Many of the authors are Christian theologians, if not missionaries,[1] some of them personally concerned by the contradictions between the Qur'ān and the Bible or in search of a common ground of dialogue. Two studies that deserve mentioning are by Roger Arnaldez (1988) and Neal Robinson (1990). In another important study focused on seven key verses, Jane Dammen McAuliffe analyzed the Qur'ānic exegesis with regard to the depiction of Christians (1991).[2] In general, these studies are exclusively based on the classical authoritative sources in Arabic language—that is, the Qur'ān and *tafsīr* and *hadith* literature.

Little interest has been paid to the image of Jesus (and Christianity) among Muslims in *our* days. Olaf Schumann, likewise a Christian theologian, has submitted a most interesting investigation[3] discussing the writings of some twentieth-century Muslim authors besides the classical texts. Coming to Rashīd Riḍā and Ṭabāṭabā'ī, McAuliffe equally treats two representatives of the twentieth century in her previously mentioned analysis which covers ten centuries of *tafsīr*. In 1986, Khoury and Hagemann published a book on modern Muslim authors' writings on Christianity with the underlying motive of detecting possible points of reference for Christian-Muslim dialogue. Similar studies were made by Hugh Goddard (1996) and Kate Zebiri (1997).[4] Again, these studies concentrate mainly on Arabic texts, whereas little research has been conducted on *Persian* sources dealing with other religions,[5] let alone *contemporary* Persian publications. This essay may be considered a modest attempt to fill in this gap.

If we look for contemporary Persian texts on non-Muslim religions we will first come across publications on Christianity and, to a lesser extent, on Judaism. Some specialists publish on Hinduism, like Daryush Shayegan, the well-known disciple and friend of Henry Corbin; a few studies on Buddhism can also be cited.[6] A number of authors deal with several religions, including Islam—under the title of the so-called great World Religions,[7] the Semitic religions,[8] or the *ahl al-kitāb*-religions, including Zoroastrism.[9]

Western Christianity

It does not surprise us that the main interest is nonetheless paid to Christianity. On the one hand, since the last two centuries, the impact on Persian economy and politics by Westerners who are Christians by definition is most important. On the other hand, in terms of religion, the Christians are viewed as the major rival, mainly because of their missionary expansionism: "In our days only two heavenly religions exist (i.e., Islam and Christianity), one of which is abrogated (i.e., Christianity). They clash notably in Asia and Africa."[10]

Due to Western colonialist and missionary activities Christianity is thus identified with the *Occident*. In fact, apart from a few books on Armenians and Assyrians as indigenous religious minorities,[11] Persian publications on Christianity discuss mainly its development in the West while they contain only brief remarks about the existence of Eastern churches.

The manifold activities deployed by occidental missionaries through educational and medical assistance in schools, hospitals, summer camps, youth clubs, and bookstores and through the modern mass media did not prosper without provoking the deep concern and the protest of the religious class. The more the Christian mission was organized, the more it appeared to them like an evergrowing network of conspiration:

> Alarm bells: Our religion and our independence are threatened. Do you know that the project of christianizing Iran was already hatched by Knox d'Arcy at the time of Nasiruddin Shah? Are you informed about the attacks launched by the American Dr. John Elder, member of the American Mission in Iran, who has published several books? Are you informed about the Christian propaganda in schools and hospitals? Do you know that Mister Christopher King(?) of the World Council of Churches came to Iran and contacted . . . the Head of the Iranian Council of Churches . . . ? Do you know that recently the rumour runs that a radio canal diffusing Christian propaganda has been uncovered in Teheran? Do you know that a widely read Iranian Newspaper has raised the importance of Christians in Iran by giving an exaggerated number—1 million instead of 200,000—and believes that one Iranian out of twenty is a Christian?[12]

The missionaries were viewed as the servants of colonialism and the message they brought was understood as an attempt to dissimulate the real motives of the foreign invaders. This correlation is voiced by a contemporary Iranian poet:

> Lined up as beggars
> We reaped with the sickle of each crescent
> Multiple harvests of poverty and hunger
> In the miracle fields of this uncrucified Jesus.
> O messiah of plunder, of hate!
> O artificial messiah!
> Where is the rain to wash off your face
> The false images, the shadows of deceit.[13]

Besides the English, American, German, French, and Swiss missionaries, the Christian presence was embodied by diplomats, businessmen, and, later on, by the engineers and experts from Europe and the United States. Following them came the culture of the consumer society: films, Coca Cola and hot dogs—yielding alienation for the elder Iranian generation and seduction for the Iranian youth.[14]

Thus, circumstances were such as to provoke rather defensive refutations of the Christian message than scholarly study.[15] In fact, Shīʿi clergy circles tried from the 1960s onward to train some sort of Muslim missionaries. At the same time, efforts were made to provide their coreligionists and notably the Muslim youth with fundamental knowledge of the "enemy's" religion and ideology, in order to immunize them from Christian propaganda.[16] For this purpose, the *Dār al-tablīgh-i islāmī* founded by Āyatullāh Sharīʿatmadārī in the holy city of Qom published a series of anti-Christian tracts, as well as monographs on Christianity and Islam.[17] Such publications were partially the result of discussion circles on non-Islamic religions and ideologies which were newly introduced in the traditional curriculum in order to match the challenge of Christian and Western indoctrination.[18] In many cases, the publications of the Muslim side can be regarded as an immediate reaction to Christian missionary publications.[19] As a matter of fact, the spreading of Christian literature was fairly advanced in comparison to other regions of the Middle East since it had shown itself to be the most effective instrument of mission among Persians.[20]

Types of Texts; Bible and Beliefs

Here I will sketch a brief survey of the main subjects of modern Persian Muslim writings on Christianity by giving special notice to new features not to be found in the "classical" heresiography (*milal wa niḥal*). Then I will discuss some original approaches as distinguished from the rather stereotyped polemical accounts and commonplaces offered by many authors.[21]

My remarks are based on a collection of some 40 printed texts dealing as a whole or in a special chapter with Christianity. They were gathered from bibliographies and from references found in some of the texts themselves. Admittedly, I was largely dependent on the indications given by the titles, so that some equally relevant texts may have gone unnoticed. Moreover, I did not include the whole of available polemical literature. Given its uniformity I have rather singled out some polemics referred to by more descriptive texts. I presume that they represent widely read samples of this category.[22] Most texts were published in the 1960s and 1980s. The respective number of copies range from 1,500 to 20,000, sometimes with several editions. Within this collection, several authors are repeatedly referred to by others. Hence, we may conclude that their writings became a sort of standard work or at least were read in circles concerned by the treated issues. Among the authors are holders of traditional titles of religious learning, as well as doctors and university professors, including some well-known personalities of public life (ambassadors, ministers), like Mahdī Bāzargān, ʿAlī Aṣghar Ḥikmat, and Muḥammad Javād Bāhunar. Within limits, this material may therefore be regarded as a representative selection.

We may distinguish three types of texts:

1. Mere refutations of Christianity or Judaism—often recognizable from the very titles, for example, "Two religions, a religion of backwardness and imperialism [i.e., Christianity] and another religion in favor of the people and nations [i.e., Islam]."[23]
2. Critical accounts of other religions, intended to furnish comparative knowledge which shall (according to the authors' expressed intention) finally lead the reader to a deliberate choice of Islam as the best religion.[24]
3. Descriptive texts which claim to rely exclusively on the sources of the respective religion and to refrain deliberately from rendering the Islamic point of view.

Certainly, these are ideal types. In fact, a polemical undertone may occasionally be noticed in descriptive texts, whereas even refutations contain descriptive passages. In all types, Qurʾānic verses, as well as verses from the Bible, are quoted. Moreover, all authors refer in some measure to Western sources. Among the latter we can distinguish some favorites which are repeatedly cited. The reasons for such a predilection are not always obvious: one factor may be that the quoted Western author sketches Islam or Iran in a positive light,[25] or that he takes a critical attitude toward Christianity;[26] another factor may simply be a book's handiness,[27] or its already existing Arabic[28] or Persian[29] translation. Obviously, some five or six manuals of history of religions translated from English and French are in current usage.

The polemic authors are eager to quote from "Christian" sources, that is, rather from enlightened critics of the Church—Voltaire, Victor Hugo, Bertrand Russell, and the like—who are supposed to corroborate their arguments, whereas descriptive texts occasionally refer to Islamic sources (*milal wa niḥal*-works, *tafsīr*, etc.). Obviously, these sources dating from the Middle Ages are supposed to provide valuable information even in our day.[30] Some authors insist on the high scholarly standard of medieval Muslim heresiography in contrast to contemporary Christian contributions.[31]

As far as the reliability of Christian sources is concerned, the polemics maintain the *taḥrīf*-thesis. Some more descriptive texts allude to it without using the term itself. Some authors declare that they will rely on Jewish or Christian sources in spite of their admittedly distorted or incomplete character. Thus, they both stick to the demands of modern scientific description and maintain the conventional Muslim standpoint.

The polemical authors add that, according to Christians, the present-day Bible is a dictation, literally revealed by God, whereas many Bible passages make a mockery of this belief.[32] Allusion is made to anthropomorphic features of Yahweh as in the story of his wrestling with Jacob and to accounts compromising the purity (*tanzīh*) of the prophets, like David violating Uriah's wife. As a further proof against its heavenly origin, our authors mention the heterogenous composition of the Old Testament by the hand of numerous authors which was extended over centuries. Regarding the Gospels, they hint at the considerable space of time between Jesus' death and the record of his sayings as opposed to the immediate, uncorrupted record of the Qurʾānic revelation.

In many texts, Christian doctrines and beliefs are not only declared to be corrupt but also their originality is denied by tracing them back to foreign (pagan) sources. The authors mention Egyptian, Babylonian, Buddhist, and Zoroastrian influences.[33] Here we recognize some sort of counterattack, given that one of the missionaries' tactics was precisely to unveil the Arab, Jewish, and Christian sources of Islam! In order to spoil Islam in Persian eyes, they even tried to depict Islam as an Arab shackle,[34] a psychologically clever argument meant to stir up the inherent Persian aversion to the Arabs.[35]

As to the subjects treated, all three types discuss the Christian doctrine of the Trinity and the diverse Christian sects with their respective doctrine on the nature of Christ at the sample of the "classical" *milal wa niḥal*—literature. Polemic authors make ironical remarks about the missionaries' futile endeavor to present the Trinity in an intelligible manner to their Muslim interlocutors—by drawing for instance a triangle on a sheet of paper. *Tawḥīd* is explicitly or implicitly viewed as the peak of religious evolution. "The majority of the Christians who consider Jesus as Son of God prevent the original creed from reaching the rank of perfect *tawḥīd*."[36] Our authors confirm the Islamic concept of the "seal of the prophets"—that is, of Islam as the peak of revealed religions—by making use of a Western model of evolution in vogue at the beginning of the century, according to which religion has developed from polytheism to henotheism before reaching the final stage of monotheism.[37]

Crucifixion; Redemption

In general, Muslim authors deny the crucifixion of Jesus.[38] The main controversial issue between Christians and Muslims besides the doctrine of the Trinity, that is, the crucifixion, reveals an interesting attitude shared by several authors. The polemical ones, of course, deny the crucifixion by pointing at the respective Qur'ānic utterance and the different versions developed in its *tafsīr* about who may have been the substitute crucified in Jesus' place. However, in a considerable number of texts the Christian and the Qur'ānic account are both rendered consecutively, while the authors do not enter into discussions about their value nor offer any synthesis.[39] I suggest that as a result of the Christian missionary efforts comprising Bible translations and the publication of commentaries and other kinds of religious literature, the biblical account has acquired a parallel status in the consciousness of cultivated Muslims besides the inherited knowledge of the Qur'ānic tradition.

Khoury and Hagemann have diagnosed the incapacity of Muslim authors to distinguish between history and its theological interpretation. So, if they want to reject the theological interpretation they first start by rejecting the historical fact.[40] An exception to this rule is the Persian author Jalāl ud-dīn Āshtiyānī.[41] In his book on Christianity he admits—at least as a hypothesis—that the crucifixion of Jesus has taken place. For him, accepting this thesis leads to suppose that Jesus rose up against the Roman Empire. Yet, in the next paragraph, Āshtiyānī insists on the vanity of its interpretation in terms of a divine sacrifice: "As to the story of . . . the crucified god, this is a primitive myth devoid of any value."[42] Thus, this author *does* distinguish between the two levels of history on the one side and the theological interpretation on the other side.

The doctrine of redemption is closely linked with the subject of crucifixion. The polemics hold that this belief weakens the sense of responsibility and therefore represents a serious social danger,[43] whereas the more descriptive texts just mention it without comment. According to the Christian missionaries, this very doctrine may serve as a starting point in dialogue with Shī'ite Muslims, given the affinity of Shī'ite creed about the cathartic effect of the martyrdom of Imam Husain to the Christian doctrine of redemption.[44] However, it is precisely this approximation which turns out to be explicitly rejected by one of our Muslim authors: "[The fathers of the Church] presented the crucifixion of Jesus as the redemption for the sins of his followers. . . . Similar ideas are sometimes to be found among certain Muslims regarding the sacrifice of religious leaders. They yield nothing but a lack of firmness and the denial of responsibility."[45]

The idea of the original sin, which entails the need for redemption, is of course equally rejected, because according to the Islamic sources, Adam showed repentance and God forgave him. Moreover, the Qur'ān clearly states that nobody can take the burden of somebody else's deeds.[46]

Jesus; The Eucharist

Let us see now how Jesus is portrayed in the Persian texts studied. The classical Islamic tradition stresses ascetism and miracle working as the essential characteristics of ʿĪsā. Yet, only one of the Persian texts refers explicitly to such a classical source, namely the *Nahj ul-balāgha*.[47] In general, the first characteristic—that is, Jesus' ascetism—is modified insofar as many authors emphasize his sociability and his participation in festivities as opposed to the retired ascetic life of John the Baptist. Nevertheless, almost all the authors underline Jesus' community with the poor and the oppressed (*maẓlūmīn*) of society. To my mind, this modification can be interpreted as a result of the more intimate acquaintance with Christian literature, notably the Gospels.

As to the second outstanding feature—that is, Jesus' capacity to perform miracles—several authors explain it as a psychological phenomenon. People were healed because of their belief in His healing force, and the daughter of Jairus was not dead but had a hysterical attack. This kind of interpretation joins a trend in Christian theology and Bible research which tries to find natural explanations to miracles in order to reconcile them with modern science. Yet, this interpretation is opposed to the Qurʾānic view which presents the miracles as worked by divine grace[48] and is also opposed to the Islamic classical theory which attributes the *muʿjizāt* as confirmative signs to the prophets of God.

Concerning the self-consciousness of Jesus, several authors hint at an alleged development which finally led him to consider himself as the promised Messiah. As one of the decisive factors which influenced this evolution, they mention the latent expectation of the Messiah among the Jews. This kind of psychological approach is clearly opposed to the Qurʾānic account, according to which Jesus announced his heavenly mission already in his cradle. Some authors even declare that Jesus called himself Son of God, thereby upsetting the Qurʾānic theology which attributes the origin of this title to the unbelievers.[49] Furthermore, one author holds that Jesus never claimed to be a prophet but that this title was attributed to him by the masses. In this respect, the author compares Jesus to Zoroaster who equally never claimed prophecy.[50] Once more, this view is openly opposed to the clear word of the Qurʾān.[51]

As stated by Guy Monnot,[52] the classical heresiographers do not seem to be interested in the observable aspects of Christianity—that is, the rituals, particularly the mass. They rather concentrate on doctrinal questions. According to Khoury and Hagemann, the same is true for modern Arab authors who hardly mention the Eucharist.[53] By way of contrast, some of our Persian texts describe a Christian mass, or at least mention the transubstantiation of bread and wine into the body and blood of Christ and the Communion. They acknowledge the transubstantiation as the "most effective act" according to Christian belief and the Communion as a commemoration of the Last Supper. In general, the Eucharist is mentioned within the context of the Christian sacraments which are correctly enumerated and briefly explained. The attention given to rituals may partially be due to the fact that Western research has revealed their pagan origin and thereby furnishes another argument against the authenticity of non-Muslim religions.

Other Issues under Discussion

Generally speaking, we notice a tendency to delineate the everyday aspects, the historical development, and the social "reality" or practice of (the Christian) religion besides the doctrines. As far as the practice of faith and religious prescriptions are concerned, the authors stress approvingly the absence of complicated rituals and laws in Christianity as opposed to pagan cults or to the Jewish religion. One author even compares the simplicity of Christian ritual prescriptions to the painstaking Shīʾite rituals of purification.[54] However, according to some polemic authors, Christians do not stick even to the few laws of their religion.[55]

According to the more polemic texts, the lack of complicated rituals and the overly spiritual orientation of the Christian teachings represents a serious disadvantage insofar as it means a lack of orientation in worldly affairs and for the guidance of society. Thus, Christianity allows worldly ideologies to fill in this gap. By way of contrast, Islam provides an all-embracing program for the solution of the diverse spiritual, as well as social and economic, problems and needs.[56]

The object of this discussion is of course secularism as applied and promoted in Western countries and praised as a model of social progress by the Western-oriented Pahlevi government. According to most authors who tackle this issue, the division of religious and political affairs is an artificial one. Its application leads to a division of society, and if the West has tried to export it, it is for the very purpose of destroying the national unity of the Muslim countries.[57]

Another main issue concerns the relationship between religion and science. Many texts start with some preliminary reflections on the role and the value of religion as such in order to prove its unabrogated validity and its important contribution to the issues of the modern age. In support of their arguments, they quote Western scientists like Albert Einstein and Max Planck who advocate the value of and the need for religion. Finally they portray Islam as the only religion up to the challenge of science. Yet exactly the same claim was supported by the Christian missionaries regarding Christianity.[58] It is vehemently rejected by pointing to the inherent contradictions and superstitions of Christianity which disqualify it for the competition in the age of science and reason.

The Persian authors we studied obviously react against the reproach that Islam stimulates fatalism and medieval backwardness as opposed to the activity, progress, and science prospering in the Christian world. Several texts of this collection deal with the relationship between the Church and science; some even dedicate a special chapter to this topic. The cases of Galileo Galilei and Michel Servet are mentioned by many authors in order to demonstrate the backwardness and violent opposition to science shown by the Church. The polemics immediately add that Islam by way of contrast is open to and congruent with science and progress. It is a "scientific religion."[59] These arguments are of course addressed not only to the Christian opponents but also to Western atheist ideologies which deny the consistency of religion and science in general.

Another issue—that is, religious tolerance and violence or pressure in the name of religion—is undoubtedly touched upon as a reaction against the Western commonplace of the so-called Sword of Islam.[60] In this respect, several texts emphasize that Christians have tried to spread Christianity by force and have oppressed non-Christians, whereas under Muslim rule non-Muslims lived in security and peace. The authors insist on the fact that this practice is the very opposite of the theory of Christian ethics. While Jesus had preached love and peace, Christians got involved in wars and oppression and thereby violated their own religion (*maẓlūm sākhtand*).[61]

History is often seen as a gradual distortion of the original religious teaching. In particular, authors allude to the abuses of clerical power (indulgence letters!), the Crusades, the Spanish Inquisition, and colonialism as opposed to the original teaching and practice of Jesus and to the truthfulness of the first Christians who endured persecution for the sake of their belief.[62] The hint at the firmness of the first Christians facing their cruel persecution occurs in several texts. For Shīʾites, it presumably evokes the destiny of their own community which is considered to be *maẓlūm* (wronged) throughout history.

In the context of the sacrament of confession, most authors deal with the movement of Reformation and Protestantism, introduced as a reaction against the abuses of this sacrament. However, as far as more recent evolutions are concerned, only one author mentions the ecumenical movement of the last decades.[63] In any case, Protestantism is viewed in a more positive light than Catholicism. According to some authors, many of its rectifications and simplifications converge with the intentions of the Qurʾān and Islam. Nevertheless, as M. Bāzargān puts it, the Protestant movement did not reach its ends and did not succeed in abolishing all superstitious and polytheistic features.[64]

Some Specific Studies

Coming to the end of our survey let us now turn to some examples of rather exceptional accounts.

Maḥmūd Rāmyār

The first text we would like to present is a book on Israelite and Christian prophecy by Maḥmūd Rāmyār.[65] The author was dean of the faculty of divinity at the University of Mashad. Born in 1922 (1301 H.S.) in Mashad, he studied Islamic Sciences at the Sipahsālār College in Teheran. He then pursued his studies in philosophy and law at Teheran University. Later on he became professor and dean of the faculty of divinity in Mashad. From 1974 to 1977 (1353–1356), he studied at Edinburgh University with Montgomery Watt where he obtained a Ph.D. degree. At the same time, he collaborated with the School of Oriental and African Studies in London. He knew French, English, and Arabic. His main research area was Qurʾānic studies—he also translated the introduction to the Qurʾān by Régis Blachère. In 1973 (1352)—thus *before* his stay in England—he published his study about the Israelite and Christian prophecy. He died in 1363/1984.

Though the author holds that the existing four Gospels are not identical with the Gospel of Jesus which circulated in the first years of Christianity, he admits that they must contain some truth, though not the entire truth. Like many other Muslim authors, Rāmyār points to the divergences between the Gospels, while admitting that nonetheless much congruence can be detected. He then goes on to describe the Christian conception of revelation:

> It means that revelation (*waḥy*) is not a literal dictation, but the meaning (*maʿānī*) settles on the intellect and the soul and with God's help, the right words are chosen. . . . Both the Old and the New Testament have an outer and an inner side, a real and a figurative sense . . . and each word has a secret and a spirit.[66] Thus, the Christian revelation has a particular meaning difficult to grasp for us Muslims. It links the human and the divine element

> together. The written word in the Gospel is a hint (*ramz*) to the Divine Word. Christians believe that the revelation of the Holy Spirit prohibits by no means the receivers from making use of possible human resources, and consequently the responsibility of *ijtihād* (individual effort) is assigned to the writer.[67]

Even though in other respects, Rāmyār is holding a rather apologetic position and occasionally does not avoid a polemic undertone, his description of the Christian concept of revelation demonstrates, to our mind, a noteworthy effort of comprehension and imparting.

Kamāl ud-dīn Bakhtāvar

From his chapter on Islam we conclude that our second author, Kamāl ud-dīn Bakhtāvar, belongs to the Shīʿi Shaykhi sect. Apart from his volume on semitic religions, he has published several other books on religion, ideology, and modern science.[68]

What strikes us first is his affirmation that heavenly laws, much like human-made ones, get paralyzed, sterile, and ineffective in the course of time. He goes on stating that the only difference between the two is that in the case of heavenly laws the distance between the foundation and the application is longer and that they are able to regulate the relationship between individuals of a society for a longer time than their human-made counterparts. As causes for the deficiency of religions, Bakhtāvar cites (1) their inadequacy to the circumstances and sometimes (2) their lack of a law for the guidance of society. At the end of this chapter, Bakhtāvar unequivocally declares that the Scriptures and religious teachings are of human origin:

> Even if in ancient times the legends of the Torah and the Qur'ān were regarded as the most logical explanation . . . , in our days . . . the creation of mankind can no longer be based on such childish suggestions. The inadequate philosophy of a religion can sometimes be unable to interpret creation in a reasonable and logical manner. This so happens because what is written in a *human* book cannot keep abreast of the enlargement of human thought and progress of knowledge. It is therefore necessary for religion to change in different historical periods and to explain the problems of mankind corresponding to current scientific standards. Otherwise the gap between science and religion will deepen and the imbalance between scientific laws and *human* teachings will undermine the roots of religious creed.[69]

However, this conclusion represents an unsolved contradiction to the author's previously mentioned thesis—that is, the gradual difference between *heavenly* laws and human-made ones.

In his account of Christianity, the same author holds some outstanding positions. Thus, he is the only one to attribute a positive value to the separation of religion and state as a characteristic feature of Christianity.[70] As he puts it, Christianity has delivered laws from the shackle of religion so as to enable men to act according to the requirements of time and circumstances. However, in his introduction, it seems like an allusion to Christianity when he quotes the lack of laws for the guidance of society as one of the possible shortcomings of religions.

Moreover, he undertakes a refutation of the Gospel of Barnabas, often referred to as equally or even more authentic than the four canonical Gospels by contemporary Muslim authors. In accordance with Western research, he mentions several anachronistic data which suggest its more recent compilation. In addition, he points out the fact that this Gospel even contains contradictions to the Qur'ānic verses. As an example, he quotes the announcement of Muḥammad by Yaḥyā according to the Gospel of Barnabas, whereas the Qur'ān clearly says that the latter announced the coming of Jesus.

Furthermore, Bakhtāvar extensively rejects the idea of *taḥrīf* (textual corruption), concerning both the Old and the New Testament. In this respect, he first points out the deep reverence for these Scriptures among Jews and Christians. As a consequence, he argues, they ought to have taken great care in transmission. It seems unthinkable that the Jews and the Christians, particularly since they suffered so much to preserve their religions, may have proceeded to manipulate their holy Scriptures. As to the Torah, he holds that Muhammad himself did not consider it to be falsified: "Maybe it will be objected, that Muhammad alluded to the book which has been burnt by the time of Nebucadnezar, but fortunately some Qur'ānic verses state that the very same book owned by the Jews of his lifetime is authentic and reliable (5:42)."[71] He then hints at the similarities between the Torah and the Qur'ān as further proof of the former's authenticity. The very existence of scandalizing accounts on behalf of the prophets in the Torah—David violating Uriah's wife, the wrestling of Jacob with God, Lot drinking wine and sleeping with his daughters—is another proof that no manipulations have taken place since they certainly would have been omitted in a manipulated text. Let us remember that most authors who point out these passages come to the opposite conclusion: that is, these passages must be the result of manipulations and deliberate distortions.

Saying that such evidence cannot be drawn from the Bible, Bakhtāvar equally corrects an old error which goes back to the Qur'ān—namely, that the Jews worship Ezra ('Uzair) as Son of God.[72]

One main argument held by the advocates of the *taḥrīf*-thesis—that is, the omission of Muhammad's name in both the Torah and the Gospel (based on S. 2: 154)—is also rejected. As to the Gospel, Bakhtāvar argues that given the oral character of Jesus' teachings, this mention may have fallen into oblivion. To uphold his thesis, he quotes St. John 21: 25, where the Evangelist concludes his record saying that Jesus did many other things which he has not reported. Given the severe admonition against any distortion of the Scripture in the Revelation of St. John 22: 18–19 it seems impossible that *taḥrīf* may have occurred. The fact that the numerous manuscripts of the Scripture show no divergences is to be considered as further corroboration of their authenticity.

Another important argument for the authenticity of the texts according to Bakhtāvar is the fulfillment of Jesus' prophecies like the decline of Rome and the destruction of the Temple. Eventually, the revelation of St. John *does* announce the coming of the Prophet of Islam, namely the Paraclete. By this argument Bakhtāvar is rejoining the common Muslim line of interpretation.

As far as the critical question of the crucifixion is concerned, Bakhtāvar is the only one among our authors to suggest some kind of synthesis between the Christian and the Muslim point of view. According to him Jesus was only crucified physically whereas his soul (*rūḥ*) ascended to heaven: "And maybe the meaning of the Qur'ānic verse 'They did not slay him, neither crucified him, only a likeness of that was shown to them' (4: 157) is that people thought they had killed Jesus, whereas his soul (*rūḥ*) and the truth manifested in his body were not crucified . . . but this spiritual truth shall last forever."[73]

Bakhtāvar's commentary on St. Paul sets him likewise apart from the majority of Muslim authors. To them, Paul is the second founder of Christianity or the inventor of Christianity in its present-day form, an argument which leads them to extensive commentaries on the additions or deformations brought to the original teaching of Jesus. Yet, Bakhtāvar only mentions the several journeys of Paul and his discussions with the idolatrists as noteworthy activities.

Hence it is not easy to determine our author's position. On the one hand, he goes so far as to suggest the human origin of the Scriptures—including the Qur'ān—and thus takes position in open contrast with Muslim doctrine. However, on the other hand, he is joining the prevailing Muslim interpretation in that he identifies the Paraclete as Muhammad. He equally rejects at length the fatherless conception of Jesus as proof of his divinity by citing the discoveries of modern biological research regarding self-reproduction (these biological arguments have already been put forward by Rashīd Riḍā as cited in Schumann).[74] Whereas the last point fits in the author's rational point of view, the reference to prophetic predictions appeals rather to believers. Is it meant to be a concession to his Muslim readers or is it an outgrowth of the author's divided mind? Bakhtāvar has dedicated his book to his friends, and not—like many of our other authors—to the Iranian youth or to the seekers of the truth. He is not referred to by any of the other texts I studied. I would thus suggest that his writings have hardly gained any influence or popularity. Nevertheless, in my opinion he represents a noteworthy voice in the chorus of modern Muslim writings on religions.

Mahdī Bāzargān

Finally, I would like to mention a recent publication by Mahdī Bāzargān, a very popular author. Born in 1905, he completed his engineering studies at the Ecole Centrale in Paris before World War II and then went to Teheran to teach thermodynamics at the university. As an opponent to the Pahlevi regime he founded the Liberation Movement (*nahżat–i āzadī–i Irān*). He advocated an active role of a modernized Islam in political life. In 1979 he became the first prime minister of the Islamic Republic.[75] His previously mentioned book is entitled *Gumrāhān* (The lost ones)—a book about the phenomenon of the Christian Inquisition with an underlying critic of the present Iranian regime. We confine ourselves to point to only one outstanding aspect of this text, which otherwise deserves a longer and separate analysis than can be provided here. We mean the effort made by Bāzargān to present not only the facts but in the same way the underlying ideas and intentions. Thus, regarding the Inquisition, the author specifies that "One must not imagine that the judges were professional executioners or seized by mental illness, but among them were saints and monks. They did it for the sake of paradise and in order to destroy Satan." Furthermore, he puts forward a more balanced view of Christian activities than the previously mentioned polemics: "Christians and their clerical institutions have done a lot of good in the field of health care and education, but likewise they did a lot of injustice regarding schism and hostility on religious grounds." As far as the sore point of occidental colonialism is concerned, Bāzargān reminds his Muslim readers that "colonialism, even though it represents betrayal and crime from our point of view, was considered by the Europeans as cultivating backward regions and civilizing ignorant savages." Even if Bāzargān is not concealing his own standpoint as a convinced Muslim who believes in the superiority of Islam and does not refrain from judgments, nevertheless, he cannot be placed at a level with the other polemics. The latter offer in many cases a superficial and outward description of the facts, borrowing selectively from Western sources what fits in their preconceived idea. Yet Bāzargān, while relying heavily on Will Durant's *History of World Civilization*, renders not only the facts but also the underlying conceptions according to his Western source material.

Conclusion

In conclusion, let us summarize the main characteristics of contemporary Persian writings on Christianity. First, we have to realize that this literature is born in the context of the Western impact on Persian economy and politics and in the context of Western Christian missionary activities. Thus, the authors react to a double challenge: on the one hand, the missionaries' claim to bring the only religion fit for the modern age; on the other hand, the materialists' claim that religion has been ruled out by modern scientific world view. Hence, some main topics touched upon by our authors—religious evolution, religion and science, religion and violence—can be interpreted as a reaction to the prejudices and reproaches adressed to Islam by Christian missionaries, colonists and orientalists. In order to corroborate their standpoint some authors arm themselves with arguments drawn from Western critics of the Church and from critical Bible research. On the other hand, the facilitated access to the Christian Scriptures brings about a modification of the Islamic picture of Jesus. Moreover, Western approaches are incorporated—like the psychological and sociological approach to the development of Jesus' self-consciousness in dependence on his environment or the psychological approach to the miracle phenomenon. Hence, while the texts continue the tradition of the classical heresiography with respect to doctrinal issues (Trinity, Christian sects), one can perceive a new focus on historical reality and social practice. In one case, this leads to a historical relativism which is extended to Islam and its holy Scripture. As a result of their acquaintance with Christian literature, single authors succeed in going beyond wrong analogies (the concept of inspiration). Instead of confronting their readers with a pure enumeration of facts, they try to render as well the underlying context and conceptions. It is due to these efforts that here and there some of the very issues separating Islam and Christianity are seen in a new light like the concept of inspiration, textual corruption (*taḥrīf*), and the Gospel of Barnabas.

NOTES

1. Hayek (1959), Michaud (1960), Räisänen (1971), and Robinson (1990).

2. R. Arnaldez, *Jésus dans la pensée musulmane* (Paris: Desclée, 1988); N. Robinson, *Christ in Islam and Christianity: The Representation of Jesus in the Qur'ān and the Classical Muslim Commentaries* (London: Macmillan, 1990); J. Dammen McAuliffe, *Qur'ānic Christians: An Analysis of Classical and Modern Exegesis* (Cambridge: Cambridge University Press, 1991).

3. D. Schumann, *Der Christus der Muslime: Christologische Aspekte in der arabisch-islamischen Literatur* (Gütersloh, 1975; rev. ed., 1988).

4. A. Th. Khoury and L. Hagemann, *Christentum und Christen im Denken zeitgenössischer Muslime* (Altenberge: Christlich-islamisches Schrifttum, 1986); Hugh Goddard, *Muslim Perceptions of Christianity* (London: Grey Seal Books, 1996); Kate Zebiri, *Muslims and Christians Face to Face* (Oxford: Oneworld, 1997).

5. As an exception, see the previously mentioned book by Jane Dammen McAuliffe based on Arabic as well as Persian sources and an earlier article by the same author: "Persian exegetical evaluation of the Ahl al-Kitāb," *Muslim World*, vol. 73, no. 2 (April, 1983), pp. 87–105, can be cited.

6. E.g., Mas'ūd Barzīn, *Gusht-i zin ustukhwān-i zin* (Teheran: Bihjat, 1362), cited in *Nashr-i dānish*, vol. 3, no. 6; Muḥammad Raḥīm Muhīnpūr, *Būdā cha mīguyad, Brahmā kīst?* (Teheran: Taḥqīqāt-i falsafī, 1340), cited in *Rāhnamā-i kitāb*, vol. 4, no. 11/12.

7. E.g., ʿAlī Akbar Turābī, *Naẓarī dar tārīkh-i adyān* (Teheran: Iqbāl, 1341).

8. E.g., Kamāl ud–dīn Bakhtāvar, *Tārīkh-i ʿaqāyid-i adyān wa mazāhib-i sāmī* (Teheran: Ābān, 1339).

9. E.g., Gulpāygānī, *Muvāzana bayn-i adyān-i chahārgāna-i zartusht, yahūd, masīḥ, islām* (Qum: ʿIlmiyya, 1364).

10. Hādī Khusrawshāhī, *Dū mazhab. Mazhab-i irtijāʾ wa impiryālism wa mazhabī dīgar dar rāh-i millathā wa tūdahā*, 3rd ed. (Qum, 1354), p. 10.

11. E.g., Ismāʾīl Rāʾīn, *Irāniyān-i armanī* (Teheran, 1349) or Muḥammad ʿAlī Tājpūr, *Tārīkh-i dū aqalliyat-i mazhabī: Yahūd wa masīḥīyat dar Irān* (Teheran, 1965).

12. M. Zamānī, *Ba sū–i islām yā āʾīn-i kilīsā*, pp. 23ff.

13. Muḥammad Riżā Shafīʾī, *Dar kūcha bāghhā-i Nīshāpūr*, pp. 65–67, cited in S. Soroudi, "On Jesus' image in modern Persian poetry," *Muslim World*, vol. 69, no. 4 (October, 1979), pp. 221–228.

14. Cf. Paul Hunt, *Inside Iran* (London, 1981), pp. 42 and 49.

15. This polemical tendency is deplored and sharply criticized not only by Western scholars but equally by some Muslims. See Mahdī Bāzargān, *Gumrāhān* (Teheran: Daftar-i nahżat-i āzādī-i Irān, 1362), p. 27.

16. Cf. Shahrough Akhavi, *Religion and Politics in Contemporary Iran: Clergy State Relations in the Pahlavi Period* (Albany: State University of New York Press, 1980). Compare the foreword to M. Zamānī, *Ba sū-i islām*, p. 8.

17. The two major aims of the center were defined as the unveiling of Christianity and the propagation of Islam.

18. M. Zamānī, *Ba sū-i islām*, pp. 6 ff.

19. See the foreword of *Ḥaqīqat-i masīḥīyat*, 3rd ed. (Qum: Dar rāh-i ḥaqq, 1355).

20. Cf. Dieter Lyko, *Gründung, Wachstum und Leben der evangelischen Kirchen in Iran* (Leiden: Brill, 1964), pp. 58 ff.

21. E.g., for what we mean by polemical accounts we may point to the *taḥrīf*-thesis; a sample for a commonplace is the frequently established opposition "materialistic Judaism versus spiritual Christianity."

22. On the different text categories, see the next paragraph.

23. See n. 10. Some are written in the form of a debate between a Muslim and a Christian or in the form of a story.

24. This suggests the Shīʿite principle of personal *ijtihād* before choosing a source of imitation (*marjaʿ-i taqlīd*).

25. E.g., Gustave Le Bon, *La civilisation des Arabes* (Paris 1884; Repr. Geneva: Minerva, 1974).

26. E.g., Bertrand Russell, *Why I Am Not a Christian; and Other Essays on Religion and Related Subjects*, ed. Paul Edwards (London: Allen and Unwin, 1957).

27. This is our guess concerning the *Petite Histoire des Grandes Religions* by Felicien Challaye (Paris: Presses Universitaires de France, 1947).

28. E.g., *The Life of Jesus* by Ernest Renan; originally published in French (Paris, 1863).

29. E.g., Challaye, *Petite histoire*. See n. 27.

30. Cf. the article on al-Bīrūnī by Mahmūd Rāmyār, "Ṭalab wa amānat-i Bīrūnī," *Nashriyya-i dānishkada-i ilāhiyat wa maʿārif-i islāmī*, no. 7/8 (Spring/Summer, 1352).

31. By way of contrast, M. Bāzargān remarks in his book *Gumrāhān*, with regard to the contemporary period that: "One ought to admit, that as opposed to the Sunna of the Qurʾān, which pays high reverence to the prophets and frequently talks about their respective nations, and as opposed to the Christian and Jewish occidentals who have broad knowledge about Muslims and the life of the prophets, Qurʾān and Islam, we Muslims are ignorant and arrogant regarding the other *tawḥīdī*-religions and the thought of their adherents" (p. 27). Nevertheless, as follows, he points to the former superiority of the brilliant Muslim over the Christian culture in the Middle Ages (p. 71).

32. For the very opposite argumentation, see the following Kamāl ud-dīn Bakhtāvar.

33. Some authors simply quote parallels, while others—the more polemic ones—maintain a direct reliance.

34. Cf. Lyko, *Kirchen in Iran* (1964), pp. 61 and 118.

35. Yet, several of our Persian authors claim that Persians accepted Islam but rejected the Arabs who had violated Islamic principles. They thus dissociate themselves from the Arabs but not from Islam.

36. ʿAlī Akbar Turābī, *Naẓarī dar tārīkh-i adyān* (Teheran: Iqbāl, 1341), p. 17. Also—in more poetical terms—M. Bāzargān, *Rāh-i tayy shuda* (Teheran, 1959), p. 187: "When reaching the Gospel after the Torah one feels a fresh breeze. It is like reaching a plain after having walked along a dark mountain path. . . . A small crescent of moon appears. . . . But more than 600 years passed till the full disc of the moon rose in the sky." The same author also expresses the opinion that the monotheistic religions have a tendency to decline toward polytheism and superstition, whereas the polytheistic ones develop toward simplicity and perfection. See *Dars-i dīndārī* (Houston, Texas, 1356), p. 55.

37. Cf. Tūrābī, *Tārīkh-i adyān*, p. 17. Also Muḥammad Javād Mashkūr, *Khulāṣa-i adyān dar tārīkh-i dīnhā-i buzurg* (Teheran: Intishārāt-i sharq, 1368), p. 14.

38. "Durchweg leugnen die muslimischen Autoren die Kreuzigung Jesu," in Khoury and Hagemann, *Christentum und Christen* (1986), p. 55.

39. An exception is Kamāl ud-dīn Bakhtāvar, *Tārīkh-i ʿaqāyid-i adyān wa mazāhib-i sāmī* (Teheran: Ābān, 1339).

40. Cf. Khoury and Hagemann, *Christentum und Christen*, p. 55.

41. Not to be mistaken with his namesake, the well-known Theosoph!

42. Jalāl ud-dīn Āshtiyānī, Muhandis, *Taḥqīqī dar dīn-i masīḥ* (Teheran: Nashr-i nigārish, 1368).

43. Cf. Muḥammad Javād Bāhunar, *Dīnshināsī-i taṭbīqī* (Teheran: Daftar-i nashr-i farhang-i islāmī 1361), p. 54.

44. Cf. Lyko, *Kirchen in Iran*, pp. 122ff.

45. Cf. M. J. Bāhunar, *Dīnshināsī*, p. 54.

46. Cf. *Ḥaqīqat-i masīḥīyat*, p. 130.

47. Ghulāmriżā Ḥamīd, *Ashkī bar pā-i Maryam-i muqaddas* (Stuttgart, 1357).

48. Cf. Qurʾān: 3, 49: "by the leave of God" (trans. A. J. Arberry).

49. Cf. Qurʾān 9:30: "the Christians say, 'The Messiah is the Son of God.' That is the utterance of their mouths, conforming with the unbelievers before them."

50. Jalāl ud-dīn Āshtiyānī, *Dīn-i masīḥ*, pp. 494 ff.

51. Cf. verses 19:30, 61:6.

52. al-Shahrastānī, *Le livre des religions et des sectes: Première partie—Islam et autres religions scriptuaires* (UNESCO, Peeters 1986), p. 75.

53. Khoury and Hagemann, *Christentum und Christen*, p. 142.

54. M. Bāzargān, *Mazhab dar urūpā* (Teheran, 1965), p. 12.

55. Cf. Muṣṭafā Zamānī, *Ba sū-i islām*, p. 14 ff. In order to demonstrate the easy contravention of their religious laws, the author reports the curious story of a party given by Bata, the Czechoslovak millionaire, attended by the German chancellor Heinrich Brüning (r. 1930–1932). The banquet fell on Ash Wednesday. Thus the Pope sent a telegram exempting them from fasting. Exactly the same story is rendered in Bāzargān, *Mazhab dar urūpā*, p. 12.

56. Cf. Bāzargān, *Mazhab dar urūpā*, pp. 22 ff. and p. 29, footnote by Khusrawshāhī. This view reminds us of the Muslim fundamentalists slogan "islām, dīn wa dawla!" (Islam is religion and government!).

57. For a more precise and comprehensive account, see M. Bāzargān, *Gumrāhān*, n. p. 122.

58. Cf. Dieter Lyko, *Kirchen in Iran*, p. 61; Andreas Waldburger, *Missionare und Moslems: Die Basler Mission in Persien 1833–1837* (Basel: Basileia, 1984), p. 140.

59. Cf. Khusrawshāhī, *Dū mazhab*, p. 7. The same author reports that the well-known Iranist Henry Corbin once qualified Christianity as a dead religion as opposed to Shīʿism which, thanks to the principle of *ijtihād*, maintains its vitality (p. 41). The same citation occurs in M. Zamānī, *Ba sū-i islām*, p. 19.

60. Cf. Muḥammad Javād Hujjatī Kirmānī, *Dar pīrāmūn-i masīḥīyat* (Teheran: Muʾassasa-i maṭbūʿātī-i islāmī), p. 35.

61. Cf. Bāzargān, *Gumrāhān*, p. 161.

62. Ibid., p. 21. Bāzargān uses the term *maẓlūm* with reference to the first Christians.

63. ʿAlī Aṣghar Ḥikmat, *Nuh guftār dar tārīkh-i adyān* (Teheran: Ibn Sīnā 1342), p. 215 ff.

64. Cf. M. Bāzargān, *Gumrāhān*, p. 116 and n. p. 130.

65. *Bakhshī az nubuwwat-i isrāʾīlī wa masīḥī* (Mashad: Našriyya-i dāniškada-i ilāhiyāt wa maʿārif-i islāmī, 1352).

66. This account reminds me of the esoteric *tafsīr* as practiced by Shīʿites.

67. *Nubuwwat-i isrāʾīlī wa masīḥī*, p. 201 ff.

68. *Mālkiyat az naẓar-i adyān wa aḥzāb; Jabr-i tārīkh; Baḥs dar māhiyat-i dīn wa qānūn; Ḥayāt wa takāmul*, titles cited in the author's *Tārīkh-i ʿaqāyid-i adyān*.

69. Kamāl ud–dīn Bakhtāvar, p. 38. Italics mine.

70. The polemics consider this separation to be an occidental import and attempt to divide Muslim unity, see as previously mentioned, p. 14. However, Bāzargān specifies that it was introduced by the Muslim intellectuals themselves. See Bāzargān, *Gumrāhān*, n. p. 122.

71. Bakhtāvar, *Mazāhib-i sāmī*, p. 79.

72. Cf. Qurʾān, 9: 30.

73. K. Bakhtāvar, *Mazāhib-i sāmī*, p. 131. This interpretation reminds us of the Docetist position according to which the physical existence and suffering of Jesus was only an appearance.

74. Schumann, *Der Christus der Muslime*, p. 119.

75. Cf. Yann Richard, *Der verborgene Imam: Die Geschichte der Schia in Iran* (Berlin: Wagenbach, 1983), pp. 127 ff.

BIBLIOGRAPHY

Persian Sources

ʿAbd al-Fānī, Muḥammad al-Mūsāvī. *Ṣad maqāla-i sulṭānī. Rāhnamā-i yahūd wa naṣārī wa muslimūn.* Teheran: Haidarī, 1957.

Āshtiyānī, Jalāl ud-dīn Muhandis. *Taḥqīqī dar dīn-i masīḥ.* Teheran: Nashr-i Nigārish, 1368.

Bāhunar, Muḥammad Javād. *Dīnshināsī-i taṭbīqī.* Teheran: Daftar-i našr-i farhang-i islāmī, 1361.

Bakhtāvar, Kamāl ud-dīn. *Tārīkh-i ʿaqāyid-i adyān wa mazāhib-i sāmī.* Teheran: Ābān, 1339.

Bāzargān, Mahdī. *Mazhab dar urūpā.* Teheran, 1965.

———. *Rāh-i tayy shuda.* Teheran, 1959.

———. *Gumrāhān.* Teheran, 1362.

———. *Dars-i dīndārī.* Houston, Texas, 1356.

Furūghī, Muḥammad ʿAlī. *Sayr-i ḥikmat dar urūpā*. Teheran, 1345.

Gulpāygānī, Ḥusain Qarnī. *Muvāzana bayn-i adyān-i chahārgāna, zartusht, yahūd, masīḥ, islām*. Qum: ʿIlmiyya, 1364.

Ḥamīd, Ghulāmriżā. *Ashkī ba pā-i Maryam-i muqaddas*. Stuttgart, 1357.

Ḥaqīqat-i masīḥīyat. Qum: Dar rāh-i haqq, 3rd ed. 1355.

Ḥikmat, ʿAlī Aṣghar. *Nuh guftār dar tārīkh-i adyān*. Teheran: Ibn Sīnā, 1342.

Hujjatī Kirmānī, Muḥammad Javād. *Jilva-i masīḥ*. Kirmān, 1342.

———. *Dar pīrāmūn-i masīhīyat*. Teheran: Muʿassasa-i maṭbūʿātī-i islāmī.

Khūʾīnī, ʿAlī Āl Isḥāq. *Masīḥīyat*. Qum, 1364.

Khusrawshāhī, Hādī. *Dū mazhab*. Teheran?, 1324.

Kasravī, Aḥmad. *Dīn wa jahān*. Teheran, 1324.

Kirmānī, Muḥammad Khān. *Husām ud-dīn: Dar isbāt-i takhrīf-i tūriya wa injīl*. Kirman: Intishārāt-i madrasa-i mubārika-i Ibrāhīmiyya, 1353.

Mashkūr, Muḥammad Jawād. *Khulāsa-i adyān dar tārīkh-i dīnhā-i buzurg*. Teheran: Intishārāt-i sharq, 1368.

Nūrī, Yaḥyā. *Barrasīhā-i taḥqīqī dar bāra-i āʾīn-i yahūd wa masīḥīyat*. Teheran, 1344.

———. *Shinākht-i taḥlīlī-i islām wa barkhī maslakhā wa adyān mānand-i yahūd, masīḥīyat, zartushtī, hindū, sīk, būdāʾī, shintūʾism, mādīgarī, bahāʾīgarī*. Teheran: Majmaʿ-i muṭālaʿāt wa taḥqīqāt-i islāmī wa majmaʿ-i maʿārif-i islāmī, 1354.

Rāʾīn, Ismāʾīl. *Irāniyān-i armanī*. Teheran, 1349.

Rāmyār, Maḥmūd. *Bakhshī az nubuwwat-i isrāʾīlī wa masīḥī*. Mashad?: Nashriyya-i dānishkada-i ilāhiyāt wa maʿārif-i islāmī, 1352.

Rażī, Hāshim. *Adyān-i buzurg-i jahān*. Teheran: Faravahar, 1360.

Sharīʿatī, ʿAlī. *Tārīkh wa shinakht-i adyān*. 1359.

Tājpūr, Muḥammad ʿAlī. *Tārīkh-i dū aqalliyat-i mazhabī: Yahūd wa masīḥīyat dar Irān*. Teheran, 1965.

Turābī, ʿAlī Akbar. *Naẓarī dar tārīkh-i adyān*. Teheran: Iqbāl, 1341.

Zamānī, Muṣṭafā. *Ba sū-i islām yā āʾīn-i kilīsā?* Qum, 1347.

Christian Mission in Iran

Bugnini, Annibal. *La chiesa in Iran*. Rome: Edizioni Vincenziane, 1981.

Dehqani Tafti, Hassan Barnaba. *Design of My World*. 1959.

———. *The Hard Awakening*. London: Society for the Promotion of Christian Knowledge (SPCK), 1981.

Hunt, Paul. *Inside Iran*. Tring (UK): Lion Publishers, 1981.

Lyko, Dieter. *Gründung, Wachstum und Leben der evangelischen christlichen Kirchen in Iran*. Leiden: Brill, 1964.

Nātiq, Humā. *Irān dar rāhyābī-i farhangī*. London: Markaz-i chāp wa nashr-i payām, 1988.

Schuler, H. C. "The approach to Shiʾa Islam." *Muslim World* vol. 17 (1929).

Waldburger, Andreas. *Missionare und Moslems: Die Basler Mission in Persien 1833–1837*. Basel: Basileia, 1984.

Waterfield, Robin E. *Christians in Persia: Assyrians, Armenians, Roman Catholics and Protestants* (London: Allen and Unwin, 1973).

Religious Minorities

Berthaud, Edmond. "Chrétiens d'Iran." *Orient* vol. 45/46 (1968), pp. 22–36.

Lang, C. L. "Les minorités arménienne et juive d'Iran." *Politique étrangère* vol. 5–6 (1961), pp. 460–471.

Mauroy, Hubert de. *Les Assyro-chaldéens dans l'Iran d'aujourd'hui*. Paris, Département de Géographie de l'Université de Paris-Sorbonne, 1978.

Menashri, David. "Khomeini's policy towards ethnic and religious minorities." In *Ethnicity, Pluralism and the State in the Middle East*, ed. Milton J. Esman and Itamer Rabinovich. Ithaca: Cornell University Press, 1988, pp. 215–232.

Richard, Yann. "Minorités." *Téhéran au-dessus du volcan: Autrement*, Série Monde H.S. no. 27 (Nov. 1987), pp. 136–140.

Schwartz, Richard Merrill. *The Structure of Christian-Muslim Relations in Contemporary Iran*. Halifax, Nova Scotia: Dept. of Anthropology, Saint Mary's University, 1985.

Yavari-D'Hellencourt, Nouchine. "Ethnies et ethnicité dans les manuels scolaires iraniens." In *Le fait ethnique en Iran et en Afghanistan*. Paris: Editions du CNRS, 1988, pp. 247–265.

Orient and Occident as Viewed by Persian Muslims

Āl-I Aḥmad, Jalāl. *Gharbzādagī*. Teheran, 1356. Transl. R. Campbell as *Occidentosis: A Plague from the West*. Berkeley, Calif.: Mizan Press, 1984.

Ḥakīmī, Maḥmūd. *Gharb bīmār ast*. Qum: Dār ul-tablīgh-i islāmī, 1353.

Mūsavī Larī, Sayid Mujtabā Ruknī. *Sīmā-i tamaddun-i gharb*—Transl. F. J.Goulding. Western Civilisation through Muslim Eyes. Guildford, U.K., 1977. (Distrib. Optimus Books).

Naraghi, Ehsan. *L'Orient et la crise de l'Occident*. Paris: Entente, 1977.

Jesus and Christianity as Viewed by Islam

Arnaldez, Roger. *Jésus dans la pensée musulmane*. Paris: Desclée, 1988.

Ayoub, Mahmud. "Towards an Islamic Christology: An image of Jesus in early Shiʾi Muslim literature." *The Muslim World*, 66, no. 3, July 1976, pp. 163–188.

Gaudeul, Jean-Marie. *Encounters and Clashes: Islam and Christianity in History*. 2 vols. Rome: Pontificio Istituto di Studi Arabi e Islamici, 1984.

Goddard, H. *Muslim Perceptions of Christianity*. London: Grey Seal, 1996.

Hayek, Michel. *Le Christ de l'Islam*. Paris, 1959.

Khoury, Th. A., and L. Hagemann. *Christentum und Christen im Denken zeitgenössischer Muslime*. Altenberge: Christlich-Islamisches Schrifttum, 1986.

McAuliffe, J. D. "Persian exegetical evaluation of the Ahl al-kitab." *The Muslim World* vol. 73, no. 2 (1983), pp. 87–105.

———. *Qur'ānic Christians: An Analysis of Classical and Modern Exegesis*. Cambridge: Cambridge University Press, 1991.

Michaud, Henri. *Jésus selon le Coran*. Neuchâtel: Ed. Delachaux Nieslet, 1960.

Räisänen, H. *Das koranische Jesusbild*. Helsinki: Finnische Gesellschaft für Missiologie und Ökumenik, 1971.

Robinson, Neal. *Christ in Islam and Christianity: The Representation of Jesus in the Qur'ān and the Classical Muslim Commentaries*. London: Macmillan, 1990.

al-Shahrastānī. *Livre des Religions et des Sectes*. Intr., transl. and notes by Daniel Gimaret, Jean Jolivet, and Guy Monnot. 2 vols. Paris: Peeters and UNESCO, 1986 and 1993.

Schumann, Olaf. *Der Christus der Muslime*. Gütersloh: Missionswissenschaftliche Forschungen vol. 10, 1975; rev. 2nd ed., 1988.

Thomas, D. "Two Muslim-Christian debates from the early Shi'ite tradition." *Journal of Semitic Studies* vol. 33 (1988), pp. 53–80.

Zebiri, K. *Muslims and Christians Face to Face*. Oxford: Oneworld, 1997.

15

Arabic Muslim Writings on Contemporary Religions Other Than Islam

A Framework for Inquiry

PATRICE BRODEUR

With the twentieth-century global Western technological hegemony and the penetration of the West's concomitant scientific discourse, not just in Islamic countries but all over the world, a symbiotic relationship has grown among many segments of humanity that were once isolated from one another. As loud as the claims of distinctiveness may be, these diverse voices betray the fact that they often have more in common with their synchronic others than with their diachronic selves within a given culture or religious community. Today, for example, many Muslims are Western scholars and many Westerners are Muslims, thereby creating an atmosphere of greater interrelatedness between our respective and yet interdependent human horizons. This essay emphasizes the a priori notion that the "interlacing of horizons cannot be methodologically eliminated,"[1] that, indeed, there is no escape from our own hermeneutical circle, bound between the movement of a composite Western tradition and that of an equally composite Islamic tradition as reflected, for example, by contemporary Arab Muslim interpreters of the Other. The increase in scholarly inquiry on the relations between the Islamic world and other cultures and religions[2] stems as much from the subjectivities of the predominantly non-Muslim western European and northern American researchers of this topic as from the subjectivities of a growing number of contemporary Muslims around the world who write about non-Muslims and their relations to Muslims and Islam. All writers, whether authors of contemporary Arabic Muslim writings on religions other than Islam or inquirers on such a topic, share a twentieth-century reality: the drastic increase in human interactions around the world. The degree of exposure to one another across cultures, underlined by the concomitant increase in competition to control the earth's resources, has led many people to question and write about their own identity. We are faced with one another as mirrors in which to recognize our own selves, to imagine our respective identities in their similarities and differences.

Contributing to the late-twentieth-century worldwide debate on the hermeneutical quest for meaning, a number of Muslim authors use writing as a means to make sense of their Islamic selves. Within this written Muslim identity discourse, a sizable number of writings on the Other can be found. Indeed, defining the boundaries of the self requires an understanding of what is non-self, that is, the Other. This Other has taken many shapes, from the ambiguous concepts of "the West," "the Christian West," "the Jewish conspiracy," "Israel," "the United States," and so on, to the varied reinterpretations of Qurʾānic concepts such as "People of the Book" (*ahl al-kitāb*), "Ignorant" (*jāhil*), "Infidel" (*kāfir*), and "Hypocrite" (*munāfiq*). The shifting boundaries between the various definitions of an Islamic self always reflect the symbiotic nature of the relation between self and Other. Therefore, as the need to understand how Arab Muslims define themselves increases with the growing number of confrontations between Muslims and non-Muslims over recent years, it has become imperative to study not only the ongoing process of Arab Muslim self-definition but also the simultaneous process of Arab Muslim image formation of the Other. This article probes into the latter by means of, first, contextualizing that body of literature comprised of contemporary Arabic Muslim writings on religions other than Islam; second, exemplifying three such cases; and third, raising the issue of the so-called outside researcher as de facto partner in the process of image formation of the Other.

As noted previously, the Other has taken many forms in modern Muslim discourse;[3] one such form is the way in which the Other has been understood through European categories of religions, as developed out of the Enlightenment discourse predicated on the dichotomy between religion and science. From this perspective, religions are believed to be separate entities that carry an essence, a uniqueness which sets them apart from other realities. In the Arab world today, the word *dīn* is translated as and has come to mean the equivalent of a "religion" with its unique essence, and the diversity of separate religions as *adyān* or *diyānāt*. The expressions "comparative religion" and "history of religions" have made their appearance in the Arabic language during the twentieth century only, as *muqāranat al-adyān* and *ta'rīkh al-adyān*, respectively. Contemporary articulations of the Muslim self thus take place within a conceptual framework that understands Islam as one religion or *dīn*—indeed, the one religion par excellence—while the Other takes the form of all other religions. Arabic Muslim writings on religions other than Islam therefore reveal one facet of the contemporary discourse on the Other among Arab Muslims, a facet which is particularly important as the process of modern Islamization continues unabated into the end of the 1990s.

Contextualizing Arabic Muslim Writings on Religions Other Than Islam

The twentieth century has witnessed a drastic increase in the exposure of Muslims to a variety of worldviews, forcing a process of reevaluation of both individual and collective selves. How has this situation affected Muslim images of religions other than Islam? How have these images in turn affected Muslim self-perceptions? No answer to these two questions is possible without first trying to understand the various social forces out of which have emerged contemporary Arabic Muslim writings on religions other than Islam, or, in short, contextualizing them.

Although the phenomenon of Muslims re-thinking themselves individually and Islam collectively is not unique to this century, contemporary Muslims have had to face the unprecedented reality of being taken, for the first time in their history, as hostages of Western colonialism, imperialism, and scientism. These three closely interwoven elements correspond more or less to the political, economic, and epistemological spheres of human activity. Various Muslim responses to each sphere seem to have been chronologically marked—first, by a gradual appropriation of the political, economic, and epistemological discourse from the West (a period of mimesis); and, second, by a period of gradual differentiation from it (a period of reconstruction). The first reaction developed primarily in the nineteenth and first half of the twentieth centuries as a result of a common pattern of mimetic attraction for the "things" of the oppressor on the part of the subconsciously oppressed. This pattern of mimetic behavior is exemplified militarily by Muḥammad ʿAlī (1769–1849) in Egypt; intellectually by al-Afghānī's famous "Answer to Renan" of May 18, 1883 (Keddie, 1972); and politically by the successful Atatürk (1881–1938) in Turkey. Coexisting with the mimetic tendency of certain circles that had more contacts with the colonial cultural discourse, traditional learning still continued with its own pace of changes which has been more difficult to measure. But both currents eventually found a shared working space, which led to the second trend: a conscious call for differentiating oneself from what pertains to "the West" and for reconstructing an Islamic discourse that will be able to challenge and compete with the dominant Western discourse.

In particular, the political, economic, and epistemological responses of Arab Muslims to their contemporary situation developed in that order, too—an order which corresponded to the struggle for first political, then economic, and finally ideological independence. To this day, these three intertwined components underlie many Arab Muslim authors' motivations to write about other religions. The same three elements also underscore the motivations of countless Muslims who have written works on Islam that have transformed the discourse of Arab Muslim self-identity from images pertaining to the predominant nationalistic ideology of Arabism in the 1950s and 1960s to the images pertaining to the flowering beliefs of Islamism in the late 1970s and 1980s. It is thus of no great surprise that the production of writings on the Other as "other religions" has risen exponentially in the 1980s in connection with the rise among Arab Muslims of more specifically religious self-representations.

Political Responses

Within the context of changing Arab Muslim self-representations, political factors have played a crucial role in modifying images of religions other than Islam, especially Christianity. But the most drastic alteration to take place this century has certainly been regarding the traditionally ambiguous Muslim images of the Jews as weak collectively yet indispensable because of their invaluable services in various fields.[4] In the 1940s and 1950s, as Muslims in many Arab countries went through a process of facing the urgent need to reappropriate their own political power, this traditional image changed drastically. Four historical events have scarred contemporary Arab Muslim consciousness. The creation of the state of Israel in 1948 and its sweeping victory during the 1967 Six Day War radically altered the relationships between Muslims and Jews. These political events forced Arab Muslims to reinterpret their understanding of Jews and Judaism in light of their new political relationship. This process of reevaluation was revitalized by the Israeli invasion of Lebanon in 1982 and the prolonged Palestinian *intifāḍa* from December 1987 until the peace negotiations. Indeed, the overwhelming majority of contemporary Arabic Muslim writings on Judaism have been motivated by this political situation of antagonism and the need for Muslims to both explain and explain away the political power of Israel, which is at once envied and abhorred.

The Westernized Arabic writings of the first half of our contemporary period have been analyzed in depth by Harkabi in *Arab Attitudes to Israel*.[5] For example, the Marxist influences are obvious in the book of anti-imperialist Nājī ʿAlūsh, *The Journey to Palestine* (1964), and in the book of the leftist journalist Aḥmad Bahāʾ al-Dīn, *Isrāʾīliyyāt* (1965). Two and a half decades ago, the principal polemical genre as surveyed by Harkabi took the forms of nationalist discourses reflecting the confrontation between Arab forms of nationalism and Jewish nationalism in the form of Zionism. This resulted in what Harkabi has called the "three Arab schools of thought": first, those that believe in the erosion and withering away of Israel; second, those who want to reduce Israel to its natural dimension; and third, those who seek to promote a continuous struggle against it.[6]

Because Islam was not the principal source of imagery for most Arab intellectuals writing in the 1950s and 1960s, Harkabi's analysis pays little attention to the relation between Islamic discourses and attitudes toward Israel and Jews in general. There is only one reference:

> The first anti-Semitic books in Arabic were written by Christian Arabs under French influence, but *Arab anti-Semitism today is of an Islamic religious character* [my emphasis]. It is no accident that this is emphasized in such books as those of ʿAqqād, ʿAlūba, Tall, al-Jiyār, Tabbāra and Rousan, or in articles in the *al-Azhar* monthly. This religious character, however, prevents the struggle against Jewry [from] being conceived as a confrontation between the slave mentality and morality and that of the master race, as it was presented by the Nazis. Nor, of course, does Arab anti-Semitism involve a war against religion, as in the Soviet Union, for example.[7]

Overlooked by Harkabi in the seventies, European Christian anti-Judaism, popularly known as "anti-Semitism," has slowly taken root into Arab Muslim soil during the twentieth century. Over the last two decades, however, this virulent form of hatred has mushroomed into a widespread popular polemical literature against the Jews, Judaism, Zionism, and the state of Israel.[8] In fact, what Harkabi had not foreseen was the complete reversal process, whereby the image of the persecuted Jew under Nazi ideology changed to that of the Jew as being the Nazi-like persecutor under Zionist ideology. This reinterpretation has dominated recent Arabic Muslim images of Jews. Furthermore, the symbol of the Islamic *jihād* has become replete with anti-Judaic rhetoric in what amounts to no less than a discursive war against one religion in particular, Judaism. All current Arab political regimes face threats from Muslims who uphold a fascist Islamic discourse in which the Other, especially the Jew, serves as the scapegoat or tool par excellence to explain all calamities and also to incriminate any Arab Muslim leadership that would dare enter into contact with *shaiṭān* (the devil).

Not just Jews have become the victims of such a use of religious symbolic language which masks the political struggles for power in countries where masses of semiliterate and often unemployed youths can be easily mobilized. The effective use of religious discourse has enabled many Muslim religious leaders to make serious inroads into the mixed secular/religious political arena characterizing most Middle Eastern regimes today. Both the 1979 revolution in Iran, and, a decade later, the 1989 military takeover in Sudan are examples of how an extreme anti-Western religious discourse can lead to the effective holding of political power, with disastrous results for minority groups such as Iranian Baha'is and Sudanese Christians and Animists.[9] The Islamic Front's construction of the Christian West as evil allowed its leader Ḥasan Turābī to rally sufficient opposition to the regime of Ṣādiq al-Mahdī to wield the influence behind the military takeover and pull the real strings of Sudanese political power to this day. Such political developments often inform the authors of Arabic Muslim books on religions other than Islam, depending on their own personal allegiances and the audience they wish to write for.

Economic Responses

As a natural corollary to the reappropriation of political power, the search for control over the means of economic production soon followed the emergence of independent political entities: the nationalization of key industries, such as oil in Iraq and the Gulf states, and water in Egypt with the 1956 Suez Crisis and the building of the Aswan Dam. These economic victories, especially the 1973 oil embargo, soon brought enough wealth to transform the nature of power relations in the Middle East, within each political regime, across the Arab world, and beyond. They also added pride to Arab Muslims' self-image, thereby potentially affecting Arab Muslim perceptions of non-Muslims. Access to an economic power base, however, does not predicate a certain attitude in one direction or another; it simply allows for a greater range of conscious choices in describing the Other, from intransigence to acceptance.

This greater freedom of choice has led to the coexistence of contradictory perceptions and behaviors among Arab Muslims. One positive example is the Jordanian initiatives for holding Muslim-Christian dialogue conferences in partnership with the Greek Orthodox Center in Chambésy, Switzerland.[10] Although such sustained initiatives reflected a unique example of official support for interreligious dialogue in the Arab world, the Jordanian initiatives were nevertheless rooted in a political rationale aimed at proving to Christians, both Western and Eastern, that the Hashimite Kingdom could take care of the needs of Christians in the Holy Land and in Jerusalem in particular. This kind of dialogue took place in the shadow of Jordan's political claim over the West Bank until June 1988. One negative example is the Saudi Arabian difficulty to recognize the right to collective worship which its many thousands of non-Muslim, generally Christian, guest workers have been denied for several decades. These two examples prove that an increase in self-esteem triggered by economic prosperity does not necessarily guarantee one kind of attitude over another regarding non-Muslims.

Epistemological Responses

At last, with greater economic and political freedom, many Muslims have begun, through the creation of their own institutions, to mobilize resources for the third and ultimate struggle for "independence": the epistemological reappropriation of "Truth" or the control over the discursive agent of meaning—that is, symbolic language. This struggle is currently taking place through a systematic effort at Islamizing Western sciences.[11] It should not be surprising if these efforts are particularly vibrant in Saudi Arabia and in the United States, where the International Institute of Islamic Thought is based.[12] The former provides the economic basis for such an intellectual movement, while the latter provides the space for a freedom of exploration and dissemination. The result is a necessary double process: acculturation into the secular scientific discourse of technological production on the one hand (e.g., with the growing emphasis on Islamic Economics),[13] and, on the other, the reinterpretation of Islamic values to explicate more meaningfully Western scientific knowledge.

From Mimesis to Reconstruction: Three Egyptian Muslims on Comparative Religion

The general trend toward epistemological independence is also at work in contemporary Arabic Muslim writings on religions other than Islam, especially among those few who have begun to grapple with comparative religion as a distinct field of science. Let us take three examples: Muḥammad Abū Zahrah (1898–ca. 1973), ʿAbdallāh Drāz (1894–1958), and Aḥmad Shalabī (b. ca 1925). By focusing on their implicit methodology which emerged from their explicit conceptions of comparative religion or history of religions, it is possible to see the differences between each author's demarcation of the limits of acculturation and his response to it. In their own respective ways, each author reflects either a process of subconscious or conscious mimesis, or else one of epistemological reconstruction.

Abū Zahrah (1898-ca.–1973)

Muḥammad Abū Zahrah grew up in the region of the Nile Delta in Egypt. Following a traditional *kuttāb* education, he completed his secondary education at al-Aḥmadī mosque in Ṭanṭā. In 1916, he entered the School of Sharīʿah at Al-Azhar in Cairo where he graduated in 1925. From 1933 to 1942, he held an appointment at the College of Uṣūl al-dīn, first as a teacher of rhetoric, then as a teacher of the history of religions, denominations, and sects. It is during this period that Abū Zahrah wrote his two books which concern us here: *Lectures in Comparative Religion*, given in 1940 and published in 1965, and *Lectures on Christianity*, which were held and appeared in 1942.[14]

In the introduction to his second book, Abū Zahrah explicates his understanding of the function of science and the methodological framework he claims to use: "As for the mission of science, it is not so much to oblige us to advance as to believe in the plain truth."[15] This passage implies a refutation of the Western notion of progress for which Abū Zahrah substitutes the core Islamic notion of having faith (*imān*) in the plain truth. Abū Zahrah's "scientific" endeavor seems to emerge naturally out of centuries of Muslim historiography with its emphasis on *isnād* transmission.[16] Since Abū Zahrah's al-Azhar training rooted him in traditional Islamic epistemology and since he never studied in Europe or in Egyptian Europeanized schools, his contact with Western epistemology must have taken place through whatever European books he might have read in Arabic translation. This may explain his superficial grasp of Western concepts and his natural tendency to use categories of interpretation already in existence within traditional Islamic epistemology. Moreover, Abū Zahrah's audience for his two books on Christianity and on ancient religions is clearly made up of students from al-Azhar. Therefore, his two books reflect a pattern of subconscious mimetic appropriation.

ʿAbdallāh Drāz (1894–1958)

ʿAbdallāh Drāz belongs to the same generation as Abū Zahrah. Born near Alexandria, Drāz did his early studies at a religious institute in Alexandria. In 1912, he received his secondary school certificate from al-Azhar, and in 1916, he received al-Azhar's highest degree (*al-shahāda al-ʿālamiyya*). While he taught in various capacities, including at the College of Uṣūl al-dīn in Cairo, Drāz learned French. This qualified him to receive in 1936 a scholarship to pursue his doctoral studies in France, which he completed only in 1947 due to the Second World War. A few months later, Drāz returned to Egypt where he began to teach the first course on the history of religions offered at Fu'ād the First University. He was later appointed to al-Azhar and soon delegated to Dār al-ʿulūm to teach comparative religion, becoming a member of the al-Azhar Academy in 1949. Four years later, he was appointed to the government's High Committee for Policies in Education and soon afterward to the Supreme Council of the ʿUlamāʾ at Cairo. In January 1958, he represented al-Azhar, together with Muḥammad Abū Zahrah, at the Pan-Islamic Conference held in Lahore, Pakistan. He delivered a lecture on the theme of "Islam's Attitude toward and Relations with other Faiths." He died soon afterward, during the conference itself. So the main difference between Drāz and Abū Zahrah was not so much chronological as circumstantial: while Abū Zahrah never studied outside Egypt, Drāz studied for 12 years in France.

In 1952, Drāz published a most interesting book on comparative religion, simply entitled, *Religion*.[17] Although he did not claim to follow any methodology directly, two introductory passages clarify his conception of the science of the history of religions. For Drāz "the science of religions has two branches: a new and original branch, as well as an old branch influenced by a renewal."[18] In his old branch, Drāz includes the descriptive studies done for each religion. This branch he calls "history of religions," the purpose of which is

> the investigation of beliefs, worship and the rest of instructions in every faith, from the reality of its sayings and of its doings. . . . This is the goal of scientific criticism which is based upon the study of

> history in order truly to ascertain the documents and their ascriptions and the study of the laws of language and the conventions of the arts to determine the meaning of texts.[19]

This definition exemplifies the historical and philological approach emphasized by Orientalists[20] and was obviously well appropriated by Drāz during his period of study in Paris. It is clear that by "old branch" Drāz implied only the late-nineteenth- and early-twentieth-century philological-historical approach to the history of religions, not the medieval Muslim investigations into "beliefs, worship and the rest of instructions in every faith" which one can find among a number of important medieval Muslim writers. If Drāz had been writing with the aim to retrieve past Muslim scholarship, he would have made his intentions more clear in this passage. The fact that he did not would imply that he worked solely from a Western European epistemological point of view. This becomes even more obvious when he writes about the "other newer and more original" branch: "[It] comes from the theoretical sciences and the numerous discoveries, whose aim is to satisfy the desire of reason in its striving for the origins of things and their general foundations, when its parts and details are ramified."[21] In these two quotes, Drāz's choice of methodology reflects his tendency to accept certain European claims of what science is and to translate them into Arabic. His book therefore belongs to a conscious mimetic appropriation which coincides with a colonized mentality.

Aḥmad Shalabī (b. ca. 1925)

Our third author, Aḥmad Shalabī, belongs to a younger generation of scholars. His education combined traditional Egyptian learning in the region of the Nile Delta, an undergraduate degree at Dār al-ʿulūm at the University of Cairo, and a doctorate degree from Cambridge University in England, earned in 1952, with a dissertation on "The History of Muslim Education," published in 1954. At Cambridge, he studied comparative religion and more particularly the works of important medieval Muslim scholars such as Ibn Ḥazm, al-Bīrūnī, Shahrastānī, and Masʿūdī with professors Arthur John Arberry, and Bertram Thomas, and Bernard Lewis in London. In 1955, Shalabī was delegated by the University of Cairo and the Muslim Congress to become professor of Islamic studies at the University of Indonesia in Jakarta. During his four years in Indonesia, he began delivering lectures and composing his series on comparative religion. Shalabī returned to Egypt to see the publication over the next four years of his four-volume series entitled *Religions Compared*.[22]

In this series, his methodological claims are often contradictory. On the one hand, there is the constant reminder that he is using the scientific method and that his approach respects the norms of science. On the other hand, his series presents a polemical rhetoric often devoid of scientific accuracy. This approach cannot be easily explained on the part of someone who must have learned the rudiments of scholarly research while doing his doctoral studies at Cambridge University in England. In the same paragraph, Shalabī can write:

> I certify indeed that I tried strongly and earnestly to make this research scientific, not religious: that is, I made it uninfluenced by my feelings and my embracing of this religion [Islam]. . . . Any knowledgeable researcher must favor monotheism and scorn polytheism and idols.[23]

Shalabī's claims to be using a scientific method closely resemble those of Abū Zahrah. Both scholars draw a direct correlation between reason (*ʿaql*) and science (*ʿilm*) on the basis of culturally inherited usages of the Arabic language, itself embedded in a wider Islamic epistemology of science. They both understand science as a method which requires the use of logical reasoning within the bounds of Islamic faith.[24] They borrow English or French words and interpret their meanings on the basis of their own cultural horizon. Moreover, both resort to the use of polemics, although Abū Zahrah's tone is less virulent and his style less politicized than that of Shalabī. But Shalabī differs from Abū Zahrah in one crucial respect: Shalabī consciously reconstructs a science of comparative religion that subordinates human reason to traditional ahistorical Islamic beliefs. Shalabī's work thus exemplifies an early attempt at an Islamic epistemological reconstruction of one branch of Western science, comparative religion.

The Impact of the Scholar

Having contextualized contemporary Arabic Muslim writings on religions other than Islam within recent Arab Muslim intellectual history and given three examples of such writings, we may now raise the issue of the so-called outside researcher as a de facto partner in the process of image formation of the Other. The predominantly European researchers who have studied contemporary Arabic Muslim writings on religions other than Islam belong themselves to a modern intellectual history that is confined primarily to Europe and North America and to westernized elites in the Middle East. They can be divided into three categories.[25] The first category, and the most important one, is *confessional*: authors who research how Muslims describe their religion—that is, the religion of the researcher. This category includes especially Christian and Jewish scholars who write from their own confessional horizons as believing Jews or Christians. It also includes Muslims who write about how their coreligionists see religions other than Islam. The second category is *national*—that is, authors who have researched how Muslims have described their nation, or their group of nations, the researcher's nation. The main case is Israeli Jews who have looked at how Muslims have interpreted Israel and by extension Judaism. Other cases include West Europeans and North Americans who have analyzed Arab Muslim usages of the ambiguous construct "the West" and by extension Christianity. The third category is *historical*—that is, authors who have researched how Muslims have described religions other than Islam as a means of making sense of the process by which ideas and images are perceived and get transmitted in a given discourse embedded in a historical reality limited by a set of unique contingencies.

One example from the confessional category is the doctoral dissertation of Hugh Goddard entitled, "Christianity as Portrayed by Egyptian Muslim Authors since 1950: An Examination in the Light of Earlier Muslim Views."[26] A survey of 70 Muslim writings on Christianity, this dissertation presents a full spectrum of the various perceptions encountered through the writings of Egyptian Muslims. After a survey of Qurʾānic, medieval, and modern Muslim views of Christianity, Goddard correctly stresses the element of continuity with the past in order to understand contemporary Muslim perceptions of non-Muslims. He writes: "Egyptian Muslim writings about Christianity after 1945 display a continuing mixture of opinion, and although there is some new material, there is also a remarkable continuity in the reproduction of older views."[27] He lists some of the more traditional contemporary views such as the historical corruption of Christianity, the truth of Islam as being forecasted in Christian sources, the link between Christianity and imperialism, Islamic hagiographical accounts of the earthly nature of Jesus, and fictional interpretations of the historic Jesus and the early Christian community.

Goddard's description of the contents of those writings is excellent. However, he does not raise any question as to why, for example, should such "reproduction" of older views be so widespread in the new material. He simply tries to mimetically translate what he finds in Egyptian Arabic Muslim books on Christianity. This approach may have been more useful if he had not superimposed a framework of analysis that stems from his own historicist Christian horizon. He divides his post-1950 material into three categories: negative, positive, and intermediate. These three categories are never defined, except in the two following and most indirect ways:

> These works are positive both in content and attitude.[28]

> In between the two categories of modern writing already discussed—the negative, rather polemical category, and the more positive group, there is an intermediate group, not explicitly positive but equally not deliberately negative.[29]

The reader is left to understand what "positive," "negative," and "intermediate" mean on their own. One must assume that Goddard shares with his primary audience, his doctoral committee in the Faculty of Theology at Birmingham University, England, an understanding of what "positive" versus "negative" representations of Christianity must mean. The outside reader, though, is only able to approximate what a "positive" or "negative" representation of Christianity might be after Goddard defines Christianity in the conclusion of his thesis:

> Christianity itself needs to be defined here. It is an imperfect term, but what is meant is "main-line," "orthodox" Christianity, the Christianity adhered to and practiced by the majority of Christians, whatever their other differences may be. It is Christianity of the Councils of the Early Church, or, to use an Anglican term, of the undivided church, and therefore particularly of the first Four Councils, and it is precisely this Christianity that the Qurʾān fails to understand.[30]

Goddard's lack of self-critical awareness weakens the value of his painstaking retrieval of much important information on how contemporary Egyptian Muslims interpret Christianity. This weakness becomes apparent on two levels. First, a Christian reader may accept Goddard's categorization and conclusions without much second thought, since they reinforce his or her stereotypes about Muslims' perceptions of Christianity. Second, a potential Muslim reader who may agree with the description of Christianity classified by Goddard as "negative" may dismiss Goddard's categorization and conclusions, accusing him of reading the "correct" or "positive" representation of Christianity on the basis of his own Christian beliefs. In fact, both kinds of readers would be doing exactly the same thing: each one would assume to hold the "correct" definition of what Christianity is on the basis of equally valid sets of beliefs. Goddard's categorization thus implies a moral judgment as to how Egyptian Muslims should interpret Christianity, a morality which has more to do with his own hopes to find Muslims capable of defining Christianity the way he suggests (and fears of the opposite), than with the more difficult task of describing what the variety of representations might indicate about the Muslims who uphold them directly. Goddard's avenue of research is not fruitful, as it can only lead to further reinforcement of stereotypes without providing us with a mechanism for better understanding the process by which Arab Muslims and non-Arab Muslim researchers interpret each other. Moreover, Goddard's kind of research can feed into how contemporary Arab Muslims write about religions other than Islam, leading to a mirroring game devoid of sufficient self-criticism to leap into a higher level of hermeneutical complexity from where both researcher and researched can be accounted for.

Conclusion

The contrasts between Shalabī on the one hand and Abū Zahrah and Drāz on the other, and between Shalabī and Goddard, raise questions about the premises upon which a study of contemporary Arabic Muslim writings on religions other than Islam should be predicated. We might ask ourselves, for example, what kind of access to non-Muslims has a Muslim author had, and vice versa? How were these encounters conditioned? Were these contacts based on business opportunities, such as simple transactions in the *suq*, educational opportunities such as in primary and secondary schools or especially university? Was it at home? in a different section of town? abroad? What kind of indirect contacts has an Arab Muslim author had with non-Muslims, or a non-Muslim researcher like myself had with Muslims? Are they the result of media exposure or street encounters that confirm or discredit popular stereotypes? Were some of these contacts framed by traumatic experiences such as attacks or war? Moreover, what audience is each writing addressed to? To the extent that the answers to these multiple questions represent experiences of the Other that have been perceived by an individual as negative, the resulting image is bound to be antagonistic. The reverse is equally true, for the motivation to write is never purely self-motivated; rather it is part of a larger social set of power relations that need to be uncovered. This applies to the writings of those Muslim authors under study, as much as to those of researchers of this topic.

To the extent that during the second part of the twentieth century there has been a merging of epistemological foundations between segments of the dominant Western cultures and segments of many dominated cultures around the world, the contemporary usage of the Western/Islamic dichotomy reflects more a constructed ideal that serves certain segments of politically motivated groups, whether Christian, Jewish, or Muslim, than a reality as such. Some writers attempt to keep the status quo in what is perceived to be the "correct" hermeneutical methodology, like Goddard's claims to be rooted in an objective historical approach that essentializes his own original context to the detriment of the contexts of the Muslim authors he investigates. Others prefer to provide an alternative reading of reality, like Shalabī's attempt to reconstruct an Islamic origin for the science of comparative religion.[31] Each writer's approach belongs to a much wider system of social forces, a *mentalité* that shapes and predisposes him or her to certain interpretations of reality. Insofar as each *mentalité* is predicated on the notion that it is not only distinct, but better than others, its usage legitimizes certain political interests that are basically incompatible with others. As examples of the two sides of a research, Goddard's and Shalabī's respective approaches would deny the fact that a merging of horizons is taking place in both cases. There is a hermeneutical competition with no winners, as each author reaps the support of an audience which already shares the presuppositions that make the arguments sound and politically useful.

This example raises the thorny question of just how much self-criticism versus other-criticism is the right balance for an academic understanding of any topic. In other words, How much of my own epistemology do I bring along and write about as a researcher, and how much do I try to discover that of the researched? Furthermore, how does my research contribute to the Other's formation of the image of his or her Other, thereby potentially constantly changing my results ad infinitum? Whether the researcher is engaged in an unconscious or conscious mimesis of his or her own context, or active in the construction of his or her own social and scientific discourse, the work of interpreting across cultures can probably never be dichotomized so easily. These given limits are imposed on our attempts to understand contemporary Arabic Muslim writings on religions other than Islam.

Through the vicissitudes of recent political, economic, and broader social events, many contemporary Muslims, whether Arab or other, have effectively enlarged their imaginative powers to re-think themselves, both individually and collectively. In the process, Muslims have collectively challenged the traditional Western enemy which did not remain unaffected. A study of President Bush's discourse during the 1991 Gulf War reveals the extent to which he revived old Christian polemical imageries that fed into, and were also fed by, old perceptions that Christians and Muslims have had of each other ever since the Crusades. The public remarks of American Vice-President Quayle at a Republican rally in August 1992 to the effect that the three evils of the twentieth century have been Nazism, Communism, and Islam, only adds an American nationalistic dimension to the deeply rooted popular western Christian cultural distortions of Islam. Both examples reflect the symbiotic nature of today's human interactions. Indeed, it is the very often confrontational contact with the Other, whomever he/she/they may be, that begins the process of reimagining the self. In turn, the modifications to the image of the self affect the image of the Other and the quality of interaction with the embodied Other. This is where researchers' writings come into play, equally vulnerable to being used by any audience for its own purposes.

The implications that the conception of the self carries for the conception of the Other are so important that it is impossible to dissociate one from the other. It is therefore vital that researchers on contemporary Arabic Muslim writings on religions other than Islam be aware of the nature of this symbiotic relationship between any writer and his or her topic. Without this greater critical self-awareness, the impact of researchers' writings may not serve cross-cultural understanding as much as it could. Yet, in a world threatened by countless misunderstandings of the Other, such understanding is desperately required. It is all the more urgent in view of the frightening increase in communalism and the resort to ethnic cleansing, the reemergence of the specter of Nazism, the continuing gender oppression, or even the ecological devastation we all witness today.

NOTES

1. G. L. Ormiston and A. D. Schrift, eds., *Transforming the Hermeneutic Context* (Albany, 1990), p. 221.

2. Jacques Waardenburg, in a letter to this author (Lausanne: March 22, 1991).

3. Images of the "West" in general will not be examined, although they are part of the immediate background to our discussion.

4. S. D. Goitein, *Jews and Arabs: Their Contacts through the Ages* (New York, 1974).

5. Y. Harkabi, *Arab Attitudes to Israel* (Jerusalem, 1976).

6. Ibid., pp. 540–541.

7. Ibid., p. 300.

8. See Bernard Lewis, *Semites and Anti-Semites: An Inquiry into Conflict and Prejudice* (New York, 1986).

9. See yearly Amnesty International reports of both of these countries.

10. I attended the third of these events held at the University of Jordan in Amman, Jordan, in the autumn of 1987. These conferences were normally held every two years, alternating between Jordan and Europe.

11. See the publication of the International Institute of Islamic Thought entitled *Islamization of Knowledge: General Principles and Work Plan* (Herndon, 1989).

12. Located at the periphery of Washington, D.C., the International Institute of Islamic Thought combines money and freedom of exploration which allows for the best process of creativity to take place. In the decade since its inception in 1981, the center has already had an important impact which will only grow with time.

13. The international conference on "Towards a Global Islamic Economy," held in Detroit, from November 29 to December 1, 1991, is just one example of this renewed vitality.

14. Muḥammad Abū Zahrah, *Muhādarāt fī muqāranat al-adyān* (Cairo, 1965); and *Muhādarāt fī al-nasrāniyya* (Cairo, 1942).

15. *Muhādarāt fī al-nasrāniyya*, p. 4.

16. See Franz Rosenthal, *A History of Muslim Historiography*, 2nd rev. ed. (Leiden, 1968); and on the methods developed by the traditionists (*muḥaddithūn*), see Claude Cahen, "L'historiographie arabe: des origines au VIIe. s. H," *Arabica*, 33 (1986): 133–198, especially pp. 136–137.

17. ʿAbdallāh Drāz, *al-Dīn* (Cairo, 1952).

18. Ibid., p. 17.

19. Ibid., p. 18.

20. See Charles J. Adams, "The history of religions and the study of Islam," *American Council of Learned Societies Newsletter* vol. 25 no. 3–4 (1974), pp. 1–10, especially p. 7; and "The history of religions and the study of Islam," in J. M. Kitagawa, ed., *History of Religions: Essays on the Problem of Understanding* (Chicago: Univ. of Chicago Press, 1967), pp. 177–193. See esp. p. 192 for a clear example of one Orientalist's impact on Muslims, that is, Goldziher.

21. Drāz, *al-Dīn*, p. 18.

22. Aḥmad Shalabī, *Muqāranat al-adyān*, 4 vols. (Cairo, 1960–1964). The volumes are entitled: Vol. 1: *al-yahūdiyya*; Vol. 2: *al-masīḥiyya*; Vol. 3: *al-islām*; Vol. 4: *adyān al-hind al-kubrā*.

23. Ibid., Vol. 3, p. 23.

24. Drāz, on the contrary, avoids contrasting reason with faith. He does not refer to Islam when he describes the Western scientific use of reason. His interpretation of scientific method does not conflict with his personal faith in Islam, at least from what we can deduce from the content of his book under analysis here.

25. There are cases where a researcher's intentionality belongs to two categories at once.

26. Hugh P. Goddard, "Christianity as portrayed by Egyptian Muslim authors: An examination in the light of earlier Muslim views," Ph.D. thesis (University of Birmingham, 1984).

27. Ibid., p. 131.

28. Ibid., pp. 197–198.

29. Ibid., p. 273.

30. Ibid., pp. 323–324.

31. If one is to judge by the number of reprints his series has gone through, his project has certainly had much appeal.

BIBLIOGRAPHY

Abū Zahrah, Muḥammad. *Muhādarāt fī al-naṣrāniyya* (1942) Cairo: Maṭbaʿat al-ʿulūm, 1942; 3rd ed. Cairo: Dār al-fikr al-ʿarabī, 1961.

———. *Muḥādarāt fī muqāranat al-adyān: al-qism al-awwal, al-diyānāt al-qadīma* (1940). Cairo: Maṭbaʿat yūsuf, 1965.

Adams, Charles J. "The history of religions and the study of Islam." In *The History of Religions: Essays on the Problem of Understanding*, ed. Joseph Kitagawa. Chicago: University of Chicago Press, 1967, pp. 177–193.

———. "The history of religions and the study of Islam." *American Council of Learned Societies Newsletter* 25:3–4 (1974), pp. 1–10.

ʿAlūsh, Nājī. *al-Masīra ilā Filasūn* (*The Journey to Palestine*). Beirut: Dār al-ʾalīʿa, 1964.

Bahāʾ al-Dīn, Aḥmad. *Isrāʾīliyyāt*. Cairo: Kitāb al-hilāl, 1965.

Cahen, Claude. "L'historiographie arabe: Des origines au VIIe s. H.," *Arabica* 33 (1986): 133–198.

Drāz, Muḥammad ʿAbdallāh. *al-Dīn: buhūth mumahhida li-dirāsat taʾrīkh al-adyān*. Cairo: al-Maṭbaʿa al-ʿālamiyya, 1952.

Goddard, Hugh P. "Christianity as portrayed by Egyptian Muslim authors: An examination in the light of earlier Muslim views." Ph. D. thesis, University of Birmingham, 1984.

———. *Muslim Perceptions of Christianity*. London: Grey Seal Books, 1996.

Goitein, S. D. *Jews and Arabs: Their Contacts through the Ages*. New York: Schocken Books, 1974.

Harkabi, Y. Arab *Attitudes to Israel*. Jerusalem: Keter Publishing House Jerusalem, 1976.

Islamization of Knowledge: General Principles and Work Plan. Herndon, Va: International Institute of Islamic Thought, 1989.

Lewis, Bernard. *Semites and Anti-Semites: An Inquiry into Conflict and Prejudice*. New York: Norton, 1986.

Ormiston, Gayle L., and Alan D. Schrift, eds. *Transforming the Hermeneutic Context*. Albany, NY: State University of New York Press, 1990.

Rosenthal, Franz. *A History of Muslim Historiography*, 2nd rev. ed. Leiden: E. J. Brill, 1968.

Shalabī, Aḥmad. *Muqāranat al-adyān*. 4 vols. (1960–1965) Cairo: Maktabat al-nahḍa al-ʿarabiyya, 1984.

16

The Muslims of South Asia (1857–1947)

SHEILA MCDONOUGH

At the time of the partition of India and Pakistan in 1947, Muslims comprised about one quarter of the population of the subcontinent. In a number of respects, the Muslim experience in India has been different from that of Muslims elsewhere. Since the tenth century, Muslims have been actively coming into India from Iran, Afghanistan, and Central Asia. The Muslims who came into India found themselves involved with a majority population of Hindus. For several centuries, differing forms of accommodation had evolved in relation to the majority population. Finally, events took a different turn when the British arrived in the sixteenth century and gradually came to dominate Indian life. In the nineteenth century, the Muslims were beginning to discover that their status was becoming increasingly insecure. As Sivan has pointed out, it has been a Muslim from this relatively insecure milieu, Mawdudi, who, in the mid-twentieth century, has articulated the most popular version of a neotraditionalist perspective.[1] Since that perspective has now become a dominant one in many movements throughout the Muslim world, it may be that the destabilizing experiences of the Indian Muslims are beginning to speak to the insecurities of Muslims in many parts of the Islamic world.

The Revolt of 1857: Sayyid Ahmed Khan

In 1857, Indian troops of the British army in India rebelled against their officers and precipitated the conflict now known as the Indian Mutiny or Revolt. With the help of Sikh troops from northern India, the British triumphed over the rebels, and, suspecting Muslim intrigue as a cause of the conflict, exiled the last Mughal emperor, shot his sons, and ruined much of the Muslim city of Delhi. They effectively destroyed the power and wealth of the Muslim aristocracy. This violent and sudden elimination of a governing class was a shock to Muslim self-understanding. One articulate witness to these events was the Muslim poet, Ghalib, who was in Delhi when the British wreaked their revenge on the defenseless city and its inhabitants.[2] In Ghalib's subtle and beautiful verses, one finds eloquent testimony to the ambiguities and sorrow of the Indian Muslim situation. Ghalib had been impressed by the cleanliness and order the British had brought to Calcutta, but he perceived their destruction of Delhi as brutal and racist. Muslims found themselves conquered by a people they could not effectively relate to by using their own standards of courtesy and diplomacy.

About 50 years after this event, a Muslim journalist, Muhammad Ali, looking back on the post-Mutiny period, tells us how his generation perceived the attitudes of their predecessors who had embodied the remnants of the Muslim governing class:

> It was the Muslim aristocracy. . . that suffered most in the terrible aftermath of the Mutiny. In fact, in its permanent results even more than in some of its terrors, it could, without any considerable exaggeration, be compared to the social upheaval that the French Revolution meant to the old nobility of France.

> The remnant of Muslim aristocracy, deprived of all influence and many of their possessions, certainly did not expect the return of the Muslim rule. Nevertheless, a whole generation kept sullenly aloof from all contact with the culture of the new rulers of India, which in their heart of hearts they still despised. . . . Few indeed can realize today the feeling of those Upper India Muslims who sulked in their tents for so long, or the difficulties of the pioneers of English education among them.[3]

Muhammad Ali explains in this way how difficult it was to get Muslims to move out of their depressed condition and to become actively involved with the new intellectual challenges the British had brought with them. He credits the efforts of Sayyid Ahmed Khan as the major cause of the eventual transformation of Muslim self-understanding, hopes, and social attitudes. Sayyid Ahmed Khan, himself one of the Muslim aristocrats who had survived the destruction of Delhi, thought that Muslims must either adapt to the new forms of learning or cease to be effective in the world. Muhammad Ali was himself a graduate of the Aligarh Muslim University. He later said that the founder of that university, Sayyid Ahmed Khan, was responsible for saving the Muslims from sinking into a condition of despair and paralysis. Sayyid Ahmed Khan believed that the future survival of the Muslims would require them to adapt to their new rulers, while maintaining their faith, and to learn whatever new skills might be necessary for survival in the new conditions. His answer to defeat was not retreat, but active quest for new knowledge. Therefore he insisted on founding a modern university for Muslims, on translating scientific materials into Urdu, and on coexistence with the British. There is not much doubt that this vigorous life-affirming spirit did much to revitalize the young Muslims who came to study at the new university.

One aspect of this new program was to reevaluate the basis for Muslim-Christian relationships. Sayyid Ahmed Khan established a journal, *Tahzib ul-Akhlaq*, with the aim of encouraging Muslims to distinguish between the basic principles of their religion (which could not be changed) and their cultural practices (which could be revised).[4] Since he believed that closer social relationships with Christians were desirable for Muslims, he urged reexamination of the attitudes and practices of his community. He believed that much Muslim behavior was based on prejudice and custom. This meant, he thought, that the Indian Muslims should try to dissociate themselves from certain cultural attitudes and practices that they had acquired from their Indian environment, such as fears of pollution from foreigners and dislike of widow remarriages. Many Indian Muslims thought it wrong to eat with Christians, but Ahmed Khan insisted that there were Hadith who affirmed the legitimacy of this practice.[5]

As part of this project of strengthening mutual knowledge and respect between Muslims and Christians, Ahmed Khan attempted to write a commentary on the Bible. He completed a commentary on Genesis 1 to 11 and Matthew 1 to 5. The pressure of his other activities prevented him from completing this work. His intention,however, remains clear, namely to encourage mutual understanding between Muslims and Christians based on scholarship. He did not think Muslims had anything to fear from such a process. He was well aware of the disparagement of the Prophet Muhammad current in many of the writings of Christian missionaries. His method, however, was to respond to misrepresentation by reasoned argument. In addition to the commentary on the Bible, he also wrote studies of the Qurʾān and Hadith.[6]

In the commentary on the Bible, he noted that there have been many versions. This fact is normally understood by Muslims to indicate the greater reliability of the Qurʾān. He indicated certain differences in the two Scriptures, such as the teaching that the creation took place in seven days according to the Bible and in six days according to the Qurʾān. His attitude to these issues was that reasonable people can agree to differ on such matters. He rejected the possibility of miracles and undertook to offer rationalistic explanations. He said, for example, that the Virgin Birth was symbolic of faithfulness to the husband. He explained the crucifixion as an event during which Jesus was put on the cross, but was removed by his disciples before he died, and was hidden by them. On the question of Christian ethics, he said that to love the enemy is not totally impossible, although he elsewhere commented that Christians have not behaved like this in their history.

Sayyid Ahmed Khan's optimism and resilience of spirit were remarkable. In spite of the humiliating defeat suffered by his immediate community, and the unpleasant experience of domination by the often racist and contemptuous British, he seemed sure that the Muslims could rise again. His knowledge of history may have helped him take a long view; he had written a history of the Muslims of Delhi, and he knew that the community had persisted through many kinds of triumphs and defeats. He actively encouraged education and the development of scientific knowledge among Muslims. Part of his long-range plan seems to have included attempting to remove obstacles to effective cooperation between Muslims and Christians in India. On the Muslim side, this meant overcoming irrational prejudices and customs which might have prevented inter-dining and other forms of social relationship between the two communities. One might look on this aspect of Sayyid Ahmed Khan's activities as the fruit of generations of training in diplomatic practices; his grandfather had been a diplomat serving the Mughal court. Sayyid Ahmed Khan's own training at home had stressed civility and courteous human relationships. Although he received much abuse for his efforts to change people, his responses were characteristically rational and good-tempered.

He tried also to educate the British so that they might adopt a more rational and civil attitude to their Indian subjects. He was encouraged in these efforts by some Englishmen who were his friends and supporters. He wrote an account for the English of the reasons for the Mutiny in which he said that the insensitivity of the rulers had been a significant factor in causing trouble. His commentary on the Bible was intended to make civil relationships between Muslims and Christians more possible. He was attempting to urge Muslims to recognize common values between the two communities. He hoped that the Christians would also become more respectful and courteous in their attitudes to the Muslim faith.

Relations with the Hindus took a less significant place in Sayyid Ahmed Khan's thought. His overriding concern was to further good relations between the Muslims and the British. He knew that the British were blaming the Muslims for the Revolt and that his community was in serious danger of repression by the rulers. Hindus were allowed to be educated along with Muslims in the university founded by Sayyid Ahmed Khan, and he was ready to encourage cultural reciprocity between the Muslim and Hindu communities. However, he was not optimistic as to what might happen to the Muslims if the British were to leave India.[7]

Early Twentieth Century

Once the Aligarh Muslim University had been founded, a number of Englishmen came to teach there. A mutually productive friendship seemed to have developed between the young English historian, Thomas Arnold, and Shibli Numani, a Muslim religious scholar who had come to teach the Qur'ān, and other Islamic subjects, to the Aligarh students. In the subsequent historical writings of both Arnold and Shibli, one can perceive some fruits of the interaction between scholars that was one significant contribution of Aligarh. In Arnold's case, for example, one finds in his book *The Preaching of Islam* arguments against the old and widespread Christian stereotype of "conversion by the sword," namely of violence as the only reason for the spread of Islam.[8]

Shibli's writings include a number of significant biographies of important Muslim leaders. These biographies contributed greatly to the self-understanding of the new generation of educated Indian Muslims. One can find in Shibli's writings references to historians like Gibbon, which indicate that the Muslim author, although critical of much Western historiography, was, nevertheless, attempting to relate his efforts in writing Muslim history to contemporary historical writing.[9] Shibli said that some Christian writers had tried to deny that the Prophet was descended from Abraham and had claimed that Muhammad got his ideas from the Christian monk Bahira.[10] These instances are typical of what Shibli perceived as distortions of the Islamic tradition by Western writers hostile to Islam, and he wanted to use scholarship to refute what he saw as malicious misrepresentations of Muslim history. He said that one of the worst characteristics of Western writings about Islam was that Western scholars seemed unable to distinguish between gossip and reliable sources. Shibli wrote a biography of the Prophet Muhammad which became extremely popular among Indian Muslims. He later tried to set up his own training institute which would, he hoped, specialize in training Muslims to write effectively.

Moving on now to 1915, we find in Muhammad Ali's *My Life a Fragment* an account of the attitudes of a young Muslim journalist who had been educated at Aligarh and subsequently at Oxford. Muhammad Ali considered that his Aligarh education, and especially Shibli's lectures on the Qur'ān, had well equipped him to confront the modern world. Muhammad Ali gives us as follows his perceptions of the contribution of Sayyid Ahmed Khan:

> With a Tacitus-like antithesis he credited Europe with every good quality in which he found his own people deficient; but for all this he never wavered for a moment in his belief in the eternal truth of Islam and the capacity of the Muslims to rise to the

> highest pinnacle of human greatness. All he wanted was to build a bridge that would connect his ancient faith with this new science, and the ideal that he placed before himself, when framing his scheme of the Muslim University of the future, is best expressed in his own words. "Science," he said, "shall be in our right hand and philosophy in our left; and on our head shall be the crown of 'There is no god but Allah and Mohammad is His Apostle'."[11]

Muhammad Ali argued that cooperation with the British had been necessary in Sayyid Ahmed Khan's time, but was no longer appropriate. He was interned in 1915 because of his "subversive" writings about the fate of Turkey. He feared that the British and their allies would capture Istanbul, which would then become Tsargrad; the Russians would have access to the Mediterranean; and the Islamic holy places might be taken by foreigners.[12] Muhammad Ali, writing early in World War I, feared that one outcome of the war might be the extinction of Muslim independence everywhere. Although events did not work out as he expected, his grasp of Western intentions toward the dismembering of the Ottoman Empire was fairly realistic.

Another active Muslim contemporary of Muhammad Ali was Jinnah. The latter had studied law in London and had become an extremely successful Muslim lawyer in Bombay. In 1915–1916, the young Jinnah managed to get the two main indigenous political organizations, the Indian National Congress and the Muslim League, to meet together and to agree on a common platform for the future independence of India. The degree of readiness to cooperate between the leaders of the Congress and the Muslim League at this point was never subsequently repeated. In the years between World Wars I and II, antagonism between the two communities continued to increase. In 1915, Jinnah was, however, considered an apostle of Hindu-Muslim unity.[13] Although he and Muhammad Ali followed different paths in the subsequent historical period, they seemed, early in World War I, to reflect a growing Muslim consensus that the period of relying on relations with the British was finished and that the Muslims of the subcontinent must begin to interact more effectively with their Hindu compatriots.

The Non-cooperation Movement

Another activist had also entered Indian politics at this period. Gandhi had returned to India from his successful nonviolence campaigns in South Africa. Immediately after the war, he entered actively into Congress politics, hoping to repeat in India some of the nonviolence campaigns that had proved effective in South Africa. Jinnah disapproved of what he considered mixing up mob emotions with serious political negotiations, and, when Gandhi came to dominate the Congress, Jinnah withdrew. Muhammad Ali made an opposite move. He became an enthusiastic coworker with Gandhi in the political struggles of 1919–1922. The Russian Revolution, and Atatürk's military successes, had frustrated Western attempts to control Turkey. Nevertheless, Muhammad Ali continued to fear European expansionism into Muslim territory, and specifically into Mecca and Medina.

The different responses of Jinnah and Muhammad Ali to Congress politics in 1919 reflect the differences in their basic approaches. Jinnah had a rationalistic understanding of religion and politics. He believed that reason should be used to help persons resolve situations of conflict. He was in favor of constitutional guarantees of individual rights and of parliamentary democracy. He thought that bringing mob religious sentiments into Indian political life would render rational constitutional negotiations very difficult, if not impossible. For this reason, he subsequently left India and went to practice law in England. Gandhi, just returned from his epic struggles in South Africa, had a sort of messianic conviction that, if the masses would follow him in nonviolent resistance, the British could be forced to leave India within a year. Jinnah thought this idea foolish. Muhammad Ali enthusiastically embraced the vision, and entered into partnership with Gandhi.[14]

The partnership of Gandhi and Muhammad Ali in the Non-cooperation struggle of 1919–1922 created many new bonds of friendship and support between Muslims and Hindus, although it also perplexed many persons in both religious traditions. Muhammad Ali believed that the independence of the Turkish Caliph was urgently important for all Muslims because the sacred places must be protected by Muslims. He founded the Khilafat Committee for the purpose of lobbying the English to maintain the independence of the Turkish Caliph. Since many Indian Muslims had fought in the British army, the British government was sensitive to these concerns. At the time, the Greeks had invaded Turkey, and Turkish independence was by no means certain. One of the most curious developments was that Gandhi became an active member of the Khilafat Committee. He was the only significant Hindu leader to do so.

Gandhi reasoned that religious matters are central to human personality. Since Gandhi wanted Muslims to work with him in building a new India, he thought that supporting them on a matter they thought religiously serious would bond them to him. Gandhi attended Khilafat meetings and was hoping to create Hindu-Muslim solidarity for the new India. Few other Hindus shared this reasoning. Most of the Muslim leaders did support the Khilafat movement, but some, including Jinnah and Iqbal, did not. The enthusiasm of Gandhi and Muhammad Ali was met with both positive response and skepticism in their communities.

From Gandhi's papers from this period, we note that Muhammad Ali and his brother Shaukat were actively involved in touring India with Gandhi and making speeches everywhere. All three were urging Indians to leave the British educational, legal, and other institutions and to refuse absolutely to cooperate with the British administration of India. Many Muslim students and teachers did leave Aligarh: they set up an independent institution called the Islamic National University, Jamia Millia Islamia. The comparable Hindu institution, the Benares Hindu University, was less willing to cooperate, but some did leave and set up another national university.

How did Muhammad Ali relate his self-understanding as a Muslim to his enthusiastic acceptance of Gandhi's cause? Gandhi had invited Iqbal to become president of the new Jamia Millia Islamia, but Iqbal refused on the grounds that he was not temperamentally suited to such a role. That Gandhi and Iqbal corresponded on this matter indicates that Muslims generally were aware of the possibility that the Non-cooperation movement might succeed in driving the English out of India.[15] Muhammad Ali then became the first head of the new institution. The curriculum he established indicated that he wanted the young Muslims, who were to be educated to participate actively in the new India, to be well grounded in the Qur'ān (as Muhammad Ali had been, thanks to Shibli's lectures at Aligarh), in Iqbal's poetry, and in Islamic history. Iqbal's Urdu poetry was an important element in stimulating Muslim revivalist enthusiasm.

Muhammad Ali

There is little doubt that Muhammad Ali was self-consciously a Muslim reformer in the tradition established by Sayyid Ahmed Khan. He saw Gandhi essentially as a political ally. He thought that cooperation with the English had been necessary in Sayyid Ahmed Khan's time, but that the different situation of his generation made cooperation with the Hindus desirable as a means to getting the English out of India. In *My Life a Fragment*, he indicated his ideas about the future:

> I felt I should now assist my community in taking its proper share in the political life of the country. . . . it should never lose sight of the prospects of the future when ultimately all communal interests had to be adjusted in order to harmonise with the paramount interests of India. I had long been convinced that here in this country of hundreds of millions of human beings, intensely attached to religion and yet infinitely split up into communities, sect and denomination, Providence had created for us the mission of solving a unique problem and working out a new synthesis. It was nothing less than a Federation of Faiths. The lines of cleavage were too deeply marked to permit a unity other than federal and yet the cleavage was not territorial or racial in character but religious, and I had been dreaming for some time dreams of a "United Faiths of India." *The Comrade*—comrade of all, partisan of none—was to be the organ that was to voice these views, and prepare the Musalmans to make their proper contribution to territorial patriotism without abating a jot of the fervour of their extraterritorial sympathies which is the quintessence of Islam.[16]

As this quotation indicates, Muhammad Ali perceived Muslims and Hindus as distinctive communities, but he thought cooperation possible. On one occasion, he precipitated angry comments when he was quoted as saying that the creed of even a fallen and degraded Mussalman is entitled to a higher place than that of any other non-Muslim, irrespective of his high character, even though the person in question be Mahatma Gandhi himself. Other Muslims had accused Muhammad Ali of being a Gandhi worshipper. Much controversy followed in the press until finally Gandhi himself wrote:

> A gentleman writes to say that the Gujrati papers report Maulana Mahomed Ali as having said in a speech that Gandhi was lower than the most wretched Muslim. . . . God knows what has happened, but at present there is misunderstanding between Hindus and Muslims all around. They do not trust each other. The Hindi and Urdu newspapers in northern India have overdone the thing. . . . In my humble opinion, the Maulana has proved the purity of his heart and his faith in his own religion by expressing his view. He

> merely compared two sets of religious principles and gave his opinion as to which was better.[17]

This controversy developed in 1924 when the period of cooperation was ending, and communal tensions were worsening, fueled by distortions in the newspapers, as Gandhi correctly pointed out. The Non-cooperation movement had been called off by Gandhi after an outbreak of violence at a police station. Muslims, and many Hindus, were angry and disillusioned by what they perceived as an arbitrary canceling of a revolution in which they had invested personal energy and sacrifice The majority of Muslims had little use for Gandhi after that. A further disillusionment came when the new Republic of Atatürk abandoned the medieval Caliphate in March 1924. The Indian Khilafat movement had no raison d'etre once there was no more Ottoman Caliph. Muhammad Ali ceased to be a unifying leader for the Muslims when the causes he had supported fell apart.

Another facet of Muhammad Ali's thought was his interest in following the approaches of Sayyid Ahmad Khan and Shibli by studying the respective histories of Islam and Christianity. He hoped to arrive at an overview of the relationship between these historical traditions. Although Muhammad Ali had opposed the continuance of British rule in India, he nevertheless perceived a need for Muslims to enter into conversation with Christian scholars so that the two groups might better understand their common history. The brief history of Islam which he outlines in *My Life a Fragment* show us something of how he thought Indian Muslims should be taught to think about their historical relationship to Christianity. These ideas were intended to be the basis for the curriculum in Islamic history that he had hoped students at the Jamia Millia Islamia would follow. He trusted that his approach would be attractive to modern youth because, as he said, "unlike Christianity, no part of our faith rested on belief in a miracle."[18] In his approach to comparative studies, he wrote:

> Islam had no apostles, no Church, and no Church Councils like Christianity to dictate her creed to the believer. It has not even a clergy and the whole spirit of Islam is consistently and relentlessly opposed to such a thing as "experts" in religion. It wants all alike to know their faith, and religion should be the province of all the faithful. That is why, unlike Christianity, it has had no "theology by committee" as Mr. Wells aptly calls it.[19]

Muhammad Ali seems to have particularly enjoyed the writing of H. G. Wells. In writing on these topics, the Muslim scholar had several aims. One was to counter the "calumnies" that some Western writers had spread about Islam, and another was to help overcome the estrangement that had existed between Islam and the West.[20] He wrote as follows about Jesus:

> It was the crying need of Israel then, and the heroic effort of Jesus to infuse love into the legalism of the Pharisee, which culminated in the soul-stirring scene enacted at Calvary which was worthy of one whom the Qur'ān describes as "illustrious in this world and in the hereafter" and "one of those near [to God]." When in the fullness of time he passed away, he left behind him an exquisitely lovable personality and an example of firmness undivorced from gentleness. . . . But he was no theologian who cared to leave to his followers the legacy of involved labyrinthine dogma as rigid as the formalism of the Pharisees themselves, or an elaborate scheme of Church Government and a hierarchy that could shame the empire-builders of Rome with its regular gradation of a cycle of fasts and feasts and rites and ceremonies and fashion plates of vestments surpassing variety and imposing effect the best efforts of heathen priestcraft . . . Muslims will not wonder at the reception they meet with at the hands of Christians if they know that fellow-Christians that dared to differ from them in the smallest particular met with nothing better. And Christians today, who think intolerance is the badge of every faith but their own, will be able to unravel the mystery of their own intolerance towards Islam that does exist, and such ample measure too, even though they are not conscious of its existence, and will, it is my earnest wish and hope, discard it once for like so many ancient and medieval superstitions that they have discarded in recent days.[21]

Muhammad Ali's message for his fellow Muslims was thus that Christianity had been made into a theology of the cross by Paul. If Christians would learn to understand how Paul had corrupted the original teaching of Jesus, Christians would come closer to understanding Jesus in the same way that Muslims did. This ought to result in better relations between Muslims and Christians. Muhammad Ali also perceived the Gospel of John as a corruption of the original message. He wrote:

> So a new Gospel was needed which would "spiritualize" the "Apostolic" teaching of the Synoptic Gospels and yet strongly react against Doketic and

> Antinomian "heresy." And the "theologian of Ephesus" who has come to bear the name of "John" and has been taken for the disciple that died long before it was compiled, produced the Fourth Gospel. He reverses the natural order that "sound doctrine" must be based on Divine Scripture, inasmuch as he sits down to write Divine Scripture which he based on the conception of "sound doctrine" entertained by a partisan in heated and turbulent polemics. It is not a Gospel in the general sense of the word, but a "theological" treatise, an interpretation of the doctrine of the person of Christ, written that the reader "may believe that Jesus is the Christ, the Son of God."[22]

Muhammad Ali's studies at Oxford had confirmed his belief in the greater reasonableness of Muslim beliefs as compared to the irrational theological conceptions of Divine Sonship and the Trinity in the Christian tradition. He seems to have been particularly interested in the writings of the German scholar Adolf von Harnack. Muhammad Ali hoped that future Christian and Muslim scholars would come to understand, as Harnack did, that the early generations of Christian thinkers distorted the original Christian message. He quoted Harnack on the struggles of the early Church against gnosticism and the Manichees:

> And so St. Paul and the author of the Fourth Gospel between them had taken more than half the journey from primary religion, which was, apparently all the concern of the Galilean disciples; to theology and the rest being taken at breakneck speed by their extravagant disciples, the Gnostics. But while this journey was being undertaken, Christianity was manifesting itself as "enthusiastic." The end of the world was held to be close at hand. Neither the story nor the sayings of Jesus were recorded by those who could have perpetuated a full and authentic account of his ministry because of their expectation of the immediate end of the world and of his second advent.[23]

Muhammad Ali repeated this account by Harnack of the reasons Jesus' teachings were not properly recorded by the early Church. It is easy to see why an intelligent Muslim would have readily concluded, as Muhammad Ali did, that these accounts confirm the Muslim view that the original teaching of Jesus has been largely obscured by the theologians. He also took from Harnack the view that mysticism and political servility had given a death blow to prophetic consciousness in the Greek Church. The Latin Church, he said, had little interest in mysticism and had made the Gospel a system of morals and then, following St. Augustine, had identified the Catholic Church with the Kingdom of Christ.

Muhammad Ali discussed at length the theological disputes of the Patristic period, and the changes brought about by the conversion of the Emperor Constantine. He quoted from Gibbon to the effect that "the prerogatives of the King of Heaven were settled or changed in the cabinet of an earthly monarch and the sword of the tyrant was often unsheathed to enforce the reasons of the theologians."[24]

These discussions of events after Nicea indicate Muhammad Ali's belief that more careful study of Christian history would readily convince Muslims of the superiority of Islam. He also hoped that such study would lead Christians to recognize, as Arnold had indicated, that the successes of Islam in the seventh century were related to the dissatisfaction among Christian people as a result of centuries of wrangling on tangled theological issues and persecutions for heresy. The perspective characteristic of this early generation of Aligarh scholars was to emphasize the irrationality and inhumane persecutions of the early Christian centuries. Muhammad Ali hoped that this perspective on their own history would lead educated Christians to take a more tolerant and accepting attitude to Muslims. As one who had been interned by the British during World War I, and subsequently imprisoned for the intemperance of his remarks, he was not naive about the realities of oppressive British rule. Nevertheless, his Aligarh and Oxford studies had led him to believe that educated persons could eventually learn tolerance and mutual respect. He died in London in 1931 where he had been taking part in the round table conference called by the British to try to find agreement about the future of the subcontinent.

Abul Kalam Azad

A younger contemporary of Muhammad Ali, and a second important Muslim leader of this generation, was Mawlana Abul Kalam Azad (1888–1958). He also had taken part in the Khilafat and Non-cooperation movements. Like Muhammad Ali, he began his career as a journalist whose Urdu newspaper, *Al-Hilal*, had similar goals to Muhammad Ali's publications. Both men had been attempting through their writings to infuse energy and purposefulness into the Indian Muslims. Azad had come from a distinguished family of religious scholars in Calcutta and had been largely educated by his own family members. He did not share the Aligarh and Oxford background of Muhammad Ali, and he was always much more consistently anti-British than his fellow Muslim journalist.

Nevertheless, Azad had studied with Shibli. After Sayyid Ahmed Khan's death, Thomas Arnold had gone to teach in Government College, Lahore, where one of his students was the young Iqbal. Shibli had left Aligarh and had established a new institution called the Nadwat ul Ulema at Lucknow where he hoped to create a new generation of articulate Muslim scholars who could write effectively for the purpose of infusing new strength into the Indian Muslims. Azad spent some time there, and learned, most certainly, to write extremely well. Azad had also had contact with Bengali revolutionaries in his youth, and had subsequently travelled in the Arab world. He had met with many Arab political activists, and he felt part of a wider community of Muslims working to overthrow Western domination.

Azad and Muhammad Ali went in opposite directions after the collapse of the Khilafat and Non-cooperation movements. We noted earlier that Jinnah and Muhammad Ali had reacted in totally different ways to the impact of Gandhi on the Congress. Now we see another example of apparently similar Muslim reformists reacting in diverse ways to a period of crisis. At a minimum, we might learn from this that Muslims, like other people, are not readily predictable. Azad's response to the crisis of the failure of these movements of the early 1920s was to move more directly into close cooperation with the leaders of the Congress party. He became, and remained to the end, a close associate of Jawaharlal Nehru. He served as one of the subsequent presidents of the Congress; he was jailed along with the other Congress leaders; and, after independence, he became one of the members of Nehru's cabinet. From the perspective of the Muslims who remained with India, he became their most important leader and representative in the early years of Congress government.

Elements of Azad's religious thought can be discerned in his commentary on the Qurʾān which he began writing while he was imprisoned by the British along with other Congress leaders in 1930. The commentary was never finished because of Azad's many political responsibilities. In his introductory remarks, he comments that new commentaries are needed which would conform more to the spirit of the first generations of Qurʾān commentators. He maintains that the later generations of commentators in the Middle Ages were often inept and that many of them allowed their partisan prejudices and idiosyncratic opinions to influence their commentaries. For this reason, in Azad's opinion, the whole enterprise of Qurʾān commentary must begin again from first principles.[25]

He characterizes such inept commentaries as *Tafsir-bi-rai*. He writes:

> Such in brief is the story of the Qurʾanic interpretation attempted in the past. But however brief this survey, it is enough to show what obstacles one has to overcome to reach the Qurʾan, or what thick veils to lift to catch a clear vision of it. The effort will involve a simultaneous survey of every nook and corner of the Qurʾan and the exercise of deep insight into the meaning of things. It is only then that the forsaken reality of the Qurʾan may put in its appearance. . . . But I may say this with confidence that I have opened a new avenue for an intelligent approach to the Qurʾan, and hope that men of understanding will notice that the method adopted by me is something fundamentally different from the method pursued in the past.[26]

What Azad understands as an intelligent approach to the problems of the modern age assumes that blind repetition of traditional beliefs and practices is unintelligent. Although not an Aligarh old boy, he shares the intellectual liveliness of Sayyid Ahmed Khan and Shibli, and he was probably influenced in his own way, as Muhammad Ali was, by Shibli's efforts to revitalize Muslim understanding of the Qurʾān. He teaches that the Qurʾān message is not sectarian, but rather offers, as all true Prophets have, a path of guidance intended for all people. Azad condemns what he calls groupism, by which he means a worship of one's particular community. For him, true religious response should strengthen the independence of the mind of the believer, and free him from idolatrous dependence on his group. He comments on verses 24–29 of Surah 2, passages dealing with Abraham: "What was the path of religion which Abraham adopted for himself and what was the path which his children followed; and what was the religion or way of life which Jacob bequeathed from his death-bed to this people? Assuredly, it was not the groupism upheld by Judaism or Christianity."[27] Azad thus insists that the Qurʾān criticizes Jews and Christians for worshipping their own groups rather than God and for failing to respond to God because of their closed minds and blind adherence to their own traditions. For Indian Muslims, he is recommending independence of judgment and freeing of the mind from blind allegiance to a group. There is not much doubt that Azad saw the communal troubles of India as a result of the groupism he lamented. The true path of Abraham, as he understood it, ought to free Muslims to become independently minded individuals, judging issues on their merits, and not accepting domination by group opinion.

Muhammad Iqbal

A third significant Indian Muslim writer of this same generation was the poet-philosopher, Muhammad Iqbal. As we noted, Thomas Arnold was one of his teachers in Lahore. Iqbal left India in 1905 and spent three years in Europe. He studied law in London and philosophy at Cambridge and in Germany. He received a doctorate from the University of Munich for a thesis on the metaphysics of the Persian mystical tradition. After his return to India, Iqbal exercized a major influence on his people's self-awareness through his poetry, which stressed the need for a revitalized Islamic spirit. His poetry in Urdu and Persian has had a profound impact on his people.

He also advised many Muslim leaders, including Jinnah, on political issues. The statement he read to the Muslim League in 1930, which stresses the need for Muslims to retain control over the cultural development of their people, is generally considered to have played a significant role in guiding the movement that eventuated in the establishment of Pakistan as an independent nation. His one published book on Islamic philosophy, *The Reconstruction of Religious Thought in Islam*, is unparalleled as an effort to restate Islamic principles in the light of process philosophy, modern cosmology, and a new understanding of Islamic history.

One thread which runs through these thinkers from Sayyid Ahmad Khan to Iqbal is a perception that Protestantism was closer to Islam than other forms of Christianity. Sayyid Ahmed Khan had observed that Luther in reinstating divorce was moving closer to Islam. The Protestant movement away from clerical celibacy, and away from legitimation of clerical authority by belief in the process of transubstantiation of the elements in the ritual of the mass, was perceived by Indian Muslim thinkers as steps toward what they understood as the rationalism and freedom from superstition of Islam. We noted Muhammad Ali's enthusiastic responses to Harnack's criticism of patristic theology. Iqbal shares this tradition. However, he had arrived in a German philosophy department shortly after the death of Nietzsche (1900), and he was greatly fascinated by that German thinker's attack on the hypocrisies and spiritual mutilations of pietistic Lutheranism. Iqbal rated Nietzsche very highly as a prophetic critic of the modern West, but he felt that Muslims as critics could go even further and affirm ideals which could transcend the dilemmas perceived by Nietzsche and other Western cultural critics.

Iqbal, who died in 1938, perceived World War I, the Russian Revolution, the Italian invasion of Africa, and the Spanish Civil War as proofs of the failure of Christianity to provide rational and practicable ideals. He wrote:

> Surely, it is high time to look to the essentials of Islam. . . . The main purpose of the Quran is to awaken in man the higher consciousness of his manifold relations with God and the universe. . . . The problem of Islam was really suggested by the mutual conflict, and at the same time mutual attraction, presented by the two forces of religion and civilization. The same problem confronted early Christianity. The great point in Christianity is the search for an independent content for spiritual life which, according to the insight of its founder, could be elevated, not by the forces of a world external to the soul of man, but by the revelation of new world within his soul. Islam fully agrees with this insight and supplements it by the further insight that the illumination of the new world thus revealed is not something foreign to the world of matter but permeates it through and through. . . . It is the mysterious touch of the ideal that animates and sustains the real, and through it alone we can discover and affirm the ideal.[28]

Iqbal thus viewed Christianity as a spiritual force which at its best had affirmed the spiritual dignity and freedom of individual human beings. As a tradition, however, he thought it had failed to affirm sufficiently the necessity of working to transform the actual social, economic, and political structures of the world in order that the perception of ideal values could be implemented by the creation of structures embodying justice. Most of his followers went to the new nation of Pakistan in order to work for these values. Some stayed in India, however, and Zakir Husain, the first Muslim president of independent India, remained an admirer of Iqbal, as well as of Gandhi, all his life.

Abul Ala Mawdudi

A fourth significant Muslim writer of this same generation was Abul Ala Mawdudi (1903–1979). Although the youngest of the thinkers we have been discussing, Mawdudi also was a supporter of the Khilafat movement. He, too, began as a religious journalist, editing a journal for the ulema. These four Indian Muslim religious thinkers were all shaped by the context of the collapsing power of Britain and the emerging force of Indian nationalism. Mawdudi published a book on *Jihad* in 1930 which has exerted a considerable influence in shaping a new form of Islamic neotraditionalism in the Indo-Pakistan subcontinent and throughout the Muslim world.

Mawdudi was most explicitly not an Aligarh old boy; his grandfather had pulled his father out of Aligarh because of the excessive Westernization, tennis shorts for example, being imposed on the Aligarh students. Mawdudi was educated primarily by the religious scholars of his own family. He went to a high school which attempted to combine Western with Islamic knowledge, and then entered a college in Hyderabad. His studies were interrupted by the death of his father, and he turned to journalism to make his living. His later education was acquired through reading and study on his own.

Mawdudi founded a movement entitled the Jama'at-i Islami which was intended to work for the implementation of an Islamic Revolution. A journal has regularly been published by the movement. The list of Mawdudi's articles and books includes 138 titles, many of them translated into many languages. Mawdudi has been the most widely read Muslim author of his generation. His perspective on relations with Christians, Hindus, and anyone else is shaped by his underlying conviction that Islam, as he understands it, is a God-given system which, if properly implemented, would solve all the problems of modernity. Mawdudi opposed both Indian and Pakistan nationalism, as forms of misguided idolatry, although he moved to Pakistan after independence. He remained a thorn in the flesh to several Pakistani governments, and was imprisoned several times. His followers run for office regularly.

One of his followers has summarized Mawdudi's perspective as follows:

> He relentlessly criticised the new-fangled ideologies which had begun to cast a spell over the minds and hearts of his brethren-in-faith and attempted to show the hollowness of those ideologies. . . . All theories or doctrines which claim that in disregard of Divine guidance, man himself has the right—be it as an individual or a group of persons, or a nation or even all humanity combined—to decide what is good or bad for mankind, are indeed to be regarded as denying the Sovereignty of God and as setting up gods other than the One True God. Submission to God means bringing the entire life of man into harmony with the revealed Will of God.[29]

From this perspective, any other point of view is idolatrous, whether it be Christian, Hindu, communist, or liberal democrat. Mawdudi explicitly opposed the idea of government by the people, since, he reasoned, if the people make the laws, they are trespassing on the prerogatives of God, who is the only acceptable lawgiver for humanity. The Islamic Revolution which Mawdudi advocated was intended to establish a political system based on revealed law.

Abid Husain

A fifth perspective from the same generation of Indian Muslims comes from the small group that remained with the Jamia Millia Islamia after the collapse of the Khilafat and Non-cooperation movements. There were three significant leaders of this group—Zakir Husain, Muhammad Mujeeb, and Abid Husain. The three came back from their doctoral studies in Europe in order to keep alive this attempt to have an Indian Muslim National Educational Institute run in accordance with Gandhian ideals. When after 1937, India gained provincial self-government, and Gandhi organized a national educational system called Basic Education, the Jamia Millia Islamia came to play a major role in training the teachers. Abid Husain has been the most prolific author of the three, and has produced a number of books dealing with the cultural role of Muslims in independent India. He argued that much cultural affinity has developed among the two peoples as a result of centuries of living together. In his words:

> Thus we have a glimpse of *Weltanschauung* of the modern educated classes of Hindus and Muslims as reflected in the philosophies of Tagore and Iqbal. We find that in the depths of the Indian mind two streams of religious consciousness spring from the same source and flow in the same channel. . . . It is only on coming to surface on the level of analytical thought that they divide themselves into two distinct rivers. . . . But we shall see presently they meet again in the wider expanse of social, moral and aesthetic life.

> Looking at the concrete aspects of the cultural life of Hindus and Muslims we find that in spite of the separatist movements of the last two hundred years most of the common factors which had been partly the causes, partly the effect of the cultural synthesis which took place in the time of Akbar the Great, are still there, and new common ground has been created by the influences of the modern Western culture.[30]

Abid Husain argued that the practical moral codes of the two communities are very much alike. Both groups stress modesty, charity, and temperance. They share musical and artistic tastes. He maintained that if the Indian Muslims are treated fairly as a minority, they can easily fit into the patterns of Indian life, which have been customary to them for a long time.

The Ulema

Thus far we have been considering differing Indian Muslim attitudes from the perspectives of individuals, most of whom have been journalists and writers. In this same historical period between 1857 and 1947, the ulema were also caught up in efforts to discover new directions for the community. A *madrassa* to train Hanafi ulema was established at Deoband shortly after 1857. Its goal was to train leaders who would tenaciously maintain the religious identity of the Muslim community. The students and teachers of Deoband played a variety of roles and made their presence strongly felt within the community. In an analysis of the role of this *madrassa*, the author writes:

> The Deobandi *ulama* issued 147,851 *fatawa* from 1911 to 1951. Rashid Ahmad Gangohi, for example, gave rulings on request that it was lawful to learn English if there was no danger to religion, that it was unlawful to take interest from a Christian, and to use money-orders and bills of exchange in which the element of interest enters. He also ruled the wearing of a cross or a *topi* to be sinful.[31]

The various groups needing support, such as the movement to establish Aligarh University, the Khilafat movement, and the Muslim League, courted the help of the ulema because they needed to prove that they had the Muslim community with them. The Deobandi ulema became particularly politically active, in a manner new to them, during the Khilafat movement because they were incensed by the threat of possible danger to Mecca and Medina. For this reason, they supported Gandhi as opposed to a group of ulema from another institution at Bareilly who rejected non-cooperation and support for Gandhi. The latter group was less influential.[32]

Shibli and Azad in the prewar period had been urging the ulema to become politically active. Many of them responded enthusiastically, and it was their support that made the Khilafat movement politically effective. The notion of Gandhi urging the political involvement of the ulema is perhaps curious, yet his own belief that religiosity was somehow a virtue led him to take this position uncritically. Paradoxically, it was Jinnah who was much more wary of religious enthusiasm. Once the ulema had acquired the new skills of political activism, they continued to play active roles in Indian politics. As we indicated earlier, most of them no longer supported Gandhi or Azad after the failure of the Khilafat movement. Some, but not all, supported the Muslim League.

Although Azad had been a key figure in urging the ulema to political activism, he could no longer count on their uncritical support after the collapse of the Khilafat movement. They continued to respect his scholarship since he was known to be a member of a family of traditional religious scholars. But his theological critique of traditional Qurʾān interpretation and his emphasis on the Qurʾān as the primary source of Muslim values were seen to be means of undercutting the traditional role of the Shariah.[33] The ulema understood themselves as the transmitters and upholders of the Shariah.

This issue of giving primacy to the Qurʾān is a significant thread in Indian Muslim thought which moves from Sayyid Ahmed Khan and Shibli through Muhammad Ali, Azad, Iqbal, and Abid Husain. The issue has many implications, including the question of whether or not any person who studies the Qurʾān might be considered a competent member of the ulema to form conclusions as to its meaning. During the century of Indian experience which we have been considering, the ulema increasingly perceived themselves as the legitimate custodians of the traditional Shariah in the context of new political realities.

Although Azad supported Nehru and the Congress party, and Iqbal had offered ideological leadership to the Muslim League, the issue of the primacy of the Qurʾān entered into both these streams of political thought, and subsequently into the political struggles of the newly independent nations of India, Pakistan, and later Bangladesh. All three are the heirs of the tradition and of the problems we have been discussing. Azad's discernment of groupism versus individual moral consciousness might be considered a key aspect of this development. From the perspective of Mawdudi and his supporters, only one human group, Mawdudi and his followers, has correct access to the Divine Plan for humanity. From this viewpoint, a devout person ought to be submissive to the spiritual dominance of this group. From Azad's perspective, a Muslim should think and make decisions on the basis of his or her own conscience, and should not be subject to groupism. One facet of twentieth-century religiopolitical thought is thus the problem of collective group consciousness versus individual morality. Indian Islam has been an arena of intense dispute on this matter.

NOTES

1. Emmanuel Sivan, *Radical Islam* (New Haven, 1985), pp. 22–23.
2. Ghalib, *Dustanbuy: A Diary of the Indian Revolt*, trans. Mirza Asadullah Khan (Bombay, 1970). See also Ralph Russell, ed., *Ghalib the Poet and His Age* (London, 1972).
3. Mohamed Ali, *My Life a Fragment* (Lahore; reprinted 1961), pp. 5–6.
4. Hafeez Malik, *Sir Sayyid Ahmad Khan and Muslim Modernization in India and Pakistan* (New York, 1980), p. 200.
5. J. M. S. Baljon Jr., *The Reforms and Religious Ideas of Sir Sayyid Ahmad Khan*, 3rd ed. (Lahore, 1964), p. 27.
6. Malik, *Sir Sayyid*, pp. 266–279.
7. Ibid., p. 250.
8. Sir Thomas Arnold, *The Preaching of Islam*, 2nd ed. (Lahore, 1913).
9. Fazlur Rahman, trans., *Allamah Shibli's Sirat al-Nabi, parts II and III* (Karachi, 1970).
10. Ibid., pp. 152, 167.
11. Ali, *My Life a Fragment*, pp. 19, 20.
12. Ibid., pp. 31, 38.
13. *Selected Speeches and Statements of the Quaid-i-Azam Mohammad Ali Jinnah* (Lahore, 1966), pp. x–xi.
14. S. R. Bakshi, *Gandhi and Khilafat* (New Delhi, 1985).
15. Sheila McDonough, "The spirit of the Jamia Millia Islamia as exemplified in the writings of S. Abid Husain," in Robert Baird, ed. *Religion in Modern India* (Columbia, Missouri, 1980), pp. 139–160.
16. Ali, *My Life a Fragment*, p. 33.
17. Bakshi, *Gandhi and Khilafat*, pp. 83, 84.
18. Ali, *My Life a Fragment*, p. 131.
19. Ibid., p. 158.
20. Ibid., p. 196.
21. Ibid., p. 200.
22. Ibid. p. 205.
23. Ibid., p. 215.
24. Ibid., p. 228.
25. Mawlana Abul Kalam Azad, *The Tarjuman al-Qur'an*, vol. 2, ed. and trans. Syed Abdul Latif (Bombay, 1967), pp. xiii–xx.
26. Ibid., p. xix.
27. Ibid., p. 50.
28. Allama Muhammad Iqbal, *The Reconstruction of Religious Thought in Islam* (Lahore; reprinted 1960), pp. 8–9.
29. *Islamic Perspectives Studies in Honour of Sayyid Abul Ala Mawdudi*, ed. Khurshid Ahmad and Zafar Ishaq Ansari (London, 1979), pp. 362–366.
30. S. Abid Husain, *The National Culture of India*, rev. ed. (Bombay, 1961), pp. 203, 206.
31. Ziya ul Hasan Faruqi," Orthodoxy and heterodoxy in India," in *Communal and Pan-Islamic Trends in Colonial India*, ed. Mushirul Hasan (New Delhi, 1981), p. 332.
32. Syed Jamaluddin, "The Barelvis and the Khilafat movement," in *Communal and Pan-Islamic Trends in Colonial India*, p. 344.
33. Faruqi, "Orthodoxy and heterodoxy in India," pp. 326–343.

BIBLIOGRAPHY

Ahmed, Aijaz, ed. *Ghazals of Ghalib*. New York: Columbia University Press, 1971.

Ahmed, Aziz. *Islamic Modernism in India and Pakistan*. London: Oxford University Press, 1967.

Ahmad, Khurshid, and Zafar Ishaq Ansari, eds. *Islamic Perspectives. Studies in Honour of Sayyid Abul Ala Mawdudi*. London: Islamic Foundation, 1979.

Ahmed, Qeyamuddin. *The Wahabi Movement in India*. Calcutta: Mukhhpedhay, 1966.

Ahmed Khan, Sir Syed. *The Muhammadan Commentary on the Holy Bible*. Aligarh: Sir Sayyid's Private Press, 1865.

———. *Series of Essays on the Life of Muhammad*. London, 1870.

Ali, Mohamed. *My Life a Fragment*. Lahore: Ashraf, reprinted 1961.

Ambedkar, B. R. *Ranade, Gandhi and Jinnah*. Bombay: Thatcher, 1943.

Argov, Daniel. *Moderates and Extremists in the Indian National Movement 1883–1920*. Bombay: Asia Publishing House, 1961.

Arnold, Thomas. *The Preaching of Islam*, 2nd ed. Lahore: Ashraf, 1913.

Azad, Abul Kalam. *India Wins Freedom*. Calcutta: Orient Longmans, 1959.

Azad, Mawlana Abul Kalam. *The Tarjuman al-Qur'an*, 2 vols., ed. and trans. Syed Abdul Latif. Bombay: Asia Publishing House, 1967.

Baird, Robert, ed. *Religion in Modern India*. Columbia, Missouri: South Asian Publishing House, 1989.

Bakshi, S. R. *Gandhi and Khilafat*. New Delhi: Gitanjali, 1985.

Baljon, J. M. S. *The Reforms and Religious Ideas of Sir Sayyid Ahmad Khan*, 3rd ed. Lahore: Ashraf, 1964.

Brown, Judith. *Gandhi's Rise to Power in Indian Politics, 1915–1922*. Cambridge: Cambridge University Press, 1972.

Dar, Bashir Ahmed. *Religious Thought of Sayyid Ahmed Khan*. Lahore: Institute of Islamic Culture, 1957.

Faruqi, Ziya-ul-Hasan. *The Deoband School and the Demand for Pakistan*. Bombay: Asia Publishing House, 1963.

Gandhi, Mahatma. *The Collected Works of Mahatma Gandhi*, vols. 14–22. Delhi: Publications Division, Government of India, 1966.

Gandhi, Rajmohan. *Eight Lives: A Study of the Hindu-Muslim Encounter*. Albany: State University of New York Press, 1986.

Ghalib. *Dustanbuy: A Diary of the Indian Revolt*, trans. Mirza Asadullah Khan. Bombay: Asia Publishing House, 1970.

Haq, Mushir-ul. *Muslim Politics in Modern India 1857–1947*. Meerut: Meenakshi Prahashahi, 1970.

Hasan, Mushirul, ed. *Communal and Pan-Islamic Trends in Colonial India*. New Delhi: Manohar, 1981.

Hardy, Peter. *The Muslims of British India*. Cambridge: Cambridge University Press, 1972.

Husain, S. Abid. *The National Culture of India*, rev. ed. Bombay: Asia Publishing House, 1961.

Hussain, M. Hadi. *A Message from the East*, translation of Iqbal's *Payam-i-Mashriq*. Lahore: Iqbal Academy, 1971.

Ikram, S. M. *Modern Muslim India and the Birth of Pakistan*. Lahore: Ashraf, 1965.

Iqbal, Allama Muhammad. *The Reconstruction of Religious Thought in Islam*. Lahore: Ashraf, 1977.

Jinnah, Mohammed Ali. *Selected Speeches and Statements of the Quaid-i-Azam Mohammad Ali Jinnah*. Lahore: Research Society of Pakistan, 1966.

Malik, Hafeez. *Sir Sayyid Ahmad Khan and Muslim Modernization in India and Pakistan*. New York: Columbia University Press, 1980.

McDonough, Sheila. *Gandhi's Responses to Islam*. Delhi: D. K. Printword, 1994.

Minault, Gail. *The Khilafat Movement: Religious Symbolism and Political Mobilization in India*. New York: Columbia University Press, 1982.

Mujeeb, M. *Education and Traditional Values*. Delhi: Meenakshi Prakasdan, 1965.

Nadvi, J. Rais Ahmed Jafri, ed. *Selections from Mohammad Ali's Comrade*. Lahore: Mohammad Ali Academy, 1965.

Nanda, B. R. *Mahatma Gandhi: A Biography*. London: Allen and Unwin, 1958.

Rahman, Fazlur, trans. *Allamah Shibli's Sirat-al-Nabi, parts 2 and 3*. Karachi: Pakistan Historical Society, 1970.

Russell, Ralph, ed. *Ghalib: The Poet and His Age*. London: Allen and Unwin, 1972.

Russell, Ralph, and Khurshid-ul-Islam, eds. *Ghalib*. London: Allen and Unwin, 1961.

Sivan, Emmanuel. *Radical Islam*. New Haven: Yale University Press, 1985.

17

Muslim Views of Hindus since 1950

ASHGAR ALI ENGINEER

There are different views on Hindu-Muslim relations in India. Because this is an extremely complex matter, no view can be wholly above controversy. Thus, the Hindus and the Muslims of India cannot be treated as entirely homogeneous communities. Different traditions in both communities play a role in determining the relationships between the communities. There are orthodox and liberal traditions; there are theocratic traditions on the one hand, and Sufi and Bhakti traditions on the other. Besides religious tensions, there are also conflicts of interests which are occasionally seen as one of the reasons for sharpening religious conflicts. In that respect, religion is often used to provide legitimation to this kind of conflict, so that what appears to be a religious conflict may, in fact, be a cover up for a conflict of interests. Of course, this does not suggest that religious conflicts between the Hindu and the Muslim communities in India have been completely avoided.

The fact that for about eight centuries Muslim dynasties ruled over India gives a certain tone to this relationship. Hence, history is seen and interpreted very differently according to the different ideological viewpoints. The liberal and nationalist traditions, for instance, read in history common interests between Hindus and Muslims. Liberal scholars tried to show how Muslim influence had a benign effect on Indian culture and how the impact of Islam generated a composite culture, which is the inheritance of all Indians today. This Muslim influence, according to these scholars, was very wide-ranging; no field—whether religion, art and architecture, music, dance, painting, or poetry—was left out. For instance, in North India, the center of Muslim rule, no sphere could escape this influence.

It is interesting to note that in this same region of the north of India, the Hindu-Muslim conflict was of a much greater intensity. Muslim invaders came from northwestern mountain passes and conquered the northern parts of India. Thus, the struggle for power between Hindu rulers and Muslim invaders took place in this region, leaving bitter memories behind. No such power struggles took place in the south, as Muslims came there mostly as traders rather than as invaders. It is interesting to note that even today, the main arena of struggle between Hindus and Muslims is in the north. Most of the communal violence takes place in this region of the country, the north being the center of Hindu communalism and of Muslim fundamentalism as much today as it was yesterday.

Moreover, this same region saw the battle for division take place in the days before 1947. The Muslim elite of the region was highly politically conscious and fought a battle to obtain its share of power. When no understanding for sharing power could be reached, division of the country between the Muslim majority areas in the north and northeast and the Hindu majority areas in the rest of the country became inevitable. This division was followed by considerable bloodshed. No fewer than a million human beings were slaughtered—a grim tragedy!

There were partition riots until 1948. During this unfortunate year, statues of Ram and Sita—two highly venerated Hindu deities—were placed inside the Babri Mosque. Subsequently, the mosque was closed because of the law and order situation so that even Pandit Jawaherlal Nehru, then prime minister (who described the installation of Hindu deities inside a mosque as a matter of shame for secular India), could not have the mosque opened. We will come back to this event further in this essay. Needless to say, this dispute proved to be a major disaster for the relationship between the two communities in contemporary India.

As pointed out earlier, partition riots continued right up to 1948. However, some skirmishes kept on occurring up to 1950. This same year of 1950 was a turning point in the Hindu-Muslim relationship since the period from 1950 to 1960 proved to be much quieter. During this decade, very few riots were reported. There were several reasons for this. First, after the formation of Pakistan, Muslims were reduced to a smaller minority. At that time, there were 40 million Muslims in India, which meant a considerable reduction in their number. Second, large numbers of Muslims were killed in partition riots on the Indian side (just as large numbers of Hindus were killed on the Pakistan side); thus, the Indian Muslims were in a state of terror. In fact, they had lost all confidence and were quite uncertain about their future in India. They could only recover from this shock and sense of insecurity by referring themselves to the declarations of reassurance given by Pandit Jawaherlal Nehru and by the great Indian scholar Maulana Abul Kalam Azad.

In this state of affairs, the Muslims could hardly assert themselves and compete with the Hindus politically or economically. Confrontation was brought about only by the self-assertion of both communities' elites. During this period, the Muslims were too subdued to provoke the Hindu ire; they thought it best to adopt a low-key posture. Another important reason was that the Muslim elite (both political and economic) had almost entirely migrated to Pakistan, so that those left behind could hardly offer any serious economic competition, at least in the so-called cow-belt (by "cow-belt" we mean the bastion of Hindu orthodoxy in the north). Thus, there was hardly any challenge for the Hindu middle classes from their Muslim counterparts. As a consequence, the decade between 1950 and 1960 was a rather quiet one.

The first major communal bombshell during the postpartition period exploded in Jabalpur in 1961. During that year, Jabalpur, a town in Madhya Pradesh, witnessed a major communal confrontation.[1] One of the reasons for this riot was an acute economic competition between two *bidi* manufacturers of Jabalpur—one a Hindu, the other a Muslim. The Hindi press sowed discord among the two parties. It all started with the daughter of the Hindu *bidi* manufacturer falling in love with the son of the Muslim *bidi* manufacturer. The Hindi press, at the request of the girl's father, described the whole affair as a Muslim boy attempting to rape a Hindu girl. The outcome was rioting, during which many Muslims were either killed or terrorized by the armed police. The Urdu press reported many stories of police atrocities. Apparently, the Muslim leadership had played no significant role in provoking violence. A team of senior journalists from Bombay investigated the Jabalpur riot and mainly blamed the Hindi press for provocation. Mr. S. B. Kolpe, a senior journalist from Bombay who visited Jabalpur, wrote:

> Most of the newspaper reports were identical, obviously emanating from the same source. On reaching Jabalpur . . . I found that two or three strangers working jointly for several national dailies were responsible for these reports which had a damaging effect on the political life of the nation as a whole. Only one of the three knew enough English to write readable reports. The others copied these with minor changes.
>
> The facts reported were collected from the local police who were not free from communal bias, and no reporter ever bothered to verify the "facts" doled out to him. Since I was known to most senior journalists in Jabalpur as an activist of the working journalists' trade union movement, I had no difficulty in mixing with the local fraternity.

The Jabalpur riot was so severe that Jawaherlal Nehru himself was shaken and took an initiative by setting up the National Integration Council to promote emotional integration in the country. Even after partition, which was thought to be a solution for the communal tangle, the two communities could not live in peace and harmony. Nehru thought that a body like the National Integration Council would succeed in bringing about some measure of accommodation between Hindus and Muslims. However, he could not know that much worse was yet to come and that the

Jabalpur riot was the beginning of a new phase of communal confrontation.

The Muslim leadership was greatly perturbed by such a fresh outburst of communal violence in post-partition India. It was far from aggressive during this phase. So far, they had looked to Nehru for protection and security. Nevertheless, with new forces emerging in the political scene, Nehru also appeared to be a helpless spectator. Some Muslim leaders like Faridi (a former socialist married to a German lady) and Syed Mahmood (a man very close to Nehru and Minister of State in the Foreign Ministery), disillusioned by the Nehrunian policy, formed the Majlis-e-Mushāwarāt, a consultative body of various Muslim groups and political parties.

The Mushāwarāt, headed by Faridi, was not a political party of Muslims in itself, but only a consultative body of all Muslim representative groups. It was the first time Muslims in postindependence India attempted to come together and pool their energies and intellectual power, not only to find a solution to the problems of the Muslims but also to exert pressure on the political system to fulfill their demands. By and large, the Urdu press welcomed the move and, to this effect, published articles and editorials. However, they were alarm signals to Hindu communalists and right-wingers. Though the Muslim masses had taken initiatives in the formation of Pakistan (the political and economic elite among the Muslims being responsible for it), all Muslims in India were seen guilty of the creation of Pakistan by communally minded Hindus. Any attempt on the part of Muslims to form a body with political implications was seen in fact as an attempt to create another Pakistan, to put it as crudely as communal Hindus did in that period.

The formation of the Majlis-e-Mushāwarāt was seen in this light by the national press, especially the Hindi press, despite declarations by the Mushāwarāt leaders asserting the contrary. The Mushāwarāt started a debate on the plight of Muslims in post-independence India, but nothing much was achieved thereby. There was, of course, no question of the organization's ability to stop communal riots. In that respect, even saner and more mature leaders like Dr. Zakir Husain, who subsequently became president of India, could not achieve much. After the death of Mawlana Abul Kalam Azad in 1958—an outstanding Muslim leader who had fought against the idea of Pakistan and had foreseen its harmful effects for the Indian Muslims—Dr. Zakir Husain became the most prominent Muslim leader. He was close to Nehru and was respected by the Muslims, although a proportion of angry Muslims, and other similar Muslims holding power in the Congress Party Ministery, saw him as a mere show figure, not good for anything.

However, Zakir Husain did what he could in these circumstances to alleviate the plight of Muslims and bring some succor to them. He was a man of great maturity and vision; moreover, he could keep Muslim militancy under control. He knew that militant and confrontationist attitudes would harm the Muslim cause by communalizing an even broader section of the Hindus. This is precisely what is happening today, but nowadays there is no mature Muslim leader of Zakir Husain's stature to restrain some of the more militant and aggressive Muslim leaders from acting without thinking of the consequences. But we will discuss this matter later on in this essay.

After Jabalpur, a chain of riots broke out in Ranchi, Jamshedpur, Aligarh, and other towns. The immediate cause was a stream of Hindu refugees arriving from what was then East Pakistan. Hundreds of Muslims were killed in these riots. In the Jamshedpur and Bhilai steel factories, some Muslim workers were thrown into steel furnaces and burnt alive. These riots continued up to 1965, when war with Pakistan broke out. Jawaharlal Nehru was alive when most of these riots took place. It was for this reason that, in his last meeting with senior LAS officers, Nehru described communalism as India's greatest international enemy. Nehru was feeling helpless in preventing these riots. All the states where riots broke out were ruled by the Congress Party, yet he could not persuade the chief minister of his own party to curb communal violence. The Majlis-e-Mushāwarāt, at best, could submit memoranda and issue statements. Though at that time Zakir Husain intervened personally, he also was unable to bring any relief. At most, Muslim leaders could threaten not to vote for the Congress Party, but there, also, Muslims had hardly any alternative. There was no strong secular opposition party which could replace the Congress Party in the states or at the center.

It was only in 1967 that an opportunity arose when some opposition parties combined and provided a united front. The Congress Party was voted out of power in some states, including Uttar Pradesh, the most populous state of the "cow-belt" where the Muslim population amounted at the time to 15%. The Muslims voted mostly against the Congress Party to express their protest against its apathy toward their plight. But then Jana Sangh, a Hindu communal party, joined the SVD (United Front) governments. This experiment was repeated again in 1989 when the Janta Dal government, led by V. P. Singh, was supported both by the left and the BJP (the new domination of the former Jana Sangh). Nevertheless, without its support, the SVD government could not have been formed.

In 1968, however, the Congress Party was rejuvenated by Mrs. Indira Gandhi. She nationalized the major banks with a stroke of the pen and won laurels from Indian people. She also provided a slogan, *gharibi hatao* (quit poverty), which electrified the atmosphere in India. Thus, she became an unquestioned leader of the Indian masses. In order to woo Muslim masses, she laid great emphasis on secularism. For her electoral win, Muslim and Harijan (now called *dalit*) votes were of crucial importance. Both Muslims and *dalits* were totally opposed to the Jana Sangh, the Hindu communal body. Although the Muslims and *dalits* readily rallied around Mrs. Gandhi, her government did not give substantial relief to Muslims. A major communal massacre took place in Gujarat, which was then ruled by that section of the Congress Party which was opposed to Mrs. Gandhi. The RSS had a strong base in Gujarat. The Jana Sangh was extremely worried by the left-wing policies of Mrs. Gandhi (for instance, bank nationalization and the slogan "quit poverty") and the more so because of her popularity among Muslims and *dalits*.

The Jana Sangh could counter Mrs. Gandhi only by engineering serious communal trouble in the country. This seems to be what they did in Gujarat. The Gujarat riots exploded on the Indian political scene with such tremendous force that the whole country's atmosphere was changed. Though law and order is the responsibility of the state, in this particular situation Mrs. Gandhi was helpless. Gujarat was ruled by the opposition of the Congress Party, and any intervention by the center would have been interpreted as politically motivated. Mrs. Gandhi (at that stage) could not afford any risky action. In any case, the Muslims suffered tremendously in Gujarat. Later on, investigations showed that more than a thousand people perished in Ahmedabad City alone (Ahmedabad City happens to be the most important city of Gujarat, its center of industry and commerce).

Ganshyam Shah, a well-known political scientist from Gujarat, depicts one of the scenes in the riot-torn city of Ahmedabad which shows the fury of the mob:

> A gruesome episode in the afternoon (of 20 September, 1969) brings out the depth of the animosity against the Muslims. A young Muslim, enraged by the destruction of his property said he would take revenge. Upon this the crowd seized him, showered blows on him, and tried to force him to shout *"Jai Jagannath."* Staying firm, the youth refused even if that meant death. To this, someone in the crowd responded that he may, indeed, be done away with. Wood from broken shops was collected, a pyre prepared in the middle of the road, petrol sprinkled on the pyre as well as on the youth, and he was set alight with ruthless efficiency. What is remarkable is that there was no resistance from any Hindu. The wails of the Muslim inhabitants of the area were drowned in the celebration of the incident by the Hindus.

So, the Jana Sangh had created a strong anti-Muslim atmosphere in the country. A resolution was passed in its conference in Ranchi demanding Indianization of Indian Muslims, thereby implying that the Muslims in India were aliens who had not adopted the Indian culture and did not respect the Hindu deities. Surprisingly, some national dailies wrote editorials in support of this demand and compared it with the demand for Indianization of services during the British period. So, Hindus strongly resented the fact that Muslims were not prepared to accept changes in their personal law. When some people demanded a uniform civil code in India, the Muslims formed the Muslim Personal Law Board to protect their Sharīʿa law, according to which they could marry up to four wives and could unilaterally divorce them.

The Muslim Personal Law Board was formed in the late 1960s and the government had to assure the Muslims that it had no intention of interfering with Muslim personal law. This was interpreted by the Hindus as an "appeasement" of the Muslims. To this day, it remains a sore point, so that the BJP has begun to describe Nehruvian secularism as a "pseudo-secularism" and describes its own version as "positive secularism."

More major riots took place around that time, the most important being the Bhivandi-Jalgaon riots of 1970 in which no fewer than 400 persons died. However, from this period until 1977, the relationship between Hindus and Muslims improved. In 1975, Mrs. Gandhi declared a state of emergency, which continued up to 1977 when general elections were declared. During the state of emergency, both Hindu and Muslim communal parties were banned and there were hardly any major riots. Nevertheless, during the 1977 elections the Congress Party was voted out of power and the Janata Party, which again included the Jana Sangh Party and other centrist parties, came to power. The Muslims had greatly suffered during the state of emergency, due to excesses in the way of enforcing the family planning measures which had been enthusiastically voted by the Janata Party. The Jana Sangh leaders, before merging with the Janata Party, took an oath at Mahatma Gandhi's Samadhi (memorial): they would renounce communalism and adopt the Gandhian program. The Muslims, tired of the Congress Party rule, accepted the professions of the Jana Sangh leaders and voted massively for the Janat Party, at least in the north where they had suffered the most. The prayer-leader of the Jam'i Masjid in Delhi, popularly known as the Shahi Imam, emerged as a strong Muslim leader who lent his support to the Janata Party.

The emergence of the Shahi Imam group was an unfortunate development for the Indian Muslims. They had neither the maturity nor the vision of earlier Muslim leaders like Maulana Abul Kalam Azad or Dr. Zakir Husain. The latter had participated in the freedom struggle and had imbibed a secular and nationalist outlook. They not only knew thoroughly what the Muslim problems were, but they were also capable of evolving a proper strategy to fight for Muslim issues. The Shahi Imam, on the other hand, had not participated in the freedom struggle nor had it shown any worthwhile knowledge of the intricate problems of the Muslims; it had no experience in evolving proper strategies.

The Shahi Imam adopted aggressive postures toward the Janata Government and was soon alienated from its leaders. The Janata Government did not last long, as there was among its constituents neither an ideological cohesion nor a unity of purposes. The communal problem surfaced once again and major riots broke out in the north in places like Jamshedpur, Aligarh, and Benaras. Once again, the Muslims were at the receiving end. At last, the Janata government fell under its own weight. The Shahi Imam, in a move of political opportunism, supported the Congress Party in the ensuing elections of 1980. The Muslims, alienated from the Janata Party government because of the outbreak of communal violence, supported the Congress Party once again. The result was that Mrs. Gandhi was voted into power. She remained unsure of Muslim support, however, and tried to woo the emerging Hindu middle castes.

There were a series of major riots, particularly in Muradabad in 1980 and in Biharsharif in 1981. Another Muslim leader, Syed Shahabuddin, began to appear on the political scene. He was brought into politics by the Jana Sangh leader, Shri Atal Bihari Vajpayes, who was then Minister of Foreign Affairs during the Janata regime. Though well informed, dynamic, and shrewd, Shahabuddin was inexperienced in politics and had the ambition of becoming the sole Muslim leader. He achieved prominence in the early 1980s. He gave aggressive comments on the Biharsharif riots and also on the conversion of a few hundred *dalits* to Islam in the southern state of Tamil Nadu, popularly known as the Meenakshipuran conversions. This event of conversion to Islam was fully exploited by the communal Hindus led by the Vishwa Hindu Parishad, RSS and BJP in order to communalize the Hindu mind in India. The aggressive stance assumed by the new Muslim leadership had a very adverse effect on Hindu attitudes and minds.

It must be remembered that a minority—be it ethnic or religious—has to adopt proper strategies for its own safety and security. If it adopts an aggressive stance, even for its legitimate demands, it ends up by further antagonizing the majority community. Even legitimate demands must be couched in a well-thought out manner. This is something which the new Muslim leadership could not properly appreciate, however. A proper strategy for minority demands becomes all the more necessary if the majority community, for historical reasons, is already hostile toward the minority community. In the case of the Muslims, there was one more reason to be added: they were seen as bearing the responsibility for the partition of the country in 1947. Nevertheless, this allegation shows how Indian Muslims have been perceived by the majority community.

The new Muslim leadership did not realize these intricacies and began to press their demands more and more aggressively. Apart from the factors mentioned affecting the relationship between Hindus and Muslims, some new factors were emerging on the political and economic scene. As pointed out earlier, immediately after the partition in 1947 the Muslims were considerably reduced in number in India (mainly due to migration and, also, to the partition riots) and were too insecure to raise any demands or adopt a high profile in politics. The new generation of Muslims, despite repeated communal riots, did not feel such constraints. By the early 1980s their number had doubled (they were 80 million according to the 1981 census) and therefore they had gained in political significance. No political party aspiring to come to power could ignore their votes. Hence, the centrist parties sought to woo them and conceded to their religious demands such as preserving Muslim personal law. The Muslims were thought to be voting en bloc, and any party securing their votes was certain to come to power. For the BJP this was highly frustrating.

So, in the 1980s a small section of Muslims in the north—especially those areas which were traditional centres of Muslim artisans like Meerut, Aligarh, Moradabad, Benaras, and Azamgarh—became prosperous by developing entrepreneurship on a small scale. This section of Muslims began to adopt a high-profile style of politics which had an adverse effect on the minds of Hindus not very well disposed toward Muslims. The section was led by the newly emerging leadership we have already hinted at. It was this same leadership which had led two major movements in an aggressive manner which made the average Hindu hostile toward Muslims. These movements were the Shah Bano and the Babr Masjid.

First we shall deal briefly with the Shah Bano movement. An old Muslim lady had filed a case of maintenance against her husband with whom she had separated. This lady, called Shah Bano, had filed this case under the secular law known as Criminal Procedure Code, Section 125. She was awarded maintenance under this law by the Madhya Pradesh High Court. Her husband filed an appeal against this judgment in the Supreme Court, claiming that the High Court Judgment was in violation of the provisions of Muslim Personal Law, according to which a divorcee was entitled for maintenance only for a period of three months, called *ʿidda* period; under the Criminal Procedure Code, Section 125, in contrast, maintenance to a divorcee is to be paid by the husband for life or until she remarries. The Supreme Court upheld the High Court judgment, arguing that it was given under a common secular law and that, as argued by the advocate of Shah Bano, it is in keeping with the Qurʾānic verse 2: 241. The Supreme Court did not accept the plea of the advocate of the Muslim Persons Law Board that it was a violation of Muslim Personal Law.

The Muslim leadership protested this Supreme Court judgment, saying that it meant interfering in Muslim Personal Law and that the Supreme Court had no right to interpret the holy Qurʾān. Liberal and progressive Muslims supported the judgment, arguing that it concerned the rights of Muslim women and that the judgment, delivered under the common criminal law of the country, must be respected. Moreover, the liberals felt that it was not a violation of the spirit of the Qurʾān. They belonged to a small minority, however. The vast majority of the Muslims was controlled by the traditional Muslim leadership. The protest movement against the Supreme Court judgment soon gathered momentum and acquired aggressive proportions. Huge numbers of Muslims came out on the streets to protest and to demand that either the Supreme Court judgment should be declared invalid or the law should be changed, exempting Muslims from the provisions of the Criminal Procedure Code, Section 125.

This aggressive protest against the Common Criminal Law of the country was strongly resented by the Hindus. Even those secular Hindus who normally had sympathy with Muslims as a suffering minority, felt greatly upset at such an aggressive protest against a secular law, and they opposed any change in the Criminal Law that would exempt Muslims from its application. They also made it an issue of women's rights. The leftist parties made the point of strengthening the secular forces in the country and opposed the Muslim orthodox view that a Muslim woman could not, on being divorced, claim maintenance beyond the *ʿidda* period. But the Muslim leadership was unbending and put tremendous pressure on Rajiv Gandhi's government to change the law. Finally, the government accepted the Muslim demand and enacted a law called Muslim Women's Law (Protection on Divorce Law) which exempted Muslims from the Criminal Procedure Code, Section 125.

Muslim leaders were jubilant that they had forced the government to change the law, thus protecting Muslim Personal Law. But they hardly realized that this was done at a tremendous price. The average Hindu was at that time highly communalized and became more hostile toward Muslims, giving more legitimacy to the demands of Hindu communalist parties and organizations. Long before the ink of the new law was dry, a new controversy arose. Under pressure from Hindu fundamentalists, the doors of Babri Masjid, closed for more than four decades, were thrown open for Hindus to worship Lord Rama whose statue had been installed inside the mosque during the partition riots in 1948 to which we alluded earlier. Some knowledgeable sources even maintain that the Rajiv Gandhi government did a tradeoff, acceding on the one hand to the Muslim fundamentalists' demand to enact the Muslim women's will and conceding on the other to the Hindu fundamentalists' demand to throw open the doors of the Babri Mosque. Whatever be the case, the fact remains that another Pandora's box was opened.

As pointed out earlier, thanks to the Shah Bano movement, the Hindu communalists had acquired a legitimacy. They now sought to further consolidate their position by intensifying the Ramjanambhoomi movement. Briefly stated, the Ramjanambhoomi movement claimed that the Hindu deity of Lord Rama had been born at the spot where the Babri Masjid stands today and that in the fourth century A.D. the Hindu ruler Vikramaditya had constructed a temple at that place in order to commemorate Lord Rama's birth. In the sixteenth century, this temple was demolished by the Mughal ruler Babar, when he conquered the province of Awadh. At his command a mosque was constructed there, which became known as the Babri Masjid.

Senior historians in India have effectively challenged the traditional Hindu point of view. They have tried to show that there is no proof that Rama was born at that place or that any temple existed at the spot where the Babri Masjid stands today. However, these historians could only have an influence over a small section of liberal and progressive Hindus. Moreover, the question was no longer merely a historical one. It had acquired serious political proportions. The BJP reaped its political harvest in the 1989 elections by increasing its number of seats from merely two in the eighth Loksabha to 80 in the ninth Loksabha. It was, by any account, a windfall vote.

In this controversy, the Muslim leadership did not play a more aggressive role than in the other conflict. They organized many meetings, rallies and conferences. Syed Shahabuddin even called for boycotting the Republic Day celebrations on 26 January 1987. Again, it had an adverse impact on the Hindu mind, since it was interpreted as a declaration of disloyalty toward the Indian Republic. Under pressure from liberal and progressive Muslims, Mr. Shahabuddin had, of course, to withdraw this call for a boycott, but the damage was done. In the course of this controversy many communal riots took place in Uttar Pradesh, Bihar, Madhya Pradesh, Rajasbhan, Gujarat, and other places. Now, the area of communalism had become so vast that even the south was affected. Riots broke out in some southern states like Karnataka, Tamil Nadu, and even Kerala, normally the stronghold of the left. In places like Bahgalpur in Bihar the casualties were very high; between 800 to 1000 persons died there, most of whom were Muslims, in communal violence between October and November 1989.

The tenth Loksabha elections in May 1991 were mainly fought on the issue of the Ramjanamohoomi-Beori Masjid; all other important and basic issues facing the people were pushed to the background. The BJP felt that it had a chance to come to power by playing up the Ramjanambhoomi controversy and, if one goes by the statements of the BJP leaders, they perhaps felt this controversy would see them into power both at the center and in some of the northern states. Although they captured power in Uttar Pradesh, they could not make it at the center.

In conclusion, we see that competitive communalism proves to be rather threatening for the country and for the Muslim minority. Even if minority communalism is defensive (though it is not always shown in the same way as the Shah Bano controversy), it provides legitimacy for a majority communalism which in turn strengthens the minority communalism. Thus, it becomes a vicious circle difficult to break. It is unfortunate that, though the Indian state is secular, religion has come to acquire a primordial place in Indian politics. Nothing could have been as great a disaster for this multi-religious and multi-ethnic society. Modern policy cannot be based on medieval concepts and doctrines, though religious faith as such, both in its individual and its corporate expression in the nonpolitical sphere, has its own importance.

NOTE

1. One can find details of this riot in my work, *Communal Violence in Post-Independence India* (Bombay: Orient Longman, 1984).

18

The Influence of Higher Bible Criticism on Muslim Apologetics in the Nineteenth Century

CHRISTINE SCHIRRMACHER

This essay traces the development of a new Muslim view of Christianity in the nineteenth century, which still has a significant impact on today's Muslim apologetical literature. The character of polemical works against Christianity has changed due to the achievement of a different view of Christian dogmas and Christianity itself in nineteenth-century Europe.[1]

Agra 1854

This new development of Muslim-Christian polemics dates back to an event in the middle of the nineteenth century. On the 10th and 11th of April in 1854 we find ourselves in the schoolroom of the British missionary agency "Church Missionary Society" (CMS) in Agra, India, among several hundred Muslims and Europeans, mostly Christian missionaries, but also a few government officials of the British colonial power. They had all gathered in order to listen to a public debate initiated by the Muslim community of Agra. The debate was carried out between the German missionary, Karl Gottlieb Pfander (1803–1865), coming out of the pietistic movement in Württemberg, Swabia, and an Indian Muslim Shīʿī theologian, Raḥmatullāh ibn Khalīl al-ʿUtmānī al-Kairānawī (1818–1891).[2] Despite the fact that this debate took place nearly 150 years ago, both of the opponents are still well remembered in the Muslim world today pertaining to matters of dialogue. The subject of discussion at this public debate, which lasted for two days, was mainly *taḥrīf* (deviation of the Christian Scriptures).

The challenger of the debate in 1854 was the Muslim theologian al-Kairānawī, who intended to publicly demonstrate the inferiority of Christianity and make it clear once and for all that Muslims should not be shaken in their faith because of the proclamation of the Christian creed by Protestant missionaries in India in the past decades.

India had been opened to Protestant Christian missionary activities by a decree of the British Parliament in 1813, and the first Anglican Bishop was secretly consecrated on the 8th of May 1814 in Lambeth Palace, Calcutta.[3] In 1832/1833 non-British missionary agencies were allowed to follow and began to establish their network of Christian missions all over India, more or less officially supported by the Britains. It is interesting enough that the Shīʿī al-Kairānawī represented himself in 1854 as the defender of the Muslim religion and obviously was accepted as such by the whole Muslim community.

Although the discussion was to include the subjects of *tatlīt* (trinity), the Qur'ān as the Word of God, and the mission of the prophet Muḥammad, the debate did not proceed further than the deviation (*taḥrīf*) of the Christian Scriptures. The discussion centered on this point of controversy: al-Kairānawī insisted that the Christian Scriptures had been abrogated and tried to prove this with examples taken out of the Bible itself, while the Christian missionaries persistently affirmed the integrity of the Old and New Testaments. After two days, the opponents separated and "both sides claimed the victory."[4] Also a few conversions to Christianity took place following the debate. Besides the well known Ṣafdar ʿAlī,[5] who was baptized in 1864, perhaps the most famous Muslim convert to Christianity in India had been ʿImād ud-Dīn (ca. 1830–1900), who was baptized in 1866 and ordained as an Anglican priest in 1872.[6] He had been involved in mosque-preaching against Christian missionary work before, and afterward he wrote several polemical works against Islam, such as the famous book *hidāyat al-muslimīn* or *taḥqīq al-īmān*.

But why is this 1854 Agra debate of such significance? Have there not been many more debates before and up until the present which have concentrated again and again on the main points of encounter between Islam and Christianity, like *taḥrīf*?

The 1854 Agra debate is a historical milestone. Experts of the religious situation of India in the nineteenth century have asserted that "there was in these days no debate on the scale of the high drama of the Raḥmatullāh-Pfander debates of the 1850s."[7] I will attempt to analyze the significance of this Muslim-Christian debate in India and its effects on future Muslim apologetical works.

Significance of Place and Time

Concerning the nineteenth century onward Jacques Waardenburg has written:

> We see another period of confrontation, now mostly political, between Muslim states and the expanding West, heir to Christian tradition. In this time we witness a growing polemics of Islam, at first linked with the national movements, against religions like Christianity, Hinduism and Judaism . . .[8]

This is perfectly true for India. In the nineteenth century Agra, the former symbol of the Mughal power, developed into one of the centers of Muslim learning and culture in India. The British government transformed it into their administrative center of the northwest-provinces. In addition, the British government allowed foreign mission agencies to enter the country. Especially in Agra, mostly British missionaries were stationed and they opened a huge orphanage after a disastrous famine in the year 1837. Several children were baptized as Christians, so that the growing influence of the Christian mission was universally recognized. In Agra itself several polemical Christian books against the Muslim creed had been published.[9] All of these facts made the Muslim population extremely aware of the presence of Westerners and missionaries as instruments of British colonialism.

So we find ourselves in the heat of Christian-Muslim tensions in Agra in the middle of the nineteenth century: the Muslim ʿulamāʾ felt threatened by the presence of European Christian missionaries and during the 1840s and 1850s underwent a severe crisis due to the decline of values of their own religion and culture. Different parties gathered in the middle of the nineteenth century in Agra, and various lines intersected at this historical turning point: (1) the representatives of India's colonial power, Great Britain, the protector of the European missionaries; (2) the German pietist and Protestant missionary Pfander himself, his co-workers, and perhaps a few of his converts; and (3) representatives of the Anglican church, who were neither against the debate nor wholeheartedly supported it. Thomas Valpy French (1825–1891) should be named, who later became the first Anglican bishop of Lahore. He was not overly convinced of the benefit or the necessitiy of open encounter and proselytizing, but having been challenged by the Muslim theologians, he was determined to defend the integrity of the Bible.[10] In addition, there were (4) Catholic missionaries in Agra, who obviously disliked the work of their Protestant colleagues and materially supported Muslims who helped them to refute the Protestant missionaries, and (5) the Muslim audience, including Shīʿīs and Sunnīs, while the Shīʿī theologian al-Kairānawī prepared himself to defend the Muslim creed against Christian mission with the help of Dr. Muḥammad Wazīr Khān, having worked since 1851 in a British medical hospital. He had received parts of his medical training in Great Britain where he collected material in order to prove Christianity to be false.

Significance of Individuals Involved in the Controversy

Karl Gottlieb Pfander (1803–1865)

The German missionary Karl Gottlieb Pfander, who was involved in the controversy, was a few decades after his death still considered as "the greatest of all missionaries to Mohammedans"[11] or "one of the most interesting figures among the Missionaries to Muhammedans of the nineteenth century."[12]

In the West, he remained nevertheless quite unknown until the very present, but especially his controversial book *mīzān al-ḥaqq* is still a current topic of debate in the Muslim world. This apologetical work, written in 1829 originally in German,[13] refutes Islam and intends to convince its readers of the supreme values of Christianity, mostly by defending the integrity of the Old and New Testaments and refuting the Muslim charge of *taḥrīf.* After its first publication in 1831 in Armenian, it was quickly translated into at least half a dozen Muslim languages, including, for example, Urdu (1840), Persian (1835), Turkish (1862), and Arabic (1865),[14] and it has had an enormous influence. This book *mīzān al-ḥaqq* is both quoted by and refuted by Muslim apologists today. It has remained a subject of controversy in the Muslim world. Twelve years after Pfander's death, a participant of the Agra debate of 1854 wrote: "He has passed away, but the stir and movement he exited has not passed. . . ."[15] *Mīzān al-ḥaqq*, the "standard work of encounter between Christianity and Islam"[16] was used by generations of Christian missionaries as an apologetical tool to refute Islam, and for this reason it was reprinted many times up until the present. Despite the fact that we also hear severe critiques concerning the work, especially in the twentieth century,[17] we can date the last Arabic and English reprints back to the year 1986,[18] and these reprints are still used today for missionary activities among Muslims.

The author of the book, Karl Gottlieb Pfander, having been stationed as a missionary of the British mission agency CMS in India from 1837 to 1857, was requested on the 10th of April, 1854, by Muslim theologians of Agra to publicly defend the Christian dogma of the integrity of the Bible. In fact, it was he who had opened the discussion by public preaching on the bazaars, by writing and distributing books for several years. It should also be noted that Pfander tried to prove the high value which the Qur'ān attributes to the Bible with the help of Qur'ānic statements. He also quoted Muslim commentators in order to hint at the difference of their judgments about Christianity: "The Christians were trying to show that in the Qur'ān itself Muḥammad shows respect for Christianity and veneration for its beliefs and teachings."[19]

Raḥmatullāh Ibn Khalīl al-ʿUthmānī al-Kairānawī (1818–1891)

Nevertheless, Pfander's opponent is much more interesting for the theme of the Muslim-Christian historical encounter.

The Shīʿī theologian Raḥmatullāh ibn Khalīl al-ʿUthmānī was engaged in the battle against the presence of Christian missionaries in India from the beginning of the 1850s, and in 1855 he had already written three polemical works against Christianity in order to defend Islam, probably with the help of the Bengali physician Muḥammad Wazīr Khān. Al-Kairānawī and Wazīr Khān belong to the most outstanding figures of Indian Muslim defense against the Christian mission in the nineteenth century. They came into contact at the beginning of the 1850s in connection with their apologetical work. In 1854 both of them took part in the public Agra debate, al-Kairānawī being the challenger and the leader of the discussion, Muḥammad Wazīr Khān acting as interpreter between the Urdu- and English-speaking participants.

The Influence of al-Kairānawī on Nineteenth-Century Muslim Views of Christianity

Al-Kairānawī's influence is not restricted to this single event in Agra. This was only a prelude to his future impact, which is due to his written works. When it comes to Muslim apologetics, al-Kairānawī certainly comes to mind. The reason for this is his famous book *iẓhār al-ḥaqq*, which he composed as a response to Pfander's *mīzān al-ḥaqq*. Written in Arabic in 1867 by request of the Ottoman Sultan Abdülaziz I (1861–1876),[20] the book has seen several translations into Turkish (1876/1877), French (1880), English (ca. 1900), and Urdu (1968)—into almost the same languages as Pfanders *mīzān al-ḥaqq* has been translated. Like *mīzān al-ḥaqq*, *iẓhār al-ḥaqq* has been reprinted up until the present. In 1964 a new edition came out, supervised by the Department for Islamic Affairs of the Kingdom of Morocco, and a foreword was added by the *adab*-professor ʿUmar ad-Dasūqī. The last Arabic editions date from the year 1978; one of the two was authorized by the late shaikh ʿAbd al-Ḥalīm Maḥmūd of al-Azhar. In 1989 a short version in English came into being, published by Ta-Ha Publishers in London.

Only a few polemical Muslim works have become as famous as al-Kairānawī's *iẓhār al-ḥaqq*. It has been stated: "The first great classic of modern Muslim polemic has never been superseded."[21] Ignaz Goldziher reported that during his visit in 1877 in Damascus, everybody was talking of *iẓhār al-ḥaqq*.[22] Undoubtedly, the book played a key role for Muslim polemics in the past, but it is still currently on the "top ten" of Muslim apologetical works. Concerning the significance of *iẓhār al-ḥaqq*, Georges C. Anawati wrote in 1969, "C'est le grand ouvrage de base qui a servi et continue à servir d'arsenal pour les apologistes musulmans de la fin du 19e siècle jusqu'à nos jours,"[23] and again in 1981, "et aujourd'hui encore, il reste le livre par excellence où les musulmans traditionalistes et peu ouverts au christianisme, puisent leurs arguments."[24]

Concerning *iẓhār al-ḥaqq* it was stated in 1976:

> The editor of the Urdu version has expressed the strong opinion that nothing written in the intervening hundred years on the theme of Islam and Christianity has replaced the books which were generated in the mind of Maulānā Raḥmat Allāh Kairānawī by the situation of extreme tension which faced the ʿulamā' of northern India in the first half of the nineteenth century.[25]

The popularity of *iẓhār al-ḥaqq* is also due to the fact that only a very cautious Shīʿī coloring can be found in the book. As far as it can be seen in the different editions from 1867 onward, the reason for this is not any revision but the original tone of al-Kairānawī himself, who only once hinted at his own Shīʿī background when dealing with ḥadīth. Therefore it could become the standard work of Muslim apologetics as well as in "orthodox" circles like al-Azhar.

The influence of *iẓhār al-ḥaqq* can be noted in the nineteenth century "reform-wing" Sunnī theologian Rashīd Riḍā's extensive use of the work when dealing with Christianity. Coming to the question of Muḥammad's mission, he quoted in the famous ʿAbduh/Riḍā Qur'ān commentary *tafsīr al-qur'ān al-ḥakīm* about 60 pages from *iẓhār al-ḥaqq*.[26] Another Muslim polemicist who used *iẓhār al-ḥaqq* is Muḥammad Abū Zahra.[27] In his "Lectures on Christianity" (*muḥāḍarāt fī an-naṣrānīya*) he referred to al-Kairānawīs commentaries on the Christian creed.[28]

Reasons for the Influence of Iẓhār al-Ḥaqq

The very reason for the immense influence of al-Kairānawīs *iẓhār al-ḥaqq* can be found in his development of a new method to prove Islam to be the only true religion. It is quite obvious that al-Kairānawī did not restrict the defense of Islam to a mere devaluation of the Christian creed or to a praise of Islam; he also took advantage of the new orientation of European theology that had occurred especially during the nineteenth century. From a former conservative standpoint in regard to the integrity of the Christian Scriptures, European theology had undergone a rapid change to a more and more critical standpoint regarding the reliability of historical and textual questions especially since the nineteenth century. Critical and liberal standpoints found their way into universities and churches. In this evolution Germany was the forerunner for the whole Christian Occident. Numerous theological liberal works appeared and found their way into the Muslim world rather quickly.

Al-Kairānawī was—ostensibly—the very first apologist in the Muslim world who referred to these books and Bible commentaries in order to fight Christianity with its own weapons. For the first time, he used different works of famous European theologians who were influenced by liberalism and historical criticism of European theology of the nineteenth century. During the Agra debate, al-Kairānawī quoted these representatives of liberalism to show the conservative missionaries that Christian theology had already produced evidence that the Bible is unreliable.

European Theology and Philosophy Influences Muslim Apologetics

This is not the only example where the Muslim world borrowed fruits of European theology or philosophy which affirmed Islam. Before the nineteenth century, there had been a movement in European theology which was called rationalism. Representatives of German rationalism—for example, Karl Friedrich Bahrdt (1741–1792) or the famous Heinrich Eberhard Gottlob Paulus (1761–1851)—maintained that Jesus Christ had been crucified, but they neglected that he had really died on the cross; a standpoint which is again an "outside" position today. Bahrdt writes at the end of the eighteenth century:

> This is my opinion on this last part of the history of Jesus. Jesus has been put to death: he underwent all the sufferings of an evil-doer, he endured the suffering of death, but he overcame death—he came from death to life—he came out of the mausoleum . . . on the third day after having been put to death

> . . . and he has shown himself to his disciples as somebody being revived from the dead.[29]

It is possible, even if not probable, that the Aḥmadīya-standpoint of Jesus having died a natural death in India after he survived his crucifixion, did not originate in Islam itself, but was fostered by developments in Europe like rationalism; Muslim apologists claimed: "European theologians and scientists have proven that Jesus Christ survived the crucifixion."

Some Christian university theologians even went so far as the climax of theological liberalism, which is, historically spoken, connected with Enlightenment, that they neglected Jesus as a historical figure or at least his deity or his being part of the Trinity. Muslim apologists have used these theories as proofs for their old affirmation that according to Sūra 4: 157–158 Jesus never died on the cross, even if he was perhaps crucified, which is doubtful.

The Gospel of Barnabas Confirms Muslim Apologists

Doubts of European theologians and philosophers concerning the death and resurrection of Jesus Christ or concerning the reliabilty of the four canonical gospels also played a key role when the "Gospel of Barnabas" was defended in numerous books and pamphlets by Muslim apologists as the only true Gospel of Jesus Christ, mostly in the twentieth century. Muslims had generally adopted the positive statements about the value of the Gospel of Barnabas of certain European critics of conservative theology of the eighteenth and nineteenth century, while at the same time Christian missionaries tried to prove that it is impossible to date this Gospel back to the first century A.D. The Gospel of Barnabas proves that Jesus Christ did not die on the cross; Judas was transformed into the likeness of Jesus and crucified, while everybody thought he was Jesus himself; so the Qur'ān is again affirmed in its refutation of the crucifixion of Jesus.

The Qur'ān is confirmed by "objective" "scientific" results: Muslim apologists name European theologians or philosophers like the well-known English deist John Toland (1670–1722), who positively mentioned the announcement of Muḥammad in the Gospel of Barnabas. Muslim apologists concentrate on European authors who, on the one hand trace the Gospel of Barnabas back to the first centuries and herewith accept its value and on the other hand doubt and critique the integrity of the Bible and the inspiration of the Old and New Testament.[30]

It is possible that al-Kairānawī himself "brought" the Gospel of Barnabas to the Moslem world for the first time in 1854 in his Urdu work *iʿjāz-i ʿĪsāwī*[31] and afterward in *iẓhār al-ḥaqq* from 1867 onward, mentioning it as an old Christian Gospel which foretells the coming of the prophet Muḥammad. In the middle of the nineteenth century, the Gospel of Barnabas was not even published as a whole. Only a few fragments were known to the Western world when al-Kairānawī used it as a weapon against the Christian rejection of Muḥammad, who had been foretold from the beginning of revelation. It is quite probable that Muḥammad Rashīd Riḍā, who defended the Gospel as the only surviving reliable Gospel of the time of Jesus, and who published the first Arabic edition of the Gospel of Barnabas in 1908 under the title *al-injīl as-ṣaḥīḥ*, was led to this Gospel through the work of al-Kairānawī. Several translations have appeared since 1908 to promote this "only true Gospel of Jesus Christ" (Urdu 1916, English 1916, Persian 1927, Indonesian 1969, Dutch 1990).

Changes of Muslim Apologetics Due to Developments in European Theology

In the nineteenth century a new wave of criticism emerged in Europe and quickly found its way into the Muslim world. In European universities all miracles reported in the Old and New Testaments were called into question; historical events were doubted; the formulation of Christology, the Trinity, the deity of Jesus Christ, and his crucifixion and resurrection were called into question in their very principles. All these doubts and critical remarks of European theology found their way into the Muslim world and were enthusiastically taken as proofs of the traditional Muslim view of a corrupted Christian Bible. This way of arguing against the reliability of the Old and New Testaments has marked the form of controversy especially since al-Kairānawī.

During the Agra debate, this method of controversy was used for the first time. Al-Kairānawī confronted the theologically conservative missionary Pfander and his friends in 1854 with the newest results of European critical research. Pfander, who had already left Europe in 1825 as a missionary, had not witnessed the important developments which had taken place in European theology in the nineteenth century. Moreover, the conservative Basel Mission

Society (Basler Missionsgesellschaft), where Pfander was educated from 1821 to 1825, had allowed its pupils to attend lectures at the theological seminary at Basel, but had tried to limit their influence on the candidates.[32] David Friedrich Strauss's world-famous book *Das Leben Jesu* (The life of Jesus) was not published until 1835, when Pfander had already been abroad for ten years. As the Agra debate took place in 1854, Pfander had already suspected that his Muslim opponents were busily studying European theological works, but he either underestimated the far-reaching effects of these studies or he did not have enough knowledge himself of these new developments. Pfander wrote concerning his Muslim opponents: "Several of their friends in Delhi have been for the last two or three years hard at work in studying the Bible, reading the controversial books we have published, and searching out our commentaries and critical writers . . . , only to obtain material for refuting it."[33]

During the Agra debate al-Kairānawī and Muḥammad Wazīr Khān presented the newest critical remarks on textual variations and on contradictions between different biblical texts of the latest theories in Europe. Al-Kairānawī seemingly inherited most of his material from Muḥammad Wazīr Khān, who received part of his medical training in Great Britain where he came into contact with European theologically critical works. In addition, al-Kairānawī received the latest European works from the Catholic missionaries in India, who strongly disliked the work of their Protestant colleagues.[34]

Several polemical works against Christianity in Agra and, later, those by the Muslim theologian al-Kairānawī presented for the first time the latest scientific research from Europe. Against this new attack, Pfander was helpless since his books responded to the traditional Muslim charges against Christianity and not to the European results of higher or lower criticism presented from the Muslim side.

Europe did not have the slightest idea about the effects of its theological evolution on Muslim countries. Protestant missions were comparatively new to them, only dating from the nineteenth century,[35] apart from single attempts in former centuries as, for example, undertaken by Henry Martyn or Bartholomäus Ziegenbalg. It can be added here that after the debate Pfander sought in Basel European authors who were refuting these theories, but only in order to demonstrate to the Muslim polemicists that the standpoint of these theologians is only one part of the prism of European theology.[36]

Apart from the Agra debate, we are able to witness that al-Kairānawī developed this method of proving the corruption of the Bible with European voices. In *iẓhār al-ḥaqq*, al-Kairānawī draws all the evidence from European sources he can procure. He quotes Luther's critical attitude concerning the pope and King Henry VIII of England and European critical remarks on the apostle Paul's devastating influence on early Christianity. He refers to doubts among theologians as to whether the Epistles of James or Judas belong to the original biblical canon; he criticizes the forming of dogmas on the first Christian councils like Nicea about 300 years after the death of Jesus Christ. Furthermore, he refers to doubts about the authorship of the books of Moses, Joshua, Judges, and others. When he comes to the genealogies of Christ, he detects "errors and contradictions," as well as "absurdities" in the narrative of Elijah being fed by ravens, and he quotes commentaries on the Bible by Eichhorn, Horne, and Henry and Scott. I could continue with hundreds of contradictions al-Kairānawī "detects" between single biblical texts.[37] In six thick volumes, *iẓhār al-ḥaqq* served as a summary of all possible charges against Christianity and was therefore used after al-Kairānawī's death as a sort of encyclopedia since al-Kairānawī extended the material of former polemicists like ʿAli Ṭabarī, Ibn Ḥazm, and Ibn Taymiyya to a great extent.

European Theology Changes Muslim Views of Christianity

Here it is obvious that al-Kairānawī has changed the former Muslim view of *taḥrīf* and the Muslim view of Christianity as a whole. According to al-Kairānawī, *taḥrīf* should no longer be understood as mere single alterations in the texts of the Old and New Testaments, which had crept into the texts throughout the process of copying them during the centuries. Apologists in former times only criticized certain biblical dogmas such as the Trinity or the dogma of the deity of Jesus Christ as the Qurʾān itself does. Al-Kairānawī expanded the Qurʾānic criticism of the corruption of the Bible to a much larger extent. Leading Muslim apologists now follow the example of *iẓhār al-ḥaqq* and take over the "results" of the textual studies of European theologians. Al-Kairānawī came to the conclusion that the biblical texts are totally distorted, corrupted, and unreliable in *all* their historical, dogmatical, and narrative passages. This is for al-Kairānawī no matter of dispute, since the Christian ʿulamāʾ of Europe themselves admit the complete distortion of all biblical texts. So al-Kairānawī and his followers feel confirmed in the traditional Muslim view that the Bible is corrupted just as the Qurʾān states. Muslim apologists have known this for centuries already, but now European theologians have confirmed it themselves through scientific studies in history, geology, and archeology.

The effect of this use of European theology can be summarized: in today's Muslim apologetical works against Christianity we find numerous results of the severe studies in textual exegesis and different sciences undertaken in the West. With this transformation of the Muslim dogma of *taḥrīf* in Christianity and the acknowledgment that European theology serves as a proof for the Muslim statements, the whole Muslim view of Christianity has changed. In former times, only certain dogmas of Christianity had to be refuted, but Christianity as a whole contained the same message as Islam. Now Christianity seems to have been proven to be corrupted as a whole: if Christian scientists and theologians in the West determine that it is untenable to believe in this collection of fanciful stories and legends originating in heathenism or Greek Platonic philosophy, it will no longer be tenable to praise this revelation. Muslim apologists only take seriously what the religious authorities of Christianity have discovered about their own creed. In contrast to this great error, Islam is the religion of understanding and intelligence. The Islamic dogmas are clear, understandable, and reasonable.

Furthermore, we witness that Muslim polemical works after the al-Kairānawī-Pfander battle always pursue this fundamental attitude: Christian theologians themselves admit that the Old and New Testament is not inspired by God as we have it today, but both parts of the Bible are full of errors, misconceptions, contradictions, and absurdities, if not willfull distortions. Thus Muslim theologians see their interpretation of the Christian Scriptures confirmed by Western scholarship.

We can witness this form of controversy today when it comes to Muslim apologetical works: Muḥammad Rashīd Riḍā used the results of European theological studies in his *tafsīr*. For him the apostle Paul is especially guilty of having introduced heathenism into Christianity. It was not until the Council of Nicea in the year 325 A.D. that the dogma of Trinity and redemption through the crucifixion of Jesus was established. With this development, *tauḥīd* was replaced by *shirk*.[38] We witness the same tendency in Abū Zahra's *muḥāḍarāt fī-n-naṣrānīya*: Jesus Christ himself preached monotheism, but this dogma was distorted by the influence of syncretism, neo-Platonic and Greek philosophy, and Roman heathenism.[39] Aḥmad Shalaby considers Christianity an unreliable mixture of heathenism, the convictions of the apostle Paul[40] and Jesus' miracles narrated in the four Gospels.[41]

Elwood M. Wherry's personal view concerning the beginning of the twentieth century was that

> The Muslims were obliged to abandon their own works and endeavour to save the day by a counter assault, in which they scrupled not [i.e., they did not scruple] to use the stock arguments of European infidelity in their effort to overthrow the authority of the Christian Scriptures. This characteristic has marked the Muslim method of controversy ever since.[42]

Summary

In the nineteenth century, a Muslim-Christian debate took place far away from the traditional centers of Muslim learning. In Agra in 1854, probably for the first time, Muslim theologians used European critical works as proofs against Christian missionaries.

The nineteenth century marks a turning point when it comes to Muslim apologetics: the Muslims developed a completely new method to prove Christianity to be the '"false religion" with the help of European sources being mainly Christian theological works (e.g., Bible commentaries).

After the publication of *iẓhār al-ḥaqq* this method of controversy became common among Muslim apologists such as Muḥammad Rashīd Riḍā and Muḥammad Abū Zahra to prove the traditional charge of *taḥrīf.*

Taḥrīf is at the center of Muslim apologetics of the nineteenth century; Christology and redemption are at the center of apologetics in the twentieth century.

This leads to a new Muslim view of Christianity, which developed during the nineteenth century. The dogmas of Christianity are not distorted any longer in fragments but as a whole.

NOTES

1. This text is based on material of my dissertation, published as *Mit den Waffen des Gegners: Christlich-Muslimische Kontroversen im 19. und 20. Jahrhundert* (Berlin: Klaus Schwarz Verlag, 1992).

2. See Avril Ann Powell, *Muslims and Missionaries in Pre-Mutiny India* (Richmond, U.K.: Curzon Press, 1993; based on Ph.D. Diss., London 1983).

3. H. H. Dodwell, ed., *The Cambridge History of India*, vol. 6: *The Indian Empire 1858–1918* (New Delhi 1932), p. 124.

4. Eugene Stock, "The C.M.S. Missions to Mohammedans," *The Muslim World* 2 (1912), p. 128; W. H. T. Gairdner, *The Reproach of Islam* (London 1909), p. 248.

5. The story of Ṣafdar ʿAlī's conversion to Christianity appeared in *Church Missionary Intelligencer* 2 (July 1866), pp. 215–221. Parts of his own report of his conversion are published in D. Rajaiah Paul, *Lights in the World: Life Sketches of Maulvi Safdar Ali and the Rev. Janni Alli* [*sic*] (Lucknow 1969), pp. 20–23, 28–30.

6. The German magazine of the Basel Mission Society EMM (*Evangelisches Missions-Magazin*) published the story of his conversion under the title "A Mohammedan brought to Christ, being the autobiography of a native clergyman in India," no. 14 (1871), pp. 397–412. This was probably a summary of his own tract dealing with his conversion in Urdu, which was republished in 1957 in Lahore and 1978 in Vanyambadi.

7. Narayani Gupta, *Delhi between Two Empires 1803–1931: Society, Government and Urban Growth* (Delhi 1981), p. 79.

8. Jacques Waardenburg, "World religions as seen in the light of Islam," in *Islam: Past Influence and Present Challenge*, ed. Alford T. Welch and Pierre Cachia (Edinburgh 1979), p. 248.

9. See Ann Avril Powell, "Maulānā Raḥmat Allāh Kairānawī and Muslim-Christian controversy in India in the mid-nineteenth century," *Journal of the Royal Asiatic Society* 20 (1976), pp. 42–63.

10. Stephen Neill, *A History of Christianity in India 1707–1858* (Cambridge 1985), p. 344.

11. Church Missionary Society, *One Hundred Years: Being the Short History of the Church Missionary Society* (London 1898), p. 78.

12. Trans. from Julius Richter, *Mission und Evangelisation im Orient* (Gütersloh 1908/1930), p. 71.

13. The original handwritten text is still to be found in the archives of the Basel Mission Society headquarters in Basel, Switzerland.

14. In Turkey, where Pfander was missionary from 1858 to 1865, "the circulation of the Mīzān seems to have brought matters to a crisis." (Pfander's letter of 16th Sept 1862 to the CMS, Doc. No. 63a; archives of Heslop Room/University of Birmingham). The Ottoman government resolved to expel all missionary agencies in consequences of the baptism of several converts to Christianity by Pfander and his coworkers in the year 1864.

15. Herbert Birks, *The Life and Correspondence of Thomas Valpy French, First Bishop of Lahore* (London 1895), vol. 1, p. 70.

16. Trans. from Horst R. Flachsmeier, *Geschichte der evangelischen Weltmission* (Giessen 1963), p. 446.

17. See, for example, Lyle L. Vander Werff, *Christian Mission to Muslims: The Record, Anglican and Reform Approaches in India and the Near East 1800–1938* (Pasadena 1977), p. 42; Emmanuel Kellerhals, *Der Islam: Seine Geschichte, seine Lehre, sein Wesen*, second edition (Basel 1956), p. 334 ff.

18. The publishers of the 1986 English edition wrote in their introduction to the book: "Perhaps the way of discussion seems questionable to some theologians in our century, but until today the book touches the central points in sincere dialogue between Muslims and Christians." "The Publishers," introduction, in C. G. Pfander, D.D., *The Mīzān-ul-Haqq, Balance of Truth* (Villach 1986).

19. Harry Gaylord Dorman, *Toward Understanding Islam* (Edinburgh 1948), p. 31.

20. Aḥmad Ḥijāzī as-Saqqā, ed., *Raḥmat Allāh al-Hindī, iẓhār al-ḥaqq* (al-Qāhira, 1978), pp. 29–30. Al-Kairānawī had to go into exile because the British government suspected him of having participated in the anti-British revolt of 1857. Al-Kairānawī fled to Mecca, and when the Ottoman sultan made his ḥajj to Mecca at the beginning of the 1860s, he was informed about the events in India of 1854. Al-Kairānawī had to stay in Mecca until his death in 1891.

21. Dorman, *Islam*, p. 44.

22. Goldziher wrote: "Während meines Aufenthaltes in der umajjadischen Chalifenstadt übte eine enorme Zugkraft auf das Lesepublikum aus das arabisch geschriebene polemische Werk iẓhār al-ḥaqq von dem indischen Muhammedaner Šeih Raḥmat Allāh gegen die mīzān al-ḥaqq betitelte Missions- und Controversschrift eines englischen Predigers des Evangeliums, welcher mit den Geschützen christlicher Theologie die Bollwerke des Islam erschüttern wollte." Ignaz Goldziher, "Über muhammedanische Polemik gegen Ahl al-kitāb," *Zeitschrift der Deutschen Morgenländischen Gesellschaft* 32 (1878), pp. 343–344.

23. G. C. Anawati, "Polémique, Apologie et dialogue islamo-chrétiens, positions classiques médiévales et positions contemporaines," in *Euntes Docete* 22 (1969), p. 420.

24. G. C. Anawati, *Les grands courants de la pensée religieuse musulmane dans l'Égypte comtemporaine*, in G. C. Anawati and Maurice Borrmans, *Tendances et courants dans l'Islam arabe contemporain*, vol. 1: *Égypte*

et Afrique du Nord (Entwicklung und Frieden, Wissenschaftliche Reihe vol. 26) (Munich, Kaiser Publishers, 1982), p. 58.

25. Powell, "Maulānā Raḥmat Allāh Kairānawī," p. 63.

26. Muḥammad Rashīd Riḍā, ed., *tafsīr al-qur'ān al-ḥakīm*, vol. 9 (al-Qāhira, 1347/1928), pp. 231–293.

27. This is mentioned by the editor of one of the newest editions of *iẓhār al-ḥaqq*: Aḥmad Ḥijāzī as-Saqqā, *Raḥmat Allāh al-Hindī*, p. 33.

28. Quotations of al-Kairānawī by Abū Zahra in his *muḥāḍarāt fī-n-naṣrānīya* (al-Qāhira 1966), p. 32.

29. Translated from Karl Friedrich Bahrdt, *Ausführungen des Plans und Zweks* [sic] *Jesu*, vol. 10 (Berlin 1784–1793), p. 187.

30. E.g., John Toland, *Christianity Not Mysterious* (London 1696) had a rationalistic understanding of the miracles narrated in the New Testament. In his work *Nazarenus* he attributes at the same time a great probability to the Gospel of Barnabas going back to the very first centuries A.D.: John Toland, *Nazarenus or Jewish, Gentile and Mahometan Christianity* (London 1718). He defended the Gospel of Barnabas against the common charge from the Christian side as being a willful forgery of a renegade of the Middle Ages: "How great . . . is the ignorance of those, who make this an original invention of the Mahometans." J. Toland, *Nazarenus*, p. 17. Or: "After this mature examination I could safely say, that this Gospel might in the main be the ancient Gospel of Barnabas." J. Toland, *Tetradymus* (London 1720), p. 148.

31. Raḥmatullāh ibn Khalīl al-ʿUṯmānī al-Kairānawī, *iʿjāz-i ʿĪsāwī* (Agra 1853; repr. Delhi 1876).

32. The attitude of teachers of the Basel Mission Seminary to the lectures at Basel University, given by one of the most famous theologians of the nineteenth century and representative of Biblical Criticism, Wilhelm Martin Lebrecht de Wette (1780–1849) is summarized as follows: "Doch trug man Bedenken, sie bei De Wette hospitieren zu lassen und sie so in die historische Kritik einzuführen. Überhaupt fürchtete man, die Zöglinge möchten aus diesen Vorlesungen nicht denjenigen Gewinn davontragen, der dem Zeitaufwand entspräche." Paul Eppler, *Geschichte der Basler Mission 1815–1899* (Basel 1900), pp. 16–17.

33. Undated letter, perhaps to Thomas Valpy French, participant of the Agra debate 1854: Birks, *Life*, vol. 1, p. 71.

34. Eugene Stock, *The History of the Church Missionary Society: Its Environment, Its Men and Its Work*, 3 vols. (London 1899–1916), vol. 2, p. 171.

35. The nineteenth century is called the "Missionsjahrhundert" (century of mission) in Europe because of the founding of numerous Protestant missionary agencies and seminaries for the education and sending of missionaries to foreign countries.

36. He asked for the books in a letter to his former school in Basel: "Um den Mohammedanern, die sich mit denselben gar sehr brüsten, zu zeigen, daß diese Neologen und Pantheisten weit über den Koran hinausgehen und also gefährliche und schlechte Hilfsgenossen seien, teils um nachzuweisen, daß Strauß und Konsorten längst ihre Widerlegung gefunden haben." Christoph Friedrich Eppler, *D. Karl Gottlieb Pfander: Ein Zeuge der Wahrheit unter den Bekennern des Islam* (Basel 1888), p. 152.

37. It is true what H. G. Dorman states for the real apologetical literature until the present time: "Through most of this material there moves a strain of suspicion and resentment. In only a few of the books is there an open friendliness in the approach. For the most part the polemists are fighting hard to win a declared battle and to overthrow the enemy. There is surprisingly little difference from the classical polemical methods of the earlier centuries." Dorman, *Islam*, p. 113.

38. Muḥammad Rašīd Riḍā, *al-manār* 10 (1325–1326), p. 386.

39. Muḥammad Abū Zahra, *muḥāḍarāt* (1942), p. 11.

40. Aḥmad Shalaby, *muqāranat al-adyān*, vol. 2: *al-masīḥīya* (Cairo 1965), p. 64.

41. Ibid., p. 62.

42. Elwood M. Wherry, *The Mohammedan Controversy* (London, 1905), p. 2.

BIBLIOGRAPHY

Anawati, G. C. "Polémique, apologie et dialogue islamo-chrétiens, positions classiques médiévales et positions contemporaines," in *Euntes Docete* (Rome) 22 (1969), pp. 375–452.

———. "Les grands courants de la pensée religieuse musulmane dans l'Égypte contemporaine," in G. C. Anawati and Maurice Borrmans, *Tendances et courants dans l'Islam arabe contemporain*, vol. 1: *Égypte et Afrique du Nord*: Entwicklung und Frieden, Wissenschaftliche Reihe Vol. 26. Munich: Kaiser-Grünewald, 1982.

Bahrdt, Karl Friedrich. *Ausführungen des Plans und Zweks Jesu*. Vol. 10. Berlin, 1784–1793.

Birks, Herbert. *The Life and Correspondence of Thomas Valpy French, First Bishop of Lahore*. London: John Murray, 1895.

Church Missionary Society, ed. *One Hundred Years, Being the Short History of the Church Missionary Society*. London: Church Missionary Society, 1898.

Dodwell, H. H., ed. *The Cambridge History of India*, vol. 6: *The Indian Empire 1858–1918*. New Delhi: Cambridge University Press, 1932.

Dorman, Harry Gaylord. *Toward Understanding Islam*. Edinburgh: T. & T. Clark, 1948.

Eppler, Christoph Friedrich. *D. Karl Gottlieb Pfander: Ein Zeuge der Wahrheit unter den Bekennern des Islam*. Basel: Verlag der Missionsbuchhandlung, 1888.

Eppler, Paul. *Geschichte der Basler Mission 1815–1899*. Basel: Verlag der Missionsbuchhandlung, 1900.

Flachsmeier, Horst R. *Geschichte der evangelischen Weltmission*. Giessen: Brunnen-Verlag, 1963.

Gairdner, W. H. T. *The Reproach of Islam*. London, 1909.

Goldziher, Ignaz. "Über muhammedanische Polemik gegen Ahl al-kitāb." *Zeitschrift der Deutschen Morgenländischen Gesellschaft* 32 (1878), pp. 341–378.

Gupta, Narayani. *Delhi between two Empires 1803–1931: Society, Government and Urban Growth*. Delhi: Oxford University Press, 1981.

Kellerhals, Emanuel. *Der Islam: Seine Geschichte, seine Lehre, sein Wesen*. Basel: Verlag der Basler Missionsbuchhandlung, second edition 1956.

"A Mohammedan brought to Christ: Being the Autobiography of a Native Clergyman in India." In *Evangelisches Missions-Magazin* (Basel) 14 (1871), pp. 397–412.

Muḥammad Abū Zahra. *muḥāḍarāt fī-n-naṣrānīya*. al-Qāhira, third edition 1966.

Muḥammad Rašīd Riḍā. *al-manār* 10 (1325–1326).

———, ed. *tafsīr al-qur'ān al-ḥakīm*, vol. 9. al-Qāhira 1347/1928.

Neill, Stephen. *A History of Christianity in India 1707–1858*. Cambridge: Cambridge University Press, 1985.

Paul, Rajaiah D. *Lights in the World: Life Sketches of Maulvi Safdar Ali and the Rev. Janni Alli* [*sic*]. Lucknow: Lucknow Publishing House, 1969.

Pfander, Karl Gottlieb. *kitāb mīzān al-ḥaqq* (1835). Jerusalem 1865. Transl. by R. H. Weakley: *The Mizan ul Haqq; or Balance of Truth*. London, 1867.

———. "Pfander's letter of 16th Sept 1862 to the CMS." Doc. No. 63a; Archives of Heslop Room/University of Birmingham (unpublished documents).

Powell, Ann Avril. "Maulānā Raḥmat Allāh Kairānawī and Muslim-Christian controversy in India in the mid-nineteenth century." *Journal of the Royal Asiatic Society* 20 (1976), pp. 42–63.

———. "Contact and controversy between Islam and Christianity in northern India 1833–1857: The relations between Muslims and Protestant missionaries in the north-western provinces and Oudh." Ph.D. Diss., London 1983.

———. *Muslims and Missionaries in Pre-Mutiny India*. Richmond, UK: Curzon Press, 1991.

"The Publishers," Introduction. In C. G. Pfander, D.D., *The Mīzān-ul-Haqq, Balance of Truth*. Villach: Light of Life, 1986.

Raḥmatullāh ibn Khalīl al-ʿUthmānī al-Kairānawī. *iʿjāz-i ʿĪsāwī*. Agra 1853; repr. Delhi 1876.

———. *iẓhār al-ḥaqq*. Istanbul 1280/1867–1868. French transl. by P. V. Carletti: *Idh-har-ul-Haqq ou Manifestation de la Vérité*, 2 vols. Paris, 1880.

Richter, Julius. *Mission und Evangelisation im Orient*. Gütersloh: C. Bertelsmann, 1908/1930.

as-Saqqā, Aḥmad Ḥijāzī, ed. *Raḥmat Allāh al-Hindī, iẓhār al-ḥaqq*. al-Qāhira: Dār al-Turāth al-ʿArabī li l-Ṭibāʿa wa l-Našr, 1978.

Schirrmacher, Christine. *Mit den Waffen des Gegners: Christlich-Muslimische Kontroversen im 19. und 20. Jahrhundert, dargestellt am Beispiel der Auseinandersetzung um Karl Gottlieb Pfanders 'mīzān al-ḥaqq' und Raḥmatullāh ibn Khalīl al-ʿUṯmānī al-Kairānawīs 'iẓhār al-ḥaqq' und der Diskussion über das Barnabasevangelium*. Berlin: Klaus Schwarz Verlag, 1992.

Shalaby, Aḥmad. *muqāranat al-adyān*. Vol. 2: *al-masīḥīya*. Cairo, 2nd edition, 1965.

Slomp, Jan. "The 'Gospel of Barnabas' in recent research." *Islamochristiana* 23 (1997), 81–109.

Stock, Eugene. "The C.M.S. Missions to Mohammedans." *The Muslim World* 2 (1912), pp. 122–132.

———. *The History of the Church Missionary Society: Its Environment, Its Men and Its Work*. 3 vols. London: Church Missionary Society, 1899–1916.

Toland, John. *Christianity Not Mysterious*. London, 1696.

———. *Nazarenus or Jewish, Gentile and Mahometan Christianity*. London, 1718.

———. *Tetradymus*. London, 1720.

Vander Werff, Lyle L. *Christian Mission to Muslims: The Record, Anglican and Reformed Approaches in India and the Near East, 1800–1938*. South Pasadena, Calif.: William Carey Library, 1977.

Waardenburg, Jacques, "World religions as seen in the light of Islam." In *Islam: Past Influence and Present Challenge*, ed. Alford T. Welch and Pierre Cachia. Edinburgh: Edinburgh University Press, 1979, pp. 245–275.

Wherry, Elwood M. *The Mohammedan Controversy*. London, 1905.

19

The Pancasila Ideology and an Indonesian Muslim Theology of Religions

KAREL A. STEENBRINK

In 1967 the Ministry of Religion of the Indonesian Republic published an edition of the Bhagavadgita—that is, the Sanskrit text along with an Indonesian translation, commentary, and introduction. The publication received three prefaces from prominent Muslims in the country. The first preface was written by Abdul Haris Nasution, speaker of the parliament. It had a political comment on the publication, related to the abortive Communist coup of September 30, 1965:

> Every negation, transgression and wrongdoing with regard to the One and Almighty God, is a betrayal of the 1945 Constitution. Therefore the People's Congress as the highest authority in our country has decided to ban Marxism, Communism and atheist Leninism. Therefore the Congress also promoted the instruction of the psychology and morality of the Pancasila-ideology with freedom for all adherents of Religions and Faiths to develop their Religion and Faith the best they can.
>
> Difference of religion does not include a conflict of religion. Surely, God, the source of all Religion, does not want a conflict. During the colonial period and in the period prior to the abortive communist coup the differences between religions were exploited and turned into conflicts, in order to disturb the religious communities. This should not occur again in the New Order. (Pendit 1967: ix–x)

The second preface was by the President Suharto of Indonesia.

> Praise and thanks be to God [Sjukur Alhamdulillah] for the finalisation of the translation of the holy book of the Hindu Religion, the Bhagavadgita by the Foundation for the Translation of the Vedic and Dhammapada Scriptures. . . . I hope that by this translation of the Bhagavadgita into our language, the whole Indonesian people may get a deeper understanding of the Hindu religion, in accordance with its ultimate values and truth.
>
> All religions that support the life of our Pancasila-State will receive a fair support from the Government, as article 29 second paragraph, of our Constitution guarantees freedom of religion and faith to all the inhabitants. (ibid., p. xi)

A third preface was written by Minister of Religion Kiyahi Haji Saifuddin Zuhri. He called the Bhagavadgita the "fifth Vedic Scripture," and he also praised God [*bersukur kepada Allah subhanahu wa ta'ala*] for the stronger position of religion in the Indonesian society of the period and the contribution of religions toward the improvement of the morality and the character of the Indonesian people.

> [This translation is] in harmony with the magnanimity and tolerance of the Indonesian people, according to the holy vocation of its philosophy, the Pancasila, that functions as its "way of life." This magnanimity and tolerance can be seen clearly in the understanding of the Indonesian people and its democratic implementation of the rules of the vari-

ous religions, Islam, Christianity, Hinduism, Buddhism and other. (ibid., p. xiii)

As statements of three prominent Muslims about the Hindu Scriptures, these quotations would sound quite strange to most Muslims since the times of Muhammad and in most Muslim countries. Apparently, Indonesian politics and the state ideology of Pancasila have influenced a Muslim theology of religions. In this contribution we want to study aspects of this recent development. We have to study aspects since the process is still under way and no final and balanced doctrine has been formulated. Only a tendency and a number of variations, as well as protests against this general tendency, can be presented here. In addition to a study of more scholarly formulated Muslim perceptions of other religions and cultures throughout history,[1] here we will concentrate on recent developments of mostly political character. As the concept of the Pancasila-ideology is very frequently mentioned in the discussions, we do not start with the religious debate and the theological concepts but with the politico-ideological context.

Pancasila: From Political Compromise Toward a Civil Religion

Between 650 and 1000 C.E., when Islam had it first great expansion and period of prosperity, the Indonesian archipelago was experiencing another conversion. During this period, this country became acquainted with the Hindu and Buddhist traditions of India. Some of its rulers were frantic builders, who employed gifted architects. Through this combination Indonesia still has the world's largest Buddhist shrine, the Borobudur of Central Java, with carved reliefs up to more than 3 kilometers long. The "Valley of Kings" of Prambanan, near Yogyakarta, shows the remains of a large number of Hindu temples, which may compete with the vast compounds of Ayodhya and Vrindavan in India nowadays. But all this is the religious past of this country. Traders and wandering mystics introduced the religion of Islam slowly since the twelfth century and nowadays, with a population of nearly 190 million, 87% of whom are Muslim, Indonesia surely has the largest number of Muslims of the world in one country.

During the process of nation-building, at the turn from colonialism toward independence in 1945, the issue of religion was very important. The founding fathers of the country then decided that for the sake of keeping the 2% of Balinese Hindus and the 8% of Christians in Batakland and the Eastern Islands within the Republic, Indonesia should not become an Islamic state. As a compromise the first President, Sukarno, formulated the *Pancasila* (literally, Five-Pillar) ideology, where the belief in the One and Only Deity is formulated as one of the five pillars for the political life of the nation. This formulation sounds quite Islamic, but is not defined as such in a parochial or denominational sense. It is inclusive and therefore also gives a legal and accepted status to all major international religions such as Christianity, Hinduism, and Buddhism.

The Pancasila ideology was not accepted in its final form with the declaration of independence on August 17, 1945, but has shown a development. In a first period, 1945–1955, this ideology was accepted as a necessary compromise between Muslim parties who wanted an Islamic State and Christians from the "outer islands" who threatened to leave the young republic. The compromise formulated not a strict Islamic but also not a secular principle. It was meant as a compromise, and therefore the formulation was rather vague: Ketuhanan yang Maha Esa should be translated as One Superior Deity rather than the more personal concept of God. During the last ten years of the first president, 1955–1965, a large number of other ideological doctrines were launched besides the Pancasila, apparently in an effort to keep the Communist party also within his government coalition, side by side with the Muslim parties. During this period many Muslims felt that the Pancasila was more or less an ideological weapon of their secular and even antireligious opponents.

This view changed after the abortive Communist coup of 1965 and Suharto's rise to power. Since then, this official ideology became one of the most effective weapons against Communism. Communism was banned in the name of the Pancasila. During the 1970s and early 1980s the ideology even became a kind of pseudoreligion or official, civil religion. Through a law of 1984, the Pancasila was declared the sole basis for all social and political organizations. All religious organizations—such as churches, the Catholic Conference of Bishops, the *Majelis Ulama*, or National Council of Muslim Divines, and the *Muhammadiyah*, the 3 million-member social and educational organization—had to include the national ideology in their charter. During the passionate debate about this bill, the government had to declare "that the Pancasila was no religion, but only a political philosophy," a clear sign of the ideological and quasi-religious eminence given to this system.

After 1984 the debate about the Pancasila has only on a few occasions received new impulses. These were invariably at moments when non-Muslims felt the threat of a more outspoken Muslim domination of political life. In 1989, after long and heated debates, a bill on Islamic religious courts was accepted. Christians protested the bill, although it did not bring actual changes for the jurisdiction of Islamic marriages and the administration of cases of inheritance. In fact, the practices as formulated by colonial laws continued. The main issue was that here a law was accepted, giving an official stamp to an institution only serving the Muslim community. Therefore this law was labeled anti-Pancasila by some non-Muslims. The general political atmosphere became somewhat more favored toward Islam, when President Suharto, often considered an adherent of Javanese syncretistic beliefs rather than an outspoken Muslim, performed the hajj in 1990. Since then, the large number of key positions held by Christians in the army and as ministers who controlled the financial and economic affairs has been reduced in favor of Muslims. But still the general policy is that religion should not be a political issue and that the Indonesian nation should be united under the ideological banner of the Pancasila. On the 17th of every month, all schools, hospitals, and government offices celebrate the national independence with a ritual, stressing the importance of this ideology. All addresses at public meetings will somehow mention this ideology. Therefore Pancasila may be compared with Shintoism or Confucianism and be labeled the civil religion of Indonesia. Here we will discuss how this civil religion has influenced the Muslim perceptions of other religions.

True Religion Restricted to Five Religions Only: Muslim Opposition to the *Aliran Kepercayaan*

The 1945 Constitution guarantees freedom of religion in article 29:

1. The state will be based upon [belief in] the One, Almighty God.
2. The state will guarantee to all citizens the freedom to adhere to their religion and fulfil their religious duties according to their religion and faith.

The significance of religion (*agama*) and faith (*kepercayaan*) has been debated since the early 1950s. In the beginning, the general opinion was that both words had the same meaning. After 1965, however, the word *kepercayaan* became more and more identified with more or less organized religious groups, not included under the formula of the five religions: Islam, Protestant Christianity, Catholicism, Buddhism, and Hinduism.[2] This formula of five religions has been expressed in the structure of the Department of Religion since 1967. From 1952 until 1967 the "religious groups" found a place within the structure of the Ministry of Religion. Since 1954 the Ministry of Justice formed as a committee PAKEM (Pengawas Aliran Kepercayaan Masyarakat: Inspection of the Religious Groups among the Society). The main goal of this committee was negative: the ministry watched these groups mainly for reasons of law and order. Especially after the 1965 coup a number of groups were forbidden by the national government, while a number of groups were forbidden by provincial authorities.

Although the Ministry of Religion also participated in PAKEM, a new government body within the ministry of religion was founded in 1971: Lembaga Kerohanian/Keagamaan, commonly called LEMROHAG. The main goals of this administrative body were the following:

1. To control the religious groups
2. To give information and guidance to members of these groups in order to bring them back to their original religion
3. To carry out research
4. To cooperate with other institutes, national as well as international (for the sake of international cooperation, the name *Religious Life and Mystics Institute* was chosen)
5. To promote religious harmony. (Badjuri 1971: 4 and 19–20)

A number of national religious groups were mentioned, followed by some international mystical groups: "Moral re-armament movement; AMORC (A Mystical Order Rosae Crusae [*sic*]); Subud; Rotary Club; Theosophical Society; IHEU: International Humanist and Ethical Union." *Bien étonnées de se trouver ensemble*! This international collection also shows that the definition of *Aliran Kepercayaan* as mystical or religious groups is rather vague.

Official criteria have never been established for the definition of religion, but in practice a religion only could be accepted within the Ministry of Religion when it had (a) faith in One God, (b) international recognition, (c) a holy scripture, and (d) a prophet. This last aspect, however, remained debated and finally was left out altogether. Some Muslims tried to restrict the definition of recognized religion to religions of revelation (*agama wahyu* or *agama samawi*) as distinct from natural religions (*agama duniawi*), but the Buddhist and Hindu communities in Indonesia had some problems in adapting themselves to this definition. The Aliran Kepercayaan generally could not find this recognition in Indonesian politics.[3]

There were some dissidents from this official political viewpoint, however. Within the Ministry of Education and Culture many officials and a succeeding series of ministers sympathized with the Taman Siswa movement of Ki Ajar Dewantara. This educational movement was very close to some forms of Javanese theosophy. The administration of the Aliran Kepercayaan therefore since the early 1970s became the duty of the Ministry of Education and Culture. From the viewpoint of the Ministry of Religion this was because these movements could be considered groups supporting traditional Indonesian arts, dance, music, philosophy, but not, strictly speaking, religion.

This viewpoint of the Ministry of Religion could not always be maintained. The 1973 People's Congress[4] defined the Kepercayaan as an independent but legitimate option within the terms of Pancasila. The interpretation of this recognition remained debated. In most places it was impossible to have the name of an Aliran Kepercayaan on one's identity card, and the same People's Congress also strengthened the position of the functionaries of the five religions in the field of marriage. In most areas, adherents of Aliran Kepercayaan had to marry according to Muslim ritual (cf. Stange 1986: 90–91).

The strong position of religion in general after 1965 and the unclear position of the Aliran Kepercayaan may be illustrated in a collection of prayers, published by Haji Zubaidi Badjuri of Lemrohag, mentioned previously. In 1974 a collection of 38 prayers, to be recited by government officials at national ceremonies was published by this body within the Ministry of Religion. Some prayers are outspoken Islamic, with many Arabic phrases, praise to Allah, and salutation to the Prophet Muhammad. There is also a prayer to be recited at the National Commemoration of Heroes in the Struggle for Independence. This prayer clearly is an effort to compose an "interreligious" prayer:

> Oh God, oh Lord, bestow reward and remuneration upon all the heroes of our nation, who died in the battle of a just fight, according to their endeavor and devotion, their weaknesses and sins . . . (Badjuri 1974: 14–15)

At several national occasions and ceremonies representatives of the five recognized religions say their prayers, sometimes also the opportunity is given to a representative of the Aliran Kepercayaan. Every week the five religions have 30 minutes on the national and regional TV and the Aliran Kepercayaan also receive their 30 minutes. In the National Holiday Park, Taman Mini Indonesia Indah, an open-air museum of Indonesian culture near Jakarta, a special area is devoted to religious buildings; the Aliran Kepercayaan were also allowed to have a house of prayer in this area.

On August 18, 1978, the Minister of Religion issued a Letter of Instruction to all Governors of the (then) 26 Provinces of Indonesia:

1. In the Indonesian Republic no ceremony of marriage, oath or burial following the rituals of Aliran Kepercayaan is recognized. On identity cards no such Aliran Kepercayaan may be mentioned as "religion."
2. Adherents of religions who (also) follow an Aliran Kepercayaan still belong to their religion. Therefore we do not recognize a ceremony of marriage according to Aliran Kepercayaan or an oath according to an Aliran Kepercayaan.

This letter to the governors was strengthened by an instruction from the president, dated September 27, 1978 (*Buku Pedoman* 1985–1986: 62–63).

Badjuri (1971: 12) mentions no fewer than 15 terms for the religious groups discussed in this paragraph: *kebatinan, kepercayaan, kerochanian, kegiatan keagamaan, aliran faham, aliran kerochanian, aliran agama, aliran kepercayaan, keyakinan, filsafat, mistik, tasauf, tarikat, kejiwaan,* and *klenik*. After 1970 the term *kepercayaan* became dominant due to its legal basis, because the word is used in the Constitution. In fact, there are still two kinds of Aliran Kepercayaan in Indonesia. One group consists of the "new religions," revivals of mostly Javanese folklore, mysticism, and tradition, very often modernized with theosophical elements or doctrines taken from modern philosophy. Besides this group there is a very different one: the tribal religions, considered as the relics of "animism" in Indonesia, mostly concentrated in the mountainous areas of the islands outside Java. These adherents of tribal religions, of course, cannot be "brought back" to their original religion, but are considered as objects of mission activities, especially for Muslims and Christians.

An example of the first group can be found in the vicissitudes of the contemporary religious movement of the Madrais in West Java, an area of its own, with Sundanese language and culture, generally considered to be more orthodox Islamic than Central Java.[5] In 1923 Madrais, a member of the lower nobility in the village of Cigugur and former student at an Islamic school (*pesantren*), declared himself the founder of a new religious movement, Agama Djawa Sunda (ADS). In a period when the conflicts between orthodox and legalistic Islam and the more mystical tendencies became sharper, and when the nobility had no political power but tried to develop a refined culture in their old palaces, Madrais started a rather sophisticated and culturally refined religious movement focusing on folklore, dances, music, and religio-philosophical meetings in his palace of Cigugur. The movement was (as with independent churches in Africa today) closely bound to the person of the founder. During colonial times, this movement was not banned by the government. Madrais died in 1939 and was succeeded by his son Tejabuana. In 1964 the provincial government of West Java banned the ADS as a subversive movement. The movement was accused of having Communist sympathies. Here we have to remember that the Indonesian army in West Java was the strongest anti-Communist group. Before the 1965 coup, Suharto, later to become president, was commander of the Western Javanese Siliwangi division. In this period the Madrais had built up strong anti-Islamic sentiments and probably joined Communist leaders for political support and survival—apparently in vain. A choice had to be made, and the ADS leader decided to become a Catholic. The Catholic priests arrived, baptized and spent a lot of development money on this first major group of Sundanese who converted to Christianity. Tejabuana and, after his death, his son Djatikusumah were still recognized as leaders of the movement by the foreign missionaries, but they were given no important functions (and not much money!) in the Catholic structures. In 1981 Djatikusumah and hundreds of his followers publicly announced they were leaving the Catholic religion and going back to the Madrais movement. They sought official recognition for their movement as an Aliran Kepercayaan. They thought that the time was suited for this action, as the palace of Djatikusumah was rebuilt with the help of the Ministry of Education and Culture and was officially inaugurated October 21, 1981, by its secretary general. As already noted, the Ministry of Education and Culture is responsible for the government control and support of the Aliran Kepercayaan. Support from this ministry did not prove to be strong enough: the military commanders of West Java issued a new prohibition of the Madrais movement. This prohibition was inspired by anti-Communist feelings and also by the general aversion from outspoken non-Islamic mystical groups under the label of Aliran Kepercayaan. So, here we see the Muslim generals of the army giving support to conversion to Christianity by a movement that still in its doctrine and practice may be considered "theosophical Muslim" (Komaruddin Hidayat 1982, Straathof 1970).

A case of a tribal religion under attack from the side of Islam and Christianity can be found in the island of Kalimantan (Borneo). Here the conversion to one of the major religions started centuries ago and accelerated in the modern Pancasila society of Indonesia—not only due to the spread of literacy, better roads, electricity, radio and TV, but also due to the requirement by the Indonesian state of membership of a major religion. In the case of the Dayak tribal people of Kalimantan, the anthropologist Douglas Miles found that the boundaries between tribal religion and universal religion were made less clear by Christians than by Muslims. Practices such as circumcision and abstinence from alcohol and pork are very strong symbols of the newness of Islam, while Christianity (even before missionaries started a theory of inculturation) has a more lenient doctrine and practice: "Christian missionaries have been preaching in Central Kalimantan for over a century and in many of their reports the same complaint recurs: those they have baptised have reverted to Paganism. . . . Islamic principles, as implemented in Kuala Karis, obstruct a convert's regression to traditional custom" (Miles 1976: 98–99). Some Dayak groups, however, tried to start a revival of an independent "animistic" religion and sought official recognition as Aliran Kepercayaan. Until now these efforts had no great success.

1971–1993: Policies of Three Ministers of Religion

1971–1978: A Weberian Scholar: H. A. Mukti Ali

The Ministry of Religion of the Indonesian Republic was founded in 1946 as a successor to the colonial offices that controlled and regulated Islam. Until 1970 this ministry was mostly dominated by traditionalist Muslims. In 1971 a modernist Muslim, H. Abdul Mukti Ali, was nominated to the post. Mukti Ali was not related to any Muslim political party. He received part of his education in Islamic schools of Indonesia and Iraq, and part at McGill University, Montreal, Canada. He participated in international meetings of dialogue under the auspices of the World Council of Churches.

For the general policy of his department he wanted to apply the theory of Max Weber (on the relationship between Protestantism and capitalism) to Indonesia and religion in general. All religions should become stimulated to participate in socioeconomic development. Religious schools were stimulated to concentrate on traditional religious learning and teaching, as well as to add training of practical skills. Foreign development organizations were invited to help Islamic schools with small-scale development projects in building, agriculture, and poultry. Mukti Ali, an outspoken Muslim, strictly separated the religious doctrines from these development projects. Religions were urged to cooperate in economic projects, but in the field of religious doctrine, all religions should show respect for different convictions.

Boland summarized his ideas on a Muslim theology of religions as follows:

> It could be said that Islam has had a kind of "theology of religions" from the very beginning. This Islamic "theology of religions" differs in one basic aspect from tendencies within Judaism and Christianity. The latter both tend to exclusiveness, either because of a nationalistic interpretation of being the chosen people, or because of the doctrine concerning Christ as the only way to salvation. Islam, however, began by thinking "inclusively": the Prophet was sent to confirm the message of his predecessors. . . . Mukti Ali advocates a dialogue on a high level by means of comparative religion, between qualified representatives of various religions. A meeting of religions, however, is not only a question of words and theories, let alone of theological discussions on strictly religious problems. According to Mukti Ali, it also includes practical co-operation. So the "meeting" or "dialogue" between adherents of various religions is also a question of daily life, of being involved in current problems of the world in which we live. (Boland 1971: pp. 205–211)

In the field of national politics Mukti Ali has to be mentioned as the minister who assisted the process of *penyederhanaan*, the reduction of four Islamic parties to one Islamic party. This new combined Islamic party was not allowed to use an Islamic name or label. Government interference within the party became very strong, and this process therefore became part of the depoliticization of Indonesian Islam. Mukti Ali was not, it is true, the main orchestrator of this process, but he supported it. Intra- and interreligious conflicts therefore were neutralized by political measures.

1978–1983: Alamsyah Ratu Perwiranegara: A Politician Promotes Law and Order between Religions

From 1978 to 1983 the post of Minister of Religion was held by Alamsyah Ratu Perwiranegara, an army general. Alamsyah surely was not a scholar, but rather a political figure. His main concern as a member of the army was national stability and law and order. He used to talk about Ireland and Lebanon as countries where religious pluralism were very negative factors. He started a threefold program of religious harmony: (a) internal harmony among various factions within a certain religion; (b) harmony between the various religions; (c) harmony between the various religions and the government. In these three fields he started a series of encounters, where representatives of groups were invited to talk and work together.

In order to sketch the background of this policy we want to elaborate here on several incidents, that took place before and during the first years of Alamsyah's period as Minister of Religion. In 1975 President Suharto had proposed the founding of a *Majelis Ulama* (Council of Islamic Scholars/Leaders): "The Catholic community already is organized through the Conference of Catholic Bishops of Indonesia, while the Protestants have a Council of Churches representing them. Also the Hindu and Buddhist communities have their representation, while there is a Secretariat for the Aliran Kepercayaan."[6] A Majelis Ulama was then founded with the double task of promoting unity and solidarity among the Muslim community and representing Islam toward the government. Haji Abdul Malik ibn Abdulkarim Amrullah (Hamka) as a well-known Islamic leader—writer of novels, popular books on religion, and a 30-volume Qur'ān commentary, and a member of the board of the modernist Muhammadiyah organization—was asked to accept the position of general chairman. He accepted it after consultations with the board of the Muhammadiyah, but he refused to receive a government salary or facilities of a car and a driver, preferring to remain as independent from the government as possible.

The execution of the task of promoting unity among the Muslims will be left out of consideration here as it is rather difficult to give a final judgment. Hamka was certainly chosen because he was a member of the board of Muhammadiyah who could also be accepted by members of the other great Islamic organization of Indonesia, the Nahdlatul Ulama.

Through the Majelis Ulama the Muslim community was represented in the Council of Consultation between Religious Communities (Badan Konsultasi antar Umat Beragama). There Hamka strongly opposed the efforts of one religion (in this case, Christianity) to make proselytes from the ranks of another religion (in this case Islam). In 1978 the Majelis Ulama strongly supported the government decision, one of the first measures taken by Alamsyah, to limit the number of foreign missionaries and to regulate foreign aid given through churches.

In 1981 the *fatwa* department of the Majelis Ulama issued a prohibition of participation in Christmas celebrations by Muslims. Especially in Protestant environments, Christmas celebrations had come into existence and non-Christians were invited to participate. The Majelis Ulama received many complaints about Muslim pupils in Christian schools who were urged to appear in pageants and to act as Joseph or Mary or as an angel in Christmas plays. Others complained that they had to sing Christmas songs at school or at Christmas office meetings. To people who complained, some Christians had answered that the harmony of religions would be endangered if they should refuse participation. Many pupils at schools dared not complain, for fear of repercussions during their examinations.

The prohibition by the Majelis Ulama which strongly rejected participation in Christmas celebration only entered the newspapers on May 5, 1981, although the decision was dated March 7. On May 6 newspapers reported that on April 23 a meeting was held between leaders of the Majelis Ulama and the Minister of Religious Affairs and that on April 30 the Majelis Ulama had made the decision to withdraw the *fatwa* from circulation. The withdrawal was signed by Hamka and not by K. H. Syukri Ghozali, head of the *fatwa* department that issued the prohibition. On May 7, 1981, Hamka wrote a letter in his magazine *Panji Masyarakat*, stating that the *fatwa* should not be considered wrong and invalid: taking it out of circulation did not diminish the value of the fatwa itself, since it was founded on the Qur'ān and the *hadith* of the Prophet. Hamka added: "Religious scholars are indeed the heirs of the prophets: from these they inherit the obligation to call for the good and to warn against evil. From these too they inherit the slander and contempt that they received. . . . Are religious scholars only teachers that can be ordered or dismissed arbitrarily? And if a meeting must be closed may one be summoned: 'Hey, nice man, just say a prayer!'"

In that same declaration Hamka twice made an odd mistake. He mentioned three things that are especially forbidden for Muslims when they attend Christmas meetings: to light a candle, to eat the bread that is considered to be the Body of Christ, and to drink the water [*sic*: twice!] that is considered to be the Blood of Christ. A general chairman of a Council of Religious Scholars should know better! By a letter dated May 19, 1981, Hamka resigned as general chairman of the Majelis Ulama. He did not wait for acknowledgment from the Minister of Religious Affairs (chairman of the Constituent Council to the Majelis Ulama) as he considered himself to be appointed only by his fellows scholars in the council.

The Minister of Religious Affairs, Alamsyah, afterward denied that he could intervene in this affair: "I cannot intervene, as I also cannot intervene in the Council of Catholic Bishops" (*Pelita*, May 25, 1981). At a meeting on August 20, 1981, the Constitutive Council to the Majelis Ulama under the chairmanship of the Minister of Religious Affairs chose K. H. Syukri Ghozali, the former head of the *fatwa* department and signatory of the *fatwa* under discussion, to be the new general chairman of the Majelis Ulama. The minister issued a letter dated September 1, 1981, in which he made a distinction between ritual and ceremonial aspects in Christmas ceremonies, as well as in ceremonies of other religions. As to ritual aspects, participation should be restricted to adherents of the religions concerned, while attendance and even participation in the ceremonial aspects are allowed also to people of other religions.

In the whole affair it was not only the issue of Christmas and the relations between Muslims and Christians that was involved. Minister of Religious Affairs Alamsyah accused Hamka of acting against the state ideology, the Pancasila, while Hamka accused the government of interfering with religion and of attempts to introduce the Pancasila as a new religion of the state.

Meanwhile Hamka died 24 July 1981 at the age of 75. According to his own wish, he was buried in a very simple way, only a few hours after he died. The Minister of Religious Affairs assisted in his burial.

We have presented this case in full detail here in order to proffer several elements of intra- and inter-religious conflicts as background for Alamsyah's program of interreligious harmony that will be presented as follows.

1983–1993: Munawir Syadzali, Internal Discussion within the Muslim Community

A third minister of religious affairs to be discussed here is Munawir Syadzali. Born in the Surakarta area of Central Java in a strongly religious family, he received a good secular education, but also a sound religious training in the Sultanate school for religious officials, *Mamba'ul Ulum* of Surakarta. After independence he pursued an M.A. in political science at Georgetown University, Washington, and started a career with the Foreign Office. In 1983–1985 he became the national promoter among Muslims of the acceptance of a law on social organizations, which formulated the Pancasila as the sole basis for social and political life. This law was the final step toward the depoliticization of Islam. One might also say that this law restricted the validity of Islamic doctrine and rules toward a limited number of aspects of society.

Munawir Syadzali also became known as a promoter of new thinking within Islam, sometimes coined as "contextualization." Several times he declared that not all the rules of the Qur'ān were valid for all times. Some precepts were valid only for the time of the Prophet. Muhammad's successor, ʿUmar, a companion and close friend of the Prophet, without hesitation changed some rules of the Qur'ān and the Prophet in an effort toward contextualization, *maslahah* or *istihsān*, to use the Western as well as the Arabic terminology.

In his policy, Munawir Syadzali paid less attention than Alamsyah to interreligious relations. He also diminished the attention given to the relation between religion and development. His prime goal was the internal promotion of the Islamic community, through improvement of the religious courts and religious education. His policy was not reactionary: he sent more than a hundred men and women of the academic staff of his ministry and the theological Islamic academies abroad for study, mostly to the Netherlands, the United States, Australia, and Canada. He organized many upgrading courses for Islamic judges, but also increased the number of women judges in religious courts. Notwithstanding a strong opposition from both Christians and more secularized Muslims, in 1989 the Parliament passed a new bill on religious courts, strengthening the legal base of this institute. During his period of office as minister, the policy of the Ministry of Religion toward mixed marriages became more strict. Until the early 1980s Muslim women still could marry non-Muslim men, by applying to the *catatan sipil*, the civil administration. In fact, the 1974 Marriage Law did not give strict rules for mixed marriages and only stated that marriages should be contracted according to the religion of the couple. Islamic law does not allow the marriage of a Muslim woman to a non-Muslim husband. Since 1987 in most areas of Indonesia, such a marriage became impossible (Pompe 1988). In this aspect, the policy of Munawir Syadzali was a return to a more strict Islamic rule in this field.

In 1993 President Suharto nominated the medical doctor Tarmizi Taher to the post of Minister of Religion for his sixth period as president and leader of the government. Taher has made his career in the army, where he built up the work of the Islamic army chaplains. Some observers consider him an example of the "return to denominationalism" of this period. The number of Christian ministers under the new cabinet was reduced from six to three (among about 40 members of the cabinet), and they lost their prominent position in financial and economic affairs. The so-called RMS (Radius Prawiro as Minister of Finance; Mooy, director of the Central Bank; and Sumarlin, Minister of Economic Affairs) were succeeded by two outspoken Muslims and one Catholic. Together with other nominations, this was considered another step in the direction of *penghijauan* (literally, "greening") of the Indonesian government, green being considered the color related to the Prophet Muhammad and Islam.

Some Cases of Government-Sponsored Encounter of Religions and Its Consequences for a Muslim Theology of Religions

As mentioned, during the fiscal year 1979–1980 Minister of Religion Alamsyah launched a new program of interreligious dialogue. This is not the place to discuss this project as a whole, but we want to mention a few aspects of this process in order to make some conclusions related to a changing Muslim theology of (other) religions. In many places the program brought together a number of qualified representatives of the major religions. The first aim was to support the government programs of Pancasila indoctrination, economic development, family planning, health care, and environmental issues.

One of the first experiences was an interreligious meeting in Ujung Pandang, the capital of the Province of South Sulawesi (*Buku Laporan* 1979). Twenty-six students were brought together: ten from the State Academy of Islamic Studies, seven from a Protestant Theological College, five from a Catholic Seminary, and four from the Medical Faculty of the State University. The represented religions held exchanges of lectures about their Holy Scripture and environmental and health problems. Then they were divided into four groups and held inspection about environmental and health issues in four villages of mixed Buginese, Makassarese, Toraja, and Javanese descent (Toraja and some Javanese "immigrants" providing the Christians among the population, the original population of Buginese and Makassarese generally being Muslims only). The four groups held inquiries in the villages and made some suggestions for improvements. On Friday and Sunday the Muslims and Christians held sermons on environmental issues in their respective places of worship. On the last day of the program (lasting five days only), the common conclusions were that this program proved the importance of religion for environmental improvement; that the program stimulated and promoted tolerance and mutual understanding; finally, that the program convinced the local people about the important relationship between religious doctrine and everyday life. In the 118 pages of the report no negative issues were dealt with. The whole process clearly was started, encouraged, and well paid for by the government in order to show good relations between the religious communities on the basis of a common interest and conviction.

In the same program research was carried out in West Lombok about relations between Hindus and Muslims (*Hubungan antara*, 1979). In this area 84.6% is Muslim, 11.3% Hindu (descendants from Balinese rulers, who colonized Lombok between 1750 and 1904), 2.2% Buddhist (mostly Chinese), and 1.2% Christian. A mixed research group of Muslims and Hindus started with a hypothesis that "the relation between the Muslim and the Hindu community cannot yet be considered as good." At the opening session of the research project some general speeches were given. The leader of the Hindu team started with an explanation of Hinduism, too curious not to be summarized here:

> Hinduism is built on five pillars (*Panca Crada*): (a) Belief in Brahman, the one and only God (*keyakinan terhadap adanya Tuhan yang Maha Esa*); (b) Atman, belief in the soul; (c) Karma Phala: man will in the life hereafter receive rewards for all his good and bad deeds; (d) Punarbhawa or reincarnation; (e) Moksa, liberation, the return of the individual soul to his Lord. In the explanation it was stated that the Hindu divines always stress, that "God is one only, but the wise men call Him with many names." Elements of faith, such as the belief in a soul, in reincarnation and in reward of good and bad acts, all have to be appreciated as stimulating for a good ethics of work. (p. 34)

Finally it was concluded that there were some occasional conflicts between the two communities, but these conflicts were usually about property, irrigation, etc., and not on religious issues, strictly speaking. Therefore, the research group concluded that the relation between the communities was good: "Both are dynamic, creative, live in peace and mutual understanding and support the national development" (p. 55).[7]

The Ministry of Religion organized a great number of such meetings and spent large funds on them. These meetings received ample attention in the press, and some 20 volumes were published with the proceedings of the meetings. These books are full of support for development programs, the Pancasila ideology, and the mutual understanding of the religious communities; sometimes they also contain descriptions of minor conflicts. It is always stressed that cooperation is possible in many practical fields, but with regard to ritual, religious ceremonies, places, and houses for prayer, as well as with regard to special theological doctrines, the special rules and beliefs of the various religions have to be respected.

Private Initiatives for the Encounter and Cooperation of Religions

The Indonesian government is the main promoter for interreligious cooperation and for mutual understanding. In the Muslim communities many are worried about the ongoing movement of conversion to Christianity, while in the Christian communities many are anxious about a loss of their privileges. The relationship between Muslims and Christians has been labeled a relation of two minorities, which are cautious about the other. While being the majority according to their number, Muslims feel economically, culturally, and sometimes even politically a minority. The economy is for a large part in the hands of Chinese businessmen, who are often closer to Christians than to Muslims. In the field of culture, Christian schools, hospitals, and newspapers are considered as meeting higher standards than Muslim ones. In the area of politics, the aspirations of part of the Muslim community to declare Indonesia an Islamic state have been rejected. Many Christians are afraid that they, being a minority, will be treated as a minority in the same sense as is the case of their coreligionists in Malaysia. This position of "two minorities" prevented movements toward broader cooperation until 1990. Related to the growing self-confidence of Indonesian Muslims since the end of the 1980s, some private initiatives for interreligious contacts have started.

Islamic organizations (as distinct from membership of Muslim brotherhoods, *ṭuruq*, or adherence to the Muslim community as such) started with the arrival of modernist/reformist Islam in 1905. In 1912 Muhammadiyah was founded in the city of Yogyakarta, and it soon obtained members in all urban and some rural areas of the country. With some 3 million members, Muhammadiyah is probably the largest Muslim organization in the whole world. Muhammadiyah is active in the fields of education, health care, administration of mosques, and *daʿwah*, the internal mobilization of the Muslim community. Muhammadiyah was partly founded as an answer to the activities of Christian missionaries, and from the beginning the organization has taken a clearly anti-Christian policy, primarily by trying to provide social and economic help for Muslims, but also through anti-Christian polemics. This Islamic defense against Christian missions is characteristic for most reformist movements. The most outspoken polemics were held by the *Persatuan Islam* of Ahmad Hassan and Muhammad Natsir. During the 1980s Natsir became active in the Dewan Dakwah Islamiyah Indonesia. Their journal *Majalah Media Dakwah* took a firm position against the moderate policies of the Indonesian government. Many issues contain cases of the "ongoing Christianization of Indonesia." The Islamic community and the government are asked to take measures against the "aggressive strategies of foreign missionaries."[8]

Since the 1920s the traditionalist *ʿulama* founded some organizations, based on the leadership of the large rural Islamic boarding schools, *pesantren*. The most important of these is the *Nahdlatul Ulama*, founded in 1926. While the reformist organizations wanted to purify Indonesian Islam from pre-Islamic elements, this Nahdlatul Ulama and similar organizations have always shown much more tolerance toward practices like the veneration of saints, holy places, and traditional Javanese rituals. They also showed a less polemic attitude toward other religions, probably because of their base in the countryside, where these new religions were still rather unknown.

During the 1980s the charismatic Abdurrachman Wahid took over the leadership of Nahdlatul Ulama, founded by his grandfather and for some time also led by his father. Abdurrachman Wahid and a small circle of intellectuals around him became close to some progressive Christian theologians who were sympathetic toward the Latin American theology of liberation. In the Indonesian context of strong anti-Communist feelings, this theology was reformulated as a "theology of development." In 1988 and 1989 the Nahdlatul Ulama held two national meetings on this topic, where representatives from all major religions were invited to discuss this theology of development and the relationship between religion and socioeconomic life. Many of the debates focused on the relation between mysticism and action, individual piety, and social engagement. Also the reinterpretation of the Scriptures was an important theme, where the concept of "contextualization" was used by Muslims and Christians alike. In his 1989 speech, Abdurrachman Wahid presented a general, "nondenominational" concept of religion rather than the Muslim intellectual heritage. The Jesuit Father Sastrapratedja took the example of the Javanese version of the Arjuna story from the Mahabharata and explained that Arjuna, fasting and meditating on a mountain and resisting all temptations of the mundane life, has to be considered an example of asceticism that prepares for action. It may be clear that these interreligious meetings were not looking to the past polemical topics between Christian and Muslims, but looked forward toward cooperation for development, in line with the government efforts in this field (Steenbrink 1989: 22–23).

One of these intellectuals, close to Abdurrachman Wahid, is Nurcholis Madjid. After a traditional Islamic education in Indonesia, he pursued Islamic studies with Fazlur Rahman in Chicago, where he defended a dissertation on the theology of Ibn Taymiyya in 1984. After his return to Indonesia, Madjid settled in Jakarta and founded the Yayasan Paramadina (the Paramadina Foundation), a center for courses, seminars, and sophisticated lectures on religion and society. Some rumors about high entrance fees and luxurious settings (prestigious hotels like Hilton, Holiday Inn, Mandarin, and Hyatt) could not prevent the solid growth of the movement. This audience hoped not only to receive a thorough instruction in a liberal and modern interpretation of Islam but also to meet other members of the highest levels of Jakarta's elite. Madjid's lectures during the period 1987–1991 were published in a 626-page volume in 1992, preceded by a new introduction of 124 pages that was written by Madjid while he was a visiting professor at the Institute of Islamic Studies of McGill University, Montreal, Canada. In this collection, entitled *Islam, Doctrine and Culture: A Critical Study of the Problems of Faith, Humanity and Modernism*, he often discusses against the background of American society, fundamentalism (rather Christian than Muslim), the history of Islam, and colonialism. His is a quest of the consequences of all these themes for the formulation and implementation of Islamic values as wordings of universal values. Certainly, this book does not present a parochial Islam but a nondenominational faith, one faith among other belief-systems, all in contact and dialogue with each other. Madjid rejected the slogan "Spirituality Yes! Organized Religion: NO!" as the summary for his proposals, but his definition of Islam as "surrender" comes close to this idea, as may be shown from an excerpt from a speech delivered in 1992:

> If we understand these concepts [i.e., of *Islam* and *hanif*], then we also understand why Abraham, the "father of monotheism" is mentioned in the Koran as someone, who was not bound to any form of 'organized religion', but is depicted as an honest and sincere seeker of the Truth (*hanif*) and one who really surrendered himself (a *Muslim* in the true sense of the word) to the Truth that is the Lord. We then also understand why the Prophet Muhammad, God's praise be upon him, was ordered by God to follow the example of the religion of the Prophet Abraham, the *hanif* and strict monotheist. (Cf. Qur'ān 3:85 and 3:67) (Madjid 1993: 19)

Besides serving his own Paramadina Foundation, Madjid is a professor at the State Islamic University of Jakarta and a senior researcher at the Indonesian Foundation for Scientific Research. He was among the persons to deliver sermons in the presidential mosque and clearly was supported by ministers of religion such as Mukti Ali and Munawir Syadzali. He is not an isolated individual, uttering some liberal ideas about religion, but until now represents a larger group. As an advisor he is also related to the newest effort to promote a liberal and modern style of Islam among the Indonesian middle class Ikatan Cendekiawan Muslim Indonesia (ICMI), founded in 1990 by the then Minister of Research and Technology, B. J. Habibie. (Hefner 1993)

Abdurrachman Wahid and some other prominent Muslim leaders cooperated in the only Christian initiative for interreligious dialogue, Dialog Antariman: Interfaith Dialogue (DIAN), also with an English name Institute for Inter-Faith Dialogue in Indonesia (INTERFIDEI), founded in 1992 in Yogyakarta by the Protestant Dr. Sumartana. Sumartana did not include the word for religion, *agama*, in the name of his institute because he wanted to stress common goals and concerns of individual believers rather than the process of bringing together institutionalized religions.

In 1990 the Department of Comparative Religion of the State Institute of Islamic Studies, IAIN Sunan Kalijaga of Yogyakarta, founded an Indonesian branch of the International Association for the History of Religions (IAHR). According to the policy of this institute, the academic study of religion should directly support the efforts for harmony and mutual understanding of religions. This is also clear from the declaration, issued from the First National Congress of Religions in Indonesia, held in commemoration of the World's Parliament of Religions of Chicago 1893, in September 1993 in Yogyakarta. At the initiative of Mukti Ali and his Department of Comparative Religion, a National Foundation for the Study of Interreligious Harmony was created.

Opponents

The promotion of interreligious harmony by the government, supported by some private initiatives, was not carried out without protest from several groups of Muslims. Previously we mentioned the case of Hamka, which was related to ceremonies of Christmas and other protests against the dominance of the Pancasila ideology as a new civil religion. The debate about the acceptance of the Pancasila as the sole basis of sociopolitical life made a number of Muslims voice their protest against this "new religion."[9]

Protests against the Suharto government have often been formulated in religious terms in the 1980s. The case of Imran, leader of an airplane hijacking in 1981, became famous in national affairs. At his trial Imran defended his action as a legitimate fight against the new polytheism of the Pancasila. God was defined in this ideology as *Ketuhanan*, an abstract word, that might indicate a plural as a similar word *gunungan* (mountain range) also indicates a plurality. In 1985 there were serious bombings on the restored Borobudur Buddhist shrine. The action was defended by mentioning the action of the Prophet Abraham, who also was forced to leave his country. A pamphlet spread in a number of mosques said that "this action was necessary in order to stop the restoration of polytheism in this country. Now these activists are labeled terrorists in the newspapers, although they just followed the example of the Prophet Abraham." Violent riots with many casualties in the harbor area, Tanjung Priok, of Jakarta in 1984 and in South Sumatra in 1989, were caused by a mixture of social, economic, and religious protest and were also partially formulated as an action against the replacement of the Islamic doctrines by the Pancasila ideology.

A prominent Muslim intellectual who fiercely opposed the imposition of the Pancasila doctrine as the sole foundation for the Indonesian state, was Deliar Noer, a political scientist. In a booklet published in 1983, he pointed out that the two founding fathers of the Pancasila ideology, Sukarno and Muhammad Hatta, both founded political parties with ideological foundations differing from the Pancasila. Sukarno founded his Nationalist Party on the *Marhaen* principle, after a petty farmer who was taken as symbol of the majority of the Indonesian people. Muhammad Hatta founded his Islamic Democratic Party on the two principles of Islam and Pancasila (Noer 1983: 42–54).

In September 1984 a Muslim activist, Abdul Qadir Djaelani, planned a petition to be sent to the parliament in order to oppose the Pancasila as the sole foundation of the Indonesian society. In mosque sermons he also uttered criticism against the state ideology. These activities were brought in relation with the Tanjung Priok riots, and therefore he was sentenced to jail in 1985. He was not the only preacher to be accused of subversion: dozens of preachers were sentenced in the 1980s for similar reasons (Baers 1988).

To add just a few recent examples to a long series of written, vocal, and sometimes even violent protests against this religious policy, we want to mention here a doctoral thesis submitted in 1989 at the State Academy of Islamic Studies of Jakarta by Harifun Cawidu and published in 1991. The thesis discusses the concept of *kufr* in the Qur'ān and Islamic theology. One of Cawidu's conclusions is that the Jews and Christians have many concepts in common with the Muslims, but still they have to be named unbelievers or *kuffār* (s. *kāfir*) as their belief often is not correct and full with deviations from truth.

A more popular example can be taken from upheaval in Muslim circles in the provinces of South Tapanuli and West Sumatra. A local publisher was blamed for several books in the field of Pancasila ideology and Islamic religion. In one of the books, used in secondary schools, a multiple-choice question was formulated as follows: "In our class, only one pupil is Muslim. We urge him to change his religion and to join ours." Of course, the right answer here is that it is not allowed to urge someone to change his religion, but still the publisher of the book was blamed for citing this example (only one Muslim in a school class). In a book on the basic principles for the Islamic religion, religious tolerance was recommended. A good example of this is the Taman Mini Indonesia Indah, an open-air museum of Indonesian culture near Jakarta, where the five religions and the Aliran Kepercayaan have their houses of prayer side by side, as already mentioned. The book concluded that "this shows the unity of the nation that can be created by building houses of prayer side by side." In another book on the instruction of the Pancasila ideology, the pupils are told about religious holidays. The pupils have to design a greeting card for classmates or other people belonging to another religion. These cards have to be put on the class walls. In a class of Muslim children, the wall was full with Christmas cards, and this evoked quite negative feelings with some Muslims (Mafri Amir 1991).

For many Indonesian Muslims, the only religion to be accepted is Islam. In a multireligious state, Christians, Buddhists, and Hindus are accepted as cocitizens, but not as coreligionists. Political statements of Muslims seem to be more liberal than theological statements. Especially in present-day Indonesia with its Pancasila ideology, many prominent Muslims utter political statements about other religions of a very liberal kind. These have to be taken seriously by all students of the Islamic religion, as they are taken seriously by Muslims themselves.

Development of Institutions for Interreligious Harmony between 1993 and 1998

At the State Institute of Islamic Studies of Yogyakarta, IAIN Sunan Kalijaga, Abdul Mukti Ali holds the chair of comparative religion. For this scholar, who was Minister of Religion of Indonesia in the period 1971–1978, the study of comparative religion is not merely an academic affair, but an intellectual exercise, leading towards a greater participation of religious people in national development and interreligious harmony. In order to stimulate these efforts, the Department of Comparative Religion at Sunan Kalijaga already founded an Indonesian branch of the IAHR in 1990. In 1993 this department took the initiative to convene a national conference, commemorating the 1893 World's Parliament of Religions of Chicago.

The conference of 1993 decided to start a new academic association. The LPKUB, Lembaga Pengkajian Kerukunan Umat Beragama, or the Indonesian Institution for the Study of Religious Harmony as it has called itself since 1995, had a quiet start. Like many other associations it started with the organization of seminars and with a new journal *Religiosa, Indonesian Journal on Religious Harmony*. The first seminar, held at Yogyakarta in October 1994, brought together students and young academics of the major religions of Indonesia to discuss the topic of the role of young religious people in national development and religious problems among young people. A second seminar in Yogyakarta in April 1995 brought together religious leaders on the national level. It was the manifest purpose of H. Tarmizi Taher, Minister of Religion in the period 1993–1998, to organize a new forum for institutionalized dialogue and cooperation besides the since 1988 existing, but not very active, Wādah (or: Badan) Musyawarah Antar Umat Beragama, Interreligious Consultative Forum in Jakarta, which in practice only came together in cases of conflicts and problems. Something more positive than conflict prevention should grow.

The journal *Religiosa*, published in English by LPKUB, seeks to communicate to the international academic and political world, partly in order to show that Indonesia is a country where religious tolerance, harmony, and freedom have a high priority. All issues (three have appeared from 1995 until early 1998) have articles written by Indonesians and foreigners, Muslims and non-Muslims, on the ideal and the efforts to promote the ideal.

We find the same lofty but somewhat constrained discourse in a recent publication by H. Tarmizi Taher, *Aspiring for the Middle Path: Religious Harmony in Indonesia* (Jakarta, Center for the Study of Islam and Society, 1997), which brings together 17 of his speeches. In a reprint of a speech in Harvard University in November 1995, the major theme of the book is explained:

> *Ummatan wasatan* (moderate and quality-oriented nation) has been the paradigm adopted to establish a new image of Islam and the Muslim world. . . . This trend of searching for a moderate and quality-oriented *ummah* has been implemented and developed by Southeast Asian Muslims for decades of their development, in particular in Brunei, Indonesia, and Malaysia. Although they are dedicated and devout Muslims, the attitude and the culture of Muslims in this region are less Arabicized. . . . Indonesia could become a leader for developing countries in the common success of material and spiritual development. (pp. 85–86)

However, it was not all a success story that can be told. In 1996 and 1997, Minister of Religion Tarmizi Taher had to go abroad several times in order to correct the image, especially in the United States, about growing problems for Christians in Indonesia. There were cases during riots in East Timor, where the Catholic population set fire to mosques, which they associated with immigrant Muslim traders and government officials and oppression by the Indonesian army since 1975. In many more cases the riots involved Christian churches and Chinese shops, attacked and burned down by Muslim mobs. In an undated paper Tarmizi Taher said:

> The problem of religious upheaval is observable in recent disturbances. The East Timor riots that broke out in November 1995 were associated with Catholicism. In these riots Catholics victimized both Muslims and Protestants and temporarily forced them to leave the province. Catholic mobs burned mosques to the ground and looted Muslim-owned shops. In Situbondo (East Java), Tasikmalaya and Rengasdengklok (both in West Java), Muslims went on a rampage burning churches and shops owned by mostly ethnically Chinese (non-Muslims).
>
> We must be cautious, however, before jumping to the conclusion that the riots are directly related

> to religious causes. As suggested by many erudite and keen observers, the roots of these riots lay not in religious problems. Sociologically, for instance, Indonesian society now is undergoing rapid social changes brought about by national development. The pace of social change is coupled with the globalization process that has also invaded Indonesia during the last decade. Consequently, certain segments of society are experiencing disorientation, dislocation and alienation, all of which is very conducive to social unrest. (p. 44)

In total, some 400 Christian churches were seriously damaged or destroyed and set on fire in the period between July 1995 and early 1998. In nearly all cases, there were yells and graffiti blaming Christians and Chinese and glorifying Islam as the national religion of Indonesia. Was this the end of a dream of harmony and tolerance? The LPKUB was charged with a thorough investigation, in cooperation with the quite critical and leftist Research Center for Rural and Regional Development of the Gadjah Mada University of Yogyakarta. The results of its inquiries were still quite vague and nebulous for outsiders, but clear enough for well-informed political observers: "Generally speaking, conflict and collective violence is part of the political violence in the society. At a higher level, violence happened at the level of state and social structure, done by state apparatus and the agents of big business. As a consequence of the development process emphasizing capital accumulation, the configuration of social stratification can change into a form facilitating the turn up of conflict." The report stressed that this terrible outbreak of riots was related to a general state of uncertainty and conflict, related to the last years of the Suharto era, when corruption reached a peak, government bureaucracy was not trusted any more, and many parties jockeyed for a good position, in preparation for the change of power. In nearly all cases of severe interreligious conflicts, the report could indicate specific political parties who paid and sent agent provocateurs to cause unrest and start riots.

As to specific religious and ethnic policies, the report blamed the government for imposing a kind of harmony rather than admitting and stimulating pluriformity and pursuing a strategy of multiculturalism: "The identity claim of ethnic minority (e.g., Dayak, Timor, perhaps Irian) should neither be answered by the way of segregation (separated identity) nor assimilation (immersed into national identity characterized by ethnic majority). What has happened until now is the way of assimilation that is culturally and politically dominated by Java. The strategy should choose the way of developing pluralism or multiculturalism."

Although a conflict-evading body, LPKUB leadership has since issued more provocative statements. Its position is now in line with that of Nahdlatul Ulama's chairman Abdurrachman Wahid, the defender of a multireligious viewpoint against Muhammadiyah leader Amien Rais, who has always stood for the proportionalist viewpoint: if the Muslims are counted as the vast majority or even about 87% of the total population, this should be confirmed in the political and social institutions of the country. Against this "proportionalist" viewpoint (which is, in fact, the traditional Muslim theory of a tolerant Muslim state), Wahid defends the true Pancasila concept of a basic equality of all religions. In Wahid's perspective the religion of the majority should not become a ruling religion, giving room to minority religions. He has therefore excluded political cooperation with Amien Rais's new party (Partai Amanat Rakyat) and defended the choice of cooperation with the secular democratic nationalists of Megawati Soekarnoputri after the coming 1999 elections.

LPKUB only entered the political observation and debate in mid-1997, some time after the start of the violent actions and the atmosphere of unrest preceding Suharto's fall in May 1998. During this recent period, we have seen another scheme of Muslim-Christian relations, starting not with interreligious dialogue in a narrow sense but with humanitarian help. In Yogyakarta, two organizations have been founded for dialogue and social action. Interfidei/Dian (Institute for Inter-Faith Dialogue in Indonesia) was started by the Protestant theologians Th. Sumartana and Elga Sarapung. Their religious discussions and meetings have concentrated on the formulation of a religious spirituality for the modern era. Their social action has focused on issues such as the poor working conditions of female workers from Indonesia in Hong Kong and Saudi Arabia, the effects of the drought of 1997, and the Asian economic crisis. LKiS, or Lembaga Kajian ilmu-ilmu Sosial (Center for the Study of Social Sciences) in Yogyakarta developed from a debating club organized by young members of Nahdlatul Ulama, mostly students or academic lecturers, into an interreligious forum and center of action, the most provocative Indonesian advocate of a "theology of liberation."

In Jakarta, some new coalitions emerged during the turbulent developments of the growing number of riots, the Asian economic crisis, and the debate about reformation after the fall of the Suharto regime. Abdurrachman Wahid and a majority within the Nahdlatul Ulama have joined a new interreligious group, MADIA (Majlis Dialog antar Iman; Council for Interfaith Dialogue) where instead of *agama* (institutional religion), the word *iman* (personal belief) is used; the leftist Catholic Jesuit priest Sandyawan Sumardi has been a prominent member of it. Muhammadiyah leader Amien Rais could for some time also be counted among the political opposition, because of his very early objection (already in 1995) to a reelection of President Suharto. He has founded an opposition movement, Musyawarah Amanat Rakyat (the Council for the Concern of the People), among whose members is the Jesuit Franz Magnis Suseno. These developments show a growing concern for interreligious solidarity and joint action for democracy and social justice.

Some Conclusions

Ash-Shahrastani noted in his study on the origins of sectarianism in Islam, also considered as the first history of Islamic theology, that theological debates in Islam from the very beginning were related to political issues, such as the imamate. Muslim theologies of religions are also connected with political issues. Such was the *Dīn Ilāhi* of the Moghul Emperor Akbar, and such is the theology of religions related to the Pancasila ideology of modern Indonesia.

The modern Indonesian Muslim theology of religions makes a sharp distinction between non-Islamic religions which may be accepted as such and those which may not. The acceptance is wider than the one mentioned as the "People of the Book" in the Qurʾān. A religious book (internationally recognized) and the confession of one God are absolute criteria. Buddhism, and Balinese and Tengerese variations of Hinduism therefore had to adapt themselves to these criteria. Tribal religions are not accepted as religions; neither are new religious movements labeled as *aliran kepercayaan*.

Aspects of religions that cannot be accepted are still allowed in a "secularized" form, as cultural manifestations and even supported by the Ministry of Education and Culture, where a more liberal trend is manifest than in the army or the Ministry of Religion.

The basic confession of Belief in One God is considered a common obligation for all Indonesian citizens. The basic practices of care for the environment, the poor, the economic development of the country, good health, and harmony between social and ethnic groups are considered common concerns for all recognized religions. Religions are not supposed to be active in practical politics. So, within the Pancasila ideology of present-day Indonesia, the social role of religion is clearly restricted but also prescribed.

For activities related to a special religion, only the fields of ritual, religious ceremonies, and regulations of marriage, divorce, and inheritance are set apart. In these fields no blending of separate religions is possible.

This policy of the Indonesian government may be considered as related to two basic Islamic doctrines: (a) the recognition of an "eternal religion," a basic doctrine, given by God to Adam and to all prophets after him; (b) the proclamation of differing laws (*sharīʿah*) to various communities.

This policy and doctrine presuppose that Islam as a religion is not dominating all aspects of man's life and human society. In fact, this doctrine involves a limitation of the validity of religious rules. This is an antifundamentalist, antitotalitarian Muslim concept of religion. It differs from the liberal Western concept of religion by the unquestioned recognition of the necessity of religion and belief in one God.

NOTES

This is an extended and updated account of my contribution to the Lausanne conference. An earlier version has been published in *Islam and Christian-Muslim Relations* 4(1993): 223–246. The last section was written in August 1998, amidst quick and turbulent changes both in Indonesian politics and in the field of interreligious relations.

1. Cf. Steenbrink 1990a, 1990b, and 1993, chapter 7.

2. On this shift of ideas between 1965 and 1970, see Steenbrink 1972. Confucianism for some time in the early 1960s also was considered as a separate religion, but finally these five were generally accepted, as is shown in the structure of the Ministry of Religious Affairs. The number of five may have a relation with the Indonesian tendency to divide the whole universe into areas of five powers (*macapat*).

3. In the international forum they found more recognition than in the national politics. David Barrett published in 1982 (p. 382) a percentage of not less than

36.4% of "New-Religionists" for mid-1975; this 36.4% is considered as Muslim by the official census. About the debate, see also Stange 1990 in his review of Woodward 1989. The government census of 1980 counted 88% Muslims, 5.8% Protestants, 2.9% Roman Catholics, 2% Hindus, and some 1.5% Buddhists.

4. A People's Congress in Indonesia (MPR: Majelis Permusyawaratan Rakyat) is the highest legislative body. It convenes only once in every five years to define the general guidelines for the national policy in the coming five years.

5. For those unfamiliar with Indonesia, it may be useful to keep in mind that the island of Java has approximately 100 million inhabitants, one third of them in the Province of Sundanese West Java.

6. Speech of President Suharto, June 21, 1975, at the opening of the first National Conference where the Majelis Ulama was constituted; quoted in U. Hasjim 1980: 320.

7. On the real conflict of West Lombok, see Lukman al-Hakim 1980. In January 1980 a Muslim high school student, riding home on his bicycle, injured a Hindu child who was playing on the road. There were some protest demonstrations between the communities during the following days.

8. A collection of these polemic articles is published in Lukman Hakiem 1991.

9. A number of examples are given in Steenbrink 1990c: 136–138.

REFERENCES

Al-Hakim, Lukman. 1980. *Hubungan pemeluk agama Islam dan agama Hindu di Paguban*. Jakarta: Departemen Agama (KITLV Leiden Microfilm 25631984).

Atkinson, 1987. "Religions in Dialogue: The Construction of an Indonesian Minority Religion." In R. Smith Kipp and Susan Rogers (ed.) *Indonesian Religion in Transition* (Tucson: University of Arizona Press, 1987) pp. 171–186.

Badjuri, H. Z. 1971. *Lembaga Kerohanian/Keagamaan (Lemrohag), suatu feasability study*. Jakarta: Departemen Agama.

———. 1974. *Kolleksi Do'a pada upacara-upacara nasional dan penting lainnya*. Jakarta: Lemrohag, Departemen Agama.

Baers, Chris. 1988. "Heilige oorlog, sociaal protest of provokatie? Indonesische moslims en politiek geweld." In Kees van Dijk (ed.), *Islam en politiek in Indonesië*. Muiderberg: Countinho, pp. 51–68.

Barrett, David B. 1982. *World Christian Encyclopedia*. Nairobi: Oxford University Press.

Boland, B. J. 1971. *The Struggle of Islam in Modern Indonesia*. The Hague: Martinus Nijhoff.

Bonneff, Marcel (ed.). 1980. *Pantjasila, Trente Anneés de débats politiques en Indonésie*. Paris: Editions de la Maison des Sciences de l'Homme.

Brown, Iem. 1987. "Contemporary Indonesian Buddhism and Monotheism." *Journal of Southeast Asian Studies* 18: 108–117.

Buku Laporan. 1979. "Buku Laporan Kerja sama sosial Kemasyarakatan di Sulawesi Selatan, 19 s/d 24 Pebruari 1979." Typescript, microfilm in KITLV, Leiden Mf. 32431979.

Buku Pedoman. 1985–1986. *Buku Pedoman Dasar kerukunan Hidup Beragama 1985–1986*. Jakarta: Departemen Agama.

Cawidu, Harifun. 1991. *Konsep kufr dalam Islam: suatu kajian teologis dengan pendekatan tafsir tematik*. Jakarta: Bulan Bintang.

Geertz, Clifford. 1960. *Religion of Java*. New York: Glencoe.

Hakiem, Lukman. 1991. *Fakta dan Data Usaha-Usaha Kristenisasi di Indonesia*. Jakarta: Majalah Media Dakwah.

Hasyim, Umar. 1980. *Ulama pewaris nabi*. Surabaya: Sitti Syamsiyah.

Hefner, Robert W. 1987a. "Islamizing Java? Religion and Politics in Rural Java." *Journal of Asian Studies* 46: 533–554.

———. 1987b. "The Political Economy of Islamic Conversion in Modern East Java." In W. R. Roff (ed.), *Islam and the Political Economy of Meaning*. London: Croom Helm, pp. 53–78.

———. 1993. "Islam, State and Civil Society: ICMI and the Struggle for the Indonesian Middle Class." In *Indonesia* (Cornell) 56: 1–35.

Hidayat, Komaruddin. 1982. "Konflik Terselubung di Kaki Gunung Ciremai." *Panji Masyarakat* 374: 28–29; 375: 43–44; 376: 40.

Hubungan antara. 1979. *Hubungan antara masyarakat beragama Islam dan Hindu di Lombok Barat, 1979/1980: Hasil studi kasus*. Jakarta: Departemen Agama, Proyek Pembinaan Kerukunan Hidup Beragama. Microfilm in KITLV, Leiden Mf. 24691980.

Johns, A. H. 1987. "Indonesia: Islam and Cultural Plurality." In John L. Esposito (ed.), *Islam in Asia: Religion, Politics and Society*. New York: Oxford University Press, pp. 202–229.

Madjid, Nurcholis. 1992. *Islam, Doktrin dan Peradaban: Sebuah Telaah Kritis tentang Masalah Keimanan, Kemanusiaan dan Kemoderenan*. Jakarta: Paramadina.

———. 1993. "Beberapa Renungan tentang Kehidupan Keagamaan untuk Generasi Mendatang." *Journal Ulumul Qur'an* 4(1): 4–25.

Mafri Amir. 1991. "Buku yang merusak iman." *Panji Masyarakat* 694 (1 Sept.): 27–29.

Noer, Deliar. 1983. *Islam, Pancasila dan Azas Tunggal*. Jakarta: Yayasan Perkhidmatan.

Patty, Semual Agustinus. 1986. "*Aliran Kepercayaan:* A Socio-religious Movement in Indonesia." Ph.D. Diss., Washington State University. Ann Arbor, University Microfilms.

Pompe, S. 1988. "Mixed Marriages in Indonesia." *Bijdragen tot de Taal-, Land-, en Volkenkunde* 144: 259–275.

Purdy, Susan Selden. 1985. "Legitimation of Power and Authority in a Pluralistic State: Pancasila and Civil Religion in Indonesia." Ph.D. Diss., Columbia University, 1984. Ann Arbor: University Microfilms.

Smith Kipp, Rita, and Susan Rodgers (ed.). 1987. *Indonesian Religion in Transition*. Tucson: University of Arizona Press.

Stange, P. 1986. "Legitimate mysticism in Indonesia." *Review of Indonesian and Malay Affairs* 20(2): 76–117.

———. 1990. "Javanism as Text or Praxis." *Anthropological Forum* 6(2): 237–255.

Straathof, W. 1970. "Agama Djawa-Sunda: sedjarah, adjaran dan tjara berpikirnja." *Basis* 20: 203–223; 258–287; 313–318; 345–350.

Steenbrink, K. A. 1972. "Het Indonesisch godsdienstministerie en de godsdiensten." *Wereld en Zending* 1: 174–199.

———. 1989. "Towards a Pancasila Society: The Indonesian Debate on Secularization, Liberation and Development." *Exchange* 54: 1–28.

———. 1990a. "Jesus and the Holy Spirit in the Writings of Nuruddin ar-Raniri (d. 1695)." *Islam and Christian-Muslim Relations* 1(2): 192–207.

———. 1990b. "The Study of Comparative Religion by Indonesian Muslims." *Numen* 37(2): 141–167.

———. 1990c. "Pancasila, Entwicklungen innerhalb der civil religion Indonesiens." *Zeitschrift für Missions- und Religionswissenschaft* 74: 124–141.

———. 1993a. *Dutch Colonialism and Islam: Contacts and Conflicts in South-East Asia 1596–1950*. Amsterdam: Rodopi.

Ward, K. E. 1970. *The Foundation of the Partai Muslimin Indonesia*. Ithaca, N.Y.: Cornell University, Modern Indonesia Project.

Woodward, M. 1989. *Islam in Java: Normative Piety and Mysticism in the Sultanate of Yogyakarta*. Tucson: Association for Asian Studies and University of Arizona Press.

20

The Debate on Muslim-Christian Dialogue as Reflected in Muslim Periodicals in Arabic (1970–1991)

EKKEHARD RUDOLPH

Throughout history, the encounter between Islam and Christianity has run through more or less peaceful stages. Starting with the late seventh century, the mainly apologetic exchange of arguments between representatives of both sides remains a significant aspect of this encounter. Despite some remarkable exceptions, theological intolerance and exclusivism may be regarded as the prevailing pattern in the Christian-Muslim relationship over the centuries.

Due to the large number of textual editions, translations, and summarizing studies currently available, we now have a comprehensive and balanced picture of the political, social, and ideological background of the Muslim approach toward Christianity in its early stages. Moreover, recent scientific studies have also helped to increase our knowledge of the contemporary Muslim understanding of Christian doctrines.[1]

Preliminary Considerations

A more or less neglected question is to what extent this approach has influenced the Islamic-Christian dialogue initiated by both Christian and Muslim institutions during the last 20 years. From the beginning of the 1970s up until the present the World Council of Churches (WCC) in Geneva, the Vatican in Rome, and some organizations and scientific institutions on the Muslim side such as the Centre d'Etudes et de Recherches Economiques et Sociales (CERES) in Tunis and the Āl al-Bait Foundation in Amman treated the idea of interreligious dialogue on diverse levels. Nevertheless, these attempts could not cover the fact that the long-standing polemical attitude on both sides and the historical and recent political experiences in the interaction of Muslims and Christians have hindered the pursuit of dialogue until now.[2]

On the Western side, we find a vast amount of literature on dialogue, on the ecumenical outlook of Christian churches and on further preliminary aspects. The question arises as to what we, in the opposite direction, know about Muslim attitudes toward dialogue, apart from the contributions of those Muslims who took part in conferences and symposia over the past 25 years. It seems obvious that official dialogue covers only a small fragment of the whole picture. The Muslim participants at the manifold meetings held in the past were often considered to be a specific intellectual elite, in comparison with other Muslims outside of these gatherings whose views are unknown to us.

In order to gain further insight into Muslim discussions concerning Christianity and interreligious dialogue, I will attempt to shed some light on a few lesser known texts that were published in Arabic periodicals in Egypt, Saudi Arabia, Qatar, Libya, Lebanon, and Tunisia and edited mainly by religious institutions (Ministeries of Religious Foundations, Supreme Islamic Councils, Muslim World League, etc.) over the past 25 years.[3]

The majority of the included articles often deal with their subject in relation to the general background of past and present Christian-Muslim or Euro-Arab relationship. The authors' interest is more or less concentrated on three topics: first, on Christian missionary activities, second, on the attitude of the Jews (in connection with Christian perceptions), and third, on theological controversies with Christian dogmas. Reflections on dialogue as such are rarely to be found. Instead, we find direct reports and speeches held at bilateral conferences or general remarks in connection with official visits and significant political events, such as the Pope's journeys. The authors of these articles and essays are mainly journalists, scholars, and intellectuals who either have a certain experience of dialogue-meetings or who refer to the topic for general reasons. This is, for example, the case with some critics associated with the Muslim World League (Mecca), who obviously aim to diminish the concept of dialogue—in the sense of *rapprochement*—and instead to strengthen the idea of an ideological *competition* with Christianity.

Egypt

I will first turn my attention to Egypt. Here the scholarly dispute and the intellectual exchange of ideas between people of different faiths have a distinct tradition and history. It was not surprising that in the late 1960s the first activities of the Vatican and its newly founded Secretariat for Non-Christians (now: Pontifical Council for Inter-Religious Dialogue) were directed toward the representatives of Azhar University, obviously one of the most influential scholarly institutions in the Muslim world. The public lecture held by the Austrian Cardinal König here on "Monotheism in the Present World" in March 1965 already marked a first step.

The official visits led by Cardinal Pignedoli, then head of the Vatican Secretariat, in Cairo in the years 1974 and 1978 gained large attention, even though the Sheikh al-Azhar never responded to the mutual invitation from Rome. Only once, in 1970, did a delegation of the Supreme Council of Islamic Affairs (Majlis al-Aʿlā li al-Shuʿūn al-Islāmiyya), which is in fact a governmental institution, come to Rome. But the encounter on both sides, intended by the Vatican to be founded merely on religious bases, seemed more than difficult at the time due to the Arab-Israeli conflict that cast a shadow on the relationship between the Christian churches and its Muslim partners.

Nevertheless, in the 1970s some large dialogue meetings organized by Christian and Muslim institutions such as the conferences in Cordoba and Tunis took place. The Cordoba meetings (1974, 1977) particularly affected the religious authorities in Egypt. Even though the Sheikh al-Azhar, the Sorbonne graduate ʿAbd al-Halīm Mahmūd, accepted the invitation to the second meeting, he cancelled his participation at the last minute. In the following year, the public in Egypt and the Arab world learned the reasons behind this decision. The well-known *Majallat al-Azhar*, which normally dealt only with general questions such as the ostensible superiority of the Islamic faith and the principal acceptance of Christians as "People of the Book" (*ahl al-kitāb*),[4] reflected the cautious attitude of the religious establishment toward these attempts of Islamic-Christian rapprochement.

In June 1978, *Majallat al-Azhar* published the invitation by Miguel de Epalza, the organizer of the Cordoba conferences, to the following third meeting—scheduled for 1979—and the negative answer, once again, by Sheikh Mahmūd. In his reply expressing his general respect for Christian-Muslim dialogue, Sheikh Mahmūd vehemently lamented the fact that Christianity had not renounced its missionary activities especially in countries with Muslim minorities such as the Philippines. By rejecting the invitation, he stressed the view that dialogue between Islam and Christianity is not at all expedient as long as the "subversive" political and religious influences of the West on the Islamic world endure.[5] Another aspect of his reply was his disappointment with the Christian attitude toward Islam and the Prophet Muhammad. He repeated what he had already declared in his book *Europe and Islam*: The Muslims bring into dialogue the veneration of Jesus Christ and his mother, Mary, while the Christians have nothing comparable to contribute.[6]

It might be surprising to recognize that the Cordoba conferences were specifically characterized by a distinct "irenic" atmosphere, in which Christian theologians and church authorities explicitly apologized to the Muslims for distorting the Prophet of Islam in the past.[7] Therefore, the Azhar's decision could only be understood in terms of diplomatic caution.

In February 1979, *Majallat al-Azhar* published an article that seemed to be a theological attestation of the prevailing Azhar policy. Under the title "It Is Not to the Advantage of Islam and to That of Christianity," the author, ʿAbd al-Fattāh Baraka, vehemently refuted the opinion, expressed by Father Georges Anawati in an open lecture held in Cairo, that Islam and Christianity are commonly based on the belief in one God. In his conclusion, he repudiated any kind of rapprochement (*taqārub*) between Islam and Christianity founded on such prerequisites because, according to him, Islamic monotheistic faith is intrinsically different from the trinitarianism of Christian faith.[8]

In an article in the previous issue of *Majallat al-Azhar* the supervisor of the journal, Zāhir al-Zughbī, declared the Christian dogma of Trinity as a falsehood, underlining at the same time the superiority and the universality of the Islamic *sharīʿa*.[9] Such statements must not be judged and evaluated as a simple repetition of traditional Islamic interpretations but must be seen in light of the serious political and ideological situation in the Arab world in the end of the 1970s which led, after the Islamic revolution in Iran (1979), to the rise of Islamicist activism throughout the Arab world.

Under the next Sheikh al-Azhar, ʿAlī Gād al-Haqq, there were no more than general statements concerning Christianity. In January 1984, he declared in an interview with the Saudi Arabian weekly *Akhbār al-ʿĀlam al-Islāmī* that the Azhar university supports Muslim presence at any international conference aimed at deepening the understanding of different religions and dealing with morals, peace, or social justice in the world. However, he vigorously refused any dialogue between Muslims and Christians on matters of faith (*hiwār ʿaqāʾidī*) because for him there is no room for discussion.[10] al-Haqq later repeated his cautious position. In June 1991, he emphasized in the same weekly that interreligious dialogue, if it takes place, should remain within the circle of academics and specialists and should, in no case, become a topic for the general public.[11] The last remark is supposed to be a rebuff to all who use the subject for their own ideological or activist purposes. However, it could also be interpreted as a plea for more rationality in the whole discussion.

Despite all the difficulties accompanying the dialogue process, we do not merely find hostile statements in the two leading Islamic periodicals in Egypt. In September 1985, the monthly *Minbar al-Islām* cited a good example for the official Egyptian point of view concerning Muslim-Christian relations. One reader posed the question as to whether the Islamic duty to establish peace with all human beings does not contradict the Qurʾānic words: "Do not take Jews and Christians as friends" (Sūra 5:51). The mufti answered that despite doctrinal differences the Prophet's behavior toward the *ahl al-kitāb* was exemplary of affection and friendship. What was forbidden, however, was any form of clientage leading to attachment.[12]

Saudi Arabia

We will now turn to Saudi Arabia. In its search for appropriate partners in dialogue, the Vatican tried to include the ruling monarchy in Saudi Arabia already in the beginning of the 1970s. At that time, the influential King Faisal seemed to be the supreme authority in the Islamic world and seemed able to promote the process of dialogue by his large influence. The visit of Cardinal Pignedoli in Riyadh in 1974 showed that this exaggerated hope was premature. The difficult question of Jerusalem alone, which rose to the top of the agenda in the discussions, revealed that a bilateral encounter excluding political issues was unrealistic.[13] Another serious obstacle were the extremely traditionalist Saudi *ʿulamāʾ* which had strong reservations in questions of dialogue and little experience in the meeting with Christian partners.

The Muslim World League (Rābitat al-ʿĀlam al-Islāmī, or RAI) based in Mecca since 1962 formed the most important platform from which Saudi Arabian intellectuals and scholars could discuss these issues. The two periodicals of the league, the monthly *Majallat Rābitat al-ʿĀlam al-Islāmī*—distributed in different issues in Arabic and English—and the weekly *Akhbār al-ʿĀlam al-Islāmī* (now *al-ʿĀlam al-Islāmī*), both have an intentional worldwide Islamic outlook.[14] The fact that a reciprocal interest in dialogue did not exist among the religious establishment was already to be seen in the reactions of the Muslim World League to the Vatican declaration "Nostra Aetate" (1965). When the text of the declaration appeared, the most widespread opinion was not to welcome its irenic content concerning Islam, but to attack the part which confesses Christian guilt concerning the Jews.[15]

However, first attempts to start the dialogue with Christianity date back to the Cordoba Conference in

September 1974. The Muslim World League sent two official delegates, one of them, Muhammad al-Mubārak, former chancellor of King ʿAbd al-ʿAzīz University in Jeddah. In December 1974, a long interview with al-Mubārak appeared in several issues of *Akhbār al-ʿĀlam al-Islāmī*, in which he justified the participation of the league. Under the significant title "Other Sides of Islamic-Christian Dialogue," the Syrian-born al-Mubārak turned his attention to possible positive results of such encounters as the presentation of the true Islamic doctrine and *sharīʿa* in Europe in contrast to the "misinterpretations of missionaries and orientalists."[16] On the other hand, the director-general of the Muslim World League, Husain Sarrāj, emphasized in the RAI weekly that the Cordoba dialogue could strengthen the worldwide alliance of true believers against atheism and materialism, as well as the alliance against Israel's policy, especially with regard to the occupation of Jerusalem.[17] Generally speaking, the main concern for the new "advocates" of dialogue within the Muslim World League is not to open up a new chapter in the Muslim-Christian relationship but to look for appropriate partners in strengthening their own position.

At the same time, the protagonists of a harsh confrontation with Christianity and the Western world tried to undermine such attempts. To these prominent "rejectionists" belonged the extremely traditionalist scholar ʿAbd al-ʿAzīz ibn Bāz and the Egyptian journalist and former member of the Moslem brotherhood, Muhammad ʿAbdallāh al-Sammān. Between September 1974 and January 1975 the latter published in *Akhbār al-ʿĀlam al-Islāmī* a series of articles entitled "Did the Crusades Really Finish?" According to him, dialogue with Christianity is nothing more than "a ruse of the international Crusade and a conspiracy against Islam."[18] This stage of discussion ended unsuccessfully for the "advocates" of dialogue. It simply revealed the enormous obstacles the different members and interest groups within the RAI would have to eradicate before they would be ready to begin constructive interreligious discussions.

The media of the RAI remained almost silent on the issue and concentrated rather on ideological demarcations from Western civilization and Christianity. This tendency continued until ʿAbdallāh ʿUmar Nasīf was appointed secretary-general of the league in 1983. In April 1984, Nasīf invited the Antiochene Orthodox bishop, Philip Salībā, to discuss with him "the problem of Jerusalem's occupation." In September 1984, he even met Pope John Paul II in Rome.[19] The periodicals of the league did not refer to such activities at length, but in its context, there emerged a controversial discussion among Saudi scholars which was reflected in *Akhbār al-ʿĀlam al-Islāmī*.

In December 1984, a special colloquium on the problem of "Christianizing" (*tansīr*) was held in Mecca. Scholars mainly from Umm al-Qurā University proposed methods on how to cope with it. In this context one of the participants labeled the dialogue conferences as reprehensible (*marfūd*), because there could not be any convergence between truth (*haqq*) and falsehood (*bātil*)—that is, between Islam and Christianity. According to him, dialogue expunges the fundamental differences between both sides and therefore must be condemned.[20] With similar arguments the journalist ʿAbd al-Bāsit ʿIzz ad-Dīn refused any kind of rapprochement one month before. He illustrated his deep-rooted mistrust of Christianity by citing an example of the conference in Chambésy (1976), where the participants had dealt with the controversial subject "Christian Mission and Islamic *daʿwa*." Despite all declarations of intent put forward during the conference, there had not been any change in the ongoing process of "Christianization."[21]

However, the opinions within the Muslim World League were divided as must be concluded from other statements published during these months in *Akhbār al-ʿĀlam al-Islāmī*. As in a public inquiry, the journal asked a number of distinguished scholars and intellectuals for their personal opinions about Islamic-Christian dialogue while, at the same time, the secretary-general of the league traveled through Europe and built up diplomatic bridges with Christian authorities.

Finally, Hasan al-Turābī, the well-known Sudanese scholar and politician—recently leader of the National Islamic Front in his country—and Roger Garaudy, the converted French philosopher, who both held close contacts to the Meccan League, emphasized the positive aspects of the dialogue between Islam and Christianity.[22] Al-Turābī pointed out that interfaith dialogue belongs to the duties of the Islamic *daʿwa*—that is, it should be held in order to change the other's attitude. But it could only lead to positive results provided there is a balance or a common basis (*ardiyya mushtaraka*), from which both sides start. According to him, the most important question is the competence or qualification (*ahliyya*) of the partners. For the Muslim, it means being very familiar with the Qurʾān and the Islamic doctrine, but at the same time it includes being familiar with the intellectual and spiritual background of Christianity. The pattern for such a "predominant strength" (*qūwa rājiha*), as al-Turābī put it, goes back to the time of the Prophet. Muhammad himself had spoken with the pagans of the Quraish and with the Christians of Najran in order to convince them of Islamic faith and to spread the *daʿwa*.

While al-Turābī emphasized the competitive character of dialogue, Garaudy turned his attention toward the responsibilities of the great monotheistic religions such as Christianity and Islam in jointly facing the dangers of modern society. In the quest for common solutions, to which Islam as "the perfect Abrahamic faith" could make a substantial contribution, interreligious dialogue is a necessity.[23] Even though this short debate on the pros and cons of dialogue did not lead to remarkable practical results, it did reveal the heterogeneous views held by the religious and intellectual establishment in Saudi Arabia toward future Islamic-Christian relations.

In recent years, the official print media of the Muslim World League dealt with the problem more or less in connection with "missionary activities" of the churches or with "hidden aims" of certain visits of the Pope to Asian or African countries.

A second topic, which considerably complicates the dialogue, is the understanding of Christian doctrines, mainly the Trinity and Jesus' death on the cross. In several issues of *Akhbār al-ʿĀlam al-Islāmī* the preacher Ahmad Deedat, a native Indian Muslim living in South Africa, emphasized the truth of the Islamic doctrine in contrast to Christian "falsifications." So he understands the encounter with Christian representatives as an ongoing competition about the "truest doctrine." Like Hasan al-Turābī, he justifies dialogue only as a part of the Islamic *daʿwa*.[24]

Besides the two official periodicals of the league, several other newspapers and journals exist in Saudi Arabia and the Gulf States which could equally be understood as "voices" of its diverse interest groups. For example, the presidency of the Sharīʿa Tribunal and of Religious Affairs in Qatar published between 1980 and 1986 the monthly *al-Umma*, whose content and outlook is comparable to the two Mecca-based journals. Despite its rather short existence, *al-Umma* gained much attention and attracted a lot of well-known Muslim contributors from different Arab countries. Among others, two former participants in Islamic-Christian conferences dealt with the dialogue problem.

In January 1981, *al-Umma* published an article by the Moroccan Sheikh ʿAbdallāh Kannūn, who took part in the Cordoba meeting of 1974. While he reiterated the exclusive Islamic position, that is, that any dialogue could only be pursued following the criteria of the Qurʾān, he pointed out that meanwhile, even in the West, Christian doctrines like the Trinity were doubtful. The critical approach, which he found in a book by British theologians—he obviously referred to *The Myth of God Incarnate* by Maurice Wiles and John Hick (1977)—appears in his understanding as a step toward Islam which he sees as a better foundation for Islamic-Christian dialogue.[25]

The second article, entitled "Muslim-Christian Meetings: Doubts and Warnings," was published in 1986. Its author, Ahmad ʿAlī Majdūb, then professor at Cairo University, surveyed the history of Islamic-Christian dialogue beginning with the Vatican declaration "Nostra Aetate" (1965) up to the second Tunis Conference (1979) in which he himself had participated. What makes his remarks so discouraging is the permanent occurrence of suppositions and inaccurate deductions in regard to these conferences which he calls mere "conspiracies" (*muʾāmarāt*). He mainly focuses on the "hidden" ideological background of the Arab and Western participants and on the supposed financial sources of such meetings. He believed to have found, for instance, a link between the Vatican and the CIA.[26] One can only speculate as to the conditions under which such a statement emerged. In any case, it shows the harsh ideological pattern in regard to Muslim-Christian relations still applied and distributed by Muslim intellectuals in Saudi Arabia and the Gulf states.

Libya

The situation seems to be somewhat different in Libya. The specific revolutionary interpretation of Islam, as Mu'ammar al-Qadhdhāfī propagated it from the 1970s onward ("Third Universal Theory"), stood in sharp contrast to the Saudian regime and the Muslim World League in Mecca.[27]

One significant characteristic of the Libyan policy, which makes the difference even more obvious, is Qadhdhāfī's attempt to gain lasting influence in the Arab world "by playing the head of Islam and the champion of the Palestinian cause in a dialogue with the church."[28] Significant for al-Qadhdhāfī's program is his "universalist understanding of religion" that gradually arose in the 1970s and found expression in the Seminar on Islamic-Christian dialogue in

Tripoli in February 1976.[29] The Seminar, which was organized by the Libyan government assisted by the Vatican-Secretariat for Non-Christians, undoubtly marked a climax in the Muslim-Christian encounter of the last decades. Nevertheless, it should have become clear from the beginning that, for the Libyan officials, the religious motives underlying the conference were subordinated to its political impact.

After 1976, the special relationship between the Libyan government and the Vatican found its continuation in mutual visits and bilateral meetings. A responsible partner for the Catholic Church soon arose in the shape of the World Islamic Call Society (Jamʿīyyat al-Daʿwa al-Islāmiyya al-ʿĀlamiyya), a government-appointed institution, which from 1982 onward has published the monthly *Risālat al-Jihād*.[30] Diverse articles on Christian subjects often focus on historical, political, or juridical aspects of the Euro-Arab relationship (Christianity and Zionism, Islam and Christian mission, Pope's journeys, religious minorities, etc.).

The inherent political and theological outlook of the Libyan *daʿwa* organization is finally expressed in two editorials that appeared in 1985 and 1986. The first entitled "A Call to the Christian World" was supposedly intended to be a remembrance of Christmas. After citing related Qurʾānic verses, the author remarks: "We consider our call for the continuation of the dialogue at this very moment more insistent than at any previous time, because of purely religious reasons and doctrinal duties on the one hand, and because of earthly and political reasons on the other." He goes on to explain that among the latter reasons are mainly dangers threatening the world, peace, and human existence—that is, "the world is at once about to fall under the control of the forces of evil and tyranny, foremost among which is the world Zionist movement." In short, the editors are warning the "unsuspecting" Christian brethren of the dangers of Zionism, whose aim is supposedly to destroy their spiritual, cultural, and historical heritage. In this context, there is no wonder that the declarations of church authorities concerning the exculpation of the Jews were much attacked, because the Libyan responsibles held the Jewish community responsible for "crucifying a whole nation"—that is, Palestine.[31]

The other editorial reviews the Tripoli Seminar of 1976 on the occasion of its eleventh anniversary. While the former text reflects the strong political motives underlining the Libyan interest in the dialogue process, the latter sheds light on the religious background of these attempts. Following diverse Qurʾānic recommendations for tolerance and peaceful encounter with Christians and Jews (*ahl al-kitāb*), which is, after all, given by the example of the Prophet, the editors also dealt with the theological problems of dialogue. These find their expression in the words of al-Qadhdhāfī himself, whose discourse at the Tripoli Seminar is quoted at length: Islam unconditionally prescribes that the Christians should return to the real Gospel and the Jews must return to the real Torah. If every believer, including the Muslims, knew their true and common origins, the problems between them could be solved. The second condition is that Christians should recognize the prophethood of Muhammad in the same way as the Muslims venerate Jesus, the son of Mary.[32] Such well-known demands unveil the real obstacles in the understanding between both sides. They often force Christian officials to use a very diplomatic vocabulary, at least, in order to save the meeting.

Under these conditions the only chance seems to be a rapprochement which was mentioned in a lecture by Taufīq Muhammad Shāhīn and published in *Risālat al-Jihād* in 1988. While dealing with the Qurʾānic view of Jesus, Shāhīn finally directs his attention to the book *The Myth of God Incarnate* in order to proclaim that even some Christian theologians approach the "truth" in regard to Jesus, the supposed son of God.[33] The use of critical Western scholars as "chief witnesses" to underline one's own position is not at all a new method. The question arises as to whether recent discussions about a new interpretation of Christian doctrines put forward in Europe and the United States might be an appropriate topic for Muslim-Christian dialogue in its present stage. Despite the unsolved basic problems, the dialogue between Libya and the Catholic Church has not yet ceased. In January 1991, the same month that the second Gulf war started, *Risālat al-Jihād* published a long report about the last bilateral meeting in Malta, which stood under the motto "Co-existence of religions: reality and perspectives."[34]

With the exception of Libya, I have mainly presented those Muslim judgments which are generally linked by the same opinion—that is, dialogue is just a theoretical option, whose advantages and dangers—if at all—have to be discussed. Let me add some final remarks on those "voices" that speak as former or recent participants of Islamic-Christian dialogue meetings. Some of them come from Lebanon and Tunisia, where a distinct tradition of dialogue between Muslim and Christian institutions and individuals has emerged in the last decades. Instead of claiming to hold the truth, its emphasis lies on the search for common bases which include religious but also a variety of practical issues.

Lebanon

The multiconfessional Lebanon, for instance, is both a center of diverse Christian denominations and of Sunnite and Shīʿite communities. In the past, interfaith dialogue often arose from initiatives by cultural and academic institutions as, for example, the Cénacle conferences.

The Sunnite authority is represented by the Supreme Islamic Council in Beirut, which has published the journal *al-Fikr al-Islāmī* for about 20 years. From the beginning, the general attitude of Islam toward non-Muslims or *ahl al-kitāb* has been one of its favorite themes. In 1980–1981, the former Mufti of Lebanon, Sheikh Hasan Khālid published a series of articles about religious foundations and historical development in the Muslim treatment of Pagans, Jews, and Christians.[35] His explanations strictly follow Qurʾānic criteria in the interpretation of Muslim-Christian relationship; however, they lack practical conclusions for this discussion.

One of the activists of interreligious dialogue in Lebanon was the university scholar Subhī al-Sālih, who was until his violent death in 1988 also Vice Mufti of his country. Returning from a Muslim-Christian conference in Cameroon in 1983 he emphasized in an interview printed in *al-Fikr al-Islāmī* that such bilateral meetings help improve the relationship between faithful people all over the Muslim and the Christian world. According to al-Sālih, the basis for this is the belief in one God and the common desire to strengthen religious values and moral principles in society and in individual life.[36]

Despite the long persistent tensions between Muslims and Christians, particularly in Lebanon, such a readiness to search for common interests is not an exceptional phenomenon. In that sense, dialogue seems to be a pragmatical issue and is considered to be a necessity in order to commonly face daily problems. However, *al-Fikr al-Islāmī* does not conceal the grave political and ideological controversies imposed on the interreligious dispute such as Israel's policy or Zionism.[37]

Tunisia

In Tunisia the discussion on Muslim-Christian dialogue has long been characterized by a certain openness that has gradually emerged in line with historical circumstances such as the special ties to the European continent. The religious authorities, as well as the Western-educated intellectual and political elite, often used the same platform to express their attitude toward Christianity and dialogue. Examples for this are the Cordoba conference in 1977 and the Muslim-Christian symposium on "Human Rights," initiated by the Center for Economic and Social Studies (CERES) in Tunis in 1982. The bi-monthly *al-Hidāya*, edited by the Directorate for Religious Affairs, published without comment some discourses of the Tunisian participants in both conferences.

Two factors may illustrate the rather unique situation with *al-Hidāya*. Its chief editor, Sheikh Mustafā al-Tārzī, former Grand Mufti of Tunisia and representative of the Islam-Directorate, held the Friday sermon in the mosque of Cordoba. It was published under the title "Islam, the Religion of Fraternity and Peace."[38] Second, the former Tunisian Prime Minister, Muhammad Mzālī, who was responsible for Islamic institutions and media, held the introductory lecture at the Tunis conference, dealing with the topic "Religion, Philosophy and Human Rights."[39]

It seems that the interreligious dialogue at that time was embedded in Tunisian politics and public life. Nevertheless, in the 1980s it became evident that Muslim-Christian relationship mostly depended on social and political stability. Tunisia had to meet with social and economic unrest and had to face—like the whole Arab region—the Islamicist appeal. While, for example, CERES as well as the "Islamic-Christian Research Group" (GRIC) in Tunis went on promoting the intellectual exchange between Muslims and Christians in Tunisia, *al-Hidāya* remained almost silent to the topic.[40] However, this phenomenon also corresponds to the decreasing number of large-scale dialogue conferences after 1982.

Conclusion

Coming to the end of this survey we can point out several conclusions: The discussion on Christianity and interreligious dialogue as reflected in the mentioned periodicals sheds some light on the current barriers to Euro-Arab communication. In general, three approaches are to be commonly found, although there are diverse shades in between:

1. *The Qur'ānic approach.* Christians are considered as "People of the Book" (*ahl al-kitāb*), but their revelation has been superseded by the message of the Qur'ān. Dialogue is only possible if Christians accept the truth of Islamic revelation and the temporality of their own Scriptures.
2. *The ideological approach.* Christianity insists on its missionary ("christianizing") efforts and supports the political interests of the West concerning Islam. Like Zionism on the Jewish side, their representatives' aim is to destroy Islam. Dialogue is impossible or can only be understood as a competition about truth and falsehood in the fundamentals of faith.
3. *The irenic approach.* Christianity and Judaism are monotheistic religions. They are linked to Islam by common bases and interests. Dialogue is both possible and necessary.

The third approach is obviously the only one that corresponds to the idea of dialogue as such because it puts aside the divergences and doctrinal differences and searches for common points of interest. Even though it often seems to be the approach of an elite, its impact and significance for the inner-Muslim discussion leaves no room for doubt. Moreover, the harsh judgments which are often destined to influence a certain Muslim public represent only one aspect of Muslim views and judgments. These must then be supplemented by the numerous voices intensely pleading for critical and rational criteria in the interreligious discussion between Jews, Christians, and Muslims.[41]

NOTES

1. For a general survey of contemporary Arab-Muslim views on Christianity, see M. Ayoub, *Muslim Views on Christianity, Islamochristiana* 10 (1984): 49ff.; A. Charfi, *L'Islam et les religions non musulmanes, Islamochristiana* 3 (1977): 39ff.; A.-Th. Khoury and L. Hagemann, *Christentum und Christen im Denken zeitgenössischer Muslime* (Altenberge 1986); and J. Waardenburg, "Twentieth Century Muslim Writings on Other Religions" in *Proceedings of the 10th Congress of the Union Européenne des Arabisants et Islamisants* (Edinburgh 1982), pp. 107–115. H. Goddard, "Works about Christianity by Egyptian Muslim Authors," *Muslim World* 80 (1990): 251–277, provides an annotated bibliography of related works by contemporary Egyptian authors. See also H. Goddard, *Muslim Perceptions of Christianity* (London, 1996) and K. Zebiri, *Muslims and Christians Face to Face* (Oxford, 1997).

2. cf. *Meeting in Faith: Twenty Years of Christian-Muslim Conversations Sponsored by the World Council of Churches*, ed. S. Brown (Geneva 1989); M. Borrmans, "The Muslim-Christian Dialogue of the last Ten Years," *Pro Mundi Vita Bulletin* (Brussels), no. 74 (1978); A. von Denffer, *Dialogue between Christians and Muslims*, 3 vols. (Leicester: Islamic Foundation, 1980); *Annotated Index of Muslim-Christian Meetings (1966–1990)*, ed. Āl al-Bait Foundation (Amman 1990). See also H. Goddard, *Christians and Muslims: From Double Standards to Mutual Understanding* (London: Curzon Press, 1995); *Déclarations Communes Islamo-Chrétiennes, 1954 c.–1995 c., 1373 h.–1415 h.* (Beirut: Dar el-Machreq, 1997); and A. Siddiqui, *Christian-Muslim Dialogue in the Twentieth Century* (London: Macmillan and New York: St. Martin's Press, 1997).

3. One of the first attempts to make those voices public in the West has been undertaken by P. Johnstone, "An Islamic Perspective on Dialogue," *Islamochristiana* 13 (1987): 131–171.

4. cf. F. Dore, *Cristianesimo e Cristiani in "Mağallat al-Azhar" 1958–1978* (Rome: PISAI, 1990).

5. *Majallat al-Azhar*, June 1978, pp. 181ff.

6. ʿAbd al-Halīm Mahmūd, *Urūbbā wa-l'Islām* (Cairo 1979), p. 186; see also "Risāla ilā al-Bābā Būlus al-sādis" (Open letter to the Pope), ed. ʿAbd al-Wadūd Shalabī (Cairo 1978), pp. 42ff.

7. ʿAbd al-ʿAzīz Kāmil, *al-Islām wa'l-mustaqbal* (Cairo 1975), pp. 135ff.; Fahmī Huwaidī, *al-ʿArabī*, no. 223, June 1977, pp. 40ff.

8. *Majallat al-Azhar*, Feb. 1979, pp. 626–638; cf. M. Borrmans, *Islamochristiana* 5 (1979), pp. 259–260.

9. Ibid., Jan. 1979, pp. 453ff.

10. *Akhbār al-ʿĀlam al-Islāmī* (AAI), Jan. 30, 1984.

11. *AAI*, June 3, 1991; cf. ibid., July 29, 1991, where Sheikh Gād al-Haqq expressed a similar opinion.

12. *Minbar al-Islām*, Sept. 1985, pp. 118–119; trans. P. Johnstone, *Islamochristiana* 13 (1987), pp. 139–141.

13. cf. M. Kramer, *Israel in the Muslim-Christian Dialogue*, Institute of Jewish Affairs (IJA) Research Report nos. 11–12 (Nov. 1986), pp. 6–7.

14. It is interesting to note that the English version of the Majalla published from 1972 onward is more open-minded concerning Islamic-Christian dialogue; cf. Zafar Ishaq Ansari, "The Muslim Dialogue with Jews and Christians," *Journal of the Muslim World League* 12 (1984), no. 3, pp. 28ff.

15. *Majallat Rābitat al-ʿĀlam al-Islāmī* (MRAI), no. 7 (Jan.–Feb. 1965), pp. 14ff.; cf. Kramer, *Israel*, p. 4.

16. *AAI*, no. 407–410 (Dec. 1974); cf. R. Schulze, *Islamischer Internationalismus im 20.Jahrhundert* (Leiden 1990), pp. 412ff.

17. *AAI*, no. 401 (Nov. 11, 1974).

18. Ibid., nos. 394, 399, 409 (Sept. 1974–Jan. 1975).

19. See Schulze, *Internationalismus*, p. 414f. Nasīf's constructive attitude toward dialogue was brought to the public in a short English article, "Muslim-Christian Relations, the Muslim Approach," *Journal of the Institute of Muslim Minority Affairs* no.1 (1986), pp. 27ff.

20. *AAI*, no. 904 (Dec. 17, 1984).

21. Ibid., no. 898 (Nov. 5, 1984). Underlining his judgment, the author quoted a statement by Khurshid Ahmad, former director of the Islamic Foundation in Leicester and participant at the Chambésy Conference, which expresses Muslim disappointment of the actual situation.

22. Ibid., no. 908 (Jan. 14, 1985).

23. About Garaudy, see T. Gerholm, *The New Islamic Presence in Western Europe* (London 1988), pp. 268ff.

24. *AAI*, no. 1115 (March 27, 1989); 1119 (April 24, 1989). In 1986–1987, Deedat's pamphlet "Crucifixion or Crucifiction?" appeared in several issues of *MRAI*. In the media of the RAI, he attracted attention also for his public competitions with Christian fundamentalists (e.g., Jimmy Swaggart); see L. Poston, *Islamic Da'wah in the West* (New York 1992), pp. 139ff.

25. *al-Umma*, no. 3 (Jan. 1981), pp. 24ff.

26. Ibid., no. 70 (June 1986), pp. 56ff.; trans. P. Johnstone, *Islamochristiana* 13 (1987), pp. 147ff.

27. See Schulze, *Internationalismus*, p. 287f.; H. Mattes, *Die innere und äussere islamische Mission Libyens* (Mainz, 1986), pp. 78ff.

28. Kramer, *Israel*, p. 9.

29. See M. al-Qadhdhāfī, *Qadiyyat ad-dīn fī'l-'ālam al-mu'āsir* (Tripolis, 1976); Mattes, *Mission*, pp. 104ff.

30. cf. Mattes, *Mission*, pp. 116ff.

31. *Risālat al-Jihād*, no. 28 (1985), pp. 8ff.

32. Ibid., no. 49 (1986), pp. 84ff.

33. Ibid., no. 72 (1988), pp. 66ff. The author refers to the Muslim paraphrase of John Hicks's book published by ʿAbd al-Samad Sharaf al-Dīn under the same title in Jeddah (1978).

34. *Risālat al-Jihād*, no. 95 (1991), pp. 8ff.

35. *al-Fikr al-Islāmī*, no. 12 (1980), pp. 10ff.; no. 2 (1981), pp. 30ff. See also his book: *Mauqif al-Islām min al-wathaniyya wa'l-yahūdiyya wa'l-nasrāniyya* (Beirut 1986).

36. *al-Fikr al-Islāmī*, no. 4 (1983), pp. 25ff.

37. As an example, see the article by Ibrāhīm Ghuwail, "Zionism and Its Danger for the Religions," ibid., no. 9 (1988), pp. 55ff.

38. *al-Hidāya*, no. 5 (1977), pp. 55ff.

39. Ibid., no. 6 (1982), pp. 14ff.

40. One exception is a lecture held by the converted French painter and writer Nāsir al-Dīn (Etienne Dinet) in 1924, reprinted in *al-Hidāya* (no. 4/1984, pp. 67ff) under the significant title "What Distinguishes the Pure Islamic Religion from the Rest of Religions."

41. See Muhammad Arkoun, "New Perspectives for a Jewish-Christian-Muslim Dialogue," *Journal of Ecumenical Studies* 26 (1989), pp. 523ff.

SELECTED LITERATURE.

ʿAbd al-ʿAzīz, Mansūr Husain. *Daʿwat al-Haqq aw al-haqīqa baina'l-Masīhiyya wa'l-Islām* (The call of the truth or the reality between Christianity and Islam). Cairo: Maktabat ʿAlā al-Dīn, 1972.

ʿAbd al-Wahhāb, Ahmad. *al-Islām wa'l-adyān: nuqāt al-ittifāq wa'l-ikhtilāf* (Islam and other religions: points of agreement and difference). Cairo: Maktabat at-Turāth al-Islāmī, 1992.

Abedin, Syed Z. "Muslim Participation in Dialogue: The Other Dimension." *Hamdard Islamicus* 15 (1992), No. 4, pp. 5–13.

Abū Zahra, Muhammad. *Muhādarāt fī al-Nasrāniyya* (Lectures about Christianity), 3rd ed. Cairo: Dār al-Kitāb al-ʿArabī, 1961.

Anees, Munawar Ahmad. "Christian-Muslim Dialogue: Myth or Reality?" *Islam and the Modern Age* 23 (1987), pp. 107–119.

Ansari, Zafar Ishaq. "Some Reflections on Islamic Bases for Dialogue with Jews and Christians." *Journal of Ecumenical Studies* 14 (1977), pp. 433–447.

Arkoun, Muhammad. "New Perspectives for a Jewish-Christian-Muslim Dialogue." *Journal of Ecumenical Studies* 26 (1989), pp. 523–529.

Askari, Hasan. "The Dialogical Relationship between Christianity and Islam." *Journal of Ecumenical Studies* 9 (1972), pp. 477–487.

Ayoub, Mahmoud. "Muslim Views of Christianity: Some Modern Examples." *Islamochristiana* 10 (1984), pp. 49–70.

———. "Roots of Muslim-Christian Conflict." *The Muslim World* 79 (1989), pp. 25–45.

Baraka, ʿAbd al-Fattāh ʿAbdallāh. "Lā hūwa li-hisāb al-Islām wa lā li-hisāb al-Masīhiyya" (It is not to the advantage of Islam and to that of Christianity). *Majallat al-Azhar* 51 (1979), no. 3, pp. 626–638.

Borrmans, Maurice. "The Muslim-Christian Dialogue of the Last Ten Years." *Pro Mundi Vita Bulletin* 74 (Sept.–Oct. 1978), pp. 1–52.

Bouhdiba, Abdelwahab. "L'Avenir du dialogue islamo-chrétien." *Islamochristiana* 15 (1989), pp. 87–93.

Brown, Stuart E., ed. *Meeting in Faith: Twenty Years of Christian-Muslim Conversations. Sponsored by the World Council of Churches*. Geneva: WCC Publications, 1989.

Busse, Heribert. *Die theologischen Beziehungen des Islams zu Judentum und Christentum: Grundlagen des Dialogs im Koran und die gegenwärtige Situa-*

tion. Darmstadt: Wissenschaftliche Buchgesellschaft, 1988.

Charfi, Abdelmajid. "L'Islam et les religions non musulmanes: quelques textes positifs." *Islamochristiana* 3 (1977), pp. 39–63.

———. "Pour une nouvelle approche du Christianisme par la pensée musulmane." *Islamochristiana* 13 (1987), pp. 61–77.

Danish, Ishtiaq. "A Conceptual Analysis of Muslim-Christian Dialogue." *Hamdard Islamicus* 13 (1990), no. 3, pp. 55–65.

Déclarations communes islamo-chrétiennes, 1954 c.–1995 c.; 1373 h.–1415 h. Textes originaux et traductions françaises. Choix de textes présentés par Juliette Nasri Haddad. Sous la direction de Augustin Dupré la Tour et Hisham Nashabé. Beirut: Institut d'Etudes Islamo-Chrétiennes, 1997.

Denffer, Ahmed von. *Some Reflections on Dialogue between Christians and Muslims*. Leicester: Islamic Foundation, 1980.

Dore, Filippo. "Cristianesimo e Cristiani in 'Maǧallat al-Azhar' 1958–1978: Riflesso e percezione di una realtà presso una differente coscienza communitaria." Theol. diss., Rome, Pontifical Institute of Arabic and Islamic Studies, 1990.

al-Faruqi, Isma'il Raji. "Islam and Christianity: Diatribe or Dialogue." *Journal of Ecumenical Studies* 5 (1968), pp. 45–77.

al-Ghazzālī, Muhammad. *al-Ta'assub wa'l-tasāmuh baina al-Masīhiyya wa'l-Islām* (Fanatism and tolerance between Christianity and Islam). Cairo: Dār al-Kutub al-Hadītha, 1965.

Ghrab, Saad. "Islam and Christianity: From Opposition to Dialogue." *Islamochristiana* 13 (1987), pp. 99–111.

Goddard, Hugh P. "Contemporary Egyptian Muslim Views of Christianity." *Renaissance and Modern Studies* (Nottingham University), vol. 31 (1987), pp. 74–86.

———. "An Annotated Bibliography of Works about Christianity by Egyptian Muslim Authors (1940–1980)." *Muslim World* 80 (1990), nos. 3–4, pp. 251– 277.

———. *Christians and Muslims: From Double Standards to Mutual Understanding*. London: Curzon Press, 1995.

———. *Muslim Perceptions of Christianity*. London: Grey Seal, 1996.

Griffiths, Paul J., ed. *Christianity through Non-Christian Eyes*. Maryknoll, New York: Orbis Books, 1990.

Hanafi, Hasan. *Religious Dialogue and Revolution: Essays on Judaism, Christianity and Islam*. Cairo: Anglo-Egyptian Bookshop, 1977.

Hāshimī, Muhammad Fu'ād. *Hiwār baina masīhī wa-muslim* (A dialogue between a Christian and a Muslim). Cairo: Maktabat al-Risāla, 1984.

Johnstone, Penelope. "An Islamic Perspective on Dialogue: Articles from Islamic Journals." *Islamochristiana* 13 (1987), pp. 131–171.

al-Jundī, Anwar. *al-Islām wa'l-'ālam al-mu'āsir* (Islam and the modern world). Cairo: Dār al-Kitāb al-Lubnānī, 1973.

Kāmil, 'Abd al-'Azīz. *al-Islām wa'l-mustaqbal* (Islam and the future). Cairo: Dār al-Ma'ārif, 1975.

Khālid, Hasan. *Mauqif al-Islām min al-wathaniyya wa'l-yahūdiyya wa'l-nasrāniyya* (The Islamic approach toward Paganism, Judaism, and Christianity). Beirut: Ma'had al-Inmā' al-'Arabī, 1986.

Khaouam, Mounir. *Le Christ dans la pensée moderne de l'Islam et dans le Christianisme*. Beirut: Ed. Khalifé, 1983.

Khoury, Adel-Theodor, and Ludwig Hagemann. *Christentum und Christen im Denken moderner Muslime*. Altenberge: Verlag für Christlich-Islamisches Schrifttum, 1986.

Kimball, Charles A. "Striving Together in the Way of God: Muslim Participation in Christian-Muslim Dialogue." Theol. diss., Harvard University, 1987.

Kramer, Martin. *Israel in the Muslim-Christian Dialogue*. Research Reports nos. 11–12 (Nov. 1986), pp. 6–7. Institute of Jewish Affairs.

Mahmūd, 'Abd al-Halīm. *Urūbbā wa'l-Islām* (Europe and Islam). Cairo: Matābi' al-Ahrām al-Tijāriyya, 1979.

Mattes, Hanspeter. *Die innere und äußere islamische Mission Libyens: Historisch-politischer Kontext, innere Struktur, regionale Ausprägung am Beispiel Afrikas*. Mainz: Grünewald Verlag, 1986.

Merad, Ali. "Dialogue islamo-chrétien: pour la recherche d'un langage commun." *Islamochristiana* 1 (1975), pp. 1–10.

Nasseef, Abdallah Omar. "Muslim-Christian Relation: The Muslim Approach." *Journal of the Institute of Muslim Minority Affairs* 7 (1986), pp. 27–31.

Rousseau, Richard W., ed. *Christianity and Islam: The Struggling Dialogue* (*Modern Theological Themes, Selections from the Literature*, Vol. 4). Scranton, Penn.: Ridge Row Press, 1985.

Rudolph, Ekkehard. *Dialogues islamo-chrétiens 1950–1993: Introduction historique suivie d'une bibliographie étendue des sources arabes*. Lausanne: Université de Lausanne, Département Interfacultaire d'Histoire et de Sciences des Religions, 1993.

Saab, Hassan. "Communication between Christianity and Islam." *The Middle East Journal* 18 (1964), pp. 41–62.

al-Sa'īdī, 'Abd al-Muta'āl. *Limādhā anā Muslim?* (Why am I a Muslim?). Cairo: Maktabat al-Adāb, 1976.

Schirrmacher, Christine. *Mit den Waffen des Gegners: Christlich-muslimische Kontroversen im 19. und 20. Jahrhundert*. Berlin: Klaus Schwarz, 1992.

Schulze, Reinhard. *Islamischer Internationalismus im 20. Jahrhundert: Untersuchungen zur Geschichte der Islamischen Weltliga*. Leiden: E. J.Brill, 1990.

Shalabī, ʿAbd al-Wadūd, ed. *Risāla ilā al-Bābā Būlus al-sādis* (An open letter to Pope Paul VI). Cairo: Dār al-Ansār, 1978.

Shalabī, Ahmad. *al-Masīhiyya: Muqāranat al-adyān*, vol. 2, 3rd ed. (Religions compared: Christianity). Cairo: Maktabat al-Nahda al-Misriyya, 1967.

Shalabī, Raʾūf. *Yā ahl al-kitāb taʿālū ilā kalima sawā . . . ? Dirāsa muqārana liʾl-Masīhiyya* (O People of the Book, come to common terms between us and you . . . ? A comparative study of Christianity). Cairo: Maktabat al-Azhar, 1974.

Siddiqui, Ataullah. *Christian-Muslim Dialogue in the Twentieth Century*. London: Macmillan, 1977.

Sulaimān, Wilyam. *al-Hiwār bainaʾl-adyān* (The dialogue between the religions). Cairo: al-Haiʾa al-Misriyya al-ʿĀmma liʾl-Kitāb, 1976.

al-Tahtāwī, Muhammad ʿIzzat Ismāʿīl. *al-Nasrāniyya waʾl-Islām* (Christianity and Islam). Cairo: Matbaʾat al-Taqaddum, 1977.

Talbi, Muhammad. *Islam et dialogue: réflexions sur un thème d'actualité*, 2nd ed. Tunis: Maison Tunisienne de l'Edition, 1979.

———. "Possibilities and Conditions for a Better Understanding between Islam and the West." *Journal of Ecumenical Studies* 25 (1988), pp. 161–193.

———. *ʿIyāl Allāh: Afkār jadīda fī ʿalāqat al-muslim bi-nafsih wa biʾl-ākharīn* (Dependants of God: new ideas on the relationship of the Muslim with himself and the others). Tunis: Dār Sirās, 1992.

ʿUthmān, Muhammad Fathī. *Maʿa al-Masīh fīʾl-anājīl al-arbaʿa* (With Jesus Christ in the four Gospels). Cairo: Maktabat Wahba, n.d.

Waardenburg, Jacques. "World Religions as Seen in the Light of Islam." In A. T. Welch and P. Cachia, ed., *Islam: Past Influence and Future Challenge*. Edinburgh: University Press, 1979, pp. 245–275.

———. "Twentieth-Century Muslim Writings on Other Religions: A Proposed Typology." In R. Hillenbrand, ed., *Proceedings of the 10th Congress of the Union Européenne des Arabisants et Islamisants*. Edinburgh: University, 1982, pp. 107–115.

al-Waqfī, Ibrāhīm Ahmad. *al-Samāha fīʾl-Islām waʾl-Masīhiyya* (Tolerance in Islam and Christianity). Cairo: Dār al-Fikr al-ʿArabī, 1990.

Zebiri, Kate. *Muslims and Christians Face to Face*. Oxford: Oneworld, 1997.

Zhuravskij, Aleksej. *Christianstvo i Islam: sociokulturnye problemy dialoga*. Moscow: Nauka, 1990.

Ziyāda, Khālid. *Tatawwur al-nazra al-islāmiyya ilā Urūbbā* (The development of the Islamic attitude toward Europe). Beirut: Maʿhad al-Inmāʾ al-ʿArabī, 1983.

SELECTED BIBLIOGRAPHY

JACQUES WAARDENBURG

The following bibliography is general in nature and is meant primarily for those who are not familiar with Asian languages. It contains a selection of books and articles that directly or indirectly deal with Muslim perceptions and judgments of other religions throughout history. It represents an independent entity. Consequently, it does not include all the titles mentioned in the notes and the more specialized bibliographies of the book. Likewise, not all the titles it includes appear in these notes and bibliographies.

Most publications mentioned are in English. A certain number are in French, and still fewer are in German. Editions of the original Arabic and Persian texts are not given, but only the translations of these texts in Western languages, as far as they exist.

The only exception is the section "Oriental Languages: Selected Modern Texts." This section presents a selection of modern Muslim texts on religions other than Islam, in Arabic, Persian, and Turkish. These texts are scholarly to the extent that they have rid themselves of strong apologetic or polemical tendencies. Texts of this period, however, which were written by Muslims in Western languages or translated into them, are to be found in the section "The Contemporary Period: ca. 1950– ca. 1995."

The next sections deal with the Medieval and Modern Periods, respectively (ca. 650–ca. 1500 and ca. 1500–ca. 1950); throughout these two sections, a distinction has been made between "Texts in Translation" and "Studies" (in Western languages). The "Original Texts" contain sources—that is, titles of translations of selected Muslim texts that deal with other religions. The "Studies" contain research about such texts and their contexts, mostly in Western scholarship. The section "The Early Period (ca. 610–ca. 650)," only offers "Studies."

"The Contemporary Period (ca. 1950–ca. 1995)" makes a slightly different distinction. On the one hand, we find "Significant Texts" written by Muslim authors during this period on the subject of religions other than Islam, which are available in a Western language. They cannot always be considered as the result of scholarly research but instead are significant statements that have a more personal or more representative character. On the other hand, here we also find "Studies," as in the preceding sections; such studies, scholarly in character, are the work of both Western and Muslim researchers.

For practical reasons, I did not make the same distinction between "Significant Texts" and "Studies" in the section "Oriental Languages." For practical reasons, too, only a small selection of the titles existing on the subject in Arabic, Persian, and Turkish is presented here. Muslim publications concerning other religions which appeared in Urdu, Indonesian, and other relevant "Islamic" languages have been omitted altogether. I can only encourage colleagues in the field to publish a full bibliography of all Muslim publications concerning other religions than Islam which exist in the "Islamic" languages.

In this bibliography we have followed the simplified transliteration of Arabic into English, as has become customary in nonspecialized publications. It has been limited to the use of an apostrophe "'" for the hamza and an opening single quotation mark "'" for the 'ayin, and to the indication of the long vowels with a macron "-". The book titles rendered in Western languages other than English that contain Arabic or Persian words, for practical reasons, have had the diacritical signs which they might have had in that particular language omitted. In a few exceptional cases, in order to avoid misunderstandings, I have replaced a French or German transliteration by the current English one.

Shortly before the final manuscript of this bibliography went to press, some books appeared with extensive bibliographies on Muslim perceptions of Judaism and Christianity. I am indebted to these books for some last-minute corrections and additions in this bibliography, and I refer the reader to Steven M. Wasserstrom, *Between Muslim and Jew: The Problem of Symbiosis under Early Islam* (1995) and Camilla Adang, *Muslim Writers on Judaism and the Hebrew Bible: From Ibn Rabban to Ibn Hazm* (1996) for more specialized bibliographies of Muslim perceptions of Judaism until about 1050 C.E. For a more extensive bibliography of Muslim perceptions of Christianity in history including the twentieth century, the reader is referred to Hugh Goddard, *Muslim Perceptions of Christianity* (1996). The first four issues of *Islamochristiana* (1975–1978) contain annotated bibliographies of Muslim writings about Christianity during the medieval period.

There exist two continuing general bibliographies of more recent Muslim writings on Islam in its relations with other religions that are extremely useful for present-day publications. One is the *Index of Islamic Literature* which since volume 7 (1986) has had a special section "Comparative Religions and Systems." The other is the *Index Islamicus* which introduced a section "Relations between Islam and Other Religions" in 1993. Both testify to the increasing interest in the study of Muslim relations with, and perceptions of, non-Muslims. After due consideration I decided not to include Muslim publications concerning the study and practice of cooperation and dialogue between adherents of Islam and other people. This subject, important as it is, falls outside the scope of the present book and this bibliography. But some Muslim publications on dialogue have been retained because they have an immediate relevance for the study of Muslim perceptions of other religions since they present a certain knowledge of other religions.

It is hardly necessary to insist that the present selected bibliography only represents a choice of titles that may be useful for interested nonspecialists. There is a growing and perhaps urgent need for an annotated bibliography on Muslim relations with and perceptions of other religions throughout history. This certainly has been my first conclusion from what follows. I only can hope that Muslim and other scholars working together, will gradually fill it. In this sense, too, the following bibliography is preliminary only.

The Early Period (ca. 610–660)

STUDIES

Ahmad, Barakat. *Muhammad and the Jews: A Reexamination*. New Delhi: Vikas, 1979.

Albright, W. F. "Islam and the religions of the ancient Orient." *Journal of the American Oriental Society* 60 (1940), pp. 283–301.

Ayoub, Mahmud. "Jesus the Son of God: A study of the terms *ibn* and *walad* in the Qur'an and tafsīr tradition." In *Christian-Muslim Encounters*. Ed. Yvonne Yazbeck Haddad and Wadi Z. Haddad. Gainesville: University Press of Florida, 1995, pp. 65–81.

———. "Dhimma in Quran and Hadith." *Arab Studies Quarterly* 5 (1983), pp. 172–182.

———. "Nearest in Amity: Christians in the Qur'ān and contemporary exegetical traditions." *Islam and Christian-Muslim Relations* 8 (1997), pp. 145–164.

Dubler, C. E. "Survivances de l'Ancien Orient dans l'Islam (Considérations générales)." *Studia Islamica*, 7 (1957), pp. 47–75.

Ferré, André. "Muhammad a-t-il exclu de l'Arabie les Juifs et les Chrétiens?" *Islamochristiana* 16 (1990), pp. 43–65.

Gil, Moshe. "The origin of the Jews of Yathrib." *Jerusalem Studies in Arabic and Islam* 4 (1984), pp. 203–224.

Goitein, S. D. "The sanctity of Jerusalem and Palestine in early Islam." *Studies in Islamic History and Institutions*. Leiden: E. J. Brill, 1966, pp. 135–148.

Griffith, Sidney H. "Images, Islam and Christian Icons: A moment in the Christian-Muslim encounter in Early Islamic Times." In *La Syrie de Byzance à l'Islam: VIIe-VIIIe siècles, Colloque 1990*. Ed. Pierre Canivet and Jean-Paul Rey-Coquais. Damas: Institut Français de Damas, 1992, pp. 121–138.

Haarmann, Ulrich. "Heilszeichen im Heidentum—Muhammad-Statuen aus vorislamischer Zeit." *Welt des Islams* 28 (1988), pp. 210–224.

Haddad, Yvonne Yazbeck, and Wadi Z. Haddad (Eds.). *Christian-Muslim Encounters*. Gainesville: University of Florida Press, 1995.

Hasan, S. al-. "A fresh look at ancient Christians of Najran and present religious dialogues." *Islamic Studies* 16 (1977), pp. 367–375.

Hirschberg, H. "Historical and legendary controversies between Mohammed and the Rabbis." *Jewish Quarterly Review* 10 (1898), pp. 100–116.

Hirschberg, J. W. *Jüdische und christliche Lehren im vor- und frühislamischen Arabien: Ein Beitrag zur Entstehungsgeschichte des Islams* (Polska Akademia Umiejetnosci, Mémoires de la Commission Orientaliste). Krakow: Nakladem Polskiej Akademii Umiejetnosci, 1939.

Horovitz, Josef. "Judaeo-Arabic relations in pre-Islamic times." *Islamic Culture* 3 (1929), pp. 161–199.

Kister, M. J. "On strangers and allies in Mecca."*Jerusalem Studies in Arabic and Islam* 13 (1990), pp. 113–154.

Kister, M. J., and Menahem Kister. "'Do not assimilate yourselves . . .' Lā tashabbahu." *Jerusalem Studies in Arabic and Islam* 12 (1989), pp. 321–371.

McAuliffe, Jane Damman. *Qurʾānic Christians: An Analysis of Classical and Modern Exegesis*. Cambridge: Cambridge University Press, 1991.

Morony, Michael G. "Religious communities in late Sasanian and early Muslim Iraq." *Journal of the Economic and Social History of the Orient* 17 (1974), pp. 113–135.

Newby, Gordon Darnell. *A History of the Jews of Arabia: From Ancient Times to Their Eclipse under Islam*. Columbia: University of South Carolina Press, 1988.

Noth, Albrecht. "Die literarisch überlieferten Verträge der Eroberungszeit als historische Quellen für die Behandlung der unterworfenen Nicht-Muslime durch ihre neuen muslimischen Oberherren." In *Studien zum Minderheitenproblem im Islam*, vol. 1. Bonn: Selbstverlag des Orientalischen Seminars der Universität, 1973, pp. 282–314.

Parrinder, Geoffrey. *Jesus in the Qurʾān*. New York: Barnes and Noble, 1965.

Peters, Curt. "Grundsätzliche Bemerkungen zur Frage der arabischen Bibeltexte." *Rivista degli Studi Orientali* 20 (1942–1943), pp. 129–143.

Peters, Francis. "*Alius* or *Alter*: The qurʾānic definition of Christians and Christianity." *Islam and Christian-Muslim Relations* 8 (1997), pp. 165–176.

Robinson, Neal. "Jesus and Mary in the Quran: Some neglected affinities." *Religion* 20 (1990), pp. 161–175.

———. "Christian and Muslim perspectives on Jesus in the Quran." In *Fundamentalism and Tolerance: An Agenda for Theology and Society*. Ed. A. Linzey and P. Wexler. London: Bellow, 1991, pp. 92–105.

Rubin, U. "The 'Constitution of Medina': Some notes." *Studia Islamica* 62 (1985), pp. 5–23.

Schmucker, Werner. "Die christliche Minderheit von Nağran und die Problematik ihrer Beziehungen zum frühen Islam." In *Studien zum Minderheitenproblem im Islam*, vol. 1. Bonn: Selbstverlag des Orientalischen Seminars der Universität, 1973, pp. 183–281.

Sfar, Mondher. *Le Coran, la Bible et l'Orient ancien*. Paris: Sfar (1 rue Cassini), 1998.

Thomson, William. "Islam and the early Semitic world." *Moslem World* 39 (1949), pp. 36–63.

Tibawi, A. L. "Christians under Muhammad and the first two caliphs." In *Arabic and Islamic Themes*. London: Luzac, 1976, pp. 53–71.

Torrey, C. C. *The Jewish Foundations of Islam* (1933). Repr. New York: Ktav, 1967.

Trimingham, J. Spencer. *Christianity among the Arabs in Pre-Islamic Times* (Arab background series). London: Longman; Beirut: Librairie du Liban, 1979.

Tritton, A. S. *The Caliphs and their Non-Muslim Subjects: A Critical Study of the Covenant of ʿUmar*. London: Humphrey Milford, Oxford University Press, 1930.

Troll, C. W. "The Quranic view of other religions: Grounds for living together." *Islam and the Modern Age* 18 (1987), pp. 5–19.

Vajda, Georges. "Juifs et musulmans selon le Hadiṯ." *Journal Asiatique* 229 (1937), pp. 57–127.

Waardenburg, Jacques. "Koranisches Religionsgespräch: Eine Skizze." In *Liber Amicorum: Studies in honour of Prof. Dr. C. J. Bleeker*. Leiden: E. J. Brill, 1969, pp. 208–253.

———. "Un débat coranique contre les polythéistes." In *Ex Orbe Religionum, Studia Geo Widengren . . . dedicata*. Pars altera, vol. 2. Leiden: E. J. Brill, 1972, pp. 143–154.

———. "Towards a periodization of earliest Islam according to its relations with other religions." In *Proceedings of the 9th Congress of the U.E.A.I., Amsterdam, 1978*. Leiden: E. J. Brill, 1981, pp. 304–326.

———. *Islamisch-Christliche Beziehungen: Geschichtliche Streifzüge* (Religionswissenschaftliche Studien, Vol. 23). Altenberge: Oros Verlag, and Würzburg: Echter Verlag, 1993.

Ward, Seth. "A fragment of an unknown work by al-

Tabarī on the tradition 'Expel the Jews and Christians from the Arabian Peninsula/lands of Islam'." *Bulletin of the School of Oriental and African Studies* 53 (1990), pp. 407–420.

Watt, W. Montgomery. "The condemnation of the Jews of Banū Qurayzah." *Muslim World* 42 (1952), pp. 160–171.

———. "The early development of the Muslim attitude to the Bible." *Transactions of the Glasgow University Oriental Society* 16 (1955–1956), pp. 50–62.

———. "The Christianity criticized in the Qur'ān." *Muslim World* 57 (1967), pp. 197–201.

Wensinck, A. J. *Muhammad and the Jews of Medina*. Berlin: Adiyok, 1982. Original Dutch text: *Mohammed en de Joden te Medina*. Leiden: E. J. Brill, 1908; 2nd ed., 1928.

Wijoyo, A. "The Christians as religious community according to the Hadit." *Islamochristiana* 8 (1982), pp. 83–105.

Wismer, Don. *The Islamic Jesus: An Annotated Bibliography of Sources in English and French*. New York: Garland, 1977.

Zahniser, A. H. M. "The Word of God and the apostleship of ʿĪsā: A narrative analysis of Al ʿImrān (3): 33–62." *Journal of Semitic Studies* 36 (1991), pp. 77–112.

The Medieval Period (ca. 660–ca. 1500)

TEXTS IN TRANSLATION

Abū Dulāf. A. von Rohr-Sauer. *Des Abū Dulāf Bericht über seine Reise nach Turkestan, China und Indien neu übersetzt und untersucht* (Bonner Orientalistische Studien). Stuttgart: Kohlhammer, 1939.

Abū'l-Maʿālī ʿAlawī, Muhammad ibn ʿUbayd Allāh. *Bayān al-adyān*. Transl., introduction, and notes by Mohamed Abdul Salam Kafafi. London, 1949. French transl. Henri Massé. "L'Exposé des Religions par Abou 'l Maāli (Mohammad ibn Obaid-Allah)." *Revue de l'Histoire des Religions* 94 (1926), pp. 17–75. Italian transl. Francesco Gabrieli. "Un antica trattato persiano di storia delle religioni—Il Bayān al-Adyān di Abū'l-Maʿālī Muhammad ibn ʿUbaydallāh. Nota presentata dal Corrisp. M. Guidi." *Rendiconti della R. Accademia Nazionale dei Lincei: Classe di scienze morali, storiche e filologiche*. Serie Sesta 8 (1932), pp. 587–644. Arabic transl. Yahyā al-Khashshāb in *Majallat Kulliyyat al-ādāb fī 'l-Qāhira* 19 (1957), pp. 11–58.

Andalusī, Saʿīd al-. *Kitāb Tabakāt al-Umam*. French transl. Régis Blachère. *Livre des Catégories des Nations*. Paris: Larose, 1935.

Bīrūnī, Abu Rayhān al-. *Kitāb ta'rīkh al-Hind*. English transl. C. Edward Sachau. *Alberuni's India: An Account of the Religion, Philosophy, Literature, Geography, Chronology, Astronomy, Customs, Laws and Astrology of India about A.D. 1030*. 2 vols. London, 1888; 2nd ed. 1910; repr. New Delhi: Chand, 1964.

———. *Kitāb al-āthār al-bāqiya ʿan al-qurūn al-khāliya*. English transl. C. Edward Sachau. *The Chronology of Ancient Nations: An English Version of the Arabic Text of the Āthār-ul-Bākiya of Albiruni, or "Vestiges of the Past."* London, 1879; repr. Frankfurt M.: Minerva, 1969.

Caspar, Robert, and Jean-Marie Gaudeul. "Textes de la tradition musulmane concernant le *tahrīf* (falsification) des Ecritures." *Islamochristiana* 6 (1980), pp. 61–104.

Gabrieli, Francesco. *Arab Historians of the Crusades: Selected and Translated from the Arabic Sources*. Transl. from the Italian by E. J. Costello. London: Routledge and Kegan Paul, 1969.

Gaudeul, Jean-Marie. *Encounters and Clashes: Islam and Christianity in History*. Vol. 2: *Texts*. Rome: Pontificio Istituto di Studi Arabi e d'Islamistici, 1984.

———, *La correspondance de ʿUmar et Léon (vers 900)*. Ed. Jean-Marie Gaudeul (Studi arabo-islamici del PISAI, 6). Rome: Pontificio Istituto di Studi Arabi e d'Islamistica, 1995.

Ghazālī, Muhammed al-. *Réfutation excellente de la divinité de Jésus-Christ d'après les Evangiles par Muhammad al-Ghazālī*. Ed. and transl. Robert Chidiac. (Bibliothèque de l'Ecole des Hautes Etudes, Sciences Religieuses, Vol. 54). Paris: Ernest Leroux, 1939. See also *Al-Ghazālī's Schrift wider die Gottheit Jesu*, Arabic translation and commentary by Franz-Elmar Wilms (Leiden: E. J. Brill, 1966).

Ghāzī Ibn al-Wāsitī. J. H. Gottheil. "An answer to the Dhimmis (Ghāzī Ibn al-Wāsitī, *Ahl al-dhimmah*)." *Journal of the American Oriental Society* 41 (1921), pp. 383–457.

Grenadino, Abū Hamīd El-. *Abū Hamīd el-Grenadino y su relaciòn de viaje por tierras eurasiáticas* (texto árabe, traducción e interpretación). Transl. C. E. Dubler. Madrid: Maestre, 1953.

Hamdānī, al-. *The Antiquities of South Arabia*. Translation from the Arabic with Linguistic, Geografic and Historic Notes of the Eighth Book of Al-Hamdānī's *Al-Iklīl*. Reconstructed from al-Karmali's edition and a MS in the Garrett Collection, Princeton University Library (Princeton Oriental Texts, Vol. 3). Transl. Nabīh Amīn Fāris. Princeton: Princeton University Press, 1938.

Hamidullāh, Muhammad. *Muslim Conduct of State*. Being a treatise of Muslim public international law, consisting of the laws of peace, war and neutrality, together with precedents from orthodox practice, and preceded by a historical and general introduction. Rev. ed. Lahore: Sh. Muhammad Ashraf, 1945.

Ibn Battūta. *Voyages d'Ibn Battūta*. Arabic text with transl. C. Defrémery and B. R. Sanguinetti. 4 vols. Paris, 1854. Repr. with preface and notes by Vincent Monteil. 4 vols. Paris: Ed. Anthropos, 1968. English transl. with revisions and notes by H. A. R. Gibb. *The Travels of Ibn Battuta*. 3 vols. (Cambridge: Cambridge University Press, 1958–1971). Compare Stephan Conermann, *Die Beschreibung Indiens in der 'Rihla' des Ibn Battuta* (Islamkundliche Untersuchungen, Vol. 165) (Berlin: Klaus Schwarz, 1993).

Ibn Fadlān, Ahmad. *Voyage chez les Bulgares de la Volga*. Introduction and notes by Marius Canard. Paris: Sindbad, 1988. See also *Ibn Fadlān's Reisebericht*. Ed. and transl. Ahmad Zeki Velidi Togan (Abhandlungen für die Kunde des Morgenlandes, Vol. 24) (Leipzig, 1939). Compare corrections by Hellmut Ritter, *Zeitschrift der Deutschen Morgenländischen Gesellschaft* 96 (1942), pp. 98–126.

Ibn Hazm. *Kitāb al-fisal* (or: *al-fasl*) *fī ʾl-milal wa-ʾl-ahwāʾ wa-ʾl-nihal*. Partial transl. Miguel Asín Palacios, *Abenházam de Córdoba y su Historia crítica de las ideas religiosas*, 5 vols. Madrid: Real Academia de la Historia, 1927–1932.

Ibn al-Kalbi, Hishām. *Kitāb al-asnām. The Book of Idols*. Transl. with introduction and notes by Nabih Amin Faris (Princeton Oriental Studies). Princeton: Princeton University Press, 1952. French transl. Wahib Atallah, *Les Idoles de Hicham ibn al-Kalbi* (Paris: C. Klincksieck, 1969). German transl. Rosa Klinke-Rosenberger, *Das Götzenbuch 'Kitāb al-asnām' des Ibn al-Kalbī* (Winterthur, 1942; privately printed).

Ibn Khaldūn (on Judaism and Christianity). *The Muqaddimah: An Introduction to History*. Transl. Franz Rosenthal, vol. 1. New York: Routledge and Kegan Paul, 1958, esp. pp. 472–481.

Ibn Munqidh, Usāma. *Memoirs of an Arab-Syrian Gentleman, or An Arab Knight in the Crusades: Memoirs of Usāmah Ibn Munqidh* (*Kitāb al-iʿtibār*). Transl. Philip K. Hitti. New York: Columbia University Press, 1927; repr. Beirut: Khayats, 1964. French transl. Andre Miquel. *Ousama, un prince syrien face aux croises*. Paris: Fayard, 1986.

Ibn al-Nadīm. *The Fihrist of al-Nadīm: A Tenth-century Survey of Muslim Culture*, 2 vol. Transl. Bayard Dodge. New York: Columbia University Press, 1970.

Ibn Taymiyya, Taqī al-Dīn Ahmad. *Al-Jawāb as-sahīh li-man baddala dīn al-masīh*. Partial English transl. Thomas F. Michel, *Ibn Taymiyya: A Muslim Theologian's Response to Christianity* (Delmar, NY: Caravan Books, 1984).

———. *Al-Risāla al-qubrusiyya*. French transl. Jean R. Michot, Ibn Taymiyya: *Lettre à un roi croisé* (*al-Risālat al-Qubrusiyya*). (Louvain-la-Neuve, 1995). See also Thomas Raff, "*Das Sendschreiben nach Zypern, Ar-risāla al-qubrusīya*, von Taqī Ad-Dīn Ahmad Ibn Taimīya (661–728 A.H./A.D. 1263–1328)," Ph.D. diss., University of Bonn, 1971.

———. Gérard Troupeau. "Les fêtes des Chrétiens vues par un juriste musulman." In *Mélanges offerts à Jean Dauvillier*. Toulouse: Université des Sciences Sociales, Centre d'Histoire Juridique Méridionale, 1979, pp. 795–802.

Izeddin, Mehmed, and M. Paul Therriat. "Un prisonnier arabe à Byzance au IXe siècle: Hārūn-ibn-Yahyā. Traduction annotée de sa description de Constantinople." *Revue des Etudes Islamiques* (1941–1946), pp. 45–62.

Jāhiz, al-. Charles Pellat. "Al-Ǧāhiz, les nations civilisées et les croyances religieuses." *Journal Asiatique* (1967), pp. 65–105.

Maghribī, Samauʾal al-. *Ifhām al-Yahūd* (*Silencing the Jews*). Ed. and transl. Moshe Perlmann (Proceedings of the American Academy for Jewish Research, Vol. 32). New York: American Academy for Jewish Research, 1964.

Maqdisī, Mutahhar Ibn Tāhir al-. *Al-Badʾ waʾl-taʾrīkh: Le livre de la création et de l'histoire*, 6 vols. Ed. and transl. Cl. Huart. Paris: Ernest Leroux, 1899–1919. See also Mahmoud Tahmi. *L'Encyclopédisme musulman à l'âge classique. Le Livre de la création et de l'histoire de Maqdisī*. Paris: Maisonneuve et Larose, 1998.

Makrīzī, Taqī al-Dīn Ahmad ibn ʿAlī al-. *Al-mawāʾiz waʾl-iʿtibār fī dhikr al-khitat waʾl-athār*. Partial French transl. U. Bourriout and P. Casanova, 6 vols. Paris, 1893–1920. Partial ed. and French transl. Gaston Wiet, 7 vols. Paris, 1911–1928. See also R. Griveau, "Les fêtes des Coptes par al-Maqrizi," in *Patrologia Orientalis*, Vol. 10 (Paris: Firmin-Didot, 1914), pp. 313–343; L. Leroy, "Les églises des chrétiens: Traduction de l'arabe d'al-Makrizi," *Revue de l'Orient Chrétien* 12 (1907), pp. 190–298, 269–279; and Leroy, "Les couvents des chrétiens: Traduction de l'arabe d'al-Makrizi," *Revue de l'Orient Chrétien* 13 (1908), pp. 33–46, 192–204.

Marwazī, Sharaf al-Zamān Tāhir al-. *On China, the Turks, and India*. Arabic text (circa A.D. 1120) and transl. V. Minorsky (James G. Forlong Fund, Vol. 22). London: Royal Asiatic Society, 1942.

Masʿūdī, al-. *Murūj al-dhahab, Les prairies d'or*, 9 vols. Ed. and French transl. C. Barbier de Meynard and Pavet de Courteille. Paris, 1861–1877; 2nd ed. 1913–1930. Rev. and corr. ed. Charles Pellat: 5 vols. of text with 2 vols. of index (Beirut, 1966–74 and 1979). French transl. Charles Pellat in Beirut and Paris: Société Asiatique and CNRS, 1962–1991. See also A. Shboul, *Al-Masʿūdī and His World: A Muslim Humanist and His Interest in Non-Muslims* (London: Ithaca Press, 1979).

Nallino, M. "Une description arabe inédite de Rome (dans le *Rawd al-Miʿtār* d'Ibn ʿAbd al-Munʿim al-Himyarī)." In *Scritti in onore di Laura Veccia Vaglieri*, vol. 1 (*Annali*, Nuova Serie). Naples: Istituto Universitario Orientali, 1964, pp. 295–309.

Nau, François M. "Un colloque du Patriarche Jean avec l'émir des Agaréens et faits divers des années 712 à 716 d'après le Ms. du British Museum add. 17193. Avec un appendice sur le Patriarche Jean 1er, sur un colloque d'un patriarche avec le chef des Mages et sur un diplôme qui aurait été donné par Omar à l'évèque du Tour Abdin." *Journal Asiatique* ser. 11, no. 5 (1915), pp. 225–279.

Palacios, Miguel Asín. *Logia et Agrapha Domini Jesu apud Moslemicos scriptores, asceticos praesertim, usitata*. In *Patrologia Orientalis*. Paris: Firmin-Didot. Vol. 13 (1917), Fasc. 3, pp. 333–431, and Vol. 19 (1926), Fasc. 4, pp. 529–624. Repr. Turnhout: Brepols, 1988.

Qāsim b. Ibrāhīm, al-. *La lotta tra l'Islam e il Manicheismo: Un libro di Ibn al-Muqaffaʿ contro il Corano confutato da al-Qāsim b. Ibrāhīm*. Arabic text and Italian transl. Michelangelo Guidi (Biblioteca della Fondazione Caetani). Rome: R. Accademia Nazionale dei Lincei, 1927. See also Ignazio di Matteo, "Confutazione contro i Cristiani dello Zaydita al-Qāsim b. Ibrāhīm," *Revista degli Studi Orientali* 9 (1921–23), pp. 301–364.

Rānīrī, Nūr al-Dīn ibn Muhammad al-. *Tibyān fī maʿrifat al-adyān*. Dutch transl. P. S. van Ronkel. "Rānīrī's Maleische geschrift: exposé der religies." *Bijdragen tot de Taal-, Land- en Volkenkunde van Nederlandsch-Indië* 102 (1943), pp. 461–480.

Rashīd al-Dīn Fadl Allāh Abu 'l-Khair. *Histoire universelle de Rašīd al-Dīn Fadl Allāh Abul-Khair*. Vol. 1. *Histoire des Francs*. Persian text with French translation and annotations by Karl Jahn. (Orientalia Rheno-Traiectina, Vol. 5). Leiden: E. J. Brill, 1951. See also Jahn, *Die Geschichte der Oğuzen des Rašīd ad-Dīn* (Vienna: H. Böhlaus, 1969); Jahn and Herbert Franke, *Die Chinageschichte des Rašīd ad-Dīn* (Vienna: H. Böhlaus, 1971); Jahn, *Die Geschichte der Kinder Israels des Rašīd ad-Dīn* (Vienna: Verlag der Österreichischen Akademie der Wissenschaften, 1973); Jahn, *Die Frankengeschichte des Rašīd ad-Dīn* (Vienna: Verlag der Österreichischen Akademie der Wissenschaften, 1977); Jahn, *Die Indiengeschichte des Rašīd ad-Dīn* (Vienna: Verlag der Österreichischen Akademie der Wissenschaften, 1980).

Sāʾid al-Andalusī. *Kitāb tabaqāt al-Umam: Livre des catégories des nations*. Transl. Régis Blachère. Paris: Larose, 1935.

Shabushtī, al-. *Vom Klosterbuch des Šabuštī*. Ed. and transl. Eduard Sachau (Abhandlungen der Preussischen Akademie der Wissenschaften. Jhrg. 1919, Philosophisch-Historische Klasse Nr. 10). Berlin, 1919. See also C. Edward Sachau, *Arabische Erzählungen aus der Zeit der Kalifen* (partly translation of al-Shabushtī). Munich, 1920.

Shahrastānī, al-. *Kitāb al-milal waʾl-nihal*. 2 vols. Ed. M. S. Kīlānī. Beirut, 1975. *Livre des religions et des sectes*, 2 vols. French translation, with introduction and notes by Daniel Gimaret, Jean Jolivet, and Guy Monnot (Leuven: Peeters, and Paris: Unesco, 1986, 1993). (Excellent bibliography on the subject, in vol. 1, pp. 84–99, and vol. 2, pp. 69–84.) Partial English translation of some fragments on Muslim schools of thought by A. K. Kazi and J. C. Flynn in *Abr-Nahrain* 8 (1968–69), pp. 36–68; 9 (1969–70), pp. 81–107; 10 (1970–71), pp. 49–75; 15 (1974–75), pp. 50–98.

Tabarī, Abu Jaʿfar Muhammad al-. *Taʾrīkh al-rusul waʾl-mulūk*. Translated as *The History of al-Tabarī*. Vol. 1, *General Introduction and From the Creation to the Flood* (F. Rosenthal); Vol. 2, *Prophets and Patriarchs* (W. M. Brinner); Vol. 3, *The Children of Israel* (W. M. Brinner); Vol. 4, *The Ancient Kingdoms* (M. Perlmann). Many volumes. Albany: State University of New York Press, 1987– .

Tabarī, ʿAlī b. Rabban al-. *Radd ʿalā ʾl-nasārā*. Transl. Jean-Marie Gaudeul as *Riposte aux chrétiens*, par ʿAlī Al-Tabarī (Studi arabo-islamici del PISAI Nr. 7) (Rome: Pontificio Istituto di Studi Arabi e d'Islamistica, 1995). Attributed to the same author: *The Book of Religion and Empire*. A semi-official defense and exposition of Islam written by order at the court and with the assistance of the caliph Mutawakkil (A.D. 847–861). Transl. with a critical apparatus from an apparently unique ms. in the John Rylands Library, A. Mingana. Manchester: 1922.

Tarjumān, ʿAbdallāh al-. *La Tuhfa, autobiografía y polémica islámica contra el Cristianismo de ʿAbdallāh al-Taryumān (fray Anselmo Turmeda)* by Miguel de Epalza (Atti della Accademia Nazionale dei Lincei, Anno 368, Memorie, Classe di Scienze morali, storiche e filologiche, Serie VIII, Vol. 15). Rome: Accademia Nazionale dei Lincei, 1971; 2nd ed. under the title *Fray Anselm Turmeda (ʿAbdallah al-Taryuman) y su polémica islamo-cristiana: Edición, traducción y estudio de la Tuhfa* (Madrid: Hiperión, 1994).

Turki, Abdelmağid. "La lettre du 'Moine de France' à al-Muqtadir Billāh, roi de Saragosse, et la réponse d'al-Bāğī, le faqīh Andalou: Présentation, texte arabe, traduction." *Al-Andalus* 31 (1966), pp. 73–153.

Warrāq, Abū ʿIsā al-. *Anti-Christian Polemic in Early Islam: Abū ʿIsā al-Warrāq's 'Against the Trinity'* by David Thomas. Cambridge: Cambridge University Press, 1992.

STUDIES

Aasi, Ghulam Haider. "Muslim understanding of other religions: An analytical study of Ibn Hazm's *Kitāb al-Fasl fī al-Milal wa-al-Ahwā' wa-al-Nihal*." Ph.D. diss., Temple University, Philadelphia, 1986.

Abel, Armand. "La polémique damascénienne et son influence sur les origines de la théologie musulmane." In *L'élaboration de l'Islam: Colloque de Strasbourg, 12–14 juin 1959*. Paris: Presses Universitaires de France, 1961, pp. 61–85.

———. "L'Apologie d'al-Kindī et sa place dans la polémique islamo-chrétienne." In *L'Oriente cristiano nelle storia della civilita*. Accademia Nazionale dei Lincei, Anno 361 (1964), Quaderno No. 62, pp. 501–523.

———. "La djizya: tribut ou rançon?" *Studia Islamica* 32 (1970), pp. 5–19.

———. "Masques et visages dans la polémique islamo-chrétienne." In *Cristianesimo e Islamismo*. Rome: Accademia Nazionale dei Lincei, 1974, pp. 85–132.

Adang, Camilla. "Eléments karaïtes dans la polémique anti-judaïque d'Ibn Hazm." In *Diálogo filosófica-religioso entre cristianismo, judismo e islamismo durante la edad media en la Península Ibérica*. Ed. Horacio Santiago-Otero. Turnhout: Brepols, 1994, pp. 419–441.

———. *Islam Frente a Judaïsmo: La polémica de Ibn Hazm de Córdoba*. Madrid: Aben Ezra Ediciones, 1994.

———. *Muslim Writers on Judaism and the Hebrew Bible: From Ibn Rabban to Ibn Hazm*, Leiden: E. J. Brill, 1996.

Ahmad Khalīfa, Muhammad Khalīfa Hasan. "Medieval Jewish-Muslim contribution to the academic study of religion: A study in the methodology of Saadia al-Fayyumi and Muhammad al-Shahrastani." Ph.D. diss., Temple University, Philadelphia, 1976.

Ahmad, Syed Barakat. "Non-Muslims and the Umma." *Studies in Islam* (Indian Institute of Islamic Studies) 17 (1980), pp. 80–118.

Ahmad, S. Maqbul, and A. Rahman (Eds.). al-*Masʿūdī Millenary Commemoration Volume*. Aligarh: Indian Society for the History of Science, 1960.

Allard, M. "Les chrétiens à Baghdad." *Arabica* 9 (1962), pp. 375–388.

Anawati, Georges C. "Polémique, apologie et dialogue islamo-chrétiens: Positions classiques médiévales et positions contemporaines." *Euntes Docete* 22 (1969), pp. 375–452.

Argyriou, Astérios. "L'épopée de Digénis Akritas et la littérature de polémique et d'apologétique islamo-chrétienne." *Byzantina* (Thessalonica) 16 (1991), pp. 7–34.

Arnaldez, Roger. "Controverse d'Ibn Hazm contre Ibn Nagrila le juif." *Revue de l'Occident Musulman et de la Méditerranée* 13–14 (1973), pp. 41–48.

———. "Les Chrétiens selon le commentaire coranique de Rāzī." In *Mélanges d'islamologie: Volume dédié à la mémoire de Armand Abel*. Ed. Pierre Salmon. Leiden: E. J. Brill, 1974, pp. 45–57.

———. *Jésus dans la pensée musulmane* (Coll. Jésus et Jésus-Christ, Vol. 32). Paris: Desclée, 1988.

Arnold, Thomas. *The Preaching of Islam: A History of the Propagation of the Muslim Faith*. Westminster: Constable, 1896; 2nd ed., New York, 1913, and Lahore: Ashraf, 1913. Latest edition, London: Darf, 1986.

Ashtor(-Strauss), E. "The social isolation of the *ahl adh-dhimma*." In *Paul Hirschler Memorial Book*. Budapest, 1949. Repr. in *The Medieval Near East: Social and Economic History* (London: Variorum Reprints, 1978).

———. "Saladin and the Jews." *Hebrew Union College Annual* 27 (1956), pp. 305–326.

———. *The Jews of Moslem Spain*. 3 vols. Translated from the Hebrew by Aaron Klein and Jenny Machlowitz Klein. Philadelphia: Jewish Publication Society of America, 1973–1984.

Atiya, Aziz S. *The Crusade: Historiography and Bibliography*. Bloomington: Indiana University Press, 1962.

———. *Crusade, Commerce and Culture*. Bloomington: Indiana University Press, 1962.

Ayoub, Mahmoud M. "Towards an Islamic Christology. I: An image of Jesus in early Shīʿī Muslim literature." *Muslim World* 66 (1976), pp. 163–188.

———. "Towards an Islamic Christology. II: The death of Jesus, reality or delusion (A study of the death of Jesus in *tafsīr* literature)," *Muslim World* 70 (1980), pp. 91–121.

———. "The Islamic Context of Muslim-Christian Relations." In *Conversion and Continuity: Indigenous Communities in Islamic Lands, Eighth to Eighteenth Century* (Papers in Mediaeval Studies, Vol. 9). Ed. Michael Gervers and Ramzi Jibran Bikhazi. Toronto: Pontifical Institute of Mediaeval Studies, 1990, pp. 461–477.

Azmeh, Aziz al-. "Barbarians in Arab eyes." *Past and Present* 134 (1992), pp. 3–18.

Baron, Salo Wittmayer. *A Social and Religious History of the Jews*. 1st ed. in 3 vols. New York: Columbia University Press, 1937; 2nd, rev., and enl. ed. in 18 vols. plus index. New York: Columbia University Press, and Philadelphia: Jewish Publication Society of America, 1958–66. (See for the Muslim medieval period in particular vols. 3, 4, and 17.)

Bausani, Alessandro. "Islam as an essential part of Western culture." In *Studies on Islam*. Amsterdam: North-Holland, 1974, pp. 19–36.

Becker, Carl Heinrich. "Christentum und Islam." In

Islamstudien, vol. 1. Leipzig: Quelle and Meyer, 1924, pp. 386–431.

Bennassar, Bartolomé, and Robert Sauzet (Eds.), *Chrétiens et musulmans à la Renaissance*. Actes du 37e colloque international du Centre d'Etudes Supérieures de la Renaissance (1994). Paris. Honoré Champion, 1998.

Bertsch, Margaret E. "Counter-crusade: A study of twelfth-century jihād in Syria and Palestine." Ph.D. diss., University of Michigan, 1950.

Bishai, Wilson B. "Negotiations and peace agreements between Muslims and non-Muslims in Islamic history." In *Medieval and Middle Eastern Studies in Honour of Aziz Suryal Atiya*. Ed. Sami A. Hanna. Leiden: E. J. Brill, 1972, pp. 50–61.

Blake, R. P., and R. N. Frye. "Notes on the Risala of Ibn-Fadlan." *Byzantina Metabyzantina* 1 (1949), pp. 7–37.

Bland, Kalman. "An Islamic theory of Jewish history: The case of Ibn Khaldūn." *Journal of Asian and African Studies* (Toronto) 18 (1983), pp. 129–197.

Blanks, David R. (Ed.). *Images of the Other: Europe and the Muslim World before 1700*. Cairo: American University in Cairo Press, 1997.

Boilot, D. J. "L'Oeuvre d'al-Bērūnī: Essai bibliographique." *Mélanges de l'Institut Dominicain d'Etudes Orientales au Caire* 2–3 (1955–1956), pp. 161–256, 391–396, respectively.

Bosworth, C. E. "Christian and Jewish religious dignitaries in Mamlūk Egypt and Syria: Qalqashandī's information on their hierarchy, titulature and appointment." *International Journal of Middle Eastern Studies* 3 (1972), pp. 59–74, 199–216. Repr. in C. E. Bosworth, *Medieval Arabic Culture and Administration* (London: Variorum Reprints, 1982), ch. 16.

———. "Al-Khwārazmī on theology and sects: The chapter on *kalām* in the *Mafātih al-ʿulūm*, in *Hommage à Henri Laoust*." *Bulletin d'Etudes Orientales* 29 (1978), pp. 85–95.

———. "The 'Protected Peoples' (Christians and Jews) in Medieval Egypt and Syria." *Bulletin of the John Rylands Library* 62 (1979–80), pp. 11–36.

———. "The concept of *Dhimma* in early Islam." In *Christians and Jews in the Ottoman Empire*, vol. 1. Ed. B. Braude and Bernard Lewis. New York: Holmes and Meier, 1982, pp. 37–55.

———. "Al-Khwārazmī on various faiths and sects, chiefly Iranian." In *Iranica Varia: Papers in Honor of Professor Ehsan Yarshater*. Leiden: E. J. Brill, 1990, pp. 10–19.

Bouama, Ali. *La polémique musulmane contre le christianisme depuis ses origines jusqu'au XIIIe siècle*. Algiers: Entreprise Nationale du Livre, 1988.

Brinner, William M. "The image of the Jew as *other* in medieval Arabic texts." *Israel Oriental Studies* 14 (1994), pp. 227–240.

Brinner, William M., and Stephen D. Ricks (Eds.). *Studies in Islamic and Judaic Traditions* (Brown Judaic Series). Atlanta: Scholars Press, 1986.

Brunschvig, Robert. "L'argumentation d'un théologien musulman du Xe siècle contre le Judaïsme (al-Bāqillānī)." In *Homenaje a J. M. Millás-Vallicrosa*, Vol. 1. Barcelona: Consejo Superior de Investigaciones Científicas, 1954, pp. 225–241.

Burns, R. Ignatius. *Muslims, Christians and Jews in the Crusader Kingdom of Valencia: Societies in Symbiosis*. Cambridge: Cambridge University Press, 1983.

Cahen, Claude. "Die wirtschaftliche Stellung der Juden in Bagdad im 10. Jahrhundert: Ein Beitrag zur Frage des historischen Anteils der Juden am Wirtschaftsleben." *Monatsschrift für Geschichte und Wissenschaft des Judentums* (Breslau) 73 (1935), pp. 361–381.

———. "Dhimma." *Encyclopaedia of Islam*, new ed., vol. 2. Leiden: E. J. Brill, 1965, pp. 227–231.

———. "Djizya." *Encyclopaedia of Islam*, new ed., vol. 2 (Leiden: E. J. Brill, 1965), pp. 559–567.

———. *Orient et Occident au temps des Croisades*. Paris: Montaigne, 1983.

———. *Turcobyzantina et Oriens Christianus*. London: Variorum Reprints, 1974.

Calder, N. "The Barāhima: Literary construct and historical reality." *Bulletin of the School of Oriental and African Studies* 57 (1994), pp. 40–51.

Cardaillac, Louis (Ed.). *Tolède, XIIe–XIIIe: musulmans, chrétiens et juifs: le savoir et la tolérance*. Paris: Ed. Autrement, 1991.

Caspar, Robert. "Le salut des non-Musulmans d'après Ghazālī." *Institut de Belles Lettres Arabes* (Tunis) 31 (1968), pp. 301–313.

Charfi, Abdelmajid. "L'Islam et les religions non musulmanes: Quelques textes positifs." *Islamochristiana* 3 (1977), pp. 39–63.

———. "Christianity in the Qurʾān commentary of Tabarī." *Islamochristiana* 6 (1980), pp. 105–148.

———. "Polémiques islamo-chrétiennes à l'époque médiévale." *Studia Religiosa Helvetica* 1 (1995), pp. 261–274.

Chittick, William C. *Imaginal Worlds: Ibn al-ʿArabī and the Problem of Religious Diversity*. Albany, N.Y.: SUNY Press, 1994.

Choksy, Jamsheed K. "Conflict, coexistence, and cooperation: Muslims and Zoroastrians in Eastern Iran during the Medieval Period." *Muslim World* 80 (1990), pp. 213–233.

Chouraqui, André N. *Between East and West: A History of the Jews of North Africa*. Philadelphia: Jewish Publication Society of America, 1968.

Christensen, Arthur. "Remarques critiques sur le Kitāb

bayāni-l-adyān d'Abū-l-Maʿālī." *Le Monde Oriental* (Uppsala) 5 (1911), pp. 205–216.

Cohen, Mark R. "The Jews under Islam: From the rise of Islam to Sabbatai Zevi." In *Bibliographical Essays on the Medieval Jewish Studies: The Study of Judaism*, vol. 2. New York: Ktav, 1976, pp. 169–232. Repr. with a supplement as *Princeton Near East Paper*, No. 32 (Princeton 1981).

Colbert, Edward P. *The Martyrs of Cordoba (850–859): A Study of the Sources*. Washington, D.C.: Catholic University of America Press, 1962.

Colomer, Eusebio. "Raimund Lulls Stellung zu den Andersgläubigen: Zwischen Zwei- und Streitgespräch." In *Religionsgespräche im Mittelalter*. Ed. Bernard Lewis and Friedrich Niewöhner. Wiesbaden: O. Harrassowitz, 1992, pp. 217–236.

Colpe, Carsten. "Der Manichäismus in der arabischen Überlieferung." Ph.D. diss., University of Göttingen, 1954.

———. "Anpassung des Manichäismus an den Islam (Abū ʿIsā al-Warrāq)." *Zeitschrift der Deutschen Morgenländischen Gesellschaft* 109 (1959), pp. 82–91.

Conermann, Stephan. *Die Beschreibung Indiens in der "Rihla" des Ibn Battuta* (Islamkundliche Untersuchungen, Vol. 165). Berlin: Klaus Schwarz, 1993.

Cuoq, J. "La religion et les religions (judaïsme et christianisme) selon Ibn Khaldūn." *Islamochristiana* 8 (1982), pp. 107–128.

D'Souza, A. "Jesus in Ibn ʿArabī's Fusus al-hikam." *Islamochristiana* 8 (1982), pp. 185–200.

Dadoyan, Seta B. *The Fatimid Armenians: Cultural and Political Interaction in the Near East*. Leiden: E. J. Brill, 1997.

Daiber, Hans. "Abū Hātim ar-Rāzī (10th century A.D.) on the unity and diversity of religions." In *Dialogue and Syncretism: An Interdisciplinary Approach*. Ed. Jerald Gort et al. Grand Rapids: William B. Erdmans, and Amsterdam: Rodopi, 1989, pp. 87–104.

Dajani-Shakeel, Hadia. "Natives and Franks in Palestine: Perceptions and interaction." In *Conversion and Continuity: Indigenous Christian Communities in Islamic Lands, Eighth to Eighteenth Centuries*. Ed. Michael Gervers and Ramzi Jibran Bikhazi. Toronto: Pontifical Institute of Medieval Studies, 1990, pp. 161–184.

———. "Some aspects of Muslim-Frankish relations in the Shām region in the twelfth century." In *Christian-Muslim Encounters*. Ed. Yvonne Yazbeck Haddad and Wadi Zaidan Haddad. Gainesville: University Press of Florida, 1995, pp. 193–209.

Djaït, Hichem. *Europe and Islam*. Berkeley: University of California Press, 1985. French original text: *L'Europe et l'Islam* (Paris: Seuil, 1978).

Dodge, Bayard. "The Sābians of Harrān." In *American University of Beirut Festival Book* (Centennial Publications), Ed. Fūad Sarrūf and Suha Tamin. Beirut: American University of Beirut, 1966, pp. 59–85.

———. "Mani and the Manichaeans." In *Mediaeval and Middle Eastern Studies in Honour of Aziz Suryal Atiya*. Ed. Sami A. Hanna. Leiden: E. J. Brill, 1972, pp. 86–105.

Donaldson, Dwight M. "Al-Yaʿqūbī's chapter about Jesus Christ." In *The Macdonald Presentation Volume*. Ed. W. G. Shellabear, E. E. Calverley, et al. Princeton, N.J.: Princeton University Press, and London: Humphrey Milford and Oxford University Press, 1933, pp. 89–105.

Dozy, R. *Le calendrier de Cordoue*, publié par R. Dozy. New ed. with French translation by Ch. Pellat. Leiden: E. J. Brill, 1961.

Dubler, C. E. "El Extremo Oriente visto por los musulmanes anteriores a la invasión de los Mongoles en el siglo XIII: La deformación del saber geográfico y etnológico en los cuentes orientales." In *Homenaje a J. M. Millás-Vallicrosa*, vol. 1. Barcelona, 1954, pp. 465–519.

Ducellier, Alain. *Le miroir de l'Islam: Musulmans et Chrétiens d'Orient au Moyen Age (VII-XIe siècles)* (Collection Archives). Paris: Julliard, 1971.

Ebied, R. Y., and L. R. Wickham. "Al-Yaʿkūbī's account of the Israelite Prophets and Kings." *Journal of Near Eastern Studies* 29 (1970), pp. 80–98.

Epalza, Mikel de. "Notes pour une histoire des polémiques anti-chrétiennes dans l'Occident musulman." *Arabica* 18 (1971), pp. 99–106.

———. "Le milieu hispano-moresque de l'Evangile islamisant de Barnabe." *Islamochristiana* 8 (1982), pp. 159–183.

———. *Jésus otage: Juifs, chrétiens et musulmans en Espagne (VIe-XVIIe s.)*. Paris: Cerf, 1987.

———. "Les symbioses culturelles à Al-Andalus." *Studia Religiosa Helvetica* 1 (1995), pp. 293–305.

Ezzati, A. *An Introduction to the History of the Spread of Islam*. London: News and Media, 1976.

Fattal, Antoine. *Le statut légal des non-Musulmans en pays d'Islam* (Recherches de l'Institut des Lettres Orientales de Beyrouth, Vol. 10). Beirut: Imprimerie Catholique, 1958.

Ferré, André. "L'historien al-Yaʿqūbī et les Evangiles." *Islamochristiana* 3 (1977), pp. 65–84.

———. "La vie de Jésus d'après les Annales de Tabarī." *Islamochristiana* 5 (1979), pp. 7–29.

Fierro, M. I. "Ibn Hazm et le zindīq juif." *Revue du monde musulman et de la Méditerranée* 63–64 (1992), pp. 81–89.

Fiey, Jean Maurice. *Assyrie chrétienne*. 3 vols. Beirut: Imprimerie Catholique, 1965–1968.

———. *Chrétiens syriaques sous les Mongols (Il-Khanat de Perse, XIIIe-XIVe s.)* (Vol. 362, Subsidia

Tome 44). Louvain: Secrétariat du Corpus Scriptorum Christianorum Orientalium, 1975.

———. *Communautés syriaques en Iran et Irak des origines à 1552*. London: Variorum Reprints, 1979.

———. *Chrétiens syriaques sous les Abbassides surtout à Bagdad (749–1258)* (Vol. 420, Subsidia Tome 59). Louvain: Secrétariat du Corpus Scriptorum Christianorum Orientalium, 1980.

Fischel, Walter J. "Ibn Khaldūn on the Bible, Judaism and the Jews." In *Ignace Goldziher Memorial Volume*, vol. 2. Ed. Samuel Löwinger et al. Jerusalem: Ruben Mass, 1956, pp. 147–171.

———. *Jews in the Economic and Political Life of Medieval Islam* (Royal Asiatic Society Monographs, Vol. 22). London, 1937; 2nd ed. with new introduction, New York: Ktav, 1969.

Forbes, A. D. W. "Liu Chih." *Encyclopaedia of Islam*, new ed., vol. 5. Leiden: E. J. Brill, 1986, pp. 770–771.

Friedlaender, Israel. "Zur Komposition von Ibn Hazm's Milal wa'n-Nihal." In *Orientalische Studien Theodor Nöldeke zum Siebzigsten Geburtstag (2. März 1906) gewidmet von Freunden und Schülern*, vol. 1. Ed. Carl Bezold. Gießen: A. Töpelmann, 1906, pp. 267–277.

Friedmann, Yohanan. "The Temple of Multān: A note on early Muslim attitudes to idolatry." *Israel Oriental Studies* 2 (1972), pp. 176–182.

———. "Medieval Muslim views of Indian religions." *Journal of the American Oriental Society* 95 (1975), pp. 214–221.

———. "Islamic thought in relation to the Indian context." *Islam et Société en Asie du Sud* (Collection Purusārtha) 9 (1986), pp. 79–91.

———. "Classification of Unbelievers in Sunni Muslim Law and Tradition." *Jerusalem Studies in Arabic and Islam* 22 (1998), pp. 163–195.

Gabrieli, Francesco. "La 'Zandaqa' au 1er siècle abbasside" (Colloque de Strasbourg). In *L'Elaboration de l'Islam*. Paris: Presses Universitaires de France, 1961, pp. 23–28.

García Gómez, E. "Polémica religiosa entre Ibn Hazm e Ibn al-Nagrīla." *al-Andalus* 4 (1936), pp. 1–28.

Gardet, Louis. "Rencontre de la théologie musulmane et de la pensée patristique." *Revue Thomiste* 46 (1947), pp. 45–112.

Gaudeul, Jean-Marie. *Encounters and Clashes: Islam and Christianity in History*. 2 vols. Rome: Istituto Pontificio di Studi Arabi e Islamistici, 1984.

Gervers, Michael, and Ramzi Jibran Bikhazi (Eds.). *Conversion and Continuity: Indigenous Christian Communities in Islamic Lands, Eighth to Eighteenth Centuries*. Toronto: Pontifical Institute of Mediaeval Studies, 1990.

Ghrab, Saād. "Islam and non-scriptural spirituality." *Islamochristiana* 14 (1988), pp. 51–70.

Gimaret, Daniel. "Bouddha et les Bouddhistes dans la tradition musulmane." *Journal Asiatique* 257 (1963), pp. 273–316.

Goddard, Hugh. *Muslim Perceptions of Christianity*. London: Grey Seal, 1996.

Göbel-Gross, E. "Die persische Upanischaden-Übersetzung des Mogulprinzen Dara Sukkoh." Ph.D. diss., University of Marburg, 1962.

Goeje, M. J. de. "Quotations from the Bible in the Qoran and the Tradition." In *Semitic Studies in Memory of Rev. Dr. Alexander Kohut*. Berlin: S. Calvary, 1897, pp. 179–185.

Goitein, S. D. *Studies in Islamic History and Institutions*. Leiden: E. J. Brill, 1966.

———, *A Mediterranean Society: The Jewish Communities of the Arab World as Portrayed in the Documents of the Cairo Geniza*. 6 vols. Berkeley: University of California Press, 1967–1993.

———. "Minority selfrule and government control in Islam." *Studia Islamica* 31 (1970), pp. 101–116.

———. (Ed.). *Religion in a Religious Age: Interfaith Relations in Medieval Islam*. Cambridge, Mass.: Association of Jewish Studies, 1974.

Goldziher, Ignaz. *Gesammelte Schriften*. 6 vols. Ed. J. de Somogyi. Hildesheim: Georg Olms, 1967–1973 (*Ges. Schr.*).

———. "Proben muhammedanischer Polemik gegen den Talmud I." *Jeschurun* 8 (1872), pp. 76–104 (*Ges. Schr.* I, 136–165).

———. "Proben muhammedanischer Polemik gegen den Talmud II." *Jeschurun* 9 (1873), pp. 18–47 (*Ges. Schr.* I, 229–259).

———. "Über mohammedanische Polemik gegen Ahl al-Kitāb." *Zeitschrift der Deutschen Morgenländischen Gesellschaft* 32 (1878), pp. 341–387 (*Ges. Schr.* II, 1–47).

———. "Über jüdische Sitten und Gebräuche aus muhammedanischen Schriften." *Monatsschrift für Geschichte und Wissenschaft* 29 (1880), pp. 302–315, 355–365 (*Ges. Schr.* II, 77–90, 91–101).

———. "Renseignements de source musulmane sur la dignité de Resch-Galuta." *Revue des Etudes Juives* 8 (1884), pp. 121–125 (*Ges. Schr.* II, 132–136).

———. "Influences chrétiennes dans la littérature religieuse de l'Islam." *Revue de l'Histoire des Religions* 18 (1888), pp. 180–199 (*Ges. Schr.* II, 302–321).

———. "Über Bibelcitate in muhammedanischen Schriften." *Zeitschrift für die Alttestamentliche Wissenschaft* 13 (1893), pp. 315–321 (*Ges. Schr.* III, 309–315).

———. "Usages juifs d'après la littérature religieuse des Musulmans." *Revue des Etudes Juives* 28 (1894), pp. 75–94 (*Ges. Schr.* III, 322–341).

———. "Islamisme et Parsisme." In *Premier Congrès*

International d'Histoire des Religions. Paris, 1900, pp. 119–147 (*Ges. Schr.* IV, 232–260).

———. "Neutestamentliche Elemente in der Traditionslitteratur des Islam." *Oriens Christianus* 2 (1902), pp. 390–397 (*Ges. Schr.* IV, 315–322).

Gottheil, R. J. H. "Dhimmis and Moslems in Egypt." In *Old Testament and Semitic Studies in Memory of William R. Harper*, vol. 2. Ed. Robert Francis Harper et al. (Chicago: University of Chicago Press, 1908), pp. 351–414.

———. "A fetwa on the appointment of dhimmis to office." *Zeitschrift für Assyriologie* 26 (1912), pp. 203–214.

———. "An answer to the dhimmis." *Journal of the American Oriental Society* 41 (1921), pp. 383–457.

Granja, Fernando de la. "Fiestas Cristianas en al-Ándalus. Materiales para su Estudio I: ʿAl-Durr al-Munazzamʾ de al-ʿAzafī." *al-Andalus* 34 (1969), pp. 1–53.

———. "Fiestas Cristianas en al-Ándalus. Materiales para su Estudio II: Textos de Turtūshī, el cadí ʿIyād y Wansharīsī." *al-Andalus* 35 (1970), pp. 119–142.

Griffith, Sidney H. "The Gospel in Arabic: An inquiry into its appearance in the first Abbasid century." *Oriens Christianus* 69 (1985), pp. 126–167.

———. "Images, Islam and Christian Icons: A moment in the Christian-Muslim encounter in early Islamic times." In *La Syrie de Byzance à l'Islam, VIIe-VIIIe siècles* (Colloque 1990). Ed. Pierre Canivet and Jean-Paul Rey-Coquais. Damascus: Institut Français de Damas, 1992, pp. 121–138.

———. "Disputes with Muslims in Syriac Christian texts: From Patriarch John (d. 648) to Bar Hebraeus (d. 1286)." In *Religionsgespräche im Mittelalter*. Ed. Bernard Lewis and Friedrich Niewöhner. Wiesbaden: O. Harrassowitz, 1992, pp. 251–273.

Grunebaum, G. E. von. *Studien zum Kulturbild und Selbstverständnis des Islams*. Zürich: Artemis Verlag, 1969.

———. "Eastern Jewry under Islam." *Viator* 2 (1971), pp. 365–372.

Guichard, Pierre. *L'Espagne et la Sicile Musulmanes aux XIe et XIIe siècles*. Lyon: Presses Universitaires de Lyon, 1991.

Haarmann, Ulrich. "Die Sphinx: Synkretistische Volksreligiosität im spätmittelalterlichen islamischen Ägypten." *Saeculum* 29 (1978), pp. 367–384.

———. "Heilszeichen im Heidentum—Muhammad-Statuen aus vorislamischer Zeit." *Welt des Islams* 28 (1988), pp. 210–224.

Habibullah, A. B. M. "Medieval Indo-Persian literature relating to Hindu science and philosophy, 1000–1800 A.D.: A bibliographical survey." *Indian Historical Quarterly* 14 (1938), pp. 167–181.

Haddad, Wadi Z. "The crusades through Muslim eyes." *Muslim World* 73 (1983), pp. 234–252.

———. "A tenth-century speculative theologian's refutation of the basic doctrines of Christianity, al-Bāqillānī (d. A.D. 1013)." In *Christian-Muslim Encounters*. Ed. Yvonne Yazbeck Haddad and Wadi Z. Haddad. Gainesville: University Press of Florida, 1995, pp. 82–94.

Haddad, Yvonne Yazbeck, and Wadi Z. Haddad (Eds.). *Christian-Muslim Encounters*. Gainesville: University Press of Florida, 1995.

Hajji, Abdurrahman A. El-. "At-Turtūshī, the Andalusian traveller and his meeting with Pope John XII." *Islamic Quarterly* 11 (1967), pp. 129–136.

Hamdun, Said, and Noël King. *Ibn Batuta in Black Africa*. London: Rex Collings, 1975.

Hamidullah, Muhammad. "Embassy of Queen Bertha of Rome to Caliph Al-Muktafi Billah in Baghdad." *Journal of the Pakistan Historical Society* 1 (1953), pp. 272–300.

Hamman, Mohammed (Ed.). *L'Occident musulman et l'Occident chrétien au Moyen Age* (Series Colloques et Séminaires No. 48). Rabat: Publications de la Faculté des Lettres et des Sciences Humaines, 1995.

Hartman, S. S. "Les identifications de Gayomart à l'époque islamique." In *Syncretism*. Ed. Sven S. Hartman (Scripta Instituti Donneriani Aboensis 3). Stockholm: Almqvist and Wiksell, 1969, pp. 263–294.

Henninger, Joseph. "Arabische Bibelübersetzungen vom Frühmittelalter bis zum 19. Jahrhundert." *Neue Zeitschrift für Missionswissenschaft* 17 (1961), pp. 201–223.

Hirschberg, J. W. "The sources of Moslem traditions concerning Jerusalem." *Rocznik Orientalistyczny* 17 (1951–1952), pp. 314–350.

Horten, Max. "Mönchtum und Mönchsleben im Islam nach Scharani." *Beiträge zur Kenntnis des Orients: Jahrbuch des Deutschen Vorderasienkomitees* 12 (1915), pp. 64–129.

Husain, Iqbal. "Perception of Hinduism in Persian literature." *Indo-Iranica* 46 (1993), pp. 121–131.

Inalcik, Halil. "The policy of Mehmet II toward the Greek population of Istanbul and the Byzantine buildings of the city." *Dumbarton Oaks Papers* 23 (1970), pp. 213–249.

Inostrantsev, K. "The emigration of the Parsis to India and the Musulman world in the middle of the VIIIth century. Translated from the Russian by L. Bogdanov." *Journal of the K. R. Cama Oriental Institute* 1 (1922), pp. 33–70.

Irani, M. S. "The story of Sanjan: The history of Parsi migration to India. A critical study." *Proceedings of the 10th All-India Oriental Conference*. Tirupati, 1940, pp. 68–85.

Irwin, Robert. "The image of the Byzantine and the

Frank in Arab popular literature of the late Middle Ages." *Mediterranean Historical Review* 4 (1989), pp. 226–242.

Jahn, Karl. *Rashīd al-Dīn's History of India: Collected Essays with Facsimiles and Indices* (Central Asiatic Studies, Vol. 10). The Hague: Mouton, 1965.

———. "Wissenschaftliche Kontakte zwischen Iran und China in der Mongolenzeit." *Anzeiger der philosophisch-historischen Klasse der Österreichischen Akademie der Wissenschaften* 106 (1969), pp. 199–211.

———. "Italy in Ilkhanid Historiography." In *La Persia nel Medioevo*. Rome: Accademia Nazionale dei Lincei, 1970, pp. 443–466.

Jeffery, Arthur. "Al-Bīrūnī's contribution to comparative religion." In *Al-Bīrūnī Commemoration Volume*. Calcutta: Iran Society, 1951, pp. 125–160.

Jomier, Jacques. "Unité de Dieu, Chrétiens, et Coran selon Fakhr al-dîn al-Râzî." *Islamochristiana* 6 (1980), pp. 149–177.

———. "Jésus, tel que Ghazali le présente dans 'al-ihya'." *Mélanges de l'Institut Dominicain d'Etudes Orientales au Caire* 18 (1988), pp. 45–82.

Kassis, Hanna E. "Muslim revival in Spain in the fifth/eleventh century: Causes and ramification." *Islam* 67 (1990), pp. 78–110.

Kaur, Guinindar. "Al-Bīrūnī: An early student of comparative religion." *Islamic Culture* 56 (1982), pp. 149–163.

Kedar, B. Z. *Crusade and Mission: European Approaches toward the Muslims*. Princeton, N.J.: Princeton University Press, 1984.

Keller, Carl-A. "L'attitude des mystiques musulmans face aux autres religions." In Carl-A. Keller, *Communication avec l'Ultime*. Geneva: Labor et Fides, 1987, pp. 195–209.

Khadduri, Majid. *War and Peace in the Law of Islam*. Baltimore: Johns Hopkins Press, 1955.

Khalidi, T. *Islamic Historiography: The Histories of Mas'ūdī*. Albany, N.Y.: SUNY Press, 1975.

Khan, M. S. "A twelfth-century Arab account of Indian religions and sects." *Arabica* 30 (1983), pp. 199–208. [al-Shahrastanī].

Khoury, R. G. "Quelques réflexions sur les citations de la Bible dans les premières générations islamiques du premier et du deuxième siècles de l'Hégire." *Bulletin d'Etudes Orientales* 29 (1977), pp. 269– 278.

King, J. R. "Jesus and Joseph in Rumi's Mathnawi." *Muslim World* 80 (1990), pp. 81–95.

Koningsveld, P. S. van. "The Islamic image of Paul and the origin of the Gospel of Barnabas." *Jerusalem Studies in Arabic and Islam* 20 (1996), pp. 200–228.

Kritzeck, James. "Muslim-Christian understanding in medieval times." *Comparative Studies in Society and History* 4 (1961–1962), pp. 388–401.

———. *Peter the Venerable and Islam*. Princeton, N.J.: Princeton University Press, 1964.

Labib, Subhi. "Die Kreuzzugsbewegung aus arabisch-islamischer Sicht." In *Medieval and Middle Eastern Studies in Honor of A. S. Atiya*. Ed. Sami A. Hanna. Leiden: E. J. Brill, 1972, pp. 240–267.

Lawrence, Bruce B. "The use of Hindu religious terms in al-Bīrūnī's *India* with special reference to Patanjali's Yogasutras." In *The Scholar and the Saint: Studies in Commemoration of Abu'l-Rayhan al-Biruni and Jalal al-Din al-Rumi* (6th New York University Near Eastern Round Table, 1974). Ed. Peter Chelkowski. New York: New York University Press, 1975, pp. 290–348.

———. *Shahrastānī on the Indian Religions*. The Hague: Morton, 1976.

Lazarus-Yafeh, Hava. "Jews and Judaism in the writings of al-Ghazzālī." In *Hava Lazarus-Yafeh: Studies in al-Ghazzālī*. Jerusalem, 1975, pp. 437–457. First published in Hebrew in *Tarbīz, A Quarterly for Jewish Studies* 33 (1963).

———. "Etude sur la polémique Islamo-Chrétienne: Qui était l'auteur de *al-Radd al-jamīl li Ilāhiyat 'Īsā bi-sarīh al-Injīl* attribué à al-Ghazzālī?" *Revue des Etudes Islamiques* 37 (1969), pp. 219–238.

———. *Intertwined Worlds: Medieval Islam and Bible Criticism*. Princeton, N.J.: Princeton University Press, 1992.

Lecomte, Gérard. "Les citations de l'Ancien et du Nouveau Testament dans l'Oeuvre d'Ibn Qutayba." *Arabica* 5 (1958), pp. 34–46.

Levtzion, Nehemia (Ed.). *Conversion to Islam*. New York: Holmes and Meier, 1979.

———. "Conversion to Islam in Syria and Palestine and the survival of Christian communities." In *Conversion and Continuity: Indigenous Christian Communities in Islamic Lands, Eighth to Eighteenth Centuries*. Ed. Michael Gervers and Ramzi Jibran Bikhazi. Toronto: Pontifical Institute of Mediaeval Studies, 1990, pp. 289–311.

Lewis, Bernard. *The Muslim Discovery of Europe*. New York: Norton, 1982.

———. *The Jews of Islam*. Princeton, N.J.: Princeton University Press, 1984.

———. "Legal and historical reflections on the position of Muslim populations under non-Muslim rule." *Journal of the Institute of Muslim Minority Affairs* 13.1 (1992), pp. 1–16.

———. "The Other and the Enemy: Perceptions of Identity and Difference in Islam." In *Religionsgespräche im Mittelalter*. Ed. Bernard Lewis and Friedrich Niewöhner (Wolfenbütteler Mittelalter-Studien, Vol. 4). Wiesbaden: O. Harrassowitz, 1992, pp. 371–382.

———. "Muslims, Christians, and Jews: The dream of

coexistence." *New York Review of Books* 39 (26 March 1992), pp. 48–52.

Little, Donald P. "Religion under the Mamluks." *Muslim World* 73 (1983), pp. 165–181.

———. "Christians in Mamlūk Jerusalem." In *Christian-Muslim Encounters*. Ed. Yvonne Yazbeck Haddad and Wadi Z. Haddad. Gainesville: University Press of Florida, 1995, pp. 210–220.

Maalouf, A. *The Crusades through Arab eyes*. London: al-Saqi Books, 1984.

Macdonald, John. "The Samaritans under the patronage of Islam." *Islamic Studies* 1 (1962), pp. 91–110.

Madelung, Wilferd. "Abū ʿĪsā al-Warrāq über die Bardesaniten, Marcioniten und Kantäer." In *Studien zur Geschichte und Kultur des Vorderen Orients: Festschrift Bertold Spuler*. Leiden: E. J. Brill, 1981, pp. 210–224.

Margoliouth, G. "A Muhammadan commentary on Maimonides' Mishneh Torah." *Jewish Quarterly* 13 (1901), pp. 488–507.

Massignon, L. "Le Christ dans les Evangiles selon al-Ghazālī." *Revue des Etudes Islamiques* 6 (1932), pp. 491ff. Repr., *Opera Minora* 2 (Beirut: Dar al-Maaref, 1963), pp. 523–536.

Matteo, Ignazio di. "Il 'tahrīf' od alterazione della Bibbia secondo i musulmani." *Bessarione* 38 (1922), pp. 64–111, 223–260. Abridged translation by M. H. Ananikian. "Tahrīf or the alteration of the Bible according to the Moslems," *Moslem World* 14 (1924), pp. 61–84.

———. "Le pretese contraddizzioni della S. Scrittura secondo Ibn Hazm." *Bessarione* 39 (1923), pp. 77–127.

———, *La divinità di Cristo e la dottrina della Trinità in Maometto e nei polemisti musulmani* (Biblica et Orientalia, Vol. 8). Rome: Pontificio Istituto Biblico, 1938.

McAuliffe, Jane Dammen. "Exegetical identification of the Sābiʿūn." *Muslim World* 72 (1982), pp. 95–106.

———. "Persian exegetical evaluation of the Ahl al-kitāb." *Muslim World* 73 (1983), pp. 87–105.

———, *Qurʾānic Christians: An Analysis of Classical and Modern Exegesis*. New York: Cambridge University Press, 1991.

———. "The Qur'anic context of Muslim Biblical scholarship." *Islam and Christian-Muslim Relations* 7 (1996), pp. 141–158.

Mehren, M. A. F. "Correspondance du philosophe soufi Ibn Sabʿīn Abd oul-Haqq avec l'empereur Frédéric II de Hohenstauffen publiée d'après le manuscrit de la Bibliothèque Bodléienne contenant l'analyse générale de cette correspondance et la traduction du quatrième traité Sur l'immortalité de l'âme." *Journal Asiatique* 7.14 (1879), pp. 341–454.

Mingana, A. "A charter of protection granted to the Nestorian Church in A.D. 1138 by Muktafi II, Caliph of Baghdad." *Bulletin of the John Rylands Library* 10 (1926).

Minorsky, V. "Tamīm ibn Bahr's journey to the Uyghurs." *Bulletin of the School of Oriental and African Studies* 12 (1947–48), pp. 275–305.

———. "On some of Bīrūnī's Informants." In *Al-Bīrūnī Commemoration Volume*. Calcutta: Iran Society, 1951.

Miquel, André. *La géographie humaine du monde musulman, jusqu'au milieu du 11e siècle*, 4 vols. Paris: Mouton, and Editions de l'Ecole des Hautes Etudes en Sciences Sociales, 1967–1988. See in particular vol. 2, *Géographie arabe et représentation du monde, la terre et l'étranger* (1975).

Monnot, Guy. "Les écrits musulmans sur les religions non-bibliques." *Mélanges de l'Institut Dominicain d'Etudes Orientales au Caire* 11 (1972), pp. 5–48. With additions and corrections, *Mélanges de l'Institut Dominicain d'Etudes Orientales au Caire* 12 (1974), pp. 44–47; repr. *Islam et religions* (Paris: Ed. Maisonneuve et Larose, 1986), pp. 39–82.

———. *Penseurs musulmans et religions iraniennes: ʿAbd al-Jabbār et ses devanciers*. Paris: J. Vrin, 1974.

———. "L'histoire des religions en Islam: Ibn al-Kalbī et Rāzī." *Revue d'Histoire des Religions* 188 (1975), pp. 23–34.

———. "Les doctrines des chrétiens dans le 'Moghni' de ʿAbd al-Jabbar." *Mélanges de l'Institut Dominicain d'Etudes Orientales au Caire* 16 (1983), pp. 9–30.

———. *Islam et religions* (Series Islam d'hier et d'ajourd'hui, Vol. 27). Paris: Maisonneuve et Larose, 1986. See in particular "L'islam, religion parmi les religions." pp. 9–23.

———. "Les Sabéens de Shahrastānī." In *Livre des religions et des sectes*, by Shahrastani, vol. 2. Paris: Peeters and Unesco, 1993, pp. 3–13.

———. "Les controverses théologiques dans l'oeuvre de Shahrastani." In *La controverse religieuse et ses formes*. Ed. Alain Le Boulluec. Paris: Cerf, 1995, pp. 281–296.

Morabia, Alfred. "La Notion de Ǧihād dans l'Islām Médiéval, des Origines à al-Gazālī." Ph.D. diss., University of Paris, 1974.

———. "Ibn Taymiyya, les Juifs et la Tora." *Studia Islamica* 49 (1979), pp. 91–122, 50 (1979), pp. 77–107.

Mourad, Suleiman A. "A twelfth-century Muslim biography of Jesus." *Islam and Christian-Muslim Relations* 7 (1996), pp. 39–45.

Nagel, Tilman, et al. *Studien zum Minderheitenproblem im Islam*, vol. 1. Bonn: Selbstverlag des Orientalischen Seminars, 1973.

Nettler, Ronald L. (Ed.). *Studies in Muslim-Jewish Relations*, vol. 1. Chur: Harwood Academic, 1993.

——— (Ed.). *Medieval and Modern Perspectives on Muslim-Jewish Relations*. Luxembourg: Harwood Academic, 1995.

Newman, N. A. (Ed.). *The Early Christian-Muslim Dialogues: A Collection of Documents from the First Three Islamic Centuries (632–900 A.D.)*. Translations with a commentary. Hatfield, Pa.: Interdisciplinary Biblical Research Institute, 1993.

Nwyia, Paul. "Un dialogue islamo-chrétien au IXe siècle." *Axes: Recherches pour un dialogue entre Christianisme et religions* 9, Fasc. 5 (1977), pp. 7–22.

Palacios, Miguel Asín. "La indiferencia religiosa en la España musulmana según Abenhazam, historiador de las religiones y las sectas." *Cultura Española* 5 (1907), pp. 297–310.

Pellat, Charles. "Christologie Ǧāhizienne." *Studia Islamica* 31 (1970), pp. 219–232.

Perlmann, Moshe. "ʿAbd al-Hakk al-Islāmī, a Jewish convert." *Jewish Quarterly Review* 31 (1940), pp. 171–191.

———. "Notes on Anti-Christian propaganda in the Mamlūk empire." *Bulletin of the School of Oriental and African Studies* 10 (1940/42), pp. 843–881.

———. "Eleventh-century Andalusian authors on the Jews of Granada." *Proceedings of the American Academy for Jewish Research* 18 (1948/9), pp. 269–290.

———. "The Medieval Polemics between Islam and Judaism." In *Religion in a Religious Age*. Ed. S. D. Goitein. Cambridge, Mass.: Association of Jewish Studies, 1974, pp. 103–138.

———. "Muslim-Jewish Polemics." *The Encyclopedia of Religion*, vol. 11. New York: Macmillan, 1987, pp. 396–402.

Peters, F. E. "Science, history and religion: Some reflections on the *India* of Abuʾl-Rayhān al-Bīrūnī." In *The Scholar and the Saint: Studies in Commemoration of Abu ʾl-Rayhān al-Bīrūnī and Jalāl al-Dīn al-Rūmī*. Ed. Peter Chelkowski (6th New York University Near Eastern Round Table, 1974). New York: New York University Press, 1975, pp. 17–27.

Pines, Shlomo. "'Israel my firstborn' and the sonship of Jesus: A theme of Moslem anti-Christian polemics." In *Studies in Mysticism and Religion Presented to G. G. Scholem*. Jerusalem: Magnes Press, Hebrew University, 1967, pp. 177–190.

———. "The Iranian name for Christians and the 'God-Fearers'." *Proceedings of the Israel Academy of Sciences and Humanities* 2 (1968), pp. 143–152.

———. "The Jewish Christians of the early centuries of Christianity according to a new source." *Proceedings of the Israel Academy of Sciences and Humanities* 2 (1968), pp. 237–310.

———. "Notes on Islam and on Arabic Christianity and Judaeo-Christianity." *Jerusalem Studies in Arabic and Islam* 4 (1984), pp. 135–152.

———, and T. Gelblum. "Al-Bīrūnī's Arabic version of Patanjali's 'Yogasūtra'." *Bulletin of the School of Oriental and African Studies* 29 (1966), pp. 302–325.

Platti, Emilio. "La doctrine des chrétiens d'après Abū ʿĪsā al-Warrāq dans son Traité sur la Trinité." *Mélanges de l'Institut Dominicain d'Etudes Orientales au Caire* 20 (1991), pp. 7–30.

Powell, James M. (Ed.). *Muslims under Latin Rule 1100–1300*. Princeton, N.J.: Princeton University Press, 1990.

Powers, David S. "Reading/misreading one another's Scriptures: Ibn Hazm's refutation of Ibn Nagrella al-Yahudi." *Studies in Islamic and Judaic Traditions*. Ed. W. M. Brinner and S. D. Ricks. Atlanta: Scholars Press, 1986, pp. 109–122.

Pulcini, Theodore. *Exegesis as Polemical Discourse: Ibn Hazm on Jewish and Christian Scriptures*. Atlanta, 1998.

Rasheeduddin Khan. *Bewildered India: Identity, Pluralism, Discord*. Delhi: Har-Anand Publications, 1995. See especially ch. 8, "Towards understanding India: Reflections of some eminent Muslims" (pp. 153–192).

Ratchnevsky, Paul. "Rašīd ad-Dīn über die Mohammedaner-Verfolgungen in China unter Qubilai." *Central Asiatic Journal* 14 (1970), pp. 163–180.

Renard, J. "Jesus and the other gospel figures in the writings of Jalal al-din Rumi." *Hamdard Islamicus* 10 (1987), pp. 47–64.

Rippin, Andrew. "Interpreting the Bible through the Qurʾān." In *Approaches to the Qurʾān*. Ed. G. R. Hawting and Abdulkader A. Shareef. London: Routledge, 1993, pp. 249–259.

Ritter, Helmut. "Zum Text von Ibn Fadlān's Reisebericht." *Zeitschrift der Deutschen Morgenländischen Gesellschaft* 96 (1942), pp. 98–126.

Robinson, Neal. "Fakhr al-dīn al-Rāzī and the virginal conception." *Islamochristiana* 14 (1988), pp. 1–16.

———. "Creating birds from clay: A miracle of Jesus in the Quran and in classical Muslim exegesis." *Muslim World* 79 (1989), pp. 1–13.

———, *Christ in Islam and Christianity: The Representation of Jesus in the Qurʾān and the Classical Muslim Commentaries*. Basingstoke, Hampshire: Macmillan, 1991.

Rohr-Sauer, A. von. *Des Abū Dulāf Bericht über seine Reise nach Turkestan, China und Indien neu übersetzt und untersucht* (Bonner Orientalistische Studien). Stuttgart: Kohlhammer, 1939.

Rosenthal, Erwin I. J. *Judaism and Islam*. London: Popular Jewish Library Thomas Yoseloff, 1961.

Rosenthal, Franz. "On some epistemological and methodological presuppositions of Al-Bīrūnī." In *Beyrunī Armagan*. Ankara: Türk Tarīh Kurumu Basimevi, 1974, pp. 145–167.

Roth, Norman. "Forgery and abrogation of the Torah: A theme in Muslim and Christian polemic in Spain." *Proceedings of the American Academy of Jewish Research* 54 (1987), pp. 203–236.

Rotter, Gernot. "Die Stellung des Negers in der islamisch-arabischen Gesellschaft bis zum 16. Jahrhundert." Ph.D. diss., University of Bonn, 1967.

Sahas, Daniel. *John of Damascus on Islam. The "Heresy of the Ishmaelites."* Leiden: E. J. Brill, 1972.

———. "The formation of later Islamic doctrines as a response to Byzantine polemics: The miracles of Muhammad." *Greek Orthodox Theological Review* 27 (1982), pp. 307–324.

———, "John of Damascus on Islam. Revisited." *Abr-Nahrain* 23 (1984–85), pp. 104–118.

———. "The Arab character of the Christian disputation with Islam: The case of John of Damascus (ca. 655–ca. 749)." In *Religionsgespräche im Mittelalter*. Ed. Bernard Lewis and Friedrich Niewöhner. Wiesbaden: O. Harrassowitz, 1992, pp. 185–205.

Said, Hakim Mohammad (Ed.). *Al-Bīrūnī Commemorative Volume: Proceedings of the Al-Bīrūnī International Congress*. Karachi: Hamdard National Foundation, 1973.

Samir, K. "Le commentaire de Tabarī sur Coran 2: 62 et la question du salut des non-musulmans." *Annali, Istituto Universitario Orientale di Napoli* 40 (N.S. 30) (1980), pp. 555–617.

Schimmel, Annemarie. "Turk and Hindu: A poetical image and its application to historical fact." In *Islam and Cultural Change in the Middle Ages*. Ed. Speros Vryonis Jr. Wiesbaden: O. Harrassowitz, 1975, pp. 107–126.

Schreiner, Martin, *Gesammelte Schriften: Islamische und jüdisch-islamische Studien*. Ed. Moshe Perlmann (Collectanea, Vol. 11). Hildesheim: Georg Olms Verlag, 1983.

———. "Les Juifs dans Al-Bērūnī." *Revue des Etudes Juives* 12 (1886), pp. 258–266.

———. "Zur Geschichte der Polemik zwischen Juden und Muhammedanern." *Zeitschrift der Deutschen Morgenländischen Gesellschaft* 42 (1888), pp. 591–675.

———. "Notes sur les Juifs dans l'Islam." *Revue des Etudes Juives* 29 (1894), pp. 206–213.

———. "Contributions à l'histoire des Juifs en Egypte." *Revue des Etudes Juives* 31 (1895), pp. 212–217.

———. "Beiträge zur Geschichte der Bibel in der arabischen Literatur." In *Semitic Studies in Memory of Rev. Dr. Alexander Kuhut*. Berlin: S. Calvary, 1897, pp. 495–513.

Schumann, Olaf. *Der Christus der Muslime: Christologische Aspekte in der arabisch-islamischen Literatur* (Missionswissenschaftliche Forschungen, Vol. 10). Gütersloh: Gerd Mohn, 1975. 2nd ed. Cologne: Böhlau, 1988.

Setton, Kenneth M. (Ed.). *A History of the Crusades*, 6 vols. Madison: University of Wisconsin, and Philadelphia: University of Pennsylvania, 1955–1989.

Shaked, Shaul. "Some Islamic reports concerning Zoroastrianism." *Jerusalem Studies in Arabic and Islam* 17 (1994), pp. 43–84.

———. *From Zoroastrian Iran to Islam: Studies in Religious History and Intercultural Contacts*. Aldershot, U.K.: Variorum Reprints, 1995.

Sharma, Arvind. *Studies in "Alberuni's India"* (Studies in Oriental Religions). Wiesbaden: O. Harrassowitz, 1983.

Shatzmiller, Maya (Ed.). *Crusaders and Muslims in Twelfth-Century Syria*. Leiden: E. J. Brill, 1993.

Shboul, Ahmad. *Al-Masʿūdī and His World: A Muslim Humanist and His Interest in Non-Muslims*. London: Ithaca Press, 1979.

Sirat, C. "Un midraš juif en habit musulman: La vision de Moïse sur le mont Sinai." *Revue de l'Histoire des Religions* 168 (1965), pp. 15–28.

Sivan, Emmanuel. "La genèse de la contre-croisade: Un traité damasquin du début du XIIe siècle." *Journal Asiatique* (1966), pp. 197–224.

———. "Notes sur la situation des chrétiens à l'époque ayyubide." *Revue de l'Histoire des Religions* 172 (1967), pp. 117–130.

———. "Réfugiés syro-palestiniens au temps des Croisades." *Revue des Etudes Islamiques* 25 (1967), pp. 135–147.

———. "Le caractère sacré de Jérusalem dans l'Islam aux XIIe-XIIIe siècles." *Studia Islamica* 27 (1967), pp. 149–182.

———. *L'Islam et la Croisade: Idéologie et propagande dans les réactions musulmanes aux Croisades*. Paris: Adrien Maisonneuve, 1968.

Skalli, Khadidja. "L'image des chrétiens dans les sources maghrébines au Moyen Age: Etude critique des sources et bibliographie." Ph.D. diss., University of Bordeaux, 1982.

Sourdel, Dominique. "Un pamphlet musulman anonyme d'époque ʿabbaside contre les chrétiens." *Revue des Etudes Islamiques* 34 (1966), pp. 1–33.

Speight, R. Marston. "Attitudes toward Christians as revealed in the Musnad of al-Tayālisī." *Muslim World* 63 (1973), pp. 249–268.

———. "The place of Christians in ninth-century North Africa, according to Muslim sources." *Islamochristiana* 4 (1978), pp. 47–65.

Steenbrink, Karel A. "Jesus and the Holy Spirit in the writings of Nūr al-Dīn al-Ranīrī." *Islam and Christian-Muslim Relations* 1 (1990), pp. 192–207.

Steinschneider, M. *Polemische und apologetische Literatur in arabischer Sprache zwischen Muslimen, Christen und Juden, nebst Anhänge verwandten Inhaltes mit Benutzung handschriftlicher Quellen*. Leipzig, 1877; repr., Hildesheim: Georg Olms, 1966.

Stern, S. M. "Quotations from apocryphical gospels in ʿAbd al-Jabbār." *Journal of Theological Studies* 18 (1967), pp. 34–57. Repr. in S. M. Stern, *History and Culture in the Medieval Muslim World* (London: Variorum Reprints, 1984), ch. 2.

———. "ʿAbd al-Jabbār's account of how Christ's religion was falsified by the adoption of Roman customs." *Journal of Theological Studies* 19 (1968), pp. 128–185. Repr. in S. M. Stern, *History and Culture in the Medieval Muslim World* (London: Variorum Reprints, 1984), ch. 3.

Stieglecker, Hermann. "Die muhammedanische Pentateuchkritik zu Beginn des 2. Jahrhunderts." *Theologisch-praktische Quartalschrift* 88 (1935), pp. 72–87, 282–302, 472–486.

Stillman, Norman A. *The Jews of Arab Lands: A History and Source Book*. Philadelphia: Jewish Publishing Society of America, 1979.

Strauss, E. "The social isolation of Ahl adh-Dhimma." In *Etudes Orientales à la mémoire de Paul Hirschler*. Ed. Ottó Komlós. Budapest, 1950, pp. 73–94.

Stroumsa, S. "The Barāhima in early Kalām." *Jerusalem Studies in Arabic and Islam* 6 (1985), pp. 229–241.

———, and G. G. Stroumsa. "Aspects of anti-Manichaean polemics in late Antiquity and under early Islam." *Harvard Theological Review* 18 (1988), pp. 37–58.

Stummer, Friedrich. "Bemerkungen zum Götzenbuch des Ibn al-Kalbī." *Zeitschrift der Deutschen Morgenländischen Gesellschaft* 98 (1944), pp. 377–394.

Suermann, H. "Orientalische Christen und der Islam: Christliche Texte aus der Zeit 639–750." *Zeitschrift für Missionswissenschaft und Religionswissenschaft* 67 (1983), pp. 120–136.

Swartz, Merlin. "The position of Jews in Arab lands following the rise of Islam." *Muslim World* 60 (1970), pp. 6–24.

Taeschner, Franz. "Die alttestamentlichen Bibelzitate, vor allem aus dem Pentateuch, in at-Tabarī's *Kitāb ad-Dīn wad-Daula* und ihre Bedeutung für die Frage nach der Echtheit dieser Schrift." *Oriens Christianus* 31 (1934), pp. 23–39.

Tahmi, Mahmoud. *L'Encyclopédisme musulman à l'âge classique: Le Livre de la création et de l'histoire de Maqdisī*. Paris: Maisonneuve et Larose. 1008.

Talbi, Mohamed. "Le Christianisme maghrébin de la conquête musulmane à sa disparition: Une tentative d'explication." In *Conversion and Continuity*. Ed. M. Gervers and R. Bikhazi. Toronto: Pontifical Institute of Mediaeval Studies, 1990, pp. 313–351.

Tardieu, Michel. "L'arrivée des Manichéens à al-Hīra." In *La Syrie de Byzance à l'Islam*. Ed. Pierre Canivet and Jean-Paul Rey-Coquais. Damascus: Institut Français de Damas, 1992, pp. 15–24.

Tartar, Georges. *Dialogue islamo-chrétien sous le calife Al-Maʾmûn (813–834): Les épîtres d'Al-Hashimî et d'Al-Kindî*. Paris: Nouvelles Editions Latines, 1985.

Thomas, David. "Two Muslim-Christian debates from the early Shīʿite tradition." *Journal of Semitic Studies* 33 (1988), pp. 53–80.

———, *Anti-Christian Polemic in Early Islam: Abū ʿĪsā al-Warrāq's 'Against the Trinity'*. Cambridge: Cambridge University Press, 1992.

———. "The miracles of Jesus in early Islamic polemic." *Journal of Semitic Studies* 39 (1994), pp. 221–243.

———. "The Bible in early Muslim anti-Christian polemic." *Islam and Christian-Muslim Relations* 7 (1996), pp. 29–38.

Tibawi, A. L. "Jerusalem, its place in Islam and Arab history." *Islamic Quarterly* 12 (1968), pp. 185–218.

Tritton, A. S. *The Caliphs and Their Non-Muslim Subjects: A Critical Study of the Covenant of ʿUmar*. London: Humphrey Milford–Oxford University Press, 1930; Repr. 1970.

Troupeau, Gérard. "Les croyances des Chrétiens présentées par un hérésiographe musulman du XIIe siècle." In G. Troupeau, *Etudes sur le christianisme arabe au Moyen Age*. London: Variorum, 1995.

Turan, Osman. "Les souverains Seldjoukides et leurs sujets non-Musulmans." *Studia Islamica* 1 (1953), pp. 65–100.

———. "L'Islamisation dans la Turquie du Moyen Age." *Studia Islamica* 10 (1959), pp. 137–152.

Turki, Abdel-Mağid. "Situation du 'tributaire' qui insulte l'islam, au regard de la doctrine et de la jurisprudence musulmanes." *Studia Islamica* 30 (1969), pp. 39–72.

———. *Théologiens et juristes de l'Espagne musulmane: Aspects polémiques*. Paris: G. P. Maisonneuve et Larose, 1982.

———. "Pour ou contre la légalité du séjour des musulmans en territoire reconquis par les chrétiens: Justification doctrinale et réalité historique." In *Religionsgespräche im Mittelalter*. Ed. Bernard Lewis and Friedrich Niewöhner (Wolfenbütteler Mittelalter-Studien, Vol. 4). Wiesbaden: O. Harrassowitz, 1992, pp. 305–323.

Udovitch, Abraham. "The Jews and Islam in the high Middle Ages: A case of the Muslim view of difference." In *Gli Ebrei nell'Alto Medioevo, 30 marzo–5 aprile 1978* (Settimane di Studio del Centro italiano di studi sul'alto medioevo, Vol. 26), vol. 2. Spoleto: Presso la Sede del Centro, 1980, pp. 655–683, discussion pp. 685–711.

Vajda, Georges. "La version des septante dans la littérature musulmane." *Revue des Etudes Juives* 90 (1931), pp. 65–70.

———. "Observations sur quelques citations bibliques

chez Ibn Qotayba." *Revue des Etudes Juives* 99 (1935), pp. 68–91.

———. "Juifs et musulmans selon le Hadīṯ." *Journal Asiatique* 229 (1937), pp. 57–127.

———. "Jeûne Musulman et jeûne Juif." *Hebrew Union College Annual* 12–13 (1937–38), pp. 367–385.

———. "Les Zindīqs en pays d'Islam au début de la période Abbaside." *Rivista degli studi orientali* 17 (1938), pp. 173–229.

———. "La description du temple de Jérusalem d'après le K. al-masālik wal-mamālik d'al-Muhallabī: Ses éléments bibliques et rabbiniques." *Journal Asiatique* 247 (1959), pp. 193–202.

———. "Ahl al-kitāb." *Encyclopaedia of Islam*, new ed., vol. 1. Leiden: E. J. Brill, 1960, pp. 264–266.

———. "Le témoignage d'al-Māturidī sur la doctrine des Manichéens, des Daysānites et des Marcionites." *Arabica* 13 (1966), pp. 1–38, 113–128.

Vernet, Juan. "Le Tafsīr au service de la polémique antimusulmane." *Studia Islamica* 32 (1970), pp. 305–309.

Vryonis Jr., Speros. *The Decline of Medieval Hellenism in Asia Minor and the Process of Islamization from the Eleventh through the Fifteenth Century*. Berkeley: University of California Press, 1971.

Waardenburg, Jacques. *Zien met anderman's ogen* [To look with someone else's eyes]. Inaugural lecture, University of Utrecht. The Hague: Mouton, 1975.

———. "L'histoire des religions dans l'Islam médiéval." In *Akten des VIII. Kongresses für Arabistik und Islamistik, Göttingen, August 1974*. Göttingen: Vandenhoeck and Ruprecht, 1976, pp. 372–384.

———. "Two lights perceived: Medieval Islam and Christianity." *Nederlands Theologisch Tijdschrift* 31 (1977), pp. 267–289.

———. "Jugements musulmans sur les religions non-islamiques à l'époque médiévale." In *Actes du 8me Congrès de l'Union Européenne des Arabisants et Islamisants (U.E.A.I.), Aix-en-Provence, septembre 1976*. Aix-en-Provence: Edisud, 1978, pp. 323–341.

———. "World religions as seen in the light of Islam." In *Islam Past Influence and Present Challenge*. Ed. Alford T. Welch and Pierre Cachia. Edinburgh: Edinburgh University Press, 1979, pp. 245–275.

———. "Towards a periodization of earliest Islam according to its relations with other religions." In *Proceedings of the 9th Congress of the U.E.A.I. Amsterdam 1978*. Leiden: E. J. Brill, 1981, pp. 304–326.

———. "Types of judgment in Islam about other religions." In *Middle East. 30th International Congress of Human Sciences in Asia and North Africa, Mexico City 1976*. Ed. Graciela de la Lama. Mexico City: Colegio de Mexico, 1982, pp. 138–140.

———. "Muslim studies of other religions: The medieval period." *Orientations* 1 (1992), pp. 10–38.

———. "Cultural contact and concepts of religion: Three examples from Islamic history." In *Miscellanea Arabica et Islamica*. Ed. F. de Jong. Leuven: Peeters, 1993, pp. 293–325.

———. *Islamisch-Christliche Beziehungen: Geschichtliche Streifzüge* (Religionswissenschaftliche Studien, Vol. 23). Altenberge: Oros Verlag, and Würzburg: Echter Verlag, 1993.

———. "Koranologie und Christologie: Ein formaler Vergleich." In *Gnosisforschung und Religionsgeschichte: Festschrift für Kurt Rudolph zum 65. Geburtstag*. Ed. H. Preissler, H. Seiwert, and H. Mürmel. Marburg: Diagonal Verlag, 1994, pp. 575–585.

Wansbrough, John. "The safe-conduct in Muslim chancery practice." *Bulletin of the School of Oriental and African Studies* 34 (1971), pp. 20–35.

Wasserstein, David. "Jews, Christians and Muslims in medieval Spain." *Journal of Jewish Studies* 43 (1992), pp. 175–186.

Wasserstrom, Steven M. "The 'Isāwiyya revisited." *Studia Islamica* 75 (1992), pp. 57–80.

———. "'The Shīʿīs are the Jews of our community': An interreligious comparison within Sunnī thought." *Israel Oriental Studies* 14 (1994), pp. 297–324.

———, *Between Muslim and Jew: The Problem of Symbiosis under Early Islam*. Princeton, N.J.: Princeton University Press, 1995.

Watt, W. Montgomery. "The early development of the Muslim attitude to the Bible." Transactions of the Glasgow University Oriental Society 16 (1955–56), pp. 50–62.

———. "Al-Biruni and the Study of Non-Islamic Religions." *al-Mushir* 15 (1973), pp. 357–361. Repr. in *Al-Bīrūnī Commemorative Volume* (Karachi: Hamdard Academy, 1979), pp. 414–419.

———. "A Muslim account of Christian doctrine." *Hamdard Islamicus* 6 (1983), pp. 57–68. Appeared under the title of "Ash-Shahrastānī's account of Christian doctrine" in *Islamochristiana* 9 (1983), pp. 249–259.

———. "Islamic attitudes to cultural borrowing." *Scottish Journal of Religious Studies* 7 (1986), pp. 141–149.

Wismer, Don. *The Islamic Jesus. An Annotated Bibliography of Sources in English and French*. New York: Garland, 1977.

Wright, G. R. H. "Tradition on the birth of Christ in Christianity and Islam." In *As on the First Day: Essays in Religious Constants*. Ed. G. R. H. Wright. Leiden: E. J. Brill, 1987, pp. 121–130.

Yarshater, Ehsan, and Dale Bishop (Eds.). *Biruni Symposium* (Persian Studies series, No. 7). New York: Iran Center, Columbia University, 1976.

Zachariadou, Elizabeth A. "Religious dialogue between Byzantines and Turks during the Ottoman expansion." In *Religionsgespräche im Mittelalter*. Ed. Bernard Lewis and Friedrich Niewöhner (Wolfenbüttler Mittelalter-Studien, Vol. 4). Wiesbaden: O. Harrassowitz, 1992, pp. 289–304.

The Modern Period (ca. 1500–ca. 1950)

TEXTS IN TRANSLATION

ʿAbduh, Muhammad. *Al-Islām wa'l-nasrāniyya maʿa al-ʿilm wa'l-madaniyya*. Cairo: Dār al-Manār, 1902; 8th ed. 1954. German transl. Gunnar Hasselblatt, "Herkunft und Auswirkungen der Apologetik Muhammad Abduh's (1849–1905), untersucht an seiner Schrift: Islam und Christentum im Verhältnis zu Wissenschaft und Zivilisation." Ph.D. diss., University of Göttingen, 1968.

Ahmad Khan, Sayyid. *Tabyīn al-kalām: The Mohammedan Commentary on the Holy Bible*. Parts I and II (Urdu and English). Ghazeepore: Private Press of the author, 1862 and 1865. Part III (Urdu) in the author's *Tusānīf-i Ahmadīyah*, Vol. 1, Parts 1 and 2. Aligarh Institute Press, 1883, 1887, pp. 2–129.

Ali, Ameer. "Christianity from the Islamic Standpoint." *Hibbert Journal* 4 (1906), pp. 241–259.

Celebi, Ewliyā. *Das religiöse Leben auf Kreta nach Ewliyā Celebi*, by Paul Hidirioglou. Leiden: E. J. Brill, 1969.

Damanhūrī, Shaykh. Moshe Perlmann (Ed. and Tr.). *Shaykh Damanhūrī on the Churches of Cairo (1739)* (University of California Publications: Near Eastern Studies, Vol. 19). Berkeley: University of California Press, 1975.

Gaudeul, Jean-Marie. *Encounters and Clashes: Islam and Christianity in History*. Vol. 2: *Texts*. Rome: Pontificio Istituto di Studi Arabi e Islamici, 1984.

Huart, Cl., and L. Massignon. "Les entretiens de Lahore entre le Prince impérial Dārā Shikūh et l'ascète hindou Baba La'l Das." *Journal Asiatique* 209 (1926), pp. 285–334.

Jabartī, ʿAbd al-Rahmān. *Ajā'ib al-āthār fī 'l-tarājim wa'l-akhbār*. French transl. Chefik Mansour Bey, *Merveilles biographiques et historiques du Cheikh Abd el-Rahman el-Djabarti*, 9 vols. (Cairo, 1888–1894). *Index* made by Gaston Wiet (Cairo: Dar al-Maaref, 1954).

Kairānawī. Rahmatullāh ibn Khalīl al-ʿUthmānī al-. *Izhār al-haqq*. French transl. Pascal Vincent Carlette. Paris, 1880. English translation *Izhār-ul-haq* (*Truth revealed*) (London: Ta-Ha, 1989).

Maghribī, Al-Husayn Ibn Muhammad b. Saʿīd b. ʿĪsā al-Lā'ī al-. *Risāla fī baqā' al-Yahūd fī ʿard al-Yaman*. Ed. and transl. Michela Fabbro in *Islamochristiana* 16 (1990), pp. 67–90.

STUDIES

D'un Orient l'autre. Les métamorphoses successives des perceptions et connaissances. 2 vols. Vol. 1: *Configurations*. Vol. 2: *Identifications*. Paris: Editions du CNRS, 1991.

Abdulkadir, A. F. M. "Early Muslim visitors of Europe from India." In *6th All-India Oriental Conference Proceedings*. Patna, 1930, pp. 83–96.

Adamovic, Milan. "Europa im Spiegel osmanischer Reiseberichte." In *Asien blickt auf Europa: Begegnungen und Irritationen*. Ed. Tilman Nagel. Wiesbaden: Franz Steiner, 1990, 61–71.

Anawati, Georges C. "Polémique, apologie et dialogue islamo-chrétiens: Positions classiques médiévales et positions contemporaines." *Euntes Docete* 22 (1969), pp. 375–452.

Ascher, Abraham, et al. *The Mutual Effects of the Islamic and Judeo-Christian Worlds: The East European Pattern* (Studies on Society in Change). New York: Brooklyn College Press, 1976.

Ayoub, Mahmud. "Islam and Christianity: A study of Muhammad ʿAbduhs view of the two religions." *Humaniora Islamica* 2 (1974), pp. 121–137.

———. "Muslim views of Christianity: Some modern examples." *Islamochristiana* 10 (1984), pp. 49–70.

Baljon, J. M. S. "Indian muftis and non-Muslims." *Islam and Christian-Muslim Relations* 2 (1991), pp. 227–241.

Baron, Salo Wittmayer. *A Social and Religious History of the Jews*, 2nd ed., Vol. 18: *The Ottoman Empire, Persia, Ethiopia, India and China*. New York: Columbia University Press, and Philadelphia: Jewish Publishing Society of America, 1983.

Binswanger, Karl. *Untersuchungen zum Status der Nichtmuslime im Osmanischen Reich des 16. Jahrhunderts, mit einer Neudefinition des Begriffes 'Ḏimma'*. Munich: R. Trofenik, 1977.

Blanks, David R. (Ed.). *Images of the Other: Europe and the Muslim World before 1700*. Cairo: American University in Cairo Press, 1997.

Borrmans, Maurice. "Le Commentaire du Manār à propos du verset coranique sur l'amitié des Musulmans pour les Chrétiens (5, 82)." *Islamochristiana* 1 (1975), pp. 71–86.

Bozkurt, Gülnihal. "Die rechtliche Lage der nichtmuslimischen Untertanen im osmanischen Reich während der Reformzeit bis Ende des 1. Weltkrieges." Ph.D. diss., University of Cologne, 1937.

Braude, Benjamin, and Bernard Lewis (Eds.). *Christians and Jews in the Ottoman Empire: The Functioning of a Plural Society*. 2 vols. Vol. 1: *The Central Lands*; Vol. 2: *The Arabic-Speaking Lands*. New York: Holmes and Meier, 1982.

Cachia, Pierre. "Themes related to Christianity and Judaism in modern Egyptian drama and fiction." *Journal of Arabic Literature* 2 (1971), pp. 178–194.

Cardaillac, Louis. *Morisques et Chrétiens: Un affrontement polémique (1492–1640)*. Paris: Klincksieck, 1977.

Carter, B. L. "On spreading the Gospel to Egyptians sitting in darkness: The political problem of missionaries in Egypt in the 1930s." *Middle East Studies* 20 (1984), pp. 18–36.

Chabbi, Moncef. "L'image de l'Occident chez les intellectuels tunisiens dans la seconde moitié du XIXe siècle (2 vols.)." Ph.D. diss., University of Reims, 1983.

Chouraqui, André N. *Between East and West: A History of the Jews of North Africa*. Philadelphia: Jewish Publication Society of America, 1968.

Cohen, Amnon. "The Ottoman approach to Christians and Christianity in sixteenth-century Jerusalem." *Islam and Christian-Muslim Relations* 7 (1996), pp. 205–212.

Cohen, Hayim J. *The Jews of the Middle East, 1860–1972*. New York: John Wiley, 1973.

———, and Tsevi Yehuda (Eds.). *Asian and African Jews in the Middle East, 1860–1971* (in Hebrew). Jerusalem: Mekhon Ben-Tsevi, 1976.

Cohen, Mark R. "The Jews under Islam: from the Rise of Islam to Sabbatai Zevi." In *Bibliographical Essays in Medieval Jewish Studies*. New York, 1976, pp. 169–229. Repr. with a supplement as Princeton Near East Paper, No. 32, Princeton University, 1981.

Conrad, Lawrence I. "Reflections by a nineteenth-century convert to Islam on Judaism and Christianity in Ottoman Jerusalem." *Islam and Christian-Muslim Relations* 7 (1996), pp. 63–73.

Davison, Roderic H. "Turkish attitudes concerning Christian-Muslim equality in the nineteenth century." *American Historical Review* 59 (1954), pp. 844–864.

Djaït, Hichem. *Europe and Islam*. Berkeley: University of California Press, 1985. Original text: *L'Europe et l'Islam*. Paris: Seuil, 1978.

Dorman Jr., Harry Gaylord. *Toward Understanding Islam: Contemporary Apologetic of Islam and Missionary Policy*. New York: Bureau of Publication, Teachers College, Columbia University, 1948.

Epstein, Mark Alan. *The Ottoman Jewish Communities and their Role in the Fifteenth and Sixteenth Centuries* (Islamkundliche Untersuchungen, Vol. 56). Freiburg: Klaus Schwarz, 1980.

Fischel, Walter J. "The Jews of Persia, 1795–1940." *Jewish Social Studies* 12 (1950), pp. 119–160.

Fischer-Galati, Stephen A. *Ottoman Imperialism and German Protestantism 1521–1555*. Cambridge, Mass.: Harvard University Press, 1959.

Forbes, A. D. W. "Liu Chih (Liu Chiai-Lien)." *Encyclopaedia of Islam*, new ed., vol. 5 (Leiden: E. J. Brill, 1986), pp. 770–771.

Forward, M. "Syed Ameer Ali: A bridge-builder?" *Islam and Christian-Muslim Relations* 6 (1995), pp. 45–62.

Friedmann, Yohanan. "Islamic thought in relation to the Indian context." *Islam et Société en Asie du Sud* 9 (1986), pp. 79–91.

Gaborieau, Marc. *Récit d'un voyageur musulman au Tibet*. Paris: Klincksieck, 1973.

Gandhi, Rajmohan. *Eight Lives: A Study of the Hindu-Muslim Encounter*. Albany, N.Y.: SUNY Press, 1986.

Gervers, Michael, and Ramzi Jibran Bikhazi (Eds.). *Conversion and Continuity: Indigenous Christian Communities in Islamic Lands, Eighth to Eighteenth Centuries*. Toronto: Pontifical Institute of Mediaeval Studies, 1990.

Ghulam, Mohammed. "Islam versus Christianity." *Moslem World* 10 (1920), pp. 76–81.

Gibb, H. A. R., and Harold Bowen. *Islamic Society and the West: A Study of the Impact of Western Civilization on Moslem Culture in the Near East*. Vol. 1 in two parts: *Islamic Society in the 18th century*. London: Oxford University Press, 1950– 1957.

Goddard, Hugh. *Muslim Perceptions of Christianity*. London: Grey Seal, 1996.

Gregorian, Vartan. "Minorities of Isfahan: The Armenian Community of Isfahan, 1587–1722." *Iranian Studies* 7 (1974), pp. 652–680.

Habibullah, A. B. M. "Medieval Indo-Persian literature relating to Hindu science and philosophy, 1000–1800 A.D.: A bibliographical survey." *Indian Historical Quarterly* 14 (1938), pp. 167–181.

Haddad, Robert M. Syrian *Christians in Muslim Society: An Interpretation* (Princeton Studies on the Middle East). Princeton, N.J.: Princeton University Press, 1970.

Haddad, Yvonne Yazbeck, and Wadi Z. Haddad (Eds.). *Christian-Muslim Encounters*. Gainesville: University Press of Florida, 1995.

Hasan, Mushirul. *Communal and Pan-Islamic Trends in Colonial India*, 2nd ed. Delhi: Manohar, 1985.

———. *Islam and Indian Nationalism: Reflections on Abul Kalam Azad*. Delhi: Manohar, 1992.

Hasluck, F. W. *Christianity and Islam under the Sultans*. 2 vols. Oxford: Clarendon Press, 1929.

Hasselblatt, Gunnar. "Herkunft und Auswirkungen der Apologetik Muhammad Abduh's (1849–1905), untersucht an seiner Schrift: Islam und Christentum im Verhältnis zu Wissenschaft und Zivilisation." Ph.D. diss., University of Göttingen, 1968.

Henninger, Joseph. "Arabische Bibelübersetzungen vom Frühmittelalter bis zum 19. Jahrhundert." *Neue Zeitschrift für Missionswissenschaft* 17 (1961), pp. 201–223.

Horn, Paul. *Die Denkwürdigkeiten Schâh Tahmâsp's des Ersten von Persien (1515–1576)*. Aus dem Originaltext zum ersten Male übersetzt und mit Erläuterungen versehen. Strasbourg: Trübner, 1891.

Hourani, Albert H. *Minorities in the Arab World*. (Issued under the auspices of the Royal Institute of International Affairs.) London: Oxford University Press, 1947.

Huart, Cl. and L. Massignon. "Les entretiens de Lahore entre le Prince impérial Dārā Shikūh et l'ascète hindou Baba La'l Das." *Journal Asiatique* 209 (1926), pp. 285–334.

Inalcik, Halil. "The policy of Mehmet II toward the Greek population of Istanbul and the Byzantine buildings of the city." *Dumbarton Oaks Papers* 23 (1970), pp. 213–249.

———. "Status of the Greek Orthodox Patriarch under the Ottomans." *Turkish Review Quarterly Digest* 6 (1992), pp. 23–49.

Jeffery, Arthur. "New Trends in Moslem Apologetic." In *The Moslem World of Today*. Ed. John R. Mott. London: Hodder and Stoughton, 1925, pp. 305–321.

Jennings, Ronald C. *Christians and Muslims in Ottoman Cyprus and the Mediterranean World, 1571–1640*. New York: New York University Press, 1993.

Johansen, Baber. *Muhammad Husain Haikal: Europa und der Orient im Weltbild eines ägyptischen Liberalen* (Beiruter Texte und Studien, Vol. 5). Wiesbaden: Franz Steiner, 1967.

Joseph, John. *The Nestorians and Their Muslim Neighbors*. Princeton, N.J.: Princeton University Press, 1961.

Joseph, Suad, and Barbara L. K. Pillsbury. *Muslim Christian Conflicts: Economic, Political and Social Origins*. Boulder, Colo: Westview Press, 1978.

Karpat, K.H. "Ottoman views and policies towards the Orthodox Christian church." *Greek Orthodox Theological Review* 31 (1986), pp. 131–155.

Keddie, Nikki R. "The revolt of Islam, 1700 to 1993: Comparative considerations and relations to imperialism." *Comparative Studies in Society and History* 36 (1994), pp. 463–487.

Kenbib, M. "Les relations entre musulmans et juifs au Maroc, 1859–1945: Essai bibliographique." *Hespéris Tamuda* 23 (1985), pp. 83–104.

Kenny, L. M. "East versus West in Al-Muqtataf, 1875–1900: Image and Self-Image." In *Essays on Islamic Civilization Presented to Niyazi Berkes*. Ed. D. P. Little. Leiden: E. J. Brill, 1976, pp. 140–154.

Kerr, David A. "Muhammad Iqbal's thought on religion: Reflections in the spirit of Christian-Muslim dialogue." *Islamochristiana* 15 (1989), pp. 25–55.

Kewenig, Wilhelm. *Die Koexistenz der Religionsgemeinschaften im Libanon* (Neue Kölner rechtswissenschaftliche Abhandlungen, Vol. 30). Berlin: Walter de Gruyter, 1965.

Khaouam, Mounir. *Le Christ dans la pensée moderne de l'Islam et dans le Christianisme*. Beirut: Ed. Khalifé, 1983.

Krämer, Gudrun. *The Jews in Modern Egypt 1914–1952*. Seattle: University of Washington Press, 1989.

Kreiser, Klaus. "Der japanische Sieg über Rußland (1905) und sein Echo unter den Muslimen." *Welt des Islams* 21 (1981), pp. 209–239.

Krikorian, Mesrob K. *Armenians in the Service of the Ottoman Empire 1860–1908*. London, 1977.

Lachèse, Jean-Philippe. "Le voyage d'un iranien en Europe à la fin du XIXe siècle." *Mélanges de l'Institut Dominicain d'Etudes Orientales au Caire* 18 (1988), pp. 359–371.

Landau, Jacob M. *Jews in Nineteenth-Century Egypt* (New York University Studies in Near Eastern Civilization, Vol. 2). New York: New York University Press, and London: University of London Press, 1969.

Laoust, Henri. "Renouveau de l'apologétique missionnaire traditionelle au XXe siècle dans l'oeuvre de Rashīd Riḍā." In *Prédication et propagande au Moyen Age: Islam, Byzance, Occident*. Paris: Presses Universitaires de France, 1983), pp. 271–279.

Leven, Narcisse. *Cinquante ans d'histoire: L'Alliance Israélite Universelle (1860–1910)*. Paris: Alcan, 1911.

Lewis, Bernard. *Islam and the West*. New York: Oxford University Press, 1993.

Lichtenstädter, Ilse. "The distinction dress of non-Muslims in Islamic countries." *Historica Judaica* 5 (1943), pp. 35–52.

Louca, Anouar. *Voyageurs et écrivains égyptiens en France au XIXe siècle*. Paris: Didier, 1970.

Mandel, Neville. *The Arabs and Zionism before World War I*. Berkeley: University of California Press, 1976.

Matteo, Ignazio di. *La divinità di Cristo e la dottrina della Trinità in Maometto e nei polemisti musulmani* (Biblica et Orientalia, Vol. 8). Rome: Pontificio Istituto Biblico, 1938.

McAuliffe, Jane Dammen. *Qurʾānic Christians: An Analysis of Classical and Modern Exegesis*. New York: Cambridge University Press, 1991.

Miller, Susan Lynn Gilson. "A Voyage to the Land of Rum: The 'Rihlah' of the Moroccan Muhammad Al-Saffar to France, December 1845–March 1846." Ph.D. diss., University of Michigan, 1976.

Montgomery, John Warwick. "The apologetic approach of Muhammad Ali and its implications for Christian apologetics." *Muslim World* 51 (1961), pp. 111–120.

Moor, Ed de. "Egyptian love in a cold climate: Egyptian students in Paris at the beginning of the 20th century." In *The Middle East and Europe: Encoun-*

ters and Exchanges. Ed. Geert Jan van Gelder and Ed de Moor. Amsterdam: Rodopi, 1992, pp. 147–166.

Motzki, Harald. *Dimma und Egalité: Die nichtmuslimischen Minderheiten Ägyptens in der zweiten Hälfte des 18. Jahrhunderts und die Expedition Bonapartes (1798–1801)* (Studien zum Minderheitenproblem im Islam, Vol. 5). Bonn: Selbstverlag des Orientalischen Seminars der Universität Bonn, 1979.

Nagel, Tilman, et al. *Studien zum Minderheitenproblem im Islam*. 5 vols. Bonn: Selbstverlag des Orientalischen Seminars, 1973–79.

Nettler, Ronald L. (Ed.). *Studies in Muslim-Jewish Relations*, vol. 1. Chur: Harwood Academic, 1993.

——— (Ed.). *Medieval and Modern Perspectives on Muslim-Jewish Relations*. Luxembourg: Harwood Academic, 1995.

Orientalist. "The Moslem doctrine of Revelation and Islamic propaganda." *Muslim World* 25 (1935), pp. 67–72.

Palmiera, A. "Corrispondenza da Costantinopoli." *Bessarione* 5 (1900), pp. 145–161.

Pérès, Henri. *L'Espagne vue par les voyageurs musulmans de 1610 à 1930*. Paris: A. Maisonneuve, 1937.

———. "Voyageurs musulmans en Europe aux XIXe et XXe siècles." In *Mélanges Maspéro*, vol. 3: *Orient Islamique* (Mémoires publiés par les membres de l'IFAO du Caire, 68). Le Caire, 1940, pp. 185–195.

Perlmann, Moshe. "A late Muslim Jewish disputation." *Proceedings of the American Academy for Jewish Research* 12 (1942), pp. 51–58.

———. "A XVIth century pamphlet against the churches of Egypt." In *Studies in Judaism and Islam, Presented to S. D. Goitein*. Jerusalem: Magnes Press and Hebrew University, 1981, pp. 175–179.

———. "Shurunbulalī Militant." In *Studies in Islamic History and Civilization, in Honour of Professor David Ayalon*. Ed. M. Sharon. Jerusalem: Cana, and Leiden: E. J. Brill, 1986, pp. 407–410.

Poonawala, Ismail K. "The evolution of al-Ǧabartī's historical thinking as reflected in the *Muzhir* and the *ʿAǧāʾib*." *Arabica* 15 (1968), pp. 270–288.

Powell, Avril Ann. "Mawlānā Rahmat Allah Kairānawī and Muslim-Christian controversy in India in the mid-19th century." *Journal of the Royal Asiatic Society* 20 (1976), pp. 42–63.

———. *Muslims and Missionaries in pre-Mutiny India*. Richmond: Curzon Press, 1993.

Reilly, James A. "Inter-confessional relations in nineteenth-century Syria: Damascus, Homs and Hama compared." *Islam and Christian-Muslim Relations* 7 (1996), pp. 213–224.

Rousseau, Richard W. (Ed.). *Christianity and Islam: The Struggling Dialogue*. Scranton, Pa.: Ridge Row Press, 1985.

Sandjian, Avedis. *The Armenian Communities in Syria under Ottoman Dominion*. Cambridge, Mass.: Harvard University Press, 1965.

Sarnelli Cerqua, Clelia. "Al-Hağarī a Rouen e a Parigi." In *Studi arabo-islamici in onore di Roberto Rubinacci nel suo settantesimo compleanno*. Naples: Istituto Universitario Orientale, 1985, pp. 551–568.

Scheel, Helmut. *Die staatsrechtliche Stellung der ökumenischen Kirchenfürsten in der alten Türkei: Ein Beitrag zur Geschichte der türkischen Verfassung und Verwaltung* (Abhandlungen der Preussischen Akademie der Wissenschaften. Philosophisch-historische Klasse, Vol. 9). Berlin: Verlag der Akademie der Wissenschaften, 1943.

Schirrmacher, Christine. *Mit den Waffen des Gegners: Christlich-muslimische Kontroversen im 19. und 20. Jahrhundert* (Islamkundliche Untersuchungen, Vol. 162). Berlin: Klaus Schwarz, 1992.

———. "Muslim apologetics and the Agra debates of 1854: A nineteenth-century turning point." *Bulletin of the Henry Martyn Institute of Islamic Studies* 13 (1994), pp. 74–84.

Schlicht, Alfred. *Frankreich und die syrischen Christen 1799–1861* (Islamkundliche Untersuchungen, Vol. 61). Berlin: Klaus Schwarz, 1981.

Schumann, Olaf. *Der Christus der Muslime: Christologische Aspekte in der arabisch-islamischen Literatur* (Missionswissenschaftliche Forschungen, Vol. 10). Gütersloh: Gerd Mohn, 1975. 2nd ed. Cologne: Böhlau, 1988.

Seferta, Y. H. R. "The ideas of Muhammad ʿAbduh and Rashid Rida concerning Jesus." *Encounter* (Rome) 124 (April 1986).

Sharma, Sri Ram. *The Religious Policy of the Mughal Emperors*, 3rd, rev. enl. ed. Bombay: Asia Publishing House, 1972.

Shayegan, Daryush. *Les relations de l'hindouisme et du soufisme d'après le Majmaʿ al-bahrayn de Dārā Shokūh* (Collection Philosophia Perennis). Paris: Ed. de la Différence, 1979.

Shepard, William E. "A modernist view of Islam and other religions [Ahmad Amīn]." *Muslim World* 65 (1975), pp. 79–92.

Spies, Otto. "Schicksale türkischer Kriegsgefangener in Deutschland nach den Türkenkriegen." In *Festschrift Werner Caskel*. Leiden: E. J. Brill, 1968, pp. 316–335.

Steenbrink, Karel A. *Dutch Colonialism and Indonesian Islam: Contacts and Conflicts (1596–1950)* (Currents of Encounter, Vol. 7). Amsterdam: Rodopi, 1993.

Stillman, Norman A. *The Jews of Arab Lands: A History and Source Book*. Philadelphia: Jewish Publication Society of America, 1979.

———, *The Jews of Arab Lands in Modern Times*. Philadelphia: Jewish Publication Society of America, 1991.

Stümpel-Hatami, Isabel. *Das Christentum aus der Sicht zeitgenössischer iranischer Autoren: Eine Untersuchung religionskundlicher Publikationen in persischer Sprache* (Islamkundliche Untersuchungen, Vol. 195). Berlin: Klaus Schwarz Verlag, 1996.

Sweetman, J. Windrow. "A Muslim's view of Christianity." *Muslim World* 34 (1944), pp. 278–284.

Tritton, A. S. "Islam and the protected religions." *Journal of the Royal Asiatic Society* 1927, pp. 475–485; 1928, pp. 485– 508; 1931, pp. 311–339.

Troll, Christian W. "Sayyid Ahmad Khan on Matthew 5: 17–20." *Islamochristiana* 3 (1977), pp. 99–105.

———. *Sayyid Ahmad Khān: A Reinterpretation of Muslim Theology*. New Delhi: Vikas, 1978.

———. "Salvation of Non-Muslims: Views of some eminent Muslim religious thinkers." *Islam and the Modern Age* 14 (1983), pp. 104–114.

VanderWerff, Lyle L. *Christian Mission to Muslims: The Record—Anglican and Reformed Approaches in India and the Near East, 1800–1938*. South Pasadena: William Carey Library, 1977.

Waardenburg, Jacques. "Twentieth-century Muslim writings on other religions: A proposed typology." In *Union Européenne d'Arabisants et d'Islamisants. 10th Congress, Edinburgh, 9–16 September 1980*. Ed. Robert Hillenbrand. Edinburgh: privately printed, 1982, pp. 107–115.

———. "Muslims and other believers: The Indonesian case. Towards a theoretical research framework." In *Islam in Asia*, vol. 2: *Southeast and East Asia*. Jerusalem: Magnes Press, 1984, pp. 24–66.

———. "Muslimisches Interesse an anderen Religionen im soziopolitischen Kontext des 20. Jahrhunderts." In *Loyalitätskonflikte in der Religionsgeschichte: Festschrift für Carsten Colpe*. Würzburg: Königshausen and Neumann, 1990, pp. 140–152.

———. *Islamisch-Christliche Beziehungen: Geschichtliche Streifzüge* (Religionswissenschaftliche Studien, Vol. 23). Altenberge: Oros Verlag, and Würzburg: Echter Verlag, 1993.

———. "Cultural contact and concepts of religion: Three examples from Islamic history." In *Miscellanea Arabica et Islamica*. Ed. F. de Jong (Orientalia Lovaniensia Analecta, Vol. 52). Leuven: Peeters, 1993, pp. 293–325.

Wajdi, M. F. E. "A twentieth century view of Christ." *Moslem World* 6 (1916), pp. 401–408.

Wiegers, Gerard. "A life between Europe and the Maghrib: The writings and travels of Ahmad b. Qāsim ibn Ahmad ibn al-faqīh Qāsim ibn al-shaykh al-Hajarī al-Andalusī (born c. 977/1569–70)." In *The Middle East and Europe: Encounters and Exchanges*. Ed. Geert Jan van Gelder and Ed de Moor. Amsterdam: Rodopi, 1992, pp. 87–115.

Wismer, Don. *The Islamic Jesus. An Annotated Bibliography of Sources in English and French*. New York: Garland, 1977.

Zolondek, Leon. "The French Revolution in Arabic literature of the nineteenth century." *Muslim World* 57 (1967), pp. 202–211.

The Contemporary Period (ca. 1950–ca. 1995)

SIGNIFICANT TEXTS

ʿAbd al-Wahhāb. *The Christ as Seen in the Sources of Christian Beliefs*. Cairo: Wahba Bookshop, 1985.

Abdul Hakim, Khalifa. "Islam's attitude towards other Faiths." *Papers from the International Islamic Colloquium, 1958*. Lahore: Panjab University Press, 1960, pp. 189–194.

Abdullah, Mohamed S. "Islamische Stimmen zum Dialog." *CIBEDO-Dokumentation* (Christlich-Islamische Begegnung-Dokumentationsleitstelle) Frankfurt, 12 (September 1981).

Akbarabadi, S. A. "Islam and other religions." In *Islam*. Ed. Z. I. Ansari, Abdul Haq et al. Patiala: Punjabi University, 1969, pp. 103–115.

Al-i Ahmad, Jalal. *Occidentosis: A Plague from the West*. Transl. R. Campbell (Contemporary Islamic Thought. Persian Series). Berkeley: Mizan Press, 1984.

Amjad, G. N. *Islam and the World Religions*. Lahore: Mufid-i-am Kutabkhana, 1977.

Anees, M. A., S. A. Abedin, and Z. Sardar. *Christian-Muslim Relations: Yesterday, Today, Tomorrow*. London: Grey Seal, 1991.

Arkoun, Mohammed. "The notion of revelation: From *ahl al-kitāb* to the societies of the book." *Welt des Islams* 28 (1988), pp. 62–89.

———. "New perspectives for a Jewish-Christian-Muslim dialogue." *Journal of Ecumenical Studies* 26 (1989), pp. 523–529.

Ayoub, M. "The Word of God and the voices of humanity." In *The Experience of Religious Diversity*. Ed. J. Hick and H. Askari. London: Gower, 1985, pp. 53–65.

Azhar, Muhammed D. *Christianity in History*. Lahore: Sh. Muhammad Ashraf, 1968.

Aziz-us-Samad, Ulfat. *A Comparative Study of Christianity and Islam*. Lahore: Sh. Muhammad Ashraf, 1984.

Brelvi, Mahmud. *Islam and Its Contemporary Faiths*. Karachi, 1965; 2nd ed. under the title, *Islam and*

World Religions. Lahore: Islamic Publications, 1983.

Charfi, Abdelmajid. "L'Islam et les religions non musulmanes: Quelques textes positifs." *Islamochristiana* 3 (1977), pp. 39–63.

———. "Pour une nouvelle approche du christianisme par la pensée musulmane." *Islamochristiana* 13 (1987), pp. 61–77.

Dangor, Suleman. "The attitudes of Muslim scholars towards new approaches in religious studies." *American Journal of Islamic Social Sciences* 10 (1993), pp. 280–286.

Déclarations Communes Islamo-Chrétiennes, 1954 c.–1995 c., 1373 h.–1415 h. Original texts and French translation. Ed. Juliette Nasri Haddad. Sous la direction de Augustin Dupré la Tour et Hisham Nashabé. Beirut: Dar el-Machreq, 1997.

Demirel, Kemal. "The High Judge: A play in two acts about the trial and crucifixion of Jesus." *Muslim World* 80 (1990), pp. 107–144.

Dennfer, Ahmad von. *Christians in the Qur'an and Sunna: An Assessment from the Sources to Help Define Our Relationship*. Leicester: Islamic Foundation, 1399/1979.

Diraz, Muhammad Abdullah. "Islam's attitude towards and relations with other faiths." *Islamic Literature* (Lahore) 10 (1958), pp. 9–16.

Droubie, Riadh El-. *A Muslim Look at Christianity and the Church*. Croydon: Minaret House, 1977.

Durrany, K. S. *Inter-Religious Perceptions of Hindus and Muslims*. Papers presented to the All India Seminar in New Delhi. Compiled with an introduction by K. S. Durrany. New Delhi, 1982.

Durrany, Muhammad Khan. *The Gītā and the Qur'ān: An Approach to National Integration*. Delhi: Nag Publishers, 1982.

Falaturi, Abdoldjavad. "Christian theology and the Western understanding of Islam." In *Hans Küng*. Ed. K.-J. Kuschel and H. Haring. London: SCM Press, 1993, pp. 326–336.

Faruqi, Isma'il Raji, al-. "History of Religions: Its nature and significance for Christian education and the Muslim-Christian dialogue." *Numen* 12 (1965), pp. 35–86.

———, *Christian Ethics: A Historical and Systematic Analysis of Its Dominant Ideas*. Montreal: McGill University Press, 1967.

———. "Islam and Christianity: Diatribe or dialogue." *Journal of Ecumenical Studies* 5 (1968), pp. 45–77.

———. "Islam and other faiths." In *The Challenge of Islam*. Ed. Altaf Gauhar. London: Islamic Council of Europe, 1978, pp. 82–111.

———. "The role of Islām in global interreligious dependence." In *Towards a Global Congress of the World's Religions*. Ed. Warren Lewis. New York: Rose of Sharon Press, 1980, pp. 19–53.

——— (Ed.). *Trialogue of the Abrahamic Faiths*. Herndon: International Institute of Islamic Thought, 1980; 2nd ed., 1986.

———. "Judentum und Christentum im islamischen Verständnis." In *Weltmacht Islam*. Munich: Bayerische Landeszentrale für Politische Bildungsarbeit, 1988, pp. 137–148.

Islam and Other Faiths. Ed. Ataullah Siddiqui. Markfield, U.K.: Islamic Foundation, and Herndon, Va.: International Institute of Islamic Thought, 1998.

Hamidullah, Muhammad. "Relations of Muslims with Non-Muslims." *Journal of the Institute of Muslim Minority Affairs* 7 (1986), pp. 7–12.

Hanafi, Hasan. *Religious Dialogue and Revolution: Essays on Judaism, Christianity and Islam*. Cairo: Anglo-Egyptian Bookshop, 1977.

Hassan, Riffat. "The basis for a Hindu-Muslim dialogue and steps in that direction from a Muslim perspective." In *Religious Liberty and Human Rights*. Ed. L. Swidler. Philadelphia: Ecumenical Press, 1986, pp. 125–142.

Hassan bin Talal, Crown Prince al-. *Christianity in the Arab World*. Amman: Royal Institute for Inter-Faith Studies, 1994.

Husain, S. Irtiza. *Parallel Faiths and the Messianic Hope (A Comparative Study)*. Aligarh: Aligarh Muslim University Press, 1971.

Hussein (Husain), M. Kamel. *City of Wrong: A Friday in Jerusalem*. Transl. Kenneth Cragg. Amsterdam: Djambatan, 1959. Compare Roger Arnaldez. "Deux chapitres non traduits de 'La Cité Inique' de Muhammad Kāmil Husayn (Traduction)," *Islamochristiana* 3 (1977), pp. 177–195.

———. *The Hallowed Valley: A Muslim Philosophy of Religion*. Transl. Kenneth Cragg. Cairo: American University of Cairo Press, 1977.

Islam et christianisme (Publ. Waqf Ikhlâs No. 16). Istanbul: Hakikat kitabevi, 1990.

Jamil, K. M. "Islam's attitude towards and relations with other faiths." *Papers from the International Islamic Colloquium, 1958*. Lahore: Panjab University Press, 1958, pp. 233–235.

Khoury, Adel-Theodor, and Ludwig Hagemann. *Christentum und Christen im Denken moderner Muslime*. Altenberge: Christlich-Islamisches Schrifttum, 1986.

Mahmud, Syed. *Hindu-Muslim Cultural Accord*. Bombay: Vora, 1949.

Manssoury, F. El-. "Muslims in Europe: The lost tribe of Islam?" *Journal of the Institute of Muslim Minority Affairs* 10 (1989), pp. 63–84.

Masdoosi, Ahmad Abdullah, al-. *Living Religions of the World: A Socio-Political Study*. English translation by Zafar Ishaq Ansari. Karachi: Begum Aisha Bawany Wakf, 1962. Turkish translation from the English. Istanbul: Yasayan Dünya Dinleri, 1981.

Maudoodi, Maulana Abu'l-A'la. "Letter addressed to H. H. Pope Paul VI." *Islamic Litterature* 14 (1968), pp. 51–59.

Mūsawī Larī, Sayid Mujtabā Rukni. *Western Civilisation through Muslim Eyes*. Transl. F. J. Goulding. Guildford, U.K.: Optimus Books, 1977.

Muzaffaruddin, S. *A Comparative Study of Islam and Other Religions*. Lahore: Ashraf, 1977.

Naraghi, Ehsan. *L'Orient et la crise de l'Occident* (Series Antidotes). Paris: Ed. Entente, 1977.

Narain, Harsh. "The concept of revelation in Hinduism and Islam." *Islam and the Modern Age* 6 (1975), pp. 32–64.

———. "Feasibility of a dialogue between Hinduism and Islam." *Islam and the Modern Age* 6 (1975), pp. 57–85.

———. "Tender mind versus tough mind." *Islam and the Modern Age* 7 (1976), pp. 33–52.

Nasr, Seyyed Hossein. "Islam and the encounter of religions." In *Sufi Essays*. London: George Allen and Unwin, 1972, pp. 123–151.

———. "The Islamic view of Christianity." *Concilium* 183 (February 1986), pp. 3–12.

———. "Response to Hans Küng's paper on Christian-Muslim dialogue." *Muslim World* 77 (1987), pp. 96–105.

———. "Comments on a few theological issues in the Islamic-Christian dialogue." In *Christian-Muslim Encounters*. Ed. Yvonne Yazbeck Haddad and Wadi Z. Haddad. Gainesville: University Press of Florida, 1995, pp. 457–467.

Qadri, Abdul Hamid. *Dimensions of Christianity*. Islamabad: Da'wah Academy, International Islamic University, 1989; 2nd ed. 1993.

Rahman, Fazlur. "Islamic attitudes towards Judaism." *Muslim World* 72 (1982), pp. 1–13.

———. "Non-Muslim minorities in an Islamic state." *Journal of the Institute of Muslim Minority Affairs* 7 (1986), pp. 13–24.

Shabasteri, M.M. "Muslims and Christians in today's world." *Iranian Journal of International Affairs* 1 (1989), pp. 15–26.

Shafaq, Sadeg Razazadeh. "Christianity and Islam." *Papers from the International Islamic Colloquium, 1958*. Lahore: Panjab University Press, 1958, pp. 200–203.

Shafiq, Muhammad. "Trilogue of the Abrahamic faiths: Guidelines for Jewish, Christian and Muslim dialogue." *Hamdard Islamicus* 15 (1992), pp. 59–74.

Siddiq, Alhaj Muhammad. "A letter to the Pope." *Review of Religions* 67 (1972), pp. 117–128.

Siddiqui, Ataullah. *Christian-Muslim Dialogue in the Twentieth Century*. London: Macmillan, and New York: St. Martin's, 1997.

Siddiqui, M. A'lāuddīn. "Islam's attitude towards other religions." *Papers International Islamic Colloquium 1958*. Lahore: Panjab University Press, 1958, pp. 204–210.

Siddiqui, M. K. A. *Hindu-Muslim Relations*. Calcutta: Abadi Publications, 1993.

Swidler, Leonard (Ed.). *Religious Liberty and Human Rights*. Philadelphia: Ecumenical Press, 1986.

——— (Ed.). *Muslims in Dialogue. The Evolution of a Dialogue* (Religions in Dialogue, Vol. 3). Lewiston: Edwin Mellen Press, 1992.

Talbi, Mohamed. "Islam and Dialogue: Some reflections on a current topic." *Encounter* 11–12 (1975). Repr. in Richard W. Rousseau (Ed.), *Christianity and Islam: The Struggling Dialogue*. Scranton: Ridge Row Press, 1985, pp. 53–73. French original text: *Islam et dialogue. Réflexions sur un thème d'actualité* (Tunis: Maison tunésienne d'édition, 1972).

———. "Musulman aujourd'hui." *Axes: Recherches pour un dialogue entre Christianisme et religions* 8 (1975/76), pp. 9–19.

———. "Islam et Occident au-delà des affrontements, des ambiguités et des complexes." *Islamochristiana* 7 (1981), pp. 57–77. English translation in *Encounter* (Rome) 108 (October 1984).

———. "Religious liberty: A Muslim perspective." *Islamochristiana* 11 (1985), pp. 99–113. Also in *Religious Liberty and Human Rights*. Ed. L. Swidler (Philadelphia: Ecumenical Press, 1986), pp. 175–188. Also published in *Encounter* (Rome) 126–127 (1986).

———. "Possibilities and conditions for a better understanding between Islam and the West." *Journal of Ecumenical Studies* 25 (1988), pp. 161–193.

———. "Le Christianisme vu par l'Islam et les musulmans." In *Un respect têtu*. Ed. M. Talbi and O. Clément. Paris: Nouvelle Cité, 1989, pp. 67–108.

———. "Dialogue interreligieux ou conflireligieux: Pour un dialogue de témoignage, d'émulation et de convergence." *Revue d'Etudes Andalouses* 14 (1995), pp. 5–33.

Vahiduddin, Syed. *Islamic Experience in Contemporary Thought*. Delhi: Chanakya Publications, 1986.

———. "Islam and diversity of religions." *Islam and Christian-Muslim Relations* 1.1 (1990), pp. 3–11.

———. "Unavoidable dialogue in a pluralist world: A personal account." *Encounters* (Leicester) 1 (1995), pp. 56–69.

STUDIES

D'un Orient l'autre. Les métamorphoses successives des perceptions et connaissances, 2 vols. Vol. 1: *Configurations*. Vol. 2: *Identifications*. Paris: Editions du CNRS, 1991.

Aasi, Ghulam Haider. "The Qur'ān and other religions." *Hamdard Islamicus* 9 (1986), pp. 65–91.

Abi-Hashem, Naji. "The impact of the Gulf War on the churches in the Middle East: A socio-cultural and spiritual analysis." *Pastoral Psychology* 41 (1992), pp. 3–21.

Abu-Rabiʿ, Ibrahim M. "The concept of the "other" in modern Arab thought: From Muhammad ʿAbdu to Abdallah Laroui." *Islam and Christian-Muslim Relations* 8 (1997), pp. 85–97.

Addleton, Jonathan S. "Images of Jesus in the literatures of Pakistan." *Muslim World* 80 (1990), pp. 96–106.

Ahmad, Syed Barakat. "Non-Muslims and the Umma." *Studies in Islam* 17 (1980), pp. 80–119.

Aldeeb Abu-Sahlieh, Sami Awad. *Non-Musulmans en Pays d'Islam: Cas de l'Egypte*. Fribourg, Switzerland: Ed. Universitaires Fribourg, 1979.

———. *Les Musulmans face aux droits de l'homme: Religion, droit et politique; Etude et documents*. Bochum: Verlag Dieter Winkler, 1994.

Ali, Javed. "Understanding the Hindu phenomenon." *Muslim and Arab Perspectives* 7 (1995), pp. 31–40, 195–204.

Amjad-Ali, Charles. "Not so much a threat as a challenge: Acknowledging the religio-cultural heritage of others." *New Blackfriars* (1990), pp. 94–103.

Anawati, Georges C. "Jésus et ses juges d'après 'La Cité inique' du Dr Kamel Hussein." *Mélanges de l'Institut Dominicain d'Etudes Orientales au Caire* 2 (1955), pp. 71–134.

———. "Polémique, apologie et dialogue islamo-chrétiens: Positions classiques médiévales et positions contemporaines." *Euntes Docete* 22 (1969), pp. 375–452.

———. "L'aspect culturel du dialogue islamo-chrétien." In *Joannes Paulus II et Islamismus*. Rome: Libreria Editrice Vaticana, pp. 144–162.

Askari, Hasan. "Christian mission to Islam: A Muslim response." *Journal of the Institute of Muslim Minority Affairs* 7.2 (1986), pp. 314–329.

Attas, S. M. al-Naquib al-. *Comments on the re-examination of al-Rānīrī's Hujjatuʾl-Siddīq: A refutation*. Kuala Lumpur: Muzium Negara, 1975.

Ayoub, Mahmoud (Ayyub, Mahmūd). "Dhimmah in Quran and Hadīth." *Arab Studies Quarterly* 5 (1983), pp. 172–182.

———. "Muslim views of Christianity: Some modern examples." *Islamochristiana* 10 (1984), pp. 49–70.

———. "Roots of Muslim-Christian Conflict." *Muslim World* 79 (1989), pp. 25–45.

———. "Islam and Christianity between tolerance and acceptance." *Islam and Christian Muslim Relations* 2 (1991), pp. 171–181.

———. "Nearest in Amity: Christians in the Qurʾān and contemporary exegetical tradition." *Islam and Christian-Muslim Relations* 8 (1997), pp. 145–164.

Balic, Smail. "Moving from traditional to modern culture: Immigrant experience of Jews, Oriental Christians and Muslims." *Journal of the Institute of Muslim Minority Affairs* 10.2 (1989), pp. 332–336.

Baljon, Johannes M. S. "Indian Muftis and the Non-Muslims." *Islam and Christian Muslim Relations* 2 (1991), pp. 227–241.

Barr, M. "ʿĪsā: the Islamic Christ." *Islamic Quarterly* 33 (1989), pp. 236–262.

Bijlefeld, Willem A. "Controversies around the Qur'anic Ibrāhīm narrative and its 'orientalist' interpretations (Encyclopaedia of Islam)." *Muslim World* 72 (1982), pp. 81–94.

———. "Christian-Muslim studies, Islamic studies, and the future of Christian-Muslim encounter." In *Christian-Muslim Encounters*. Ed. Yvonne Yazbeck Haddad and Wadi Z. Haddad. Gainesville: University Press of Florida, 1995, pp. 13–40.

Boom, M. van den. "Dr. Hasan Hanafi: From dogma to revolution. With a selection from the writings of Dr. Hasan Hanafi." *Exchange* 18 (1989), pp. 36–51.

Borelli, John. "The Abrahamic traditions in trilateral dialogue: A selected bibliography with annotations." *Ecumenical Trends* 20 (1991), pp. 27–29.

Borrmans, Maurice. "Future prospects for Muslim-Christian coexistence in non-Islamic countries in light of past experience." *Journal of the Institute of Muslim Minority Affairs* 10.1 (1989), pp. 50–62.

Bouhdiba, Abdelwahab. "L'avenir du dialogue islamo-chrétien." *Islamochristiana* 15 (1989), pp. 87–93.

Breiner, Bert. "Christian-Muslim relations: Some current themes." *Islam and Christian Muslim Relations* 2 (1991), pp. 77–94.

Brodeur, Patrice C. "Contemporary Muslim approaches to the study of religion: A comparative analysis of three Egyptian authors." M.A. thesis, Institute of Islamic Studies, McGill University, Montreal, 1989.

Butler, R. A. "The image of Christ in recent Muslim literature." *Bulletin of the Henry Martyn Institute of Islamic Studies* 14 (1965), no. 3, pp. 3–11; no. 4, pp. 3–13.

———. "A Muslim's view of Christianity: Ghulam Ahmad Parvez." *Encounter* (Rome) 8 (October 1974).

Cachia, Pierre. "Themes related to Christianity and Judaism in modern Egyptian drama and fiction." *Journal of Arabic Literature* 2 (1971), pp. 178–194.

Caspar, Robert. "Le Concile et l'Islam." *Etudes* 324 (1966), pp. 114–126.

Cerbella, Gino. "Il dialogo tra Christiani e Musulmani nel pensiero di Ahmad Taleb." *Africa* 26 (1971), pp. 219–223.

Charfi, Abdelmajid. "L'Islam et les religions non musulmanes: Quelques textes positifs." *Islamochristiana* 3 (1977), pp. 39–63.

Chartier, Marc. "La rencontre Orient-Occident dans la pensée de trois philosophes égyptiens contemporains: Hasan Hanafī, Fu'ād Zakariyya, Zakī Nagīb Mahmūd." *Oriente Moderno* 53 (1973), pp. 605–642.

———. "Penseurs musulmans contemporains (2): La pensée religieuse de Kāmil Husayn." *Institut de Belles Lettres Arabes* 37 (1974), pp. 1–44.

———. "Muhammad Ahmad Khalaf Allāh et l'exégèse coranique." *Institut de Belles Lettres Arabes* 39 (1976), pp. 1–31.

Chittick, W. C. "Appreciating Knots: An Islamic approach to religious diversity." In *Inter-Religious Models and Criteria*. Ed. J. Kellenberger. Basingstoke: Macmillan, 1993, pp. 3–20.

Cohen, Mark R. "Islam and the Jews: Myth, countermyth, history." *Jerusalem Quarterly* 38 (1986), pp. 125–137.

Corbon, Jean. "Le dialogue islamo-chrétien dans la conjoncture du monde chrétien de 1950 à 1980." *Islamochristiana* 11 (1985), pp. 177–189.

Corm, Georges G. *Contribution à l'étude des societés multi-confessionnelles: Effets socio-juridiques et politiques du pluralisme religieux* (Bibliothèque constitutionnelle et de science politique, Vol. 42). Paris: R. Pichon and R. Durand-Aurias, 1971.

Cragg, Kenneth. "Ismail al-Faruqi on dialogue." In *Christian-Muslim Encounters*. Ed. Yvonne Yazbeck Haddad and Wadi Z. Haddad. Gainesville: University Press of Florida, 1995.

Déjeux, Jean. "L'image des Chrétiens dans les romans et les receuils de nouvelles maghrébins de langue française de 1920 à 1978." *Islamochristiana* 5 (1979), pp. 193–220.

Djaït, Hichem. *Europe and Islam*. Berkeley: University of California Press, 1985. French original text: *L'Europe et l'Islam* (Paris: Seuil, 1978).

Doi, ʿAbdal-Rahmān. *Non-Muslims under Shariʿah*. Brentwood, Md., 1979.

Duran, Khalid. "Die Muslime und die Andersgläubigen." *Der Islam: Religion–Ethik–Politik*. Ed. Peter Antes et al. Stuttgart: Kohlhammer, 1991, pp. 125–152.

Engineer, Asghar Ali. "The Hindu-Muslim problem: A cooperative approach." *Islam and Christian-Muslim Relations* 1 (1990), pp. 89–105.

Expert-Bezançon, Hélène. "Notes biographiques sur le docteur Kāmil Husayn, médecin et humaniste égyptien (1901–1977)." *Institut de Belles Lettres Arabes* 48 (1985), pp. 19–43.

———. "Regard d'un humaniste égyptien, le Dr Kāmil Husayn, sur les religions non-musulmanes." *Islamochristiana* 14 (1988), pp. 17–49.

Faruqi, I. H. Azad. "The Qur'ānic view of other religions." *Islam and the Modern Age* 18 (1987), pp. 39–50.

Ford, Peter F., Jr. "Ismaʿil al-Faruqi on Muslim-Christian dialogue: An analysis from a Christian perspective." *Islam and Christian Muslim Relations* 4 (1993), pp. 268–282.

Franz, Erhard. *Minderheiten im Vorderen Orient: Auswahlbibliographie*. Hamburg: Deutsches Orient-Institut, Dokumentationsleitstelle Moderner Orient, 1978.

Ghrab, Saād. "Islam and Christianity: From opposition to dialogue." *Islamochristiana* 13 (1987), pp. 99–111.

Goddard, Hugh P. "An annotated bibliography of works about Christianity by Egyptian Muslim authors (1940–1980)." *Muslim World* 80 (1990), pp. 251–277.

———. "Modern Pakistani and Indian Muslim perceptions of Christianity." *Islam and Christian-Muslim Relations* 5 (1994), pp. 165–188.

———. "The persistence of medieval themes in modern Christian-Muslim discussion in Egypt." In *Christian Arabic Apologetics during the Abbasid Period*. Ed. S. K. Samir and J. S. Nielsen. Leiden: E. J. Brill, 1994, pp. 225–237.

———. *Christians and Muslims. From Double Standards to Mutual Understanding*. Richmond, U.K.: Curzon Press, 1995.

———. *Muslim Perceptions of Christianity*. London: Grey Seal Books, 1996.

———. "Christianity from the Muslim perspective: Varieties and changes." In *Islam and Christianity: Mutual Perceptions since the Mid-20th Century*. Ed. Jacques Waardenburg. Leuven: Peeters, 1998, pp. 213–255.

Green, D. F. *Arab Theologians on Jews and Israel*. (Selected from the official English translation from the Fourth Conference of the Al Azhar Academy of Islamic Research, Rajab 1388/September 1968). Geneva: Ed. de l'Avenir, 1971; 3rd ed. 1976.

Griffiths, Paul J. (Ed.). *Christianity through Non-Christian Eyes*. Maryknoll, N.Y.: Orbis Books. 1990.

Gunaimi, Mohammad Talaat, al-. *The Muslim Conception of International Law and the Western Approach*. The Hague: Martinus Nijhoff, 1968.

Haddad, M. Y. S. "Arab perspectives of Judaism: A study of image formation in the writings of Muslim Arab authors, 1948–1978." Doctoral diss., University of Utrecht, 1984.

Haddad, Yvonne Yazbeck. "Christians in a Muslim state: The recent Egyptian debate." In *Christian-Muslim Encounters*. Ed. Yvonne Yazbeck Haddad and Wadi Z. Haddad. Gainesville: University Press of Florida, 1995, pp. 381–398.

———. "Islamist depictions of Christianity in the twentieth century: The pluralism debate and the depiction of the other." *Islam and Christian-Muslim Relations* 7 (1996), pp. 75–93.

Haekal, M. H. "La cause de l'incompréhension entre l'Europe et les musulmans et les moyens d'y remédier." In *L'Islam et l'Occident*. Paris: Les Cahiers du Sud, 1947, pp. 52–58.

Hamdūn, Muhammad Ahmad. "Islamic identity and the West in contemporary Arabic literature." Ph.D. diss., Temple University, Philadelphia, 1976.

Hasan, Qamar. *Muslims in India*. New Delhi: Northern Book Centre, 1988.

Hassab Alla, W. "Le christianisme et les chrétiens vus par deux auteurs arabes." In *Islam and Christianity: Mutual Perceptions since the Mid-20th Century*. Ed. Jacques Waardenburg. Leuven: Peeters, 1998, pp. 159–211.

Hefner, Robert W. *Hindu Javanese: Tengger Tradition and Islam*. Princeton, N.J.: Princeton University Press, 1985.

Institut d'Etudes Islamo-Chrétiennes, Université Saint-Joseph. *Déclarations Communes Islamo-Chrétiennes*, de 1954c./1373h. à 1995c./1415h. *Textes originaux et traductions françaises*. Dir. Augustin Dupré la Tour et Hisham Nashabé; textes présentés par Juliette Nasri Haddad. Beirut: Dar el-Machreq, 1997.

Johns, Anthony H. "Let my people go! Sayyid Qutb and the vocation of Moses." *Islam and Christian-Muslim Relations* 1 (1990), pp. 143–170.

Johnstone, Penelope. "Christ seen by contemporary Muslim writers." *Encounter* (Rome) 87 (August 1982).

———. "Articles from Islamic journals: An Islamic perspective on dialogue." *Islamochristiana* 13 (1987), pp. 131–171.

Jomier, J. "Quatre ouvrages en arabe sur le Christ." *Mélanges de l'Institut Dominicain d'Etudes Orientales au Caire* 5 (1958), pp. 367–386.

———. "Un regard moderne sur le Coran avec le Dr Kamel Hussein." *Mélanges de l'Institut Dominicain d'Etudes Orientales au Caire* 12 (1974), pp. 49–64.

Kewenig, Wilhelm. *Die Koexistenz der Religionsgemeinschaften im Libanon* (Neue Kölner rechtswissenschaftliche Abhandlungen, Vol. 30). Berlin: W. de Gruyter, 1965.

Khan, Ibrahim H. "The academic study of religion with reference to Islam." *Scottish Journal of Religious Studies* 11 (1990), pp. 37–46.

Khaouam, Mounir. *Le Christ dans la pensée moderne de l'Islam et dans le Christianisme*. Beirut: Ed. Khalifé, 1983.

Khatīb, ʿAbd al-Karīm al-. "Christ in the Qurʾān, the Taurāt and the Injīl." *Muslim World* 61 (1971), pp. 90–101.

Khoury, Adel-Theodor, and Ludwig Hagemann. *Christentum und Christen im Denken zeitgenössischer Muslime*. Altenberge: Christlich-islamisches Schrifttum, 1986.

Khoury, Paul. *L'Islam critique de l'Occident dans la pensée arabe actuelle: Islam et sécularité* (Religionswissenschaftliche Studien, Vols. 35/1 and 35/2), 2 vols. Altenberge: Oros Verlag, and Würzburg: Echter Verlag, 1994 and 1995.

Kimball, Charles Anthony. "Striving together in the way of God: Muslim participation in Christian-Muslim dialogue." Th.D. diss., Harvard Divinity School, 1987.

Klein, Menachem. "Religious pragmatism and political violence in Jewish and Islamic fundamentalism." In *Studies in Muslim-Jewish Relations* vol. 1. Ed. Ronald L. Nettler. Chur: Harwood Academic, 1993, pp.37–58.

Lakhsassi, Abderrahmane. "The Qur'an and the 'other'." In *Theoria → Praxis: How Jews, Christians, and Muslims Can Together Move from Theory to Practice*. Ed. Leonard Swidler. Leuven: Peeters, 1998, pp. 88–118.

Lewis, Bernard. *Islam and the West*. New York: Oxford University Press, 1993.

Manssoury, F. El-. "Muslims in Europe: The lost tribe of Islam?" *Journal of the Institute of Muslim Minority Affairs* 10.1 (1989), pp. 63–84. See "Reply" by J. S. Nielsen, in ibid. 10.2 (1989), pp. 559– 560.

Massey, Keith A. J., and Kevin Massey-Gillespie. "A dialogue of creeds." *Islamochristiana* 19 (1993), pp. 17–28.

Massouh, Georges. "Les thèmes chrétiens dans les oeuvres des chefs religieux musulmans pendant la guerre libanaise (de 1975 jusqu'à 1996)." Doctoral diss., Institut Pontifical des Etudes Arabes et Islamiques, Rome, 1997.

McAuliffe, Jane Dammen. *Qurʾānic Christians: An Analysis of Classical and Modern Exegesis*. New York: Cambridge University Press, 1991.

Merad, Ali. *Charles de Foucauld au regard de l'Islam*. Paris: Ed. Chalet, 1976.

———. "Un penseur musulman à l'heure de l'oecuménisme: Mahmūd Abū Rayya." *Islamochristiana* 4 (1978), pp. 151–163.

Michel, Thomas F. "Enseignement de la foi chrétienne dans les facultés de théologie de Turquie." *Se Comprendre* 35 (1990), pp. 1–5.

———. "Social and religious factors affecting Muslim-Christian relations." *Islam and Christian-Muslim Relations* 8 (1997), pp. 53–66.

Miller, Roland E. "The dynamics of religious coexistence in Kerala: Muslims, Christians, and Hindus." In *Christian-Muslim Encounters*. Ed. Yvonne Yazbeck Haddad and Wadi Z. Haddad. Gainesville: University Press of Florida, 1995, pp. 263–284.

Misconceptions about Islam: Correspondence between K. Raghupathy Rao and T. Abdullah. Madras: T. Abdullah, 1991.

Mooren, Thomas. "Einige Hinweise zum apologetischen Schrifttum des Islam in Indonesien." *Zeitschrift für Missionswissenschaft und Religionswissenschaft* 66 (1982), pp. 163–182.

Moussalli, A. S. "Islamic Fundamentalist perceptions of other monotheistic religions." In *Islam and Christianity: Mutual Perceptions since the Mid-20th Century*. Ed. Jacques Waardenburg. Leuven: Peeters, 1998, pp. 121–157.

Mushir-ul-Haq. "Muslim understanding of Hindu religion." *Islam and the Modern Age* 4 no. 4 (1973), pp. 71–77.

Naraghi, Ehsan. *L'Orient et la crise de l'Occident*. Paris: Entente, 1977.

Nasr, Seyyed Hossein. "Islam and the encounter of religions." In *Sufi Essays*. London: Allen and Unwin, 1972, pp. 123–151.

———. "Comments on a few theological issues in the Islamic-Christian dialogue." In *Christian-Muslim Encounters*. Ed. Y. Y. Haddad and W. Z. Haddad. Gainesville: University Press of Florida, 1995, pp. 457–467.

Nazir Ali, M. *Frontiers in Muslim-Christian Encounter*. Oxford: Regnum Books, 1987.

Nettler, Ronald L. *Past Trials and Present Tribulations: A Muslim Fundamentalist's View of the Jews*. [Sayyid Qutb]. (Vidal Sassoon International Center for the Study of Antisemitism, Hebrew University of Jerusalem). Oxford: Pergamon Press, 1987.

———. "A post-colonial encounter of traditions: Muhammad Saʿīd al-ʿAshmāwī on Islam and Judaism." In *Medieval and Modern Perspectives on Muslim-Jewish Relations*. Ed. Ronald L. Nettler. Luxembourg: Harwood Academic, 1995, pp. 175–184.

Nieuwenhuijze, C. A. O. van. *Cross Cultural Studies*. The Hague: Mouton, 1963. (See in particular "Frictions between presuppositions in cross-cultural communication." pp. 192–221).

———. "Muslim-Christian encounters: Some factors at play." *Islam and Christian-Muslim Relations* 1 (1990), pp. 233–243.

———. *Paradise Lost: Reflections on the Struggle for Authenticity in the Middle East*. Leiden: E. J. Brill, 1996.

Noer, Deliar. "Evangelical activities in Southeast Asia: The case of Indonesia, Malaysia and the Philippines." *Indonesia's Crescent* 3 (1993), pp. 1–25.

Nolin, Kenneth E. "Truth: Christian-Muslim (A Review-Article)." *Muslim World* 55 (1965), pp. 237–245.

Nüsse, Andrea. "The ideology of Hamās: Palestinian Islamic fundamentalist thought on the Jews, Israel and Islam." In *Studies in Muslim-Jewish Relations*, vol. 1. Ed. Ronald L. Nettler. Chur: Harwood Academic, 1993, pp. 97–125.

Osman, F., et al. "Jesus in Jewish-Christian-Muslim dialogue." *Journal of Ecumenical Studies* 14 (1977), pp. 448–465. Repr. in L. Swidler (Ed.). *Muslims in Dialogue: The Evolution of a Dialogue* (Lewiston, NY: Edwin Mellen Press, 1992), pp. 353–376.

Pinault, David. "Images of Christ in Arabic literature." *Welt des Islams* 27 (1987), pp. 103–125.

Rafique, M. *Sri Aurobindo and Iqbal: A Comparative Study of Their Philosophy*. Aligarh: Aligarh Muslim University, 1974.

Rasheeduddin Khan. *Bewildered India: Identity, pluralism, discord*. Delhi: Har-Anand, 1995. See especially ch. 8, "Towards understanding India: Reflections of some eminent Muslims" (pp. 153–192).

Rosen, Lawrence. "A Moroccan Jewish community during the Middle Eastern crisis." *Peoples and Cultures of the Middle East*, vol. 2. Ed. Louise E. Sweet. New York: National Press, 1969, pp. 388–404.

———. "Muslim-Jewish relations in a Moroccan city." *International Journal of Middle Eastern Studies* 3 (1972), pp. 435–449.

Rousseau, Richard W. (Ed.). *Christianity and Islam: The Struggling Dialogue* (Modern Theological Themes: Selections from the Literature, Vol. 4). Scranton, Pa.: Ridge Row Press, 1985.

Rudolph, Ekkehard. *Westliche Islamwissenschaft im Spiegel muslimischer Kritik: Grundzüge und Merkmale einer innerislamischen Diskussion* (Islamkundliche Untersuchungen, Vol. 137). Berlin: Klaus Schwarz, 1991.

———. "Muslimische Äußerungen zum Dialog mit dem Christentum (1970–1991)." *CIBEDO* (Christlich-Islamische Begegnung-Dokumentationsleitstelle): *Beiträge zum Gespräch zwischen Christen und Muslimen* 2–3 (1992), pp. 33–46.

———. *Dialogues islamo-chrétiens, 1950–1993: Introduction historique suivie d'une bibliographie étendue des sources arabes*. (Cahiers du Département Interfacultaire d'Histoire et de Sciences des Religions, Université de Lausanne, Nr. 1). Lausanne, 1993.

———. "Muslim approaches towards Islamic-Christian dialogue: Three decades in retrospect." In *Encounters of Words and Texts: Intercultural Studies in Honor of Stefan Wild* (Arabistische Texte und Studien 10). Ed. Lutz Edzard and Christian Szyska. Hildesheim: Georg Olms, 1997, pp. 149–158.

Sachedina, Abdulaziz A. "Jews, Christians, and Muslims according to the Quran." *Greek Orthodox Theological Review* 31 (1986), pp. 105–120.

———. "Islamic theology of Christian-Muslim Relations." *Islam and Christian-Muslim Relations* 8 (1997), pp. 27–38.

———. "Is Islamic revelation an abrogation of Judaeo-Christian revelation? Islamic self-identification in the classical and modern age." In *Islam: A Challenge for Christianity*. Ed. H. Küng and J. Moltmann. London: SCM, 1994, pp. 94–102.

Scharlipp, Wolfgang-Ekkehard. "Die alttürkische Religion und ihre Darstellung bei einigen türkischen

Historikern." *Welt des Islams* 31 (1991), pp. 168–192.

Schumann, Olaf. *Der Christus der Muslime: Christologische Aspekte in der arabisch-islamischen Literatur* (Missionswissenschaftliche Forschungen, Vol. 10). Gütersloh: Gerd Mohn, 1975. 2nd ed. Cologne: Böhlau, 1988.

———. "Das Christentum im Lichte der heutigen arabisch-islamischen Literatur." *Zeitschrift für Religions- und Geistesgeschichte* 21 (1969) pp. 307–329.

Schwartz, Richard Merrill. *The Structure of Christian-Muslim Relations in Contemporary Iran* (Occasional Papers in Anthropology, No. 13). Halifax, Nova Scotia: Department of Anthropology, Saint Mary's University, 1985.

Scott, David. "Buddhism and Islam: Past to present encounters and interfaith lessons." *Religion* 42 (1995), pp. 141–171.

Shayegan, Daryush. *Le regard mutilé*. Paris: Albin Michel, 1989.

Shepard, William. "A modernist view of Islam and other religions [Ahmad Amīn]." *Muslim World* 65 (1975), pp. 79–92.

———. "Conversations in Cairo: Some contemporary Muslim views of other religions." *Muslim World* 70 (1980), pp. 171–195.

Shepherd, Margaret. "Trialogue: Jewish, Christian, Muslim." *Christian Jewish Relations* 14 (1981), pp. 33–40.

Smith Kipp, Rita, and Susan Rogers (Eds.). *Indonesian Religion in Transition*. Tucson: University of Arizona Press, 1987.

Solihin, Sohirin Mohammad. *Copts and Muslims in Egypt: A Study in Harmony and Hostility*. Leicester: Islamic Foundation, 1991.

Soroudi, S. "Jesus' image in modern Persian poetry." *Muslim World* 69 (1979), pp. 221–228.

Steenbrink, Karel A. "The study of comparative religion by Indonesian Muslims." *Numen* 37 (1990), pp. 141–167.

Stümpel-Hatami, Isabel. *Das Christentum aus der Sicht zeitgenössischer iranischer Autoren: Eine Untersuchung religionskundlicher Publikationen in persischer Sprache* (Islamkundliche Untersuchungen, Vol. 195). Berlin: Klaus Schwarz, 1996.

Troll, Christian W. "Christian-Muslim relations in India: A critical survey." *Islamochristiana* 5 (1979), pp. 119–145.

———. "Salvation of non-Muslims: Views of some eminent Muslim religious thinkers." *Islam and the Modern Age* 14 (1983), pp. 104–114.

———. "Islam in a pluralistic society: The case of Maulana Abul Kalam Azad." *Salaam* 9 (1988), pp. 3–16.

———. "Sharing Islamically in the pluralistic nation-state of India: The views of some contemporary Indian Muslim leaders and thinkers." In *Christian-Muslim Encounters*. Ed. Yvonne Yazbeck Haddad and Wadi Z. Haddad. Gainesville: University Press of Florida, 1995, pp. 245–262.

Vahiduddin, S. "Comment le Coran conçoit l'harmonie et la réconciliation entre les confessions religieuses." *Islamochristiana* 6 (1980), pp. 25–31.

Vogelaar, Harold S. "Religious pluralism in the thought of Muhammad Kāmil Hussein." In *Christian-Muslim Encounters*. Ed. Yvonne Yazbeck Haddad and Wadi Z. Haddad. Gainesville: University Press of Florida, 1995, pp. 411–425.

Waardenburg, Jacques. "Twentieth-century Muslim writings on other religions: a proposed typology." In *Proceedings of the Union Européenne des Arabisants et Islamisants, 10th Congress, Edinburgh, September 9–16, 1980*. Ed. Robert Hillenbrand. Edinburgh, 1982, pp. 107–115.

———. "Muslimisches Interesse an anderen Religionen im soziopolitischen Kontext des 20. Jahrhunderts." In *Loyalitätskonflikte in der Religionsgeschichte: Festschrift für Carsten Colpe*. Ed. Christoph Elsas and Hans G. Kippenberg. Würzburg: Königshausen and Neumann, 1990, pp. 140–152.

———. *Islamisch-christliche Beziehungen: Geschichtliche Streifzüge* (Religionswissenschaftliche Studien 23). Altenberge: Oros Verlag, and Würzburg: Echter Verlag, 1992.

———. "Some North African intellectuals' presentations of Islam." In *Christian-Muslim Encounters*. Ed. Yvonne Yazbeck Haddad and Wadi Z. Haddad. Gainesville: University Press of Florida, 1995, pp. 358–380.

———. "Critical issues in Muslim-Christian relations: Theoretical, practical, dialogical, scholarly." *Islam and Christian-Muslim Relations* 8 (1997), pp. 9–26.

———. *Islam et Occident face à face: Regards de l'histoire des religions*. Geneva: Labor et Fides, 1998.

——— (Ed.). *Islam and Christianity: Mutual Perceptions since the Mid-20th Century*. Leuven: Peeters, 1998.

———. "Observations on the scholarly study of religion as pursued in some Muslim countries." *Numen* 45 (1998), pp. 235–257.

———. *Islam et sciences des religions. Huit leçons au Collège de France*. Paris: Les Belles Lettres, 1998.

———. "L'Europe dans le miroir de l'islam." *Asiatische Studien—Etudes Asiatiques* (1999).

Wahba, Magdi. "An anger observed." *Journal of Arabic Literature* 20 (1989), pp. 187–199.

Wasserstrom, Steven M. (Ed.). *Islam and Judaism: 1400 Years of Shared Values*. Portland, Or.: Institute for Judiac Studies in the Pacific Northwest, 1991.

Waterfield, Robin E. *Christians in Persia: Assyrians, Armenians, Roman Catholics and Protestants.* London: Allen and Unwin, 1973.

Watt, W. Montgomery. "Muslim-Christian encounters: Perceptions and misperceptions." *Muslim World* 57 (1967), pp. 19–23.

———. "Thoughts on Muslim-Christian dialogue." *Hamdard Islamicus* 1, no. 1 (1978), pp. 1–52.

———. "Cultural identity in Islam and Christianity." *Journal of Ottoman Studies* 7–8 (1988), pp. 71–82.

———. "Islamic attitudes to other religions." *Studia Missionalia* 42 (1993), pp. 245–255.

Wild, Stefan. "Judentum, Christentum und Islam in der palästinensischen Poesie." In *Der Islam im Spiegel zeitgenössischer Literatur der islamischen Welt.* Ed. J. C. Bürgel with M. Chenou, M. Glünz, and M. Reut. Leiden: E. J. Brill, 1985, pp. 259–297.

Wismer, Don. *The Islamic Jesus. An Annotated Bibliography of Sources in English and French.* New York: Garland, 1977.

Zebiri, Kate. "Relations between Muslims and non-Muslims in the thought of Western-educated Muslim intellectuals." *Islam and Christian-Muslim Relations* 6 (1995), pp. 255–277.

———. *Muslims and Christians Face to Face.* Oxford: Oneworld, 1997.

Oriental Languages: Selected Modern Texts

ARABIC

Proper names starting with ʿayin (ʿa and ʿu) are listed at the beginning of the alphabet.

Anonymous

Muʿāmalat ghayr al-muslimīn fī ʾl-Islām. 2 vols. Amman: Al-Majmaʿ al-Malakī liʾl-Buhūth, Muʾassassat Āl al-bayt, 1989.

"Mughālatāt wa haqāʾiq hawla wāqiʿ al-masīhiyīn fī ʾl-duwal al-islāmiyya wa wāqiʿ al-muslimīn fīʾl-duwal al-gharbiyya." *Risālat al-Jihād* (Tripoli) 8, no. 83 (1989), pp. 7–11.

Authors alphabetically (starting with *ʿayin*)

ʿAbd al-ʿAzīz, Mansūr Husayn. *Daʿwat al-haqq aw al-haqīqa bayna ʾl-masīhiyya waʾl-islām.* Cairo, 1963; 2nd enl. ed., 1972.

ʿAbd al-Fattāh, Nabīl, and Diyāʾ Rashwān (Eds.). *Taqrīr al-hāla al-dīniyya fī Misr 1995.* Cairo: Markaz al-dirāsāt al-Siyāsīya waʾl-istirātījiyya biʾl-Ahrām, 1996.

ʿAbd al-Wahhāb, Ahmad (?). *Al-masīh fī masādir al-ʿaqāʾid al-masīhiyya: Khulāsat abhāth ʿulamāʾ al-masīhiyya fīʾl-gharb.* Cairo: Maktabat Wahba, 1978.

ʿAbd al-Wahhāb, Ahmad. *Al-islām waʾl-adyān: Nuqat al-ittifāq waʾl-ikhtilāf.* Cairo: Maktabat al-turāth al-islāmī, 1992.

ʿAbduh, Muhammad. *Al-islām waʾl-nasrāniyya maʿa al-ʿilm waʾl-madaniyya,* 8th ed. Cairo: Dār al-Manār, 1373.

ʿAmmāra, Muhammad. *Al-Islām waʾl-wahda al-qawmiyya,* 2nd ed. Cairo: al-Muʾassassa al-ʿArabiyya liʾl-Dirāsāt waʾl-Nashr, 1979.

ʿAqqād, ʿAbbās Mahmūd al-. *Allāh. Kitāb fī nashʾat al-ʿaqīdat al-ilāhīya.* Cairo, 1947; 7th ed., Cairo: Dār al-Maʿārif bi-Misr, 1976.

———. *ʿAbqarīyat al-masīh.* Cairo: Matbaʿa Dār Akhbār al-Yawm, 1953; 2nd ed., *Hayāt al-masīh fīʾl-tarīkh wa-kushūf al-ʿasr al-hadīth* (Cairo: Dār al-Hilāl, 1958); 3rd ed., *ʿAbqarīyat al-masīh* (Cairo: Dār Nahdat Misr liʾl-Tibāʿa waʾl-Nashr, 1973).

ʿAwwā, Muhammad Salīm al-. *Al-Aqbāt waʾl-Islām: Hiwār 1987.* Cairo: Dār al-Shurūq, 1987.

ʿAzm, Sādiq Jalāl al-. *Naqd al-fikr al-dīnī.* Beirut: Dār al-Talīʾa, 1969.

ʿUthmān, Fathī. *Maʿa ʾl-Masīh fīʾl-anājīl al-arbaʿa.* Cairo: Maktabat Wahba, 1961; 2nd ed., Cairo: Al-Dār al-Qawmiyya liʾl-Tibāʿa waʾl-Nashr, 1966.

Abū Rayya, Mahmūd. *Dīn Allāh wāhid: Muhammad waʾl-masīh akhawān.* Cairo: ʿĀlam al-Karnak, 1963; 2nd ed., *Dīn Allāh wāhid ʿalā alsinat jamīʿ al-rusul.* Cairo: ʿĀlam al-kutub, 1970.

Abū Zahra, Muhammad. *Muhādarāt fīʾl-nasrāniyya* (1942); 2nd ed, Cairo: Dār al-Kitāb al-ʿArabī, 1949; 3rd ed., Cairo: Dār al-Fikr al-ʿArabī, 1961; 5th ed. with the same publishers, 1977.

———. *Al-diyānāt al-qadīma.* Cairo: Dār al-fikr al-ʿarabī, 1965.

Ahmad, Ibrāhīm Khalīl. *Al-ghufrān baynaʾl-islām waʾl-masīhīya.* Cairo: Dār al-Manār, 1989.

Badrān, Abūʾl-ʿAynayn. *Al-ʿAlāqāt al-ijtimāʿiyya baynaʾl-muslimīn wa ghayr al-muslimīn fīʾl-sharīʿa al-islāmiyya waʾl-yahūdiyya waʾl-masīhiyya waʾl-qānūn.* Beirut: Dār al-Nahda al-ʿArabiyya, 1980.

Baraka, ʿAbd al-Fattāh. "Lā huwa li-hisāb al-Islām wa lā li-hisāb al-Masīhiyya." *Majallat al-Azhar* 51 (1979), pp. 626–638.

Bedoui, Fawzi. "Mulāhazāt hawla manzilat al-adyān ghayr al-islāmīya fīʾl-fikr al-islāmī al-muʿāsir." *Islamochristiana* 17 (1991), pp. 1–14.

Bint al-Shāti. *Qirāʾa fī wathāʾiq al-bahāʾiyya.* Cairo: Markaz al-Ahrām, 1986.

Drāz, Muhammad ʿAbdallāh. *Al-dīn. Buhūth mumahhida li-dirāsat taʾrīkh al-adyān.* Cairo: Al-Matbaʿa al-ʿālamiyya, 1952; new ed., Cairo: Matbaʿat al-saʿāda, 1969.

Fadlallāh, Muhammad Husayn. *Al-Hiwār fī ʾl-qurʾān,* 5th ed. Beirut: Dār al-Taʿāruf liʾl-Matbūʿāt, 1407/1987.

Ghannūshī, Rashīd al-. *Huqūq al-muwātana: Wad'iyyat ghayr al-muslim fī'l-mujtama' al-islāmī*. Tunis, 1989.

Ghazālī, Muhammad al-. *Al-ta'assub wa'l-tasāmuh bayna'l-masīhīya wa'l-islām: Dahd shubuhāt wa-radd muftarayāt*. Cairo: Dār al-kutub al-hadītha, n.d. (ca. 1976).

Hilmī, Mustafā. *Al-Islām wa'l-adyān: Dirāsa muqārana*. Cairo: Dār al-Sahwa, 1990.

Himāya, Mahmūd 'Alī. *Ibn Hazm wa-manhajuh fī dirāsat al-adyān*. Cairo: Dār al-Ma'ārif, 1983.

Husayn, Muhammad Kāmil. *Qarya zālima*. Cairo: Maktabat al-Nahda al-Misriyya, 1954; 4th ed. 1974.

———. *Al-wādī al-muqaddas*. Cairo: Dār al-Ma'ārif, 1968.

Huwaydī, Fahmī. *Muwātinūn lā dhimmiyūn: Mawqi' ghayr al-muslimīn fī mujtama' al-muslimīn*. Cairo: Dār al-Shurūq, 1985.

Ibrāhīm, Sa'd al-Dīn. *Ta'ammulāt fī mas'alat al-aqalliyāt*. Cairo: Markaz Ibn Khaldūn, 1992.

al-Ijtihād (Beirut). Special issues Nos. 28–32 on Muslim-Christian relations (Summer 1995–Summer 1996).

Ja'far, Muhammad Kamāl Ibrāhīm. *Al-Islām bayna'l-adyān: Dirāsa fī turuq dirāsāt al-dīn wa ahamm qadāyāh*. Cairo: Maktabat Dār al-'Ulūm, 1977.

Khālid, Hasan. *Mawqif al-islām min al-wathaniyya wa'l-yahūdiyya wa'l-nasrāniyya*. Beirūt: Ma'had al-Inmā' al-'Arabī, 1986.

Khālid, Khālid Muhammad. *Ma'an 'alā 'l-tarīq: Muhammad wa'l-masīh*. Cairo: Dār al-Kutub al-Hadītha, 1958; 4th ed., 1966.

Khālidī, Mustafā, and 'Umar A. Farrūkh. *Al-Tabshīr wa'l-isti'mār fī'l-bilād al-'arabiyya* [*Missionaries and Imperialism, being an account of Mission work in the Arab World as a medium of cultural expansion and a preparation for political intervention*]. Saida: Al-Maktaba al-'Arabiyya li'l-Tabā'a wa'l-Nashr, 1953; 2nd ed., 1957.

Khatīb, 'Abd al-Karīm al-. *Al-Masīh fī 'l-qur'ān wa 'l-tawrāt wa'l-injīl*. Cairo: Dār al-Kutub al-Hadītha, 1966.

Khazrājī. A. U. al-. *Bayna 'l-masīhiyya wa'l-islām*. Ed. M. Shama. Cairo: Maktabat Wahba, 1972.

Khūrī, Yūsuf Quzmā (Ed.). *'Īsā wa Maryam fī 'l-qur'ān wa'l-tafsīr*. Amman: Al-mahad al-malikī li'l dirāsāt al-dīnīya; Dār al-Shurūq, 1996.

Murjān, Muhammad Majdī. *Al-Masīh insān am ilāh?* Cairo: Dār al-Nahda al-'Arabiyya, 1970.

———. *Allāh wāhid am thālūth?* Cairo: Dār al-Nahda al-'Arabiyya, 1972.

Qaradāwī, Yūsuf al-. *Ghayr al-muslimīn fī'l-mujtama' al-islāmī*. Cairo: Maktabat Wahba, 1977; new ed., Beirut: Mu'assassat al-Risāla, 1985. Turkish transl. Beşir Eryarsoy, *Müslümanlar gayri Müslimlere nasil davrandi?* Istanbul: Ihya Yayinlari, 1985.

Qudāt, Amīn al-, et al. (Ed.). *Adyān wa firaq*. Amman, 1990.

Sa'd al-dīn, Laylā Hasan. *Adyān muqārana*. Amman: Dār al-Fikr li'l-Nashr wa'l-Tawzī', 1985.

Sahhār, 'Abd al-Hamīd Jūda al-. *Al-Masīh 'Īsā b. Maryam*. Cairo: Dār Misr li'l-tibā'a, 1951.

Sammāk, Muhammad al-. *Al-Aqalliyāt bayna'l-'urūba wa'l-Islām*. Beirut: Dār al-'Ilm li'l-Malāyīn, 1990.

Saqqā, Ahmad Hijāzī al-. *Allāh wa sifatuh fī'l-yahūdiyya wa'l-nasrāniyya wa'l-islām*. Cairo: Dār al-Nahda al-'Arabiyya, 1978.

Shalabī, Ahmad. *Muqāranat al-adyān*, 4 vols.: *al-Masīhiyya* (1960); *al-Islām* (1961); *Adyān al-Hind al-kubrā: al-Hindawiyya, al-Jayniyya, al-Budhiyya* (1964); *al-Yahūdiyya* (1965). Cairo: Maktabat al-Nahda al-Hadītha, 1960–1965; 4th/5th ed. 1974–1977. These books were translated into various "Islamic" languages.

Sharfī, 'Abd al-Majīd al-. *Al-Fikr al-islāmī fī 'l-radd 'alā 'l-nasārā ilā nihāyat al-qarn al-rābi' 'ashar*. Tunis: Al-Dār al-Tūnisiyya li'l-Nashr, and Algier: Al-Mu'assassa al-Wataniyya li'l-Kitāb, 1986.

Sharqāwī, Muhammad 'Abdallāh al-. *Fī muqāranat al-adyān: Buhūth wa dirāsāt*. Cairo: Dār al-Ma'ārif, 1990.

Sulaymān, Samīr (Ed.). *Al-'Alāqāt al-islāmiyya al-māsihiyya: Qirā'āt marji'iyya fī 'l-hādir wa'l-mustaqbal*. Beirut: Markaz al-Dirāsāt al-Istrātījiyya wa'l-Buhūth wa'l-Tawthīq, 1994.

Talbī, Muhammad. *'Iyāl Allāh. Afkār jadīda fī 'alāqat al-muslim bi-nafsih wa-bi'l-ākharīn*. Tunis: Dār Sirās, 1992.

Waqfī, Ibrāhīm Ahmad al-. *Al-samāha fī 'l-islām wa'l-masīhiyya*. Cairo: Dār al-Fikr al-'Arabī, 1990.

Zaydān, 'Abd al-Karīm. *Ahkām al-dhimmiyyīn wa'l-musta'minīn fī dār al-islām*. Mu'assasat al-risāla (Maktabat) al-Quds. Baghdad: Matba'at al-Burhān, 1963; 2nd ed., 1976.

Ziyāda, Khālid. *Tatawwur al-nazra al-islāmiyya ilā urūbbā*. Beirut: Ma'had al-Inmā' al-'Arabī, 1983.

Zughbī, Muhammad 'Alī al-, and Hāshim Daftardār. *Al-Islām wa'l-Masīhiyya fī Lubnān*. Beirut: Mu'as-sassat Matābi' al-Ma'tūq, 1978.

PERSIAN

(See also the bibliography of Isabel Stümpel's contribution, ch. 14.)

Bāhunar, Muhammad Javād. *Dīnshināsī-i tatbīqī*. Tehran: Daftar-i nashr-i farhang-i islāmī, 1361/1982.

Bakhtāvar, Kamāl ud-Dīn. *Tārīkh-i 'aqāyid-i adyān va madhāhib-i sāmī*. Tehran: Ābān, 1339/1960.

Gulpāygānī, Husayn. *Muvāzana bayn-i adyān-i chahārgāna zartusht, yahūd, masīh, islām*. Qum: 'Ilmīya, 1364/1985.

Hikmat, ʿAlī Asghar. *Nuh guftār dar tārīkh-i adyān*. Tehran: Ibn Sīnā, 1342/1963.

Mashkūr, Muhammad Javād. *Khulāsa-i adyān dar tārīkh-i dīnhā-i buzurg*, 3rd ed. Tehran: Intishārāt-i sharq, 1368/1989.

Rāzī, Hāshim. *Adyān-i buzurg-i jahān*. Tehran: Farvahar, 1360/1981.

Rizāzāda Shafaq, Sādiq. *Translation of a Selection of Thirteen Upanishads into Persian, with annotations*. Tehran: Shirkat-i Intishārāt-i ʿIlmi wa farhangī, 1345/1988.

Sharīʿatī, ʿAlī. *Tārīkh va shinākht-i adyān*, 2 vols. Tehran (?), 1359/1980. Turkish transl. Abdullah Sahin. Istanbul: Seçkin Yayıncılık, 1988.

Turābī, ʿAlī Akbar. *Nazarī dar tārīkh-i adyān*. Tehran: Iqbāl, 1341/1962.

TURKISH

History of Religions in General

Demirci, Kürşat. *Dinler Tarihinin Meseleleri*. Istanbul: Insan yayınları, 1997.

Kahraman, Ahmet. *Dinler Tarihi*. Istanbul, 1993.

Sena, Cemil. *Tanrı Anlayışı*. Istanbul, 1978.

Tümer, Günay and Abdurrahman Kücük. *Dinler Tarihi*. Ankara: Ocak Yayınları, 1988; 3rd ed. 1997.

Yavuz, Hilmi. *Dinler Tarihi Ansiklopedisi*. Istanbul, 1976.

Religions in Turkey

Ancient Turkish Religion

İnan, Abdülkadir. *Tarihte ve Bugün Şamanizm*. Ankara, 1972.

———. *Eski Türk Din Tarihi*. Istanbul, 1976.

Ogel, Bahaeddin. *Türk Mitolojisi*, 2 vols. Ankara, 1993.

Ottoman Times

Bozkurt, Gülnihal. *Gayri Müslim Osmanlı Vatandaşlarının Hukuki Durumu (1839–1914)*. Ankara, 1989.

Eryilmaz, Bilal. *Osmanlı Devletinde Gayrimüslim Tebaanın Yönetimi*, 2nd ed. Istanbul, 1996.

Küçük, Abdürrahman. *Dönmeler ve Dönmelik Tarihi*. Istanbul, n.d. (ca. 1962). New ed., Istanbul, 1994.

Ozşuca, Neyir. *Bahai Dini*. Ankara, 1989.

Sever, Erol. *Yezidilik ve Yezidilerin Kökeni*. Istanbul, 1993.

Sociology of Religion

Atacan, Fulya. *Sosyal Değişme ve Tarikat Cerrahiler*. Istanbul: Birinci Bası, 1990.

———. *Kutsal Göç: Radikal Islamcı Bir Grubun Anatomisi*. Istanbul: Bağlam Yayınları, Birinci Basim, 1993.

Bulaç, Ali. *Din ve Modernizm*, 3rd ed. Istanbul: Beyan Yayınları, 1992.

Cakir, Rusen. *Ayet ve Slogan: Türkiye'de islami oluşumlar*. Istanbul: Metis Yayınları, 1990; 6th ed. 1993.

Kırkıncı, Mehmed. *Darü'l-Harb Nedir?* Istanbul: Cihan Yayınları, 1990.

Paksu, Mehmed. *Dārü'l-Harb Tartişması*. Istanbul: Yenı Asya Yayınları, 1987.

Tozduman, Aysel Zeynep. *Islām ve Batı Gözüyle Insan*. Istanbul: Seha Nesriyat, 1991.

Christianity

Albayrak, Kadir. *Keldaniler ve Nasturiler*. Ankara, 1997.

Altindal, Aytunç. *Türkiye ve Ortodokslar*. Istanbul, 1995.

Asrımızda Hıristiyan-Müslüman Münasebetleri (lectures). Istanbul: Ilmī Nesriyat, 1993.

Aydin, Mehmet. *Müslümanların Hıristiyanliğa Karşi Yazdiği Reddiyeler ve Tartişma Konulari*. Konya: Selçuk Üniversitesi Basimevi, 1989.

———. *Hristiyan Genel Konsilleri ve II. Vatikan Konsili*. Konya: Selçuk Üniversitesi Basimevi, 1991.

———. *Hıristiyan Kaynaklarina göre Hıristiyanlik*. Ankara: Türkiye Diyanet Vakfı, 1995.

Aygil, Yakup, *Hıristiyan Türklerin Kısa Tarihi*. Istanbul, 1995.

Benlisoy, Yorgo, and Elçin Macar. *Fener Patrikhanesi*. Ankara, 1996.

Bilge, Yakup. *Sürynailer: Anadolu'nun Solan Rengi*. Istanbul, 1996.

Çelik, Mehmet. *Süryani Tarihi*, vol. 1. Ankara, 1996.

Eröz, Mehmet. *Hıristiyanlaşan Türkler*. Ankara, 1983.

Kazici, Ziya. *Kur'an-ı Kerim ve Garp Kaynaklarına göre Hıristiyanlık*. Istanbul, 1971.

Kücük, Abdürrahman. *Ermeni Kilisesi ve Türkler*. Ankara, 1997.

Kuzgun, Şaban. *Dört İncil: Farklılıkları ve Çelişkileri*, 2nd ed. Ankara, 1996.

Şahin, Süreyya. *Fener Patrikhanesi ve Türkiye*. Istanbul, 1980; repr. 1995.

Sırma, İhsan Süreyya. *İslāmiyet ve Hıristiyanlik* ("Islam and Christianism," in Turkish, English, French, and German). Istanbul: Düsünce Yayınları, 1980; 3rd ed., Istanbul: Beyan Yayınları, 1991.

Yeşilyurt, Süleyman. *Türk Hıristiyanların Patrikhanesi*. Ankara, 1995.

Yildirim, Suat. *Mevcut Kaynaklara göre Hıristyanlık*. Ankara: Diyanet Isleri Bakanliğa Yayınları, 1988.

GENERAL INDEX

kuffār (infidels), 41, 56, 291
kufr (unbelief), 4, 19, 186, 193, 198, 217, 291

Lahore, 27, 257, 258, 271
Libya, 301–302
Low Countries, the, 75
Lull, Ramon, 18, 46
Luther, Martin, 275

Mahabharata, 289
al-Mahdī (caliph), 38, 42
Maimonides, 55, 169, 190, 191
Majūs, 106, 162. *See also* Zoroastrians
al-Malik al-Kāmil, 141
Mamluk Egypt, 160–180
al-Ma'mūn, 42, 218, 220
al-Manār, 77, 78
Mani, 35, 37, 39, 203, 209
Manicheans (Manichees), 29, 30, 36, 37–40, 44, 56, 198, 256
Manicheism, 37, 38, 40, 79
Martí, Ramón, 46
Martyn, Henry, 275
Mawdudi, Abul Ala, 259
Mazdak and Mazdakites, 30, 35
Messiah and Messianic Age, 109, 149
millat Ibrāhīm (religion of Abraham), 12–14, 58
millet system, 72
Ministry of Religion (Indonesia), 282, 283, 284–290
mission and *da'wa*, 300
missionaries, 91, 235, 251, 289
missionary expansionism, 47, 227
missionary religions, 59
missions, 71, 85, 275, 298, 301
  to India, 270–276
mobads (Zoroastrian priests), 207
Moghul empire, 35, 70–71, 92, 250, 252, 271
monasticism, 114
monk(s), 133, 141, 190, 217–219
  and Christian ascetics: as seen by Muslims, 182–184, 191
monotheistic religions, 47–49, 90, 304
monotheists without revelation, 26
Moses, 7, 147–150, 152
Mount Sinai, 147, 150
Muhammad, 9–16, 123
"Muhammadan" Bible exegesis looking for announcement (*a'lām*) texts, 53
Muhammadiyah, 286, 289
Muhammad's relations with
  Christians in N.W. Arabia, 12–16
  Jews in Medina, 11–12
  polytheists in Mecca, 10–12
Mukti Ali, H.A., 284–285, 292
mushrikūn (polytheists), 35, 56

Muslim apologetics
  in Arabic (8th–9th c.), 128–131
  in Persian (20th c.), 231–232
Muslim approaches to Christianity in modern period
  changes in apologetics, 274–276
  kinds of approaches, 304
  modern texts on Christianity in Arabic, 77–79, 88–89, 240–249
  modern texts on Christianity in Persian, 227–235
Muslim-Christian dialogue, 63 n. 64
  contemporary Muslim views of, 89, 90, 227, 297–304
  Muslim positions on dialogue: in Egypt, 298–299; in Lebanon, 303; in Libya, 301–302; in Saudi Arabia, 299–301; in Tunisia, 303
Muslim-Christian perceptions in medieval period, 46–49
Muslim-Christian polemics in medieval period, 41–46, 128
  al-radd al-jamīl, 45, 50, 65 n. 101
Muslim-Christian relations in medieval literature
  Kitāb al-aghānī of al-Iṣfahānī, 213–217, 219–220
  Kitāb al-diyārāt of al-Shabushtī, 217–219
Muslim-Christian relations in modern Indonesia, 288–290, 293–294
Muslim-Christian spirituality in medieval period, 181–192
Muslim-Hindu relations
  during 1550–1918, 70–71, 74, 192–193
  during 1918–1947, 253–261
  during 1947–1995, 85, 92–93, 263–269 (Indonesia 288)
  medieval, 28–29, 187
Muslim identity, 88, 126, 240–241
Muslim immigrants, 74, 87, 88, 92
Muslim interest in other religions in medieval period, 31–34
  major attitudes in medieval Islamic civilization, 20–21
  plurality of cultures and religions, 31–32
  practical interest in non-Muslims paying *jizya* in Muslim societies, 18, 23, 161
Muslim-Jewish historical relations (medieval period), 51, 55–56, 98 n. 44
Muslim-Judaic polemics (medieval period), 52–55, 143–154
Muslim judgments of other religions in medieval period in general, 56–59
Muslim League (India), 253, 258, 260
Muslim life under Christian authority (Sicily), 137–142
Muslim minorities, 92, 263–269, 298
Muslim modern studies of other religions, xii n., 89, 93, 94, 290

MUSLIM AUTHOR INDEX